ENGLISH BREAD AND YEAST COOKERY

Elizabeth David, whose cookery books have inspired and influenced a whole generation, developed a taste for good food and wine when she lived with a French family while studying French history and literature in Paris at the Sorbonne. After returning to England, Mrs David made up her mind to teach herself to cook, in order to reproduce for herself and her friends some of the delicious foods she had learned to appreciate in France. She found not only the practical side but also the literature of cookery of absorbing interest and has been studying it ever since. Mrs David has lived and kept house in France, Italy, Greece, Egypt and India, learning the local dishes and cooking them in her own kitchens. Her first book on *Mediterranean Food* appeared in 1950. In 1951 she published *French Country Cooking*, and in 1954, after a year of research in Italy, *Italian Food*, which became a Book Society recommendation. This was followed by *Summer Cooking* (1955), *French Provincial Cooking* (1960) and *Spices, Salt and Aromatics in the English Kitchen* (1970). All these books are published as Penguin Handbooks. In 1973 Mrs David severed all connection with the business trading under her name. Since then she has concentrated on study and experiment for *English Bread and Yeast Cookery*, for which she won the 1977 Glenfiddich Writer of the Year Award. In 1976 she was awarded the O.B.E.

Elizabeth David
English Bread and Yeast Cookery

With illustrations by Wendy Jones

Penguin Books

Penguin Books Ltd, Harmondsworth, Middlesex, England
Penguin Books, 625 Madison Avenue, New York, New York 10022, U.S.A.
Penguin Books Australia Ltd, Ringwood, Victoria, Australia
Penguin Books Canada Ltd, 2801 John Street, Markham, Ontario, Canada L3R 1B4
Penguin Books (N.Z.) Ltd, 182–190 Wairau Road, Auckland 10, New Zealand

—

First published by Allen Lane 1977
Published in Penguin Books 1979

—

—

Made and printed in Great Britain by
Richard Clay (The Chaucer Press) Ltd
Bungay, Suffolk
Set in Monotype Ehrhardt

TO JILL NORMAN, AFFECTIONATELY

Contents

xi · ACKNOWLEDGEMENTS

xv · LIST OF PLATES

xvii · INTRODUCTION

Part I: History and Background

3 · OUR BREAD GRAIN:
WHEAT, RYE, BARLEY, OATS AND PEASE

17 · MILLING:
The beginnings. The watermills and the windmills. Stone milling. Bolting the flour. Roller milling. Bleaching of flour. The millers and the Government Flour Order, 1953. The millers and the myth of the extraction rate. Have we a choice? What is choice and who makes it? Hand milling.

45 · BREAD FLOURS AND MEALS:
The structure and content of a grain of wheat. Buying flour for bread: stone-ground 100 per cent wholemeal or whole wheat-meal; wheatmeals with husk and bran removed; 'Farmhouse' bread flour; strong plain white bread flour; bakers' white bread flour; bakers' wheatmeal or brown flour; bakers' wholemeal or wholewheat flour; granary meal; household flour; American all-purpose unbleached flour; Graham meal and Graham flour; French bread flour; barley meal; rye meal; oatmeal; cornmeal or maize meal; cornflour or cornstarch; rice and rice flour; potatoes and potato flour; miscellaneous bread flours; buck-wheat and buckwheat flour; proprietary bread flours; bread mixes; self-raising flour; Vienna flour; patent flours; semolina

meals; bran in bread and in diet; wheat germ in bread and in diet; National flours.

89 · YEAST:

The yeast plant and its food. Yeast manufacture. Ale barms, brewers' yeasts and home-made yeasts. Using compressed or bakers' yeast. Yeast and the flavour of bread. Sugar and yeast. The yeast dies. Buying and storing yeast: to freeze compressed yeast; to test compressed yeast. Using dried granular yeast. Buying and storing dried yeast.

119 · SALT

125 · LIQUIDS AND FATS USED IN BREADMAKING:

Water. Milk. Buttermilk and sour milk. Cream. Butter. Lard. Oil. Vegetarian fats.

133 · EGGS, DRIED FRUIT, SUGAR, SPICES AND FLAVOURINGS USED IN YEAST CAKES AND BREADS:

Eggs. Dried fruit, spices and sugar. Sugar. Brown sugars. Molasses and black treacle. Golden syrup. Spices. Lemons. Flavouring essences.

153 · MALT EXTRACTS

155 · BREAD OVENS:

Brick ovens in use: the radiation of heat; judging the temperature; home baking in the eastern counties; the fuel; the fuel and the firing; the iron door . . . and the wooden door; the earthenware ovens of the West Country; a Cornish clay oven, and 'baking under'; the village bakeries: Sussex, Dorset, Essex – repairing the oven; the village bakery: a survival; pastry-cooking in the brick oven; taking dough to the baker's oven. The iron side-oven: the criticisms and the complaints; coal ranges: their slaves. Baking in gas and electric ovens.

191 · THE BREAD FACTORIES

197 · SHAPES AND NAMES OF ENGLISH LOAVES

206 · MOULDS AND TINS FOR BREAD AND YEAST CAKES:

Earthenware bread moulds and pots. Moulds and tins for yeast leavened cakes.

217 · STORAGE OF MEAL AND FLOUR

221 · STORAGE OF BREAD:
The freezing of bread

226 · WEIGHTS OF LOAVES AND THE ASSIZE OF BREAD

233 · WEIGHTS, MEASURES AND TEMPERATURES:
The conversion of British imperial weights and measures
(avoirdupois) into metric and vice versa; table of solid and
liquid measures. Linear measurements; table of linear measurements. The old dry measures for flour and grain; table of old
dry measures. Dough temperatures; table of dough temperatures. Oven temperatures; table of equivalent oven temperatures.

241 · WEIGHING AND MEASURING EQUIPMENT:
Scales and jugs. Measuring spoons. Thermometers.

246 · THE COST OF BAKING YOUR OWN BREAD:
Composition of flour used in breadmaking

Part II: Recipes

255 · BREAD

320 · BAPS AND ROLLS

329 · MANCHETS AND MAYN AND PAYNDEMAYN

341 · CRUMPETS AND MUFFINS

362 · NOTES ON FRENCH BREAD

384 · THE PIZZA AND THE PISSALADIÈRE

398 · QUICHES WITH YEAST DOUGH

403 · SAUSAGE IN BRIOCHE CRUST

407 · YEAST LEAVENED PANCAKES AND OATCAKES

418 · DUMPLINGS AND DOUGHNUTS

424 · REGIONAL AND FESTIVAL YEAST CAKES
AND FRUIT BREADS

473 · YEAST BUNS AND SMALL TEA CAKES

496 · FRENCH YEAST CAKES

515 · SODA BREADS

528 · BAKESTONE CAKES OR BREADS

540 · TOAST

549 · BIBLIOGRAPHY AND FURTHER READING LIST

557 · INDEX

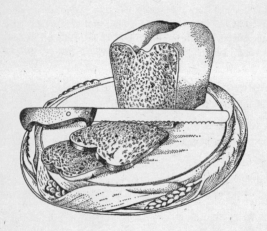

Acknowledgements

During the five years I have spent working on this book I have received much help from a great many people, and in very diverse ways. Librarians, museum officials, millers, bakers, have been generous with their time and extraordinarily patient and courteous in providing information. I'd like to thank them all.

In a category unique to herself my sister Felicité Gwynne of Sandoe Books in London has been the imaginative finder-and-provider-in-chief of books for study. Without her remarkable eye for the relevant book I might perhaps have finished writing my own sooner, but I certainly wouldn't have learned or enjoyed so much while I was doing it. I could say the same I think for my editor, Jill Norman. I have dedicated the book to her because she has nursed it along chapter by chapter and stage by stage, has supervised every aspect of its production, has certainly worked on it as hard and become almost as involved in its subject as I myself. Together we have visited mills and talked to millers, we have both tested many times all the bread flours and meals used for the recipes in this book; it has been a happy collaboration.

Three more friends I thank here for most understanding and constructive help are April Boyes who has accompanied me to museums and libraries all over London and a great deal further afield, and has enormously assisted me with my search for books, information and likely illustrations. As a trained librarian she has been able to track down books which I would have had great difficulty in locating. It's difficult to thank her enough. In Wales, Jean Bolland has done the same, driving me to mills, museums, libraries, bakeries, local markets – and as a bonus provided the cleaned-out old brick oven in her own house for me to try my hand at the ancient way of baking bread. Nothing could have been more instructive or more enjoyable or indeed more fruitful for this book than my visits – rather prolonged, some of them – to South West Wales.

On visits to France, Elizabeth Savage drove me hither and yon to talk to bakers, to find different kinds of bread flour, brioches, and related goods. Once we made a little pilgrimage to East Sussex to talk to kind Mrs Louie Mayer who was taught to make bread by Virginia Woolf. (It was on this particular drive, I think, that we passed a bakery – somewhere near Croydon?

– enticingly called The Crusty Loaf and sporting a big placard announcing 'oven fresh bread'. On getting out of the car to investigate we found the shop window crammed with wrapped, sliced loaves from the factory. That was in the early days of my work on this book. I was a bit surprised then by the display of cynicism. I wouldn't be now. I'd know that any shop with a name like that almost certainly belonged to one of the big bread factories.)

Among many other people who have given me special and much-needed help and information are Miss Rita Ensing, Chief Librarian at Kensington Public Library; Mr George Ort of the National Association of Master Bakers; Mr Lockyer of Clapton Mills, Crewkerne, Dorest; Mr Jordan of Holme Mills, Biggleswade, Bedfordshire; Mrs Lickley of White Mill, Carmarthen; Mr Denis Moore, M.A., of the City of London School; Mr J. Brown of B.F.P. Ltd; Mr N. W. Miller of Ruddle's Brewery, Rutland; Mrs Margaret Phillips, who undertook the tedious, necessary job of converting my quantities into metric equivalents (although for the table she used I take sole responsibility); Miss Jenny Skidmore, who got through the daunting task of typing my manuscript with speed and impeccable accuracy; and Wendy Jones, who spent so many hours in my kitchen (and a great many more in her own home) doing drawings of bread and buns and muffins, loaf tins, yeast cake moulds, bread crocks, griddles and bakestones. That brings me to two old friends, Mr Derek Hill and his cook and housekeeper Gracie McDermot. I am grateful to both of them for taking so much trouble to ensure that my Irish soda bread and Donegal oatcake recipes were given as Gracie has made them all her life in Donegal.

In France I've had – not for the first time – much good advice and assistance from a friend of long ago, Mr Bob Bucher, one-time owner of a favourite hotel at Duclair on the Seine, now a wine merchant in Rouen, and from his schoolmate, M. Rivière, now a miller and Master Baker at Honfleur.

I should add that although I have endeavoured to quote faithfully from all those whose help I have sought and who have so generously given it to me, responsibility for the interpretation I have put upon their words remains my own, and mine only.

Many years ago a reader, Mrs Caroline Simmonds of Littleover, Derby, wrote to me asking if I would be interested in seeing her family receipt book, dating back to about 1800. I would indeed. Mrs Simmonds then typed out the whole long manuscript for me, and has allowed me to quote several recipes from it. I thank her for her generosity and interest.

For the rest, I have drawn much counsel from books written by professional bakers for their colleagues in the trade. Among those I have quoted frequently are the splendid works of John Kirkland, Walter Banfield, William Jago, Frederick Vine and W. J. Fance. With the exception of Mr Fance's fine book, all are long out of print and considered outdated. To the bakery trade no doubt they are. To the household breadmaker they are still valuable.

Libraries with specialist collections on food technology are the places to look for them. Bibliographical details will be found in the list on p. 549.

Eliza Acton's very interesting *English Bread Book*, published in 1857, was directed at the domestic market at a time when household breadmaking was already in decline (I wonder if there was ever not such a time). It is not that Miss Acton is by any means the only domestic cookery writer upon whose work I have drawn – a number of much earlier works proved equally illuminating – it is just that among those I have quoted, Miss Acton's voice predominates. It is her sense of the vital detail which makes her work unique. That I owe her a particular debt is manifest in nearly every chapter of my book.

I could, but will not, go on for quite a while with lists of the books – diaries, memoirs, accounts of household life – sometimes well known, just as often obscure, which have given me insight into the history and the background of the whole vast, absorbing subject of bread and its baking. All are fully acknowledged in the text and nearly all are listed in the bibliography. I hope that they may prove as fascinating to new readers as they have been to me. To make an end, I'd like to say how grateful I am to the Windmill and Watermill Section of the Society for the Protection of Ancient Buildings, first for their very existence, and then for the sympathetic help I have received from the Section's officials and from its publications.

I didn't realize, when I embarked on a book about English bread, how largely our supplies of good flour for household breadmaking depend upon the survival of a few independent millers and their modest mills, some of them still using water power and French burr stones to grind their flour in the ancient way, bolting it in the old meal dressers which don't destroy its character and vitality. In this book I have mentioned a few such mills, and I am grateful that I am able to buy their products. The restoration of another watermill, Felin Geri near Newcastle Emlyn in South Wales, very properly earned an Architectural Heritage Award for its young owners. It gives me pleasure to record also that two East Sussex mills which for me have youthful memories and family associations have recently been restored to useful working lives, largely through local and voluntary effort. They are the handsome nineteenth-century tower windmill at Polegate and the much older little watermill at Michelham Priory, now in the keeping of the Sussex Archaeological Trust.

Elizabeth David
April 1977

For permission to reproduce recipes and other copyright material in this book I am indebted to the following authors and publishers:

From *Give Me Yesterday* by James Williams, to Gomer Press; *An Hour-Glass on the Run* by Alan Jobson, to Robert Hale; *Five Miles from Bunkum* by Christopher Ketteridge and Spike Mays, to Associated Book Publishers; *Corn Country* by C. Henry Warren, to Batsford; *The Isle of Wight Cookery Book* to the Isle of Wight Federation of Women's Institutes; *A History of English Ale and Beer* by H. A. Monckton, to The Bodley Head; *Home Baked* by George and Cecilia Scurfield, to Faber and Faber; *A London Home in the Nineties* by M. Vivian Hughes, to Oxford University Press; *Ask the Fellows who Cut the Hay* by George Ewart Evans, to Faber and Faber; *The Story of Bread* by R. Sheppard and E. Newton, to Routledge and Kegan Paul; *Good Appetite My Companion* by Victor MacClure, to the Hamlyn Publishing Group; *The Surrey Cookery Book* to the Surrey Federation of Women's Institutes; *Lakeland Cookery* to the Dalesman Publishing Company; *Northumbrian and Cumbrian Recipes* by Patricia Donaghy, to Oriel Press; *The Geordie Cookbook* by Peggy Howey, to Frank Graham; *Sussex Recipe Book* by M. K. Samuelson, to the Hamlyn Publishing Group; *A West Country Cookery Book* by Kathleen Thomas, to Wheaton; *Shropshire Cookery Book* to the Shropshire Federation of Women's Institutes; *Ryedale Recipes* to Pierson Smith Enterprises; *A London Girl of the Eighties* by M. Vivian Hughes, to Oxford University Press; *Breadmaking* by Edmund Bennion, to Oxford University Press; *Cornish Recipes Ancient and Modern* to the Cornwall Federation of Women's Institutes; *The Valley* by Elizabeth Clarke, to Faber and Faber; *Our Daily Bread* by Doris Grant, to Faber and Faber; *The Technology of Breadmaking* by William Jago and William C. Jago, to Turret Press; *Guernsey Dishes of Bygone Days* by J. Stevens Cox, to Toucan Press; *Chart of Composition of Flour Used in Breadmaking* to the Flour Advisory Bureau; *Recollections of Virginia Woolf* to Peter Owen; *Through Yorkshire's Kitchen Door* to the Yorkshire Federation of Women's Institutes; *The Housekeeping Book of Susanna Whatman*, ed. Thomas Balston, to Geoffrey Bles; *Up to Date Breadmaking* by W. H. Fance and B. H. Wragg and *Manna* by Walter Banfield, to Maclaren and Sons; *Buying Oatcakes in the Potteries* by Philip Oakes, to the *Sunday Times*.

List of Plates

1. Man crushing grain, Egypt, 2250 B.C.; reproduced by permission of the Trustees of the British Museum.

2. Grain crushing bowl, *c.* 3000 B.C., found in the Lebanon; reproduced by permission of J. Allan Cash.

3. Woman crushing grain, Rhodes, mid fifth century B.C.; reproduced by permission of the Trustees of the British Museum.

4 and 5. Two rotary querns; Jewry Wall Museum, Leicester.

6. Roman bakery at Pompeii, first century A.D.; Radio Times Hulton Picture Library.

7. A farmer's wife taking grain to the mill; misericord in Bristol Cathedral, 1520.

8. Watermill with eel traps; from the Luttrell Psalter, *c.* 1340; reproduced by permission of the British Library Board.

9. Floating mills; from *The Romance of Alexander*, fourteenth century (MS. Bodley 264); reproduced by permission of the Bodleian Library.

10. The watermill at Michelham Priory, Sussex.

11. Millwright dressing a French burr stone; from *Corn Country* by C. Henry Warren (Batsford).

12. Roman millstone found in Leicestershire; Jewry Wall Museum, Leicester.

13. Bakers at work; Egyptian tomb model, *c.* 1900 B.C.; reproduced by permission of the Trustees of the British Museum.

14. Portable earthenware bread oven from Dardanus, early fifth century B.C.; reproduced by permission of the Trustees of the British Museum.

15. Portable earthenware cooking bell, Athenian, 500–480 B.C.; American School of Classical Studies, Athens.

16. Fifteenth-century French baker and pastrycook at work; from *The Kalender and Compost of Shepherds*, Troyes, 1480.

17. The local baker, sixteenth-century misericord in the Church of Estouteville-Ecalles, Normandy; from *The Hidden World of Misericords* by Dorothy and Henry Kraus (George Braziller, New York, 1975; Michael Joseph, London, 1976).

18. Gravel-tempered clay wall oven found in a Glamorganshire farmhouse; the Welsh Folk Museum, St Fagans, Cardiff.

19. Terracotta bread oven from León, Spain. Photograph by Anthony Denney.

20. Gravel-tempered clay wall oven; Colonial National Historical Park, Jamestown, Virginia.

21. Cast iron pot used for baking bread; the Welsh Folk Museum, St Fagans, Cardiff.

22 and 23. Iron door and domed brick interior of oven built into the wall of a Carmarthenshire farmhouse; photographs by W. R. Peregrine, Cawdor Studio, Llandeilo, Dyfed.

24. Belling Classic fan oven.

Introduction

It's nearly four hundred years since a certain 'Ever Famous Thomas Muffett, Doctor in Physick,' wrote a treatise entitled *Health's Improvement* or *Rules Comprising and Discovering the Nature, Method and Manner of Preparing All Sorts of Foods Used in This Nation*. Ever famous? Ignorantly, I had never heard of Dr Muffett until, revising the final chapters of this book, I was loaned a copy of *Health's Improvement*.

Thomas Muffett, it turned out, was an eminent Elizabethan, a physician and writer on medical and scientific matters, something of a poet. Born in 1553, five years before the Queen's accession, his life span coincided with that of her long reign. Graduating from Caius College, Cambridge, Muffett became a successful practising doctor and eventually a Fellow of the College of Physicians. Working within the immediate circle of the Queen's ministers and friends, he attended notables such as Sir Francis Walsingham and Anne, Duchess of Somerset, widow of the Lord Protector, in 1591 went to Normandy as physician to the forces serving under the Earl of Essex, made friends with Sir Francis Drake (who showed him a dead flying fish, and bread made in Brazil from 'the root of a herb resembling purcelane'). Travelling in Italy, Spain and France, the Doctor studied the silkworm, subsequently relating his findings in a long poem *The Silkwormes and their Flies*, published in 1599. His learned work on the natural history of insects was, like *Health's Improvement*, published after his death.

In his later years, still under fifty, Dr Muffett was befriended by Mary Herbert, Countess of Pembroke, that same great and famous lady who was 'Sidney's sister, Pembroke's mother', and for a time he lived with the Herbert family at Wilton. Eventually the Earl of Pembroke granted him the nearby manor of Bulbridge where he lived until his death in June 1604, aged only fifty-one.

Half a century after Muffett's death a Dr Christopher Bennett, another member of the College of Physicians, took over from Muffett's family, probably from his daughter Patience, the unpublished manuscript of *Health's Improvement* (written, it is thought, about 1595), enlarged it, wrote a brief preface, and in 1655 had the book published by Samuel Thomson at the Sign of the White Horse in St Paul's Churchyard.

'Tis a Piece for my Palate', wrote Christopher Bennett in his Preface, 'not likely to disrelish any, where so much pleasure is interlarded with our profit. I may safely say, upon this subject I know none that hath done better.'

Thomas Muffett's work is a piece for my palate too. 'A gossipy collection of maxims concerning diet', says the *Dictionary of National Biography*. An odd verdict. Conversational would have been the more accurate description. What the Doctor did was to set down his opinions and observations – many of them are still not generally known – concerning the foods in common and not-so-common use in his day, describing their various properties and the manner in which they should be prepared. He is erudite and entertaining company (had he not been it is unlikely he would have attracted the cultured Herberts) and when it comes to his precepts concerning the 'Variety, Excellency, Making, and true use of Bread', his summary of the points he intends to enlarge upon tallies closely with the one I made when planning my own book. This is not particularly surprising. The essentials pertaining to bread were the same then as they are now. That is, they are the same for the bread we make at home. For commercial bread and baking many things would have to be added, both in the way of ingredients and of essential machinery. Indeed there wouldn't be much about the manufacture of bakery bread that Dr Muffett and his contemporaries would recognize, least of all perhaps the bread itself.

Here is that table of essentials as he saw them:

'Things to be observed in the well making of Bread – whereof we must have great choice and care:

1) of the Wheate itself	6) of the Dough or Past
2) of the Meal	7) of the Moulding
3) of the Water	8) of the Oven
4) of the Salt	9) of the Baking
5) of the Leaven	

'All which circumstances I most willingly prosecute to the full, because as Bread is the best nourishment of all other, being well made, so it is simply the worst being marred in the ill handling.'

Writing of a subject so ancient and so universal as the baking of bread it is hard for a modern author to find fresh words to express his views and his observations. Over and over again I have found that something I have been struggling for days to put on paper has been said long before, and in rather more graphic words than I could achieve. 'Wherefore do ye spend money for that which is not bread?' demands the Prophet Isaiah. I doubt if I could ever convey my feelings about shop bread quite so devastatingly. Of one of the particular pleasures of working with yeast Miss Alison Uttley has achieved almost the last word when she writes that when as a child she watched the dough rising it was 'like a lively white cushion, growing bigger and bigger'.[1] It would be hard to better that, and it would be even more difficult to improve on the words used by Thomas Muffett when he set out his maxims. From these, taking some liberties with the order of the text, I have made extracts which seem to me of more than antiquarian interest; they constitute a kind of A B C of bread-making, memorably and stirringly written. Small wonder. It is not to be forgotten that Thomas Muffett was the contemporary of Ben Jonson and Edmund Spenser, of Shakespeare, Raleigh, Sir Philip Sidney. Their English was also his. The food he wrote about was familiar to them. The bread he described was their daily bread as well as his. Given the circumstances of his life the likelihood is that he knew and conversed with them all.

From the choice of grain and the manner of its milling to the shaping of the dough into loaves and the way to cut them before consigning them to the oven, Dr Muffett deals in sequence with each of the points noted in his preliminary table. When it comes to the meal and flour he expresses the opinion, familiar today but unusual for his time, that bread made from a medium coarse meal containing a part of the bran – by no means all of it as is now advocated by the wholefood movement – was both easier to digest and more nutritious than the manchet bread, made from finely bolted almost white flour, eaten by the rich and privileged. At the same time he makes an odd distinction between 'the inmost crumbs of bread . . . most nourishing and fittest for hot and cholerick persons' and 'the crumbs next the crust . . . fittest for phlegmatic dispositions, . . . unto whom sometimes we allow the crust itself or else the crumb toasted before the fire'. Quite a bit of such lore, worked out on the principle of opposites, is scattered throughout

1. *Recipes from an Old Farmhouse*, 1966.

Health's Improvement. It was common at the time. In plenty of ways we are no less superstitious today.

One point of special interest is the Doctor's paragraph concerning leaven. Although ale yeast was commonly used in Elizabethan England, the Doctor gives instruction only on the use of a leaven to be made from wheat flour. Whether this was to be a spontaneous ferment or one aided by barm he does not say, stressing only that it must be of a proper ripeness, but not so ripe as to produce sour bread. Because of its tendency to turn sour a natural bread ferment or leaven was often used as a symbol of decay, something corrupt, and indeed Muffett refers to it as 'the mother and daughter of corruption, souring all if it be too much'. In another paragraph however he pronounces that 'unleavened Bread is good for no man', so he regarded the leaven as vital to good bread.

'Of the Variety, Excellency, Making, and true use of Bread

'*Concerning the Wheate* : . . . the sorts of this Country are especially two, the one red called *Robus* . . . and the other very white and light called *Siligo* whereof is made our purest manchet. Wheat nourisheth exceeding much and strongly: the hardest, thickest, heaviest, cleanest, brightest and growing in a fat soil, is ever to be chosen; for such wheat is most nourishing . . . Chuse ever the yellowest without, and smoothest . . . white and full within, clean thrasht and winowed, then clean washt and dryed, afterwards grossly grinded (for that makes the best flour) in a Mill wherein the grind-stones are of French Marble, or some other close or hard stone.

'*The Meal* must neither be so finely grinded (as I said) least the bran mingle with it, nor too grossly, least you lose much flour, but moderately gross, that the Bran may be easily separated, and the fine Flour not hardly boulted. You must not presently mould up your meal after grinding, lest it prove too hot; nor keep it too long lest it prove fusty and breed worms, or be otherwise tainted with long lying. Likewise though the best manchet be made of the finest flour passed through a very fine boulter, yet that Bread which is made of courser Meal is of lighter digestion and of stronger nourishment.

'*The Water* must be pure, from a clear River or Spring, not too hot . . . not too cold . . . but lukewarm.

'*The Salt* must be very white, finely beaten, not too much, nor too little, but to give an indifferent seasoning.

'*The Leaven* must be made of pure Wheate, it must not be too old least it prove too soure, nor too new least it work to no purpose . . .

When a just proportion is kept betwixt them both Leaven corrects the Meals imperfection, making all together a well rellished mass called Bread which is justly termed the staff of life . . . Loaves made of pure Wheaten-meal require both more leaven and more labouring, and more baking, than either course cheate,[1] or than Bread mingled of meal and grudgins.

'*The Dough* of White Bread must be thoroughly wrought, and *the manner of moulding* must be first with strong kneading, then with rouling to and fro, and last of all with wheeling or turning it round about, that it may sit the closer; afterwards cut it slightly in the midst round about, and give it a slit or two through from the top to the bottome with a small knife, to give a vent every way to the inward moisture whilst it is in baking.

'*The Loaves* should neither be too great nor too little: for as little loaves nourish least so if the loaves be too great the Bread is scarce thoroughly baked in the midst. Wherefore the Francklins Bread of England is counted most nourishing, being of a middle sise, between Gentlemens Roules or little Manchets, and the great loaves used in Yeomens houses.

'*The Oven* must be proportionable to the quantity of Bread, heated everywhere alike, and by degrees; not too hot at the first, lest the outside be burnt and the inside clammy; nor too cold, lest the Bread prove sad and heavy in our stomachs.

'Last of all *Concerning the baking*: it must not stay too long in the oven, least it prove crusty, dry and cholerique; not too little a while for fear it be clammy and of ill nourishment, fitter to cram Capons and Poultry, than to be given to sick or sound men.

'Bread being thus made strengtheneth the stomach and carries truly with it the staff of nourishment.

'In the Lords Prayer we ask for all bodily nourishment in the name of Bread because Bread may be justly called the meat of meats . . . Bread is never out of season, disagreeing with no sickness, age or complexion, and therefore truly called the companion of life.'

We know now of course that bread made from any flour containing gluten does disagree with the minority, and that coeliacs in particular

1. Cheate or chet bread was made from wheat flour dressed through a coarser bolting cloth than was used for manchet flour. It would have been the equivalent of our 85 per cent or 90 per cent wheatmeal bread. Grudgins or gurgeons were the coarsest particles of husk and bran.

must adhere to a gluten-free diet, so Dr Muffett's final words mustn't be taken too literally. What else is there to add to them? Nothing much, other than the reflection that if bread *is* to be a life companion, then we had best be choosey about it, or to use the Doctor's own earlier phrase, we should have great choice and care of the bread we eat; that is the essential concern of the book I have written.

Part I: History and Background

Our Bread Grain:

WHEAT, RYE, BARLEY, OATS AND PEASE

'Whereas one adviseth to sow this or that grain at one season, a second to set this or that at another, it must be conceived relatively, and every Nation must have its Country Farm; for herein we may observe a manifest and visible difference, not only in the seasons of the harvest, but in the grains themselves. For with us Barley-harvest is made after wheat-harvest, but with the Israelites and the Egyptians it was otherwise.'

Sir Thomas Browne (1605–82),
Of the Divisions of the Seasons and Four Quarters of the Year

'They now till wheat up to March, having the different sorts of seeds to suit – not like it was some thirty years ago when all must go into the ground at a particular time, merely two or three sorts. Now there is no end of the sorts, so that neither miller nor farmers can tell one from the other in grain, and not half of them in stalk.'[1]

Cecil Torr, *Small Talk at Wreyland*, Series II, 1921

It is estimated that in this country we eat – or at any rate we buy – 11 million large loaves per day. A large loaf weighs 28 oz. If I've done my arithmetic correctly that makes 19¼ million pounds of bread. For every ounce of it – a thin slice – an ounce of grain has been grown, harvested, transported (a large percentage of it from overseas) to the big mills, cleaned, dried, conditioned, ground into flour, treated, stored and finally delivered to the bakeries and the bread factories.

For every one of the 11 million 28 oz loaves we buy, 20 oz of flour have been used, and for each 20 oz of flour a farmer, somewhere, has produced grain from enough wheat to cover between 2 and 6 square yards of his land, just how much wheat can be grown per acre depending upon conditions, methods of farming, climate, variety of wheat.

How did the cultivation of wheat first come into being? How did it

1. This extract was written by Cecil Torr's grandfather on 24 December 1848.

swell into an industry so vast that today world production, so it is estimated, is in the region of 350 million tons annually, only 4 of those
millions being our own share? How did our annual wheat consumption
grow, allowing for animal food and seed, to 8 million tons, and how on

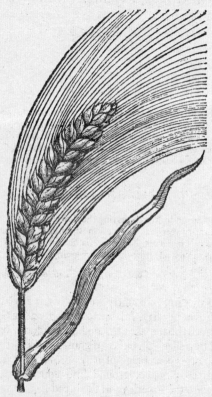

Bright wheat. 'This kind of wheate is the most principall of all other, whose eares are
altogether bare or naked, without awnes or chaffie beard.' *Gerard's Herbal*, 1597.

earth does each of us account every year for 200lb of grain or 150lb of
white flour? And if those figures sound unlikely, they represent a considerable decline over the past eighty years or so. In the early years of
this century bread consumption was an average of 1lb per head per
day, representing something like 240lb of flour which in turn means

6 bushels (360lb) of grain per head per annum for bread alone, not counting cakes, biscuits and other flour confectionery, home-baked and commercial.

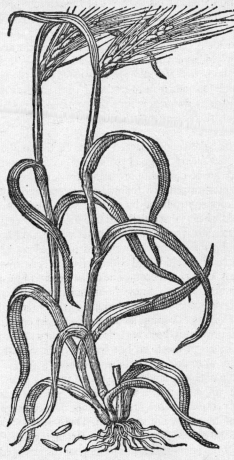

Naked barley. 'Like to that which is called French Barley,' Gerard says, 'and also like to *Zea*, otherwise called *Spelta*.' *Gerard's Herbal*.

The traditional demand for white bread is very easily understood when it is remembered that until the end of the eighteenth century wheat was by no means the common English bread corn. In areas where wheat was plentiful the bread was probably good, sweet and, once the art of bolting or sifting out the bran had been mastered, even comparatively light; but in the north and the Midlands, oats, rye or the mixed crop of rye and wheat called maslin or monkcorn were the staple cereals of the rural population. In bad harvest years even maslin was too scarce and expensive, and the poor made do with a substitute bread of peasemeal or ground beans. 'If the world last a while after this rate', wrote the Tudor parson William Harrison in his *Description of England* (1577), 'wheate and rie will be no graine for poor man to feed on.' In the West Country and parts of Wales barley was at this time the common bread cereal. Sustaining and nutritious these breads no doubt were. They were also dark, coarse, heavy and dry.

It was not that the country lacked wheat. In the southern half of England there was plenty. In good years we exported grain to Europe, but for the majority of our own population it was too expensive. Only in the mid eighteenth century, following the great agricultural innovations and reforms introduced by such men as Coke of Norfolk and Jethro Tull, did wheat substantially replace the rye, barley and oats of the past. Vast new areas were now put under wheat. On his own lands in West Norfolk, for centuries considered unsuited to wheat, Coke showed that it could be cultivated with perfect success; by the end of the century East Anglia had become one of the richest wheat-producing areas in the country. 'Such was now the artificial improvement of land', writes G. M. Trevelyan,[1] 'that in the course of the eighteenth century, Englishmen of all classes became so dainty as to insist on refined wheat bread that had previously been regarded as a luxury of the rich. This new demand began in the town but spread to the country, even to paupers.' There were growing numbers of those paupers. Following enclosure of the common lands many agricultural families, who now had no strip of land of their own to cultivate, no place to graze a cow or even to keep a pig, no free fuel, and little hope of regular employment, were thrown on the bounty of the parish. There wasn't much of it. If enclosing the land made for more efficient farming, greater yields and more profits for the landowners, it left the poor dispossessed, poverty-stricken and bitter.

By the end of the eighteenth century our population had grown to

1. *Illustrated English Social History* (Volume 3), Longmans Green 1949–52; Penguin Books, 1964.

such proportions – it had doubled during the course of a century – that even the greatly increased grain production was inadequate for our needs. Our traditional exports of wheat ceased. We became an importing country. As will presently be explained, the wheat and the flour we imported did much to influence our future taste in bread.

*

Thomas Traherne, in his *Centuries of Meditations*, wrote that when a child it seemed to him that 'the corn was orient and immortal wheat, which never should be reaped nor was ever sown. I thought it had stood from everlasting to everlasting'. Magical and mysterious words, as the golden corn was magical and mysterious to Traherne. The origin of wheat still seems almost mysterious. We know that it was from somewhere in western Asia that our grain cereals came to Europe. How or when we scarcely know even today. Perhaps it was as long ago as 8,000 years. To Britain it came rather later.

Grain was first cultivated when man started to settle in one place in order to ensure the continuity of his food. It was the beginning of community life, the first step towards our civilization. In a dramatic article published in the *Journal de Genève* during the last war,[1] Professor Eugène Pittard stressed the almost inconceivable change which this represented:

'From being a hunter, man became a farmer and a shepherd. He moved from the nomad state to that of the settler . . .

'The greatest, the most significant of all days in history are about to be recorded in the annals of Europe (as they were sooner or later in the rest of the world). No social revolution – on whatever conceivable scale – can be compared with that about to take place. Somewhere, in Asia Minor, men still those of pre-history have begun to domesticate animals; they have selected among wild plants those which were to become our grain cereals: wheat, barley, millet. They have started to cultivate them in order to ensure their continuance . . . They are therefore the instigators of the most momentous development in all History . . . Again, no social change, either in time or in space, can be compared to this one.'

Botanically, bread wheat, *Triticum vulgare*, probably derived from the accidental crossing of two varieties of wild grass. Even this is supposition, no single wild ancestor of wheat having yet been discovered. All

1. June, 1944.

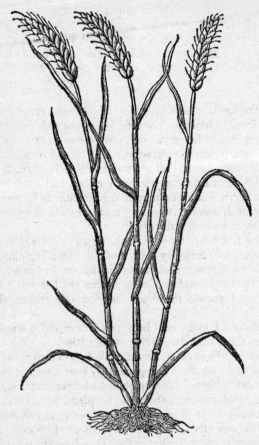

Starch corn. Another variety of spelt, one of the early cereals of southern Europe. As its name implies it was also grown specifically to make starch. (Think of all those Tudor and Jacobean ruffs.) The original Italian pasta, recorded in the sixth century, is said to have been make from spelt meal. *Gerard's Herbal.*

we know is that thousands of years ago, in those pre-history days, wheat, barley and millet had already been singled out as the most reliable cereals for cultivation and for storage throughout the winter. All three became important crops to the Egyptians – as we know, they were skilled brewers and bakers – and in the Mediterranean world wheat exported from Alexandria was much prized for the good bread it made. It is thought to have been this variety, later known to us as emmer wheat, which was the ancestor of our European grain. From Kurdistan its progress has been traced via Asia Minor to Egypt, thence northward and westward to south-eastern and central Europe, north again to Scandinavia and westward to Britain. Here it arrived during the Neolithic or New Stone Age, about 3400 B.C. Galloping through the centuries – some thirty of them – past the Bronze Age and its revolutionary metal farm implements, and on to the Iron Age of approximately 500 B.C., the famous lake villages of Meare and Glastonbury in Somerset yielded identifiable grains and much evidence of agricultural activity. Those strange and ingenious men of the lakes must have cultivated their grain up on the ancient hills above their settlements in the watery lowlands. They grew barley, oats, beans, as well as wheat. When the conquering Romans came the foundations of an agricultural Britain were well established. During the four centuries of their occupation the island became, as every schoolchild learns, one of the great granaries of the Roman Empire. After they left, the invaders from the north largely destroyed Britain's agriculture. The rye which subsequently became the main cereal crop of large areas of the country was introduced later by the Saxon and Scandinavian conquerors who came from areas where rye had already for centuries been the predominating bread grain.

From the early three or four forms of wheat – emmer was succeeded in Britain and much of Europe by club wheat or *Triticum compactum* – the world has now developed some 30,000 variations. Very broadly speaking they fall into four main categories. Into the first two come spring wheat, sown in the spring and cut in the autumn of the same year, and winter wheat, sown in the late autumn and harvested early in the following autumn. Traditionally, it was the long-maturing winter wheat which was the more highly prized. When modern methods of farming were beginning to develop it was realized that spring wheat was potentially just as valuable. Much depends upon the climate. In Canada, for example, the famous Manitoba wheat upon which we now rely so largely for our bread is all spring-sown. In the short, hot summer the grain matures and ripens quickly, whereas the long, icy winter and frozen soil would be altogether too extreme for wheat. Here, in our damp, mild climate, the farmer can cultivate both spring and winter wheat; he can sow winter wheat from September to February, his spring wheat in March and April. Early August to mid-September is harvest time.

The second main distinction to be made between wheats concerns the pigmentation of the bran coatings of the berry or grain. With some exceptions, red, amber and yellow wheats – such as the durum variety grown mainly for pasta-making – are high in the gluten-forming protein which gives dough its maximum elasticity and expansion, producing the nice big handsome loaves to which we first became accustomed towards the end of the eighteenth century when we started importing American wheat and flour. White-skinned varieties of wheat are predominantly soft, or low in protein, yielding flour now considered more suitable for biscuits, cakes, and household baking generally than for bread. Most of our home-grown wheat comes from these strains. In our climate, the hard wheats don't flourish, such red wheats as we do grow being of medium strength. One of them, planted in western Canada in the 1840s by a Scottish pioneer farmer called David Fife, became famous as Red Fife. In its turn Red Fife was one of the ancestors of Marquis, a highly productive strain first evolved in the 1800s by Doctor A. P. Saunders. It was Marquis which eventually earned for Canada her position as the granary of the British Empire.

In Britain between the wars, in an effort to help the farmers and make the country more self-sufficient in bread wheat, a variety called Yeoman was much boosted as yielding a good all-round flour, suitable for bread.[1] Similar efforts are again being made. Yield and resistance to disease are the most important factors in the strains being tried out.

Wheat was taken to North America by the early settlers and colonists. As we know, it flourished beyond anyone's wildest hopes. When in the last decades of the eighteenth century it became vital for us to import rather than export flour and wheat, it was mainly to America that we then turned – although Russia and central Europe also sold us a certain amount – and it was flour from American wheat which seems to have set the millers and the bakers on the way to that preoccupation with 'strong' flour and the volume of a loaf which has now become almost an obsession. It is not, of course, merely a question of looks. It is primarily one of yield and value for money. As long ago as 1806 a domestic cookery writer, Mrs Rundell, was recommending her readers to buy American flour, because it 'requires almost twice as much water to make it into bread as is usual for English flour, and therefore it is more profitable: for a stone (14lb) of the American will make 21½lb of bread; but the

1. See National Flours, p. 82.

best sort of English flour produces only 18½lb'.[1] An extra 3lb of bread for every 14lb of flour was – and is – quite a consideration. Some of the modern wheats we are now importing from Canada, our main source of supply for hard wheat, give a much higher yield than those of the nineteenth century, and when calculated in bulk quantity, the difference in yield between a sack (280lb) of flour from high- as compared with low-protein wheats is important. The performance of fermented dough made from a strong flour is also altogether more satisfactory than that of dough made from a soft flour. Then, of course, there's all that lovely water that the customers pay for. Given all the circumstances, the millers and the bakers are scarcely to be blamed for their preference for imported strong wheat, though even at its best it doesn't make such sweet-eating bread as does our own home-grown grain. It is undeniable that, on the whole, the soft wheats have the best flavour. Much depends, though, upon the proportions of different wheats used by the miller in his grist, on the way the flour is treated, and on the way your dough is made. The various high-gluten flours packed for the retail trade certainly do help to make household breadmaking easy. What is utterly dismaying is the mess our milling and baking concerns succeed in making with the dearly bought grain that goes into their grist. Quite simply it is wasted on a nation which cares so little about the quality of its bread that it has allowed itself to be mesmerized into buying the equivalent of eight and a quarter million large white factory-made loaves every day of the year.

It is not my intention now to go any deeper into the melancholy question of our commercial bread, of what the millers do to our wheat and the bakers to our flour. All this is discussed in other chapters. What I propose to do here is to quote the observations of one of our greatest naturalists, Gilbert White of Selborne, on a year's grain-growing in Hampshire in the eighteenth century; with their echoes of Shakespeare's 'rich leas of wheat, rye, barley, vetches, oats and pease',[2] these notes evoke a picture most essentially and intensely English. Gilbert White, author of the famous *Natural History of Selborne*, one of that wonderful breed of country parsons who have enriched our literature with their diaries and their meticulous records – William Harrison of Essex, from whom we learn so much of Tudor England, was another – kept his journals for nearly a quarter of a century, from 1768 to 1793. He noticed and noted everything going on around him. Such details as the exact 'delicate soft tinge of green rye', 'the millers complain for

1. *A New System of Domestic Cookery.* 2. *The Tempest,* iv. 1. 60.

want of water', and again 'the water is so scanty in the streams that the millers cannot grind barley for mens hogs', 'Farmer Knight's wheat of a beautiful colour', 'oats and barley ripe before wheat', 'boys bring wood-strawberries: not ripe', 'the poor begin to glean wheat', recur year after year. Yet every entry still tells us something, every change in the weather is significant. Read in sequence, each year's journal becomes a saga of suspense.

Here is what happened to the wheat, rye, barley, oats and pease as observed by Gilbert White in this corner of southern England in the year 1768, a year, it would seem, of more than usually capricious English weather:

'Jan 12   Wheat, being secured by the snow, looks finely.

'Feb 23   Great rain. Prodigious floods in Yorkshire.

'Feb 28   Wet continues still: has lasted three weeks this day.

'March 7–8 The ground and paths drie very fast. Wheat is fed down by sheep. Beans are planted in yᵉ fields. Pease sown.

'June 17   Wheat that was lodged [beaten down] rises again.

'June 29   The ears of wheat in general are very long.

'July 6–7   No sun for several days. Bad time for corn.

'July 18   The country is drenched with wet, and quantities of hay were spoiled.

'Aug 1   Rock-like clouds. Oats and pease are cutting.

'Aug 11   Wheat harvest is pretty general. The male and female flying ants, leaving their nests, fill the air.

'Aug 13   Sweet harvest weather.

'Aug 19   White wheat begins to grow. Plums ripe.

'Aug 24   Much wheat bound up in the afternoon. Goldfinch sings. Oats are cutting.

'Aug 26   White dew. Peaches ripen. Barley begins to be cut. Much wheat housed.

'Sep 3   Much wheat still abroad. Hop-picking becomes general: there is a vast crop.

'Sep 7   First blanched endive. Some wheat standing still.

'Sep 17   Wheat still abroad. The fields are drenched with rains and almost all the spring corn is abroad. Sheep die.

'Sep 19   First blanched Celeri. Wheat still abroad: oats and barley much grown.

'Sep 24   Much wheat still out, and spoiled. Much barley and oats spoiled.

'Sep 27   People are now housing corn after 27 days interruption.

'Oct 1   Harvest pretty well finished this evening. Some wheat out at Harting.[1]

'Oct 28   Some wheat is now sowing.

'Nov 13   Wheat continues to be sown. Elms are still in full leaf.

'Nov 23   The ground in a sad drowned condition. The low fallows can never be sowed.

'Dec 2   Thunder and hail. Incredible quantities of rain have fallen this week.

'Dec 9   Wells run over at the bottom of the village.

'Dec 10   Paths get firm and dry. People sow wheat again briskly.

'Dec 15   Wheat comes up well.

'Dec 27   Weather more like April than ye end of December.

'Dec 31   A wet season began about 9th of June, which lasted thro' haymaking, harvest and seed-time, and did infinite mischief to the country.'

Gilbert White's Journals, ed. Walter Johnson,
Routledge & Kegan Paul, 1931; reprinted by David & Charles, 1970

A point arises now. The ancient rituals of ploughing and sowing and reaping, the gruelling work at harvest time, the thanksgivings and feasting when the corn was safely gathered in, the allusions to the white wheat and the red wheat, to the millstreams running dry so that no grain could be ground, the tales of dishonest millers, the portrayals of the poor humble gleaners bent double over their task of scratching the few last ears of wheat from the cornfields after the landlord's grain had been harvested – all these are more or less familiar to us through the works of our poets and writers. From William Langland to Shakespeare, from Chaucer to John Bunyan (whose grandfather Thomas Bonyon was a baker at Elstow in Bedfordshire), from the Jacobean translators of the Bible to the eighteenth-century Parson Woodforde, all and scores more, travellers, diarists, chroniclers of the farming scene, have in some way recorded the years' cycle of growing and harvesting. Curiously, though, none of them has much to say about how, once the farmer had threshed his grain, he conveyed it to the mill to be ground into flour.

The story of milling is told, in so far as I am able to tell it, in the next chapter. Some part of it, though, belongs here; that part of it which concerns the farmer who had wheat for sale rather than simply for his

---

1. Just over the Hampshire–West Sussex border. One of Gilbert White's married sisters lived there, and he owned land in the neighbourhood.

own subsistence. How much access had such farmers to the markets and the mills? The question was a vital one. Road transport was precarious, expensive and very slow. Until the establishment of the canal system in the eighteenth century opened up internal communications, it might be said almost that the mills came to the farmer rather than the other way about. Once the feudal and ecclesiastical landlords had lost the manorial rights which included the milling of all the grain grown on their lands, independent mills proliferated. In grain country there was at least one in every village, often more. The grain rarely had to be carried farther than a short horseback ride. The mills weren't only in the countryside. Every town situated on a river had its quota of watermills. Wherever a river was navigable grain could be brought in by water, and it was in such towns that the chief cornmarkets of the country came into being. In London, Queenhithe and Billingsgate were the ancient ports for the landing of grain. Bakers and merchants who bought their corn at Queenhithe could get it transported as far as Newgate, Fleet Bridge or Cripplegate for a charge of one penny. No doubt if they so wished they could also get it ground in the vicinity, for the Thames was always well supplied with mills, both wind and water driven. In the thirteenth century, for example, there were tide-operated floating mills on the river, and in the sixteenth century there was a great complex of granaries, bread ovens and watermills at London Bridge, the granaries and ovens being on the Bridge, the mills – according to Stow[1] – moored under 'the two Arches, next London'. The Bridge-house, as this establishment came to be known, belonged to the City of London, and for a time became the centre of its corn administration. Eventually mills, granaries and ovens were all destroyed in the Great Fire of 1666.

Many market towns were ringed with windmills. In the early years of the seventeenth century London had at least ten (just as Paris had windmills on the surrounding fortifications and on the heights of Montmartre), some in outlying districts such as Mary-le-Bone to the west and Camberwell to the south, others close to the confines of the city at Walbrook, and one at Southwark, not far from Shakespeare's Globe Theatre. Also on the south bank of the Thames were two between Battersea and Vauxhall and one opposite the Strand.

These mills were essential to the towns. To a certain extent – and provided that the rats could be kept at bay – grain could be stored in the ear.

1. John Stow, *Survey of London,* 1598; ed. John Strype 1720, Vol. I, pp. 62–3 and Vol. II, pp. 24 and 465.

Ground flour couldn't. Because of the oil contained in the germ – and no doubt many impurities due to imperfect cleaning of the wheat – ground meal tended to turn rancid in a relatively short time. It was also subject to the ravages of weevils and mites, and, like grain, of mice and rats. The only solution was to grind the grain at frequent intervals. In times of war and of the internal strife which raged in this country throughout the Middle Ages, the maintenance of a supply of flour for bread was vital to the warring barons and their armies.

At the time when the old mills were disappearing fast, an Edwardian naturalist – another in that line of English writers of which there can never be enough – put the whole matter in a way which brings home just what the situation, and the continuity, of the mills meant:

'The old town and city mills often survived longer than the country ones, and those on the Thames longer than those on smaller rivers. The corn and barley which was taken to market in the town was easily transferred to the town mill, and thence by water to the place of consumption . . .

'Some of these [Oxford] mills were standing long before abbeys or colleges were founded, and were part of their endowments. They are the oldest link between London life and country life left in Oxford, or indeed in England. For a thousand years the corn grown on the hills beyond the Thames meadows has been drawn to their doors. Saxon churls dragged wheat there on sledges, Danes rowed up the river to Oseney and stole the flour when they sacked the abbey, Norman bishops stole the mills themselves . . .

'The Knights Templars had a mill at Cowley, and the King himself one on the Cherwell, which was given to the Hospital of St John, who swapped it with Merton. Later on these mills helped King Charles' army vastly, for all the flour needed for the Oxford garrison was ground inside or close to the walls.'

W. J. Cornish, *The Naturalist on the Thames*, 1902

It was the partnership of a colliery-owning nobleman, Francis Egerton, third Duke of Bridgewater, and James Brindley, an apprentice mill-wright turned engineer, which was responsible for the building of the canals which were to revolutionize our inland transport. Bridgewater provided the capital, Brindley, who never learned to write or make drawings, turned out to be an engineer of astonishing genius and vision.

Conceived originally as a means of linking up the Duke's Yorkshire colliery at Worsley with Manchester and then Liverpool, the first great canal was built during the 1760s and completed in 1772. The Grand Junction Canal, linking the rivers Mersey and Trent, followed in the 1770s. By the end of the century the network of new canals had changed both the nature of our commerce and the aspect of the country. Barges laden with grain had become as familiar a sight on the inland waterways as the coal barges. Thomas Pennant, a naturalist friend of Gilbert White's and another observer of the agricultural scene, thought the opening up of internal communications between Liverpool, Bristol and Hull even more significant from the point of view of grain distribution than from that of coal 'for cheap transport prevents the monopolisers of corn from exercising their infamous trade and the line of canal being through countries abundant in grain it affords a conveyance of corn unknown in past ages'.[1]

Unhurried canal transport certainly was. It was also cheap. So for that matter was sea transport. In the 1920s, when the railways had largely superseded the canals as a means of internal freight haulage, it was cheaper for American farmers to send wheat 700 miles from St Louis to the port of New Orleans and thence across the Atlantic to Britain than it was for an English farmer to send his wheat by rail freight across three counties from Somerset to London, a distance of about 200 miles.[2]

Neither distance nor speed were very relevant considerations when it came to the carrying of grain. As recently as the 1930s wheat was arriving here in the great four-masted barques taking part in the annual race to bring Australian grain to British ports. Seeing those ships in all their splendour of sail coming up the Channel was one of the sights of the time. So potent was the glamour of the ships that we didn't give much thought to their cargoes, accepting it as normal that wheat should be shipped here in so archaic a manner. The true reason was that although the loading of a cargo of 4,000 tons of wheat in the Australian ports often took as long as six weeks and the passage to England four months, the ships were manned by low-paid crews, many of them amateurs doing the voyage for the sailing experience, and so economically run that the owners, the farmers, the grain dealers and all concerned could still make a good profit on the deal. The final grain race from Australia to Britain took place in 1939, the great ships reaching port towards the end of that last summer of peace.

1. *Tours in Wales, 1778–81,* 1782. 2. R. Moelwyn-Hughes, *Cheap Bread,* 1930.

Milling

THE BEGINNINGS

'It is important to realise that whenever one reads of a mill in the Old Testament or in Homer one must picture a saddle quern . . . for no other type was then known.'

Dr E. Cecil Curwen, 'Querns', *Antiquity*, June 1937

Early man didn't mill grain. He crushed or bruised it, using a pounding stone on a slab, sometimes fixed, sometimes portable, and with a natural or water-worn hollow. Gradually, with use, the base or bedstone wore down until the hollow became cup-shaped. The rounded pounding stone was now no longer practical, so a cone or pear-shaped pounder was evolved. This was the first mortar and pestle. The meal obtained by the early methods can scarcely in any sense have been meal as we know it. Hard, unwashed grain, often mixed with acorns, beech mast and chestnuts, it would have contained grit, chips from the grinding stones and the coarse outside husk barely broken up. Nobody had yet thought of sifting the crushed meal. Teeth in the skulls of Stone Age men show signs of the wear and the damage caused by the primitive bread baked from stone-crushed grain.

After the pounding stone and mortar came the saddle quern (Plate 1). This has been called the first grinding device, but was in reality still more of a crusher, although a better one than the stone and mortar. It consisted of a broad, curved under stone and an elongated upper stone, more like a modern rolling pin than a pounder; this was dragged and pushed backwards and forwards on the grinding surface, which sloped at an angle of about twenty degrees, so that in order to operate the grindstone, it was necessary to kneel behind the millstone and lean over it, exercising a great deal of shoulder and elbow power. In ancient Egypt this task was performed by slave women, hence the allusion in Exodus, otherwise difficult to understand, to the 'maidservant that is behind the mill'. As for our childhood images – and for that matter those of Cecil B. de Mille – of blind Samson toiling round and round the treadmill, they are, says Dr Curwen (quoted above), about as realistic as the notion of King Alfred burning cakes in a gas oven. It was the work of a slave girl labouring at the saddle quern which Samson was made to do when the Philistines consigned him to grind grain in the prison-house.

At what date the next step in the evolution of milling took place is not known, although it is certain that between 100 and 50 B.C. rotary millstones or querns were in general use in Britain (Plates 4 and 5). These, the remote ancestors of today's surviving stone mills, were small and of such limited capacity that it seems likely that every dwelling needed its own quern. All over the country, archaeologists have brought quantities of querns to light. At the Iron Age site of Hunsbury in Northamptonshire alone no fewer than one hundred and fifty were discovered. Consisting of two round granitic or lava stones varying from 15 to 20 inches in diameter, from 6 to 8 inches thick, and looking sometimes rather like a small beehive, sometimes more like two roughly made, misshapen cheeses standing one upon another, the Iron Age querns in fact represented an immense, a gigantic, improvement in the working of stones and the grinding of grain, for the upper stone was ingeniously hollowed on the underside to fit the equally well fashioned convex grinding surface of the lower. From a socket in a central hollow in the base stone projected a spindle which passed through the centre of the top stone. The central hole was made some 3 inches in diameter, large enough for the grain to be fed through as the millstones were turned. The wooden handle to turn the mill was fixed through a hole or groove at the side of the stone, or sometimes, if the top of the stone was flat, in its upper surface. The Iron Age rotary mills had horizontal handles. Later versions, probably introduced by the Romans, had handles fixed vertically to the stones. Although these must have been easier to work, meal grinding was still a very slow and laborious process. As anyone sufficiently interested can see for themselves by visiting the Jewry Wall Museum in Leicester or the Barbican House Museum in Lewes, where reconstructed querns can be worked by visitors, only a small amount of grain could be fed in at one time, and in the absence of any channel or gutter into which the ground meal could fall, every scrap had to be scooped by hand from the surrounding surface. In this respect, the later Saxon and medieval pot querns, in which the upper stone revolved inside a hollow cylindrical stone so that the ground meal collected in the bottom, seems to have been more practical. Yet in spite of the apparent clumsiness of the primitive querns, similar devices remained in use for home-milling long after the establishment of the manorial watermills and windmills, and, in isolated areas such as the Hebrides and the Shetland Islands, were used and even being made as recently as the early years of this century. Indeed there seems to be no reason why so useful a piece of equipment as a hand mill of some kind for the home-milling of grain on a small scale should ever entirely die out.

THE WATERMILLS AND THE WINDMILLS

'The sound of water escaping from mill-dams, etc., old rotten planks, slimy posts, and brickwork – I love such things . . . those scenes made me a painter, and I am grateful . . .'

John Constable in a letter to Archdeacon Fisher, 23 October 1821[1]

'The rush of water, and the booming of the mill, bring a dreamy deafness, which seems to heighten the peacefulness of the scene. They are like a great curtain of sound, shutting one out from the world beyond. And now there is the thunder of the huge covered wagon coming home with sacks of grain.'

George Eliot, *The Mill on the Floss*, 1860

The water wheel came to us from Rome via Greece and Asia Minor. In the earliest water-powered mills the wheel was laid horizontally in the water, the vertical shaft pivoting on a stone set in the bed of the stream. The hurst, or framework supporting the millstones, was built over the water, the wheel and grinding stone revolving at the same speed. From these mills the Romans evolved the vertically set water wheel with its gearing system much as we know it today. Surprisingly, since we know for certain that the Romans installed water-powered corn mills in their colonies – notably in southern France – it is only in very recent years that evidence of Roman watermills left behind in Britain has come to light (the sites of two mills in the vicinity of Hadrian's Wall are now believed to be almost certainly of Roman origin), and we can only surmise that the barbarian invaders who followed the Romans, and who regarded the harnessing of the forces of nature to man's use with superstitious terror, systematically destroyed all the mills they found. At some stage between these invasions and the arrival of the Normans, the principle of the water-powered mill was rediscovered, and its potential

1. *John Constable's Correspondence*, ed. R. B. Beckett, 1962.

appreciated. By the time of the Domesday survey of 1086 there were nearly 6,000 recorded watermills serving 3,000 communities south of the Severn and the Trent.

Windmills are not recorded until over a century later. Curiously, their origins have never been determined with any certainty, the theory favoured by modern historians being that the idea evolved as a natural

A Seistan windmill of the tenth century. From *The Cosmography of Dimashqi, c.* 1300, reproduced in Rex Wailes's *Horizontal Windmills.*

progression from the watermill, some alternative to water power having been found essential for times of drought or of extreme cold, when the rivers either dried up or froze and there were no means of driving the millstones. Another possible source of origin of the windmill, as of the oldest known watermills, is the Middle East, in this case Seistan in eastern Persia. In this region the wind blows incessantly during nine months of the year and always from the same quarter. The inhabitants of Seistan, it was noted by the tenth-century Baghdad geographer al Ma'asud, were extraordinarily adept at utilizing wind power. The windmills they had built appear to be the earliest known to us. They worked on the principle, very different from the one subsequently evolved in Europe, of vanes set horizontally atop a vertical shaft enclosed in the mill tower, the wind reaching them through long vertical openings diagonally set in the enclosing structure.

According to Rex Wailes, the great windmill expert, the stones in the Seistan mills were in an upper storey and the vanes or sails below. The whole works were enclosed in shield walls so that the wind entered only from one side. Mr Wailes thinks that in effect these mills were little more than wind-driven versions of the old hand querns.[1]

Information about the Persian windmills, so the theory goes, began to filter through to northern Europe via twelfth-century Eastern trade with the Baltic, thence to Holland and to Britain, in which two countries the first windmills began to appear almost simultaneously towards the end of the century. The likelihood of the Persian windmill having been adapted by European engineers, just as the Persian watermill had been adapted by the Romans, is however no more than a theory favoured by some authorities, discounted by others, who maintain that the European windmill was almost certainly an independent invention of the Gothic North.[2]

No sooner were windmills established – the invention was seized upon by the lords of the manorial lands and by the church – than they seem to have become an integral part of the landscape and of our agricultural country, so much so that even now, when they have long outlived their function, it is difficult to visualize a time when they were not there. Certainly they captivated the imagination of our earlier artists far more than did the watermills.

By the fourteenth century the windmill had begun to feature with extraordinary frequency in illuminated manuscripts, books of hours, psalters, and even in the stone and wood carvings decorating country churches (Plate 7). No harvest scene or pictorial chronicle of country life was complete without the farmer on his way to the windmill, his sack of grain slung across the back of his horse. Even today the windmill remains a symbol, instant and basic, recognizable by every child,

1. Rex Wailes, *Horizontal Windmills*, 1968.
2. John Reynolds, *Windmills and Watermills*, 2nd edn, 1974.

and there are flour-milling businesses which still use it on their packaging, however inappropriate it may be to the contents; it is an easy one to portray, even if the crudely drawn conical tower and four sails in no way represent a working construction. For that matter how many artists did get the details right, or show the sails set so that they would actually turn? 'When I look at a mill painted by John', said Abram Constable after his brother's death, 'I see that it will *go round* which is not always the case with those by other artists.' This of course was because John Constable had had youthful training in his father's mills, both wind- and water-driven, before he came to the decision that he must paint rather than enter the family business. Nobody, therefore, knew better than he that although the windmill looks like a simple construction it is in reality of some complexity. The miller's trade involved long hours and a craftsman's experience and skill. He, or the manager who supervised the running of the mill, needed to be conversant with a great deal more than just the basic mechanical workings of his gear. He had to judge the quality of the grain he bought or was required to grind, supervise its storage and cleaning and watch over every stage of its grinding and dressing. He was required also to be something of a meteorologist, forever watching the sky like the look-out man on a ship, interpreting the local weather portents, setting his sails accordingly. Lacking understanding of the movement of clouds and air currents his mill would not operate to the best advantage, nor with safety. A freak squall, for example, might drive the sails round too fast, the millstones inadvertently left unfed with grain would overheat, the friction would strike sparks as they revolved and in no time the wooden structure of the mill would be on fire. Many a windmill was destroyed by some such accident. A severe gale could be equally disastrous, bringing the whole building crashing to the ground. When the wind died the mill was becalmed, no grain could be milled, there would be a shortage of flour in the neighbourhood and the miller lost his customers to the nearest rival able to operate his mill. An additional hazard, ever increasing to keep pace with the growth of the country's population, was the building of new houses, and commercial or public construction work. A tall building erected close to a windmill often meant that the wind no longer reached the mill. In theory, the wind that turned the mill was held to belong to the owner of the land on which that mill stood; in feudal days the lord of the manor automatically owned also the milling rights on grain grown by anyone living upon and tilling the land within his manorial domain, and the wind or water which turned his mills was

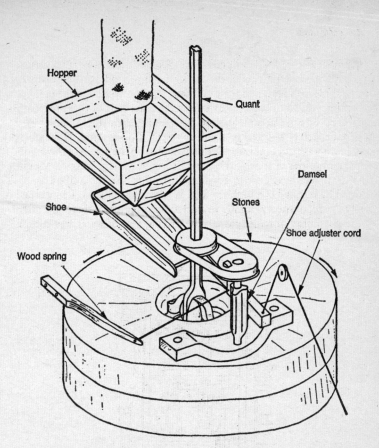

Hopper

Quant

Damsel

Shoe

Stones

Shoe adjuster cord

Wood spring

Inside a windmill. The millstones are enclosed in a casing, and the drawing shows how the grain reaches them. From sacks stored in the upper storey of the mill the grain travels via a cylindrical chute into a wooden hopper, thence into the shoe. The damsel agitates the shoe (in earlier mills the quant which turns the upper stone served this purpose) and the grain is shaken into the centre eye of the upper stone. Thence it falls between the two stones and emerges at the outer edges as ground meal. Bins or sacks on the lower floor receive the meal as it falls through wooden spouts. If to be sold as wholemeal it would be put into sacks. If to be separated it would go to a dressing or bolting machine, a cylinder of fine-mesh metal in which horizontal brushes revolve. Most mills also had a grain-cleaning machine, called a smutter.

Polegate tower mill, East Sussex, where this diagram was made, was built in 1817 and worked until 1965. Under the auspices of the Eastbourne and District Preservation Trust it has now been restored to working order. Diagram by David Jones, reproduced by permission of Mr Lawrence Stevens from *Polegate Windmill Souvenir Guide*.

safe enough from human interference. As the feudal system collapsed, the mills passed into independent ownership, land was increasingly sold off in small plots and the traditional legal protection of the mill became impossible to enforce. As late as the latter part of the nineteenth century, Acts of Parliament were passed to prevent the building of a house or factory so close to a mill as to rob it of its wind. How much attention was paid to this legislation is shown by the action of the municipal authorities of Lewes, the county town of Sussex, when they built the town gaol next door to a windmill. In this case the mill owner riposted by raising his mill thirty feet. Where watermills were concerned rights were, in theory, legally protected but in practice there was often little possibility of remedy when the driving flow of water was cut off.

Sketch of watermill machinery. The sacks of grain are lifted to the upper storey of the mill by means of a sack-hoist (top and bottom right). The stones are inside the casing, centre right. As in a windmill the grain reaches them via a chute and a wooden hopper, and the ground meal falls into the sleeve, bottom right. The drawing shows in simplified form how the mill turns. A horizontal shaft connects the big water wheel, far left, with the pit wheel; this meshes with the small wheel called a wallower, and connects by a vertical shaft with the great spur wheel which in turn meshes with the stone nuts (beneath the stone-casing) and drives the stones below. Sketch by Philippa Miller.

In the city of Winchester, for example, there were at one time twelve mills on the river. Few of them can have had enough water power to work satisfactorily. There must have been many a dispute between the owners. Readers of *The Mill on the Floss* will recall how Mr Tulliver, the miller, is ruined by an unsuccessful lawsuit against an upstart local landowner who plans to dam a stretch of the river for irrigation purposes, thereby depriving the Tulliver mill of its legitimate share of water power. When Mr Tulliver loses his case he, his family and his business disintegrate. One of the most famous watermills in the country, Flatford on the Suffolk Stour, referred to by Constable in the letter quoted on p. 19, and painted by him many times, was part of the substantial corn-milling business owned by his father and in later years run by Abram, his younger brother. The Constable business had prospered largely because, in the early years of the century, the branch of the Stour on which the mill was built had been made navigable by barge. This meant that the flour could be loaded on to barges lying at the mill's own wharf and shipped to London by water rather than carried by road to the local towns and villages. Flatford Mill had been in operation for some 200 years when the Stour canal was closed to commercial traffic seventy years ago.[1] Owing to its associations, the mill itself was preserved and is now in the safe keeping of the National Trust. Thousands of Flatford's counterparts, which owed their prosperity and their subsequent decline to similar circumstances, have vanished. Like the windmills, they succumbed, although not quite as completely, to competition from the roller mills. The first of these to be established in the British Isles was opened at Glasgow in 1872. By the end of the century the windmills and the watermills had already become an anachronism.

Today, a century after the roller-mill revolution, we have become very conscious of the need to preserve, restore, rescue from final disintegration our few surviving historic watermills and windmills and whenever feasible to put them back into operation.[2] These eleventh-hour enterprises are valuable and valiant. They deserve support, as indeed do all the independent millers who cater for the health-food and wholefood organizations. Our supplies of flour for the bread we bake

1. Part of this canal was recently (1975) re-opened for the use of pleasure boats.
2. The Wind and Watermill section of the Society for the Protection of Ancient Buildings publishes a number of informative booklets on windmills and watermills of all descriptions and also supplies a list of mills, some working, which can be visited by the public.

at home depend upon them. From a few lines on a bag of flour milled by one such old-established family firm we learn that in the small county of Bedfordshire alone there were once 400 operative mills. By 1970 there was only one supplying bread flour to the public. Will that one survive as an independent business or will it be swallowed up, as so many have been, by one or other of the juggernaut combines?

STONE MILLING

'Whiteness is all, today.'

C. Henry Warren, *Corn Country*, 1940

Many householders who bake their own bread look for the announcement 'stone milled' on the bags of flour they buy. The words indicate that the contents have not been deprived of the natural properties of the grain by the drastic action of high-speed rollers. The stone-milled meals and flours we buy are ground much as they were in the latter days of the wind- and the water-powered mills, the result being basically as it has been for hundreds of years, except that the cleaning of the wheat prior to milling has evolved to a high degree, and that wheat varieties have changed, and continue to change as new types are tried out.

The millstones used in our few surviving old mills are very large, measuring 4 to 5 feet in diameter and weighing anything from 15 hundredweight to $1\frac{1}{2}$ tons each; they are also extremely hard, the emery stone from which they are cut being, with the exception of the diamond, the hardest substance known to us. The commonest stones, called burrs, were French, from La Ferté-sous-Jouarre in the Marne valley. These stones, a silicious conglomerate with a permanently rough surface, were imported from France in sections.[1] Welding these together was part of the skilled work of the millwright. Our own Derbyshire millstone grit was another stone frequently used. This carboniferous stone, well known to coal miners as one of the lower strata in the coal measures – when they reached the millstone grit they knew that the seam was

---

1. 'Grinding stones in pieces, dressed with rays' were shown at the Great Exhibition of 1851. They were exhibited by the firm of Gaillard Senior from La Ferté, and were described in the catalogue as being in great repute not only in France and England but also in America. The discovery of the blocks of stone was 'a matter of difficulty and uncertainty, giving employment to a large number of persons' (*Official Description and Illustrated Catalogue of the Great Exhibition 1851*, vol. III, p. 1187). The vein of burr stone at La Ferté has now run out. It has become difficult to find stones suitable for the grinding of wheat for bread flour.

worked out[1] – occurs also in outcroppings in the Midlands and was used by Iron Age men to make many of the quern stones found in their settlements such as Hunsbury in Northamptonshire and Breedon in Leicestershire. Another stone used for early querns and picturesquely known as 'pudding stone' is a conglomerate which derives its name from the rounded bits of quartzose rock, white and red, embedded like plums in the surrounding mass of finer silicious particles which form the main body of the 'pudding'. A number of such stones, found locally, are to be seen in the collection of the old Jewry Wall Museum at Leicester; others have been unearthed at Wroxeter in Shropshire. The pudding-stone conglomerate occurs on the west bank of the Severn, and is also found underlying the mountain limestone in the neighbourhood of Symond's Yat on the Wye.[2] In the Somerset lake villages of Glastonbury

A reconstruction of the bakery and mills discovered in the ruins of Pompeii (see Plate 6). Alternatively, horses or donkeys could be harnessed to the mills. The massive stones were hewn out of local lava. From *Living in Pompeii* by R. J. Unstead, illustrated by Laszlo Acs (A. and C. Black, 1976).

1. George Ewart Evans, *The Farm and the Village*, 1969.
2. J. Buckman, *Materials of Roman Querns*, c. 1880.

and Meare the quern stones found were, again, of stone locally available such as Old Red Sandstone, or silicified rock from the neighbourhood of the Mendip Hills.[1]

These latter stones were too soft to be satisfactory for the grinding of grain, and although the gritstone and silicious rock are harder and more efficient there is evidence that both before and during the Roman occupation it was in any case customary first to partly roast the grain, so that the husk was loosened and the inner grain hardened or made more brittle. In this manner grinding was facilitated whatever the stones used, the grain emerging quite finely ground rather than simply crushed or flattened. Dr Cecil Curwen, the great authority on querns already quoted at the head of this chapter, proved the point for himself. Having first dried and oven-baked 16 oz of wheat (reduced to 14 oz by the drying-out process) he ground the cooled grain in one of the Hunsbury querns, with, he reported, 'greatly increased efficiency' and with surprisingly little waste – in a few minutes he had obtained 13 oz of flour from the 14 oz of grain. As Dr Curwen writes, without first hand experience the performance of the old querns cannot be assessed or be understood and his own enlightening experiments are described in some detail in his paper 'More about Querns', published in *Antiquity*, Volume XV, 1941.

By far the hardest of all the millstones, and probably the least common in England, were the black Andernach lava stones from near Coblenz on the Rhine (Plate 12). These are believed to have been introduced to Britain by the Romans, who had evolved methods of cutting and grooving stones far more effective than those used on the earlier quern stones found in this country. Although only about 15 to 20 inches in diameter, and small compared to modern millstones, the radial grooving on some of the Romano-British lava stones appears to have been of some precision and, although less intricate, not unlike that on nineteenth-century stones. It was surely imported black lava stones, alternatively called blue or Cullen (Cologne) stones, which were meant by Gervase Markham when he declared in his recipe for manchet loaf[2] that 'the black stones make the whitest flower', a statement which reads suspiciously like an old wives' tale until it is realized that the precision of the grooving and the extreme hardness of the lava stone meant

1. Sir Arthur Bulleid and H. St George Gray, *The Lake Villages of Somerset*, 6th edn, 1968 (first published 1924).
2. *The English Hus-wife*, 1615. The recipe is quoted on page 335.

that an experienced miller could set the stones very close together, and the meal could be ground very fine; subsequently given the maximum bolting or sifting, the flour achieved would have been the whitest then feasible.

Once the watermills and windmills began to be established and milling became a trade rather than a purely household or manorial concern, it must have been realized that various types of millstone and more or less complex grooving were appropriate to different grain. The hardest stones will take the finest grooving, so these were used for wheat, the larger the stones the greater being the output of flour. Using 4-foot burr stones a miller could grind 5 bushels or 300lb of wheat per pair of stones per hour, the resulting meal yielding 180lb of finely dressed or bolted flour. The total capacity of an average mill with three pairs of stones is not quite straightforward to calculate because one pair would almost certainly be of secondary quality – softer stone, such as Peak or Derbyshire millstone, suitable for the grinding into coarse meal of barley, oats, and other grain for animal feed. The yield from these stones would be about 10 bushels or 600lb of coarse meal per pair per hour. If a mill had only 3-foot stones, then the yield would be reduced by about one-third.[1] In view of the great economic difference made by the size of the millstones, it is hardly surprising that the mill owners attempted to use ever larger stones, to the point where the tremendous centrifugal force engendered as they revolved was known, as *Cassells Domestic Dictionary* dramatically puts it, 'to tear them asunder'.

We see then that those words 'stone ground' on our flour bag labels are of ancient significance. To our ancestors the stones were as important as the power which turned them. The radial grooving on the grinding faces of both stones was and is a vital factor. Along these grooves the grain is driven by centrifugal force towards the outer circumference where it is delivered pulverized into a more or less coarse meal according to the degree to which the top stone, revolving on its spindle, is raised from or lowered to the fixed base or bedstone. With use the grooving gradually wears down, becomes ineffectual, and after approximately every hundred hours of milling has to be renewed, a process known as dressing, and involving a high degree of craftsmanship. In the prosperous days of the windmills and watermills the dressing of the stones

1. John Vince, *Discovering Watermills*, 2nd edn, 1976. This excellent little booklet is obtainable from the publishers at Cromwell House, Church St, Princes Risborough, Aylesbury, Bucks.

was usually performed by a travelling millwright, who would sit all day, his elbow propped on a cushion of sawdust, patiently chipping away at a stone until it was ready to be replaced (Plate 11), the dressing of a pair of stones taking about eighteen hours. (The mill meantime would not be idle, for few mills had less than two pairs of stones in use at one time, some as many as five or even seven.) Today the craft of the millwright has all but died out, so in our few surviving stone mills it is likely to be the miller himself or a member of his family who dresses the stones – yet another of the aspects of milling which make it difficult for anyone not born into the trade to appreciate the degree of experience and expertise necessary to the miller and his associates.

BOLTING THE FLOUR

The sifting or bolting of the ground grain is a process of milling which changed radically during the eighteenth century, a change which certainly accelerated the demand for bread made from finer, whiter flour, and which must also have been largely responsible for the development of fine pastry-making and for the very marked increase in the number of recipes for light cakes, buns, biscuits and flour confectionery generally which appear in the cookery books of the second half of the century.

Bolting cloths were originally made of a tough canvas, linen or woollen fabric. Using these, it cannot have been possible for millers to produce flour of anything approaching the degree of fineness and whiteness we now know. (Many small cultivators who took their grain to the mill to be ground carried out the sifting operation at home, as and when the flour was needed, the quantity of bran sifted out depending on the purpose for which the flour was to be used. This saved the extra charge made by the miller for bolting the meal, and also ensured that the grower received back his rightful measure of milled grain. The millers were forever being accused of dishonest dealing in this respect. Whichever way it was looked at, the miller did well out of the small farmer. By keeping back a measure of his customers' bran he could feed his own livestock or he could re-sell the bran.)

With the mid-eighteenth-century improvement in weaving techniques it was discovered that fine silk could be made into a hard-wearing gauze for sieving meal. This yielded a whiter, higher-extraction flour than could be obtained with the old canvas or even fine woollen or linen bolting cloths. Eventually, silk or millers' gauze became, and until recently remained, essential to the milling trade. The different grades of mesh had to be exact and constant, requiring a high degree of skill from the weavers. For the finest flour a mesh of something like 130 holes to the inch was used, and eventually the great roller mills became dependent on the silk weaving trade for their fine bolting drums – known as the 'silks' – for white flour. It is only during very recent years that a form of nylon good enough to replace the silk has been evolved. There were, of course, plenty of exceptions to the use of silk bolting cloth. Fine linen also remained in use. A beautiful example of a linen bolter, preserved in the Science Museum, South Kensington, London, is so fine that it is difficult to imagine how even silk could have produced finer flour. At Clapton Mills near Crewkerne in Dorset a fine copper gauze mesh on cylindrical wooden frames has been used, so the owner told me, since long before he can remember. No white flour, however, is produced at Clapton. In common with many millers still using the stone grinding method, Mr Lockyer finds it more practical to buy in strong unbleached white flour for those of his customers who need it for breadmaking. Another mill where the bolter or meal dresser dates back to the last century is Felin Geri – the mill on the River Ceri – at Cwm Cou near Newcastle Emlyn in South Wales. This mill, dating originally from 1604, has been restored by the present owners and is now producing stone-ground bread flour on a commercial basis. Visitors are shown most amiably and efficiently the workings of the mill.

Basically then, such stone-milled flour as we can now obtain is produced, if not, as is sometimes claimed, in the way known a thousand years ago, at least in a manner which would make it recognizable to our early-nineteenth-century forbears, in whose times flour with an extraction rate of less than 80 per cent would have been a rarity. Even in the whitest and finest stone-milled flour, obtained by bolting the meal over and over again until only the fine grain from the endosperm remains, the yellow flecks of the vital wheat germ are still clearly discernible and there is still a proportion of fine branny particles, so the flour is only relatively white. Flour is never naturally white-white. It is artificial bleaching which makes it so.

Depending upon whether you think that flour's only function is to be preternaturally white and bacteriologically totally pure or whether you think that it is more proper for the bread you eat to be made from flour retaining rather more of its original nature, you could say that the colour of stone-milled 'white' flour is poor and unappetizing or, in the second case, that it is a wholesome and enticing one.

ROLLER MILLING

With the invention of the roller mill in the second half of the nineteenth century the long search for a means of producing uniformly white flour was over. For centuries and centuries primitive man had striven to find the most effective method of grinding his grain, choosing his milling stones by trial and error, transporting them long distances, working them patiently and painfully, first turning them laboriously by hand, then using animal power to turn the cumbersome machinery, later learning to harness the forces of nature, the water and the wind, to drive his mills, eventually applying steam power and at last electricity to the grinding of his grain. Now one at least of his traditional aims has been achieved, and by a means which owes little to his early struggles.

Whereas in stone milling the grain is crushed, the action of the great mechanically driven rollers produces a drastically different effect. Once the wheat is matured, blended, then dry-cleaned and wet-cleaned by a series of complex operations, the milling proper starts. Break rollers shear open the wheat berry, freeing the endosperm or starchy part of the grain. This is then separated from the bran and the rest of the 'offal'. The wheat berry has now become a granular semolina, to be pulverized into flour, graded through fine meshes, and ultimately chlorine-bleached, processed, 'improved' and packed into sacks or bags.

The bran extracted during milling may be made into animal feed or into various patent foodstuffs, or be re-blended with the white flour to make a proprietary brand of 'brown' flour to sell to bakery plants for 'wheatmeal' bread. The wheat germ, if extracted separately, may be used for a patent wheat-germ food, or, as explained in the chapter on flours and meals, returned to white flour to make a 'wheatmeal' bread flour of, say, 85 per cent extraction, or perhaps sold to the blenders of meal for proprietary wheat-germ breads. The bulk, however, of bran and germ goes into the main stream of the 'offal' to be sold as animal food. It is not economic for the great roller-milling concerns to separate out the different components of the grain.

BLEACHING OF FLOUR

Chlorine bleaching of the processed flour is also expedient, for the giant milling combines own the plants which manufacture the white wrapped loaf, and artificial bleaching produces flour better suited to high-speed mechanical dough mixing than natural unbleached flour. Bleaching is by no means a necessity, and in some countries – France is one of them – is prohibited. It is not carried out solely in order to obtain whiter-than-white flour. It is also a method of instant maturing or ageing of the flour, and matured flour, so long as it has been deprived of its germ, has long been recognized as giving the most satisfactory performance for machine-made dough. To a certain extent flour whitens during storage. Not sufficiently, however, to suit English millers and bread and biscuit manufacturers, so the flour is bleached with a chemical which speeds the ageing process. When we remember that one of the bleaches widely used during the immediate post 1914–18 War period and for the succeeding thirty years was called agene we immediately understand its function. (This bleach is now banned in England. It was suspected, although not proved by the medical profession, of causing serious nervous disorders.) At the same time as maturing and bleaching the flour, chemicals destroy its natural vitamin B content. This is just one of the 'nutrients' required by our present laws to be put back into bread flour in synthetic form.

THE MILLERS AND THE GOVERNMENT FLOUR ORDER, 1953

After the last war, successive British governments, unable to control the millers or the demand engendered by them for ever-whiter bread, stepped in and decreed that some at least of the vital elements removed from wheat by the high-speed roller-milling system be returned to our bread flour. This compromise, which to many of us appears a feeble one, was arrived at in the immediate post-rationing period of the early 1950s, when flour milling was released from the controls imposed in 1941 and in force until 1953. At this period a curious situation arose, one that is worth remembering when it is reiterated over and over again that the public wants white bread, and that the milling–baking combines are only giving the public what it wants, and what it has always wanted. In 1953, then, a Government Flour Order permitted the millers, for the first time since the early years of the 1939 War, to mill flour to any extraction rate they pleased. Two important provisos qualified this order. First, flour of any extraction rate below 80 per cent was to be restored as much as possible to 80 per cent level by the addition of synthetic vitamins and 'nutrients'. Second, the National loaf, made from

80 per cent or higher extraction flour, was still to be subsidized,[1] while bread made from white flour would not be eligible for the subsidy. It was up to the public and the bakers to choose. Overwhelmingly, both chose the National loaf. After some two years during which the 1953 Flour Order was in force, consumption of the unsubsidized white loaf was no more than 0·8 per cent of the total amount of bread baked in the country. It looked as though the claim that the majority would buy white bread regardless of cost was disproved, and that the popular loaf was the cheaper one, whatever its colour. Unfortunately the whole operation was invalidated when it dawned on the government that the millers had increasingly been claiming the subsidy on the milling of National flour of 80 per cent extraction while at the same time passing off virtually white flour as National flour, so drawing a subsidy to which they were not entitled. Once again the millers had the upper hand. The government gave in, reporting[2] that the 1953 Order was unenforceable, that the public demand for white flour was genuine, and that so long as the prescribed 'nutrients', the vitamins, the calcium, the iron, the nicotinic acid and the rest, were added to white bread flour the nation's health would be safeguarded.

THE MILLERS AND THE MYTH OF THE EXTRACTION RATE

It has been much put about that in order to produce massive quantities of flour by roller milling, it is essential to extract something like 25 per cent of the outer part of the wheat grain and its germ. This is not exact. A basic extraction rate of 95 per cent can easily be achieved with roller milling, and within limits the millers can produce any extraction rate of flour they choose. To *store* flour for any length of time it is necessary, so the millers claim, to extract the germ or vital part of the berry. It is the oil from the crushed germ which inhibits the keeping quality of flour; the realization that the germ could be completely eliminated and the storage potential of milled grain thus enormously increased was surely just as responsible as were the whiteness and uniform quality of the flour produced for the phenomenally rapid spread of roller milling during the final decades of the nineteenth century. In those days cold

---

1. Bread had been subsidized since early in the Second World War.
2. *Report of the Panel on the Composition and Nutritive Value of Flour* (*The Cohen Report*), H.M.S.O., 1956.

storage and grain stores maintained at controlled temperatures had not been developed. Now, a century later, the original argument would appear to be invalidated. Of course there are other reasons for maintaining the extraction rate at the lowest feasible level. One of them is that the particles of bran and untreated wheat germ in dough don't suit the mechanical processes used in the bread factories where the bulk of our bread is produced.

HAVE WE A CHOICE?

Now, I do not think, as do wholehearted wholefood campaigners, that all the ills of this country stem from the eating of white bread and the lack of bran in roller-milled white flour. I do think that there should be far more choice, and above all, that every responsible person should know what he is choosing. We are faced with an ironic situation. For centuries the working man envied the white bread of the privileged. Now he may very soon grow to envy them their brown wholewheat bread. This is certainly every bit as inaccessible to the majority as was the fine white manchet bread of the sixteenth century, perhaps more so. For while it is true that, legally, wholewheat bread bought from a baker must contain 95 to 100 per cent of the grain, and (1976) carry a maximum price of only 6p more than that of the white wrapped loaf of equivalent weight, there are very few bakers who make or sell the genuine article.

It should be, and is not, generally understood that what is sold by bakers as 'wheatmeal' or 'brown' bread is quite distinct from wholemeal, should not be designated as such and should be 2p cheaper for a 28 oz loaf. Many people who buy those brown loaves are under the impression that they are buying wholemeal while what in fact they are buying is or may be, *quite legally*, a loaf of white flour with o·6 per cent fibre plus caramel colouring, or it may be white with added wheat germ or a malted meal, or just possibly a quite genuine 85 per cent wheatmeal.

In view of the widely differing content of brown flours and brown bread as sanctioned under the Regulations,[1] it is curious that these are thought by our legislators to be so clearly defined that bakers are not required by law to label their products or to state what flour they have

1. *The Bread and Flour Regulations*, Statutory Instrument, 1963, no. 1345; see the *Food Standards Committee Second Report on Bread and Flour*, H.M.S.O., 1974.

used for any given loaf. So the customer, not surprisingly, has little idea of what she is buying. In the 1974 survey of the bread industry conducted by a Manchester University research team,[1] it was found that out of ninety-three shops visited, only thirty-two had 'brown' or 'brownish' loaves for sale. Of these thirty-two, five only were accepted by a public analyst as being made from genuine wholewheat flour. Among the loaves rejected was one made from white flour coloured with caramel.

Caramel, of course, is a permitted colouring for bread. It is the only permitted one – so for the time being we are protected from blue or pink or green bread – but it is widely used and is even legally permitted in 100 per cent wholemeal bread. So are quite a few other unexpected additives. To quote the *Food Standards Committee Second Report on Bread and Flour* (1974) 'While consumers may purchase wholemeal bread in the belief that it contains no additives, it is in fact permitted to contain all the yeast stimulating preparations . . . preservatives, emulsifiers and stabilisers which are permitted in white bread and in addition caramel is permitted for standardising the colour . . . all these types of additives are used by some if not all bakers. Thus while consumers may rely on wholemeal flour to contain no additives, the same cannot be said for wholemeal bread.'

For those, then, who are determined to eat bread made from authentic 100 per cent wholemeal or even 85 per cent wheatmeal, there is precious little alternative but to buy the flour and bake it themselves.

WHAT IS CHOICE AND WHO MAKES IT?

It was during the 1950s that the millers bought out the British bakery industry. What happened, briefly, was that Mr Garfield Weston, Canadian head of a powerful biscuit and flour confectionery group known as Allied Bakeries, started buying up the more vulnerable bakery businesses throughout the country. These provided his company with valuable outlets for his products, increasing also its production facilities by using existing bakery plant. In time Mr Weston decided to by-pass the British milling trade and import his own flour direct from Canada. The loss of so large-scale a flour customer as Allied Bakeries – by this

1. T.A.C.C. Report (*Bread. An Assessment of the Bread Industry in Britain*), 1974. See also note on p. 56, and Bibliography.

time they had acquired control of the Aerated Bread Company with its manufacturing plant, its teashops and retail outlets – was a serious blow to the millers. Before long two of the most powerful milling firms in the country, J. Rank Ltd and Spillers Ltd, retaliated by establishing their own bakery plants, thus maintaining assured outlets for the flour products of their mills. These companies also went shopping for the minor plant bakeries and family businesses. At the same time many of the smaller milling firms found themselves succumbing to the unequal competition and went out of business or allowed themselves to be taken over.

By the end of the decade all three of the new major baking concerns had set about ensuring that their products would be available in grocery shops and dairies throughout the country, thus creating thousands of hitherto untapped retail outlets for their mass-produced bread. It was no longer necessary for the housewife to go to the bakery on her daily shopping round. She could buy a wrapped loaf at any corner shop. With the early 1960s came the spectacular growth of supermarkets and self-service stores. Commercial television also came. Proprietary brands of bread manufactured by the great milling concerns – Mother's Pride, Wonderloaf, Sunblest – became household names. J. Rank Ltd swallowed the old-established Hovis business and the familiar McDougall milling concern. Rank Hovis McDougall and their Mother's Pride white loaf came to be synonymous with all that was – and is – the total antithesis of homely basic bread. As *Which?* observed mildly in its issue of June 1975, 'if you like wrapped sliced bakery bread you'll find it difficult to make something similar at home'.

By the mid 1960s the notorious Chorleywood Bread Process[1] had been evolved. Unknown to the general public the instant factory loaf had superseded the plant loaf of the 1950s. Does Chorleywood bread represent a further deterioration in quality? It certainly does not lack detractors. One example, perhaps an extreme one – those who feel strongly about the white factory loaf tend to feel very strongly indeed – was a Mr Maurice Frohn, a London consultant surgeon, who wrote to the *Daily Telegraph* (6 June 1973) that 'not only does the white loaf do no good, it is actually harmful to the body. Every encouragement should be given to the abolition of this foul food . . . the white loaf is not even fit to be given away.'

Now, criticisms such as Mr Frohn's, and many less forcibly expressed,

1. See the note on p. 108.

are dismissed by the spokesmen and the apologists of the milling–baking industry as emotive, unrealistic, alarmist, mischievous. The bread produced in its factories, the milling industry claims, is incontrovertibly what the overwhelming majority wants. They support their claim by telling us that two out of every three loaves bought today by the British housewife are loaves processed by one of the three major combines.[1] When these companies send out their market researchers with questionnaires, what are the reasons given by housewives for their choice? They are 'availability', 'convenience' (which means, I think, that the slices are the appropriate size and shape for toast and sandwiches) and 'hygiene'. These are reasons which include no mention of anybody buying the bread because they actually like it, and reasons which appear also to imply a bored indifference to the bread itself. It happens to be there in the shop, so it is bought. The customers like it being wrapped in paper and they like the shape. Is that choice? What yardstick of comparison is offered? And what choice is left to the minority, which is after all quite a substantial minority? That this minority is also an articulate one, and that it can scarcely be shrugged off as biased, irresponsible and ignorant (it does after all include a growing body of medical opinion) was candidly admitted by the Flour Advisory Bureau when it stated in an advertisement issued to the national Press in April 1975 that 'the white loaf, which represents over 80 per cent of the bread bought in Britain, hardly ever gets a good word said for it'. It might be inferred from this statement that the Flour Advisory Bureau is itself a biased body. So in a sense it is. It is the milling industry's own paid public relations agency. Its advertising copy went on to tell us how good is the white loaf, how packed with proteins, minerals, iron, vitamins and – again – all those 'nutrients' handed to us in exchange for 16p,[2] the then cost of a 28 oz sliced, wrapped white loaf. Somewhat reluctantly – or so it appeared – and in parentheses, the copy added that 'brown and wholemeal of course are extremely good nutritionally, and may be chosen by people requiring extra roughage'.

*

What we really need to discover is what would happen were there freedom of choice uninhibited by considerations either of price or of availability, and choice unprejudiced by massive one-sided advertising campaigns. In view of the fiasco of the 1953 effort, described on pp. 33–

1. Now only two. In 1978 Spillers French withdrew from the baking industry.
2. 25p by November 1978.

34, no government is likely again to provide us with such a choice. The whole-food organizations and the independent bakers are not rich enough to launch million-pound advertising campaigns. Any movement towards more interesting, more authentic bread and a genuine choice must come from the public itself. (That is, if we are not forced by economic circumstances to reconsider the whole question of the waste inherent in our present milling and animal feeding systems.) That a genuine choice *was* once a reality is very well demonstrated by the following passage, quoted from a chronicle of childhood and youth in a remote village of West Wales during the Edwardian era, at a period in our social history when the old ways and the new coincided, when a humble village family of two adults and six growing children was able to appreciate the products of both the roller-mill and the stone-mill systems. The passage provides ample evidence, too, that just because flour was roller-milled and white it did not follow that the bread made from it was anything like the sad substance which in 1974 received the official and financial blessing of a Labour government.

'Mother always baked in a big oven heated by billets of oak, ash, or sycamore, with the occasional old apple tree. Ash was a splendid burner, green or dry, but oak steadied the temperature . . . In all my travels I have never eaten either bread or butter equal to those my mother made, not even fresh French *baguette* with Breton *demi-sel* spread on it. The average loaf was anything from 18 inches to two feet in diameter. Enough bread would be baked to last the household a week at least. She baked pure white Spillers "As You Like It" flour, and also mixed oatmeal and barley flour, so there would be three kinds of bread from which to choose. Large slices of this bread with all the air pockets filled with the salted butter – and the cawl with meat and vegetables in it – composed a meal fit for royalty.

'In my childhood we took the oats, the wheat and the barley to the local mill, and after discussion with the miller, we arrived at the exact kind of fineness best suited to our taste, and the exact amount of husk, if any, to be left in the final product.'

James Williams, *Give Me Yesterday*, 1971

And one more equally relevant quotation, also of childhood memories, this time of East Anglia, in a slightly earlier period, and from a book which will be quoted often in these pages:

'Broom [the village grocer] also sold flour, which he kept in a huge wooden hutch and ladled out with a nice smooth shiny wooden scoop.

This was weighed up on beam scales suspended over the counter. If you wanted less than a stone of flour at a time you went to Broom, but if more then to the mill. Paper in those days was scarce, so customers had to provide their own wrappings, which when it came to flour was a pillow case.'

Allan Jobson, *An Hour-Glass on the Run*, 1959

Oh for a neighbouring mill to which I could take a pillow case, you will perhaps say. Until you have searched and inquired you cannot be so sure that there is not within reach one from which you could buy bread flour by the stone at a substantial saving on the price charged by the specialist retail shops for the equivalent quantity (14lb) packed in 3lb bags. Surprising survivals and revivals are to be found, such as – at the time of writing – an operative stone mill in London's Old Kent Road, where grain is milled daily for the bread baked by the Ceres Bakery which supplies many wholefood shops with wholewheat bread and which has its own retail shop in North West London. In South Wales, two or three miles from Carmarthen at the White Mill, once water-powered but now electrically driven, three grades of stone-ground flour can be bought. Mrs Lickley, the miller's wife (the mill has been in her family for generations) makes her own blend of 100 per cent wholemeal and strong white flour. This is the flour Mrs Lickley herself prefers for bread and, should there be none ready when you call at the mill, she will blend and pack it for you while you wait. Many a time I have brought White Mill flour back to London with me, and have also used it for bread to be baked in the old brick oven at Ty Isaf, shown in Plates 22 and 23.

HAND MILLING

'My bread is sweet and nourishing, made from my own wheat, ground in my own mill, and baked in my own oven.'

Tobias Smollett, *Humphrey Clinker*, 1771

In the days of the great feudal estates the peasant farmer was obliged to take his grain to his overlord's mill to be ground. His dues were paid in kind. (In many cases he had no alternative but to pay also to have his bread baked in the manorial oven.) In order to escape the imposition, some of the more humble families ground their grain at home, using their primitive pot querns. Eventually the landowners – among the most powerful was the Church – contrived repressive measures making the home grinding of grain illegal. Handmills and querns were confiscated and broken up – hence the rarity of complete querns of the medieval period – and it was only in remote and inaccessible areas such as the Hebridean islands that hand milling persisted uninterrupted until recent years.

As the feudal system died out and milling became a commercial enterprise, the restrictive laws against household milling became

Victorian household handmill. The hopper, *a*, and the grinding cylinder, *b*, were made of steel. Dressing or bolting could be effected simultaneously with the grinding. The ground meal, falling into the box at *c* was carried into a dressing cylinder set horizontally and at an incline, extending from *d* to *e*. Canvas of four different degrees of fineness of mesh covered the cylinder so that as it revolved the meal could be separated into four different grades, the bran falling into the drawer at *i*, the finest flour or 'firsts' at *f*. Into *g* and *h* went the 'seconds' and 'thirds'. The divisions were removable. If you wanted bread meal with only the coarsest bran sieved out, you took out the divisions on each side of the box *g* and mixed up the two grades of flour in the drawer. A mill of this type, to grind one bushel an hour, cost £10. From Walsh's *Manual of Domestic Economy*, 1861 edition.

equally obsolete. If farmers and cottagers chose to mill their own grain there was nothing to stop them. Many rural households and farms kept a grain mill or a grain-crushing device which would at least serve for grinding oats and barley for animal feed if the local mill broke down, and this could be used for household bread meal in an emergency. Often the miller was suspected of cheating over the yield of flour from the grain entrusted to him, of adulterating his flour, of mixing inferior grain in his grist, in short, of petty malpractices of a dozen kinds; even when he was perfectly honest it was scarcely possible for him to keep each small amount of grain brought to him for milling separate from the next man's, so if any farmer with only a bushel or two of wheat to be ground wanted to be quite sure of getting bread meal and flour from his own wheat then he had no alternative but to have it ground on his own premises. William Cobbett, for example, used a hand-operated mill 'turned by a man and a stout boy' for both his bread flour and the meal for his pigs. He reckoned that the cost of grinding 6 bushels of wheat was only one day's labour at 4s 6d for the man and the boy. If necessary his mill could also be turned by 'any little horse, pony or even ass' (*Cottage Economy*, 1821–3).

In his *Manual of Domestic Economy Suited to Families Spending from £100 to £1000 a Year* (1856), J. H. Walsh, F.R.C.S., goes into detail on the subject of handmills, examines the cost, the labour, the pros and cons of the household milling of wheat. Admitting that the labour involved was very considerable and that the cost of the labour to operate a handmill, calculated at 6d an hour – the time taken to grind 1 bushel – would be much the same as that charged by most millers. Walsh concluded that 'by its use there is a certainty of having a genuine article, which cannot be the case with wheat sent to the public mill'. The mill illustrated and described in detail by Walsh was ingenious. It had a built-in cylindrical bolting drum or 'dressing apparatus' through which three grades of flour plus the bran could be produced simultaneously, each falling into different compartments of a box-like drawer underneath the bolting drum. The cost of a mill large enough to grind and sift 1 bushel per hour (there were larger and smaller ones also to be had, and they could be bought with or without the dressing apparatus) was £10. Walsh's illustration is reproduced on p. 41.

Some forty years after the publication of the Walsh manual, which pre-dated the roller-mill revolution by two decades, an eminent doctor and dietician called Sir Henry Thompson was again advocating the purchase of a handmill, but on grounds rather more familiar to us today. In his widely read book *Food and Feeding*,[1] Sir Henry strongly recommended whole wheatmeal bread containing a proportion of oatmeal as being nutritionally superior to any other.[2] It was obvious that anyone wanting such bread would have to have it baked at home, but the requisite meal, although to be bought in most towns, was 'by no means always in such perfect condition as it ought to be'. This probably meant that it was often stale and musty. The remedy was a handmill made by Kent & Co.[3] and a supply of 'the best white wheat', from which 'meal of any degree of coarseness desired' could be ground.

Today, the reasons put forward by the advocates of hand milling are much the same as those advanced by Sir Henry Thompson, with the added benefit, at least to those who buy wheat from wholefood stores, that the grain will be organically grown, that it will almost certainly be home-produced soft wheat unblended with imported hard wheat, and that it will have a good flavour. With a handmill you can grind your grain as coarsely as you please – I find that most 100 per cent wholemeal is too finely ground – and you can grind small quantities as and when you need it, so that your bread will always be made from freshly milled meal, a point considered of some importance where wholemeal is concerned. On the market at present (1975) are at least three types of household mill for grains: an iron mill looking something like an outsize mincer, a high-powered and expensive electric mill, and another hand-operated mill, ingeniously designed and beautifully made, with two small adjustable grinding stones of Naxos emery granules embedded in a stabilized magnesite cement. This elegant and solid little mill is of French manufacture.

I do not myself go in for grinding my own grain. It is an activity confined mainly I think to those who want only 100 per cent wholemeals for their bread, and to enthusiasts who have their own grain to grind. It has to be remembered that in any household needing bread flour less heavy than 100 per cent wheatmeal the further task of sifting out the coarsest part of the bran would have to be considered.

Anyone interested in buying a handmill should be able to obtain details and price through the Ceres Mail Order Organization, 269 Portobello Road, London W11, or from Hofels Pure Foods Ltd, Woolpit, Suffolk.

1. 12th edn, 1901 (first published *c*. 1882).
2. One of Sir Henry's excellent recipes is quoted on p. 522.
3. The firm which also produced the rotary knife-cleaning machine now often to be seen in museums of domestic life.

English agents for the French SAMAP stone handmill and electric mill mentioned above are Springhill Farms (Dinton) Ltd, 38 Buckingham Street, Aylesbury, Buckinghamshire. Good explanatory brochures with clear photographs are available for both mills.

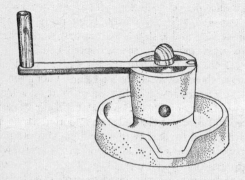

Modern French handmill with composition stones. In appearance and action they are a small scale version of the French burr stones in the mechanical mill for wholemeal shown on p. 50. Reproduced by courtesy of Springhill Farms (Dinton Ltd), Aylesbury, Bucks.

Bread Flours and Meals

'The wheat berry is a complex little storehouse of food.'

Ronald Sheppard and Edward Newton, *The Story of Bread*, 1957

'He [York Ketteridge] was a most kind and understanding man who knew about wheats, their differences in height, colour and yield. He would snatch a couple of near-ripened ears, rub them in his horny hands to shed the husks, then blow into his cupped hands to winnow husks from grain. Husks clung to his whiskers as he tossed the grain into his mouth. Wheat is life, boy. Don't let no silly bugger tell you different.'

Christopher Ketteridge and Spike Mays, *Five Miles from Bunkum*, 1972

'In wheat and some other grains, there are glutenous proteins which form the substance called gluten when the dough is made. . . . This gluten is important because when developed it forms the skin of myriads of tiny balloons which hold the gas produced by wheat activity. If the gluten were not formed in dough any gas produced would simply escape and the dough could not be aerated or made light.'

Walter Banfield, *Manna*, 1937

The words of Walter Banfield, master baker and author of a lively and lucid work written for professional bakers, make it very clear why the best flours for English bread – at any rate for English bread as we have become accustomed to it – are milled from a hard grain wheat with a high gluten content. These so-called hard or strong wheats with a gluten content of 12 to 15 per cent yield flours which give the dough greater expansion, absorb more water and produce bread with a better structure and a greater volume than soft wheat flours with a gluten content of only 8 to 10 per cent.

In England very little hard wheat is grown – our climate is not propitious to it – so our own product, which has good flavour, is blended with Canadian, American or Argentine hard wheat. The mixture of wheat before milling used to be called the grist. Now it is more often known as stock. What precisely these blends are at any given moment depends upon what is available on the market, which in turn is governed by the world's wheat harvests and consequent supplies.

From the home breadmaker's point of view, it should be understood that an edible English loaf *can* be made from an ordinary brand of household flour as sold by the local grocer. This flour is very white because it has been bleached, and it is nearly always a soft blend, used mainly for cakes and pastry. Therefore bread dough made from it will not be so springy and the resultant loaf will not have the quality, the texture or the volume of one made from flour blended expressly for household breadmaking. Nor – and this is due to modern technology – will it have any noticeable flavour. But although convinced wholefood and health-food addicts would probably say that a loaf made from ordinary commercial white flour, however or wherever baked, whether at home or by an independent baker or in a bakery plant, is worse than worthless, I still think that given just a little knowledge and experience the housewife should be able to make a more appetizing loaf at home, whatever the flour, than any to be bought in the general run of commercial bakeries. So in times of shortage or high prices of imported hard wheat, there is no need to give up. Indeed, I doubt that anyone who has learned to make their own bread with success, and whose household and family eat it with enjoyment, could be induced to give up. A way round the difficulties is always to be found. French bakers, after all, have adapted their bread techniques to their own soft flour, although not in a way which can be copied for home breadmaking or using the ovens of domestic cookers. There are other ways. It is, for example, possible to obtain concentrated gluten extract in powder form from millers or wholesalers to the bakery trade; add it to soft flours in the proportion of 1 to 1½ oz per pound of flour; proprietary wheat-germ extracts add life to dough made with emasculated flour; and flours can be mixed, so that a small proportion of expensive stone-milled whole wheatmeal or strong plain unbleached flour blended with ordinary household flour can do something to give good texture and quality to bread dough and flavour to the loaf. Malt extracts provide another flavour and texture improver, one which I find rather cloying and over-assertive; but these are questions of personal taste.

The next point of importance about flours for home-made bread is some understanding of the different types of meal and flour (approximately, meal is coarse, flour is fine), whether milled from wheat, rye, barley or other grain.

THE STRUCTURE AND CONTENT OF A GRAIN OF WHEAT

Here it is necessary to explain that, inside the 'complex little storehouse' which is the wheat berry, is, first, the germ or embryo which will sprout and grow into a new wheat plant. The germ represents only 2 per cent of the grain, but is rich in protein, vitamins and oil.

Next to the germ is the endosperm, which is the heart of the grain and the part which supplies the starch. This accounts for 85 per cent

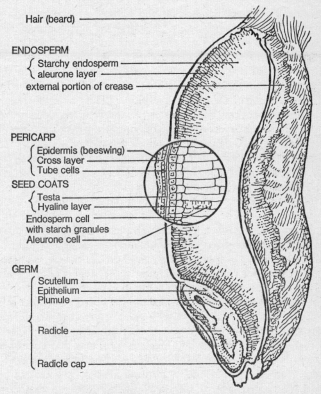

The structure and content of a grain of wheat. The different layers of bran coating can be seen quite clearly. The bulk of our flour comes from the white area, the starchy endosperm. Although the germ represents only 2 per cent of the grain, many people feel that to remove it from flour is the equivalent of discarding the yolk from an egg and eating only the white. Reproduced by courtesy of the Flour Advisory Bureau.

of the grain, and is the only part which survives in our modern roller-milled white bread flour.

All round the germ and the endosperm is the protective casing of bran, making up the remaining 13 per cent of the grain's content. The bran, a complicated structure, consists of four main layers of skins, each of them providing a part of the fibre considered so important in bread made from stone-milled wholemeals and wheatmeals and flours, but missing from bakers' white bread. Of those four layers of bran, there is one called aleurone, lying next to the endosperm. The aleurone layer, containing important vitamins, fat and minerals, makes up half the total quantity of bran, and is considered by many nutritionists to be by far the most necessary half. By the millers and bakers it is viewed without enthusiasm. The aleurone skin is attached to the endosperm but cannot easily be assimilated with it because it is also attached to the outer skins of the grain. As the millers put it, 'these skins would discolour the flour badly and also spoil its baking qualities'.[1] (This means for factory baking, not for conventional processes.) So the aleurone, along with the germ and the outer layers of bran, goes into wheatfeed, the Orwellian word for animal food derived from milled wheat grain.

It is the extraction of all but a scarcely perceptible trace of bran from our flour, and the consequent absence of fibre in our bread, which gives rise to the warnings so urgently expressed by wholefood campaigners. It is indeed difficult not to feel dismay over the drastic impoverishment of our bread flour. The replacement of lost vitamins and minerals by synthetic equivalents is held by the government – and some dieticians – to be an adequate solution; but it does not of course deal with the lack of fibre content. In 100 per cent wholewheat flour there is approximately 2 to 2·5 per cent of fibre, and in 70 per cent reinforced white flour it is reduced to the vanishing point of 0·12 per cent.

The importance at present attached to bran fibre in daily diet is discussed further on in this chapter, as is also the vital part played by the wheat germ in the flavour and savour of bread. Here it is sufficient to note that it was only in the mid nineteenth century that doctors and dieticians began to agitate for the inclusion of wheat bran in household bread. Before this period bran was much disliked, and was not considered wholesome. Except for the lowliest bread, and in times of famine, the bran was fed to the animals. 'Bread having too much bran

---

1. *The Milling of Wheat*, leaflet issued by the National Association of British and Irish Millers, 21 Arlington Street, London s w 1.

in it is not laudable', wrote Andrew Boorde in his *Dyetary of Helth* (1542), and that seems to have been very much the general opinion about the matter for at least 300 years, although fairly early in the nineteenth century, during the years of grain shortage, an economical way of increasing the bulk and improving the flavour of bread was to boil bran, use the water from it – called bran tea – for making up bread dough, and still use the bran for the horses or pigs. In seventeenth- and eighteenth-century rural France this was common practice, and was feasible, as in England, because any farmer who took his own grain to the mill received it back with all the bran intact. The sifting, or bolting, was done at home.

The popular feeling about ordinary brown bread, as it had been for generations and indeed as it has persisted until today, was recorded by Henry Mayhew in his famous book on the working people of nineteenth-century London:

'One of my elder informants remembered his father telling him that in 1800 and 1801, George III had set the example of eating brown bread at his one o'clock dinner, but he was sometimes assailed as he passed in his carriage, with the reproachful epithet of "*Brown* George". This feeling continues, for the poor people, and even the more intelligent working men, if cockneys, have still a notion that only "white" bread is fit for consumption.'

Henry Mayhew, London Labour and the London Poor, 1851

Writing in 1857 Eliza Acton evidently regarded the dietary significance of whole wheatmeal bread as still something of a revelation. Having made some rather over-emphatic statements concerning the strengthening nature of wholemeal bread and its value to persons of sedentary habits and to invalids as well as to 'those whose toil is heavy and exhausting', caution returns and in a qualifying footnote she observes that 'it may possibly not suit all eaters equally, but it seems at least worthy of a trial'.[1] This appears a sensible way of approaching the matter.

To make good bread from whole wheatmeal, although always said to be so easy, demands rather more care and understanding than making it from a more finely milled flour. In compensation, it has or should have a wonderful true wheaty flavour, and all the minerals, fat and vitamins, as well as the bran, of wheat which has not been tampered with in any way.

1. *The English Bread Book*, 1857.

BUYING FLOUR FOR BREAD

To anyone setting out to buy bread flour without previous knowledge
or experience much confusion can be caused by the different nomen-
clatures adopted by the flour combines and the millers, as also by the
health-food and wholefood merchants, and since many of these nomen-
clatures depend upon proprietary variations it is not easy to sort them
out. Roughly, though, wheat flours and meals sold for home breadmaking can be classified as follows:

Stone-ground 100 per cent wholemeal or whole wheatmeal

This is the whole grain of the wheat, from which nothing has been
extracted and to which nothing has been added, ground in the old way

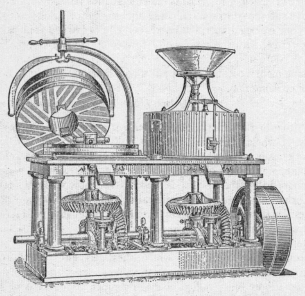

French burr stone mill for wholemeals illustrated in Grant's *Chemistry of Breadmaking*, 1912. 'A genuine wholemeal,' said Grant, 'contains the whole of the materials
of the wheat berry; frequently, however, the coarsest bran is removed, yielding a
finer meal and a more palatable and digestible loaf without serious loss of the mineral
salts.'

between specially cut and dressed circular stones. (The process is described more fully in the chapter on milling. See also Plate 11.)

In England this meal is usually – although there are quite a few exceptions – milled from home-grown soft wheat blended with a proportion of hard Manitoba grain. In spite of the blending with high-gluten wheat, bread made from it has little volume because the presence of the large particles of bran from the outside of the berry inhibits aeration, so it is on the heavy side and, although considered so healthy by convinced wholefood disciples, is not necessarily everybody's salvation. While to me today's commercial white bread is as repulsive as pig to a devout Mohammedan, I am not convinced that wholemeal provides the ideal alternative. Wholewheat flour well-milled from clean, sweet, organically grown grain unblended with imported hard wheat *can* make wonderful bread. Unfortunately, it does not often follow that the bread is as good as its raw material. Even when it is well made, it is not necessarily the kind of bread everyone wants every day.

When wholemeal has been stone-ground this will be stated on the bag. If there is no such statement then the chances are that the meal in question is a reconstituted one, of 95 per cent extraction rather than a true 100 per cent wholemeal. In other words it is a roller-milled flour, unbleached, to which the bulk of bran and the wheat germ extracted by roller milling have been returned. Because of the presence of the wheat-germ oils – small in proportion though these are – whole wheatmeals do not keep as well as fine roller-milled flours from which the germ has been extracted. So it is essential to store wholemeals in a very cool dry place, and not to buy very large quantities at a time.

When meal has been ground from organically grown wheat this is stated on the bag, and when a proportion of hard wheat has been used in the blend this too will be announced. The hard imported wheat has not however been organically grown. This point, together with the reason for the blending of the different grains, is now stated on some packages. This helps to inform the customer and at the same time forestalls somewhat trivial criticism of the kind which caused a *Sunday Times*[1] journalist to imply that there was something deceitful about the mixing of Manitoba wheat with the organically grown soft English product. Prewett's, the firm under fire, made matters no clearer by telling the *Sunday Times* that, if the Manitoba wheat were not used, the bread made solely from organically grown English wheat would

1. 24 March 1974.

'taste like cake'. To the ordinary public – and indeed to journalists – this statement is bewildering. The real issues are volume and keeping quality versus flavour. Undoubtedly organically grown soft wheats have the better flavour. Equally certainly the flour they yield makes flat loaves which quickly go stale.

Wheatmeals with husk and bran partially removed

These meals or flours vary in wholegrain content from 81 to 90 per cent, according to the custom of the millers concerned, or to the majority preferences of his customers. Wheatmeals are unbleached, and will vary in colour and also in gluten content according to the wheat used. If they are strong flours this will be stated on the bag, as, for example, in the case of Prewett's strong brown bread flour. The percentage of wholegrain is also usually stated on the bag, and as with 100 per cent wholemeal there will be an indication of whether or not the wheat has been organically grown, and if it has been stone-milled this too will be announced, as in Prewett's 81 per cent Millstone flour. In the case of a blend of soft and hard wheats it should be taken that the strength or high-gluten content comes from imported Canadian (Manitoba) or American wheat which is not organically grown. As already explained above this puts off the hard-line wholefood addict but to the rest of us the small proportion – rarely more than 25 per cent because these types of meal or flour require less assistance from high-gluten wheat than do the coarse meals – is welcome because it will make a better and lighter loaf with very little sacrifice of flavour.

It must here be emphasized that according to our present legislation all wheat flours with the sole exception of 100 per cent wholemeal must contain added chalk in the proportion of 14 oz per sack or 280 lb of flour, iron, vitamin B_1 or thiamine, in synthetic form, and nicotinic acid or nicotinamide.[1] Some millers, such as Prewett's, admit the added chalk on their packages. Others are silent on the matter. The laws are considered to be so clearly defined that detailed labelling is not at present legally necessary.[2] As with fluoride in our water, the chalk and the vitamins are introduced into flour for our benefit, not for that of the baker or cake manufacturer. That, whatever the extraction rate of the flour,

---

1. The vitamins and iron, or nutrients as they are collectively called, are required to be added in quantities which bring their levels to those found naturally in flour of 80 per cent extraction rate.
2. The question of ingredient listing is now (1978) under reconsideration.

these additives should be considered beneficial to public health, strengthens the argument of wholefood believers in favour of bread made from meal from which nothing has been extracted and to which it is not therefore necessary to add anything.

Wheatmeal and brown flours as used by the bakers are not necessarily of the same extraction rate as those sold for household baking. They are described further on in this chapter.

Flours of 81 to 90 per cent extraction rate can be mixed according to individual preference, perhaps with a white flour to produce a lighter, finer, pale brown loaf, or with a proportion of 100 per cent whole wheatmeal to make bread with a sufficient bran content and a fine flavour but less pudding-like texture than the usual wholemeal loaf. Another variation, useful when a good wholemeal may be difficult to find, is a small proportion of medium-ground oatmeal mixed with an 80 to 90 per cent wheatmeal, which will yield a loaf with a nice bite and a good flavour. A mixture of rye meal and 85 to 90 per cent wheatmeal makes a loaf which would have been familiar to our ancestors of three centuries ago, when wheat and rye was still the traditional mixture of grain which under the name of maslin was used in England for the bread commonly eaten by the majority. In some areas indeed this type of bread persisted until the latter half of the eighteenth century. To us, bread of this rather dense texture but attractive flavour is a welcome change, interesting and odd. To our ancestors it was daily food. Is it surprising that lighter, whiter bread seemed preferable?

'Farmhouse' bread flour

This is a proprietary brand of 81 per cent whole wheatmeal, unbleached, stone-milled and packed by the firm of Allinson. It makes very good dough and produces an appetizing pale brown loaf, light and moist, with good volume. Another similar flour, and a good one, from the firm of Jordan at Holme Mills in Bedfordshire (a mill still driven by the original water wheel), bears the name of Country Cookbook plain flour. It is unbleached, 85 per cent wheatmeal, not stone-milled, but ground, as stated on the bag, 'by slow moving rollers, to minimize damage to its natural vitamin and enzyme content'. When you open the bag, the flour looks attractively creamy, flecked with the smallest of straw-yellow particles. These indicate that the germ, the life of the wheat, has not been destroyed by the rollers. When dough from this flour is made up it turns a deeper, true wheat colour. It makes beautiful bread, with an exceptionally subtle flavour and scent of wheat, and it provides a refutation of the notion that only stone milling produces worthwhile flour with a true wheaty taste. The explanation is in the slow movement of the rollers used at Holme Mills. The speed of approximately 200 revolutions per minute doesn't over-heat the grain; there is no danger of the oil in the germ becoming rancid, which is more or less what happens when the giant, high-speed rollers – they operate at something like 650 to 800 or even more revolutions per minute – of the great industrial milling companies set to work on the wheat grain. Roller milling, like so many of the remarkable inventions of the nineteenth century, has been abused. Its powers have grown beyond control.

Stone-milled flours such as Farmhouse and Millstone are recommended by wholefood enthusiasts for cakes and pastry-making. I don't quite see the logic of this. If the soft and hard wheats have been blended to make flour expressly for bread, then why use it for cakes and pastries which do not require strong flour and indeed are by no means improved by it? In this context it may be relevant to bear in mind a comment made in the *Which? Good Food Guide 1974*, concerning the Guildford branch of Cranks wholefood restaurant. 'The stoneground pastry here' – the very words are sufficiently leaden – 'is harder than in w 1' (the London branch). In other words if you use brown flour for pastry,[1] don't expect it to be light, or even very appetizing. If the aim is to put people off eating cakes and pastries, a kinder and less wasteful way of doing it would be to provide evidence – I am sure there is plenty of it – of the very marked way in which the demand for sweet pastries, pies and sticky cakes will drop in households where the bread is home-baked, good, *varied* and so satisfying that little need is felt for rich and sugary confections. If the health-food and wholefood restaurants are doing their job well, do their customers need sweet pastries?

There remains the question of savoury pastries, such as the pizza, and of all the breakfast cakes and teacakes and pancakes based on yeast doughs and batters, the spice breads and buns, the butter-enriched brioche-type delicacies, and so many other nice things described in this book. For most of these I use unbleached strong white flour, but there is nothing to stop anyone who prefers to do so making the same doughs with a wheatmeal of 81 or 85 per cent extraction. I do not recommend

1. The millers of wholewheat flours pack 81 per cent extraction flour, stoneground from low-gluten wheat, which they recommend for cakes and pastry. This makes more sense than using bread flour.

these for brioche or pizza doughs, nor for light yeast cakes such as Sally Lunns and Bath buns, but for fruit and spice bread they are very successful. They are of course more expensive than plain white household flour.

STRONG BREAD FLOUR
(PLAIN)
LOCKYER&SON, Clapton Mills, CREWKERNE.
7 lb. Net   Tel. 321

Strong plain white bread flour

'The judging of bread by its whiteness is a mistake which has led to much mischief, against which the recent agitation for "whole meal" is, I think, an extreme reaction.'

W. Mattieu Williams, *The Chemistry of Cookery*, 1885

Strong plain bread flour is usually milled from a blend of soft or medium-soft wheats, which may be home-grown or imported, with hard wheats, usually from Manitoba. The extraction rate of white bread flour is 70 to 73 per cent, which is to say that in the milling process all but negligible traces of bran and germ are automatically sifted out from the ground grain. What remains is the endosperm, or protein and starch cells of the wheat berry, by this time in the granular form known as semolina. These are the grains which are eventually ground into the fine white flour we know. Some strong white flours sold for home bread-making are bleached, some are not. The latter, which are cream-coloured rather than white, make notably better bread. And when I say better, I mean that it tastes nicer and looks more attractive and more natural. Nutritionally there isn't much difference.

A good blend of strong plain unbleached flour will produce a well-risen, rich creamy-coloured loaf rather than the dead grey-white of bakery-plant bread, and is good for nearly all types of yeast cookery – spice cakes, brioches, buns, pizza doughs, muffins, crumpets, baps and leavened pancakes.

As an economy it is often possible to use a fifty-fifty mixture of strong bread flour and plain household flour, particularly in those doughs for quickly cooked breads such as baps and muffins which are usually given a relatively short rising time.

A high-gluten flour is considered right for puff pastry, and *can* be used for sauces and ordinary short pastry, although there is no particular advantage in so doing – see above – since it is more expensive than household flour.

Strong plain white bread flour keeps well, and since a mixture of this flour with a proportion – according to taste – of 100 per cent whole wheatmeal makes a beautiful, sweet-smelling and very wholesome loaf, it is hard to see why so many health-food and wholefood stores should take so bigoted and high-handed an attitude towards white flour that they will not stock it in any form. Perhaps if the people who buy the stock and run these establishments knew just a little about bread-making and the properties and performance of different flours and would train their staff, shopping would be made easier and quicker, and the customers would not be intimidated or exasperated – according to temperament – by nanny-type chatter of what is or is not 'good for you'.

Bakers' white bread flour

'The resources of science have been ransacked to cheapen and adulterate practically every foodstuff that is consumed in large quantities.'

Frederick Hackwood, *Good Cheer*, 1911

'British bread is the most chemically treated in Western Europe.'

T.A.C.C. Report, 1974[1]

If you are on good terms with an independent baker it is just possible that he might let you buy a few pounds of his flour from time to time,

1. Technology Assessment Consumerism Centre Report, *Bread. An Assessment of the Bread Industry in Britain*, Intermediate Publishing Ltd (P.O. Box 6, Kettering, Northants.), 1974.

and this would be cheaper than buying proprietary bread flour from a health-food or wholefood shop. But it must be taken into account that flour supplied to bakeries has not only had many of its natural properties removed by roller milling but has also been subjected to chemical bleaching. As well as the obligatory additives, various dough improvers and dough-maturing agents – these mean improvers from the baker's point of view, not that of the consumer – have also been added. Sometimes ascorbic acid, or vitamin C which acts as an oxidant,[1] is added to the flour by the baker. This additive is the only 'improver' permitted in all the original Common Market countries with the exception of Holland, where five bleachers and improvers are allowed.[2] With our ten improvers and bleaching chemicals, we are still well ahead.

Having made experiments in baking bread from white flour kindly supplied to me by a baker, I think it relevant to report that I found it all too easy to produce a professional-looking loaf with splendid volume, dead-white flaky crumb and total absence of flavour or character. So anyone who can obtain bakers' flour would be well advised to keep it for blending purposes, to give volume to wholemeal loaves, or to make yeast cakes in which spices and fruit will compensate for the non-flavour of the flour.

Bakers' wheatmeal or brown flour

'Brown bread as sold by the bakers is seldom a genuine article, but is made up by mixing bran or pollard with inferior flour.'

J. H. Walsh, *A Manual of Domestic Economy,*
new edn, 1861 (first published 1856).

The complaints made about commercial brown bread by the dieticians and doctors of the latter half of the nineteenth century are familiar. What in those days was considered a dubious practice on the part of the millers and/or bakers is one now legally sanctioned by the government. According to the present Regulations governing the content of bread and flour, 'wheatmeal' and 'brown' are interchangeable terms for any flour containing not less than 0·6 per cent of crude fibre or bran. This compares with 2 to 2·5 per cent found in 100 per cent wholemeal,

1. See the recipe for short-time bread dough on p. 267.
2. T.A.C.C. Report (see quotation above).

and is about the percentage found in a wheatmeal of 80 per cent extraction. Into the same category of 'brown' flours come proprietary mixes such as Hovis with its added wheat germ, and the malted Bermaline meal, the latter being available in retail shops as well as to the bakery trade. Low-grade white flours with permitted caramel colouring plus the required percentage of added bran and of course the obligatory chalk and synthetic vitamins and minerals are also covered by the terms brown and wheatmeal. As J.H.Walsh wrote, 'bread baked from this kind of mixture rapidly becomes dry, and is quite lacking in that sweet nutty flavour which is due to all the elements of pure wheat'. It is scarcely surprising that 'brown' bread is so often disliked and rejected, and that the average consumer is indifferent to the distinctions to be made between wholemeal, wheatmeal and just 'brown' breads. If bakers themselves are aware of the distinctions – they could scarcely not be – their shop assistants often are not. To them the words wholemeal and wheatmeal are synonymous, so the customers are frequently, and not necessarily deliberately, misled. For this reason, among others, the Food Standards Committee in its *Second Report on Bread and Flour* (1974), recommended that the term wheatmeal be outlawed and brown retained. Understandable though it is, the Committee's recommendation does seem to me a faulty one. To abandon a traditional, associative and descriptive term in favour of one so amorphous and indecisive can only open the way to further confusion and obscuring of the facts. What should be changed is the ruling concerning the content of the various wheatmeals, not their nomenclature. For a start, wheatmeal should surely contain a percentage of the natural germ? Of this there is no mention in the Regulations. (Those of us who make our own bread quickly learn to appreciate the differences between say 81 per cent or 85 per cent wheatmeal and 100 per cent wholemeal and to recognize the distinctions to be made between various types of brown flour. It is hard to believe that those who buy their bread are not equally up to mastering a few of the same simple facts.) A third category to cover white flours with added treated wheat germ, malted meal, bran and so on could be created to cover the made-up flours and breads.

Among somewhat smug criticisms frequently levelled at housewives is the one that even those who buy 'brown' bread because 'it's good for the children' don't know the difference between wheatmeal, wheatgerm, and wholemeal bread. This is often true. It is nothing for anyone to feel superior about. If the housewife is not told that the differences exist how is she expected to know what questions to ask? In this country there is no legislation covering the listing of ingredients used in any given type of bread (what a long list it would be, even for wholemeal), and astonishingly there are no flour labelling laws. It is up to the public to educate itself on this point.

It is curious to reflect that while every prepared foodstuff on sale in this country, from baked beans to tinned pears, from sardines to pheasant in port wine, must by law carry on its label a list of its contents, no such protection is extended to the consumer of what politicians are still given to describing as 'the basic food of the people'.

It is difficult not to agree with the T.A.C.C. Report quoted above when it concludes that 'the other countries of the Community, if they are wise, will not break bread with the British'.

Bakers' wholemeal or wholewheat flour

One hundred per cent wholewheat flour from which nothing has been taken away and to which nothing has been added would not be the correct description of the wholewheat flours used in commercial baking. That is to say that the first part of the description would be or should be accurate, since the Bread and Flour Regulations of 1963 lay it down that 'wholemeal shall contain the whole of the product derived from the milling of cleaned wheat'. That it is the whole wheat and nothing but the whole wheat cannot however be claimed. According to the Regulations, 'wholemeal bread may contain all or any of the yeast stimulating' preparations, acids, diluents, preservatives, emulsifiers, stabilizers and the lecithin as permitted in white and brown flours and breads. In addition caramel colouring can be added to wholewheat flour 'to standardise the colour'.

It is comforting to know that no additional iron, vitamin B_1 or nicotinic acid – the nutrients added to all other flours – are required in wholemeal, such 'nutrients being naturally present and not added'. No *creta preparata* or chalk is at present added to wholemeal (out of deference, it would seem, to those consumers who crankily prefer their wholemeal natural), and no flour or meal derived from any grain other than wheat is permitted in commercial wholemeal flour or bread. This latter regulation seems a rather odd one to emphasize. Wholefood bakers such as the Ceres Bakery in Portobello Road, London W 11, and the Springhill Bakery at Dinton near Aylesbury, pride themselves on bread made with a mixture of wholemeals milled from different grains.

Granary meal

Granary is the proprietary name of a blend of wheatmeal, rye flour and pieces of malted grain, or sprouted wheatflakes as they are known to the blenders. The sweetish taste and slightly sticky texture of bread made from granary meal is liked by a great many people, as witness the weekly production of three quarter million granary loaves by the British bakery trade. Granary Foods Ltd, of Burton-on-Trent, have superseded Mapletons, the health-food firm, as suppliers of granary meal both to the trade and to household breadmakers. Although the company supply their own recipes to the bakers, who are supposed to adhere to them, bought granary bread does inevitably vary from baker to baker, a circumstance which leads the public – as indeed it led me – to assume that granary bread was a generic term applied to any loaf made with malted meal and whole bits of wheatkernel.

Bread from granary meal is very easy to make up at home, and provides encouragement to beginners. It also keeps well. It is not, however, what I would call everyday bread, and in making up the dough I usually blend in a proportion of strong white flour or 85 per cent wheatmeal so that the malt flavour is toned down.

Household flour

'This flour is made from the "pick of the world's" finest wheat, just the way it's always been: selected, blended and milled by McDougalls, using today's most modern methods. McDougalls flour is as fine and as white as can be, which makes it a part of the pleasure of cooking.'

Flour bag label, 1974

By the term household flour is meant, throughout this book, the all-purpose plain white flour which you buy from the grocer or the self-service store. It will almost certainly be a soft flour, roller-milled, refined, bleached. As already explained, for the sake of economy or when you run short of strong flour it is perfectly feasible to mix household and bread flours or to make the kind of bread, such as baps or muffin loaves, for which household flour is quite successful. Neither McDougalls nor any other miller or flour packer would make the slightest claim that this type of flour is good for breadmaking. (As can be seen from the quote above, mention of its taste is carefully avoided because it doesn't have any nor does anyone expect it to have.) Indeed they would probably far rather we didn't try to make bread with it.

Years ago, when I made inquiries of McDougalls on this point, they refuted, through their public relations agent, the likelihood of household flour making 'bread of an edible nature'.

In the Midlands and the north of England, where home bread-making and yeast cookery generally have never died out, it is easier to find bread flour than in other parts of the country, since high-gluten-content flours packed by some of the big flour-milling combines (McDougalls among them) are stocked by many grocers – and at less fancy prices than those exacted by wholefood and health-food stores. These flours are bleached and treated in much the same way as bakers' bread flour, and in my experience suffer from a similar lack of flavour. When comparing prices of ordinary household flour and high-gluten bread flour, it must always be remembered that the latter absorbs more water and makes a bigger loaf, so that pound for pound you get more bread for your money. But unless you buy flour and bake bread on a large scale it is not easy to calculate just what the differences may be – probably something within the region of an extra 2½lb of bread for every stone (14lb) of flour.

American all-purpose unbleached flour

Although American flour is not, so far as I know, to be found in English shops, those who use American recipes may find it helpful to know that their all-purpose flour means a flour of medium strength which can be used for bread and cakes. It is nearer to our unbleached strong plain flour than to ordinary plain household flour, and I have found that its performance is very little different from that of the plain bread flours which I normally buy. It is, by the way, 'enriched' with additives, which are listed on the bag I have as 'malted barley flour, niacin, iron, thiamine, riboflavin'. There is also a thoughtful explanation of the term unbleached flour. It means, say the packets, flour which is not bleached.

Graham meal and Graham flour

These are the American equivalents of our wholewheat meals and flours. They derive their name from the nineteenth-century Doctor Sylvester Graham who propounded the importance and the beneficial effects of bread made from flour containing the whole content of the wheat grain, with particular emphasis on the bran.

French bread flour

Although, like American flour, French bread flour cannot at present be bought in England, so many people believe that if only they *could* buy it they would then automatically be able to make French bread that I have gone into the question at some length in the chapter entitled 'Notes on French Bread'. The way to set about buying bread flour in France, and what to ask for, is noted in the same chapter.

Barley meal

> 'Here all the summer could I stay,
>   For there's a Bishop's Teign,
>   And King's Teign,
> And Coomb at the clear Teign's head;
>   Where, close by the stream,
>   You may have your cream
> All spread upon barley bread.'

John Keats,
Poems Written at Teignmouth

'The people lived on very coarse diet. The food on farms consisted of "Sopen", barley bread which was almost black and generally very mouldy. It was considered a waste to eat fresh bread.'

Miss R. M. Evans, writing in *Transactions of the Cardiganshire Antiquarian Society*,
vol. xii, 1937

Miss Evans was writing of the seventeenth and early eighteenth centuries in Cardiganshire. Keats's lyrical enjoyment of barley bread spread with clotted cream, and Miss Evans's down-to-earth description of the poor Welsh farm labourers' diet in previous centuries seem typical of the conflicting attitudes of poet and social historian.

Among the important staple meals for breadmaking, after wheat, the two most common in England until the mid nineteenth century were barley and rye.

Meals and flours milled from the barley grain, which is low in gluten content, make a rather flat loaf, the colour is greyish, and bread made entirely from barley quickly goes dry, but the flavour is good, with an unmistakably earthy tang – anyone who has ever eaten a good barley or Scotch broth will recognize the taste and the aroma – so barley flours can be mixed with white or brown wheat flours to make a loaf with more volume, and a better colour and keeping quality. A mixture of coarsely milled barley meal and 85 per cent wheatmeal makes delicious bread. A recipe is on p. 297. Bread made from a mixture of barley flour and oatmeal is mentioned by James Williams in the passage from *Give Me Yesterday*, quoted on p. 39.

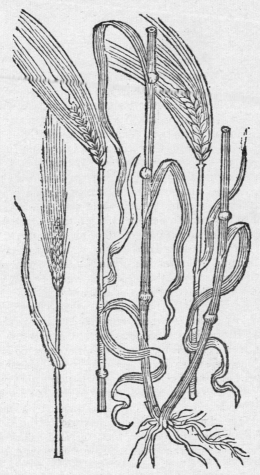

Common barley. 'The most usuall Barley' in Gerard's time, and the one then commonly used for malting. *Gerard's Herbal.*

In Wales, Scotland and some parts of northern England barley bannocks or flat, griddle-cooked bread, made in much the same way as oatcakes, were for long far more common than oven-baked loaves, although in households where there were the old primitive clay ovens, as in Devon, Cornwall and parts of Wales, barley loaves were popular. Barley-flour pastry is said to have been used for the crust of the Christmas goose pies made in Cumberland. Barley-meal pancakes leavened with yeast are particularly delicious.

Barley is perhaps best known and recognized today as the original source of malt and the one most generally used.

Malting is the process whereby the cleaned grain is steeped in cold water until it has absorbed some 42 to 45 per cent of moisture, which is sufficient to induce germination. It is then drained and spread in a long, 2 to 3 foot high heap, called a 'couch', and left until, as the temperature of the moist grain rises, germination begins. The grain, now spread evenly and approximately 6 inches deep over the floor of the malting house, is left to grow or sprout for about ten days. During this stage the grain is known as a 'piece'. The 'piece' is regularly sprinkled with water, ploughed and turned so that the temperature is controlled and the acrospires, or embryo green shoots, start growing under the barley skin. In this manner, uniformity of growth is ensured, the aim of the maltster being to achieve growth of the acrospire to approximately two-thirds of the length of the grain, while the rootlet growth is kept to a minimum. When the maltster judges that the embryo shoots have reached the right point, the 'piece' is once more thickened up into a heap, to be left for twelve to twenty-four hours. Next, the 'green' malt is moved to a drying kiln. It is now ready for the drying process. This consists of drawing first cold, then warmer, and finally hot air through the grain. The drying lasts over a period of three to four days. It is this process which checks further germination of the grain and creates the typical malt flavour and sweetness, the final flavour being determined by the degree of curing, which takes approximately eight hours.[1]

Almost any grain can be malted, barley, wheat and rye being the three most commonly used for the process. The craze for adding malted meal or malt extract to bread seems to have started during the last two decades of the nineteenth century, when the food values and tonic properties of malt extract and malt sugar were discovered. Writing in

---

1. For much of this information on the malting of barley, I am indebted to Mr N. W. Miller, production director of Ruddle's Brewery in Rutland.

the late 1890s, the compiler of *Law's Grocer's Manual* observes that 'malt would seem to have become a boon and a blessing not to babes alone but to speculators as well. Besides malt bread, malt coffee, and malt sugar, there are various other preparations designated as malted: malted cocoa, malted marmalades, malted preserves, malted jellies, etc.'

Malted meals, malted foods and malt extracts can be bought at health-food stores, and the latter also at chemists.

Rye meal

'Maslin bread is made half of wheat and half of rye. And there is also maslin made, half of rye and half of barley.'

> Andrew Boorde, *The Dyetary of Helth*, 1542

'Bake it in rye paste, and when it is cold fill it up with butter, after a fortnight it will be eaten.'

> From a recipe for making beef 'like red Deer to be eaten cold',
> *The Compleat Cook*, 1658 (first published 1655)

Although rye was for centuries one of the staple grains of the English farmer, often sown and grown in conjunction with wheat to make the crop known as maslin (hence maslin or meslin – i.e. mixed – bread), the use of rye flours for breadmaking in this country has diminished to the point where it is virtually only in bakeries catering for Jewish or Polish communities that rye bread is baked in any quantity or variety. The grain is subject to a fungus disease called ergot. If diseased grain gets into the meal, bread made from it can cause internal bleeding. Also, according to *The Baker's ABC*,[1] 'weariness, giddiness, a voracious appetite, a sensation of creepiness, followed by gangrene and death'.[2]

Although rye has a good gluten content it is gluten of a different and inferior nature to wheat gluten, making rye meal difficult to handle and unstable when used on its own (it must have been a hard task to make it into pastry as directed by that *Compleat Cook* quoted above). Consequently nearly all rye breads – with the exception of pumpernickel and one or two Dutch breads – are made with a mixture of wheat flour.

Rye gives a very delicious and rather powerful flavour to any bread dough with which it is mixed, so a little goes a long way, especially given the characteristic density of texture which even a small proportion of rye will produce in a loaf.

1. Ed. John Kirkland, 1927.   2. In Britain ergot is rare.

Anyone new to breadmaking who would like to use rye meal would be best advised, I think, to start by making a tin loaf such as the one described on p. 293. Once familiar with the feel and the performance of rye, it is a simple matter to increase the proportions, and attempts at

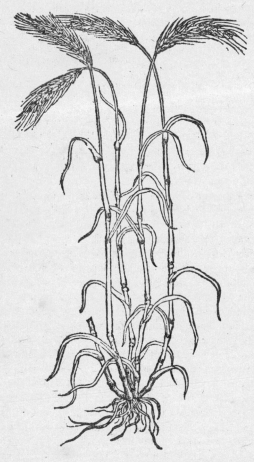

Rye. When our own rye and wheat harvests failed, we imported rye from Germany and Poland. This happened in 1596 'when there was a generall want of corne, by reason of the abundance of rain that fell the yeare before'. The year 1596 has come down to us as the worst of the whole century for grain shortage. *Gerard's Herbal.*

the more characteristic torpedo- or cylinder-shaped rye loaf are likely to be more successful, although these are never entirely easy to bake because rye meal dough cracks and spreads.

Dark and light rye meals, the latter easier to handle but with less flavour, are to be found in the usual health-food stores, although few of them offer a choice. To my taste, the best, a dark one, is Mrs Horsfield's, and for those who prefer the light meal Prewett's market a stoneground rye. Both are packed in 1 lb bags. Rye meal is not one to store for any length of time.

Sourdough rye bread is a great German, central European, Scandinavian and Jewish favourite. The famous San Francisco sourdough bread[1] is more usually made with wheat flour, as in the old French tradition. Sourdough rye breads, made on a basis of a starter or leaven kept from one breadmaking to the next, and each time renewed by the paying back into the original of a portion from the new batch, probably stemmed from the natural propensity of rye dough to acquire a mildly and attractively sour taste and aroma. Two other characteristics of rye bread are the addition of spices such as caraway, dill or cumin seeds (the latter particularly successful) and the shiny polished appearance on the crust of rye loaves, achieved by two or three successive brushings of the loaf with a thickish starch paste. This can be made with potato flour or cornflour (cornstarch) and water in the proportion of $\frac{1}{2}$oz of starch mixed with $\frac{1}{4}$ pint of boiling water. The crust is brushed with this mixture before the loaves are put in the oven, and again when they are taken out. The familiar look is, I have found, not easily achieved with bread baked in an ordinary domestic oven.

Apart from its fine savour in bread, dark rye meal gives a characteristic flavour to many of the gingerbreads or honeycakes of central Europe, and to the dry crispbreads, such as Ryvita, of Scandinavian countries. Among the most delicious of those which I have eaten are the biscuits or rye-cakes made on the Danish island of Bornholm.

Oatmeal

'Corn and oats is much the same as saying people and horses.'

F. Braudel, *Capitalism and Material Life 1400–1800*, 1973

There is no appreciable gluten content in oatmeals, so they are used in

1. See pp. 295–6.

breadmaking only in very small proportions, to give flavour and add to the fat content (oatmeal is rich in fat).

So-called oaten breads are nearly always flat, griddle-baked bannocks or oatcakes, although recipes for yeast-leavened oatmeal muffins appear in eighteenth- and nineteenth-century English cookery books, and Yorkshire oatcakes were often made with a natural or sour leavening.

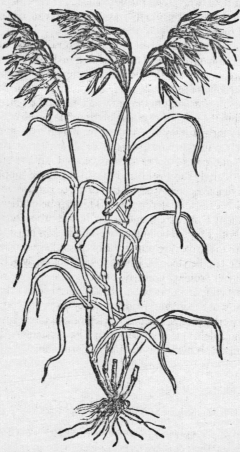

Common oats. In Lancashire, Gerard writes, 'it is their chiefest bread corn for Iannocks, Haver cakes, Tharffe cakes, and those which are called generally oten cakes.' *Gerard's Herbal.*

There are many grades of oatmeal, fine, medium and pinhead – also known as small, middle and rough respectively – being the most common. Of these, fine and medium are the best for adding to bread dough and also for making oatcakes.

Rolled oats, often used for Yorkshire parkin and for strewing on the crust of brown loaves before baking, are steam-treated groats or husked grain crushed into flakes by mechanical rollers.

A small proportion of medium or fine oatmeal gives an exceptionally good flavour to wheatmeal and wholemeal bread.

Although oatcakes and flat oaten breads have long-lasting qualities, the meals in their uncooked state do not store well – probably owing to the fatty content, which easily acquires a bitter taste – so it is advisable to buy only small quantities at a time.

The French historian Braudel, quoted above, when equating corn with people and oats with horses, of course knew perfectly well that for many centuries oats made the staple meals of Scotland, of the English midland and border counties and, with barley, of Wales. In these regions oaten bannocks or haver cakes, cooked on the bakestone or griddle, took the place of the rye or wheaten loaves of more cultivated areas of England and Europe. What is hard for us to realize today, when the keeping and breeding of horses are rich men's luxuries, is that, in the days of which Braudel was writing, horses were one of the first essentials of European life. They were needed for nearly every form of transport, for ploughing, for war – and feeding them was just as important as feeding people. So the oat crops were of great importance. They still are. In England today 90 per cent of all oats grown are used for animal food.

Cornmeal or maize meal

This is the yellow meal ground from so-called Indian corn (the Italians call it Turkish corn – *grano turco*) which also provides us with the familiar corn-on-the-cob.

Although increasingly grown for animal food, maize is not yet an important English crop, but in northern Italy it is grown in great quantity, both for animal feeding and to grind into the meal called *polenta*. Boiled in a great pot, stirred with a hefty wooden stick until stiff, turned out on to boards, then cut into strips or wedges and grilled or toasted, *polenta* still very often takes the place of bread, and accompanies fish, meat and game dishes. Unless very expertly made, *polenta* can be very stodgy, and to me has too soft a taste to make a satisfactory substitute for bread. Several varieties of maize are grown in Italy, among them one which produces beautiful coppery red grains and another which yields a white meal.

In south-western France cornmeal, or *farine de maïs*, was once popular as a kind of porridge, and was also made into cakes and galettes. It is now used mainly for animal food, notably for pigs, poultry and the force-feeding of geese which are fattened for the sake of their livers.

Jean-Paul Clébert in his book *The Gypsies*[1] tells us that the Kalderash, or tinsmiths and coppersmiths, consume large quantities of a maize cake called *ankrusté*, perfumed with cumin and coriander seed. The Kalderash (the name derives from the Romanian *caldera*, a boiling pot or cauldron) came originally from the Balkans. According to themselves they are the only authentic gypsies. Under the name *mamaliga* maize meal is still one of the staple foods of Romania. It is prepared in much the same ways as Italian *polenta*.

In the United States cornmeal is much loved, and cornmeal muffins and other flat hot breakfast breads are almost legendary. Spoon bread, another famous American speciality, is more like a rather solid soufflé than bread (the recipe I have insists on white cornmeal for this dish), and Johnny cakes are a kind of cornmeal muffin. Interesting recipes for these and many other cornmeal breads are to be found in Gertrude Harris's *Manna : Foods of the Frontier* (101 Productions, San Francisco, 1972).

In American recipes for home breadmaking, cornmeal is often recommended for dusting and sprinkling on baking sheets, in greased bread tins and on dough to be rolled out or otherwise manipulated. It is, presumably, the high starch content which makes it useful as a drying meal.

To the Mexicans, maize meal is a staple food. Anyone who wants to learn about the way they use it should read Diana Kennedy's *The Cuisines of Mexico* (1972), and *The Tortilla Book* (1975), the latter a remarkable study of the Mexican national pancake. Both books are published by Harper & Row, New York.

Cornflour or cornstarch

This is the very fine starch of the corn grains, familiar to us as a sauce thickener and, all too much so, as the basis of the terrible white starch puddings or blancmanges of schooldays, and as the foundation of the

[1]. Penguin Books, 1967.

equally dreaded gelatinous custards. English cornflour, as opposed to American cornstarch, was often actually made from rice, a very English way of causing confusion. In the back of Dr A. H. Hassall's famous book on *Food, its Adulterations and the Methods for their Detection* (1876) appears a full-page advertisement for 'Colman's British cornflour (prepared from rice)'.

Rice and rice flour

Several nineteenth-century English writers, among them Eliza Acton and Lady Llanover, considered rice bread one of the best, and best-keeping, of all breads. Boiled rice was used, in varying proportions, to add bulk to scarce and expensive wheat flour; sometimes the water in which the rice was boiled was used for mixing the dough. A good recipe for rice bread, which is first class for sandwiches, is on p. 290. In times of famine during the sixteenth, seventeenth and eighteenth centuries rice flour was used in western Europe to mix with other flours for bread. Cooked rice is more effective, makes more bulk, and a much moister loaf than the grain in flour form. The Greeks made a bread from rice called *orinde* which was highly thought of.

Rice flour (not to be confused with ground rice, which is much coarser) is another and perhaps the best of the very fine white starch flours used for dusting dough at the moulding stage. These starch flours are especially useful when a fat-enriched rather sticky dough is to be handled; they dry the surface of the dough without adhering to it, so any surplus can easily be brushed off and the dough itself has not then been affected or made patchy by the addition of extra flour.

To the bakery trade, dusting flours are known as cones; they were much used at one time for filling the wooden trays or boxes in which certain types of buns and muffins were moulded. The appropriate sized impressions were made in the thick layer of cones with a cutter or a cup, and the portions of dough were dropped into them, shaped, well dusted on the top and left to rise or prove for the second time. When ready, the muffins were lifted carefully on to the heated griddle or hotplate. Cones for this type of moulding were sometimes ordinary flour dust of the cheapest grade. For dusting during the second proving of more serious goods such as cottage and other oven-floor loaves, rice-flour cones were used. I have been told by Miss Rita Ensing, whose father was a London Master Baker, that the bottom crusts of loaves proved in rice cones had a slightly gritty texture, peculiarly attractive.

Potatoes and potato flour

During the grain shortages of the Napoleonic Wars and of the early decades of the nineteenth century and again in the early 1840s before the repeal of the Corn Laws, potatoes, boiled and mashed, were very frequently mixed with flour to produce bread with extra bulk. A small proportion of mashed potato is also of great help in keeping bread moist (second only to rice in this respect, Miss Acton thought), and in addition gives a characteristic and, I find, peculiarly attractive flavour to bread. This is probably something to do with the interaction of the yeast with the potato, always a fertile fermenting ground. Even when grain was plentiful, Victorian bakers often used a small proportion of potato mash in their dough expressly as a fermenting agent rather than with intent to deceive as was generally supposed. Potatoes figure in the majority of recipes for home-made yeast. An excellent nineteenth-century potato-bread recipe is given on pp. 288–90, and is really worth a trial.

Potato flour is a very fine starch, known in France as *fécule de pommes de terre*, or just *fécule*, and used mainly to bind soups and sometimes sauces. Potato starch, like cornstarch, is useful for dusting, and is the best starch for making a glaze for rye loaves (pp. 67 and 294–5).

Miscellaneous bread flours

Chickpea flour (often referred to as lentil flour) and brown wheat flour are used for the various flat, hot breads, *nan* and *chupattees*, and for the poppadums of Indian and Pakistani cooking. These flours can be bought in Indian and Pakistani shops. Wholewheat flour is called *atta* and chickpea flour is interchangeably *gram* flour or *besun*.

Soya flour, extracted from soy beans, is used in much the same way as malted meal, and is regarded as a valuable enriching agent in bread dough. It can be bought from health-food stores. An emulsified form of soy bean extract is used in the bakery trade as a dough improver.

In times of dire shortage of grain, many kinds of root vegetables such as parsnips and beetroot as well as potatoes have been used for bulking out bread. '. . . the artificer and poore labouring man', wrote William Harrison in his *Description of England* (1577), 'is driven to content him-selfe with horsse-corne, I mean, beanes, peason, otes, tares and lintels.' In times of famine in central and southern Europe acorns, normally fed to the pigs, as they were in England, were frequently made into bread. In poor tropical areas beans, sago, locust beans, cassava root, even bananas, can be and are made into forms of bread. Millet grains and cracked wheat are favoured by health-food disciples. Cracked wheat, which is the whole grain lightly crushed, was used for frumenty, one of the oldest of English dishes, a kind of porridge enriched with eggs and milk, and coloured with saffron. It was made for feast days and was also the proper accompaniment to venison. A few years ago an attractive-looking proprietary brown loaf, baked in a flower-pot shape, the outside scattered with cracked wheat grains was commonly sold by London bakers and dairy shops. This loaf seems to have vanished, but at least one proprietary bread meal (see granary bread, p. 283) contains a small proportion of the cracked whole grains.

Buckwheat and buckwheat flour

'Buckwheat is not really a cereal at all, but belongs to the Polygonacie family of plants, of which the rhubarb, the common dock, and several other weeds are also members. It grows two or three feet high, with a knotty branching stem of a reddish colour. Its leaves are ivy-shaped, its flowers are white and hang in bunches, and bees are particularly fond of them. The plant is an annual of easy culture, growing on the poorest soils, sandy heaths, moorlands, and requiring very little attention or manure. . .

'The seeds resemble beech-nuts, whence the name (*bock*, beech) and make very good food for milk cows, hogs, poultry, as well as game . . . throughout the United States buckwheat is largely made into cakes or crumpets, and eaten for breakfast hot from the baker's. These cakes have great renown, but being deficient in gluten, the flour cannot well be made into bread.'

Law's Grocer's Manual, 2nd edn, *c.* 1902

Although little known nowadays in England, buckwheat was certainly grown to a small extent in the midland counties in the eighteenth and nineteenth centuries. The seed was used to feed pheasants as well as poultry, and probably pigs. Recipes for leavened buckwheat pancakes, called bockings, appear in two or three early nineteenth-century cookery books, and are evidently still remembered, since similar recipes are recorded in modern collections published by the National Federation of Women's Institutes. These English recipes seem to be quite distinctive, and are not copied from their American counterparts, nor from Russian blinis, the famous yeast-leavened buckwheat pancakes eaten with sour cream, melted butter and salt herring or caviar.

In northern France buckwheat, called *sarrasin* (saracen grain), is still grown to a small extent, and the flour used to make the regional Breton pancakes called *galettes de sarrasin* or *galettes bretonnes*. These are very thin and often made as large as 12 inches in diameter. They are not usually yeast-leavened. Buckwheat is cultivated also in Belgium.

Proprietary bread flours

Probably the most popular and widely known of these, in England, is Hovis, originally known, according to the Hovis advertising agents, as Smiths Old Patent Germ Bread, and launched some time during the 1880s. The great selling point of Hovis is its wheat germ, added back in concentrated form to white flour, and its mild flavour. The wheat germ for Hovis meal is said to be prepared for blending by being cooked with salt. The meal is sold to the bakers ready mixed for making up into dough, so the quality of the bread does to some extent depend upon the bakery you buy it from. The Hovis company is now part of the huge Rank Hovis McDougall group, and Hovis meal is not sold in retail shops.

Among many similar proprietary brands, launched at various times during the past fifty years or more, are Daren, Turog and Vitbe. All these meals made, or make, moist, light brown breads, with the sweetish flavour produced by the cooking of the germ before it is blended with ordinary white flour. In the case of Turog, the rather crude caramel flavour and darker colour are the results of roasting the germ at a high temperature. Bermaline is a malted meal available to the general public through health-food stores. I find that on its own it makes too sweet a loaf, but a small proportion has a beneficial effect on the volume and performance of wheatmeal and white bread doughs.

Bread mixes

Bread mixes which can be bought by the general public are mostly of the Irish soda-bread type, with the chemical raising agents already mixed in. They make useful standbys in case one might run out of yeast or need to make bread in a great hurry, although it would seem rather less space-consuming to keep a small supply of bicarbonate of soda and cream of tartar and make up one's own soda bread with whatever brown or wholemeal flour may be to hand. Scofa meal is another bread mix – it comes either brown or white – which makes quite an attractive, coarse and rough scone-type loaf, not, as far as I am concerned, one for every day, but a very great improvement on the white flannel loaf of the bakery plant. A proportion of buttermilk or sour milk used instead of water to make up dough from bread mixes produces a better loaf.

Various yeast bread and roll mixes have recently been launched on the British market. For further information about them see pp. 118–19.

Self-raising flour

Although self-raising flour – flour mixed by the millers or packers with their own blend of chemical raising agents – has little part in the recipes in this book, it is a mistake to think that it must not or cannot be used for yeast baking. For example, Prewett's pack an unbleached self-raising flour which on more than one occasion when I have been short of bread flour I have used with perfect success for baps and muffin loaves, and even, mixed with whole wheatmeal, for ordinary bread. A similar blend can also be used for soda bread.

It is interesting to learn that both self-raising flours made with chemical raising agents and bread mixes blended with dried yeast particles have been known for over a century. In the Patent Office published records are several such formulas – in experimental form – three of them submitted in April and May of 1871. Two of these incorporate ½lb of a form of powdered dried yeast to 60lb of clean grain. The yeast and the grain were to be ground together, care being taken to keep the temperature of the meal in grinding below blood heat. 'The flour thus prepared is to be made into dough with water, and without yeast or other fermenting agent.'

The raising part of self-raising flours is a mixture of cream of tartar and bicarbonate of soda, the standard proportion being two of the former to one of the latter – which is more or less the composition of proprietary baking powders. Sometimes rice flour is blended with the chemicals to keep them dry. The proportion of raising agents to flour is determined by the milling companies who market the flour. For household use the proportion will be small in relation to that blended for sale to bakeries. This is to take into account the diverse cooking purposes for which household self-raising flour is often used – for cakes, scones, puddings, suet crusts, biscuits, pancakes – and if the taste of soda is evident in any of these confections the result is not attractive. The chemicals used in baking powders and self-raising flours don't retain their strength for ever, so cooks who use these ingredients only occasionally would do better to buy them in very small quantities from a chemist rather than in the unnecessarily large tins and other containers in which proprietary brands are packed.

Vienna flour

In late nineteenth-century and pre-1914 twentieth-century English cookery books quite frequent mention is made of Vienna flour, and advertisements for various proprietary brands figure heavily in the bakery trade publications of the time. 'Vienna' flour was in reality high-quality Hungarian or Romanian flour, roller milled, fine, of medium strength and creamy white, good for 'Vienna' bread and for puff pastry and yeast cakes.

On the desirability of Vienna flour, and its particular attributes, the following passage provides interesting evidence:

'Undoubtedly the best flour for the purpose [puff paste] is Vienna . . . in the first place, flour for paste should be of good colour and finely ground, not too soft or harsh. It should have a good percentage of gluten, but that gluten must not be so strong that it will pull the rounds into ovals and the ovals into rounds . . . although I have used some few brands of American flour for pastry, the great majority of the flours sent to this country are ground only with the idea that they will be turned into bread, for which they are alone suitable . . .'

Frederick T. Vine, *Savoury Pastry*, 1900

The import of Hungarian and Vienna flours virtually ceased with the disintegration of the Austro-Hungarian Empire after the First World War.

Patent flours

'Top patent', 'long patent', 'short patent' are terms familiar to the bakery trade, but not often encountered by the general public. These names were originally used, in the early days of roller milling, to designate fine flour from which all outside parts – offal, as the millers call the bran, germ, etc. – of the wheat berry were extracted, only the endosperm or semolina, finely milled, remaining. Today the terms are used mainly by millers to denote their own particular blend or grade of extra fine white flour, the bulk of it being of 50 to 65 per cent extraction rate and used for fancy breads such as milk and Vienna loaves and various special rolls in which a very white crumb is considered important. The white bread flour of 70 to 75 per cent extraction used by the bakers for ordinary bread is known as 'straight-run'.

Semolina meals

Although to us semolina means either the milky-starchy puddings of schooldays or the filling but much more delicious *gnocchi alla romana*, bubbling with Parmesan and butter, of Italian cooking, to millers semolina is the major part, the heart or endosperm, of the wheat berry, which provides the bulk of their flour.

When first separated from the bran and the rest of the wheat offal (see 'Patent flours' above) the semolina emerges in granules, of varying degrees of fineness, according to the methods by which it has been milled. When ground to an intensive degree, the result is the finest wheat flour. In stone milling (see pp. 26–30) semolina is made 'by keeping the stones a little farther apart than for flour-making, then carefully sifting the meal thus produced' (John Kirkland, *The Bakers' ABC*, 1927).

Semolina meals as we know them are not normally used in bread doughs.

A confusion which may arise in the minds of those familiar with Italian pasta products and their manufacture is, again, the use of the words *semola* or *semolino di grano duro*, or hard-wheat semolina, which appear on the packets of all the good Italian pasta products. To make pasta which will dry successfully, without splintering, and cook firmly rather than collapsing into a mush, an exceptionally hard-grain, high-gluten variety of wheat called durum is used; and because flour in semolina form absorbs less water than the finely ground product it makes a dough which dries out quickly. This makes it preferable for mass-manufactured pasta, although it is the durum wheat itself which is the really important factor in commercial pasta products – in France, for example, it is a legal requirement for *pâtes alimentaires* – and if no mention of durum wheat or *grano duro* appears on a packet of Italian pasta it is inadvisable to buy it.

The semolina meals we buy in packets from the grocer vary in degrees of fineness, and can be milled from any good hard wheat, not necessarily durums, but always high-gluten grain. The Italian words *semola* and *semolino* derive from *simila*, the Latin for fine flour – fine, that is, in the sense of best quality. Some people do, I believe, use semolina for home-made pasta. I prefer a good strong plain unbleached bread flour, which makes excellent pasta dough. I don't recall ever seeing an Italian cook or housewife making her pasta with semolina.

Durum wheat flours are considered too tough for breadmaking on their own, but are sometimes used for blending.

Bran in bread and in diet

'Bran bread or brown bread is considered by Baron Liebig and other chemists to be much more wholesome than white bread, not only because it contains a greater amount of nutriment, but also because the gritty particles that are present in it produce a slight irritation in the alimentary canal, and so cause it to be slightly aperient in its effect.'

Cassell's Domestic Dictionary, c. 1880

Wholefood supporters make very large claims for the beneficial effects of bran, and warn us that a lack of fibre in the diet 'is believed to be a contributary cause of the increase in diseases like coronary thrombosis, ulcers, diabetes, digestive diseases and appendicitis'. It all sounds very over-stated until you realize that at least some of the assertions are based on serious medical research, for which three respected surgeons have been responsible during the past ten years. In 1966 Surgeon Captain T. L. Cleave published a book, *Diabetes, Coronary Thrombosis and the Saccharine Disease*, in which he and G. D. Campbell, his co-author, propounded the beliefs summarized above. Five years later, Neil S. Painter, Senior Surgeon at Manor House Hospital, London, wrote in the *British Medical Journal* ('Aetiology of Diverticular Disease', 17 April 1971) that, out of seventy patients suffering from diverticular disease and put on a high-residue diet containing wholemeal bread, plenty of vegetables, and a supplement of about six teaspoons of bran daily, sixty-two showed marked relief of the symptoms or complete recovery over a period of three and a quarter years' treatment. The following month Mr Painter, in collaboration with Mr Denis Burkitt, a surgeon working for the Medical Research Council, returned to the subject. In the *British Medical Journal* of 22 May 1971, the two surgeons published a paper, 'Diverticular Disease of the Colon: A Deficiency Disease of Western Civilization'. In this paper Messrs Painter and Burkitt asserted their belief that around 1880 the British diet was depleted of fibre sufficiently to damage the colon. 'The evidence suggests', they wrote, 'that the refining of flour and other cereals is the primary cause of diverticulosis, while the consumption of refined sugar at the expense of bread further increased the loss of dietary fibre.' Concluding their long and important article, Painter and Burkitt observed that 'it is worth remembering that the rise in the death rate from diverticular disease was halted in Britain only during war and immediate post-war years, when white bread was not available and refined sugar was strictly rationed. Perhaps a return to this high-residue diet would achieve more than all our surgical endeavours.'

The Painter and Burkitt findings were disturbing. It goes without saying that they were sharply contested by the milling trade, their researchers and their spokesmen at the Flour Advisory Bureau. One of the very relevant contentions of this body was that we don't necessarily have to eat wholemeal bread in order to get a satisfactory proportion of fibre into our diet, and that, taken overall, the fibre content of our present diet is not significantly lower than it was before the advent of the roller mill and the all-conquering, all-white, no-germ, no-bran loaf. To this criticism the wholemeal/bran advocates were able to reply that there is evidence that as a laxative cereal fibre is superior to fibre from fruit and vegetables.

The controversy will of course continue, there will be further contradictory findings and claims, the millers will go their profitable ways churning out the white flour for the white loaf which accounts for 75 per cent of the bread sold in this country, and the ardent disciples of the pro-bran school will also go their ways, proclaiming their beliefs without accepting the possibility of an alternative. 'White bread and white flour are, literally, destroying us', cries Miss Barbara Cartland in an article published in a health-food periodical.[1] On the other side of the fence are those nutritionists who believe, or appear to, that we are truly fortunate to live in the age of reinforced white flour and the factory loaf. Miss Dilys Wells, for example, lecturer in nutrition and graduate of Queen Elizabeth College, London, has stated that 'today flour and bread are better than ever before . . . it is doubtful whether the interests of the consumer could be more fully protected than by the current legislation.'[2] My own reaction to Miss Wells's assertion is that if you believe that you'll believe anything.

*

1. *Here's Health*, October 1975.
2. *Our Daily Bread*, London, Newman Neame Ltd, 1969; booklet obtainable from the Flour Advisory Bureau.

The English obsession with constipation and the roughage to remedy it is not shared in other European countries. It is true that in central Europe and in Scandinavia more brown bread, especially rye, is eaten than in England, but in France and Italy this is far from the case. French and Italian bread are both predominantly white. Possibly the much greater quantity of fresh fruit and vegetables commonly consumed in these countries supplies some of the roughage as well as the vitamins in which the English diet is sometimes lacking. However that may be, those who pin their faith on bran usually eat it in the form of breakfast cereal. If extra bran is needed for bread, it is to be bought in health-food shops. Were one stuck with nothing but tasteless soft white flour with which to make bread, bran would be valuable for blending; the result would be rather a dry loaf, though, and somewhat reminiscent of the nondescript 'brown bread' of the bakeries. The real taste of the wheat is in the germ.

Wheat germ in bread and in diet

'. . . it has been left to our own refined age to prefer a bread made of wheat from which the very germ has been extracted – only to be sold again as a patent food without which, as the advertisements unashamedly profess, we may look in vain for a long and healthy life.'

C. Henry Warren, *Corn Country*, 1940

'Father was really the Master Baker in the bakehouse . . . though white bread was the rule, because nearly everyone asked for it, Father was no believer in it. "We take out the germ and nourishment of the wheat and feed it to the pigs" he would say, "and keep the rubbish for ourselves. Who would ever think of trying to fatten a pig on white flour?"'

H. S. Joyce, *I was Born in the Country*, 1946

'The pigs have the best of it.'

Mr W. Jordan, of Holme Mills, Bedfordshire, talking to the author, in January 1975, of the 'middlings' of bran, wheat germ and other 'offal' left from the milling of white flour and which goes to make up animal food

It is the extraction of the wheat germ from our bread flour which to many of us seems to constitute the most unnecessary and the saddest of all the offences for which the roller mills are to be blamed. The germ represents only a very small percentage of the grain, and it is a vital one. Just as it is unnecessary to bleach bread flour, so it is expedient rather than necessary to extract the germ. The great milling concerns, using today's high-speed rollers find it more profitable to sell the bran and germ for animal food than to separate them out through the bolting drums and return a percentage of germ to bread flour which would have only a limited appeal.

Few people now know or care whether or not the bread they eat contains that part of the wheat which is its life. Even the little yellow specks of germ to be seen in 81 per cent and 85 per cent wheatmeal make this type of flour unpopular with the majority. At one time flour such as this was the whitest obtainable. It made the luxury bread of the rich. No sooner had the invention of roller milling put it within reach of all than chemical bleaching and more ruthless extraction methods created a demand for flour and bread which was whiter than white.

Curiously enough, among those who do mind about the content of their bread, bran seems to represent a more important component than the germ. Owing, perhaps, to the efforts of the wholefood campaigners, the sale of 100 per cent wholemeals is at present on the increase, while the 81 to 85 per cent extraction flours are the least popular. To me these are the flours which make the best everyday bread. While obviously they contain less bran than 100 per cent wholemeals, they retain a high percentage of the wheat germ which gives bread much of its flavour and character, as well as nutritional value. As the Bemax advertisements say, pure natural wheat germ is 'one of nature's most concentrated sources of protein, iron and vitamin B'. What these ads. fail to say is that Bemax isn't strictly 'natural' wheat germ because in order to ensure its keeping qualities the germ is cooked, and natural enzymes therefore destroyed.

Restoring to denatured flour some of the extracted natural elements in concentrated or synthetic form may go a good way towards compensating for its lost nutritional qualities. Little can be done to restore the wrecked flavour except by returning the germ itself to the flour. This of course was discovered by the inventors of the original Hovis meal, whose blend has been imitated at different times by so many other firms. The popularity of Hovis bread owes more, I fancy, to its sweetish taste and its moist texture than to its content. This is little understood by the majority of customers, although some perhaps buy it because they have a vague idea that 'brown' bread is 'good' for them, and they find Hovis more palatable than most of the 'brown' breads of commerce. It is also the most readily available and most widely advertised.

It is an instructive and useful experiment to make a wheat-germ bread at home. It is also quite an expensive one. At the time of writing (1975) a 3 lb bag of 85 per cent wheatmeal or of strong plain white flour costs about 26p, and a 12oz packet of Jordan's pure wheat germ, 20p. It is obviously cheaper to buy wheatmeal which already contains the germ (and a percentage of bran) than to add this back to white flour, but for times when it may be difficult to buy supplies of wheatmeal I find it a good idea to keep a packet or two of the germ. Proportions I use for one large loaf are 2 to 3oz of germ to 18oz of flour.

Apart from its valuable nutritional qualities and its good savour, wheat germ is considered a most useful dough 'improver', helping to produce loaves with nice open crumb, good volume and excellent keeping quality. According to Walter Banfield, added germ is 'an admirable help in the production of shapely cottage bread' – but too much will have an adverse effect on the dough, so don't be tempted.

Wheat germ in uncooked form, i.e. as sold in packets by health-food stores, should be kept in a cool dry place. The salad drawer of the refrigerator is usually about the right temperature.

National flours

During the 1930s a great national campaign to buy British and Empire produce was launched. This embraced all kinds of foodstuffs from butter and cheese to Australian dried fruit, South African oranges, Jamaican bananas, New Zealand chilled lamb and flour milled from British wheat. In the effort to promote this produce recipes were issued by the Ministry of Agriculture and Fisheries, published in newspapers and magazines and circulated to the Townswomen's Guilds and the Women's Institutes. National Mark flour, milled entirely from British-grown grain, was widely advertised. As bread flour it was not popular, perhaps because it was not white enough, was too soft to make a well-risen loaf, and also perhaps because the recipe for making bread from it, devised by the National Bakery School, was written in terms daunting to any but a professional baker. With its talk of dough thermometers and precise temperatures the recipe must have been responsible for putting off many a housewife from the idea of baking her own bread. The Ministry's advertisements for National Mark flour make interesting reading today. Below are extracts from an advertisement published in a Women's Institute cookery book of the period:

'WHY YOU SHOULD USE NATIONAL MARK FLOUR

'By force of habit and suggestion the consuming public has come to regard whiteness as the test of quality of flour and bread. Yet pure white

USE NATIONAL MARK ALL-ENGLISH FLOUR AND WHOLEMEAL.

Milled entirely from home-grown wheat. Unbleached by artificial means, and free from all chemicals except self-raising materials.

NATIONAL MARK STRAIGHTS
(Blue label),
and
NATIONAL MARK PATENTS
(Green label), for biscuits, pastries, etc,

NATIONAL MARK SELF-RAISING
(Red label), for cakes, scones, buns, sponges,
puddings, and general household purposes.

NATIONAL MARK WHOLEMEAL,
for digestive biscuits, brown scones, etc.

NATIONAL MARK (YEOMAN) STRAIGHTS
or
NATIONAL MARK (YEOMAN) PATENTS
for bread.

Support English wheat-growers by insisting on National Mark flour and bread made from that flour.

Look for the National Mark

on the Bag.

Issued by the Minister of Agriculture and Fisheries.

National Mark Flour advertisement, *c.* 1930.

is not the normal colour of natural wheat flour, nor of bread made from such flour, and can generally be obtained only by artificial bleaching. Unbleached wheat flour as it leaves the mill generally approaches the colour of rich cream and seems to preserve the natural bloom of the freshly-milled grain in all its attractiveness. . .

'The fields of England grow excellent wheat, and the grain when threshed is sweet, clean, fresh, and free from pests. Flour made entirely from English wheat is obtainable under the NATIONAL MARK, which guarantees that flour bearing this trade mark is derived exclusively from English wheat and milled to a definite standard of quality, that it has not been bleached by artificial means, and that, apart from certain constituents added to the self-raising variety in order to make it rise, it is free from any added substances. National Mark flour therefore preserves the full characteristic colour and flavour of good, clean, home-grown wheat, and can be relied upon to give satisfaction.'

The Isle of Wight Cookery Book, 5th edn, *c.* 1930

The National Mark flour of the 1930s (see also p. 83) is not to be confused with the National flour of the 1939–45 War and of the long years of rationing and shortages which followed. This flour, with an average extraction rate of 85 per cent – sometimes lower, sometimes higher, according to current supplies of wheat – looked something like the so-called farmhouse flour which we buy today for home bread-making, and on nutritional grounds contained added calcium carbonate. The loaf made from wartime National flour was launched in March 1941, amid fanfares from the Government and the Ministry of Food as 'the most nourishing bread there could be, not as dark as brown and not as white as white, but very good for you'.[1] Good for you as the National loaf may have been it was much disliked, partly because it was often badly baked and lacked volume owing to the low gluten content of the flour, and partly because there was no choice. To make things worse, there was a long period during which it was an offence to sell a newly baked loaf, so the bread was always dry and stale. Although in retrospect the bread made from National flour seems a great deal more acceptable than today's commercial white loaf, it was no doubt the long years of

1. Two years later, André L. Simon, writing in the introduction to the 'Cereals' volume of the Wine and Food Society's *Concise Encyclopaedia of Gastronomy* (1943), pointed out that while, after three and a half years of total war, wine was exceedingly scarce and olive oil totally unobtainable, we still had unrationed bread, better bread, he thought, than before the war, 'even if its looks be darker'.

BREAD

INTO BATTLE

The housewife deserves a bouquet for the part she is playing in the War effort, but she is falling down on one thing—the daily waste of bread. Too many crusts are being thrown away, or put into the pig bin. Wheat takes the lion's share of our shipping space. And even if waste of bread is as little as half an ounce per head of the population each day this means eight families of four waste a loaf a day, a town of 12,000—the size of Horsham—a sack a day and the whole country a shipload every twelve days—thirty ships a year! A whole convoy! Bread into battle—YES INDEED!

HOW TO KEEP THE LOAF FRESH

Make sure the loaf is quite cold before putting it away. The best way to keep bread fresh is to wrap it in a clean, dry cloth and store in a well ventilated place in a cupboard. Remember, bread must have air. If you keep it in a bin, be sure the bin is well ventilated; even with ventilation holes, keep the lid tilted. Keep the bin scrupulously clean. Wipe it out every day. Wash it out once a week and dry it thoroughly.

TO AVOID DRY LOAF ENDS

When you get to the last three inches of your loaf, place it crumb side down on the bread board—

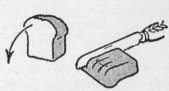

and cut this way. You'll eat the crust while it's fresh and you won't cut your fingers.

Wartime, 1939–45. Ministry of Food leaflet, 1944.
(Bread wasn't rationed until *after* the war.)

that dry, uninteresting loaf which helped to confirm the majority of English people in their taste for bread that is whiter than white, no matter what its taste, texture or content.

As can be seen, then, the desirability of using only or mainly home-grown wheat or of blending it with imported hard wheat for bread is a question of propaganda and of historic necessity as much as of habit or taste. In times of prosperity the big milling and baking combines tell us that we do not like bread made from home-grown wheat. It is not bread, it is cake, they say, forgetting that until the latter part of the eighteenth century all our bread was made from soft wheat, and that for long periods during the nineteenth century we subsisted mainly on our own cereal crops.

Eat Less Bread

Waste None

ASSIST THE GOVERNMENT BY DISPLAYING THIS IN A CONSPICUOUS PLACE IN YOUR HOME.   *Inserted in "The Connoisseur," July, 1917*

Wartime, 1914–18; government poster, 1917.
Reproduced by permission of the Radio Times Hulton Picture Library.

As we have seen, when money for foreign imports is short or when a national crisis demands the utmost support for home industry and farming, the government takes over the propaganda from the millers and the bakers, launching campaigns which stress the excellence of British wheat, the delicious flavour and the wholesome qualities of bread made from our own soft flour. After the harvest of 1974 there were signs that another such campaign might be on the way. That year a recently

Eat *more* BREAD

It is cheap
It is nourishing!

Nowhere in the great wheat - producing countries of the world can you buy good, fresh, wholesome bread as *cheaply* as you can here in Great Britain.

It is baked in spotlessly clean bakeries by skilled bakers who know how to make bread light, delicious and nourishing. Eat more white or brown bread, it is all highly nutritious and recommended by the best medical authorities.

British BREAD

Your best and cheapest food
**Give the children more bread—
it's good for them.**

Between the wars; Ministry of Agriculture, and Fisheries, *c.* 1930.

developed wheat variety, Maris Huntsman, produced record crops of up to 4½ tons per acre. It was estimated that if 50 per cent of Britain's bakers were to install new microwave baking machinery then being researched at Chorleywood, they could make 'acceptable' bread using only soft wheat flour, thereby saving 800,000 tons of American wheat at a cost of £108 per ton. There were snags attached to the scheme. One was that tins or other metal containers hinder the microwaves, 'leaving the interior of the loaf doughy', and some solution of this problem was still to be found. Another snag, not published at the time, was the quality of the high-yield wheat. One miller I questioned on this point was carefully non-committal. Another said flatly that it was rubbish.

In the autumn of the following year it was reported in the *Guardian* (5 November 1975) that the European Commission, dealing with Common Agricultural Policy, had suggested that the guaranteed E.E.C. price for wheat suitable only for animal feed should be considerably lower than the price for wheat suitable for bread. Unfortunately the Commission found itself up against various national tastes, traditions and prejudices in the matter of which wheats are suitable for bread and which are not. Among the wheat varieties under discussion was Maris Huntsman. In several countries it had been rejected as unsuitable for bread. The British and the Dutch however had accepted it as 'a perfectly adequate ingredient for the supermarket loaf'.

Acceptable, adequate – chill words to describe our daily bread, our companion of life. Even so, as applied to the British factory loaf they seem to me much exaggerated. It will be interesting to see the efforts of the milling industry to sell us bread made from flour which is more suitable for cake, or at any rate for cattle cake.

Yeast

'The flavour and sweetness of your bread depends in so great a measure upon the yeast used in its manufacture that I must claim your indulgence if I seem to treat it at undue length.'

Frederick T. Vine, *Practical Breadmaking*, 1897

'The components of yeast are the same as those in the flour from which it gains its nourishment.'

The Encyclopaedia of Practical Cookery,
ed. Theodore Francis Garrett, 1899

'Whilst the results of fermentation were apparent, the way in which it worked was a complete mystery, and we can only assume it was for this reason that writers of old gave the subject a wide berth.'

H. A. Monckton, *A History of English Ale and Beer*, 1966

Who discovered yeast in the first place? Where did it come from? Out of the everywhere? In a sense. The air is full of wild yeasts, they are all around us. They are on leaves and tree bark and in the soil and on the skins of fruit. They are carried by insects and birds, and in dust particles. That much we know. How or when the first leavened bread came into being we do not know. We can only surmise that it happened when a mixture of meal and water, left longer than usual on a warm day, had started to ferment before it was put to bake. The resulting bread was found to be lighter and more appetizing than the usual hard, flat cake. Before long early man must have discovered that given similar conditions the ferment would recur. From there it would have been no more than a step – although a step that perhaps took many generations to achieve – to the discovery that a lump of fermented dough kept back from one day's baking could be used to ferment a fresh mix of dough. Gradually the system of storing a piece of leaven and keeping it alive by refreshing it with newly made dough became normal routine. The leaven was stored in clay jars, and evidently lasted some while before it was discarded as being too sour or too weak to work and a fresh batch started. By the time we hear of the Israelites in captivity in Egypt something like this seems to have been general practice. When they left Egypt 'they took their dough before it was leavened . . . it was not leavened because they were thrust out of Egypt and could not tarry'. Or was it because they couldn't carry jars of leaven as well as 'their kneading troughs . . . bound up in their clothes upon their shoulders'?[1] How much had the Israelites learned from the Egyptians? Had they discovered how to use a kind of barm or liquid yeast from fermented liquor? Probably. As we know, the Egyptians were wine-makers and brewers as well as bakers. Brewing operations and the preparation of bread dough were carried out in the same place.[2] What more likely than that the fermenting liquor sometimes spilled over, reaching the kneading troughs and the dough itself? Eventually someone must have realized why bread made from such dough, although it may have been thought to be spoiled, rose better and was more satisfactory than that made with only the straight grain leaven, spontaneously fermented, and so the first barm-raised bread was developed.

The interdependence between the grain and the yeast, between bread and fermenting liquor, was certainly established – surely in some such way – in the earliest times and has persisted throughout history. This circumstance, together with its very mystery, accounts perhaps for the curiously ambivalent attitude towards leavened bread and leaven generally as expressed in both the Old Testament and the New; 'a symbol of silent pervasive influence, usually of that which is corrupt', my Concordance explains. We know that St Paul used it as a figure of speech signifying corruption.[3] That attitude died hard. In seventeenth-century France, the Paris Faculty of Medicine spent months debating the question of beer leaven and whether the bakers should be permitted to use it, eventually coming up with the solemn decision that it was injurious to health and should be forbidden. (Apart from a decree passed by the Paris parliament and shortly afterwards rescinded, nobody took much notice. The ancient spontaneous leaven and sourdough systems were all right for bread made from coarse brown meal, but for

1. Exodus xii, 34, 39.
2. A wooden model of a combined brewhouse and bakehouse found in a tomb of the Middle Kingdom period, *c.* 2000 B.C., is to be seen in the British Museum.
3. 1 Corinthians v, 7.

the fine light bread liked by the gentry, a good barm was needed.) In more recent times, one of the factors making for the success of Dr Dauglish's famous aerated bread was that being unfermented it was believed by many people to be more wholesome than ordinary bread. A ferment indicated a kind of decay, a corruption, and was therefore suspect. It was still a few decades before the pendulum swung the other way, and yeast became a health-food fad. Yeast is rich in vitamins, and when vitamin-mania was at its height yeast pills, yeast extracts and patent yeast foods proliferated, not live or bread yeasts it is true, but yeasts just the same. There are even those who hold that the more yeast you put into bread the more nourishment it gives you, much to the detriment of the bread they make. It is more to the point to discover how little yeast you can manage with than how much.

The precise nature of yeast, whence it comes, the reasons for its being, remained a mystery for thousands of years. From the beginning of the seventeenth to the middle of the nineteenth century chemists and scientists tried to discover the secrets. The invention of the microscope in about 1600 enabled researchers to see yeast cells invisible to the naked eye; scientists working on the theory of fermentation soon understood that the cells of beer and wine yeasts multiplied in a sugar solution, but few people believed that these cells were alive. The great Liebig, one of the most renowned of nineteenth-century food chemists, insisted that it was the decomposition of the cells which caused fermentation, and could not accept that yeast was a plant. It was Pasteur who established beyond doubt that it was the dust, or bloom, on the skin of the grape and not its juice which makes wine ferment, that yeast is a living plant, that only active living cells can bring about alcoholic fermentation. In as few words as possible, this very complex process can be described as the breakdown of starch and sugar into alcohol and carbon dioxide.

THE YEAST PLANT AND ITS FOOD

'When mixed with moistened flour yeast converts the starch into sugar and this sets free carbonic acid gas which in its efforts to escape spreads through the mass of dough, making it light, porous, and spongey.'

Law's Grocer's Manual, 2nd edn, *c.* 1902

'Yeast performs two functions in a dough: it produces gas which aerates the dough and the finished bread; and it aids in the maturing or conditioning of the dough.'

Edmund Bennion, *Breadmaking*, 4th edn, 1967

'The great thing about baking with yeast is the difficulty of failure.'

George and Cecilia Scurfield, *Home Baked*, 1956

In Chaucer's England one of the names for yeast or barm was goddis-goode 'bicause it cometh of the grete grace of God'.[1] These words imply a blessing. To me that is just what it is. It is also mysterious, magical. No matter how familiar its action may become nor how successful the attempts to explain it in terms of chemistry and to manufacture it by the ton, yeast still to a certain extent retains its mystery.

Forced to reduce it to a few facts – and many people who bake their own bread do want to know what is this substance which performs the ever-recurring leavening miracle – yeast is a plant, a plant with a single active cell. There are many species. The one used for bakers' yeast is called *Saccharomyces cerevisiae*. When cultivated in propitious conditions, that is in warm moist surroundings, and properly fed, the single cells of this fungus-like plant put out buds which in time break away from the parent cell, and in their turn create more buds. Well-fed yeast cells will reproduce a whole generation every five hours, making about thirty generations in one week. These cells are much too small to be seen by the naked eye. One hundred and fifty thousand millions of them, it is estimated, go to make up 10 grams or $\frac{1}{3}$ oz of modern compressed yeast; and it is now known that they are made up of a quantity of complex chemical substances which keep them alive.

The foods that suit yeast are those which in themselves contain the elements of natural ferment, for example damp grain, warm mashed potatoes, moistened flour and the natural sugar which develops in dough as it ferments. Sugar in fact is essential to yeast growth, but must be administered in moderation. In most things, indeed, yeast prefers moderation – warmth, a steamy atmosphere, its favourite foods in small doses – and it responds best when allowed to take its time over the fermentation process.

When yeast cells are neither fed nor warmed, and so long as they are kept cold and dry, they will remain dormant, but alive, ready to return to active growth when released into propitious surroundings. In correct

1. *The Brewers Book*, Norwich, 1468-9. See *The Oxford English Dictionary*.

storage conditions, at a temperature of 40°F or 4°C, compressed bread yeast remains alive and healthy for three or four weeks from the time it leaves the distillery before it gives up and starts to decompose. If frozen, it will survive for three months. Air-dried in granules its life can be prolonged for three years or more.

YEAST MANUFACTURE

Bakers' yeast as we now know it is manufactured only in factories specializing in production of this particular type of yeast on a massive scale. Originally, when the distillation of baking yeast was first developed in the mid nineteenth century, the basis was a wort or infusion of grain – wheat, rye, malted barley – or of potatoes and sugar. Nowadays bread yeast is nearly always grown on a solution of molasses and water, the processes by which it is produced being highly automated and controlled from the laboratory rather than in the distillery itself.

Each production cycle starts in the laboratory, where a pure yeast culture is kept growing in ideal conditions. Every week a small quantity of this culture is put into a flask containing a sterilized and purified molasses solution. For food the culture is given ammonium salts which supply the nitrogenous matter and the phosphates necessary to all plant growth. Within twelve hours the initial batch of new yeast is transferred from its flask to a larger container, of about 2 gallon capacity, where it is fed with more molasses solution and nitrogen salts. It is also given air. This minimizes the alcohol production, ensuring that the maximum amount of the sugar content will be used up in the formation of fresh yeast cells.

At the third stage of fermentation the process of transference to a larger vat and of more feeding of the yeast is repeated. Through four or five successive stages the growth of the liquid ferment proceeds until the small initial volume of molasses solution and yeast culture has grown into 5 tons of fermenting liquid. Called the mother or seed yeast, this ferment – it does not yet at all resemble yeast as we buy it – is divided up and channelled into three separate tanks in which it will feed fresh ferments. Eventually each tank will produce 15 tons. The initial 5 tons will have turned into a dramatic 45 tons.

At each stage of the yeast growth temperatures are rigorously checked and controlled and a series of filterings, coolings, dilutions, reheatings and acidity-testings combine to make a process of far greater complexity than might be inferred from this sketchy outline of the first stages of the production cycle. The aim of this control is to produce commercial yeast with characteristics identical to those of the parent culture.

Once the yeast growth is arrested, the yeast formed in it is present as a suspension of cells in the liquid residue of the molasses solution. The yeast and the fermentation liquor must now be washed and separated. The operation is carried out in centrifugal separators running at high speed. When the process is completed the spent liquid is at the top of the separating tank, the mass of thick white creamy yeast at the bottom. The yeast cream is now filtered into storage vessels and maintained at a low temperature – about 36°F or 2°C – until the extraction of excess water from the yeast cells by rotary vacuum filters leaves the yeast cream in flakes. It will not be the yeast we know until it has been fed into packing machines to be compressed, extruded, cut into blocks and wrapped for dispatch to cold stores all over the country, where the wrapped blocks are kept at 40°F, 4° to 4·5°C. From the stores the yeast is delivered to the bakers and the bread factories. In Britain two manufacturers alone are responsible for our entire annual output of some 50,000 tons of bread yeast.

It is satisfying to reflect that however bewildering the assembly of vats and tanks, filters and fans, pipes and compressors and dehydrators, however scientific the control and gigantic the scale of production, the process of yeast manufacture is still one which relies on a living organism, the yeast itself, for its continuing cycle of reproduction.

*

It was in the middle years of the nineteenth century that compressed yeast, also confusingly called dried yeast and German yeast, began to appear in England. During the preceding thirty years or more there had been many attempts to produce a form of solidified yeast which would be more stable and less bitter than ale and beer yeasts and more efficient than those obtained from a solution or wort of fermented grain, potatoes, flour, sugar, hops, malted barley – there were any number of variations – and drawn off into bottles to be stored in the brewhouse or bakehouse. These yeasts were as temperamental as ale barms. Their strength was uncertain, so were their keeping qualities. Methods of preserving yeast in an active state were ingenious, primitive and laborious. The most common way was to spread coat after coat of wellwashed yeast, whisked up into fresh water, on a large clean wooden platter or in a tub. When each coat was dry, another was brushed on, until eventually a layer 2 to 3 inches thick was achieved. Between each coating, the platter or tub was turned upside down, to protect the yeast from dust, but also to allow enough air to get under to dry it. According to accounts this yeast would keep several months, and 'when you have occasion to use it, cut a piece off and lay it in warm water, stir it together and it will be fit for use'.[1] This was for bread and cakes. For brewing there was the ancient method of dipping handfuls of birch twigs in liquid yeast, hanging them up to dry – 'take great care no Dust comes to it' – and keeping them until the next brewing session, when one of these small brooms was thrown into the wort. 'You must whip it about in the wort, and then let it lye. . . . When the vat works well, take out the Broom and dry it again, and it will do for the next Brewing.'[2]

The old method of preserving baking yeast in a solid form no doubt provided the basis for the numerous experiments, made during the late eighteenth century and the beginning of the nineteenth, involving the drying out and pressing of yeast on a commercial scale. Finally, it was Austrian chemists who evolved the system of producing and compressing yeast in spirit distilleries, and Dutch distillers who took the lead in expanding production of the new yeast. At first nearly all our compressed yeast was imported from Holland, and bakers were wary of it. Its advantages were perhaps not then so great as they now seem to us. Without refrigerators it did not keep well. A great deal must have been wasted, and its strength seems to have been as variable as that of the old barms. Often it was bulked out with starch, chalk, and even in one instance cited by Theodore Garrett[3] with 30 per cent of pipe clay. By the turn of the century, however, British distilleries were taking over production of yeast for the home market. The journals of the period carry a good deal of advertising for yeast. It goes without saying that all the products advertised were claimed to be of the purest quality.

The dozen yeast distilleries established in the British Isles by 1900 were, according to Law,[4] producing 68 million pounds of yeast annually (we were importing a further 28 million. We ate more bread in those days than we do now). A Belfast distillery, whose Balloon brand of yeast carried the slogan 'Never Done Rising', was one of two recommended by Law as suppliers to the baking trade. The second was in Hull. The East London distillery which produced Domo yeast must

1. Hannah Glasse, *The Art of Cookery Made Plain and Easy*, 1747.   2. ibid.
3. *The Encyclopaedia of Practical Cookery*, 1899.
4. *Law's Grocer's Manual*, 2nd edn, c. 1902.

Balloon yeast was much advertised in bakery trade journals and publications. From Frederick Vine's *Biscuits for Bakers*, 1896.

have been festooned with the gold and silver and bronze medals won
at bakery exhibitions and trade shows; Tiger was a bread yeast long
before it was something we put in our petrol tanks; and a certain Walter
Hepworth of Harwich was selling a very fine production of yeast
grown upon wort prepared from malted rye 'undoubtedly as pure and
vigorous as yeast can be, one pound being sufficient to leaven four sacks
of flour', so it was asserted by Theodore Garrett. When for household
breadmaking we are told to use 1 oz of yeast for 3½ lb, how could 4 oz
be stretched to leaven 280lb of flour? Well, yeast being what it is,
Garrett was not talking through his chef's bonnet. He was just talking
in terms obscure to all but professional bakers. In those days bread
doughs were given much longer and slower fermentation than today's
high speed doughs. That is one of the reasons why the bread had more
character, a better developed flavour. A slowly built-up dough, made
in three successive stages and taking sixteen hours altogether from
initial mixing of the sponge to the dividing up and moulding stage, is described in detail by Walter Banfield.[1] For a sack of flour Banfield used
only 6oz of yeast to make this dough, on what is known to bakers as
the quarter-sponge system, rarely used today. A summary of the method
will be found on p. 107. It is very instructive. So is Edmund Bennion's[2]
summing up of the way yeast reproduces itself in dough. It isn't quite
the expected one. Where the yeast quantity is less than 2 per cent, says
Bennion, it has been estimated that it reproduces by 50 per cent; when
the yeast content exceeds 2 per cent there is no growth. What this
means in terms of domestic breadmaking is that 1 oz of yeast to 3 lb 2 oz
of flour is the maximum necessary, and that given time and the right
conditions for growth a half or even a quarter of that amount will
eventually do the same work just as effectively.

ALE BARMS, BREWERS' YEASTS AND HOME-MADE YEASTS

'As we brew so must we bake.'

Popular saying

'After the beer had cooled, the yeast which floated on the top was skimmed off by
a fleeter (the same instrument used to remove the cream from the milk) and put into
stone bottles ready for baking, with a little clear water.'

Allan Jobson, *An Hour-Glass on the Run*, 1959

1. *Manna*, 1937.   2. *Breadmaking*, 4th edn, 1967.

Although there is evidence that both Greek and Roman bakers fermented some of their bread with new wine must, wine yeasts are not generally considered propitious to bread. Even in predominantly wine-growing countries barms from grain and malt-based liquors were the traditional leavenings for bread. These yeasts were of variable and unpredictable strength and, to judge from written evidence, more often than not they were very bitter.

Until the early decades of the nineteenth century, the majority of English domestic cookery books included, as a matter of course, instructions for brewing. Housekeepers were expected to be as familiar with the routines of brewing and wine-making as they were with baking, and the cookery writers repeatedly warned their readers to take care that the barm they used to leaven their bread and cakes was not bitter, or stale, or too strongly flavoured with hops; the quantities they specified were of necessity uncertain and inconsistent because the barm itself varied from household to household, from one brewing, one month, one week, one day even, to another. The manner of its use varied accordingly, and the old instructions strike modern readers as hopelessly haphazard and erratic. It could hardly have been otherwise. Quantities are usually given in liquid measures, but now and again in spoonfuls of washed and purified yeast (barms are the liquors in which yeast grows, not, properly speaking, the yeast itself, so when used in liquid form it must have been fairly weak and slow-working). Three-quarters of a pint of 'new Ale-Yeast' to $3\frac{1}{2}$lb of flour is demanded in one of Sir Kenelm Digby's[1] recipes; in another he instructs that 'a quart at least of thick barm of ale be left to settle to have the thick fall to the bottom which will be when it is about two days old'. This was for 14lb of flour, but how potent the resulting yeast was or how much of it had settled would only have been clear to someone experienced in brewhouse methods, and observant enough to differentiate between the action of barms in which the yeast rose to the surface of the fermenting liquid and that in which it fell to the bottom, forming a sediment. The former, the common one of English ale fermentation, came to be known as high yeast, and was the one most generally used for bread. The second, low or sedimentary yeast, was produced by the fermentation at a low temperature of light beers and continental lagers. The slow action of this type of barm evidently resulted in heavy, damp, sour bread.

Whichever kind of barm was to be used for bread, clearly the most

1. *The Closet of the Eminently Learned Sir Kenelm Digby Knight Opened*, 1669.

crucial point was the washing of the yeast in an effort to eliminate the bitter taste. All the cookery writers of the seventeenth and eighteenth centuries made this point. Hannah Glasse,[1] for example, left her pint and a half of 'good ale yest' – 'but take care that it be not bitter' – lying overnight in a gallon of water. In the morning the water was poured off. The yeast that was left was then stirred into a mixture of 3 quarts of water to 1 of milk. This was for a 'French' bread or roll dough to be made on a basis of a peck and a half or 21 lb of flour. The dough was to be left to ferment while the oven was heating, in other words for about two hours. So many cookery authors of the second half of the eighteenth century copied Hannah Glasse's bread recipes almost word for word, and without making any original observations on methods and quantities, that little further in the way of useful detail is to be discovered from them until the appearance of Mrs Rundell's immensely popular *New System of Domestic Cookery*, first published in 1806. Mrs Rundell provided clear directions for brewing up home-made yeast, and told her readers how much to use for a 7 lb loaf, but to the inexperienced the detail was still inadequate.

It is not until 1845 and the publication of Miss Acton's *Modern Cookery* that we find decisive instructions and definite directions for the making of bread and the management of yeast. What a blessing this book must have been to the baffled housekeepers and cooks of the time.

'The yeast bought from a public brewery is often so extremely bitter that it can only be rendered fit for use by frequent washings, and after those even it should be cautiously employed', wrote Miss Acton, and instructed that as soon as it was brought home the yeast was to be mixed with a large quantity of cold water and left overnight in a cool place. Next morning the water was drained and the yeast again mixed up with fresh water and left to stand for several hours before the water could be poured off clear. The process could be repeated for several days, with daily changes of water in winter and twice daily in hot weather. In this way, Miss Acton found, yeast could be preserved fit for use very much longer than it would otherwise be. 'Should it ferment rather less freely after a time a *small* portion of brown sugar stirred to it before the bread is made will quite restore its strength.'

Miss Acton's quantities and methods are given in precise terms: 1 pint of yeast if unwashed, or ½ pint if purified, to a half bushel, or 28 lb,

1. *The Art of Cookery Made Plain and Easy*, 1747.

of flour. She allowed only about two hours or a little more for the fermentation of her bread dough. When she made her own favourite recipe, called Bordyke bread[1] after the Tonbridge house in which she lived and wrote her book, she used 2 tablespoons only of 'solid well purified yeast' to a gallon, or 7 lb, of flour. Like so many experienced bakers, she was emphatic on the effect of using too much yeast. 'Very rapid fermentation, which is produced by using more than the necessary quantity of yeast, is by no means advantageous to the bread, which not only becomes dry and stale from it, but is of less sweet and pleasant flavour than that which is more slowly fermented.' Sooner or later everyone who bakes his own bread must come to the same conclusion. The difference made by slow fermentation and a much reduced quantity of yeast is hard to credit until trial and error have demonstrated that the true essence of good bread lies in that slow ferment and unhurried ripening of the dough.

During 1845, its first year of publication, Eliza Acton's *Modern Cookery* was reprinted twice, and for the third printing, from which her directions concerning yeast are quoted, she had already made revisions and improvements. By 1855 she had revised the whole book. Her re-written chapter on bread now included notes on German yeast, which had 'very generally superseded the use of English beer yeast in London and other places conveniently situated to receive quickly and regularly the supplies imported from abroad'.

During the decade which had passed since the original publication of her book, Miss Acton must have made many experiments, for in 1845 she had noted that although she had heard it 'answered remarkably well' she had not had the opportunity of testing it. It is evident that she was delighted with the new yeast. 'It makes exceedingly light bread and buns and is never bitter.'

Apart from ale barms, beer yeasts and the new distillery or compressed yeasts, nineteenth-century bakers and housekeepers used specially brewed ferments from which they extracted their yeast for bread. Such yeasts were often known as patent yeasts. There are scores of different recipes and methods to be found in published cookery books, and many variations appear in MS. receipt books. They really were used and were successful. Professional bakers, of course, knew all about them. Their trade depended upon the skilful management of

---

1. See *The Best of Eliza Acton*, ed. Elizabeth Ray, Longmans, 1968; Penguin Books, 1974.

their barms and yeasts, and they were slower to appreciate the new distillery yeast than were household bakers.

The home brewing of ale and beer was declining fast – the high prices of raw materials and the taxes imposed as a result of the Napoleonic wars had made it expensive – and far fewer households had their own ale barm to draw on, so quite often breadmaking was abandoned except by those who could depend on a supply of compressed yeast from a brewery or who were prepared to make their own barm. With less experience than the bakers, and fewer facilities for keeping the brew and surveying its progress the task was sometimes daunting. The untoward bursting of yeast bottles and the popping of corks in the night were evidently fairly common occurrences. Mrs M. Vivian Hughes, victim of a late-Victorian self-sufficiency effort in the matter of making her own yeast to leaven her own bread, recorded her experiences and subsequent reversion to bakery yeast. The passage is quoted further on in this chapter.

The basis for home-made yeasts was a mash of grain, malted barley or rye, sometimes flour, sometimes boiled potatoes; anything and everything that would give a good ferment and convert into sugar and then alcohol was called into use for the making of barms. Hops were usually included, more as a preservative, or preventative of sourness, than as a stimulant. Most of the barms needed to be implanted with existing yeast from the previous brew. Others were made on a wort left to ferment spontaneously. Bakers who used this kind of leaven called it 'spon' or virgin barm. Scottish bakers preferred what they called Parisian barm, based on flour and malt. They had a high reputation for their barms. Until well on into the twentieth century and even after the First World War, there were still a few bakers making their bread with barm rather than with compressed distillery yeast; people accustomed to bread leavened with barm held that its flavour was much more interesting than that produced by modern yeast. It is one of those lost tastes.

Among the quantities of yeast recipes for household use given in cookery books of the past 200 years, Mrs Rundell's is one of the clearest. Her book was so popular, ran into many editions and was in print for so long that her yeast recipes may well have been the ancestors of any number of the variations found in later cookery books and in nineteenth-century MS. receipt books.

Mrs Rundell's yeast

'Thicken two quarts of water with fine flour, about three spoonfuls; boil half an hour, sweeten with near half a pound of brown sugar; when near cold, put into it four spoonfuls of fresh yeast in a jug, shake it well together and let it stand one day to ferment near the fire without being covered. There will be a thin liquor on the top, which must be poured off; shake the remainder, and cork it up for use. Take always four spoonfuls of the old to ferment the next quantity, keeping it always in succession.

'A half-peck loaf [based on 7 lb of flour] will require about a gill [i.e. ¼ pint].'

A New System of Domestic Cookery, new edn 1807 (first published 1806)

Mrs Rundell also made a potato leaven fermented with, presumably, her own yeast. One pound of potatoes boiled to a mash were left to get half cold, then well mixed with a cupful of yeast. 'It will be ready', Mrs Rundell said, 'in two or three hours and keeps well.' She added that when this leaven was used twice as much as of beer-yeast was needed.

In the Gibson/Pegus MS. receipt book, from which recipes are quoted on pp. 446 and 460, two potato leavens are described as 'yeast for white bread', while the 'yeast for brown bread' noted by Mrs Gibson is very similar to Mrs Rundell's. Potato leavens were started with yeast from the original batch, as in Mrs Rundell's formula. Sometimes they were made on a small scale for immediate use to leaven one batch of bread, sometimes for keeping. These recipes date from 1840 to 1850.

In Lady Clark of Tillypronie's cookery book (1909) several home-made yeast recipes collected between 1858 and 1895 from a variety of sources give an idea of the importance attached to good yeast in a household where all the bread was made at home. Although Lady Clark could obtain brewery yeast, and most of her recipes needed it for a starter, she clearly preferred bread leavened with a home-made barm. In 1893 she notes the Tillypronie method for tin bread leavened with spirit yeast, i.e. German or compressed yeast, which could be obtained by post direct from the distillery in Fife.

Here are some of Lady Clark's recipes. The first is interesting in that ginger was often used as a yeast stimulant. There seems to be no scientific basis for the belief in its efficacy, and modern bakers regard it as no more than superstition. But evidently it worked. The recipe was given to Lady Clark by a Mr Nightingale of Leahurst, but is not dated. Lady Clark certainly made use of it, for she gives a recipe for bread leavened with it, and this must have been a loaf that was made regularly for she called it Birk Hall bread, after the Scottish house where she and Sir John Clark lived for many years. (In more recent times, Birk Hall became the property of Queen Elizabeth the Queen Mother.)

Ginger yeast

This recipe was marked 'Excellent' by Lady Clark.

'Over 2 oz of hops, 2 or 3 of ground ginger and ¼ peck [3½ lb] of fresh malt, pour 2 gallons of water and boil all for ½ hour, then let it stand for 6 hours. Strain it off, and add flour to make it as thick as cream.

'Add ½ pint brewers' yeast to start it. Let it stand all night and bottle it next morning.

'This will make nice cottage loaves, bread very white, crust very crisp, baked on the oven bottom, as well as buns, rolls and tin bread. The ginger keeps it sweet and good, and the bread rises well and pretty quickly. The breakfast buns made with it rise beautifully.'

The Cookery Book of Lady Clark of Tillypronie, 1909

Note: For Birk Hall bread, Lady Clark's cook used ½ pint of ginger yeast to 4 lb of flour. The dough was fermented for two hours, then kneaded and put into one large tin and left to prove until it rose to the top. For oven bottom loaves – evidently there was a brick-built oven at Birk Hall – the risen dough was shaped, probably into cottage loaves, and put into the oven without further proving.

In another recipe, for Mrs Thomas's Bread, 6 tablespoons only of the ginger yeast are mixed with ¼ lb of warm mashed potatoes and 4 lb of flour and some water. This was left to rise for five or six hours according to the temperature, broken down and kneaded with extra flour and water, and left overnight in a cool pantry. Next morning half the dough was kneaded and put into a tin for bread, the other half was mixed with a little milk and butter and made into rolls for breakfast. Lady Clark gives other bread and yeast recipes in which potatoes play an important part. She noted that potatoes, by increasing the fermentation in the sponge, make the bread lighter, and also that they make a little yeast go far. Inevitably, there occurs the customary note: the less yeast that bread will rise with the better it will be.

Notes in other yeast recipes given by Lady Clark make the point that it is important that the bottles or jars in which the yeast is kept should not be corked for some hours, and then only loosely, or the bottle will burst. In the unlikely event of anyone in these days wishing or needing to make their own yeast, this is quite a point, and one which many recipes failed to make clear. Hence, no doubt, the cork-popping of Mrs Vivian Hughes's home-made yeast as recounted in a characteristically good-humoured passage:

'An old friend of Arthur's, Dr Daniell, learned in physics and indeed everything else, was quite excited about the bread, wanted to hear exactly how I made it, but was shocked at my having to send out for the yeast. "Why not save time and trouble, not to mention expense, by making your own?" he urged. So, following his directions, I cooked two pounds of potatoes, mashed them up in water and all, poured them into an earthenware pan, and when they were cooled to about blood heat, placed a slice of toast to float on the top with an ounce of yeast spread on it. (After all, one had to *begin* with a bit of yeast.) After some hours the whole panful became yeast, and we bottled it and put it away, using from it as required. Economical, labour-saving, efficient. But Arthur said it must stop, because his nerves couldn't stand it. It was frequently his custom of an evening to be sitting up late for work after I had gone to bed, Emma had ceased singing, and all was quiet. Once, at about midnight, he was startled by what he called an infernal explosion. One of the bottles of yeast had burst its cork forth. So we returned to the pennyworth of yeast at the baker's. Another pestiferous visitor, a "notable housewife", informed me in a superior way that no bread was really home-made unless brewers' barm was used. So I bought a little covered tin can (such as navvies use for their tea) and made expeditions to a brewery for a pennyworth of barm. We could perceive no difference in the quality of the bread, and I found the barm so temperamental and uncertain in its raising power that I soon returned to the original yeast, of which a pennyworth lasted for three bakings.'

M. Vivian Hughes, *A London Home in the Nineties*, 1937
(Part 3 of *A London Family 1870–1900*, 1946)

The following recipe, also recorded by Lady Clark of Tillypronie, is something like the bakers' 'spon' or spontaneous barm. It is a convincing recipe, although why it should 'only make tin loaves' is a puzzle. Perhaps the dough aerated with it was best when rather soft.

'Times' yeast (Lledr Cadog, 1858)

'To be used when you cannot get brewer's yeast.

'The advantage of this yeast is, that you make it for yourself without requiring any other yeast to start it; you must have *patience* in making it. It should keep good some weeks; then make a fresh supply, not using any of the old.

'It only makes tin loaves, but the bread should honeycomb, and makes excellent toast.

'The vessel it is made in should be a wide earthenware milk bowl, capable of holding about 6 qts., and the mixture is to be kept about "new-milk-warm" during the entire time of making – namely, *from Monday morning till Thursday evening* – and this is done by letting it stand at a proper distance from the kitchen fire.

'On Monday morning, then, begin by boiling 2 ozs. of the best hops, choose yellow hops, not green – which are bitter – in 4 qts. of water for ½ hour, stirring occasionally, then strain it and let it cool to "new-milk warmth", then put in a small handful of salt and ½ lb. of brown sugar. Beat up 1 lb. of the best wheat flour with some of the liquor, and then mix all well together. Set the bowl by the fire, covered over with a flat dish, where it may stand till Wednesday morning, being occasionally stirred.

'On Wednesday morning add 3 lbs. of potatoes, merely boiled and mashed whilst hot with nothing added to them, cooled down to the same temperature as the contents of the bowl (about "new-milk warm"). It is shortly after this addition that fermentation may be expected to commence, and as it proceeds the mixture must be frequently stirred. It very soon assumes the appearance of the finest brown-coloured brewer's yeast, rising to a crown.

'By Thursday evening its powers will be completely established, and it may then be strained, and put into bottles, stirring it to the last moment. Do not cork the bottles for some days, until the yeast has done working – and when you do cork them, it must be loosely; never cork them tightly.

'It is now ready for use. When new it is weak, and more is then required to raise the bread than when this yeast is 6 or 8 weeks old. Shake the bottle well up always, before using its contents, and keep it in a cool place. It should keep above two months at least, and is best and strongest the latter part of the time.

'The dough should be left in the pan all night to rise before the kitchen fire, and when made into loaves and put into the tins it will again require 2 or 3 hours to rise before going into the oven.

'The bread takes a considerably longer time to rise in the sponge, and again after being made into dough, than if made with ordinary yeast.'

The Cookery Book of Lady Clark of Tillypronie, 1909

(This recipe is signed 'D.S.Y.', who adds, 'I make all my bread from rough wheatmeal, which is the most wholesome of all. I use seltzer water bottles, filling them two-thirds full only of yeast, and when bottled, I put them at once in a cool place.')

USING COMPRESSED OR BAKERS' YEAST

'Unless you have experimented you cannot realise the difference in the flavour, volume, tenderness and texture between a bread dough allowed to rise slowly and gently and a dough quickened by the use of too much yeast or heat.'

Dorothy Allen-Gray, *Fare Exchange*, 1963

Today's bread yeasts are of high strength. They are reliable and they work fast. Most of us tend to use more than is necessary, either because recipes for home-baking are based on old ones adapted from the days of slow-working and more chancy yeasts, or because we are in a hurry to get the dough ready for the oven, or most commonly of all because we find the potential leavening powers of yeast difficult to credit. Although, for example, the rough rule that 1 oz of yeast will leaven 3 to 4 lb of flour is a fair enough general guide, that is not at all to say that it would be necessary to increase the quantity even if four or five times as much flour were being used. It would depend on the fermentation period allowed – the longer this is, the smaller the proportion of yeast – and on the temperature, and on the techniques used for making the dough. This would be mixed in two or three successive stages, all the yeast being used to make the first batch, called the sponge, in effect a quite ordinary dough. After a partial fermentation, this batch would be used as the implant, so to speak, for the second build-up of the dough, to which in turn the remaining flour, water and salt would be added, the whole given a further fermentation period. For a dough made in this way and fermented over a total period of say 16 to 24 hours depending on the temperature, 1 oz of yeast would easily be enough for 14 lb of flour. The old professional bakers' way of making a long-term dough on a large scale, using only 6 oz of yeast to 280 lb of flour is described below. To anyone new to breadmaking the whole process will no doubt sound daunting and tedious, and indeed there is no call to go through so many hoops to produce a few decent loaves of bread. Yet, even though we would not find it practical to use the old methods, there is much to be learned from an understanding of them. For one thing, rising times of dough cease to present any kind of problem. You realize that those given in recipes can and should be regarded as mainly for guidance, that in practice they are widely adjustable and can be regulated according to the amount of yeast you use and within certain limits according to the temperature at which the dough is fermented.

An understanding of the way dough develops when left for a long period with a minimum of leavening soon follows a few experiments. The understanding is one very relevant to the success of household breadmaking. It is also relevant that the long-term doughs were particularly popular in Scotland, where in the past bakers had a much higher reputation for good bread than did their English colleagues, and this was certainly due to a great extent to the very thoroughly and slowly fermented dough leavened with the least possible amount of yeast or barm.

So although now considered archaic by the majority of professional bakers, a summary of Walter Banfield's formula for Scotch pan or batch bread[1] seems to me well worth a study. At the very least it provides to the sceptical a good demonstration of the way in which a very little leaven can indeed be made to leaven a very large lump.

Dough-mixing on the quarter-sponge system

The dough is made in three stages, starting with a dough mixed to an average consistency for breadmaking, going on to a much more liquid sponge-batter, and ending up with, again, a normal dough. Three different grades of flour, the first two of high gluten content, the third a soft blend, were specified by Banfield.

Total ingredients for the dough are: flour 280 lb, yeast 6 oz, salt 7 lb, water 15½ gallons, malt extract 8 oz.

The initial sponge is made with 64 lb of the flour, the entire 6 oz of yeast, 8 oz of the salt, and 3¾ gallons of the water allowance (i.e. one quarter of the total, on the average ½ pint per pound of flour). Mixed at

1. *Manna*, 1937.

a temperature of 70°F, 21°C, the sponge is left to ferment for fourteen hours. By the end of this time the temperature of the dough should have risen to 76°F, 24°C.

At the second stage the 'quarter' is broken down and integrated into another 100lb of flour, 11 gallons of water, 1¾lb of salt and the malt extract. All but ¾ gallon of the water allowance is now used up, and the 'quarter' has become a batter sponge. At a dough temperature of 80°F, 27°C, it will be ready for the next stage in one hour.

At the third stage the remaining 116lb of flour, 4¾lb of salt and ¾ gallon of water are added to the batter sponge. This dough is left for a further hour at 78°F, 26°C. It is then ready for kneading, dividing and moulding into square batch loaves, that is loaves to be baked side by side in large square pans, so that the sides will be crumby and there will be top crusts only.

Banfield's comment on this typical Scottish method of dough-making and baking, still current in his day, was that it produced 'lovely eating bread'. The large bread factories in the Scottish cities, he noted – it was the mid 1930s – were then already using faster processes 'but not necessarily producing better bread'.

It may be noted that the quantity of salt specified by Banfield is rather high for a baker's dough. This was because the taste in Scotland was always for a saltier bread than was liked in the south. The method by which the salt is added to the dough at different stages is instructive. In the first sponge there is sufficient salt – ⅛oz to the pound of flour – only to keep the dough sweet during its long initial fermentation. At the second stage the proportion is increased to something over ¼oz per pound of flour, and the real seasoning comes only during the final stages of fermentation.

At the other extreme from this informative recipe of Banfield's, in which the dough is given a total of sixteen hours' fermentation without counting final proof, are today's high-speed doughs, made in the bread factories according to the wholly mechanized Chorleywood Process[1] evolved in the 1960s, by which 80 per cent of all bread sold in this country is now produced. The rapidity with which the dough is fermented and matured by these machine processes – less than an hour from first mixing to readiness for the oven – necessitates the use of yeast in the proportion of 6lb per sack, i.e. sixteen times as much as in Banfield's three-stage, long-term method.

1. In the Chorleywood Bread Process the maturing of the dough is replaced by a few minutes of intense mechanical agitation in special high-speed mixers.

The Chorleywood Process is, again, an extreme case which does not – at any rate not yet – have much bearing on the way we bake bread at home, although it does of course have a good deal of bearing on our reasons for doing so. Banfield's method, on the other hand, *is* relevant. So are the figures for yeast quantities and fermentation times given by another Master Baker, W. J. Fance, whose *Up-to-Date Breadmaking*[1] is the current handbook for bakers. We can learn a great deal from these bakery methods and formulas.

For example, a dough to be made in two stages instead of Banfield's three, and with a total of five hours' fermentation, needs 2 lb of yeast to the sack of flour. A two-stage dough to be given, all told, only one and a half hours' fermentation would need 3¾ lb of yeast to the sack. A basic straightforward dough to be made up and fermented all in one operation, approximately as most of us make our household bread, and given three hours' fermentation, needs 3 lb of yeast to the sack. The same straight dough given fifteen hours' fermentation would need only 14 oz of yeast. (All proportions are based on 280 lb of flour and a dough temperature of 78°F, 26°C. Average salt quantity is 5 lb, reduced to 4¼ lb for the short process, one-and-a-half-hour dough.)

How then to calculate yeast quantities for the relatively small amounts of bread we make at home? It is not necessary, nor even particularly helpful, to divide down bakery quantities until they reach amounts realistic for domestic baking, but the examples quoted surely make certain points clear enough. We know that 1 oz of yeast will aerate 3½ lb of flour in two to three hours, so it is easy to accept that 1½ to 2 oz will be as effective for 7 lb of flour fermented for the same time and at the same temperature, and that 3 oz of yeast will be sufficient for 14 to 15 lb of flour, and this is indeed the average quantity and timing given in domestic recipes of the 1900–14 era. If, however, the same doughs were to be left overnight, or all day, say for eight to ten hours, half the amount of yeast would in each case be sufficient.

To me it seems both convenient and practical to give bread doughs a long fermentation. Rather like meat steeping in a marinade it is looking after itself while you are asleep or busy with other jobs. What could be less troublesome?

Quite often I use ¼ oz of yeast to aerate 1¼ lb of flour made up into a dough left for eight to ten hours, and sometimes, after a quick kneading, left for another two hours. In my experience this works even with an

1. W. J. Fance and B. H. Wragg, *Up-to-Date Breadmaking*, 1968.

enriched dough for fruit and spice bread, as for example in the recipe for Devonshire cake on page 442. I must add that using this method for rich cake and fruit bread doughs is against every accepted rule.

YEAST AND THE FLAVOUR OF BREAD

The reason for using decreased proportions of yeast is not primarily one of economy – although in view of the retail prices exacted for yeast that too is a consideration – but because the longer fermentation times given to the dough result in bread with better flavour and texture, a vastly improved crust and a loaf which will stay fresh and moist. What has to be remembered is that given time, moisture and warmth the flour itself undergoes a form of natural fermentation and ripening, and this process materially adds to the acidity of the dough, affecting the ultimate flavours of the bread. Without a certain amount of natural acidity bread, like wine, is insipid. Acidity accounts in part for what Banfield describes as the bread flavour of bread. It is this flavour which the scientists of the plant bakeries cannot get into instant bread by any means at all. It would be surprising if anyone were deluded into thinking they have succeeded in doing so. A technological triumph factory bread may be. Taste it has none. Should it be called bread?

When bread is to be baked in some quantity, it is useful to know about the two-stage dough, or sponge and dough method, but for normal household breadmaking it is not necessary. Nor for that matter is the initial ferment or sponge often advocated in the past for home-made bread. Because of the slow-working yeasts of earlier times the initial sponge was usually left for a minimum of two hours, sometimes longer, so that the ferment was working quite vigorously by the time the second portion of flour was added. Although modern yeast has made this system unnecessary, some recipes still instruct that the dough be started off with a sponge, but one made with only a small proportion of flour, and left for no longer than fifteen minutes. There is little point in this except as a mild fermentation boost. So little time and flour are allowed that there is no development or ripening of the gluten. That gluten ripeness is all. Again, the question of flavour is involved. This is a point that household bread recipes fail to emphasize. Unless, then, an initial sponge is to be made with a good half of the flour and left for a minimum of two hours, it can be forgotten. It makes extra work where one mixing and a straightforward dough would be just as effective. It should be added though that low-gluten wholemeals, except when used in conjunction with a larger proportion of strong white flour or 85 per cent wheatmeal, do not benefit from lengthy fermentation.

SUGAR AND YEAST

Many household bread recipes, and invariably those printed on flour packets, instruct that sugar be added to the yeast. Except in the case of dried yeast, which is dealt with on p. 114, this is not good practice. The idea is that sugar is a yeast food, but modern compressed yeast simply does not need it; the minute it comes into contact with the tepid liquid it starts coming back to active life, and as soon as it begins to work, which is when the flour is moistened, and it finds itself in nice damp warm surroundings, it starts its job of converting the flour starch into its own form of sugar. The yeast doesn't need any more – and, if prolonged, direct contact between sugar and yeast is destructive of the yeast cells.

THE YEAST DIES

A last word on the working of yeast in bread dough: at a temperature of 130°F, 54°C, or thereabouts, yeast cells die. They are killed when that degree of the heat of the oven penetrates to the centre of the loaf. Until then there should still be sufficient spring or aeration potential left in the dough for it to go on rising in the oven. The small amount of alcohol produced by the yeast is driven off during baking.

BUYING AND STORING YEAST

'Brewers' yeast and bakers' yeast were one and the same thing . . . brewsters (female brewers) were under obligation to provide yeast for baking, at the regulation price.'

H. A. Monckton, *A History of English Ale and Beer*, 1966

It is tempting to speculate whether the fifteenth-century law referred to by H. A. Monckton was made necessary by ill-tempered brewsters either unwilling to part with yeast for baking, or exacting extortionate prices for it. Today it is the bakers who do not willingly – or even unwillingly – supply yeast to the public. Selling it is a nuisance to the bakery assistants. They may 'oblige' with an ounce or two, as they put it; they may make a rule that you can only buy it in the afternoon; they may refuse to sell less than a pound at a time. There is no agreed retail price. Charges vary wildly. My own local bakery in Chelsea, where I have bought yeast regularly since the early 1950s, was recently taken over by a provision merchant. Having first doubled the price of his yeast, it was then decreed that his assistants could not sell less than a pound block at a time (and then only after 4 p.m.); finally he – or his ladies – clamped down altogether. This may be an extreme case, but judging by reports from friends and colleagues, refusal of yeast by the bakers has become the rule rather than the exception, at any rate in London and the south. In Yorkshire, and many northern and eastern counties, it is taken for granted that yeast be supplied for household baking. Sometimes the butchers sell it – their cold cabinets make storage easy – and, at any rate in the north east, the smaller super-markets are beginning to stock wrapped blocks of about $1\frac{1}{2}$ oz, a sensible and convenient amount, packed and distributed by one of the big factories. In London, health-food stores have at last begun to understand that if they sell fresh yeast they will also sell twice as much bread flour and at the same time keep their customers happy – and visiting the shop at frequent intervals.

Danish friends to whom I have mentioned the problems of buying fresh yeast in London are amazed. Almost every food shop in Denmark, they tell me, sells yeast as a matter of course – and for the Danes yeast cookery holds no mysteries. All Danish schoolchildren, boys and girls alike, are obliged to do a minimum of a year's cookery course, bread-making being compulsory.

Some $1\frac{1}{2}$ oz packs of yeast sent to me from Copenhagen remained fresh for about three weeks. I don't suggest that we all start sending to Denmark for yeast, although sometimes it would seem to be an easier solution than trying to buy it in London, but whatever your source of supply, it's a good idea to find out on what days the yeast is delivered. The fresher you can buy it the better. It should always be in one piece, not crumbly, and it should be an even creamy beige in colour, smooth and fresh-smelling. If it has crumbled and looks grey and dry, it is stale; it may still do its work, but will not do it well. The bakery ladies will of course tell you that the crumbled yeast is perfectly usable. What they do not appreciate – they do not know anything about yeast or how to keep it – is that once a block of yeast is broken up or crumbled, it starts to dry out and rapidly loses potency. For example, 4 oz of yeast in one piece will remain in usable condition at least four times as long as the equivalent quantity in small particles.

Assuming, then, that you have contrived to buy a small block of fresh yeast, unwrap it as soon as you get it home. Put it in a plastic storage box with a well-fitting lid in which you can make one or two small air holes. These provide just enough ventilation to prevent the moisture in the yeast evaporating and condensing inside the box, but not so much as to over-expose the yeast to air. Store the yeast in the refrigerator, in the coldest spot. The ideal temperature is 40°F, 4° to 4·5°C, rather lower than most people keep their refrigerators, but even at 42°F, 5°C, I have found that a small block of yeast, say 4 oz, will keep in good condition for a fortnight to three weeks, provided that the rest is returned to the refrigerator immediately you have taken out what you need.

To freeze compressed yeast

Sometimes it is convenient to buy a block of yeast and cut up at least part of it for freezing. Unfortunately, one kilo blocks of yeast have now replaced the old one pound size packed and delivered by the manufacturers. For any kind of household baking two pounds plus is a lot of yeast to buy at one time. When it proves impossible to persuade a bakery or a health-food shop to sell half or a quarter of a kilo, sharing with friends who have a roomy deep freeze is about the only solution.

Usually I cut the yeast into ounce pieces, wrap them separately and then pack them all into a couple of bags, so that they are easy to lay hands on rather than scattered all over the freezer. Don't forget to label and date the bags, and to get the yeast into the freezer just as soon as possible after you get it home.

Frozen yeast is not perhaps ideal – the freezing process does do slight damage to the cells, as does air drying – but many people accustomed to compressed yeast prefer to use it frozen rather than resort to dried yeast, and certainly I have found it a highly valuable standby. It will remain in good condition for at least three months, and I have used it successfully after nearly a year.

It is very necessary to allow frozen yeast a little time, say fifteen minutes, to come back to life by putting it in tepid water, just as for dried yeast. The time it will take depends, obviously, on the temperature of the room. The important points are not to put it in hot water and not to use it before it has fully dissolved. If you have to take too large a piece out of the freezer, it should be fairly easy, given a small sharp saw knife, to cut through it and put back the piece you don't need. Alternatively, it will keep for two or three days in the refrigerator. After that it will decay fairly quickly.

A short-term way of preserving yeast moist and fresh when partially thawed out, or indeed when in its fresh state, is to cover it with cold water and store it in the refrigerator or in a cold larder. When the time comes to use it, pour off the excess water and cream the yeast with fresh water in the usual way. There are those who maintain that this is in any case a more effective way of using yeast than the normal straightforward method of creaming it and immediately incorporating it into the flour. Certainly I have found it perfectly satisfactory.

To test compressed yeast

A baker's test for compressed yeast used to be to half fill a cup or tumbler with warm water (100°F, 38°C), dissolve an ounce of sugar in it, then add an ounce of yeast. The yeast sinks to the bottom, but if in good condition should rise to the top in two minutes. 'Should it take much longer than that, the less you have to do with it the better.' I have never had occasion to use this test – it comes from Robert Wells's *Bread and Biscuit Baker's Assistant* (1929) – and think it probably just as easy to judge by smell and look whether yeast is fit for use.

USING DRIED GRANULAR YEAST

When compressed or German yeast was first becoming known in England, many people thought it was dried and for a long time referred to it as such, which makes for confusion when one looks up older recipes; and it does not help that baking powder mixes were also sometimes called, and indeed advertised as, dried yeast or yeast powders.

The granular yeast we buy now really is yeast, active yeast, and it really is dried, hot-air dried so that all moisture is driven off.

Anyone who has always used compressed or fresh yeast for leavening bread dough finds it hard to believe that in dried granular form it will be efficacious. In fact its leavening powers are very high, and for this very reason bread aerated with it is often unsuccessful because most people use too much – often the instructions on the packet are at fault – or else they will not be bothered to wait for the granules to reintegrate and come back to active life before mixing their dough.

Now that independent bakers whose bread is baked on their own premises are so rapidly disappearing, and that those who do survive train their shop assistants to give surly answers when asked to sell yeast, people who bake their own bread regularly will find it essential to know how to use dried yeast, so although nearly all the recipes in this book specify bakers' yeast – because that was what I was in the habit of using – I have now switched almost entirely to dried yeast. I have found nothing wrong with the results except when the proportion of yeast was too high – the same applies to fresh yeast – or the reactivating inadequate.

First, then, always bear in mind that dried yeast is at least twice as potent, weight for weight, as compressed yeast. The instructions on packets are emphatic enough on this point, but fail to say that if you use more than necessary your bread will very quickly go dry and stale. So although the rule of halving the quantity of fresh yeast specified in a recipe is a good enough general guide, in practice I find that for ordinary straightforward bread the allowance is if anything too high, unless it is for dough which is to be given a very short rising time, or perhaps one rising only. For doughs to be given two risings over a period of, say, three hours, and for which 1 oz of fresh yeast is normally used, $\frac{1}{3}$ oz of dried granules will be sufficient. For a loaf made with $1\frac{1}{4}$ lb or 20 oz of flour – the amount specified in many of my recipes, and which yields a 28 oz to 2 lb loaf – a scant $\frac{1}{4}$ oz (7 g) or 1 level British standard teaspoon of granules is enough. For a dough to yield three loaves of the same size, and based on $3\frac{3}{4}$ lb of flour, I find 2 teaspoons rather than 3 are sufficient.

When it comes to measuring very small quantities, such as the equivalent of $\frac{1}{4}$ oz of fresh yeast for a pizza or a small cake, a saltspoonful or a $\frac{1}{4}$ teaspoonful of granules is equal to $\frac{1}{8}$ oz. I know that it is difficult to believe that so minute a quantity will do the trick, so for the first time you just have to have faith. After all, if something does go wrong a little boost of extra yeast can be added. But I have not yet known this to be necessary.

For doughs heavily enriched with butter, eggs, sugar and fruit, I find that the regulation half quantity of dried to fresh yeast is about right. Again, though, this varies with the length of time you intend to leave the dough to rise. Fruit breads and cakes are not so adversely affected by an overdose of yeast as is ordinary bread, because the fruit and fat, plus sugar and eggs, alter the structure of the dough; cooking time is relatively short, and the weight of the enriching ingredients prevents the dough ever being too gassy and overblown.

To reactivate dried yeast the best way is to put a little warm water in a cup, sprinkle in the yeast, give it a stir, leave it for ten to fifteen minutes, until a slightly frothy cream has formed.[1] Whisk it for a few seconds, then mix your dough in the usual way.

I find that the initial rising of dough leavened with dried yeast is usually fairly fast – except in very warm weather it is best to help it out, as with fresh yeast, by warming the flour – but that it takes longer to regain volume the second time round. Possibly a little more patience *is* needed than with fresh yeast dough. The waiting, when it is feasible, is always worthwhile. One of the best loaves I have ever achieved with dried or any other yeast was with a dough left to rise overnight in a cool kitchen, then kneaded and shaped into a 4-inch-deep loaf tin. It took four hours, twice as long as I had calculated, to rise to the top of the tin. It was a difficult dough, a mixture of coarse barley and wheatmeals. The beautiful honeycombed crumb of the loaf when finally it was baked was something worth waiting for. So was its marvellous flavour; and the loaf remained fresh and delicious for five days, unusually long for barley bread. It was an encouraging lesson.

As dried yeast returns to active life in its warm water it tends to give out a beery smell not present in compressed yeast. This is due, so yeast producers say, to the effect of the drying process on the cells. It does not mean that the yeast derives from a brewery type of wort. Dried granular yeasts are, basically, produced in the same way as compressed yeasts, although slightly different yeast strains are used.

BUYING AND STORING DRIED YEAST

Packets of dried yeast can be bought from many delicatessens as well as from health-food shops and food counters of department stores. Some shops also sell 4oz tins.

The majority of English dried yeast packages contain 1oz, or the equivalent of 2oz of fresh yeast, although BE-Ro, the brand which carries the most reliable instructions, is sold in ½oz sachets. Other packers' instructions usually allow for twice as much yeast as is needed. No doubt this accounts for a great deal of poor quality bread, and as a consequence a widespread distrust of dried yeast. Granular yeasts may well vary in performance, but given that there are only two bread yeast

1. If you need reassurance, add a pinch of sugar to the warm water – but my experience has now convinced me that the sugar is quite unnecessary.

manufacturing companies in the whole of the United Kingdom and that only one of them produces the dried granular yeast we buy, the variations can only be minimal, and are more likely to be due to the age of the yeast than to its original strength or working capacity.

American active dry yeast as it is always called – it wouldn't be much use if it were inactive – is packaged in sachets containing a $\frac{1}{4}$ oz (7 g). American cookery writers nearly always specify their yeast quantities in terms of so many packages, and their flour in cup measurements, so it is useful to know the contents of a package as well as that of an American cup, which holds from 4 to 5 oz of flour according to the way you measure. Cup measuring is a very unsatisfactory method compared to weighing on scales.

In France I have bought dried yeast from bakeries. It is packed in 8 gram sachets, approximately $\frac{1}{3}$ oz. The instructions – and I have found them correct – tell you that this is enough for 500 grams to 1 kilogram, or 1 lb to 2 lb 2 oz, of flour, depending upon the type of dough to be made; in other words, $\frac{1}{3}$ oz is enough for 2lb of plain bread dough, or 1 lb of enriched, brioche-type dough.

British bakers neither use nor sell dried yeast.

Packets and tins of dried yeast should be stored in a cool dry place. I keep mine in the least cold part of the refrigerator. Although in my experience dried yeast keeps for at least a year, there is no means of knowing how long the shop has had it in stock when you buy it. In the United States dry yeast packages are stamped with the recommended final date of use. Although this doesn't necessarily mean that the yeast isn't still active – I have used it a year after the expiry date and found it quite normal – the system does provide a useful protection for the customer. Given our traditionally carefree attitude to such matters, it would be surprising if any similar rule were ever enforced here. Even without it, to have a supply of dried yeast in store gives a welcome sense of security and of liberation from those bakery ladies who sometimes will and more often will not sell fresh yeast.

A slightly different form of dried yeast has recently been developed by a Dutch manufacturer with an affiliated British company. Sold under the trade name of Fermipan, the advantages of this new yeast are high activity, what is known as 'good bread flavour', and above all that the reactivating process, involving pre-mixing with water and sugar, is by-passed. Fermipan goes straight into the flour – only half the specified quantity of ordinary dried yeast is needed, quarter the quantity of fresh yeast – and the dough is made up with water as usual.

The attributes of the high-activity yeast have made it especially suitable for use in the so-called 'complete' bread mixes – not to be confused with soda bread mixes – to which the housewife need add nothing but water. Three such mixes are at present (1977) on the market. They are stocked by Co-op shops, Sainsbury's and some of the larger supermarket chains. Expensive though these mixes are in comparison with basic home-made bread, as an emergency store they are most certainly not to be despised. And if they can help to show beginners how easy it is to handle bread dough, so much the better. There are white and brown versions. There is now (1978) also a granary mix which comes complete with a sachet of high-speed dried yeast.

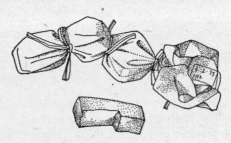

Fresh yeast packed for freezing.

Salt

'The use of salt is a very interesting discovery on the part of the unscientific baker. The baker found out the value of it long ago, and also in this case before there was any science to tell him of it . . . The salt (he discovered) might be compared to the bridle, and the yeast to the whip, that the one was a check on the other, and that by a judicious use of salt at the different stages, one could guide and arrest the fermentation.'

> J. Thompson Gill, *The Complete Bread, Cake and Cracker Baker*,
> 5th edn, Chicago, 1881

It is, then, not only because it gives the necessary flavour, or rather corrects insipidity, that salt is so important to bread. It is also in the context of its action on the yeast and the dough during the fermentation or rising period, and for its ultimate effect on the baked loaf, particularly the crust, that salt has to be considered.

First, the flavour. Those early bakers started putting salt in their bread to improve its flavour, then slowly began to appreciate, through observation, that varying amounts of salt made the dough behave differently and affected the quality as well as the taste of the loaves.

So although the amount of salt we put in our bread should, ultimately, depend on taste, individual or collective, practical application of this theory is not so straightforward a matter.

Quite apart from the widely differing salt-toleration, or salt requirements, of each individual, the strength of the ultimate salt flavour in any batch of bread will depend to some extent on the flour used – new flour absorbs more than old flour – on the kind of dough made and on the length of time it is left to ferment.

Broadly speaking, the shorter the rising time the *more* yeast and the *less* salt are needed, but this is an over-simplification because proportions of both are determined by the volume of dough concerned. The larger the batch, the relatively smaller the proportion of yeast, so the balance of salt must be adjusted, at any rate in theory, to the time calculated for the fermenting or rising of the dough.

I say in theory because when it comes down to a small batch of home-baked bread, it really is not necessary to make elaborate calculations. A few experiments will surely show what is the proper quantity of all the ingredients, their relation to rising times, and to the ultimate flavour and texture of the bread. When it comes to finding out what went wrong with a loaf or a batch of bread, made apparently in every respect identically with your last successful one, then is the moment to try to remember whether perhaps your salt was carelessly measured, or if you guessed at the quantity instead of weighing it as usual.

So how much to use?

On the whole, professional bakers can't be taken as guides where salt is concerned. Their opinions and beliefs differ just as widely as do those of household cookery writers, with the added factor of cost to be considered. To the home cook a spoonful of salt is a small matter. Multiplied by 200 or more it adds up to a very material increase. For example, one baker will tell you that to the sack of flour (280lb) 4lb is the permissible limit, while another advises 7lb. This latter quantity divides down to $\frac{1}{2}$oz of salt per pound of flour, which is more than most household cookery writers advise, and a little less than I use myself. To me, bread with a very low salt content is virtually uneatable, and in my calculations for the rising time of the dough the extra salt I put in is allowed for. It is worth remembering that a proper proportion of salt helps the retention of moisture in the baked loaf, and that too much makes for a hard crust.

The very marked discrepancies found in the proportions of salt given by responsible writers, both professional and domestic, can be explained by two main factors. One is the necessity of producing a loaf neutral enough to be acceptable to the majority. To the majority in England bread is a substance to spread butter on, and the butter traditional to the majority is salted. If this seems a small point, it is a very relevant one. Those who prefer unsalted butter, as I do, need more salt in their bread. I have tested this theory and found that it works out – up to a point.

The second factor to be taken into consideration is tied in with the unreliable method of calculating small quantities by exact division of bulk quantities. So when somebody works out that $\frac{1}{2}$oz of salt is sufficient to season a dough made with 3lb of flour, it surely means they have broken down a bulk formula already rather low in salt content by as exact a division as was possible, and the result makes very little sense.

Taken to its extreme, this method reduces the salt to vanishing point. Certainly it is not uncommon to see bread recipes calling for less than a teaspoon of salt to a pound of flour, which produces virtually unsalted bread. Some people, it has to be admitted, do like this, as for example do the majority of Italians, whose bread is so often a disappointment owing to its lack of salt (in Italy, salt is a State monopoly, and expensive).

If dividing down bulk quantities is an unreliable method, multiplying up small ones can equally be a trap.

As explained in the chapter on yeast, the proportion required of the latter decreases as the bulk of the flour is increased and can again be reduced when the fermentation period is prolonged. Normally, 1 oz of yeast is sufficient for up to 7 lb of flour, and 2 to 2½ oz for 10 to 11 lb. For the larger amount of dough, i.e. one made with 10 to 11 lb of flour, it would be right to multiply the basic quantity of salt by seven, giving say 5 oz to 11 lb of flour. Still considered quite a high proportion, this is right for my taste, and is not so much that it will noticeably alter the rising time of the dough or its subsequent performance – assuming, that is, that the initial rising time allowed for your dough is 2½ to 3 hours at a temperature of 70°F, 21°C.

For a quicker-rising dough it is necessary to increase the yeast allowance by, say, an ounce without increasing the salt. For an overnight or eight-hour rising the yeast can again be decreased without reducing the salt content. It would be the high proportion of salt which would slow up the action of the yeast, and prevent the dough over-fermenting or developing a sour taste.

The very short rising and proving times, often as little as 40 minutes all told, sometimes given on flour-packet recipes, can only be explained by the minimal salt content of the dough.

So much for the quantity of salt for bread dough. What of the quality and the kind, and how to use it?

First, all old-fashioned English bakers are agreed that 'proprietary salts as prepared for household or restaurant use should not enter the bakery'. Walter Banfield's words,[1] not mine, and by 'proprietary salts' he meant salt to which magnesium carbonate had been added to keep it dry and make it free-running. In those days (pre-1939) cooking salt, unadulterated and sold in blocks of varying weights – the minimum as I remember being 2 lb – was cheaper than so-called table salt. Now it is

1. *Manna*, 1937.

more expensive, in some cases very much more so. Pure salt, like any other untampered-with foodstuff, has to be paid for. (It is curious how unwanted additives make things cheaper.) So if anyone feels that it is an unnecessary expense or trouble to buy or to find pure salt, then by all means use free-running table salt for bread. I used to think that the small amount of chemical in free-running salt would affect the yeast and the dough in some adverse way. Now I see that, at any rate in small batches of bread, it makes little difference, although the quantities may need careful checking.

I do myself use only pure salt for bread because I use it for all cooking and for the table, but I do not pay fancy prices for it. I find myself increasingly out of patience with the salt wholesalers and packers, with the prices they charge and with those 'kitchen shops', health-food stores and delicatessens who put so exaggerated a mark-up on so basic a commodity. The customers who pay these foolish prices are not without blame. As long as they like to buy their kitchen condiments, herbs and spices in sets of matching jars with matching labels, all showily arranged in a wooden rack or cabinet, then they must accept that they are paying for the packaging and the presentation regardless of the quality or quantity of the product. There are also the incurably gullible customers who think that the price of a commodity has something to do with its food value, or with its health-giving properties. Knowing the way that such beliefs are exploited in the trade, I would not myself feel like contributing to the profits of the packers, nor to those of the importers and distributors who hold exclusive English rights to the sea salt produced by French companies, and who may therefore charge what they please to the retail shops whose customers believe that there is some particular virtue in salt from the Mediterranean. Very often this is beautiful, sparkling, very pure salt. (Or, in view of the pollution in the Mediterranean, is it?) Certainly to use so expensive a product for the seasoning of bread is unnecessary.

Anyone who makes bread in any quantity finds himself getting through a deal of salt. What salt then to use? Since, with the exception of the famous Maldon salt from Essex on the east coast – again a luxury – there is now no sea salt extracted from English or Scottish waters, I use Cheshire rock salt sold in $1\frac{1}{2}$lb blocks or 2lb bags or 6lb clear plastic jars, the latter being the best value[1] and the most convenient. This salt

1. In the autumn of 1974 a 6 lb jar of Cheshire rock salt cost me 42 p from a country provision shop. In a London kitchenware shop the following week I saw 3 to 4 oz bags of sea salt priced at 45 p.

is produced by the old Liverpool firm of Ingram Thompson (mention of 'Liverpool salt' occurs quite often in eighteenth- and nineteenth-century cookery books) whose salt works are at Northwich.[1] This firm's packaging is minimal and their wholesale prices fair, so if you find you are paying too much for rock salt or 'crystal' salt it is probably because middlemen have bought it in bulk and are charging the retailer more than is fair for packaging and labelling, and it is advisable to try a big department store, a chain grocery, even a supermarket, which buys in bulk direct from the producers or, more properly, processors. Other pure cooking salts, probably processed by one of the big chemical companies, may well turn up in big stores and branches of chain groceries, and probably at a very reasonable price. It is always worth asking.

For those who prefer sea salt to rock salt, the least expensive at present available is imported and packed by a company called Granose, producers and purveyors of vegetarian and health foods certainly since the 1930s, probably longer. This company's Mediterranean sea salt is packed in containers reminiscent of those used for scouring powders, so at least you are not paying much for the packaging. The salt itself is coarse and only partially purified, excellent for cooking but less convenient for breadmaking and flour mixtures generally because it needs either a good deal of vigorous pounding (it *could* be electrically ground, though) or dissolving in water and then filtering.

This brings us to the question of the best way of getting the salt into the flour or the dough. Should it be incorporated directly into the flour or dissolved in the water measured out to mix the dough? Of this decision Walter Banfield asks, 'Which do you prefer, a penny or two halfpennies?' Well, it depends on the salt. If coarse crystals are used it is essential to dissolve them in the water to ensure even distribution of the salt, and also to eliminate the risk of undissolved salt crystals in the dough. Once any crystals are mixed into the flour, nothing will dissolve them; they will be present, like ice particles in an ice cream, in the finished loaf, and although salt crystals on the crust of a loaf or a roll are enticing, in the crumb they are the reverse. Using the powdery Cheshire rock salt there is little risk of this, so I add the salt directly to the flour.

Apart from its importance in bread, salt helps to bring out the flavours

1. Messrs Ingram Thompson and Sons Ltd, Lion Salt Works, Marston, Northwich. Names of retail stockists will be sent on request to this company.

in sweetened mixtures such as bun, brioche and pastry doughs, cake and spiced bread batters. In these cases, the quantity used is small, but its presence is important.

I keep my rock salt or sea salt for breadmaking and all cooking in wide, glazed stoneware (*not* porous earthenware) jars, uncovered, by the side of the stove. There is really no necessity for special salt boxes, salt jars and the like. Provided that the container you use is large enough to get your hand into, that it is not porous earthenware nor any kind of metal – glass is splendid for salt, but the usual storage jars are too narrow for convenience – and that it is always readily accessible, there is no problem.

One final, cautionary paragraph from Banfield's *Manna* concerning salt in relation to bread:

'When extra salt is added, perhaps under the misapprehension that the more salt one uses the better the bread will taste, a loaf of bread is produced that is more savoury than flavoury, and any flavours of the cornfields and the subtle flavours resulting from combinations of the products of fermentation which should produce true bread flavour cannot be appreciated by the palate.'

Mr Banfield, of course, was right. It *would* be agreeable to think that some of the flavours of the cornfields linger in our daily bread. But in reality it is patient maturing of the dough, just as much as its proper seasoning and the taste of the grain, which distinguishes memorable bread from just good bread. This question is dealt with in the chapter on yeast.

Liquids and Fats
Used in Breadmaking

WATER

For plain ordinary everyday bread the only liquid needed is water. The quality of the water, whether it is hard, soft or medium soft – the latter is supposed to make the better dough – and its purity do of course make a difference to the bread, and this is just one of the factors that explain the differences between bread made in different districts from precisely the same flour and by identical methods. On the whole, though, I don't think the quality of the water has such a marked effect on bread as it does, say, on coffee, tea, broth, soups and boiled vegetables. Water softeners may provide the answer to many cooking problems but, although soft water does in my experience make a very lively bread dough easy to handle, it doesn't necessarily make the bread itself any better. A water filter would be every bit as much to the point as a softener.

Aerated water is said to make good dough, and indeed during the mid nineteenth century a Doctor Dauglish patented a system of making bread from dough enclosed in a container and aerated under pressure with nothing but highly carbonated water. This bread achieved a certain commercial success, and is still made. The company which exploited it, known as the A.B.C. or Aerated Bread Company, opened a number of London tea-rooms selling light meals at popular prices. Launched in 1861, these A.B.C. tea-shops preceded the Jo Lyons establishments by over thirty years. They were cheap without being very cheerful. Under the aegis of Allied Bakeries, the giant combine which acquired the A.B.C. during the 1950s, some of the tea-shops still survive, and the A.B.C. factory in Camden Town still churns out its aerated bread. Dull and flavourless though it is, it has its faithful adherents.

The temperature of water for the mixing of bread dough should, normally, be approximately 98° to 108°F, 37° to 43°C, or a little warmer in very cold weather, and is rarely used hotter than 120°F, 49°C. Very hot water has an adverse effect on the starch in the flour, as well as on the yeast.

In exceptionally hot weather, or in tropical climates, iced water can be used to slow up over-rapid generation of heat in the dough. According to Walter Banfield, crushed or solid ice from the refrigerator serves just as well. Of this he makes the following assertion: 'Adding solid ice assists the production of French bread, with its desirable irregular, "holey" texture. A rather strange effect follows the use of ice. Bread so made possesses an extremely thin crust, almost wafer-like, so that it is occasionally referred to as the egg-shell crust.'[1] Interesting, and worth noting. Banfield is the only professional English baker I have yet come across who has admitted in his writings that the 'irregular, "holey" texture' in French bread is 'desirable' or even acceptable. The majority of bakers writing for their colleagues or pupils devote pages and even chapters to the importance of a uniform crumb, and refer constantly to the holes in bread as if they were a dangerous plague. One friend of mine, who makes beautiful bread, maintains that 'the holes are the best part', and the joy of filling the 'air pockets . . . with . . . salted butter' is mentioned by James Williams in the passage from *Give Me Yesterday* quoted on p. 39.

Snow, incidentally, is often suggested in old country recipes for aerating pancake batter, in the same way that some cooks use beer, or whisked egg whites. Living in London, and not fancying the muddy slush from the streets, I have never tried the snow trick. But ice, why not? About $1\frac{1}{4}$ lb of ice would be needed to make the equivalent of 1 pint (20 oz) of water.

Another effective trick to know about when you need to slow down the rising of yeast dough is the 'peggy tub' system described on pp. 311–12, in which the dough is immersed in a tub of water and left to rise. My American colleague and friend James Beard[2] calls this 'waterproofing' and, as it must be of ancient origin, there are probably many more names for it. A peggy tub was simply a Victorian version of a kind of wash tub. John Kirkland, in *The Modern Baker, Confectioner and Caterer*,[3] quotes Pliny on a kind of bread introduced into Rome from Parthia in Asia Minor: '"It is not very long since we had a bread intro-

1. *Manna*, 1937.
2. *Beard on Bread*, New York, Knopf, 1973; London, Michael Joseph, 1976.
3. London, 1907, new and revised edn 1923.

duced from Parthia, known as water bread from a method of kneading it, of drawing out the dough by the aid of water, a process which renders it remarkably light and full of holes like a sponge. Some call this Parthian bread."'

The water, or any mixture of liquids used for mixing flour into dough, is known to bakers as 'liquor', and, as I have already written in the chapter on different flours and meals, and repeated in many of the recipes, the question of the quantity of liquor or liquid which any given flour will absorb is something which everyone has to discover for himself. In this respect, quantities in a recipe can be no more than an approximation. This variability is particularly marked in the case of whole wheatmeal.

In the modern wrapped white loaf of the bakery plant the ratio of water to flour is much higher than it was in pre-war bread. Up-to-date machinery and mixing processes have enabled the factories to increase the amount of water per sack, or 280 lb, of flour, from the once-normal 14 gallons to 17 gallons. In home breadmaking ½ pint of water per 1 lb or 1 lb 2 oz of flour is the average proportion. In the factory product it is ¾ pint to 1 lb of flour. That is higher than the permitted limit in the U.S.A. and in Australia. In Britain, however, we have at present no statutory regulation covering the water content of our bread.

MILK

Milk is second to water in importance for the mixing of dough. A moderate proportion, say one of milk to three of water, is said to prolong the life of a loaf of bread. Eliza Acton was particularly insistent on this point. I have made the experiment dozens of times and cannot say that I have found any marked difference in the keeping qualities of milk-enriched bread, although the milk does, I think, improve the quality of the crumb, particularly in whole wheatmeal bread. This is due to the fat content of the milk. Lard, butter or cream will produce the same effect.

For any small breads which should have a soft rather than a crisp crust, such as rolls, baps and muffins, a half and half mixture of milk and water, or even all milk, makes a great difference. Made entirely with water these breads develop a tough crust. Baked in an oven designed especially for breadmaking this doesn't happen to nearly such a marked degree, but in the oven of an ordinary household cooker heated by gas or electricity – solid-fuel ovens are more satisfactory in this respect – small breads bake so quickly that the crust is formed before the inside dough is properly developed or cooked. It is of little use to try to counter-act this by baking at a greatly reduced temperature because the rolls will not then rise in the oven, and the end product will be sad and heavy. The milk in the dough provides a good solution, and has long been used to make soft breads, as for example in the seventeenth-century manchet bread given on p. 335.

Commercial milk breads are made with various milk powders or con-centrates. Unless these are full milk rather than skimmed or de-fatted products, the bread made with them should not be designated 'milk bread'.

BUTTERMILK AND SOUR MILK

Buttermilk is the residue of milk or cream left in the churn from the making of butter, and is very often used for mixing Irish soda breads, for scones and for other chemically aerated breads. It is the lactic acid action on the bicarbonate of soda which helps to lighten the dough, and also gives a nice taste and texture to unfermented breads. Sour butter-milk is best for unfermented bread, while for any yeast bread it should be fresh and sweet.

It would be a tall order nowadays to try to find true fresh buttermilk, but the cultured buttermilk launched on the English market in the early 1970s by one of the big dairy combines is very adequate for bread and scone mixing. Cultured buttermilk is no novelty. A formula given in John Kirkland's *Bakers' ABC* of 1927 is quoted in the chapter deal-ing with buttermilk bread, scones and griddle cakes made with chemical raising agents. Now and again in old country recipes one comes across the term 'churn milk'. This means buttermilk.

Sour milk is, or was, often used in the same way as buttermilk, but when modern pasteurized milk goes sour it can have a very strong unattractive and mouldy smell, so it is important to try it before using it. Yogurt would probably serve the same purpose as buttermilk and sour milk. Remember, though, that commercial yogurt is very acid, and that a little goes a long way. Cultured soured cream, as sold by the dairy combines, is another possibility.

CREAM

In this book there are a number of enriched yeast dough, pastry and batter recipes which call for cream instead of butter. This is partly because many, surprisingly many, of the older English recipes for such delicate confections as wiggs, and the earlier versions of Sally Lunn cakes did specify cream – several such recipes are quoted in this book – but mainly because I find that cream is very often more satisfactory than butter, making a lighter batter or yeast pastry, with a smoother texture. It is also a good deal quicker and easier to work with. Very thick, ripe, matured – which doesn't mean sour – cream, as used to make the finest butter, is the ideal for working into yeast pastries, but this implies the most expensive Jersey cream, which isn't always easy to find, and does seem rather extravagant. Cream from the dairy combines is a deal cheaper, and although not so rich-tasting has approximately the same fat content, which by present English law must be a minimum of 48 per cent. Single cream, with a minimum fat content of 18 per cent, can be used instead of double cream in many recipes, but allowance must be made for the difference in consistence, as it will make a thinner, more liquid batter or dough, while double cream is much more akin to butter in its effect.

Clotted cream is occasionally specified in West Country recipes, and very delicious it is, so thick and rich that it is a joy to use – but, unless you live in Cornwall, Devon or Dorset, that *does* come expensive, as it must be either ordered by post or bought from a specialist provision store. And the so-called clotted cream marketed by the big dairy combines is a pitiful travesty of the real thing. True Cornish clotted cream should contain up to 60 per cent of fat with a minimum content of 55 per cent. Florence White, in *Good Things in England* (1932), claims that the dough for Sally Lunns should *only* be made with clotted cream, never butter, and that, once cooked, they should be split and spread with more clotted cream.

Seventeenth-century French recipes for special white breads, which must have been much like our manchet bread of the same period, sometimes call for *fromage blanc* or *fromage frais*. This was used instead of butter, and would have been more like thick cream, or clotted cream, than what we call white cheese.

BUTTER

'Butter should smell as sweet as a nosegay.'

Mrs Rundell, *A New System of Domestic Cookery*, 1806

When a fat is to be added to bread dough, it is unanimously agreed by bakers that butter is the best one to use. Certainly butter does something to dough which gives the baked loaf a good-looking crust and the crumb a fine flavour; and a butter-enriched roll dough, such as in the Vienna roll recipe on p. 325, is wonderfully easy and enjoyable to work with.

To ordinary everyday bread I seldom add fat of any kind, other than a little milk or oil. The use of the latter is explained below.

When a dough or batter is to be heavily enriched with butter or other fat it is often worked in after the straight dough has risen for the first time. This is because the fat globules, in coating the flour grains, make them sticky, forming a barrier which gets in the way of the yeast and impedes its action. Once the yeast has done its work and spread throughout the whole mass, the addition of the fat presents less of a problem.

LARD

This means pure pork lard. Most purveyors of bread flour for home-baking print recipes on their packets which include a small proportion of butter or vegetable oil or lard, more often the latter, and never more than 2 oz per 3 lb of flour, sometimes less. Lard is thought to improve the keeping qualities of the loaf. Except that it may make the crumb just a little more moist, and does perhaps improve the texture of whole wheatmeal bread, I do not find it particularly effective. The English obsession with the storing of bread stems from the days when ovens were not part of the cooking stove proper and, because of the work involved and the expense of the fuel, were fired only once a week, in some households only once a fortnight, for the baking of a very large batch of bread and other dough products. Hence all the lardy cakes, the yeast dumplings, the buns and small cakes which were made from any extra dough not used for bread.

For these lovely cakes and rolls, lard *is* essential to achieve the proper texture, richness and weight. There is no such thing as a really light lardy cake. For all that, dough cakes and their like are not as heavy, and nothing like as rich, as today's Christmas cakes, plum puddings and many of the fatty and sugary pastries sold by bakeries and cake shops.

From the lardy cake recipes given in this book – some of them are to be found in the chapter on regional and festival breads, others in the section on manchets, as that is what they were called in some districts – it will be seen that the lard is nearly always worked into plain dough after the first rising or proving, as explained for butter.

It is essential to use very clean pure lard for any kind of bread or cake. The slightest taint or rancidity in lard communicates itself to dough in a most disconcerting manner. If you cannot lay hands on pure pork lard, don't attempt lardy cakes.

OIL

To me this means olive oil. In the Italian manner I add it sometimes to the dough for plain rolls and other small breads. It has a wonderful effect on the dough, making it exceptionally easy to knead, and giving it a particular litheness. A very small proportion, no more than 2 scant tablespoons to $1\frac{1}{4}$ lb of flour, is ample. Instead of lard for English muffin dough, a little oil, although unorthodox, does wonders, while for pizza dough it is, as the Italians know, infinitely preferable to butter. Dough to which olive oil has been added, even in very small proportions, never forms a skin, and doesn't develop a sour taste even if over-proved or otherwise neglected.

I would not use my best, heavy, fruity olive oil for dough – that would be the equivalent of tipping Château Margaux into the cooking pots – but a decent light olive oil, probably blended, but genuine. Such oils are usually to be bought much more cheaply from a multiple chemist such as Boots than from specialist provision stores, with the exception of Italian shops in the Soho quarter of London and the equivalent districts in other large cities.

Alternatives to olive oil are sesame-seed, sunflower-seed and tasteless arachide or peanut oil. Corn oil has its adherents. To me, that's just what it is, an adherent. I don't like the way it sticks to the palate and I don't like its taste or its smell. To many, however, these are quite inoffensive. Each must decide for himself. It is in any case seldom necessary to buy oil especially for bread or any other dough. So long as it is without any trace of rancidity, which would be communicated to the dough, you use the oil you have in the store cupboard. Unless, that is, you plan to make pizza or something of that kind regularly and on a large scale.

VEGETARIAN FATS

Among those who make their own bread are great numbers of vegetarians. They will know better than I which brand of fat suits them and their bread dough. Those new to breadmaking and in need of advice as to vegetarian fats and alternatives to milk, cream and butter would perhaps do best to consult a vegetarian cookery book, or the Vegetarian Society, 53 Marloes Road, London W8 6LD and Parkdale, Dunham Road, Altrincham, Cheshire.

Eggs, Dried Fruit, Sugar, Spices and Flavourings Used in Yeast Cakes and Breads

EGGS

'It is well to remember that a single musty egg will spoil a ton of cake or anything else it is put into.'

Frederick T. Vine, *Saleable Shop Goods*, 6th edn, 1898

In English spice cakes, breads, buns, tea cakes, yeast pastries and light cakes such as Sally Lunns, eggs are used in very modest quantities. Confections with a high content of eggs, such as brioches, tend to go dry more rapidly than those with a smaller proportion. One point to remember in this context is that when increasing the proportions of a recipe given in small quantity, it is not necessary, nor desirable, to multiply the number of eggs by the same amount as you may do for the flour. For example, the Sally Lunn recipe on p. 467 calls for ½ lb of flour, ½ oz of yeast and 2 eggs. To double it, you use 1 lb of flour, but still only ½ oz yeast, and 3, not 4, eggs. Experienced cooks will scarcely need to be told so basic a kitchen fact, but beginners so often fall into the trap of doubling or multiplying every ingredient that I have thought it worth stressing, as in the matter of salt explained on p. 121, and equally of yeast, which is gone into at some length on pp. 106–10.

Sometimes, in old recipes and in those worked out in bulk by professional bakers, eggs are specified by liquid volume rather than by number. One pint (20 fluid oz) of beaten egg is approximately the equivalent of a dozen average eggs. Incidentally, it is sometimes thought that in the seventeenth and eighteenth centuries hens' eggs were seldom larger than today's bantams' eggs and that this accounts for the apparently lavish quantities often specified in old recipes. I can find no evidence to support the theory, any more than there is evidence for the similar claim that lemons were much smaller than they are today. The paintings of domestic scenes and still-lifes of those periods show that both lemons and eggs, as related to the scale of other objects represented, were much the sizes that they are today. You don't have to go further than the works of the most obvious seventeenth-century painters – de Heem, Velazquez – and, for the eighteenth century, some of Chardin's most famous pictures, to see that this is the case. And when recipes are analysed it is seen that the number of eggs is rarely out of proportion to the weight or volume of the other ingredients.

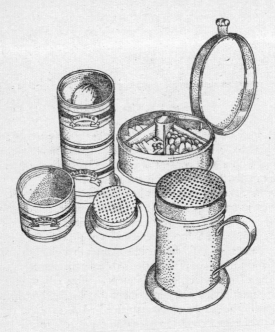

DRIED FRUIT, SPICES AND SUGAR

'He [the village grocer] could be a bit tight, for he had been known to cut a raisin in half to achieve the just balance, screwing up his mouth as he did so.'

Allan Jobson, *An Hour-Glass on the Run*, 1959

Dried fruit and sugar both figure quite largely in the buns, spice and dough cakes and fruit breads given in this book, although sugar plays a much smaller part than the fruit, which supplies its own sugar content.

Both fruit and sugar can be incorporated directly into a dough, as in the hot cross bun and the saffron cake recipes on pp. 477 and 440 respectively, or left until the dough has had its first rising as in the spiced cake recipe on pp. 457–9 and the Simnel yeast cake recipe on p. 455. In these cases it is advisable to warm the fruit before working it in. This will help to ensure that it is evenly distributed, and that it will not have a deadening effect on the dough, which does not take kindly to the addition of a large proportion of cold and heavy ingredients. Work the fruit in thoroughly, and carefully, with your hands when this is feasible. Spoons or spatulas and the blades of electric mixers split or cut the fruit, the juice runs out, and the end result will be blotchy, messy-looking slices. A 'broad pudding-stick' is recommended by E. Smith (*The Compleat Housewife*, 1727) for the incorporation of dried and warmed currants into the dough.

The candied peel of citrus fruits – lemon, citron and bitter orange – and candied angelica stems and sometimes cherries go to make up the 'mixed peel' often specified in English recipes, both old and modern. With the exception of angelica these peels are tough and gummy, and if bought in the piece rather than ready mixed should be cut up as small as is feasible before being worked into the dough. I find it a good idea to substitute stem ginger in syrup for candied peel. It is softer, I prefer the flavour – in small doses – and it blends better into the dough. In fact the peel can often be omitted altogether by those who don't like it. For those who decide to use ginger, a little of the syrup from the jar makes a useful addition. Another alternative to candied peel can be dried apricots, cut into slivers after a short steeping in water just to soften them. They look more attractive, taste more interesting and are less sugary than candied peel.

Almonds occur seldom in the recipes in this book. When they do, they are an important ingredient, adding moisture as well as a particularly good flavour and an attractive texture. Ready ground almonds from a shop are often stale, and when feasible it is best, and cheapest, to blanch and skin the almonds yourself, although it is not always strictly necessary to skin almonds for grinding. With today's electric blenders and coffee mills, the grinding should present no problem; a little rose water, as explained further on in this chapter, may be needed to prevent the almonds from oiling, and also for mixing them to a paste as is specified in the recipe for the Countess of Kent's spice cake given on p. 457.

Most of the dried fruits specified in the recipes in this book are the conventional currants, sultanas and raisins. Many more modern recipes provide for dates, prunes and apricots for fruit breads, so anybody who would prefer one, or a mixture, of these, plus perhaps the walnuts favoured by vegetarians, has only to substitute the appropriate quantities of the fruit of their choice. Prunes should be soaked until they are soft enough for the stones to be easily extracted, without waste, and for the fruit to be cut into pieces. As explained above, apricots need only a very brief steeping – some varieties indeed can be used as they are, and simply cut into strips, not too small. Preserved dates are delicious in bread, and highly nutritious, but sticky and troublesome to stone. Fresh dates are equally good, but in this country a luxury, more likely to be kept for dessert than used in cooking.

The various dried grapes, the currants, raisins and sultanas made familiar to English kitchens through our Levantine and Mediterranean trade long before the days of Australian, South African and Californian imports, are trouble-free and need no preparation beyond warming, as explained above. This wasn't always so. In the past an immense amount of labour was necessitated on account of the rough and ready methods by which the fruit was picked, dried, packed and exported. Raisins, often described in old recipes as 'raisins of the sun', had to be stoned, a tedious and sticky task. For anyone who may be faced with having to perform it, the following instructions given in the 1902 edition of *Law's Grocer's Manual* will prove useful:

'To stone or seed Raisins by Hand – Pour boiling water over them and let them stand five or ten minutes. Drain, and rub each raisin between the thumb and finger till the seeds come out clean. Dry the raisins before using, and rub them in flour before putting them into cake, to prevent their sinking to the bottom. If chopped, flour should be scattered over them, to prevent their adhering together.'

Raisins were bought in large quantities by households where wine was made, while the expensive Málaga and Valencia muscatel raisins, dried on the stalk and packed in boxes, were imported for the Christmas and New Year festivities.

Currants were all imported from Greece and the Greek islands – their name is derived from Corinth – and until late in the nineteenth century the entire Greek crop was absorbed by the British market. Exported in cases, the fruit harboured bits of stalk, grit, soil and other foreign matter including no doubt dead flies as well as a good deal of dust, so the cleaning was a very real necessity.

Over and over again, in the recipes of the seventeenth, eighteenth and nineteenth centuries, the reader is warned not to omit a careful drying and, as already explained, warming of the currants before they were added to a yeast dough. 'Then have ready twelve pounds of currants very well washed and pick'd, that there may be neither stalks, nor broken currants in them. Then let your Currants be very well dried before the fire, and put warm into your Cake', writes Sir Kenelm Digby. And again, 'Take three pounds of raisins stoned, and twelve pounds of Currants very well washed and dried again; one pound of Dates slic'd, half a pound of green Citron dried and sliced very thin.'[1]

By the end of the nineteenth century special machines had been evolved for fruit cleaning, so that sifting and picking the currants clean was no longer quite the arduous task it had been, but they were still sold loose by the grocer, and even if they didn't have to be rubbed round and round in a sieve until the fingers bled, as described by Allan Jobson,[2] they still needed washing and drying.

Sultanas, or Smyrna raisins, were a later addition to the dried fruits of the English kitchen. They were, and are, the product of a sweet seedless grape, and evidently presented no cleaning problems, for at first they were treated as a dessert delicacy (plumped up with brandy, wrapped in lemon leaves and presented in little parcels, locally grown seedless sultanas are still one of the treats of southern Italy), and they do not appear in recipes until the mid nineteenth century, when presumably it began to be appreciated that although they had less character than raisins and were more expensive than currants, they were a great deal less trouble than either. I still think that currants and raisins do more for cakes and fruit breads than sultanas, which tend to be insipid.

Sometimes, in old Cornish and other West Country recipes, figs or 'figgys' are specified. Don't be misled into running out to buy dried figs. In this context figs nearly always mean raisins or currants. These are also the plums in plum pudding and 'plumb' cake.

SUGAR

'The best Sugar is hard, solid, light, exceeding white and sweet, glistring like snow.'

Dr Thomas Muffett, *Health's Improvement*, written *c.* 1595, published 1655

1. *The Closet of the Eminently Learned Sir Kenelm Digby Knight Opened*, 1669.
2. *An Hour-Glass on the Run*, 1959.

'Plenty of sugar should always be kept ready broke in the deep sugar drawers in the closet storeroom. There is one for spice, one for moist sugar, and two for lump sugar. The pieces should be as square as possible, and rather small.'

The Housekeeping Book of Susanna Whatman[1] *1776–1800*,
ed. Thomas Balston, 1956

'After refining white sugar is of purity over 99·9% and is the purest food supplied for human consumption. It is purer than London tap water.'

Sugar, ed. J. A. C. Hugill, 1949

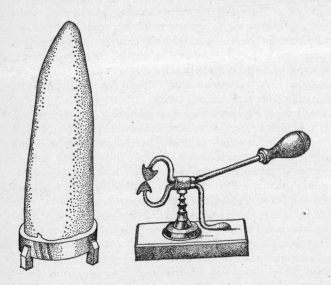

The weight of a sugar loaf could vary from 5 lb to 40 lb, according to the moulds used in the refinery. As late as 1938 Tate and Lyle were importing sugar loaves from the continent.

Sugar cutters also varied in size. For domestic use they were usually about 16 inches long and 7 inches high. Smaller ones were used for cutting up chunks cut by the grocer from a large loaf.

Apart from all the labour involved in the cleaning and stoning of fruit and the chopping of candied peel (much of this had probably been home-preserved), the sugar also represented hours of work.

1. Susanna Whatman was the second wife of John Whatman, founder of the famous Whatman paper mills in Kent.

Large and prosperous households bought their white sugar in tall, conical loaves, from which pieces were broken off with special iron sugar-cutters. Shaped something like very large and heavy pliers with sharp blades attached to the cutting sides, these cutters had to be strong and tough, because the loaves were large, about 14 inches in diameter at the base, and 3 feet high. 'I pray that you will vouchsafe to send me another sugar loaf, for my old is done', writes Margaret Paston from Norfolk to her husband in London (*The Paston Letters*, 1422–1509). In those days, sugar was used with great care, and one loaf lasted a long time. The weight would probably have been about 30 lb. Later, the weight of a loaf varied from 5 lb to 35 lb, according to the moulds used by any one refinery. A common size was 14 lb, but the finest sugar from Madeira came in small loaves of only 3 or 4 lb in weight.[1]

White sugar was already, in the early seventeenth century, 'double-refined' in English refineries. Before that, sugar in varying degrees of refinement had been largely imported from Europe, mainly from Italian and Baltic refineries which received their raw sugar from India, Persia and North Africa. In the mid sixteenth century, in the 1550s, only two sugar refining establishments existed in the whole of England. A hundred years later, after raw sugar had begun to arrive in quantity from the West Indies, and many a great English fortune had already been founded on the sugar business, there were fifty refineries in London alone, but it took another century before sugar refining had grown into a major British profit-making trade.

For ordinary sweetening purposes, white sugar, most of which was only relatively white – Dr Muffett's 'best Sugar . . . glistring like snow' would have been rare and very expensive – was roughly pounded in a mortar, and for filling the china and silver casters of well-appointed households was reduced to a fine powder. For the icing of cakes it had to be further 'searced' or sieved through fine gauze, lawn or silk. This labour must have been exceptionally arduous, as will be appreciated by anybody who has ever tried to reduce cube sugar to powder, or even to restore caked and lumpy icing sugar to its powdery state without the aid of an electric blender. And the standards demanded seem to have been high. The icing on the cakes had to be pure white and smooth, the cook was continually exhorted to take care not to allow the iced cake, when put into the oven to set or dry, to take colour or scorch. In one recipe Sir Kenelm Digby requires that the finished article resemble

1. Thomas Muffett, *Health's Improvement*, 1655.

'silver between polished and matte or like a looking glass'. One wonders how often the elegant ideal was achieved.

Up till late Victorian times household sugar remained very little changed and sugar loaves were still common and continued so until well into the twentieth century, but white sugar was no longer the precious commodity it had been in the early days of sugar refining (in the fifteenth century the retail price of white sugar was about 17d a pound,

Japanned tin sugar box, nineteenth century.

the equivalent of at least £3 or £4 of today's money), so lump sugar could be bought by everybody from the grocer, who performed the task of cutting it from the loaves while the customer waited. In carefully equipped larders and store cupboards Susanna Whatman's wooden chest with its 'deep sugar drawers' had been superseded by deep japanned tin boxes, in which a supply of lumps from the loaves could be kept. At the bottom of the box there was a sheet of perforated tin, and beneath this a drawer to catch the sugar dust from the lumps. Relatively cheap though sugar had become housewives were still careful to look after it, and the packers still wrapped their sugar loaves in the blue paper which had become traditional since it had first been used because it reflected a white light on the sugar crystals, making the loaves look less yellow.[1]

During the latter decades of the nineteenth century caster and icing or confectioners' sugar had become current, but the process whereby cubes of sugar could be produced in uniform size and massive quantity, although originally evolved by German refiners, was still, in England, the exclusive patent of the Tate Sugar Company, who had acquired it from the German inventors.

BROWN SUGARS

'As yet they made but bare muscavadoes, so moist and full of molasses, so ill-cured that they were barely worth the bringing home to England.'

Richard Ligon, *A True and Exact History of the Island of Barbadoes*, 1657

Moist brown sugars 'of a baser sort', as they were still considered by the Victorians, could and would have been used by the less well-off for sweetening fruit cakes and puddings, but for anything light and delicate such as fine yeast buns, wiggs, Sally Lunn cakes, and of course for confectionery, fruit-preserving and cake icing, the sugar had to be white. Gradually, even in fruited doughs such as those for hot cross buns, white sugar replaced brown, as Walter Banfield wrote, 'on the grounds of showmanship'. Again, as with flour, the whiter the sugar, the more highly prized – and again we find the reversal in our own day of the relative status of the refined and unrefined products. The once lowly brown sugar, the 'pieces' – also known as 'yellows' – or partly refined sugar in a moist state, not 'stoved' or dried out, and the delicious treacly 'foots', the sugar which settled to the foot of the raw molasses cask, are now much sought after by the minority, and are more expensive than white sugar. Under the old name of muscovado – the word is derived, it is said, from the Portuguese *mazcavado*, meaning 'impure, unrefined'[2] – the authentic unpurified 'foots' sugars, like wholewheat flours, have become favourite props of the wholefood business. Delicious as

1. Another explanation of the blue paper is that it preserved the whiteness of the sugar. The first seems the more likely.

2. Another interpretation of the word is that it derives from the Spanish *más acabado*, meaning 'more finished', i.e. it was more refined than when mixed with the molasses.

the true brown cane sugars are, they can't have been very attractive in tea, and they do distort the flavour as well as the colour of the fruit in jams and preserves. And would one really want brown sugar with fresh strawberries? The answer to the dangerous over-consumption of sugar which as a nation is one of our greatest health hazards is not so much to substitute one kind of sugar for another but rather to eat drastically less of it, whether directly in cakes and pastries, with fruit and in tea or coffee, or indirectly in soft drinks, jam and confectionery.

The main sources of our muscovado sugars, once used for commercial British wine-making and brewing, and still used – when procurable – for the curing of hams and other salted meats, were the West Indian islands of Barbados, Trinidad and Jamaica.

Another sugar frequently mentioned in eighteenth-century recipes is 'Lisbon'. Originally this came from Portuguese territories, the Azores, Madeira and Brazil – 'two and a halfe pounds of right Brazil sugar' is called for by one late-seventeenth-century cookery writer – and was shipped to England, probably to Bristol, via Lisbon. This sugar was processed on the plantations, the loaves being divided into three portions, the base being more or less white, the centre yellow and the top of the cone brown. Although only partially refined, Lisbon sugar was evidently considered to be particularly desirable, for the recipes often specify 'fine' or 'the finest' Lisbon sugar, indicating whether the white or the brown was to be used. Eventually the name Lisbon came to denote a process or manner of refining sugar rather than any particular provenance.[1] It was also known as 'clayed' sugar.

Demerara sugar, originally cane sugar from the Demerara district of the British Guiana (now Guyana) territory on the mainland of northern South America, was a natural product of the cane juice, and the term came to denote many different soft crystal sugars. Nowadays so-called Demerara, the pale brown sugar so popular in the coffee bars of the 1950s, is just as likely to be coloured beet sugar as a natural cane product.

Although it is often thought that the preponderance of beet sugar consumed in this country dates from the First World War and the years immediately following, trade figures show that already in 1901 the product of the cane accounted for only one quarter of our total yearly sugar consumption.

As a yeast food, sugar is believed by many people to be essential to breadmaking, and since this point is inseparable from the discussion

1. Geoffrey Fairrie, *Sugar*, 1925.

of yeast itself, notes on the subject are included in the chapter on yeast.

MOLASSES AND BLACK TREACLE

'Five or six spoonfuls of the best Malassoes you can get. Spanish cute,[1] if you can get it, is thought better than Malassoes.'

Sir Hugh Plat, *Delightes for Ladies*, 1609

Correctly speaking, molasses is the drainings of crude unrefined sugar, whereas treacle is the dark brown, viscous, uncrystallizable syrup drained from sugar during the refining process. For the purposes of sweetening fruit and malt breads and giving them that moist and squashy quality so much liked by children, the two are interchangeable. True molasses is, generally, only to be found in wholefood stores, whereas proprietary brands of black treacle are sold by good groceries and provision stores. Only very small proportions of black treacle are used in commercial bread. Walter Banfield recommends 2 oz to 14 lb of meal.

GOLDEN SYRUP

This is Tate & Lyle's proprietary invention, a mixture of refined sugars and, in their words, 'super-saturated solution together with non-sugars which give it colour, flavour, and properties which are characteristically its own'.

When golden syrup or black treacle are to be substituted for the sugar specified in any of the spice and fruit cake recipes in this book, the best way to measure them in approximately the same terms is to coat the weighing tray of your scales with flour before pouring in the treacle or syrup. In this way it will not stick to the tray. Work it into the dough with the fruit, as directed for the sugar in the recipe. Speaking for myself, I prefer to use honey, which gives a more subtle and delicate flavour to bread and yeast cakes than treacle or golden syrup.

1. Probably from *massecuite*, the raw sugar as shipped for refinement. In other words Sir Hugh knew very well – or his informant did – that the sugar itself was better for his purposes – brewing a kind of whisky – than the crude residue in its viscous form.

SPICES

'My old school-fellow, Smith, the Grocer, of Margaret Street, has been frequently heard to declare that whenever Mrs Nollekens purchased tea and sugar at his father's shop, she always requested, just at the moment she was quitting the counter, to have either a clove or a bit of cinnamon to take some unpleasant taste out of her mouth; but she never was seen to apply it to the part so affected, so that, with Nollekens's nutmegs, which he pocketed from the table at the Academy dinners, they contrived to accumulate a little stock of spices, without any expense whatever.'

John Thomas Smith, *Nollekens and his Times*,[1] first published 1828

Two main categories of spices are used in the recipes in this book. For breads, they are caraway, dill, cumin, fennel and anis seeds; and for spice cakes and buns, they are the sweet spices, which comprise cinnamon, cloves and nutmeg, sometimes blended with coriander seeds or allspice (Jamaica pepper or pimento berry) or with both, the latter often being used in small proportion in the blends sold as cake, pudding or just 'mixed' spice. The mild peppery taste of the Jamaica pepper adds a fillip to the sweeter spices. My own sweet spice blend, given on p. 430, includes a little true pepper. This makes a better-balanced and longer-

English silver spice caster, 4 inches high. Early seventeenth century.

1. Nollekens was the celebrated eighteenth-century sculptor, born in 1737 and active until his death in 1823. Both he and his wife were notorious for their parsimonious habits. The Smith who recorded the life of Nollekens had been his apprentice. A modern edition of the book was published by the Turnstile Press in 1969.

lasting mixture than the Jamaica pepper. Incidentally, the alternative name of allspice given to this berry makes for confusion with mixed sweet spice, so that quite often when 'allspice' figures in recipes – usually the more modern ones – I think that mixed spice is meant. In older recipes the authors specified Jamaica pepper, so there can be no doubt as to their intention.

Caraway seeds, the great English favourite, were sometimes used in conjunction with the mixed spices, often in the form of 'comfits', tiny, sugar-coated sweets, enclosing the seed. Coriander and aniseed were treated in the same way, the art of comfit-making having developed early in the seventeenth century, when the sugar refineries established in London, and gradually in other English ports, began to make white sugar more easily available for confectionery. The use of comfits in cakes and buns must have been an interesting way of introducing sugar into the dough, giving a crunchy effect. Caraway comfits are nearly always specified in eighteenth-century recipes for Bath cakes and buns, both for mixing into the dough and for strewing over the cakes when they were baked.

Never one of my own favourites, I have included caraway seeds only in recipes in which they are entirely traditional and characteristic. They can always be omitted by those who dislike them. On this point Sir Harry Luke, in *The Tenth Muse* (Putnam, 1954), wrote to the effect that people only *think* they dislike caraway because they confuse it, or associate it, with aniseed. Very possibly, but this doesn't account for those who, as I do, like aniseed but not caraway. And I don't think that anyone familiar with both is likely to confuse them. In fact, I think that it is the hardness of caraway seeds, as well as their associations with the dust-dry seed cakes of childhood, which is repellent to many people. Their taste and aroma are pleasant enough, and used with caution, and in a good light springy dough, rather than in an ordinary cake batter, it must be conceded that caraways have their charm.

Dill, aniseeds and cumin are more Scandinavian, central European and, in the case of cumin, North African and Levantine addictions, than English ones, although aniseed comfits were once popular. Fennel seeds are, or were, much liked in northern and north-eastern France, and also in Italy. The Athenians were fond of a bread they called Alexandrian, presumably made from Egyptian wheat flour, and flavoured with fennel or cumin seeds. I have included various recipes using one or other of these spices in this book because to me they are more beguiling than the tough little caraways. It is all a matter of taste. 'In Germany,' writes

Eliza Acton in her *English Bread Book* (1857), 'aniseed is commonly mixed with bread. Indeed it is sometimes quite difficult to procure any that is free from it; and it is very distasteful to some eaters when flavoured with it.'

Poppy seeds and sesame seeds are used more for strewing over the crust of loaves just prior to baking than for flavouring the bread itself. The former are characteristic of the white, plaited Jewish loaves called chollahs, and of many varieties of mid-European rolls and breads, the latter of Middle Eastern, Greek and North African breads. Some English wholewheat loaves sold in health-food stores are also decorated with sesame seeds, perhaps because any form of sesame is thought to be so health giving. Neither poppy nor sesame seeds are called for in any of the recipes in this book, and anyone who likes to use them will, obviously, find it a simple matter to substitute them for the fennel, aniseeds or dill used in or on some of the breads given.

Ginger is a spice only occasionally specified in the traditional recipes for home-made English yeast cakes and breads, although this is an unexpected omission. Ginger is one of the oldest of English favourites among spices, appearing from very early days, and in lavish quantity, in sauces, meat, fish and game dishes and later, as we know, in cakes and biscuits, and in fizzy drinks. Ginger was supposed also to have medicinal virtues,[1] and in addition is or was regarded as a yeast stimulant. This property of ginger – whether actual or supposed – was familiar to early American cooks and housewives, and in a volume of interesting American recipes called *Manna: Foods of the Frontier*, published by 101 Productions, San Francisco, in 1972, Gertrude Harris advises a pinch of ginger added to dried yeast to speed its return to active life. If it has been found to work, why not try it?

The use of 'stem' ginger in syrup as an alternative to candied peel for adding to fruit and spice doughs is mentioned on p. 135. It is advisable to keep a small supply of dried ginger in root form (once known as 'race' ginger, according to the *Oxford English Dictionary* from *rais* or *raiz*, the Spanish word for ginger, deriving from *radix*, *radicem*, a root, although strictly ginger is not a root but a rhizome) for grating, as well as ground ginger, which quickly loses its potent aroma, making it difficult to judge of the amount needed for flavouring any given recipe.

1. Eliza Acton gave a recipe (*Modern Cookery*, 1845) for a ginger loaf or rolls made with 2 oz of ground ginger to 2 lb of flour, made up with ½ oz of yeast and 1 pint of milk and water mixed. She claimed that this bread was of excellent effect in cases of diarrhoea and related 'disturbances of the stomach', especially in travelling.

Among the most costly of spices used in early English cooking, and one which has survived – that is in our true native cooking – almost solely in yeast cakes and buns, is saffron. Originally treated as a colouring rather than a flavouring agent, it was used lavishly in sauces and for almost any category of dish, whether fruit, flesh, fowl or fish, sweet cream or savoury stew, whenever it was felt that a fine yellow colour would be appropriate.

As is well known, there was once a flourishing English saffron industry. 'Common or best knowne Saffron groweth plentifully in Cambridge-shire, Saffron-Walden, and other places thereabout, as corne in the fields', wrote John Gerard in his *Herbal* published in 1597. Some sixty years later in October 1654 John Evelyn, on a visit to Audley End, the great house built by the Earl of Suffolk, noted in his diary that the saffron of Saffron Walden was at that time 'esteemed the best of any foreign country'.[1]

Gradually, as the cultivation of English saffron declined, during the first half of the nineteenth century, the use of saffron all but died out, surviving in the West Country in saffron buns and the famous saffron cake, which is really another yeast-leavened and fruit-enriched bread. When, during and after the 1939–45 War, saffron was replaced in those regional specialities by a harmless yellow dye called anatto, it was soon appreciated by those familiar with the originals that saffron was a very great deal more than just a colouring agent.

For a true saffron cake so little saffron goes so far that surely the expense could not now be grudged. It should be noted, though, that saffron is usually weighed by the *grain* (237 to the ounce; a grain was based on the weight of a grain of wheat) and that the best way to buy it is in whole filaments. These are the dry stigmas of *Crocus sativus*, the beautiful mauve autumn-flowering crocus. To use them, put the required quantity on a fireproof plate in a warm oven for a few minutes, until they have started to dry out, and can be crumbled between the fingers. For cakes, pour a little warm milk or water over them and leave them to infuse until the liquid is a fine deep yellow. The little strands *can* be strained out, but for saffron cake are usually left in, probably as a visible sign that true saffron has been used.

Saffron appears occasionally in eighteenth-century recipes for wiggs and also in Sally Lunn cakes. There are those who dislike saffron and its

1. *The Diary of John Evelyn*, edited by William Bray, Everyman edn, 1907, Volume I. The first record of Walden's prefix seems to be 1582.

pungent aroma as others dislike caraway or aniseeds, or for that matter cloves or ginger. The sixteenth-century writer Andrew Boorde, author of the famous *Dyetary of Helth* (1542), mentions the bread rolls at that time made for the tables of Roman patricians: 'Many little loaves joined together, the which doth serve for great men, and it is saffroned: I praise it not.'

I find saffron delicious, and fancy that I would have liked those Renaissance saffron rolls all joined together. They must have been a pretty sight.

There is by the way no historical evidence whatever to support the widespread legend that saffron was introduced to Cornwall by Phoenician traders in search of tin. According to historians there is indeed no evidence whatever that any Phoenician ever landed on British shores.

Until the nineteenth century the majority of large households would have bought their spices in whole form, while the less well-off probably obtained them ready-ground in small packets from pedlars and other itinerant salesmen or at markets and fairs. It was widely known that ready-powdered spices were open to abuse by the spice-grinders and wholesalers. Inferior quality spices could be easily passed off in powdered form, they could be adulterated, and they quickly lost their scents and potency. So the cinnamon bark, the whole cloves, the peppercorns, the allspice berries, the mace, all had to be pounded in a mortar or ground in a primitive hand mill made on the lines of early coffee mills, and very often sieved. Again, as with sugar-pounding, this was tough and arduous work, spices often being required for the preservation of meats as well as for cakes and everyday cooking. Nutmegs were used in quantity, and not necessarily grated. There were frequent directions to use 'a nutmeg slic'd', which seems to have meant that it was scraped with a knife, and used in little pieces. The elegant little silver nutmeg graters of the eighteenth and early nineteenth centuries were not for kitchen use. They were kept for the master or the lady of the house to grate nutmeg into their hot punch, their comforting ale possets and wine caudles, and to carry with them on journeys. Since we have the evidence of Nollekens the sculptor filching the nutmegs from the table at Academy dinners possibly the guests provided their own pocket nutmeg graters.

Spices were stored in a variety of cabinets, drawers and more or less elaborately decorated and valuable boxes, to be handed out to the cook by the housekeeper or the lady of the house.

By the nineteenth century, kitchens had their own spice boxes, either of japanned tin, divided into sections for the different spices, and with a compartment for a small nutmeg grater, or of hand-turned wood, arranged in tiers, each fitting neatly into the next, and with its appropriate label painted on. These boxes could have as many as six different tiers, for ginger, cloves, mace, allspice, cinnamon, nutmeg. Occasionally there would be a small, flat grater for the nutmegs, attached to the inside of the lid, a neat and practical device.

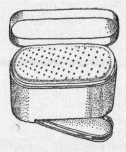

Pocket nutmeg grater, 2 inches by 1 inch. The nutmeg is kept in the bottom half of the box.

For sprinkling cinnamon on hot toasted and buttered muffins and crumpets there were china or silver casters, called muffineers. Again, like sugar casters, these were for the drawing-room and the dining-room rather than for the kitchen.

Sometimes spices were used to make flavoured or scented sugars, just as we make vanilla sugar today by storing a cut vanilla bean in a jar of caster sugar. Sir Hugh Plat, writing in 1609, gave a formula for musk-scented sugar, and another for clove or cinnamon sugar. Musk was a rare and highly prized perfume derived from a secretion in an abdominal gland or 'musk pouch' of a species of mountain deer, *Moschus moschiferus*, found in central Asia, from the Himalayas to Pekin. The substance from each gland, when coagulated and dried, weighed no more than 2 oz, often as little as ¼ oz. Other species of deer yielded an inferior musk, and in the later years of the nineteenth century a relatively cheap substitute was found in the secretions of the so-called musk rats, at that time killed in millions for their skins, which were made into furs. Musk was, we know, tremendously potent (it is still used in perfumery), and even in those days of strongly scented and spiced foods, only the smallest quantities – a grain or two – are called for, however large the cake. 'Muske sugar', Sir Hugh tells us, 'was sold for two shillings the pound.' His formula for spiced sugar is quoted on p. 432.

Nowadays, although it is unlikely that bought powdered spices will be adulterated, they may still easily be of inferior quality (the substitution of cassia[1] for cinnamon is a common dodge), and since they are commonly packed and retailed in quantities too large for any household which doesn't live entirely on heavily spiced foods, and since over the months – years even – that they are stored in kitchen cupboards they lose their aromas, it is almost impossible to specify exact quantities for any recipe.

For those who like to grind their own spice, now so easy and quick with the aid of a small electric coffee grinder kept especially for the purpose, a formula is given on p. 430.

LEMONS

Although not used a great deal in the recipes in this book the peel or zest of fresh lemons is one of the best of flavourings for light yeast cakes. In one old recipe, called Mrs Tashis' Little Puddings, given on p. 489, it was, and is, used to very good effect. Lemon-flavoured brioches and Sally Lunns are equally delicious.

When using lemons for the sake of their grated rind, it is best whenever possible to buy the rough-skinned variety. Smooth-skinned lemons are very difficult to grate. In the past, a piece of rough sugar, cut from the sugar loaf, was used as a grater, and the sugar wonderfully scented with the oil from the lemon peel was used for sweetening the cake. It was an effective method, and persisted long into the days of sugar cubes. These have now become so small that it would be virtually impossible to use them for this purpose. They dissolve before the lemon can yield up any of its essence. A piece of broken glass, advocated by several eighteenth-century writers for the grating of lemon peel, would be a hazardous alternative, and one I wouldn't care to attempt, while the little instrument known as a lemon zester is effective only with very coarse-skinned lemons. There remains the old basic grater. A stainless steel one is the best since it will not blacken the zest as it is grated. The coarse grating

---

1. Cassia comes from a tree similar to the true cinnamon; often known as Chinese cinnamon, the scent is similar but coarse in comparison. Cassia buds as well as bark were used. Cassia is always cheaper than cinnamon.

surface is more effective than the fine one, so long as it is very lightly applied, and it is easy to clean.

Nowadays, it is advisable to rinse lemons for grating in warm water, then rub them dry, before using them. So many are sprayed, or coated with a film of preservative before shipment.

FLAVOURING ESSENCES

Scented waters distilled from roses, orange blossoms, and sometimes carnations, were used as agents to prevent the oiling of almonds when being pounded or ground, and to moisten sugar for cake icing, as much as for their perfume, which could hardly have stood up to the fruit and the stronger spices which went into many of the cakes for which the recipes are given in this book.

Rose water for the kitchen is to be bought in Cypriot, Greek and Indian groceries, and sometimes from chemists. Orange-flower water – the finest is distilled from the blossom of the *bigarade* or bitter orange tree – is used much more in French and Spanish cooking than in our own. It is not called for in any recipes in this book.

Concentrated essences and extracts of herbs and spices such as oil of cloves, of mace or nutmeg, of rosemary, lavender and sage, together with a great variety of such things as cinnamon water, spirits of honey, syrup of violets, marigold and cowslip vinegars, were kept in the medicine closets or still-rooms of big houses, not only for medicinal use but for cosmetics, soap and the flavouring of wines and cordials. Some of these essences would surely have been interchangeable with kitchen ingredients. For all that Sir Kenelm Digby, Mrs Glasse, Mrs Raffald, Mrs Rundell and many another of the recipe writers quoted in this book directed their readers to pound and sieve, to beat and grate and strain, I wonder if their instructions were always obeyed to the letter. A little oil of nutmeg, a few drops of tincture of cinnamon . . . what a deal of work they would save, and would they not give as good a flavour or aroma to a cake or spiced loaf as the powdered spices? At any rate that is surely how the use of spice essences, already common in late-Victorian commercial baking, originated. Then, again, that question of colour, or showmanship as Banfield put it. Essences didn't darken the dough for spiced loaves and buns as did the powdered spices, and of course they were less trouble and cheaper in the end. In his *Saleable Shop Goods* (6th edn, 1898), Frederick Vine, a regular contributor to the *Baker's*

Journal, advised the trade that spiced goods with a light coloured crumb would bring in a greater return and show better profits than when powdered spices were used. Not all his colleagues agreed. The contributor on bread and bun making to *Law's Grocer's Manual* at the same period, giving formulas for mixed spice for hot cross buns, allows that these may be taken as the basis for essences, but adds that 'the powders are preferable as giving that amount of brown colouring necessary for hot cross buns'.

Malt Extracts

These come in a dry and in a viscous form. John Kirkland declares that 'the use of malt extracts is largely due to the attempt to provide the subtle flavour supposed to have been lost through the exclusion of germ and bran cereal from modern roller-milled flours'.[1]

I think that one may be excused for considering that this worthy attempt has not been very successful. Subtle is not the word which springs to mind as descriptive of the flavour of malted bread. Curiously, for many people, a taste for the overwhelming flavour of malt amounts almost to an addiction – or is it simply that too much flavour in bought bread is often the only alternative to none at all? – while for those like myself, tormented in childhood by the enforced administration of those viscous malt extracts which were supposed to ward off colds, flu and any number of ills, a prejudice against malted bread is equally strong.

This said, it must be admitted that, used in small doses, malt in some form does have a marked effect on the moist feel, the volume and the crust of a loaf as well as on its keeping qualities, and, although the experts say that malt is not a particularly good yeast food, a dough made with a proportion of malted meal 'grows' very satisfactorily, and the resulting loaf always has an appetizing appearance.

A number of friends have told me that when they buy bread they go for the type called 'granary' because it looks 'more like the real thing'. One up to the manufacturers, or perhaps they should more properly be called meal blenders. Granary bread is made from a malted meal, and the 'real' look is achieved mainly by the addition of a scattering of whole cracked wheat grains in the meal mix.

Malt extracts made specifically as 'improvers' for bread are sold in health-food stores. So are malted meals. Directions for using them will

1. *The Modern Baker, Confectioner and Caterer*, 1907.

be on the packet or tin. Basically, 1 tablespoon of dehydrated malt extract per 2lb of flour is dissolved in $\frac{1}{4}$ pint of boiling water, which is then made up with tepid water to the necessary amount for mixing the dough. Those who prefer to use the viscous type of malt extract – to be bought from multiple chemists such as Boots – maintain that the best way to use it is to rub it into the flour, exactly as for rubbing in lard or butter.

A formula for baker's malted bread popular in the eighties of the last century was obtained, he says with some difficulty, by W. Mattieu Williams, author of *The Chemistry of Cookery*, published in 1885. This formula, at that time bang up to date, for it had been revised only the previous year, specified 6lb each of wheatmeal and wheat flour, 6oz of malt flour, 2oz of German yeast, 2oz of salt and 'water sufficient'. 'Make into dough, without first melting the malt, prove well, and bake in tins.'

Mr George Ort, of the National Association of Master Bakers, who has a prosperous family bakery business at Leighton Buzzard in Bedfordshire, told me that he considers malt the most useful of all bread 'improvers'. He advises that it be used in its dehydrated form and claims that, when added to dough in the correct, very small proportion, its taste is undetectable in the finished bread. I do certainly agree with Mr Ort that malt enhances the bloom on the crust of a loaf. I have also found that the cuts on a slightly malted dough open out exceptionally well.

Bread Ovens

The earliest method of baking bread was to place lumps of dough, unleavened, on hot stones in the embers of a wood fire, and leave them to cook until they were hard. In other words it was the bakestone system, and after countless thousands of years it still survives, although in the slightly more evolved form of the iron or other metal griddle heated over peat, coal, gas or electricity.

Baking on stones was followed, according to Dr Alfred Gottschalk,[1] as early as the Bronze Age in Europe by the method of inverting a pot over the bread and surrounding this pot oven with hot embers. By this means the bread was protected from the ashes, and the covering pot drew the dough upwards, so that, even before the discovery of leavening, it would rise slightly, and lighter bread resulted. The inverted-pot system was certainly still quite commonly used in Britain less than a century ago. Lady Llanover[2] gives a precise description of this type of pot bread as baked in her day in South Wales, and Frederick Vine,[3] a professional baker, gives an account of the same form of baking, witnessed by him in Devonshire, carried out by a family who used the chaff saved from the winnowing of their own grain as fuel to heat the covering cauldron.

In Cornwall, two traditional variants on the 'baking under' system still survived in the later years of the nineteenth century. Some households used a 'kettle', actually a three-legged round iron crock or bowl, others favoured a 'baker', the name given to a plain round pot rather like an outsize frying pan. Whichever type of covering pot was used, the prepared dough was laid on a stout round iron griddle, ready heated on a

---

1. *Histoire de l'alimentation et de la gastronomie depuis la préhistoire jusqu'à nos jours*, 1948.

2. *Good Cookery*, 1867. The passage is quoted on p. 307.

3. *Practical Breadmaking*, 1897. See p. 306.

trivet thrust into the centre of the open hearth with the burning peat or turf underneath.

Cornish kettle bread, usually made from barley meal – wheat bread was only for special occasions – was originally a kind of sourdough made on the basis of a leaven kept from the previous week's baking, but in later days was more like the Irish 'cake' bread aerated with soda and buttermilk. Baking this bread for a feast day can have been no easy task. According to one historian, it was not unusual to see a single buttermilk cake, destined for the annual parish feast, as large as a coster's cart-wheel, baked beneath one huge 'baker', and carried by two women to the scene of the festivities.[1]

Another baking utensil similar in effect to the inverted iron pot was the dome-shaped clay cooking bell evolved by the earliest potters of Greece (Plate 15). This again, or something very like it in metal, has survived until today, and very useful it is.

Ovens proper seem to have come into being as a means of combining the hearth or baking stone and the covering pot in one single fixed construction, some of the earliest ovens having an opening at the apex through which the bread could be introduced. The opening was sealed with stones or pieces of clay, and live embers piled up all round and over the oven. The crude beehive-shaped or tunnel-like clay ovens with a front opening which developed later provided a more satisfactory way of feeding the bread into the oven. As in the more evolved brick-built ovens of the Roman world (a good example is the one to be seen in the ruins of Pompeii, Plate 6, and illustration on p. 27), the early clay ovens were fired from the inside and the ashes swept out before the loaves were put in to bake. The opening was stopped up with stones, or perhaps with a rough door luted round with wet potters' clay so that the maximum heat was sealed in. In his *Modern Baker and Confectioner* (1907), vol. 1, p. 23, John Kirkland records that stopping all round the oven door with clay was still in his day the usual practice in all bakehouses with ovens of the old 'pot' type – i.e. the brick-built oven with tile floor, as distinct from the archaic little clay oven, which probably originated sometime between 3000 and 1800 B.C. Like the Athenian cooking bell and the primitive quern, the rough clay oven had its counterparts for several thousand years, among its descendants being our own seventeenth-century Devon gravel-tempered clay wall ovens

1. A. K. Hamilton Jenkin, *Cornish Homes and Customs*, 1934. See also the account quoted from *Cornish Recipes* on p. 308.

(Plates 18 and 20), of which two rather battered specimens are preserved in the Bideford Public Library and Museum, others at the Welsh Folk Museum at St Fagans, near Cardiff. These crude ovens differ hardly at all in form from those of the Neolithic Age. Produced in the potteries which flourished in and around Barnstaple from the sixteenth to the early part of the twentieth century, they were the common bread ovens of West Country cottages, and considerable numbers were also exported farther afield, to Wales, Ireland and, during the seventeenth and eighteenth centuries, to America.[1] According to Llewellyn Jewitt, author of *The Ceramic Art of Great Britain* (1883), the Bideford and Barnstaple clay ovens were, and for generations had been, 'in much repute in Devonshire and Cornwall, and in the Welsh Districts and the bread baked in them is said to have a sweeter and more wholesome flavour than when baked in ordinary ovens'. Built into the side wall of the open hearth so that from the front only the opening was visible, these primitive-looking ovens were still being produced in Barnstaple potteries as late as 1890.[2] Another West Country district known for its clay or 'cloume' ovens was Calstock in south-east Cornwall. It was probably one of these – and a rather larger one than the Bideford examples – which is described by the Cornish countrywoman in the passage quoted on p. 178. Heavy and crude, with their bulging heads, small openings and roughly fashioned loose doors, the old West Country ovens have an ancient and moving beauty of their own. They were made by potters familiar with their purpose, they were used by generations of cottage families to whom the weekly bread bake was a necessity of life as well as part of its normal rhythm.

The manufacture of the Devon ovens was confined, as we have seen, to the West Country, and their use limited to small-scale baking, the most common form of English household bread oven being the type built with a domed, beehive roof, and so constructed that they formed a deep recess in the kitchen or bakehouse wall, the opening being sideways on and adjacent to the open hearth. While the oven was being fired the door was usually, although not invariably, left open so that the smoke escaped through the front aperture into the main chimney. Many such ovens must remain abandoned and walled up in farmhouses and

1. C. Malcolm Watkins, Paper 13 (pp. 17–59), from *North Devon Pottery and Its Export to America in the 17th Century*, United States National Museum Bulletin 225, Smithsonian Institution, Washington, D.C., 1960.
2. They are more fully described later in this chapter, see pp. 177–9.

manors, country inns, vicarages and rectories not modernized out of all recognition. Sometimes a new owner, tearing out the superimposed plaster walls and partitions, the iron ranges of the Edwardian era or the imitation log fires of the 1930s, will discover the original open hearth and the brick-built oven intact in the side wall. They are of extraordinarily skilled construction, these ovens, the bricks precisely placed to form the arched crown, the floor or sole sometimes of small glazed bricks, sometimes of large flagstones. There are no side flues, no temperamental complications. Once cleared out, one of these old brick ovens will be ready for firing and for baking just as it was for centuries, before the commercial bakery took over the job of supplying our daily bread.

In districts where there was plenty of scrubwood, furze, blackthorn from the hedgerows, gorse from the downs, heating the oven cost very little. You had to collect the wood and bundle it into faggots, or pay a labourer to do the job, and there had to be a dry storage place for it, but it was fuel which was not of much use for any other purpose, so in terms of money baking was cheap. It took time, though, and considerable physical strength and effort to mix and ferment and knead and shape half a bushel, or 28 lb, of flour into loaves ready for the weekly bake; few farmers' wives or anyone with a household of any size would bother to fire the bread oven to bake less than that amount at a time, and many a farmer's wife, responsible for feeding the farm workers as well as her family, needed to bake at least a bushel at one firing. After the bread was drawn, cakes and puddings and pies went into the oven, which retained the heat for several hours.

It was the installation of iron kitchen ranges, in place of the open hearth fire, the spit in front of it and the separate bread oven in the wall at the side or in the bakehouse, which radically altered English cookery techniques. Spit-roasting and bread-baking were the two basic traditions doomed by the accelerating changes of the late eighteenth and early nineteenth centuries. Where bread-baking was concerned, the ancient methods did of course persist in less industrialized areas as long as the lack of public bakeries made them a necessity; and until well into the second half of the nineteenth century there were hundreds of villages and even sizeable towns where such facilities were few and far between. As late as 1831, for example, the town of Sheffield, with a population exceeding 91,000, had only fifty-three bakers. At the same period, in newly built farm cottages, just as in smaller town dwellings, cooking facilities were often limited to the combined kitchen–living-room stoves or 'kitcheners', consisting of a hob, a little barred grate and an oven so small that it is difficult to see of what practical use it can have been to a family with growing children to be fed. These ovens were, it is true, fairly deep, so that the small openings are deceptive, but even making allowances for this point, bread-baking would not have been a very practical proposition in cottage kitcheners. In those days of large families and severely restricted diet, bread was the staple food. Coal, unlike the wood for the old ovens, was expensive. It was scarcely worth while stoking up the oven to the necessary heat just to bake a day or two's supply of bread at a time.

So to whom, it has to be asked, was William Cobbett addressing himself when he berated agricultural workers for squandering their wages on bought bread, or, in Cobbett's view the ultimate sin, for feeding their children on boiled potatoes? Today his theatrical cries of outrage make embarrassing reading: 'How wasteful, then, and indeed how shameful for a labourer's wife to go to the baker's shop, and how negligent, how criminally careless of the welfare of his family must the labourer be, who permits so scandalous a use of the proceeds of his labour . . . Servant women in abundance appear to think that loaves are made by the baker as knights are made by kings.'[1] How did Cobbett propose to enlighten those labourers and servant women? Intoxicated with his own rhetoric, he appears to have lost sight of them altogether. Disregarding the cramped conditions in which most cottagers lived, ignoring their pitifully limited cooking facilities – not to say their illiteracy, which would in any case have prevented them from appreciating his efforts – he failed to mention that even communal ovens were few and far between, that the inconveniences attached to conveying the dough to the nearest bakery were often so great as to make the proposition quite impracticable and that even to buy their bread meant a weekly trip to the nearest market. No wonder the hastily boiled potatoes which were such anathema to Cobbett provided the easiest and cheapest means of staving off hunger. Effectively, the cottage part of Cobbett's economy was figurative only. What he had to say applied mainly to prosperous farmers and smallholders of some substance, whose establishments automatically included a bakehouse and a brewhouse. Even then, his instructions as to the mixing of the dough and the firing of the oven, although vivid and often quoted, are far from realistic. Fifteen to twenty minutes' fermentation for 56 lb of flour mixed to dough on

1. *Cottage Economy*, 1821–3.

the basis of a previously prepared sponge is a good deal short of adequate. Equally so is fifteen minutes for the firing of an oven large enough to hold fourteen 4lb loaves and in which the heat had to be maintained for two hours. These instructions would surely have produced the kind of bread described by Eliza Acton as 'heavy or bitter or ill-baked masses of dough which appear at table under the name of household or home-made bread . . . and inspire a prejudice against it which, in some instances, can never be surmounted'.[1] Miss Acton hits yet another nail squarely on the head. Don't let us run away with the romantic notion that because bread was baked at home it was always necessarily good. And, heavens, how stale and dry it must often have been.

Under such circumstances it is no surprise that unless Mother was a good manager and a competent baker her family would grow to dislike home-made bread and turn to the fresher, lighter, whiter products sold by the professional bakers. As Frederick Vine wrote in the last years of the nineteenth century, 'the cry goes up for white, silky, palatable bread, in the place of that dark heavy, tasteless variety, like mother makes . . . when she cannot help it'.[2] As for those anxious to achieve the proper skills of bread-baking there seem to have been precious few people to teach them. What were the cookery writers doing about the problem? In the second half of the nineteenth century two eminent professional chefs, authors of many works on classy cookery, were among the well-meaning writers who turned their attention to the needs of the poorer classes.

Alexis Soyer, the great innovator, the reformer of army cookery during the Crimean campaign, a highly inventive and resourceful man, lost his touch when it came to addressing a humble audience in print. His *Shilling Cookery for the People*, published in 1855, is patronizing and long-winded. Solemnly he informs the aspiring bread baker that 'the oven should be well heated and sufficiently large to bake the quantity of dough you make at one time'. Charles Elmé Francatelli, despite his name an English-born chef, who had worked briefly for Queen Victoria, followed Soyer with *A Plain Cookery Book for the Working Classes*, published *c*. 1862. Where bread was concerned he was even less realistic than Cobbett and Soyer. Can he have supposed that it was enlightening to anybody to be told to 'heat your oven to a satisfactory degree of heat with a sufficient quantity of dry small wood faggots'? Francatelli's little

1. *Modern Cookery*, 1845.   2. *Practical Breadmaking*, 1897.

manual was priced at 6d, Soyer's twice as much. Poor value, both of them, to anyone in search of instruction. If neither of the gentlemen concerned knew how to fire a brick oven, nor how many loaves could be loaded into an oven of any given capacity, it seems surprising that they did not seek information from a professional baker: even more surprising that neither thought of giving directions for baking bread on a small scale and making the best use of the limited facilities available to working-class families living in two-room cottages and overcrowded lodging houses.[1] Both of them could have learned from Mrs Esther Copley, whose practical and business-like *The Complete Cottage Cookery*, published in 1849, price one shilling, gave clear and simple instructions for making bread, managing a brick oven, and also for baking bread in the iron side oven (Plate ??) By this, Mrs Copley meant the oven built into the brickwork surround of the 'kitchener' grate or range then much in use in farmhouses and cottages – Mrs Copley calls it a York-shire grate – or installed as an integral part of the range itself. More considerate than Cobbett who in his customary rumbustious tones declared that if 'a young woman bake a bushel once a week, she will do very well without phials and gallipots', Mrs Copley suggested that a half-peck (7 lb) or at the most a peck was quite enough for the inexperienced to deal with at one time. Some of Mrs Copley's directions are quoted further on in this chapter.

Realistically, Eliza Acton in her *English Bread Book* of 1857, asserts that '*not only are there no ovens in vast numbers of our cottages, but many a small village is entirely without one*', although she still thought it valid, as indeed it was, to give directions for firing brick ovens, both large and small, claiming that for the baking of half a bushel of bread (eight or nine large loaves) in a cottage brick oven the cost of fuel should not be more than 4d, 'at least in counties where wood is to be obtained at a reasonable price'. Most writers of the time told their readers, none too helpfully, that the solution to the problem of an unsatisfactory oven, or indeed no oven at all, was to make their dough and take it to the baker

1. Soyer does write at some length of an invention to be known as Soyer's Aerial Cooking Stove. Among its many attributes this would 'make cottage bread lighter, and contain more nutriment than when baked in a large oven in which considerable evaporation takes place'. Beyond singing its praises in his most flowery style and promising that the apparatus 'will be dedicated to all classes but more particularly to the masses', he gives no hint as to the construction of his aerial pygmy, as he called this little marvel. It sounds an ingenious device. Sadly, it seems never to have become airborne.

or the communal oven to be baked. Not Eliza Acton. Having made the experiment a number of times she seems to have reached the conclusion that the advantages of the baker's brick oven were outweighed by the inconveniences and uncertainties attendant upon getting the dough to the bakery and consigning it to the care of the baker. Like anyone who has mixed and kneaded and tended their dough, she preferred to see it through to the end.

Surprisingly, the young Mrs Beeton, whose *Book of Household Management* (1861) was aimed at all classes of household, had nothing to say about the benefits or otherwise of home bread-baking, most of her recipes and precepts being taken, on her own acknowledgement, from Miss Acton. Of ovens, Mrs Beeton, like Miss Acton, observed that 'brick ovens are generally considered the best adapted for baking bread . . . iron ovens are more difficult to manage, being apt to burn the

Section of an Eagle coal-fired range. The heat in the pastry and bread oven could be diverted from bottom to top by pushing in or pulling out the knob of a reversing damper. Although the diversity of pies, puddings and loaves baking simultaneously is a manufacturer's fantasy, the Eagle pastry oven was a genuine improvement on its predecessors and was much imitated. The Eagle manufacturers also claimed that the coal consumption of their range was only three hundredweight per week compared to the seven hundredweight of their imitators. From Charles Herman Senn's *New Twentieth Century Cookery Book*, 5th edn, 1913.

surface of the bread. To remedy this a few clean bricks should be set at the bottom of the oven, close together, to receive the tins of bread.'

The regret for the vanishing brick ovens, the dislike of the temperamental iron ranges, the optimistic belief that a few bricks or tiles placed beneath the bread tins (a tiled oven roof would have made more sense) would prove efficacious in producing the same kind of bread as had emerged from the old wood-fired ovens, all persisted. It seems curious that so many people accepted the coal-devouring, smoke-belching, attention-demanding ranges with such apparent docility. In the country, although not in large towns, there was still plenty of wood to burn, it was still cheaper than coal, it was certainly cleaner. But coal-burning ranges represented Progress and Progress was on the march.

By 1906, when Herman Senn, a professional chef of Swiss origin, and great experience, edited and almost entirely re-wrote the largest-ever edition of Mrs Beeton's book (she herself had died five years after its original publication, at the age of twenty-nine), gas and electricity were fast replacing coal ranges in town dwellings. And for the better, Senn thought. His instructions for baking bread are detailed. He explained the need for an airtight oven and emphasized the importance of the retention of steam vapour from the point of view of achieving bread with a good crust. Senn too harked back to the tiled oven floor . . .[1]

That the difficulties of bread-baking in the iron oven of the old closed ranges were perhaps exaggerated – or at any rate only relative – is shown by contemporary accounts, as for example that of Mrs M. Vivian Hughes describing, in *A London Family 1870–1900*, her discovery of the simplicity of the whole process. This illuminating passage will be found on p. 255. Mrs Hughes began her married life, to a hard-up young barrister, in a Bayswater flat seventy steps up from street level. For the first time she found herself faced with a huge iron range, and not an idea of how to cope with it: 'I had got up early, lit the fire, filled the kettle, arranged slices of bacon in the pan, only to be met by smoke billowing forth at me from my "fire". In despair I called out to Arthur for help. He just shoved a damper or two about, and that impish range, seeing a man on the job, gave up its tricks and blazed up brightly.' It was in the oven of this temperamental range, and without instruction, that Mrs Hughes baked her first bread. It was so much better than the London bakers' bread that neither she, nor her children

1. Extracts from Senn's descriptions and opinions of the newest ovens of his day are quoted on pp. 188 and 189.

as they grew up, ever again willingly ate bought bread. A familiar story.

Today's oil- and gas-fired iron ranges are clean and trouble-free compared to the old coal-burning monsters. Their ovens, deep and capacious, are well insulated, solid. Bread bakes pretty well in them, better than in the ovens of domestic gas and electric cookers, which are too small, and getting smaller. With few exceptions, manufacturers are designing cookers with more 'hob' or boiling and simmering facilities and less oven space. Can it be true that today's women need only to reheat frozen food and to boil soup and potatoes (how Cobbett would have disapproved) and ignore the advantages of leaving a slowly simmering stew, a cheap and rapidly assembled casserole of meat and vegetables in an automatically controlled oven while they attend to other matters, go out shopping, spend the day at work? It seems to me that, as with the imposition of closed iron ranges upon people who didn't particularly want them and certainly didn't understand them, what suits the manufacturer is attributed to the customer's demand. Smaller ovens mean a saving on materials. A couple of inches here and there, who is going to mind or notice? In fact the *depth* of the oven is of great importance in relation to the size and number of items, whether it be a question of casseroles, baking dishes, cake tins or loaves, which can be fitted in for one baking session. That extra inch or two may mean that you can bake six loaves at a time on one shelf instead of only three.

A little extra spent on a cooker constructed of solid materials also pays off. Oven doors should shut properly, the heat should be sealed in, expensive energy concentrated, not wasted.

One category of cooking stove, not yet mentioned, which played an important part in English kitchens, particularly in the country and in the colonies, was the oil- or paraffin-fired cooker. Cheap to buy and to run, costing next to nothing to install, these comparatively lightweight steel cookers, the Albionette, the Valor Perfection, the Rippingille, the Florence, were surprisingly efficient. They did require understanding and sympathetic management. If they didn't get it, they smoked, they smelt awful, your pans were blackened, your food tasted of paraffin. Like paraffin heaters, these cookers could also be dangerous. Well looked after they were useful. In the ovens, little more than galvanized steel boxes set over two burners, joints were cooked, bread was baked, soufflés rose in a spectacular manner. In the oven of one such oil cooker, the Florence, Virginia Woolf baked her cottage loaves and in turn taught her young cook, Louie Mayer, to make them. Mrs Mayer has told me that she started the bread in a cool oven, that the loaves rose well as the temperature of the oven increased, that she made two large loaves at a time, usually twice a week, and that when eventually the Florence was

Cost of this family oil stove was £4 4s without the special utensils to fit on the hot plates. The oven measured 14½ inches by 14 inches by 13½ inches. Baking meat, bread and pie simultaneously would have been economical but bad practice. Steam from the joint and the bread would make the pastry soggy. Probably the illustration was just to show how much you could cram into the oven. From Cassell's *Book of the Household*, Vol. 1, 1889.

replaced by an electric cooker she continued to bake her bread by the same method.

I have tried Mrs Mayer's method in my own gas oven. It works well, and produces much better cottage loaves than I was able to achieve before learning of the cool oven system from Mrs Mayer. It was, incidentally, the system recommended by the manufacturers of oil stoves, and no one who has made even the briefest study of the mixing and baking of dough will be surprised at the apparent contradiction of more usually accepted methods.[1] The subject is one which is a morass of inconsistencies and conflicting theories. What does emerge, though, is that much unnecessary fuss is made about the techniques of household bread-baking on a small scale, and that, as far as the oven is concerned, understanding of its tricks and idiosyncrasies is the crucial ingredient. Anyone determined enough can make *some* kind of good bread in almost any oven, providing it will eventually reach and maintain a heat of approximately 400°F, 205°C.

When it comes to precise descriptions of the traditional brick bread ovens, how they were constructed, fired, cleaned out, and sealed during baking, and of household baking routines generally, the excerpts which follow, most of them recorded at first hand, tell us vividly enough how our bread was baked from medieval times until well on into the nineteenth century. Later extracts bear witness to the general dissatisfaction with the performance of closed range ovens, at least in respect to the baking of bread. In Herman Senn's description of an early twentieth-century gas cooker it is clear that the domestic baking of bread was still a factor to be taken into serious consideration. Today that consideration is rarely manifested, although there are hopeful signs that the manufacturers of electric cookers are concerning themselves with the possibility of a demand – or with creating one – for domestic ovens well geared to the baking of bread, and are becoming (for good reason) less obsessively preoccupied with the weekly joint and the once-yearly 20 lb turkey which for so long have been the criteria by which ovens have been advertised, if not very seriously judged by the customer.

The fan ovens introduced in 1971 by the Belling cooker manufacturers achieve, it is claimed, 'such amazingly even heat distribution that you can put the food on any shelf you wish . . . and fill every one of the shelves right to the sides . . . the fan circulates hot air to every corner of the large oven' (Plate 24). A Sunday supplement double-page spread advertising this oven showed a colour photograph of twelve pan loaves baking simultaneously on three shelves. What struck me as amazing about the advertisement was not so much the adaptation of an efficient system of hot-air circulation to domestic ovens – there is nothing extra-ordinarily new in the principle – as the implication that the English housewife is once again sufficiently interested in the baking of bread to

1. It isn't so much of a mystery as it appears. From what Mrs Mayer told me, it is clear that her bread was baked from slightly under-proved dough; and loaves from under-proved dough rise best in an initially cool oven. But it must be an oven which is heating up steadily and fairly rapidly.

be enticed by an oven more convenient for the purpose than the one incorporated in the routine electric cooker. In these cookers it is necessary to change the position of the loaves during baking, and the same drawback applies to the majority of domestic gas cookers, although slightly less so to the gas-fired Aga range.[1] This, and the depth of the ovens, are among the advantages of this particular cooker. I should add that I am not rolling a log for the Aga, nor for the Belling, nor for any other specific cooker. I bake all my bread in the oven of a four-burner household gas stove. Admittedly for its size it is the heaviest on the market. It is, and has to be, a good all-round cooker. Although it would be agreeable to have a separate bread oven, it is not necessary nowadays to set bread baking apart from other forms of daily cooking. Many people who bake their own bread get it all over in a once-weekly session, as housewives did in the brick oven days, only now the loaves are stored in the freezer, and home-made bread need never be stale or dry.

BRICK OVENS IN USE

'When he [grandfather] was a boy the fear of Napoleon had not yet departed from the countryside. They expected him any hour. Grandfather would tell about precautions taken in the village, some being told off to break down the brick ovens. Had not the little Corporal said that an Army marched on its stomach?'

Allan Jobson, *An Hour-Glass on the Run*, 1959

'In the building of your oven for Baking, observe that you make it round, low roofed, and a little Mouth; then it will take less fire, and keep in the Heat better than a long oven and high roofed, and will bake the Bread better.'

Hannah Glasse, *The Art o Cookery Made Plain and Easy*, 1747

1. The Aga was the patented invention of Dr Gustav Dalen, blind Swedish physicist and Nobel prize-winner. Launched in Sweden in 1924, in England in 1929, the Aga was the first closed iron range designed on the heat storage system. Insulating covers over the hot plates retained the heat of the ovens. It was continuous-burning, clean, easy to control and to re-fuel. The original Aga ranges were fired with anthracite nuts. During the decade following the end of the Second World War the oil-fired Aga was developed. This is the one most widely used in country areas lacking a gas supply. In towns the gas-fired Aga, launched in the late 1960s, is growing in popularity. The largest Aga ranges have three ovens, one for roasting, one for baking, one for slow simmering. The manufacturers of the early Agas claimed that, using the roasting and baking ovens, twelve 2 lb loaves could be baked simultaneously. Their recipe is quoted on p. 301.

'The oven should be round, not long; the roof from twenty to twenty-four inches high, the mouth small, and the door of iron, to shut close.'

Maria Eliza Rundell, *A New System of Domestic Cookery*, 1806

The radiation of heat

In the first description, below, of how brick ovens were heated, W. Mattieu Williams makes entirely clear the effect of the heat radiating from the arched roof of the oven on to the surface of the bread. The final sentence of the passage quoted is a very exact description of the cottage loaf of my own childhood.

'The old-fashioned oven, such as was generally used in Rumford's[1] time, and is still used in country houses and by old-fashioned bakers, is an arched cavity of brick with a flat brick floor. This cavity is closed by a suitable door, which in its primitive, and perhaps its best form, was a flat tile pressed against the opening and luted round with clay. Such ovens were, and still are, heated by simply spreading on the brick floor a sufficient quantity of wood – preferably well-dried twigs; these, being lighted, raise the temperature of the arched roof to a glowing heat, and that of the floor in a somewhat lower degree. When this heating is completed (the judgement of which constitutes the chief element of skill in thus baking) the embers are carefully brushed out from the floor, the loaves etc., inserted by means of a flat battledore with a big handle, called a "peel", and the door closed and firmly luted round, not to be opened until the operation is complete.

'Baked clay is an excellent radiator, and therefore the surface of bricks forming the arched roof of the oven radiates vigorously upon its contents below, which are thus heated at top by radiation from the roof, and at bottom by direct contact with the floor of the oven. The difference between the compact bottom crust, and the darker bubble-bearing top crust of an ordinary loaf is thus explained.'

W. Mattieu Williams, *The Chemistry of Cookery*, 1885

1. Count Rumford (1753–1814) was an Anglo-American scientist, military administrator and inventor. Born Benjamin Thompson, he was ennobled by the Bavarian government for services to their war department, for his agricultural reforms and nutritional teachings. He also laid out the famous English Garden in Munich. In England he founded the Royal Institution, and was largely responsible for the development of nineteenth-century kitchen ranges. His efforts to perfect coal-burning grates were equally influential on the construction of fireplaces.

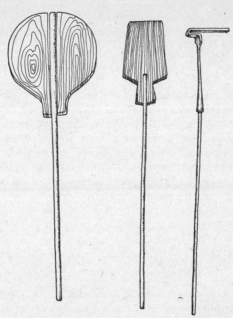

Wooden peels for feeding loaves into the oven and removing them when baked. On the right is a rake for clearing the ashes from the oven when it was sufficiently heated.

Judging the temperature

There were several methods of judging the heat of a brick oven, not all of them as subtle as the 'watch and tell-tale' pebble described on p. 171, but probably as effective. Striking sparks from the floor or the roof of the oven is a recurring hint, probably almost as old as the ovens themselves. The flour test was another well known method. Not everybody specifies new flour, as does the John Timbs manual.

'You put in your sticks and sets them alight, my dear, and then when they're all burnt up and the oven be all hot through, then you draws out all the fire from the oven, and then you takes a bit of stick and you strikes the floor of the oven with 'un and if sparks fly then you knows 'tis just right heat for baking your bread or cake.'

Kathleen Thomas, *A West Country Cookery Book*, 1961

'The oven is known to be properly heated to receive the bread, when a little of the newest flour, thrown in on its floor, blackens without taking fire: old flour will not suit the test.'

Lady Bountiful's Legacy, ed. John Timbs, 1868

A little more precision as to the initial temperature required for bread-baking in the brick oven was provided in the 1906 edition of Mrs Beeton's *Book of Household Management*, edited by Herman Senn. If it could be tested with a thermometer, wrote Senn, the heat of the oven would be found to vary from 400° to 500°F, 205° to 260°C, and by the time the bread was taken out it would have dropped to 200° to 250°F, 94° to 121°C, 'the heat having been practically used up in baking the bread, part of it passing off into the atmosphere'.

Home baking in the eastern counties:
Essex and Suffolk,
making the dough, the management of the oven
a device for judging its temperature

In the next passage there is more detail as to the techniques and the routine of baking in the brick oven. One important point was the copious swabbing out of the oven as soon as the heat was judged to be right and the embers had been cleared. The damp floor of the oven, combined with the natural vapour generated by the moisture in the dough itself, created the atmosphere of steam so important to the successful baking of bread. According to a *Domestic Dictionary* of 1842 (by Merle and Reitich) a method of giving the steam an extra boost, practised by German bakers, was to throw a little water on some lighted braise. This was placed in the oven, the vapour rising from it giving their fine white rolls 'a peculiar colour'.

'Bewhiskered, weather-stained and nearing sixty, grandfather Reuben Ford tethered his plough team to a five-barred gate to eat his dockey (elevenses). His sharp shutknife conveyed to his mouth a sliver of cheese topped with raw onion, and he pointed to the lower half of a cottage loaf made the day before by Granny Ford in the "bakus" behind our twin cottages, Brick and Stone Villa. "With half a quartern o' that, a mite o' cheese and an' owd onion I can larst the day," and he washed down a mouthful with a gulp of home-brewed ale.

'Bread was our staple diet. Every cottage house-wife was taught by her mother the art of mixing, firing, kneading and watching, to make loaves and bakestones in brick ovens. There was an immediate restoration of energy from a hunk or two, with or without butter, cheese or the hard butcher's dripping.

'For the fortnightly ritual of baking Granny Susannah Ford prepared her dough overnight, placing careful measures of white wheat flour in her kneading trough, the keeler. Secret measures of salt and water were added and a little mysterious "something" to the yeast, a family secret. When thoroughly mixed the wooden lid of the keeler was pressed down

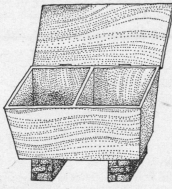

The lid of the dough trough was used for kneading and moulding. Trough was pronounced 'trow' to rhyme with dough.

and covered with warmed sacks to assist fermentation. By morning the rising dough would have forced off the lid. Pressing firmly but gently all over the sacking with the flat of her hands to expel the gases, Susannah would then get busy shaping and moulding on the upturned well-floured lid; a tidy lump for the base, a small one for the top, and the shape of the cottage loaf was formed.

'Meanwhile Reuben, after feeding Overhall Farm's horses, brought the oven to baking heat. The correct temperature was of paramount importance. Deep inside the clay-plastered oven was placed an ignited faggot of dead and well-dried blackthorn or whitethorn. Carefully directed jets of air from hand bellows drew the fire to an even white heat on which branches of whitethorn were continually thrust until they became white hot. The right time for putting the dough in the oven was determined by a glance at the "watch and tell-tale", a small pebble specially selected from the fields, which changed colour with variations of temperature. This was built into the oven. When it became fiery red embers were raked into the recess below the oven which was then cleaned with a mop made of sacking tied round a pole and saturated with water. One at a time each loaf was placed in the oven with a peel, a long spoon or circular board mounted on a wooden handle, and left to bake. Granny then scrubbed down the keeler (a much-prized gift from the wheelwright on her wedding day) and would stand sniffing the wonderful smell of baking bread; by this she knew when it was properly baked. Then sliding a steel-bladed peel under the loaves, she removed them one at a time to the deal table to cool. Her fortnightly baking was over, and we would get hot bread to sample, smelling of wheat and heat-softened cheese.

'But there were other rituals to be observed. Not a bit of the oven's heat could be wasted for faggots were cut by hand and carried from woods and hedgerows, or were sixpence a piece to buy. Therefore King Edward potatoes were placed in the heart of the glowing embers. Never since have baked potatoes tasted so good.'

Christopher Ketteridge and Spike Mays, *Five Miles from Bunkum*,[1] 1972

From the next passage, those on pp. 174–5, and indeed from many others quoted in this book, it is clear that in East Anglia the old brick ovens remained in use until well into the twentieth century, probably until the days of rationing during the 1939–45 War.

East Anglia has always been, and to some extent remains, a comparatively isolated and unindustrialized area of the country. Norfolk, Suffolk and Cambridgeshire are wheat-growing and sheep- and pig-rearing counties; almost every village had its mill, good flour was easy to come by (Norfolk and Cambridge flours were famous) and traditions of cooking and baking seem to have remained intact long after they had been destroyed in areas subjected to the industrial upheavals of the early nineteenth century. Possibly the baking lore of East Anglia owes something to the Flemish weavers and the wool merchants who first settled there in the thirteenth century and for 400 years exercised so much influence on the architecture and the crafts of the area. Flemish bakers were known in western Europe for their skill.

'Prissy's family of ten had two bakes a week, using altogether five

1. Bunkum is a local Essex name for Saffron Walden. The village described by the authors is Ashdon.

stones of flour. The flour was often mixed with the whey left after making butter or cream cheese at the farm. The yeast was saved from the last brewing of beer; it was called *barm* and was kept in a cool earthenware jar on the floor of the larder. It would keep up to six months without going sour. But before Prissy mixed the dough she had to make sure she had plenty of fuel to heat her oven. This had to be heated by burning the fuel inside it. Apart from the door there is no outlet in a brick oven: the chimney is at the front just outside the oven-door and when the fuel is burning the oven-door is left open and the smoke escapes through that. The fuel used was most commonly *whin* faggots – the *bones* of *sere* or dry gorse – bound with elm withes. The process of making them was described by Prissy: "You tied the whin faggots with green ellum withes. You put your foot on the bottom of a withe then you could rave the top of it like an S." Broom was sometimes used for fuel: so also was heather. The heather was first stacked and pressed into bundles: it was preferred by some folk because, they said, it gave more heat. The fuel was thrust into the oven with a long-handled fork kept specially for the purpose. This fork was also used to stir up the embers until they burned completely out, leaving no smoke at all. It took about an hour for a brick-oven to become properly heated for the dough. The bricks would change in colour from black to red as they got hotter; and when a handful of flour, thrown lightly against the side of the oven, burned up with a blaze of sparks, the housewife knew that her oven was hot enough for baking.

'But before the dough went in the oven the ash would be scraped out and stowed in a hole beneath the oven. This was done with an ordinary garden-hoe or with the *peel*, a long-handled spade-like tool used to slide in the tins of dough. While the oven was being heated the dough would have been rising in an earthenware pan covered with a cloth and placed near the oven. Just before the oven was ready the dough was placed into tins or kneaded into the shape of cottage loaves which were baked on the actual floor of the oven.

'The actual placing of the dough into the oven was called *a-settin' in*. It was a job that had to be done quickly and smoothly so that the oven-door was open for as little time as possible. When the housewife was *a-settin' in* everything else had to wait; even the doctor calling to examine one of the children would have to see the oven door closed before he could get her attention.

'The bread would be done in about an hour. Often, however, the housewife took advantage of the heated oven to bake other things, risking the fact that by opening the door the bread might go *dumpy* or flat. One housewife in this village cooked her weekly joint of meat in the same oven as the bread. The meat, which took about two hours to cook, was placed at the back of the oven; then came the bread; and in front of the bread, at the edge of the oven, she placed two or three tins of Suffolk rusks which were done in about ten minutes and could quickly be withdrawn.

'Small pieces of charcoal – the embers left from the fuel – often adhered to the loaves of bread that had not been baked in tins. These bits of charcoal gave an extra flavour to the bread according to the old people who are generally very critical of modern shop-bread. They say that no bread has the flavour of the home-baked bread. It was made from stoneground flour with all the goodness of the wheat grains left in it; and, therefore, it was much more sustaining than the present day bread. It needed to be, for a meal in these days would often consist – apart from a hunk of cheese – almost entirely of bread, and before the coming of breakfast cereals many country children started their day with a "mess of bread and hot skimmed milk".'

George Ewart Evans, *Ask the Fellows Who Cut the Hay*, 1956

The fuel: East Suffolk

'At the beginning of the present century Aaron Ling, Prissy's father, used to spend most of his time making whin faggots on the Heath. He charged one shilling for making twenty faggots and one shilling for carting them. But as entries from the accounts of the overseers of the poor show, the use of gorse or broom as fuel was a very old practice. It is even much older than these eighteenth-century documents indicate. The closed type of oven was known in biblical times, as is shown by a verse in *Matthew* (Chapter vi): ". . . the grass of the field which today is and tomorrow is cast into the oven" – a verse which could be puzzling were it not realized that grass in this context meant that it was used as a fuel. But closed ovens similar in principle to the ones existing here are still used in Egypt and parts of the Middle East.'

ibid.

'About a hundred faggots a year was the usual estimate of fuel needed for a cottage or a small farmhouse – two for each bake; and little allowance was made for any special bakes. Faggots for heating the brick-oven were an important part of the household economy, and had carefully to be budgeted for. On many farms, those workers with the extra skills and responsibilities – the head horseman, the shepherd and the stockman – were supplied with faggots as part of their perquisites.'

ibid.

The fuel and the firing:
advice from Esther Copley and Eliza Acton

'The fuel for heating an oven should be very dry, and such as will heat through quickly. The stalky part of furze, and the brush-wood of faggots answer the purpose best. If larger wood is used (such as beech spokes and billets) they should be split in pieces about the thickness of a spade-handle. Coals are altogether improper; so also are all knotty roots or greenwood. From one hour to an hour and a half is the time required for heating an oven; nothing but experience can give aptitude and exactness in determining the proper heat; when this is attained, every thing should be placed quite ready, that the business now to be proceeded with may be accomplished in the least possible time. Take out the fire, sweep the oven very clean, by means of a rag mop fastened to a long handle. Put in the loaves with a peel, that is, a flat shovel with a long handle; it must be dusted with flour, between each time of putting in a loaf. Yet the whole operation of taking out the fire, cleaning the oven, putting in the bread, and shutting the door, should not take up five minutes; as much less as possible. The heating of an oven costs from sixpence to a shilling, according to its size, and to the price of fuel; neighbours can generally accommodate each other, and thus a saving is effected to all parties. But, observe, the longer the time elapses between the heatings of an oven, the longer it takes to bring it to a sufficient heat.'

Esther Copley, *The Complete Cottage Cookery*, 1849

'I have known a very large brick oven, heated in the middle of the day with one full sized faggot or rather more, and a log or two of cord-wood[1] which was added when the faggot was partly consumed, still warm enough at eight or nine o'clock in the evening to bake various delicate small cakes, such as macaroons and meringues, and also custards, apples etc. . . .

1. Cord-wood was another name for cut wood, or logs, once measured by the cord.

'Elm, or beech or oak is the best of all fuel. When no cord-wood is at hand the necessary quantity of large faggot or other wood must be used instead.'

Eliza Acton, *The English Bread Book*, 1857

The iron door ...

'Remains of cottage ovens are still to be found, where the buildings have not yet been messed up to meet the requirements of an urban-minded County Council anxious only to keep the number of "reconditioned" cottages up to the theoretical standard laid down by Whitehall. These ovens are either built into the cottage or, in the case of communal ovens, erected in an outhouse nearby. The best thing about the old craftsmanship was that it was employed on services intimately connected with the needs of everyday life. Thus, in the case of these cottage ovens, where they opened into the wall of the wide, open fireplace, the door was often fashioned in a truly beautiful style: not at all ornate, but with a grace in all its lines and a comeliness in its proportions dictated first by necessity. Its most obvious attraction, perhaps, was the strong, slim latch with which it was securely fastened to let no heat escape – an instance of the local blacksmith's craft that was often comparable to those other latches on the old, leaded windows, delicate in line and yet well able to resist the pull of the strongest wind.'

C. Henry Warren, *Corn Country*, 1940

... and the wooden door

Surprisingly, perhaps, the door of the brick oven was sometimes made from a heavy block of wood instead of clay or iron. In the famous Pinto collection of wooden bygones, now housed in the Birmingham City Museum and Art Gallery, there is a magnificent oak oven door found at Chard in Somerset. Wonderfully incised on one side with the figure of a mermaid combing her hair, the door measures $15\frac{1}{4}$ inches across and $11\frac{1}{2}$ inches in height and probably dates from the seventeenth century. According to Mr Edward Pinto, the door doubled as an ornamental print, presumably for gingerbread. In his great work on *Treen and Other Wooden Bygones* (1969), Mr Pinto tells us that in country districts 'it was not unusual to use a piece of hardwood which dropped into a groove in the brick cill of the oven floor and was secured at the top by a turn-button'. He adds that the wooden panel was usually perforated with a few vent holes, and that although – as might be expected – it became charred on the back with use, it probably lasted indefinitely.

Mention of a wood oven door in use is made by Miss M. K. Ashby, writing of her childhood in the Warwickshire village of Tysoe, and describing the weekly Saturday bread baking in the brick oven:

'. . . the girls made and fed the fire, while mother kneaded the dough. When the loaves were in and the big oak block pushed against the oven's mouth, they fetched and carried for their mother while she shredded the white lard, marjoram-scented, into dough for lard cakes.'

M. K. Ashby, *Joseph Ashby of Tysoe, 1859–1919,*
Merlin Press, 1974 (first published Cambridge University Press, 1961)

Surviving Spanish clay ovens of the type shown in Plate 19 always have wooden doors lined with a sheet of metal to prevent charring from the heat.

The earthenware ovens of the West Country

In the first part of this chapter I have written of the primitive earthenware ovens made in the Devon potteries of Bideford, Barnstaple and Fremington, and at Calstock in Cornwall. These ovens had their counterparts in Europe and the Mediterranean countries but were unique in Britain. Awkward cargo though they must have made, they were much exported to the ports of South Wales, to Ireland and in early colonial times to America,[1] so it is of interest to learn how they were constructed, and why they worked so effectively and so economically. (If only some potter with a large enough kiln would revive them, how useful they would be.) The following extracts condensed from Llewellyn Jewitt's *Ceramic Art of Great Britain* (1883) seem to indicate that they were something of a curiosity even to him:

'Pot works appear to have existed at Bideford since the fourteenth century . . . the great speciality of the productions of Fremington, as of Bideford, are the fire-clay ovens, which are made in considerable numbers and of various sizes, for baking from one peck up to twelve. They are of peculiar shape and so constructed as to retain the heat for a considerable time. The bottom is flat, and the walls, which are of great strength and thickness, are arched so that the heat is thrown upon the

---

1. See footnote 1, p. 157.

bread in every direction. In front is a loose fire-clay door made to fit with exactness; or occasionally a cast-iron door is fixed. The ovens are heated with gorse, or wood, and one bundle of either is said to be sufficient to thoroughly bake three pecks of dough.

'These ovens are simply enclosed in raised brickwork leaving the mouth open to the front. They are ornamented in a primitive manner with impressed and incised lines, and the mark used is the proprietor's name.'

That these fireclay ovens were not invariably built into the wall but sometimes left free-standing is attested by Dr Richard Pococke, the eighteenth-century traveller. Like Celia Fiennes before him, Dr Pococke noted down every unusual or unfamiliar detail of rural life encountered on his journeys:

'They make great use here [about Penzance] of Cloume ovens, which are earthenware of several sizes, like an oven, and being heated they stop em up and cover em over with embers to keep in the heat.'[1]

Dr Pococke also noted, in the very western parts of Cornwall, the pot ovens: 'a round piece of iron which is heated, on which the bread is put, and then it is covered over with a pot, on which they heap the embers to keep in the heat.' In some households both the clay oven and the 'baking under' system were used, according to how large a batch was to be baked. The following account of both methods was sent to the editor of *Cornish Recipes Ancient and Modern*[2] in response to an appeal for descriptions of old ways of baking bread, cakes, pasties and such like.

A Cornish clay oven, and 'baking under'

'You ask me to write and tell you what a "clome ob'n" is like. Well, I will do my best.

'I take it that you never saw one. That is a pity, for I dunno which will be the hardest, to describe it or to imagine it from the description. You must know that years and years ago, before Watts, his name, invented steam, or coal mines were discovered, that people still ate bread, at least, perhaps not so much as they do to-day. I believe they used to eat more oatmeal, and more "fry teddied"; still what bread there was had to be baked somehow, and I believe the first and oldest way of baking

1. *The Travels through England of Dr Richard Pococke 1750*, Camden Society Publications, 1888 (new series No. 42).

2. Compiled by Edith Martin for the Cornwall Federation of Women's Institutes, 11th edn, 1934 (first published 1929).

bread, or anything else, was by means of a "flat ire" in the open chimbley.

'I have baked on it scores of times before we had one of the new fashioned "apparatusus", and my mother never baked on nothing else, except in the "clome ob'n". We only heated the latter for a big baking, say once a week or so.

'The "flat ire" was "etted up" quicker, and was plenty big enough for a few pasties or a roast, or tart, or anything we might want for dinner or tay.

'We first of all put the "flat ire" on the brandis (a three-legged iron affair) and then we lit a fire under it of sticks and "brimbles", furze and anything that would give a clear "ett", and after about twenty minutes or so the "ire" would be white 'ot, and the fire would be allowed to die down, when we would take out the brandis, and "drop the ire" (a round heavy sheet of iron with a handle at each side) among the ashes, wiped off whatever ashes was on it, and drop our loaf of bread, or whatever we were going to bake, right in the centre. The "baker" (it looked like a huge iron frying-pan without a handle) was then turned over on it and red-hot ashes piled up all over and that was all there was to do.

'If it was a loaf of bread it took about an hour, and lovely bread it would be, too.

'Now I will try to tell 'ee how to "Ett a Clome Ob'n".

'The oven (or ob'n) is simply a hole in the wall of the chimbley, there must be hundreds of them walled up in Cornwall, for every old house had one, and I daresay some have still got them.

'They are oval in shape and are roofed over with a hard white substance which gave it the name of "clome". It took about an hour to "ett", and the fire had to be kept burning clear all the time the fire was *in* it of course, and at first it would all turn black, but gradually it would grow white.

'Blackthorn was the favourite fuel for heating it with, and the ashes had to be kept raked out, so the bottom would get hot as well as the sides and roof. When it was white 'ot to the very door, the ashes were thoroughly cleaned out and the tins of bread and plum cake put in (our oven would hold ten tins), the door was shut and red ashes piled around it to keep out any draught, and there you were, nothing more to do till it was ready to come out an hour later, a lot less trouble and a whole lot cleaner than blackleading a new-fashioned apparatus to my mind.'

St Kea Women's Institute

The village bakeries: Sussex

'Not all cottages, of course, even in the hey-day of home-baking, baked their own bread; but until the steam bakery took much of the virtue out of bread-making, there were almost as good and wholesome loaves sold at the village baker's shop as were baked at home.'

C. Henry Warren, *Corn Country*, 1940

The foregoing descriptions of firing the household bread ovens, mixing the dough, baking the bread, are graphic and moving. They convey the sense of rhythm of a way of life unchanged for generations, of housewifely duties cheerfully and capably performed. Perhaps, though, it should be remembered that these passages were written by men or women in middle age or older, recording the memories of childhood or youth. In such records, factual though they are, a certain sense of nostalgia for the past is difficult to avoid. The smell of new bread (even the most unskilfully made bread smells good in the oven), the special treats for the children, the drama of household baking day are emphasized. The inconveniences, the heavy labour, the intense heat of the oven, the smoke and the grime, the total lack of hot or even running water for cleaning up are forgotten. As an antidote it is instructive to learn what the professional baker, firing his oven and baking his bread daily, not just once a fortnight, had to say about his task. A first-hand record is quoted in Ronald Sheppard and Edward Newton's *The Story of Bread* (1957). It came from a book written by an old Sussex baker, Fred Lester of Mayfield:

'The wood we used was house faggots (not many know what they are now). These were put whole into the oven – an awful struggle generally to get them through the door. One was laid straight across the back of the oven and one down either side – three altogether. These were put in the oven overnight so that they got nice and dry, otherwise they did not burn when lighted in the morning (first job). Very often the whole place would be filled with choking, eye-smarting smoke in which atmosphere we had to work.

'When three faggots were burnt down and the hot ashes spread over the bottom of the oven, another faggot was burnt in the mouth of the oven to make an even heat. After that the ashes were all raked out and taken in buckets to be emptied outside. Then a pail of water would stand on the floor in front of the oven and a long pole with a swinging sack tied on the end of it, this being called a "scuffle". The sack was soaked in the pail, put in the oven and swung round and round until all the oven bottom was quite cleared of ashes. This made the oven ready for setting the bread in . . .

'I have forgotten to mention the very unpleasant job of getting the ashes out. The one doing that would be stripped except for trousers and unbuttoned shirt. These ashes would be scorching hot, and as the wood oven was close to the back door, which had to be kept open during the operation, if it happened to be a wet windy day, what with the smoke and fumes the man doing this did not have a very enjoyable time. Sometimes the whirling "scuffle" would fetch out a hot coal which would go down inside the man's shirt. Then there were fireworks and language.'

Fred Lester, *Looking Back*, Mayfield, 1951

The village bakeries: Dorset

As the next passage tells us, the baker's day was a very long one, his work exacting. Although his bread was probably worth ten times – in terms of flavour and the enjoyment it provided – today's equivalent, his profits were small.

'There was no place quite so welcome on a cold day as the bakehouse; it was always warm and cosy in there. Local people often stopped during a shower to take refuge in the stables, which opened right on to the main road; but, if it was really cold weather, many of those who would claim any sort of acquaintance with Father, turned off the road and went into the bakehouse to enjoy the warmth and have a chat before continuing their journey.

'The bakehouse was a low, square building with a window looking straight out on to the river. The oven stood nearly opposite the door of the bakehouse. A stout iron door closed its mouth and inside was a deep and low cavern paved with flat stones. It was heated chiefly with faggots of furze cut on the downs and kept in stacks on the spare ground between the mill and the river. The next best fuel to gorse was thorn, plenty of which could be obtained when the big hedges in the meadows were being cut. Most of this fuel could be bought very cheaply, as it was useless for general household purposes; a nominal charge to cover the cost of putting it into faggots was all that was demanded. When faggots had burnt themselves out, the door of the oven was opened and any embers that remained were raked out by means of a long-handled iron tool, curved at the end into a half circle. These embers were thrown into a recess at floor level below and slightly to one side of the oven. Sufficient heat remained in them to stew things slowly and frequently an iron pot filled with small potatoes stood over them. The cooked potatoes were used as food for the pigs and poultry. A second implement was used to clear out the small embers still remaining in the oven and to cool the floor slightly. This consisted of a long pole to which was attached a short length of chain and a piece of sacking. The sacking was dipped in water and then pushed and turned about over the floor of the oven until every glowing cinder had been "douted" and swept out. The oven was now ready to receive the batch of loaves.

'The dough had been made and put to rise first thing in the morning. On three sides of the bakehouse were long wooden bins raised on short legs from the floor. One of these contained cake tins and other sundries, another contained flour, and the third was used as a receptacle for the dough whilst it was rising. When removed from the bin, the dough was placed on the lid of the next bin and kneaded by an action of the wrist that closely resembled the movements of a cat's feet as it works them when comfortably seated on one's knee: we also spoke of our cats as "kneading" when they did this. As the kneading proceeded, lumps of dough were torn off and flung upon the scales, and it was surprising how frequently an experienced man could remove exactly the amount to make a loaf. This lump was again torn apart, the largest portion remaining under the left hand. After further kneading, the smaller right hand portion was put on top of the larger left hand lump and a final dig given with the knuckles to produce the depression always found in the centre of the top of a cottage loaf. Loaves were made in two sizes and, when I first knew anything about the bakehouse, only cottage loaves were produced there; loaves baked in tins came into fashion considerably later.

'The loaves were introduced into the oven by means of long-handled wooden spades known as peels, and were removed by the same means. The peels and rakes, when not in use, rested on an iron framework suspended from the roof of the bakehouse.'

H. S. Joyce, *I was Born in the Country*, 1946

The village bakeries: Essex – repairing the oven

'Periodically a very necessary but highly uncomfortable task was performed for the baker, the renewing of the lining of his furnace. Old fire lumps had to be cut and replaced with new ones, and in addition a man would often have to work inside the oven renewing brick paving in the floor. The oven was no more than eighteen inches from floor to crown and the terrific heat prevented him from staying inside more than a minute at a time, after which he would come out quickly, streaming with sweat and gasping for air. In he would go again, lying prone to do his work, his body blocking out the light and his legs protruding from the oven door. The heat precluded the use of a candle. This work was done in between baking times, but even at weekends when there was no baking the oven could not be cooled sufficiently to make conditions bearable. Whenever Chris repaired furnace and oven, which he has done several times, usually a severe cold followed the ordeal.'

Christopher Ketteridge and Spike Mays, *Five Miles from Bunkum*, 1972

The village bakery : a survival

In the *Sunday Times* of 22 June 1975 appeared an account of a Devon baker, Gerald Collier of Branscombe, who is probably the last surviving baker in England to use a wood-fired, brick-built oven.[1] Mr Collier, who inherited the bakery and the fifteenth-century cottage in which it flourishes from his father, mixes his dough in the evening, gets up at four o'clock in the morning to light his oven – like most brick ovens it takes two hours to reach the right temperature for bread – and bakes altogether 120 loaves large and small, per day, using a half sack (140 lb or 70 kg) of flour at a time and mixing his dough with well-water. To Brian Jackman, the *Sunday Times* reporter, he spoke of his oven in the terms one has grown to expect from owners of obsolete but beautiful machinery, old ships, vintage cars . . . : 'She's a fine old oven . . . she's hard work but she's part of our life. I shouldn't change her now, not even if I was offered a new one. I don't know why but we always speak of her as a lady. We also use her to cook our Christmas dinner. She cooks turkeys beautifully.'

Compared to people who live in deep country and can still get their firewood for almost nothing, Mr Collier pays quite heavily for his oven fuel. Provided by local farmers, it was reported by Brian Jackman that the charge was 16p per bundle, and that five bundles are needed to fire the oven. Eighty pence a day may not be very much as compared with

1. I have since heard of another, in the splendidly named village of Brightwell-cum-Sotwell, Oxfordshire. Here and there others will perhaps come to light.

the cost of other fuels, but is all the same high in relation to the profit to be made on a small oven load of 120 loaves.

The bakery and cottage, which have been in the Collier family for over a century, are now in the safe keeping of the National Trust.

Pastry-cooking in the brick oven:
dry heat and a falling temperature

As we see from the recollections quoted in the foregoing pages, and in the passage from Eliza Acton, it was common practice to put pies, pastries and fancy breads into the oven when the household bread was already partly baked. By this time the fierce heat had dropped a little, and the steam engendered by the damp dough and the swabbing out of the oven had dispersed. The atmosphere was now the dry one most propitious for the finishing off of the bread. It was also the best one for pastry. How many cooks today still do not realize that a steamy oven makes soggy pastry?

In large and well-equipped households there were often two full-size brick ovens in simultaneous use, one for the ordinary household bread, the second for pastry and the small, fine, white manchet loaves and rolls which were baked at a lower temperature. On the Continent, the second brick oven for pastry seems to have been a tradition going back at least to the fifteenth century. A woodcut in a much-copied French Almanach printed at Troyes in 1480 shows two identical ovens in use. Raised pies, similar in appearance to our own pork pies, are being fed into one, round loaves into the other (Plate 16); and in one of his translations of French, Italian and Spanish manuals of husbandry our own seventeenth-century Gervase Markham provides a good description of an opulent country gentleman proudly showing off his newly built kitchen quarters and his bakehouse with its two fine ovens.[1] Two and a half centuries later we find that great French chef Jules Gouffé, author of *Le Livre de cuisine* and *Le Livre de pâtisserie*,[2] observing that for pastry nothing to date had been good enough to replace the brick and tile oven: '. . . cast iron and forged iron ovens may serve very well for an army on the move . . . but I can see no merit in them from the point of view of baking fine quality pastry.' Emphasizing the importance of *dry* heat for pastry, Gouffé complained that in iron ovens, as he knew them, steam dropped back on to the pastry.

1. *Maison Rustique; or The Countrey Farme*, 1616.
2. 1867 and 1873 respectively.

Taking dough to the baker's oven:
the advantages, and the disadvantages

'Persons who live near to an honest baker may find it quite as economical to send their bread to his oven; the usual charge is a half-penny a loaf. The dough must be covered with a flannel or thick cloth, and carried very quickly, as the cold air checks its rising.

'If given out to be baked, the dough is usually sent in one lump, and the baker divides it into loaves.'

Esther Copley, *The Complete Cottage Cookery*, 1849

'It is most of all in many of our villages that better accommodation is required than now exists for baking generally, and for baking bread especially; for great discouragement to the makers often attends the sending it to a common bakers' oven, should there chance to be one at hand, which in many instances there is not. It is a real grievance to the poor but industrious housewife to have the dough which she has prepared carefully and well, given back to her either underbaked or burned, or partially spoiled by standing for hours in the heated air of the bake-house after it was ready for the oven.'

Eliza Acton, *The English Bread Book*, 1857

THE IRON SIDE-OVEN

It was during the middle years of the nineteenth century that so many farmhouses and cottages which had hitherto escaped the attention of the improvers were updated and furnished with built-in grates and ovens to replace the old open hearth and the wall oven (Plate 22). In *Welsh Country Upbringing*,[1] the Rev. D. Parry Jones, aged eighty-three at the time of writing his book, refers to the innovation:

'In my mother's early days the grate was taken out in summer when they used logs only, and brought back at the beginning of winter. Before I can remember, a fixed grate with boiler on one side and an oven on the other had been built.'

The new grates and the boiler on one side did of course bring some comfort in the form of hot water – although far from constant – and a

1. Batsford, 1948.

hob on which a pot could be conveniently kept simmering for hours at no extra cost, but for the baking of bread as well as the roasting of meat the side-oven was chancy, and extravagant with fuel. 'A good fire must be kept up the whole time of baking', warned Esther Copley, 'for if once the process slackens, an injury is done which no subsequent heat can remedy . . . and the bread, when it comes to be used will seem insufficiently baked – *puddingy*.' Other writers were sharper with their criticisms and complaints.

Iron ovens : the criticisms and the complaints

Emma Roberts, writing in the 1841 edition of Mrs Rundell's *A New System of Domestic Cookery*, first published 1806; says: 'For the baking of bread there can be no doubt that the fireproof brick oven is the best.' Emma Roberts, however, adds that she herself had used an iron oven for thirty years.

'They are . . . we should say, . . . far from economical as regards the proportion of fuel required to heat them . . . The strong smell, too, emitted from the iron ones and diffused often entirely through a house, is peculiarly unpleasant.'

Eliza Acton, *Modern Cookery*, 1845 edn

'A brick oven heated with wood, is far superior to any other for baking bread, as well as for most other purposes. The iron ovens, now commonly attached to kitchen ranges – the construction of which has within these few years been wonderfully improved – though exceedingly convenient, from the facility which they afford for baking at all hours of the day, do not in general answer well for *bread*, unless it be made into very small loaves or rolls, as the surface becomes hardened and browned long before the heat has sufficiently penetrated to the centre of the dough.'

Eliza Acton, *Modern Cookery*, 1855 edn

'The iron oven at the side of the grate, if of a large size, will bake a couple of loaves on each shelf; but they are seldom equally baked on both sides, and the result is not to be compared with the brick oven. Iron ovens are also made to be heated with a separate fire and flue, but even they are not good bakers of bread.

'Gas ovens do not answer well for bread, as they dry it too much by the draught of air necessary for the proper combustion of the gas.'

J. H. Walsh, *A Manual of Domestic Economy*, 1856

'The iron ovens attached to kitchen-ranges in most cases, will spoil the bread attempted to be baked in them, as it will be either unevenly baked or altogether burnt. If, therefore, a family possess not a brick oven, the bread should be sent to the baker's.'

Lady Bountiful's Legacy, ed. John Timbs, 1868

In view of such wholehearted dislike of the iron ovens, whether part of the grate itself or built into the surrounding brickwork, it is interesting to find that in our own day it is coming back into use. The flight of so many town dwellers to remote country farms and cottages, the need for economy in the matter of fuel and the increasing and sometimes ferocious rejection of factory bread have all played their part in such revivals:

'There was a sirloin of beef slowly roasting . . . in the bread oven built in alongside the range. One hundred and fifty years ago the Coalbrookdale[1] bread unit would have been the latest thing for a small farm and a large family. It is designed to burn wood or peat. We use wood and from cold it will reach 450 degrees.

'. . . It is unbelievably economical, using only half a wheelbarrow-load of logs a day and the bread it makes has to be tasted to be believed.'

Thurlow Craig in the *Sunday Express*, 2 November 1975

Coal ranges: their slaves

One of the worst aspects of the old coal ranges was the arduous cleaning and the maintenance they required. In *The New Century Cookery Book* (1901), Herman Senn gives thorough and detailed instructions as to laying and lighting the fires, explains how to use the dampers to regulate the heat, how to clean the flues and remove the accumulated soot, how to sweep out the ashes and cinders from the grate and hearth, how to scour the inside of the ovens with hot water and soda, and finally how to

1. The Coalbrookdale iron foundry was in Shropshire. Many of their ranges and ovens are still to be found in the Midlands, and in Wales, where they were very popular. See Plate 22.

black-lead and polish these beautiful iron tyrants. Many had brass trimmings, and these too had to be cleaned and polished. It all reads rather as if it were the daily routine of the crew of a warship in Nelson's day. The marvel is that the cook and the kitchen staff, when any, had time or stamina enough left for food preparation and cooking. Indeed knowledge of cookery was by no means the most essential qualification for a cook. Given, as Senn concludes, a range with perfect construction, perfect draughts and flues and perfect working (how often were these conditions fulfilled?) 'success depends further upon the management of the fire, dampers and flues used, and upon the skill of the cook as a stoker'.

A range such as Senn was describing, the Eagle, is to be seen in the original kitchen of the Sir John Soane Museum in Lincoln's Inn Fields. One of the guardians there, a Durham man, told me that in the oven of a very similar range his mother used to bake sixteen loaves at a time, twice a week. In the Midlands and the north of England bread-baking remained a domestic tradition – and to some extent still does – whatever the difficulties. Coal, in the days of the iron ranges, was readily available and cheap to any family involved in the coal industry. All the same, cooking and baking *did* mean slaving all day over a hot stove. Except that if the slave were less than devoted and competent, the stove sulked and wasn't hot. The unskilled stoker would find that her bread and pies and cakes were heavy, her meat half-baked. When the fire smoked the sauce-pans and boiling pots were blackened, ashes blew into the potatoes and the soup. A section of an Eagle range is illustrated on p. 162.

BAKING IN GAS AND ELECTRIC OVENS

Gratefully we turn to the era of gas and electricity. Herman Senn too welcomed it. Gas-fired kitchen stoves had been on the market for just fifty years when he published his *New Century Cookery Book* (1901). They had evolved and improved out of all recognition during the forty years since Walsh criticized them in the passage quoted on p. 187. The French admired and envied our technical knowledge in this field. Alfred Suzanne, chef at different times to the Duke of Bedford and to the Earl of Wilton, was openly pained by British achievement in a domain which he considered properly belonged to the French. 'It is surprising', he wrote, 'that France, the culinary nation *par excellence*, has allowed herself to be outdistanced by England in the construction of gas cooking apparatus; for it is indisputable that the use of gas in the kitchen offers great advantages from the point of view, first of economy, then from considerations of cleanliness and of speeding the work.'[1] Describing the newly installed gas cookers in the then Duke of Westminster's London kitchens Suzanne tells us that the special pastry oven, built of brick and lined with iron, was constructed in such a fashion that it would retain its heat for two hours after the gas had been turned off.

Electric stoves were slower to develop than their gas counterparts, although Senn, while still regretting the brick oven, wrote of both with enthusiasm:

'Where it is necessary to bake bread in a town there is nothing that will be so satisfactory for this purpose as an electric or gas oven, failing one specially designed for baking bread . . . Most of these ovens are provided with a tiled "sole" or bottom, and therefore bake excellent cottage and other breads that are desired to have a sweet crusty bottom. Usually bread baked in and on tins or metal has a tough crust that is not generally liked, and to avoid this defect it is advisable to procure some new red house-tiles and fit them into the bottom or shelf of the oven. By this means a more satisfactorily-baked loaf will be obtained than by baking it on the iron . . .

'The unsuitability of the modern oven is principally due to thinness of the sides and the fact that it is not airtight; consequently all the steam escapes, rendering the bread dry and the crust hard and chippy, and not moist and crisp like baker's bread or bread baked in a large brick-built oven. For it should be remembered that it is absolutely necessary to keep all the steam in the oven when baking bread, for the vapour assists the crust to assume the brightness and gloss seen on new bread, known as "bloom".'

Mrs Beeton's Book of Household Management, ed. Herman Senn, 1906

With the nineteenth-century commercial bakers' preoccupation with steam, with the volume and the whiteness of a loaf regardless of its other qualities, the traditions of domestic and professional baking diverged. Whereas for hundreds of years the housewife and the baker had used essentially the same equipment and closely related methods, the development of ovens with steam injectors, of mechanical kneaders and dough dividers, rapidly made bakery equipment and bakery bread

1. *La Cuisine anglaise*, 1894.

something totally outside the experience or indeed the understanding of the housewife.

Many family bakers in towns and villages did of course continue to use their old brick ovens, converting them to the use of gas or coal in places where wood was scarce, and here and there some of these ovens survive. (I have seen a brick-built oven, now gas-fired but otherwise just as prescribed by Hannah Glasse, in use in a London bakery supplying bread to a wholefood shop.) They must seem almost as astonishing to the younger generation of factory-trained bakers as the high speed mixers and mechanized ovens of the latter are to the ordinary housewife accustomed to a simple gas or electric cooker. The ovens of the great multiple bakeries and the bread factories scarcely concern us here, but because it seems to me important that we should have at least some notion of the way our bread is produced, and why it is like it is, a description of a big bakery of the 1950s, with a note about the developments of the 1970s, is included in the next chapter.

Before the invention of mechanical kneaders, bakers used a wooden brake to knead dough. Some were hand-operated, others consisted of a long stout pole firmly fixed to the wall at the back of the low table in a fork-like swivel, so that the pole was loose enough to allow of free working up and down and from side to side. These brakes were ridden like a seesaw. This is really a brake for biscuit dough, but the principle for bread dough was the same. From Frederick Vine's *Biscuits for Bakers*, 1896.

The Bread Factories

'To describe some of the tackle sold as bread in London as anything else than batter would be to stretch a point in its favour.'

Frederick T. Vine, *Practical Breadmaking*, 1897

There is today a lot of bread that is steam-cooked or boiled rather than baked.'

Walter Banfield, *Manna*, 1937

For the past 200 years or more complaints about the poor quality of our bread have been frequent and forcibly expressed. Millers and bakers alike have been periodically accused of frauds upon the community. Bread flour was commonly mixed with alum, chalk (so it is now, by law, to provide us with extra calcium) and even according to one over-wrought pamphleteer with ground down human bones. That story was perpetuated for posterity in Smollett's *Humphrey Clinker* when Matthew Bramble asserted that 'the bread in London is a deleterious paste, mixed up with chalk, alum, and bone-ashes; insipid to the taste and injurious to the constitution'. 'The good people', he continues with obvious truth, 'are not ignorant of this adulteration; but they prefer it to whole-some bread because it is whiter than the meal of corn. Thus they sacrifice their taste and their health . . . and the miller or the baker is obliged to poison them and their families, in order to live by his profession.'

'*Que votre pain est mauvais,*' said a French friend to Eliza Acton, who observed in her *English Bread Book* (1857) that our bread was 'noted both at home and abroad for its want of genuineness, and the faulty mode of its preparation'. Some thirty years later we have Sir Henry Thompson, eminent surgeon and dietician, complaining that London bakers' bread was 'unpalatable and indigestible'. He did not suppose that any 'thoughtful or prudent person would, unless compelled, eat it habitually'.[1]

Sir Henry was writing during the period following the introduction of roller milling with its resulting white loaf for all. Many doctors and dieticians were voicing Sir Henry's opinion, as indeed they still are.

W. Mattieu Williams, a writer of popular treatises on scientific matters and author of *The Chemistry of Cookery* (1885), took a more moderate and perhaps for that reason more effective line than many of his contemporaries when he pointed out that the quantity of alum used in bread flour actually amounted to 1/160th of an ounce per pound of bread, and that it could scarcely amount to adulteration. All the same, he took an amiable dig at the bakers for their preoccupation with the appearance rather than the quality of their bread and for their insistence

'I've been giving them sliced bathroom sponge and they haven't noticed yet.'

Cartoon by Bryan McAllister, the *Guardian*, 3 December 1974. The occasion was a strike of workers in the bread factories. For several days the country was deprived of the bulk of its supply of sliced bread. Queues besieged the independent bakeries. There was panic buying of bread flour and yeast.

1. *Food and Feeding*, 12th edn, 1901 (first published *c*. 1882).

on using alum for its whitening action and its effect on the crumb of the loaf: 'One of the technical tests of quality is the manner in which the loaves of a batch separate from each other. That they should break evenly and present a somewhat silky rather than a lumpy fracture is a matter of trade estimation. When the fracture is rough and lumpy . . . the feelings of the orthodox baker are much wounded. The alum is said to prevent this impropriety, while an excess of salt aggravates it.' He adds mildly that in the matter of adulteration (today we don't have anything so crude as adulterants; we have additives and improvers and nutrients) there were two guilty parties, the buyer who demands impossible or unnatural appearances and the manufacturer who supplies the foolish demand. We are back where Smollett left us, with cause and effect, chicken and egg.

That obsession with whiteness is of ancient origin, far older than Smollett's day. Together with the baker's natural professional pride and his preference for a loaf with good presentation rather than one with good flavour – there is no reason why we shouldn't have both but we've forgotten what bread flavour is – it landed us with commercial bread such as was denounced by those gentlemen quoted at the head of this chapter. Neither was a doctor or dietician or wholefood crank or propagandist writing for effect. Both were professional bakers.

In our own day, scientists and their technological achievements have combined with commercial interests, compliant governments and the public's own indifference to give us the factory bread we now have. No doubt we deserve it. We certainly asked for it, and the milling–baking combines gave it to us. At any rate that's their story.

One interesting point which emerges from the criticisms of the past is that so many of them appear to have been directed at London bread rather than at that of the country bakers. Nobody could make that particular complaint today. Our bread is the same everywhere. How this uniformity was achieved, far back in the 1950s, is explained in the following account, written at a time when, even in a factory, bread dough was given a minimum of two hours' fermentation before it was mechanically kneaded, scaled off and moulded for final proving. The whole process took about three hours and was then still recognizable as a twentieth-century development of traditional methods of breadmaking. In the bread factories controlled by the big milling combines that has now changed. As explained in a final note, the bulk of our sliced wrapped white bread – accepted by the government as the standard loaf – is made on the instant dough principle, taking about ninety minutes from the start of dough-mixing to the finished product. The company which pioneered the plant bakery in England was H. W. Nevill Ltd. Their organization, described below, is of modest size compared to the factories now operated by the giant combines responsible for the manufacture of Mother's Pride, Sunblest and Homepride.

'In the plant bakery, as in the modern flour mill, the visitor is usually surprised to find that there are few workers. Machinery is employed to the maximum so that from start to finish the process is almost entirely automatic . . .

'Flour is elevated from the lofts to the flour plant where it is blended and sifted and weighed, 560lb at a time, into one of the two high-speed mixers. These two machines mix 6,724lb of flour (more than the family baker uses in a week) into dough every hour, and are in fact capable of exceeding this. The machines are automatically switched off when the dough has been mixed for the required time. The newly mixed dough is emptied from the mixers into dough bowls mounted on wheels and left to stand for two hours. The dough is then wheeled to a revolving pan kneader and mixed for a further nine minutes. At this stage salt and fat are added. After standing long enough to mature fully the dough is fed into a dividing machine which automatically scales off the dough pieces at any required weight. One divider can deal with 2,640 dough pieces in an hour. The dough pieces are then fed into a machine which gives them their first moulding and passes them on to the first prover which allows them to recover from their mechanical handling.

'Next follows the final moulding and two pieces of dough are twisted together to make one loaf. The twisting is done to give the loaf a better appearance and colour internally and to improve the surface of slices of bread for buttering. When twisted, the pieces are placed in tins and passed through the final prover, a chamber in which temperature and humidity are automatically controlled, for 40 to 45 minutes, by which time the yeast has worked and brought the loaf to the required size for baking.

'Baking takes place in a 12-sack travelling plate oven, 75 feet long and 8 feet wide and with a capacity of 2,640 loaves an hour. The oven is heated by thermostatically controlled oil burners. Bread discharged from the ovens travels on chutes to the dispatch department where, after cooling, it is sliced and wrapped in wax paper.

'Although the whole sequence of operations is carried out with the minimum of human assistance each stage is controlled by skilled technicians.

'That is typical of the way bread is produced in the factories today. Almost every year brings further improvements to the machinery, all of which make possible further economies in cost.'

Ronald Sheppard and Edward Newton, *The Story of Bread*, 1957

Since the above description was written, the famous Chorleywood Process, evolved in the early 1960s, has fundamentally changed the method by which the great bread factories mass-produce their wrapped loaves. The Chorleywood system, named after the milling and baking industry's research centre in Hertfordshire where it was evolved, can be briefly defined as 'the replacement of the conventional period of dough maturing by a few minutes of intense mechanical agitation in high speed mixers'. After this initial treatment the dough is sufficiently matured to be divided, and to go straight into the tins for a short proof period before consignment to the ovens.

Today about two-thirds of British bread is made by the Chorleywood Process, which is to say that it is produced by the three giant milling-baking concerns of Allied Bakeries, Rank Hovis McDougall, and Spillers French.[1] The points made by the bread industry in support of the Chorleywood Process are that it enables the factories to make use of flour milled with a substantial proportion of low-protein English wheat in the blend, saving expensive imports, and that the new process also economizes labour, reduces production costs, and results in an increased yield of bread per sack of flour. This is because, even using a fairly high percentage of soft flour, the dough will absorb much more water – an extra gallon per 280lb of flour. Of any advantage to the bread itself nobody has anything much to say. One Master Baker and technical expert, Mr John Scade,[2] observes a little less than enthusiastically, that 'bread quality has good consumer acceptance'.

Could it be that the technological achievements of the bakery scientists have removed bread just that much too far from the image of a real loaf as it once was?

Whatever the cause, a recent ploy in the battle to increase or at least to maintain sales is the installation of 'live' bakeries within the retail shops owned by the factory bakers, and in supermarkets and food stores, the enticement being the offer of 'crusty' loaves and rolls hot from the oven. What journalists are fond of describing as 'the heady aroma' of freshly-baked bread brings in the customers, and the sight of hot loaves

1. See note, p. 38.
2. *Cereals*, Oxford University Press, 1975 ('Value of Food' series).

sends them into a spin. Some of them, to be sure, come down to earth fairly smartly when required to pay an extra 2p or 3p per loaf for the pleasure of carrying it home unwrapped. Those who fall for the hot and crusty line regardless of price soon perceive for themselves that while its aroma may be as heady as the scent of a beanfield in midsummer its taste is suspiciously like that of the supermarket loaf, its texture still that of boiled wool. For all that your bread shop may be decked out as a wholesome little old country bakery with smell to match, the dough has been made by methods very little different from the ones used in the great big shining factory. And it is a fact of life that *all* bread, home-made, factory-made, bakery-made, good, indifferent, and just plain awful, gives out a glorious smell while it's baking and for a few minutes after being drawn from the oven. To buy bread on its smell while hot is asking for disillusion. How soon will the customers discover this? Will the make-believe bakers prosper? It will be interesting to watch the progress of the hot and crusty movement.

1978

During the three years since the above notes were written the hot and crusty movement has taken off in quite a big way. Mr Don Miller, the Australian who opened the first hot-bread shop in Britain (at Hemel Hempstead) in 1973, launched his fiftieth shop in 1978. Three of these shops, including one in Central London, are called hot-bread kitchens and have restaurants on the premises. More are planned by the fast-expanding Don Miller group. Sandwich bars and establishments called doughnut diners are also looming.

Don Miller's idea has been much copied, both by smaller firms throughout the country and by supermarket operators. Hot-bread bakeries within the giant stores are multiplying. The following extracts from a news item concerning a Safeway superstore newly opened at Hammersmith are taken from the *British Baker* of 17 November 1978. They give a fair enough idea of the actual meaning of hot and crusty:

An in-store bakery . . . is sited near the front of the superstore so that the smell of freshly-baked bread is an immediate attraction to customers . . . the small bakery is equipped with a bread plant and both rack and multideck ovens. The range of crusty bread being made includes bloomers, French sticks, split tins and farmhouse, as well as rolls.

In other words, factory bread.

Shapes and Names of English Loaves

'A loaf may be any irregular mass of bread with no describable shape; or it may be a carefully shaped article, the particular shape settling the name by which it is to be known.'

The Bakers' ABC, ed. John Kirkland, 1927

'The shape of the loaf rather than the size of the loaf is a guide to baking time.'

Walter Banfield, *Manna*, 1937

The differing shapes of loaves should indicate that they have been made with doughs which even when basically identical have been differently treated in the proving and the cutting as well as in the shaping, thus producing loaves with characteristic tastes, textures and crusts. Although in England – I don't include Scotland – today there is still quite a variety of shapes, there are scarcely more than four types of dough used for basic daily bread, so that unless one lives within easy reach of a Continental, Jewish or Greek bakery, or a very exceptional English one, there is little choice as far as the taste of the loaves is concerned. There are bakery-plant white loaves wrapped and sliced, or wrapped and unsliced. There are white loaves made in round shapes and cylindrical shapes, occasionally in cottage shapes, and of course in tins. There are white loaves made in the semblance of Vienna or French *baton* or *baguette* bread. There are brown wheat-germ loaves, meaning Hovis, baked in tins, sometimes wrapped and sliced, sometimes not. There are ordinary brown loaves, which may be but more often are not made of whole wheatmeal, baked in round shapes and in tins.

Milk loaves, fruit loaves and rolls come under the heading of fancy bread, and, as far as the rolls and the milk loaves are concerned, the English bakers' fancy seems to extend in the first case to round or long, brown or white, in the second to a choice between oblong tins and oval tins, although the latter must be fast becoming obsolete for lack of the tins.

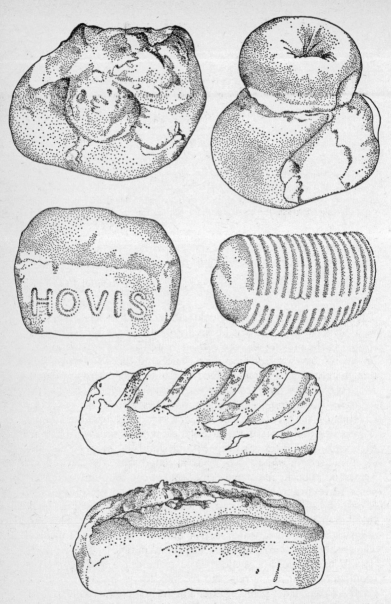

From top left, clockwise: coburg, cottage, crinkled or musket loaf (baked in a double cylindrical mould), bloomer, split tin, Hovis.

Currant or fruit bread is always, I think, made in the routine oblong tins.

A few small variations occur in the appearance of tin or pan loaves, according to the manner in which the bread rises above the top of the tin, and whether the crust has been left by the baker to form in a plain domed shape or whether it has been cut along the centre to allow outward expansion and more crust area. This type of loaf is known as a split tin. Then there are farmhouse tins, rather wider and shallower than the routine ones; these are usually recognizable because they have the word 'farmhouse' impressed on the sides, just as Hovis has its name impressed on every loaf. Farmhouse loaves originated, I think, in the seventies or eighties of the last century, when many thoughtful people, led by medical writers and dieticians, were becoming perturbed by the deterioration in the nutritional content of our daily bread, due to the popular obsession with ever whiter and whiter flour. At that time a farmhouse loaf bought from the baker meant one made from a brown wheatmeal (not whole wheatmeal) similar to the flour sold today as 'farmhouse' for home-baking. The attraction of consciously countrified names for factory products was already well understood a century ago, and by 1900 Frederick Vine, who wrote for a bakery trade journal, was telling his readers that farmhouse-imprinted loaves looked rather false. Besides, he said, they cost the baker more because owing to the impress the tins needed greasing more often than plain ones. Today, a so-called farmhouse loaf is usually made from ordinary white flour. Other variations on tin loaves, called brick and sisterbrick, are baked close together in one wide tin, so that on the sides where the loaves have merged and are subsequently broken apart there are no crusts. In Scotland the term for loaves set close together in one large tin so that the sides merge as they bake is 'batched bread' and in England loaves and rolls baked in this way, whether in tins or without them, are usually described as 'crumby' or 'crummy'. A typical Scottish batch loaf is a spectacular high-rise pan loaf, baked in so-called square tins, although as the tins are not square this is just one more among the thousand and one contradictions and confusions connected with every aspect of breadmaking and baking. Further confusion is to be found in Wales, where a batch loaf is round and bun-like in shape, and baked separately, in other words crusty rather than crumby.

All bread baked in the old manner, without tins, is known as 'crusty' because the loaves have an all-round crust, so that while to journalists and cookery writers the term 'crusty' in association with bread is an evocative or emotive word, to bakers it signifies just a method of baking, which by no means always lives up to the promise seemingly implied by the name.

Among the most common of English crusty breads is the Coburg and its variations, round loaves with cuts in the crust which take different forms, some bakers producing a Coburg with four distinct corners, others a loaf with just one spreading cut, as on a round roll – this one is called Danish by some bakers; others again may make a plain round Coburg without cuts but with small holes – as in a biscuit the holes are made with a docker, a dangerous-looking utensil consisting of sharp heavy spikes driven into a bun-shaped piece of wood. This docked loaf, and a similar one but quite plain, is sometimes called a cob, often thought to be a contraction of Coburg, but in fact of much earlier origin, since cob was an old word for head, and a cob loaf a small round loaf of coarse brown meal, weighing no more than 12oz. Shakespeare uses the term as one of contempt and abuse: 'Thou cobloaf', says Ajax to Thersites in *Troilus and Cressida*[1] meaning that Thersites is a pinhead, and an oafish one at that.

In some parts of the country the four-cornered Coburg was – possibly still is – known as a skull. A Welsh cob loaf, however, is quite different in shape, and can best be described as a square oval with a rounded top, usually with a central cut – more like the English farmhouse loaf, but baked crusty, not in a tin.

Perhaps it doesn't do to assume that the obvious explanation of the name Coburg is that it was first used in the nineteenth century out of compliment to Queen Victoria's consort, Albert of Saxe-Coburg-Gotha. No baker seems able to account for the name, and research may well reveal some earlier origin. Certainly Coburg was the name of a fabric in use before Prince Albert's day, woven from mixed and rather coarse yarns and used for coat linings and very often for cheap black mourning garments. So the Coburg loaf, which is nothing more than a variation of the basic round loaf as made for centuries by all bakers, may well have been one made from mixed and coarsely ground meals. Or it may owe its name to any one of the many German bakers who settled in London during the latter decades of the nineteenth century and since it was also sometimes known as a Brunswick loaf this seems the most probable answer. What is surprising is that the Coburg has retained its name in spite of the frenzy of two world wars during which most German

1. Act II, scene 1.

names were hastily changed or anglicized, the Coburg Hotel, for example, becoming the now famous Connaught, the Battenberg family transformed into Mountbatten (although Battenberg cake is still with us), and the reigning royal family swapping Coburg for Windsor. There was I believe an attempt among bakers to follow the royal example, but old food names change and evolve gradually, with the language, not by deed poll or royal decree.

A further variation on the Coburg is, or was, a pan Coburg, a loaf baked in a shallow round tin, so that the main part of the loaf, cut into the cross or four-cornered shape, rises in the oven and spreads out into a spectacular looking soufflé-like top. Also known as a 'cauliflower', this is a nice loaf for home baking, and a good one for anybody who would like to attempt a change from the routine tin loaf but finds it daunting to embark on the entirely hand-moulded one. In other words, a halfway loaf. The method of setting about making it is given on p. 278.

Yet another version of the Coburg is the attractive little rumpy or porcupine loaf, so cut that when baked the crust appears like a chequerboard. According to Frederick Vine[1] this, and an alternative long version of it, were called undersellers' loaves and were popular in London East End bakeries, and 'in any other locality where cheap bread is the general rule'. Eliza Acton's name for the porcupine is a college – as distinct from a cottage – loaf; she gives a very precise description of the manner of making the cuts, as follows:

'*Crusty, or College Loaves* – These are more frequently made in private families than for sale. The dough for them should be tolerably firm, and be first moulded and slightly cut round in the usual manner; and then, with a sharp knife, the tops should be divided into large dice of equal size, the paste being cut down nearly half through to form them. They will spread open in the baking, and furnish plenty of nice crisp square crusts for amateurs.'[2]

In effect this loaf is similar in appearance to those beautiful and usually very large round French country loaves which keep their freshness so much longer than the *baguette*, and to me are very often better. The English version is rarely nowadays to be found, but one crusty loaf still popular is the bloomer, a long plump loaf with squarish ends and evenly spaced diagonal cuts on the whole crust surface. Again, there seems to be no certain explanation of the name. One country baker I asked replied that it was because it was a loaf which was left to

1. *Practical Bread Making*, 1897.   2. *The English Bread Book*, 1857.

'bloom', i.e. rise or spring in the oven, instead of being confined within a mould. When so many other loaves are made on the same system if not in the precise shape, this explanation seems not very helpful. Nor am I very convinced by the claim made by many people that the bloomer loaf owes its name to Mrs Amelia Bloomer, the American lady who is said to have invented or popularized bloomers as the most practical wear for bicycling. I wonder if a more likely explanation is that, bloom being a word much used in the baking trade to describe the particular sheen or lustre on good crumb, and good flour, the bloomer loaf derived its name from one of these aspects, either of its composition or its appearance. Good quality Australian flour was known as 'bloomery' and at one time it was understood that the bloomer loaf was of a special quality, made from high-grade flour and enriched with milk and butter or lard. It is also possible that the name and the shape are of much earlier origin and derive in some way from a 'bloom' or thick bar of iron smelted in the first forge in an iron works through which the raw iron was passed after it had been melted from the ore. These forges were called bloomeries, and according to the *Oxford English Dictionary* were already in full operation in Furness in the thirteenth century. Another possible derivation, one purely conjectural on my part, just could be from the Greek *arton oktablawmon*, a loaf divided into eight pieces, *blawmos* meaning a morsel of bread and *arton* a loaf. Such loaves are said to have been the equivalent of the Roman *quadrate* and, as we know from remains found in Pompeii, these were round loaves divided by radial cuts made before the loaves went into the oven, so that when baked they would easily break into portions, rather like certain of our tea cakes and scone loaves. Hesiod, in the seventh century B.C., mentions an eight-piece loaf broken into four pieces[1] – that at any rate is what the construction seems to mean, the reference being considered obscure by the lexicographers. I don't think it would be obscure to a baker. The number of cuts or divisions in a loaf usually depends upon its size, and you can just as easily break it into two portions at a time as into one. That part of it doesn't seem much of a puzzle. The bloomer being a long loaf rather than a round one is perhaps less easy to explain. Not that such metamorphoses are by any means unknown. And proof that the Greek eight-portion loaf was necessarily a round one seems to be

1. *Works and Days*, line 442. I am indebted to Mr Denis Moore, M.A., of the City of London School for tracking down the reference and explaining it to me. The interpretation I have put upon it is, however, my responsibility, the Lexicon holding Hesiod's words to be 'an obscure conjunction of epithets'.

lacking. One thing we do know is that in modern Greece there is a popular loaf not unlike the English bloomer and the French *bâtard* – a long, thick, boat-shaped one, divided by pre-baking cuts into slices or fingers. This loaf, sprinkled with poppy seeds, can be bought in London – from Greek bakeries and provision shops. It makes delicious but very un-English toast.

Whatever the origin of its name today the bloomer appears to be made from an ordinary standard white bread dough, not an enriched one. In some bakeries it is called specifically a London bloomer, and Rita Ensing, already quoted elsewhere in this book, told me that in her father's Battersea bakery it was also known as a 'curly'.

By far the most characteristic and distinctive shape among English breads, one now unique I think to this country, is the cottage loaf, two round loaves baked one on top of the other, the top one always being smaller than the bottom one. This loaf, like all our hand-moulded bread, was baked on the floor of the old brick oven of the cottage, the farmhouse or the village bakery. The joining together of the two loaves was possibly an improvised way of economizing baking space in a small oven. Eliza Acton gives the following excellent description of the cottage loaf, and it is interesting to find that in the mid nineteenth century when she was writing, the cottage loaf was the commonest of the bakery loaves:

'The common shape of bakers' loaves is given by dividing the portion of dough intended for one loaf into two parts of unequal size, the smaller one being little more than a third of the whole. These are made into the form of very thick cakes, and then placed one on the other, care being taken that there should be no flour between them, and then pressed together, and a deep indentation made in the centre of the upper one, sometimes *by the baker's elbow*.'[1]

It is, alas, extremely difficult, all but impossible, to reproduce this beloved loaf either in modern bakery ovens or in those of domestic cookers. When, on the rare occasion, a spectacular looking cottage loaf in a bakery tempts one into buying it, the disillusion is all the greater. Today's white bakery dough, for all that it may be hand-moulded and well baked, just does not have character or flavour. Some of the difficulties and problems in the making of a cottage loaf are described on p. 286. It is as hard to achieve the right shape and texture, crust and crumb, of an authentic cottage loaf as it is to reproduce true French

1. *The English Bread Book*, 1857.

baguette bread. In France, incidentally, there was at one time the equivalent of a cottage loaf, and it must have been recognized that it was a tricky one to make, for in the mid seventeenth century one of the tests for every Paris baker before qualifying as a Master Baker was to make a loaf known as a *pain brayé et coiffé*, in other words dough kneaded in the break[1] and made up with a bonnet on the top; it sounds uncommonly like a cottage loaf, and what else after all is the brioche but an enriched and refined version of the same loaf?

A variation on round cottage bread was a loaf called a 'cottage brick', two brick-shaped loaves baked one on top of the other; this one, I have

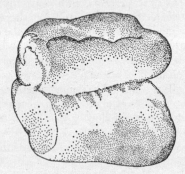

Cottage brick.

learned from London bakers, was more popular and more commonly made in London than the round cottage. A third version was the pan cottage, baked in a shallow round tin, with the main bulk of both bottom and top loaf towering above the tin – an odd-looking hybrid.

Interestingly, although the true cottage loaf has all but disappeared, and efforts made in modern bakeries to reproduce it result in futile travesties, to the English the cottage loaf remains the basic symbol of homely, wholesome bread. The shape would still be instantly recognized by any Englishman anywhere, even had he never set eyes on the real thing. As a racial memory it will die hard.

In the second category of familiar English loaves are those made with meal or flour to some degree brown or beige. In a more restricted way these follow the same pattern as white flour loaves. There are two basic shapes, tin loaves and cobs or round bun-like types. Loaves made from

1. See Gervase Markham's manchet loaf, p. 335.

proprietary meals are usually baked in tins with the brand name impressed on the side. At one time there were several varieties of these proprietary beige breads made from patented mixes containing malted meal and/or concentrated sterilized wheat germ. Some of these breads had good flavours, and were baked in shapes which gave them more personality than the routine tin loaf of which Hovis is the obvious example. There was an appealing oval malted loaf – was it Veda? – and another which was flower-pot-shaped; we still have Bermaline, a light malt bread, and a fourth, also still with us, made from a wheat-germ meal called VitBe, in an ordinary tin loaf shape.

In bakeries which cater for foreign communities, many more varieties and shapes of brown breads are to be found, such as torpedo-shaped rye loaves in a choice of light or dark meal, and round ryes with a chequered and floured crust. In such bakeries there may also be the familiar Jewish chollah, a plaited white loaf scattered with poppy seeds – the plaiting is a very simple matter and anyone accustomed to working with dough can achieve it with ease. (I like the Master Baker who wrote: 'I learnt plaiting from four pieces to twelve on a railway journey, using the fringe of the window-strap pieces.'[1])

In Cypriot and Greek shops can be found characteristic round white loaves, rather flat, and thick, long ones liberally strewn with sesame seeds. These are called finger loaves, from the manner of cutting them before they go into the oven. Both these breads are good when they are fresh – although the sesame seed one is too sweet for my taste – but like French bread very quickly become stale; they are made, I think, with ordinary soft and cheap flour. The be-all and end-all of bread is not, however, or at any rate not to me, that it should remain fresh for a week but that it should be edible in the first instance, and that there should be variety of taste and texture as well as of shape. This is evidently not the opinion of the majority of consumers and certainly not that of the wrapped-loaf manufacturers, although it could be claimed that they do provide variety in their own way. Their bread can be bought in two or even three different sizes and in whole or sliced form. In the case of the latter there are three different thicknesses of slice to choose from, thin, medium and thick. One for sandwiches, one for toast, one, presumably, for bread and butter. Further, there is a coloured loaf, the Hovis, in three different styles, unwrapped, wrapped, wrapped and sliced. There is even a roly-poly-pudding-shaped Hovis, sliced and wrapped, and miniature Hovis tin loaves to serve as rolls.

1. H. Gribbin, *Vienna and Other Fancy Breads*, c. 1900.

Moulds and Tins
for Bread and Yeast Cakes

'As soon as a loaf is taken from the oven, the loaf begins to sweat. That is, there is still a lot of moisture in the form of steam which every loaf must lose as it cools. Therefore it is vital that all loaves baked in containers should be removed from them as soon as they are withdrawn from the oven. Otherwise the steam which cannot escape condenses, producing a wet, water-sodden crust.'

Walter Banfield, *Manna*, 1937

Bread baked in pans or tins of uniform shape and capacity was a late development. Indeed, it seems to have been mainly a British one, Holland being the only other European country in which the method is in general use. In France only soft sandwich loaves and rusk bread are baked in tins, provided with a sliding cover so that almost crustless tops and perfectly even shapes are achieved. All other French loaves are, or were until the invention of dough-moulding machines, fashioned by hand, proved upside down on cloths or in canvas-lined baskets, turned over on to the wooden peel, cut, fed into the oven and baked, as they were in the rest of Europe, without benefit of tin or mould. Notable exceptions are the German and Dutch pumpernickel breads, which are special cases.[1]

Before the advent of mass-produced factory tinware English household bread was either baked in earthenware crocks, glazed on the inside only, or the loaves were hand-moulded and fed into the oven on wooden peels in the ancient manner, as was our bakery bread. In the seventeenth century, deep tin or wooden hoops and, more rarely, round iron cake pans were used for yeast cakes, and there were earthenware dishes for pies, 'broad tins' for gingerbread, tin patty pans, plates and oven sheets

1. Pumpernickel bread is made from rye meal. It is baked very slowly, in shallow rectangular containers.

Typical English loaf tins. The wide one at the top is a popular shape for fruit and spice loaves. Bottom left is the one for a pan coburg or cauliflower loaf (see recipe). The shallower one, right, is a French cake tin which can be used instead.

for small cakes, biscuits and confectionery, glass plates and dishes for drying out fruit and sugar pastes, alabaster moulds for sweets, and occasionally wooden dishes for moulding rolls or small loaves – Robert May (see p. 314) specifies these – but until the turn of the eighteenth century no mention is made in cookery books of tins for bread-baking. That they were in use long before that, probably in the early years of the century,[1] seems certain, but it is Mrs Rundell, writing in the second edition of *A New System of Domestic Cookery* (1807), who makes the earliest English cookery book reference I have yet found to tin loaves: 'If baked in tins the crust will be very nice', says Mrs Rundell.

It is curious to reflect that without those tins we might never have had the sliced wrapped loaf. Dear Mrs Rundell, would she have been quite so pleased with the innovation had she foreseen where it was to lead? And how was it that only the Dutch and the English took readily to bread baked in tins while the system was obviously rejected by the rest of Europe? Of course, at the time it must have seemed wonderfully convenient – it still does – to settle a batch of dough comfortably into space-saving tins, simply cover them with a cloth and transfer them into the heated oven when the dough had risen for the second time. This meant much less handling in the shaping of the dough; the tricky notching, cutting or 'scotching', as the earlier writers called this part of dough management, could be dispensed with; and if the dough had been made up too slack no harm would be done; it would be confined within the walls of the tin and so could not spread and flatten out, but would spring upwards.

By the early nineteenth century domestic cooking methods had already much changed. In the towns coal ranges with ovens were being installed in kitchens, so the separate bakehouse with its special bread oven was often abolished, and housewives or their cooks no doubt found that in the new ovens bread baked in tins or crocks was more satisfactory than the old hand-moulded 'crusty' loaves, the all-round

1. Hanging in the Silver Gallery of the Victoria and Albert Museum is an interesting still-life said by the museum's experts to be in the style of E. Collier, a Dutch painter who flourished during the last four decades of the seventeenth century, and died possibly in 1702, possibly 1712. The painting shows various pieces of English silver, one hall-marked 1688 and all identifiable as dating from the end of the seventeenth century. There is also a handsome mound of butter, and a white loaf quite unmistakably baked in a rectangular pan or tin. The picture could have been painted in England or in Holland. Another Dutch painting, dated 1668, of a peasant interior by Adriaen van Ostade also shows a loaf – a brown one – which appears to have been baked in a mould or tin. The picture is in the Queen's collection.

exposure to high heat in a small space without radiation from above causing a hard crust to develop before the inner part of the loaf had properly grown. As can be seen from some of the contemporary descriptions quoted in the chapter on ovens, many a housewife discovered that the ovens of the new iron ranges called for techniques of bread-baking rather different from those used for the traditional dome-shaped brick oven.

EARTHENWARE BREAD MOULDS AND POTS

In spite of the new tins and the new ovens, which certainly didn't become common until after the middle of the nineteenth century, most householders continued to make their bread as they had always done, often taking the prepared dough to a communal oven or to a local bakery to be baked. When Eliza Acton[1] did this at Tonbridge she put her dough into large round earthen crocks, rather shallow, wide at the top and with sloping sides. The tin loaf was given short shrift by Miss Acton. 'The loaves technically called bricks, which are baked in tins,' she remarks, 'are of convenient form for making toast or for slicing bread and butter.' There are people who still maintain that terracotta crocks are better than tins. Writing in the 1930s, Walter Banfield, for all his experience and skill as a professional baker, held the opinion that earthenware pots, preferably glazed and of suitable shape, 'invariably yield a more flavoury loaf . . . baking in pots is quite a common practice amongst farm people and country housewives . . . remember that a loaf baked on the hearth or tile is considered by many people to be better flavoured than one baked on a metal sole.'[2]

The Greeks – need it be said? – knew all about baking bread in earthenware moulds.

Earthenware baking pans or moulds seem to have been devised by an Athenian baker named Thearion, who had them made by the local Attic potters. The moulds were originally intended for special white loaves baked in honour of religious festivals. Later the use of moulds or pans for white bread evidently became a household custom. 'Pans which Thearion invented', 'white-bodied loaves in dense array' and again 'baking pans of various shapes' all occur in a few lines from *Omphale*, a lost comedy by Antiphanes, fourth century B.C. In another fragment,

1. *The English Bread Book*, 1857. 2. *Manna*, 1937.

this time from Aristophanes' *Old Age*, also fourth century B.C., we get 'hot loaves . . . pot-baked loaves . . . very white loaves'.[1]

There seems also to be evidence – from the writings of Pliny – of Roman 'pan bread' and 'mould bread'. If these methods were ever transmitted to Britain then they must have died out after the departure of the Romans. What remained – and survived until recent times – was the ancient use, long pre-dating Roman civilization, of the primitive iron cauldron for pot bread baked *underneath* the pot, with hot embers or burning peat piled all round and over the pot. This method – as distinct from baking in an upright, covered pot over direct heat – is described by Lady Llanover in the passage quoted on p. 307. From many years of close observation Lady Llanover knew just how the basic foods of her beloved South Wales were prepared and cooked. Her descriptions are to be taken as accurate. Another first-hand record of the same basic system of under-the-pot baking, this time in an oven, is that of the lively Cornish lady quoted on p. 178.

The old method, or one closely related to it, was appropriated and adapted to their own use by Victorian bakers when they evolved 'under-tin' bread for sandwich loaves and some types of brown bread. Kirkland, in *The Modern Baker, Confectioner and Caterer* (1907), gives a formula for a plain brown loaf of coarse meal 'made to satisfy the ideas of those who prefer this kind of bread', which was given a homely appearance by being rolled in broken wheat when moulded, '*whether to be baked under covers or in open tins*' (my italics). I fancy that this was the loaf which was baked underneath a tin shaped like a flower pot. Household bakers utilized ordinary earthenware flower pots to bake similar bread, only they used them upright rather than inverted, so that the dough rose above the top of the pot, and when turned out the loaf looked like an outsize castle pudding or rum baba. The best way to bake bread in a flower pot, i.e. underneath it, is described in the recipe on p. 309.

Bread can be baked under tins in just the same way as under flower pots, but whereas clay pots produce loaves with good side and top crusts, under-tin bread tends to be soft and steamy. The method was used by bakers to make neat and evenly shaped loaves for sandwiches, the result being rather too reminiscent of the bakery-plant loaf for my taste. The same applies to sandwich bread baked in covered tins.

1. Both these fragments are from J. M. Edmonds, *Fragments of Attic Comedy*.

MOULDS AND TINS FOR YEAST LEAVENED CAKES

When it comes to choosing moulds for the yeast-leavened cakes described in this book it is as well to remember that while bread shrinks from the sides of the mould, making it easy to turn out, cakes do this much less, so that an earthenware or china mould which is at all elaborate or patterned is very difficult to use with success unless it is exceptionally well moulded and sharply defined. Curiously enough, although

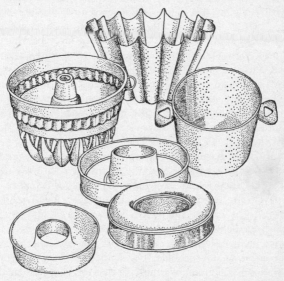

Top left and clockwise: Austrian kugelhopf mould, aluminium; French fluted brioche mould, heavy steel, double tinned; French charlotte mould, heavy steel, double tinned; two views of true French savarin mould with rounded base; English savarin or ring mould, aluminium.

decorative earthenware cake moulds were, and to some extent still are, popular in eastern France, Austria and Germany, in English cookery literature there is little mention of them. That they were used in the fifteenth century and earlier, most probably for gingerbread, seems fairly certain (a terracotta cake mould with the figure of St Catherine with her wheel, dating from that time, is preserved in the London Museum) but by the end of the sixteenth century earthenware moulds seem to have fallen out of favour. When they made their great come-back 200 years later it was for the creams, the flummeries and the elaborate jellies of the eighteenth and nineteenth centuries.

For the cakes of the seventeenth century onwards tin or iron hoops were increasingly used and are mentioned with great frequency in the cookery books. These hoops were similar to our modern flan rings but much deeper (cake hoops about 4 inches in depth are still made for the bakery trade, to be used for wedding, Christmas and other celebration cakes). The hoop was placed on an iron or tin sheet, and a layer or two of paper, floured, was put at the bottom. The sides of the hoop were buttered. These or similar directions occur over and over again in E. Smith's *The Compleat Housewife*, first published in 1727, which gives recipes for forty cakes, the large ones nearly all being yeast-leavened. In her preface this author says that her book was the fruit of upwards of thirty years' experience, so her recipes and methods must often date back well into the previous century, for quite often the reader is directed to bake the cake 'in a paper hoop' – and paper was a great feature in the kitchens of those days.

Wooden hoops were also fairly common. Some cooks, the seventeenth-century Sir Kenelm Digby among others, evidently preferred them to tin, perhaps because they didn't rust, and so were easier to store. Probably they would have been rather like the frames of our present-day drum sieves. Writing a century after Digby, Elizabeth Raffald calls them 'garths' and advises her readers that for large cakes they are better than 'pot or tin', in which the cakes, so Mrs Raffald found, were liable to burn more easily. Alternatively, spice cakes were baked like bread, without moulds. 'For the better baking of it put it in a hoop', says Sir Kenelm Digby, implying that the hoop was an alternative; and in the early part of the nineteenth century, Mrs Johnstone, author of the famous Margaret Dods's *Cook and Housewife's Manual*, thought that her Irish spiced fruit bread was more impressive if baked to look like a large household loaf than when turned out of an ornamental mould. It would certainly have looked more authentic, since the old Irish fruit breads were baked in the iron pot, like ordinary bread.

One late-seventeenth-century housewife, Rebecca Price, whose MS. receipt book[1] was kept from 1681 until well into the eighteenth century,

1. Rebecca Price, *The Compleat Cook or The Secrets of a Seventeenth Century Housewife*, compiled and introduced by Madeleine Masson, original research material by Anthony Vaughan, Routledge & Kegan Paul, 1974.

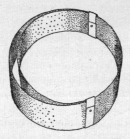

Expanding cake hoop, untinned steel, French.

notes that for one of her cakes 'the tin hoop must be at ye full bigness', which can only be taken to mean that she had an expanding hoop. If so, the method of making these was forgotten, and has only lately been rediscovered and expanding hoops launched as a novelty by a French tinware manufacturer.[1] Rebecca Price certainly needed the full bigness of her hoop. Her yeast fruit cake was made with nearly 20lb of ingredients, moistened with rose water, 'orringe' flower water, cream and sack, spiced with cloves, cinnamon, mace, two nutmegs, and scented with musk and 'ambergreece'. This same splendid lady, for fifty-seven years châtelaine of the manor house at Houghton Regis in Bedfordshire, also refers to a pan as an alternative to a hoop. So she had both. Her kitchen was well equipped and carefully ordered. Incidentally, that word pan, denoting what we now call a cake tin, has been retained, like

Hinged cake tin, lightweight tinned steel, German.

1. I have not seen these expanding hoops on sale in England.

so many old English cookery terms, in America, where all tins are pans except tins with food or drink in them, which are cans.

In Rebecca Price's time tins would probably have been made by a local tinsmith – at Elstow, fifteen miles from Houghton Regis, the youthful John Bunyan had learned his father's trade of tinsmithing – or, if there was not one within easy reach, by a travelling tinker who would have made regular calls in an area where there were good customers. Any special requirements in the way of household or kitchen equipment could be explained, and he could also carry out repairs to existing utensils. As late as the 1930s these travelling tinkers were to be encountered in England, Scotland and Wales. Dorothy Hartley describes in *Made in England* (1939) how a tinker made a special cooking pot for her. He had a primus for soldering, and, marking a heavy sheet of tin, 'bent up the shape, secured the seam, bent over the wire of the rim, bottomed and handled and completed the job with the simplest apparatus, and the greatest skill. It took him about half an hour.' Other things made by the travelling tinker, says Miss Hartley, included baths for babies, wash-basins and wash-up bowls, cake tins, flat tins for ovens, toasting tins, toasting forks (of twisted wire, sometimes with wooden handles) . . . baking tins, dripping tins, small Dutch ovens to stand before the fire . . .

Then there were the blacksmiths. They too were called upon to make kitchen implements and utensils in great variety, from roasting spits and chimney cranes to oven rakes, salamanders and cake pans. In the bakehouse of the late-seventeenth-century Scottish Duchess of Hamilton there is a record of iron pans with loose bases, perhaps for large cakes or raised pies, or for some confection such as the famous Scotch Bun, and these would probably have been made for the Duchess's baker by the estate blacksmith, as were many of the kitchen utensils in use in Hamilton Palace.[1] Some 200 years later we find Lady Llanover going off to her local blacksmith in South Wales and ordering double boiling pots of large capacity, to be made to her own design and measurements.[2] In this way many an innovator could get his designs and fantasies turned into reality, sometimes with useful results.

Anyone living within easy reach of a pottery and on good terms with the potters could do the same when it came to bowls, cooking pots, pans for bread and so on. Although, potters being what potters are and surely

1. Rosalind K. Marshall, *The Days of Duchess Anne. Life in the Household of the Duchess of Hamilton 1656–1716*, 1973.
2. Lady Llanover, *Good Cookery*, 1867.

always have been, special shapes would have been more difficult to achieve and certainly would have taken time. When Thearion the Athenian baker wanted new moulds for special bread to 'honour holy festivals' one may be sure that he didn't get them without a deal of discussion with the Attic potters, and countless visits to them to ensure that the moulds would be ready in time to bake for the feast day. Potters do what they please, and when, and what suits their kilns and their firing routine. As Dorothy Hartley wrote of the Buckley potteries in Flintshire, where dairy bowls, jugs and oven dishes constituted the main output, 'sometimes they would set to work and make a whole lot of heavy bread pans and jars'. Just as suddenly, of course, this whole oven-load would vanish, perhaps sold to a big shop in the nearest market town, and it might be six months or longer before another batch would be fired.

A studio potter, as opposed to a commercial establishment turning out utilitarian earthenware, will today often be pleased to attempt a shape specially ordered, but the earthen pans best for baking bread in, and for a cover while it is baking, are of crude unglazed terracotta, or for storage glazed on the inside only, rather than the weighty, heavily glazed, non-porous stoneware usually turned out by the 'art' potters. If you do decide to use earthenware dishes or pans for bread, remember that it is essential to grease or oil them very copiously, or the bread will stick at the bottom.[1] The bowls I use as covers are described in the recipe for baking 'under-cover bread'. They can be found in many kitchen shops. But something in the shape of the Athenian cooking bell of Plate 15 would be much more convenient.

About buying tins for every kind of bread and yeast cake there should be no problem. They are to be found in great variety in kitchen and hardware shops and in department stores. For both bread and cakes the choice of material is between tin and aluminium. The latter is a good heat conductor, easier to clean, and correspondingly more expensive. Good quality, heavy tin is on the whole, I think, preferable to aluminium, but much of the tinware now on the market, both imported and home-manufactured, tends to be thin and shoddy, is difficult to keep clean and rusts easily. If you do have difficulty in finding heavy-quality loaf tins it is always worth looking in the classified yellow pages of the telephone directory to discover the whereabouts of the nearest supplier of bakery equipment. The heavy black steel pans used by bakers are a good buy

1. See the method of preparing a flower pot for bread-baking, p. 309.

when you can find them. These are no longer to be obtained in the baffling variety described by Walter Banfield when he wrote, in the 1930s, that 'the square, 2 lb tin alone can be purchased in about a hundred different sizes'. It is however still true that 'what is known as a square tin is not exactly square'.

Non-stick cake tins, bun sheets and baking sheets make sense to me, although apart from these the only non-stick utensil in my kitchen is a blini pan of Finnish manufacture, to be seen in the drawing on p. 408.

As a fancy mould, about the most useful, as well as the best looking, is an Austrian or German kugelhopf tin, with decorative markings, a central funnel and a siliconized interior which makes the turning out of cakes trouble-free. Earthenware kugelhopf moulds, still made in Alsace, are decorative, but tricky in use. Savarin, brioche and charlotte tins, dariole moulds and removable-base tart tins are suggested in various recipes in this book. None of them should be difficult to find. They are stocked by most of the shops specializing in good class kitchenware, as also by the kitchen and hardware departments of large stores. Woolworths and Timothy Whites are likely places to look for fairly priced basic equipment such as loaf tins and well-made meat tins which can be used for a large loaf or spiced fruit cake. Before buying look carefully at tins and moulds to see that they are well moulded, and have no shoddy seams or badly finished corners which will dent and buckle when you try to clean them.

Very bright shiny tins which reflect too much heat for a satisfactory baking performance can be 'seasoned' by being left dry and ungreased in a hot oven, 400° to 450°F, 205° to 230°C, for about three hours, until they have acquired a dull or oxidized surface. I can't say that I have ever found it necessary to do this seasoning for bread pans. In my experience they acquire the requisite surface in the course of the first few bakings. Nowadays, unless you have a solid fuel oven, it would be very expensive to leave an oven heated at 450°F, 230°C, for three hours just to oxidize the surface of two or three tins.

Anything unusually large in the way of a bread or cake tin, and special loaf tins such as those with covers, can usually be ordered direct from the Portsmouth firm whose address is given on p. 357, and who also make muffin or crumpet rings, not easily obtainable elsewhere. No specialist retail shops are listed in this book. To keep such a list up to date is not feasible and an obsolete list is the reverse of a service to the reader.

Storage of Meal and Flour

It is only in households where bread is baked in quantity and variety, and flour bought in bulk, that storage bins and a place to put them become a problem.

Of the different varieties of flour, those milled so that they retain the whole grain, i.e. wholemeals, whether of wheat, rye or barley, need the most care. This is because the presence in the meal of the oil from the germ of the grain, small in proportion though it is, reduces the keeping qualities of wholemeals, giving them a tendency to develop a rancid taste and smell, although the insistence by some purveyors of wholefoods that wholewheat meal should be used within a maximum of five weeks of milling seems to me exaggerated. On many an occasion I have used Irish stone-milled meal stored for several months, and have found the bread made from it if anything better and sweeter-tasting than that made from meals bought directly from a mill and used within a week. So

Brown japanned steel flour bin stands flat against the wall.

much depends upon the wheat itself and the conditions in which it has been milled and stored before it reaches the customer that it is impossible to lay down rules as to its keeping qualities.

White flour, given that it is stored in a cool, clean, dry place, and protected from insects and mice, will keep for a long time and presents few storage problems. It was this attribute which was one of the contributing factors to the instant and universal popularity of white flour once it had been discovered that roller milling made the separation of the germ – as well as the bran – from the starch a comparatively quick and cheap process.

Since the household storage of meals and flours must of necessity depend on individual circumstances, the following suggestions are for general guidance only:

The sixteenth-century kitchen at St Fagans Castle, Cardiff. A massive oak meal chest stands below the dog-wheel which turned the roasting spit in front of the left-hand fireplace. The slatted oak bread cart or crate suspended from the ceiling was made late in the seventeenth century and came from Penrhyn Old Hall, Carmarthenshire. Sometimes Welsh bread crates were lowered and raised by pulley. They were used for the storage of oatcakes as well as bread. From *Life and Tradition in Rural Wales* by J. Geraint Jenkins (Dent).

1. All meals and flours must be kept dry and cool.

2. Even when you keep your flour in the bags in which it is packed for sale, it is a good idea to store the 100 per cent and 85 per cent wholemeals in a container separate from the one used for plain white flour. In this way, if something should go wrong with your wholemeal, it will not contaminate the rest of your flour store. It is all too easy for a musty taste, not to mention insect pests, flour mites and weevils, which usually originate in wholemeals, to be transmitted from one small bag of meal to an entire batch of different flours.

3. Keep flour bags standing *upright*, one in front of the other, not stacked one on top of the other.

4. Meal should be allowed to breathe. Hence the oak meal chests (see the illustration of the kitchen at St Fagans opposite), the wooden flour kegs, and the cotton flour bags, in which flour and meal were formerly stored and packed. Metal flour bins, products of the late nineteenth century, are perfectly good for white flour, less so for wholemeals. One alternative is some sort of porous or ventilated container such as an earthenware crock, as used for bread storage. Another solution would be a covered linen basket. This is a method I have not tried, since I do not store meal in quantity, but the idea, based on one learned from a Welsh historian, Miss R. M. Evans, and her writings on the domestic customs of eighteenth-century Wales, is an agreeable and, it seems to me, a sensible one. The people of Cardiganshire, noted for their basket-making, Miss Evans tells us, made large hampers from oat straw to store their oatmeal, and another kind from barley straw to store barley meal.[1] The belief among the Welsh country people was that meal kept best in its own environment, and straw from oat and barley crops provided the answer.

As opposed to baskets and crocks, the Scurfields[2] recommend 'any dry mouseproof container – a small dustbin will take 5 stone nicely' and claim that even wholemeal will stay in perfect condition for three or four months and longer. So, basketwork, hamper, wooden chest, earthenware or stoneware crock, enamelled or japanned steel bin, mouseproof dustbin (but preferably not a plastic one) – take your pick, and don't try to store any wholemeals indefinitely.

5. Should a paper bag of flour get torn, by all means transfer the

1. *Transactions of the Cardiganshire Antiquarian Society*, vol. xii, 1937.
2. George and Cecilia Scurfield, *Home Baked*, 1956.

contents to a polythene or other plastic bag, *so long as an air hole is left open at the top of the bag*. Flour sealed into plastic will sweat.

6. The recommended temperature for storage of flour for immediate use is between 60° and 70°F, 15° and 21°C. For bulk cold-storage, flour can be kept in good condition for a year or more at a temperature of 38° to 40°F, 3° to 4°C. Untreated, that is unbleached, flour will improve in quality and become whiter as it ages. About two years' storage is considered the safe limit for white flour.

Storage of Bread

'To put hot bread at once into a cool atmosphere is almost bound to make it heavy.'

Florence Jack, *Cookery for Every Household*, 1914

Among the vital points to remember about the storage of bread are, first, that the larger the loaf the longer it stays fresh; next, that a loaf should never be wrapped up or put away until it is perfectly cool; and that unless it is to be consigned to the deep freeze it keeps best if it is allowed to breathe. A loaf enclosed in, for example, a sealed polythene box or bag may appear to retain its moisture for a day or two but is in fact giving it out; this moisture is condensing in the airtight container and dampening the crust; the rapid formation of mould is inevitable. The same happens, although not quite so quickly, when bread is stored in a non-porous, highly glazed stoneware crock *unless* there is an air-hole in the cover, or unless the cover can be raised slightly, allowing air into the crock. This can be achieved by sticking tiny wedges of cork at intervals round the rim of the crock, so that the cover rests on them.

On street-market stalls and in antique shops one sometimes comes across the old Doulton stoneware storage crocks for bread. It is a rare occurrence to find one complete with its cover. This is because the people who made these crocks, familiar with the problems of bread storage, evolved specially designed lightweight steel covers, slightly domed and perforated with small air holes in the centre. These covers provided a very practical solution to the problems both of ventilation and of weight. Unfortunately they were not rust proof, and few have survived.

As practical as the old metal-covered stoneware crocks, lighter, and much cheaper were the common porous earthenware variety, the crock glazed on the inside only and the cover only on the outside. These crocks, called bread pans, were made in potteries specializing in rough

clayware such as flower pots, dairy bowls, earthenware pans for bread-baking, and all manner of animal-feeding dishes and crocks. Although they cracked and chipped easily, bread pans were cheap to replace. Prices quoted in a catalogue dated 1900 range from 3s to 9s 6d including the covers. There were six sizes, from 12 inches to 20 inches in diameter. Such crocks have now become rarities, almost museum pieces – as indeed have ordinary clay flower pots – the only pottery whose interior-glazed terracotta or clayware crocks are nationally distributed being Brannams of Barnstaple in Devon. Brannams' products are usually to be found in the kitchen, hardware or china departments of such stores as those of the John Lewis group. Brannams' terracotta crocks are far from cheap and deliveries are irregular. It must be remembered that they are bulky, take up much space in the kiln, and are therefore un-economical to produce. They are, however, solidly made and very much tougher than the old lightweight covered flower-pot type of crock, which incidentally is still occasionally to be found, although only by making an expedition to the premises of one of the few surviving pro-ducers of terracotta garden pots, such as the Harris family's establish-ment at Wrecclesham near Farnham in Surrey, or the Fareham pottery in Hampshire.

For bread storage, it is a help to stand earthernware crocks on a triangular wooden pot stand or a brick so that air circulates round them. It is essential that bread crocks be frequently and meticulously cleared of crumbs, which generate mould. If you feel that the regular cleaning of the crock is too much bother there isn't much point in using one at all.

Metal containers, such as enamelled steel bins and roll top boxes are

quite efficient for bread storage, although I find the latter difficult to keep clean and free of crumbs.

As an alternative to crocks and bins, a clean dry cloth wrapped round a loaf makes an effective protection. So does a porous earthenware bowl inverted over the loaf on a board or earthenware platter. For a cut loaf I find this the most effective of all short-term keeping methods, its disadvantage being the obvious one of the space it occupies.

In France bread is rarely stored from one day to the next. If it is, the long loaves are kept upright, like walking sticks, uncovered, in a tall basket. Round *pains de campagne* are stored in a cupboard, as indeed were their counterparts in England and most other European countries, until the old farmhouse food cupboards with carved and ventilated

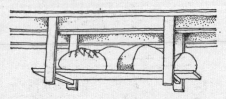

The bread rack from a Norman farmhouse is similar to those used in Yorkshire for storing oatcakes, but for drying the oatcakes were first hung over leather thongs strung like washing lines between the supports of the shelves.

doors all disappeared into museums or were bought by private collectors probably unaware of the original purpose of these beautiful pieces of furniture. Taking into account, however, the quantity of bread baked at each firing of the oven, a storage cupboard, although a very necessary piece of equipment, would have been large enough only for the short-term storage of a few loaves, probably those already cut. For bulk storage some other solution had to be found. In Wales I have seen a splendid device, a huge wide cradle or crate of slatted wood suspended like a hammock from the ceiling. Two such bread crates are to be seen at the Welsh Folk Museum at St Fagans, near Cardiff, one in the great kitchen of the castle (see p. 218). In Normandy, a similar device on a smaller scale consisted of shelves, also slatted and suspended from the ceiling. Both systems seem to be very practical. So was the bread creel, the hammock-like device slung between cross bars hanging from the ceiling and used in Yorkshire for the storage of oatcakes. The creel is described in the chapter on bakestone breads.

THE FREEZING OF BREAD

The deep freeze is surely the best bread bin to date. If wrapped and consigned to the freezer just as soon as it has cooled, a loaf will retain its moisture intact, and when thawed will be difficult to distinguish from bread freshly made. The crust does of course suffer a bit, but less, I think, than it does when the loaf is stored in a crock or a metal container.

In effect, it is perhaps the deep freeze which has contributed most to the present revival of domestic breadmaking. We all know that it isn't going to be feasible to bake a new loaf whenever we may happen to want it, but it *is* possible always to have a fresh loaf or two in reserve. Many people who have a large enough freezer now do a weekly bake, rather as housewives did in the days of the brick oven. They find that good bread fully justifies the space it occupies in the freezer.

The sooner, after it has cooled, that a loaf is put into the freezer the fresher it will remain. Whatever wrappings you choose, see that they are well closed. Label and date them.

A large loaf takes three to four hours to thaw out at room temperature – a loaf still half-frozen in the centre is not an enticing proposition – but the process can be speeded by giving it a final half hour or so in a low oven, or you can transfer it straight from the freezer (having first unwrapped it) to a medium oven and let it re-bake for 30 to 40 minutes depending on the size of the loaf. Re-baking will if anything improve the bread, although only on a temporary basis. If it has to last for any length of time then it is best to let it thaw slowly. It is a good idea to take the loaf out of its freezer bag and wrap it in a towel while it thaws, otherwise moisture from the bag condenses on the loaf, making the crust leathery.

For cutting sandwiches, especially very thin ones, it is an advantage if the loaf is still slightly under-thawed.

Tin or pan loaves are the most practical for freezing, but small soft-crusted baps freeze well. So do fruit and spice loaves.

The refrigerator, by the way, is not a good place to store bread. The usual temperature of a refrigerator does indeed delay mould for a time, but is also just the one to draw out moisture.

Weights of Loaves
and the Assize of Bread

'Famous merchants, that far countries ride
With all their great riches and winnings,
And artificers that at home abide . . .
. . . What may avail all your imaginings
Without proportions of weight and just measure?
'Masons, Carpenters of England and of France
Bakers, Brewers, Vintners with fresh liquor
All set at nought to reckon in substance
If poise or weight do lack, or just measure.'

John Lydgate (*c*. 1370–*c*. 1451),
Measure is Treasure

As early as 1202, in the reign of King John, and thirteen years before
Magna Carta, laws were formulated to regulate the price of bread and
to fix the amount of profit allowed to the baker. The Assize of Bread
which grew out of the original laws was established in 1266, during the
closing years of Henry III's reign. For over four and a half centuries the
basic principles of the 1266 system controlled the weights and prices of
bakers' bread.

The Assize system was a complex one. The bakers, much bedevilled
by the constant changes involved and frequently prosecuted for selling
loaves which failed to conform with the weights as required by their
local Assize laws, understandably felt it to be unjust and oppressive.

To explain it as shortly as possible, what the Assize set out to do was
to regulate the *weight* of a penny loaf according to the prevailing price
of wheat and the grade of flour used. At any given moment therefore the
penny loaf would have three different weights, each being made from a
different quality of flour. First came the so-called white loaf, made from
flour as finely bolted as was then possible. Next was the 'wheaten' loaf,
made from more coarsely bolted meal. This one was half as heavy again

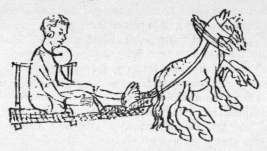

A London baker convicted of selling underweight loaves is 'drawn upon a hurdle from the Guildhall to his own house, through the great streets, where there may be most people assembled and through the great streets that are most dirty, with the faulty loaf hanging from his neck'. (*Liber Albus* or *White Book of the City of London*, 1419). Illustration from the *Assisa Paris*, 1266; Corporation of London Records Office.

as the white loaf. Third was the penny loaf of household bread, the largest and heaviest of the three, made from unbolted meal 'as it cometh from the mill', or what we should call wholemeal bread. As an example of the relative weights of a penny loaf, in the year 1329, when the price of wheat was around 6s a quarter (8 bushels) the white loaf was to weigh 3lb 13oz, the wheaten 5lb 12oz and the household 7lb 11oz.

Today, bakers' bread flours are submitted to rigorous quality tests before they leave the mill, and very often again before a new consignment is used in the bakery. The amount of water they will absorb is a known factor, the loss of weight in baking of a given batch of dough can be calculated, the temperature of the ovens is uniform. Yet in 1976 a professional baker can still assert publicly 'that the final weight of a loaf of bread is in God's hands as much as the baker's'.[1] It's easy to appreciate then, that, given the variable quality and unpredictable performance of meals and flours in the days of the Assize, not to mention the difficulty of assessing the oven heat, the necessity of achieving loaves of required weights imposed an unenviable task upon the bakers. To stay on the safe side of the law, they can hardly have done other than sell overweight loaves, thus reducing the already modest profit legally allowed them.

Apart from the three main categories, there were rougher breads made from mixtures of rye meal and wheat bran, some of them without any wheat flour at all. Gervase Markham[2] gives the composition of a bread

1. From a letter published in the *Guardian*, February 1976. The writer signed himself E. S. Gaskell, 'an old retired baker'. 2. *The English Hus-wife*, 1615.

which is 'the coarsest Bread for man's use: you shall take of Barley two bushels, of Pease two Pecks, of Wheat or Rye a peck, a peck of Malt'. In earlier times bread of this type, described by Markham as for the 'hind servants', would have been baked by the brown-bread bakers, who were allowed to bake bread from dough brought to them by house-wives, and also made pease-meal bread for horses, but were in a differ-ent category from the white-bread bakers, upon whose province they were not permitted to impinge. As a separate entity the brown-bread bakers had, however, virtually ceased to exist by the time Gervase Markham was writing his books.

Up to a point the Assize regulations were clear enough. But prices of corn varied throughout the country and fluctuated from month to month, so the weights of penny loaves produced by London bakers would probably differ from those in, say, Norwich or Winchester, the legally required weights being liable to change every three months, or whenever the local magistrates thought fit to set an Assize. Even very minor changes in the price of wheat could in theory be applied to the weight of bread, for the Assize table was calculated in stages of 6d at a time and ranged from 6d to £5.

What makes for confusion when we attempt now to equate the weight and the price of any given loaf in say the latter half of the fifteenth century with the equivalents in our own time, is not only that it was the price of grain rather than that of ready-milled flour which was the governing factor, but that the actual weight of a bushel of wheat could vary between 60lb and 72lb, and a bushel of oats or a bushel of barley were both different again (see table on p. 238). To complicate matters a little more – no doubt at the time it seemed in the natural order of things – weights of bread were initially reckoned by the pennyweight and shillingweight rather than by the ounce. These were fractions of the troy pound established at the time of the 1266 laws, and were based on the weight of one grain of wheat, well dried and taken from the middle of the ear.[1] On this basis there were reckoned to be 24 grains to a penny-weight, 12 pennyweights or 288 grains to a shillingweight (three fifths of an ounce), 480 grains to an ounce, 5,760 grains or 12 ounces (20 shillingsweight) to the pound troy. Looked at in the terms of what became, and for so long remained, our sterling currency of 12 pennies to the shilling, 20 shillings to the pound, troy weights are quite easy to grasp. Unfortunately there is also the question of avoirdupois weight

1. The Greeks based their weights on barley – 12 barleycorns to the obol – and the Chinese on the millet grain.

which for a long time coexisted with troy weight and was often confused with it. In the avoirdupois pound there were – and are – 437½ grains to the ounce and 7,000 grains or 16 ounces to the pound. The troy pound in other words was the equivalent of approximately 14½ ounces avoirdupois.[1]

If that sounds complicated I should add that in the early decades of the Assize there were farthing loaves and halfpenny loaves and that the latter were tied to the troy weight of the bread in such a way that if, say, 24 loaves weighing 30 shillings each (2 lb) were selling for 20 halfpennies, then they were reckoned to be underweight because in number they exceeded by four, or one fifth, the number of halfpennies in the selling price. 'Accordingly the weight of each loaf will have to be increased by one-fifth of its weight,' says the Assay clerk, observing that 24 loaves each weighing 40 shillings weigh 48 pounds; while 20 loaves, each 48 shillings in weight, weigh exactly the same. 'But this original number of halfpennies being 20, the number of loaves is now made equal with that of the halfpennies, the weight of them in the whole being the same as before.' It seems a long way round to go to say that it was the weight and price of the unit which had to be adhered to rather than the overall weight and price of any given batch of loaves. I have, I'm afraid, greatly oversimplified. Medieval methods of calculation and the manner of expressing them were of a tortuousness which would do credit to any modern Excise official drawing up an amendment to the VAT regulations for the building trade.

When the Assize of Bread was first established the bakers bought their own wheat direct from the farmers, paid a miller to grind it, and bolted it themselves, the law allowing them to keep the bran for their own profit and use. Over the next three centuries, as milling slowly developed into a separate trade, the bakers began to buy ready-milled flour direct from the millers or through a factor or middleman. Calculating the weight of bread according to the price of the grain was no longer realistic. By the end of Elizabeth I's reign in 1603 the system had become unworkable, and, as is normal in such circumstances, another century passed before the obsolete law was changed, and an alternative system, already in common practice, recognized as legal.[2]

By the new laws introduced in 1709 two distinct systems of selling bread were established. Bakers could choose to adhere to a modified

1. Since 1878 troy weights have been used only for gold, silver, precious stones and pearls.
2. See note on p. 339 concerning the 'penny loaf' as specified in recipes.

version of the old system of baking and selling by weights changeable according to the price of flour, or they could bake their bread to standard weights, the price being set according to the weight of the loaf. The first system was still known as Assize Bread, the second, confusingly, as Priced Bread. Bakers were obliged to bake and sell by one system only, and once they had made their choice could not chop and change.

The most commonly baked size of Priced Bread was the quartern, or quarter-peck, loaf, weighing at that time not 4 lb as has generally and understandably been supposed, but 4 lb $5\frac{1}{2}$ oz, the weight of bread officially calculated to be the yield from a quarter peck or $3\frac{1}{2}$ lb of flour. There were also peck loaves weighing 17 lb 6 oz, and half-peck loaves of 8 lb 11 oz. It was reckoned therefore that the 280 lb sack of flour was to yield 347 lb of bread. At the time, our bread flour was milled almost entirely from our own home-grown low-protein wheat, so the yield of bread per sack was low by today's standards, when modern bakery machinery and high-gluten flour enable bakers to get between 385 and 390 lb of bread per sack.

At times of shortage in particular the Bread Laws could still be seriously enforced. Writing on 22 April 1800, a period when bad harvests at home and the Napoleonic wars in Europe had caused severe grain shortages, Mrs Edward Boscawen, describes how her son-in-law, the Duke of Beaufort, 'has been well employed in the County, as he always is. He has caused all the bakers' loaves in every parish to be suddenly weighed, and fined those that were short in weight, so now no one dares to defraud the poor, which was a practice gaining ground and wanted this unexpected prevention.'[1]

Mrs Boscawen added that at the same time the Duke had instituted strict regulations to prevent the waste of flour in his own large household: 'It is amazing what a difference is established by that means. I tell you that because the famine is sore in the land.'

By the early years of the nineteenth century, when the increase in urban populations had caused a corresponding expansion of the profes-

---

1. Brigadier-General Cecil Aspinall Oglander, *Admiral's Widow. The Life and Letters of the Hon. Mrs Edward Boscawen from 1761 to 1805*. London, the Hogarth Press, 1943.

Incidentally, it was at about this period that in order to economize flour the gentry were instructing their cooks to bake their great meat and game pies in earthenware containers made by the Staffordshire potters, notably Josiah Wedgwood, in imitation of pie crust.

sional bakery trade, the original Assize system was admitted to be irredeemably obsolete. In 1815 the 1266 laws were at last repealed. The standard weight loaf remained, but without price control. Further Acts, passed in 1822 and 1836, abolished the standard weights and introduced another liberating regulation. This time, although the baker was still to sell his bread by weight, it could be any weight so long as it was clearly stated. In other words the baker was obliged to 'weigh his loaves in the presence of the party purchasing the same, whether required by the purchaser so to do or not.' (This regulation was subsequently modified to one which obliged the bakers to weigh their loaves before sale only when required by the customer to do so.) Every baker's shop was compelled to display weighing scales in a conspicuous position, and bakers' delivery carts and carriages were to carry 'correct Beam and Scales with proper weights, in order that all Bread sold by every such Baker or seller of Bread may from Time to Time be weighed in the Presence of the Purchaser or Purchasers thereof'.

The wording of the 1822 Bill also made it perfectly clear that the only legal weights used for loaves were to be those of the 16 ounce avoirdupois pound, or fractions or multiples of it, that the old standard peck and half-peck, quartern and half-quartern weights as applied to bread were now illegal, and that it was also illegal to use those terms in relation to the sale of bread. The 1822 Bill however applied only to London and districts within ten miles of the Royal Exchange; when in 1836 the London Act was made general throughout England and Wales (it was not accepted in Scotland) the clause concerning the old denominations was omitted, presumably inadvertently, with the result that in the country as a whole the old terms persisted, and many bakers, the public and even the magistrates thought that the old weights were still the legally required ones. Gradually the old denominations had come to be taken literally as implying the *actual* weight of the loaf bought, irrespective of the amount of flour which had gone into it. When, therefore, quartern and half-quartern loaves are mentioned in later nineteenth-century and early twentieth-century books it is safe enough to assume that 4 lb and 2 lb loaves are meant.

Although other attempts were made, chiefly in the 1878 Weights and Measures Act, to clear up the confusion, it remained until the middle of the 1914–18 War. By that time the bakers had at least had nearly a century of comparative freedom from controls, and even if some of them appeared to be unaware of the true legal situation the years of liberation cannot have been other than beneficial to the baking trade and to the public who had a far greater choice than ever before both of types of bread and of bakers from whom to buy it.

In 1916, the first war-time Food Controller, Lord Devonport by name, decreed that bread was once again to be sold only in units or multiples of 1 lb. That regulation obtained until after the end of the 1939–45 War when, in 1946, shortage of grain caused the government to reduce the unit weight of loaves from 1 lb to 14 oz. The 4 lb loaf then became $3\frac{1}{2}$ lb, the 2 lb loaf 28 oz and the 1 lb loaf 14 oz. Whatever other purpose the reduction served, it effectively killed off the traditional denominations. Although there may still be those who suppose that the 28 oz loaf weighs 2 lb, and the $3\frac{1}{2}$ lb loaf 4 lb, quarterns and half-quarterns are for the history books. Now, with the introduction of metrication, the legal weights and denominations of our bread will again be changed. The standard large or 28 oz loaf will be 800 grams, the 14 oz loaf 400 grams.

In comparison with the problems presented in the past by the simultaneous usage of troy pounds and avoirdupois pounds, pints and gallons dry and liquid, pints and gallons imperial and pre-imperial, not to mention such anomalies as Scottish pints varying from $3\frac{3}{4}$ to 4, $4\frac{1}{2}$ or 5 imperial pints according to district, North of England gills of $\frac{1}{2}$ pint as opposed to the legal and official $\frac{1}{4}$ pint, the sack of flour weighing 4 bushels in the Midlands, while in London and the rest of the country it was 5 bushels, the transition from imperial to metric measures should be relatively straightforward. If the experience of the past is anything to go by, it will also be a very long time before the old measures fall into disuse and the old denominations are forgotten.

Weights, Measures and Temperatures

The following table of conversion for English measurements into metric terms is the one I have worked out for the purposes of this book. I think it is a more realistic one for a cookery book than that suggested by the Metrication Board, which for easy calculation reduces the ounce from 28 grams to 25. This means that the British pound weight is calculated at 400 grams instead of 450. By the time you have converted say 5 lb of flour (or meat, or potatoes) into metric terms you are well over ½ lb out on the original quantity. True, the rest of the ingredients in the recipe are reduced *pro rata*, so the formula retains its balance. But what of other factors, such as the size of saucepan, mould, cake tin to be used? The timing of the cooking? The number of servings?

Speaking as one who has for many years been accustomed to the transposition of metric measures of weight and volume into English terms and vice versa, I find the process perfectly straightforward provided that the long-accepted equivalent weights be adhered to. To be sure, some rounding off is necessary – up in some cases, down in others – only a modicum of commonsense being required to produce a clearly set out and balanced formula. It is obvious that nobody is going to have any patience with a recipe specifying precise metric equivalents down to the final gram, any more than anyone ever accepted pedantically exact conversion of a metric recipe into English terms. Who is likely to measure, for example, ⅝ of a pint, or 224 grams? Well, reckoning on 28 grams to the ounce, 224 grams is ½ lb. You don't have to be a genius to see that 225 grams is an easier quantity both to measure and to remember. That means a gain of 1 gram only. If you round up to the nearest ten, you will sometimes lose, or gain, from ⅛ to ⅓ oz. These are trivial differences and where cooking is concerned can be disregarded. (Most people's cooking measurements tend to be haphazard anyhow.)

It is only, I find, when dealing with the smallest quantities, such as in this book are specified for salt and yeast, that there is any problem of calculation or of weighing and measuring. In these cases it is best to calculate the ounce as 30 grams, and if in a recipe as small a quantity as $\frac{1}{4}$oz is specified, treat it as 10 grams or $\frac{1}{3}$oz. Salt and dried yeast can, after all, be measured in teaspoons or tablespoons. Fresh yeast is more difficult, but I should be surprised to hear that household bakers mind all that much about the accuracy of their yeast measurements, or, given the inexactitude of most domestic scales, that they are in a position to mind.

When it comes to liquid measurements, the Metrication Board has decreed that the litre of 1,000 grams be divided into millilitres (ml) or thousandths of a litre. In France, Italy, Belgium, Switzerland, Spain, and the Scandinavian countries, measures of wine, spirits, milk, cream, water, soup, and as far as I know any other liquid you care to think of, are expressed in units – where fractions of litres are called for – of decilitres (tenths of a litre) and centilitres (hundredths of a litre). These are the measures which are used in the dispensing of wine and spirits, and which are common usage in all the Continental cookery books I have ever worked from. The millilitre unit was one I had never encountered until it began to crop up in English tables of measurements. Why this further botheration should be introduced it is hard to see. I propose to disregard it. My own system is to use grams for liquid measurements as well as for solid ones. For cookery purposes and indeed all others so far as I know, the liquid gram is precisely the same as the millilitre. There are a thousand of each of them in a litre, so why not use the shorter and more familiar of the terms? For those not yet accustomed to the metric system, this obvious but disregarded point makes the conversion of recipes that much easier and more comprehensible. In the light of a table drawn up on this system, American measures also fall easily and clearly into place. It all becomes quite simple, and would have been simpler still had we retained, as the Americans did, our pre-1825 system of measurement, when the liquid pint was 16 oz and the equivalent of the avoirdupois pound. There was of course – there still is – the troy pound, which was 12 troy oz, or the equivalent of $14\frac{1}{4}$oz avoirdupois. At one time bread was weighed by the troy system. But that is another story. It is explained in the chapter on the Assize of Bread.

Table of solid and liquid measures

Imperial or avoirdupois		U.S.	Metric	Rounded to most convenient 10 grams	
			1 g	1 millilitre	
⅙ oz	1 teaspoon	1 teaspoon	5 g		
¼ oz			7 g	1 centilitre	10 g
½ oz	1 scant tablespoon	1 tablespoon	14 g		15 g
1 oz			28 g		30 g
2 oz			56 g		60 g
3 oz			84 g		85 g
3½ oz			98 g	1 decilitre	100 g
4 oz	¼ lb	½ cup liquid	110 g		120 g
5 oz	¼ pint (1 gill)				
		1 cup flour	140 g		150 g
6 oz			168 g		170 g
7 oz			196 g		200 g
8 oz	½ lb	1 cup liquid	224 g		225 g
9 oz			252 g	¼ kg/litre	250 g
10 oz	½ pint	2 cups flour	280 g		280 g
11 oz			308 g		310 g
12 oz	¾ lb		336 g		340 g
13 oz			364 g		365 g
14 oz			392 g		400 g
15 oz	¾ pint		420 g		420 g
16 oz	1 lb	1 pint / 2 cups liquid	448 g		450 g
17 oz			476 g		475 g
18 oz			504 g	½ kg/litre	500 g
19 oz			532 g		530 g
20 oz	1 pint, 1¼ lb	4 cups flour	560 g		550 g
24 oz	1½ lb		672 g		675 g
25 oz	1¼ pints		700 g		700 g
27 oz			756 g	¾ kg/litre	750 g
28 oz	1¾ lb		784 g		780 g
30 oz	1½ pints		840 g		840 g
32 oz	2 lb	1 quart	896 g		900 g
35 oz	1¾ pints		980 g		980 g
35½ oz			994 g	1 kg/litre	1,000 g
36 oz	2¼ lb		1,008 g		1,000 g
40 oz	2 pints or 1 quart		1,120 g		1,120 g

LINEAR MEASUREMENTS

Recipes in this book do not call for any great range of sizes in the way of bread and cake pans, tart tins, and fancy moulds; dimensions and capacity of those specified require no very complex transposition from inches to centimetres, so a brief conversion table should provide an adequate guide.

For those setting out to buy new equipment it is worth noting that French and other European manufacturers reckon sizes of frying pans, saucepans and cake moulds by the *top* measurement, saucepans also by capacity. A litre saucepan of straightforward pattern, for example, always measures 14 cm or $5\frac{1}{2}$ ins across the top, and the next size up, 16 cm or $6\frac{1}{2}$ ins, holds 1·5 litres, the equivalent of just on 3 pints. Omelette and pancake pans are sold by size. The 18 cm size, a good one for yeast-leavened pancakes, measures 7 inches at the top, 5 ins at the base; if you want to make slightly larger pancakes then buy a 20 cm pan, which is also the best size for a two-egg omelette.

Table of linear measurements

Metric (cm)		English (ins)
2·5		1
5		2
15·5		6
18		7
20·5		8
23		9
25·5		10
28		11
30·5	(1 foot)	12
91·5	(1 yard)	36
100	(1 metre)	39·5

THE OLD DRY MEASURES FOR FLOUR AND GRAIN

In the following table the dry measures shown are those habitually used by English bakers, millers and flour merchants during the past 150 years. Some of them are of much older usage, dating back to the original Assize Laws of 1266. Mention of dry measures occurs often in quoted passages and occasionally in recipes in this book. A bushel, it should be understood, varied in weight according to whether it was a heaped measure or a stricken one. The rules for the former were that the grain or flour was to be heaped in the form of a cone at least 6 inches above the rim of the bushel measure. For a stricken measure the goods were

A household flour or grain measure, turned wood.

levelled off or struck with a round stick, straight and of the same diameter from end to end. A bushel measure, according to the 1826 Act, was to contain 80 lb avoirdupois weight of water; it was to be 'round, made with a plain and even bottom', and a diameter of $19\frac{1}{2}$ inches 'from outside to outside'.

It should be noted that the average weight of 60 lb of wheat to the bushel applied only to home-grown grain. According to James Grant, author of *The Chemistry of Breadmaking* (1912), some of the bread wheats we were at that time importing from Europe weighed up to 67 lb per bushel.

Table of old dry measures for flour and grain

Flour measures		Weight (avoirdupois)	Average yield in bread (19th century) (avoirdupois)
1 pint	=	14 oz	1 lb 2 oz
1 quart or half-quartern	=	1 lb 12 oz	2 lb 3 oz
1 quartern or half-gallon	=	3 lb 8 oz	4 lb 6 oz
1 gallon, half-peck or half-stone	=	7 lb	8 lb 12 oz
1 peck or stone	=	14 lb	17 lb 8 oz
2 pecks or half-bushel	=	28 lb	35 lb
4 pecks or 1 bushel	=	56 lb	70 lb
1 bag	=	140 lb	175 lb
1 barrel (U.S. and Australian measure)	=	196 lb	—
1 sack	=	280 lb	350 lb
1 sack Midlands measure	=	200 lb	—

Grain measures

1 Winchester bushel	=	60 lb
1 London bushel	=	56 lb
1 quarter, wheat	=	480 lb (or 8 Winchester bushels)
1 coomb or comb, wheat	=	240 lb (or 4 Winchester bushels)
1 coomb or comb, barley	=	224 lb
1 coomb or comb, oats	=	148 lb

DOUGH TEMPERATURES

In breadmaking certain temperatures, other than those of the oven, are important to the successful performance of the yeast and the fermentation of the dough. That is to say that they are important to professional bakers, and even if the majority of household breadmakers prefer not to be bothered with them, relying on their experience, instinct, common-sense rather than on thermometers, it is nevertheless useful to know what those temperatures are. The following conversion table shows those that are crucial.

Table of dough temperatures

Degrees Fahrenheit		*Degrees Celsius*
32	Freezing point	0
40	Temperature for refrigerated storage of yeast	4
50 ⎱	Cold or cool room temperature	⎰ 10
60 ⎰	for slow fermentation of dough	⎱ 15
70 ⎱	Surrounding or room temperature	⎰ 21
75 ⎰	for normal fermentation of dough	⎱ 23·5
76 ⎫		⎧ 24
78 ⎪		26
80 ⎬	Temperature of dough during fermentation	27
82 ⎪		28
90 ⎭		⎩ 32
98·4	(Blood heat)	⎧ 37
100 ⎫		38
105 ⎬	Temperatures for doughing liquid	41
108 ⎭		⎩ 43
130	Yeast is killed	54
212	Approximate *interior* temperature of loaf when drawn from the oven	100

OVEN TEMPERATURES

Oven temperatures specified in recipes are those registered in the centre of the oven, and to which the oven should be heated. In most domestic ovens temperatures are higher at the top and lower at the bottom. According, therefore, to whether the baking of a loaf, a pizza, a brioche, a spice cake is carried out below or above the centre shelf of the oven the *actual* temperature may differ by several degrees from that given. Occasionally, when the discrepancy is very marked I have noted the point in the recipe.

Whatever the claims made by cooker manufacturers and fuel boards, even the most inexperienced of cooks will appreciate that vagaries and

idiosyncrasies of domestic ovens must be allowed for, temperature
tables be taken as approximate, and temperatures specified in recipes
regarded as for guidance.

Table of equivalent oven temperatures

Solid fuel	Electricity		Gas
Very slow⎤	230°F	110°C	¼
Very slow ⎬	265°F	130°C	½
Very slow⎦	285°F	140°C	1
Moderate⎤	300°F	150°C	2
Moderate	320°F	160°C	2½
Moderate	330°F	170°C	3
Moderate⎦	350°F	180°C	4
Fairly hot⎤	375°F	190°C	5
Fairly hot⎦	400°F	205°C	6
Hot	425°F	220°C	7
Very hot⎤	450°F	230°C	8
Very hot⎦	465°F	240°C	9

Weighing and Measuring Equipment

For bread doughs, cakes and any kind of pastry accurate quantities and the proper proportions of ingredients are important. Reliable scales and a measuring jug of not less than 2-pint/1-litre capacity, and marked in ounces and grams, are necessities.

SCALES AND JUGS

I prefer old fashioned scales with weights and a capacious weighing tray for the ingredients. This type of weighing scale is very finely balanced; it is accurate, and treated with care will remain so for a lifetime. Disadvantages, apart from the high cost, are its weight and the space it occupies.

Among cheaper and lighter alternatives the choice is wide. One that I have used and found reliable is an ingeniously designed version of the spring-balance kitchen scale, made by Salter. This has a 4 pint/2 litre capacity plastic weighing bowl deep enough to double as a mixing bowl, and a switching device which enables you to return the mechanism to zero after each ingredient has been weighed. Grams and ounces, pounds and kilograms are clearly marked, and the scales will weigh from ½ oz/15 grams up to 5 lb/2·5 kilograms. Like all scales, these will repay careful handling. The balance is delicate. Rough treatment or overloading may well disrupt it.

Since spring-balance kitchen scales are rarely calibrated to weigh under ½ oz – on the Salter half ounces are not marked so it's more guess work than accurate – if you often need to weigh small amounts it is quite a good idea to have a letter scale. I have found mine very handy, especially for spices as well as for small quantities of yeast. Modern spring-balance letter scales, marked, of course, in grams and ounces,

Scales and weights, flour scoop, measuring jug, cup for yeast. In front of the big bowl is a stainless steel utensil for scraping up the dough on the kneading table or board. It's also useful for dividing or cutting dough.

are cheap, and are to be found at stationers and office supply shops such as W. H. Smith and Ryman.

Our measuring jugs are inadequate, too small and too vague. A half-pint measure seems useless to me, and measures marked on the outside, like the popular and cheap Pyrex glass jugs, don't give accurate readings for small quantities. Enamelled jugs get chipped. Plastic jugs are hideous, they don't last, and they are not accurate. That leaves stainless steel. These are expensive, they are reasonably well marked, and they are durable. The only commonly available one in this country is also ungainly, the handle uncomfortable to hold. So it really is a question of how reliable, convenient and accurate you require your measure to be, and of whether or not you mind it being unprepossessing. An unsatisfactory choice. Why doesn't someone design and market a range of measuring jugs, and for that matter spoons and cups for U.S. measures, in laboratory glass? Measuring glasses and beakers in this tough, fine, very clear glass do already exist of course, but for laboratory use are made without handles, obviously unsatisfactory for domestic use. What is wanted is something in the manner of Melitta glass coffee jugs.

There is, it should be said, a perfectly simple, and up to a point satisfactory, alternative to a measuring jug for the water and/or milk used in dough mixing. This is to weigh it. In English measurements a pint of water weighs $1\frac{1}{4}$ lb or 20 oz, in U.S. terms a pint, or 2 cups, of water weighs 16 oz, and in metric terms a half litre is 500 grams in weight. Bakers habitually weigh rather than measure the liquor for their dough, and in their recipes it is always expressed in weight rather than in volume. The method is held to be the more accurate one.

The Salter scale described above, with its capacious bowl, makes it less trouble to weigh the water than to measure it, and there is now a similar scale with a Pyrex glass bowl – of smaller capacity – on the market.

Notes: 1. Chemists' measuring glasses are useful and accurate for measuring liquid ingredients in small amounts.

2. If you use scales with weights it is a good idea to keep the smaller weights, so easily mislaid, in a separate container. Always, always, put them away as soon as your ingredients are weighed: although it is easier now to buy spare weights than it was before the days of kitchen shops, there are often delays in delivery from the manufacturers, and it is maddening to be left without a crucial ounce or half-ounce weight.

3. When weighing small amounts see that both weight and ingredients are in the *centre* of their respective trays or weighing surfaces.

MEASURING SPOONS

Throughout this book I have used American tablespoons and teaspoons for measuring small quantities of both dry and liquid ingredients. Their capacity is slightly less than that of the old standard English equivalents, but virtually identical with the new ones approved by the Metrication Board. These hold 15, 10, 5 and 2·5 millilitres or grams respectively. I have found that a modern English soup spoon of a common pattern has precisely the same capacity as the U.S. standard tablespoon, i.e. $\frac{1}{2}$ fluid oz or 14 grams, or millilitres as the Metrication Board has decreed that fluid grams are to be called. To me, and to any cook accustomed to the metric system, grams remain grams whether liquid or solid.

For dry ingredients all measurements are *level* unless otherwise specified. Note that the teaspoon is the one marked 5 ml.

THERMOMETERS

Some people find cooking thermometers an unnecessary nuisance, others consider them indispensable. I am a convert to the latter school, particularly where yeast doughs are concerned. I have a room thermometer in my kitchen and among others two oven thermometers (for comparison of temperatures in different parts of the oven) and a dough thermometer. This latter little piece of equipment I use just as often for testing the temperature of the water or milk used to make up my dough as for its specific purpose, which is for it to be thrust into the made-up dough to ascertain the temperature at which it is fermenting, and to the baker this is the vital point. For domestic breadmaking, I find that on the whole it is sound enough to get the temperature of the water right, without fussing too much about the fermenting temperature of the dough.

The dough thermometer I use is a simple spirit one, the kind used by bakery students, about three times as thick as an ordinary clinical thermometer, and registering from 10°F to 120°F. For testing the temperature of dough-mixing liquid I find it much more satisfactory than the so-called Universal thermometer sold in kitchen shops, because it is both easier to read and to handle, particularly for small quantities. Like a clinical thermometer it has a neat little case and is easy to clean and to store. I keep mine safely stowed away in an ancient pencil box in a corner where it is always accessible.

Dough thermometers such as the one I use are made by the famous English firm of Brannan, and are to be found at establishments supplying equipment to the baking trade and to technical college students. The one I go to is Mathews at 214 Borough High Street, London SE1. For local sources look in the classified yellow pages of the telephone directory.

Some people use an ordinary clinical mercury thermometer for testing dough and water temperatures. If you choose to do this, remember that they are fragile, and if you leave one thrust into the dough it will probably get submerged as the dough rises, so don't forget it's there before you start the breaking down and kneading process, or you may have to throw away the whole batch.

Oven thermometers, also made by Brannan, can usually be bought in kitchenware departments of large stores and in kitchen shops. There are two variations, one which stands on the shelf, and one which hangs on its edge. On the whole I find the latter the more satisfactory, since it is easier to see and you don't have to move it to take a reading.

The Cost of Baking Your Own Bread

'Without wishing in the slightest degree to disparage the skill and labour of bread-makers by trade, truth compels us to assert our conviction of the superior wholesomeness of bread made in our own homes.'

Eliza Acton, *Modern Cookery*, 1855 edn

When it comes to buying special flours for bread the price may seem high in relation to that of the bought loaf. Although valid comparisons are almost impossible, it is quite useful to make an assessment on a weight for weight basis, of how much flour goes to make up the loaf you bake yourself, what that loaf weighs, and what you pay for one of equal weight at the bakery or in the supermarket.

A pound of flour makes about 1 lb 6 oz of bread, the water used to make up the dough adding an average of half as much again to the weight of the flour. Some of the water is driven off during baking, and there are small amounts of other ingredients – salt, fat – to add to the total weight.

The easiest calculation goes like this: 1¼lb or 20oz of flour (4 cups U.S.) plus 10 to 12oz of water and, say, 1½oz of extra ingredients make 34oz or 2lb 2oz of dough. When baked this yields a loaf weighing a minimum of 1¾lb or 28oz, which is also the present legal weight of the bakers' large loaf. (I have made many checks on the weights of my dough and baked loaves and find that they vary surprisingly little.)

To compare the basic cost of home-baked bread with the retail price of the shop product it would be necessary to make the calculations in large quantity. As a guide, in a small-scale bakery it is reckoned that the average yield from a 280lb sack of high-gluten flour is 220 to 224 large loaves. This adds up to 380 to 390 lb of bread. In the factories the yield is higher and so is the ratio of water to flour; then there is all the gubbins in the way of improvers for the dough, for the crumb, for the crust, there is fat in the form of hardened vegetable oils, a very high proportion of yeast and a low one of salt. Factory bread doesn't have very much crust because that would upset the slicing machine, and it retains more moisture than a home-made loaf or a bakery one. So the bread factories are charging for quite a lot of water, but then at home, baking in small batches, we have the high cost of oven fuel to add to the price of our bread, and our time and labour, in all probability unpaid. We used to benefit slightly from the flour subsidy (withdrawn in May 1977) but not of course from the one still paid to the bakers. In 1976 the latter worked out at $1\frac{1}{2}$ p per 28 oz loaf, or £50.5 million for the whole year.

'O.K., I'll try anything once.'
Drawing by Alan Dunn; *c.* 1972, The New Yorker Magazine, Inc.

All in all, it could quite easily be proved that home-made bread does in the long run work out more cheaply than bought bread (no doubt you could equally well prove the contrary should you be so minded), especially when flour is bought in bulk and several loaves baked in one session, and the deep freeze has made that feasible even for relatively small households. Out of a stone or 14 lb of flour, for example, the yield should be eleven large loaves, and I think it very relevant to bear in mind that it is rare for home-made bread to be wasted, whereas a

Approximate composition of flour used in breadmaking (at 15 per cent moisture content)

Flour	Assumed Extraction rate %	Protein %	Fat %	Carbohydrate %	Crude Fibre %	Dietary Fibre	Ash %
Wholemeal	100	12·0	2·4	64·3	2·0	11·2	1·5
Brown	85–90	11·8	1·6	68·5	1·09	7·87	1·37*
White	72	11·3	1·0	71·5	0·12	3·15	0·66*
Wholemeal (from all-British wheat)	100	8·9	2·2	67·0	1·8	11·2	1·5

Ca = Calcium
Fe = Iron
Na = Sodium
K = Potassium
Mg = Magnesium

Cu = Copper
P = Phosphorus
Cl = Chlorine
Mn = Manganese

very large proportion of bought bread ends up in the dustbin because it is not valued or in any way respected.

So much for price comparisons. Long before you've finished doing the sums you realize that what counts is the value of decent bread to you and to the people you are responsible for feeding, and what that is, it's up to us to work out for ourselves.

Personally, I find it difficult not to come to the conclusion that, given the appropriate flour, the bread we bake at home is likely to be more satisfactory from a nutritional point of view, more honest and better value for money as well as much more interesting in flavour than nearly all bread bought from the bakery and the supermarket. Necessarily

Fe mg/100 g	Thiamine mg/100 g	Nicotinic Acid mg/100 g	Riboflavin mg/100 g	Na mg/100 g	K mg/100 g	Mg mg/100 g	Ca mg/100 g	P mg/100 g	Cl mg/100 g	Mn mg/100 g
·5	0·40	5·5	0·12	3·3	329	129	0·625	345	37	3·4
·6	0·42	4·2	0·06	4·0	280	110	0·35	270	45	2·5
·2‡	0·31‡	2·0‡	0·03	3·0	130	36	0·22	130	62	0·8
·0	0·29	4·8	0·12	3·4	361	106	0·65	340	35	2·8

The addition of chalk at the rate of 235–390 mg/100 g is compulsory to all flours except wholemeal.

* Including 0·24 per cent derived from added chalk.

† Including 125 mg/100 g derived from added chalk.

‡ Part of the iron, thiamine and nicotinic acid is derived from added nutrients.

Issued by The Flour Advisory Bureau.

excluded from this comparison are the guaranteed 100 per cent wholemeal breads from wholefood shops and bakeries, which are undoubtedly as wholesome as can be. That the bread is often heavy, brick-like and generally lacking in appeal seems to be irrelevant to the customers, who perhaps buy it in the belief that it constitutes of itself a passport to good health.

Those who bake their own bread from 100 per cent wholewheat flour don't get any nutritional benefit which they wouldn't find in the equivalent loaf from the wholefood shop, but with a little practice they will surely be able to produce something rather more attractive and probably cheaper. Here, though, price comparison is more difficult than with ordinary commercial bread. According to the present bread regulations, wholemeal loaves come into a miscellaneous category which includes milk bread and various proprietary and diet breads; the maximum permitted price of a large wholemeal or milk loaf is at present (1977) 6p more than that of the cheapest 28 oz standard white wrapped loaf and the 14 oz loaves are priced *pro rata*, but if the baker concerned chooses not to claim the subsidy he can charge what he pleases, which accounts for a good deal of confusion and discrepancy in the price of wholemeal bread sold in wholefood shops. The smaller 8 to 10 oz loaves come into a category to which the bread subsidy does not in any case apply – they are outside the legally required 14 oz unit weight – and the price in a wholefood bakery or shop would be only ½p less than that of the 14 oz loaf. To counteract this anomaly, the bakers very naturally restrict the smaller sizes to the making of their own specialities, such as fruit, malt, nut, honey and other such breads for which they can charge accordingly. Prices of 100 per cent wholewheat flours and meals packed for household baking vary a good deal, so do their quality, but roughly you need 10 oz of meal to make a loaf weighing 14 oz.

As far as the food value of bread flours is concerned, the table on pp. 248–9 should help to show the differences in content between low-

The hog and wheatsheaf.

Design by Eric Gill for paper bags for the Hampshire House Bakery, Hammersmith; wood-engraving, 1915. Reproduced by permission of the Victoria and Albert Museum.

extraction white flour with its obligatory reinforcements and 100 per cent wholewheat flour from which nothing has been extracted and to which, if for retail sale to the public, nothing has been added.[1] In between are the intermediary grades of extraction.

Here I think it only right to note that to me, and I think to many people, variety and change in the matter of daily bread are as important as its nutritional content. If you bake your own, using different flours and meals in varying ways, it helps towards the very important understanding of the properties, the performance and character of each one, so in the long run variety makes for great improvements in the quality of the bread you bake. Or so I have found.

1. For wholewheat flour as used by commercial bakers see the chapter on meals and flours.

Part II: Recipes

A tall earthenware pancheon, glazed only on the inside, like a bread crock, was always considered the best shape for mixing and raising yeast dough. From the eighteenth century until the mid twentieth bread pancheons were traditional products of many English and Welsh potteries. This one came from Wales.

Bread

'In the Old Book it sais the Cook must bake her bread in the morning time enough for breakfast. She should bake Wednesdays and Saturdays, clean her Larder and Pantries Mondays and Fridays, and rise Tuesday to wash her own things, Thursday morning wipe her pewter or do any other early job.'

The Housekeeping Book of Susanna Whatman 1776–1800, ed. Thomas Balston, 1956

THEN WHAT ON EARTH DO THEY DO TO THE BREAD IN THE SHOPS?

'Many a bit of country lore I picked up from Emma. One of these described the ideal wife:

> She could make, she could bake,
> She could brew, she could sew,
> And found time to teach her three sons to say "No".

Brewing was out of my scope, and so were the three sons at the moment, but what about baking? I determined to have a try at this. My cookery book was discouraging, making it seem that to cook a loaf of bread was like carrying out some chemical experiment, referring to weights (I possessed no scales) and even to Fahrenheit. So I harked back to my recollections of having seen it done scores of times in Cornwall and Wales without having paid attention to the actual details. I remembered how often mother used to send me out when I was a little child to buy a pennyworth of yeast at the baker's, for her saffron cake. So I sent Emma out on a like errand. She had never made bread, but recalled a saying of her mother's – "All that bread wants is time and warmth." I started in with some flour; the yeast and the oven did their work; and with beginner's luck I produced some lovely rolls. These were placed on the table within reach of Arthur at dinner.

'"Good roll, this," said he, trying one. "Where do you get them? A new baker?"

'"Yes," said I, as casually as my bursting pride would allow me, "I made them myself."

'"Do you mean to tell me," he exclaimed, "that this thing is only flour and water?" Holding it up in amazement, he added, "Then what on earth do they do to the bread in the shops?"

'To this day I have never gone back from that exciting discovery, and except in emergencies have produced my own bread for over thirty years, the family strongly objecting to "boughten" bread. People dislike the idea of trying this for themselves because of the "time it takes". The bread certainly wants time, I assure them, but not *their* time; it doesn't ask to be watched, and can be trusted alone in the house; the actual labour in making a batch takes about six minutes from start to finish. But they shake their heads in a melancholy way as they ask for another slice.'

M. Vivian Hughes, *A London Home in the Nineties*, 1937
(Part 3 of *A London Family 1870–1900*, 1946)

· A BASIC LOAF ·

This basic recipe is for one large loaf weighing 28 to 30 oz or 800 to 850 g. It is made with 81 per cent or 85 per cent wheatmeal, i.e. flour from which 15 to 19 per cent of the grain has been extracted by the milling process but which retains the germ of the wheat and hence the most vital part of its flavour, plus the germ oil and vitamins. A percentage of the bran also remains. An alternative to the wheatmeal is a mixture of one part 100 per cent wholemeal and two parts strong plain white flour – or if you prefer it, all strong white.

The tin should be of the size known as a 2 lb loaf tin, 4 to $4\frac{1}{2}$ inches in depth with a capacity of 3 to $3\frac{1}{2}$ pints.

Ingredients are 20 oz of wheatmeal or 16 oz of strong plain unbleached white flour and 4 oz of 100 per cent wholemeal, $\frac{1}{2}$ oz of bakers' compressed yeast or $\frac{1}{4}$ oz of dried yeast, $\frac{3}{4}$ oz of rock salt or sea salt, approximately 12 oz of water at blood heat, and oil or fat for the tin.

Equivalent metric quantities: wheatmeal 550 g, or strong plain unbleached flour 450 g and 100 per cent wholemeal 120 g, bakers' compressed yeast 15 g or dried yeast 10 g, rock salt or sea salt 20 g, water at blood heat approximately 340 g, oil or fat for the tin. Tin size : a kilo loaf tin 8 cm in depth with a capacity of 1·5 to 2 litres.

Put the flour and salt into a bowl, mix well, cover the bowl with a heat resistant plate or dish, and put it in a *very* low oven for about 5 to 7 minutes so that the flour is warmed. But not too much so.

In the meantime, put the yeast in a cup, pour enough tepid water over to just cover it. By the time the flour is warmed the yeast will be soft

enough to mix to a cream. If you are using dried yeast you can add a pinch of sugar to the warm water, although with modern yeasts sugar is not necessary. Give the yeast a good 10 minutes to return to active life.

Pour the creamed yeast into the centre of the flour. Add some of the tepid water and stir it round with the yeast, using a wooden spoon. Now pour in the rest of the water and mix the dough with your hands. If it is too sticky and wet to work, sprinkle in more flour, until you feel that the dough is becoming lithe and elastic. Work it for a minute or two, until it comes away easily from the sides of the bowl. Form it into a ball, sprinkle it with flour. Cover the bowl with a sheet of polythene and the dish or plate, which should have been left warming in the oven. By this means both the bowl and the cover are warm, the dough itself generates its own warmth as the yeast works, and unless the weather is very cold it should not be necessary to find a special warm place to leave the dough to rise. If you have no suitable cover for the bowl, use just the sheet of polythene, which helps to generate the damp steamy atmosphere propitious to the dough. To envelop the whole bowl in a polythene bag, as is so often advised nowadays, is an unnecessary and clumsy method. And if you have young children please don't leave large polythene bags lying about. They are dangerous.

In $1\frac{1}{2}$ to 2 hours the dough will have expanded to more than twice its original volume. It will look puffy and spongy. Break it down by giving it a good punch with your fist. Then gather it up and slap it down hard in the bowl several times. Sprinkle it with flour and knead it by pushing it out and then folding it over on itself in a roughly three-cornered fashion; then repeat the process two or three times. The punching down and kneading, or knocking back as it is also called, redistributes the gas bubbles produced by the yeast, helps the gluten to develop and reinvigorates the yeast so that it will renew its work and form new air balloons. With such a small amount of dough, the knocking back and kneading process takes only 3 or 4 minutes. A larger batch obviously takes longer and is harder work, which can be done, if you like, with the dough hook of an electric mixer.

Have ready the warmed tin, greased with a little oil or fat.

Shape the dough, so that the folds are underneath, and put it into the tin. At this stage the amount of dough looks totally inadequate for the size of the tin. But cover it with a sheet of polythene or a damp cloth and leave it in a warm place. Almost immediately it will start coming back to life, and in about 45 minutes – sometimes less, sometimes more – it will have risen to the top of the tin. If the dough has been well kneaded, the second proving is usually quicker, and the volume achieved greater, than in the initial rising.

Bake the loaf in the centre of a good hot oven, 425° to 450°F, 220° to 230°C, gas nos. 7 to 8, for the first 15 minutes, reducing the heat to 400°F, 205°C, gas no. 6 for the next 15. Shake the loaf from the tin, return it, on its side, to the oven, now reduced to about 350°F, 180°C, gas no. 4, and leave it for a final 15 to 20 minutes. When it is sufficiently baked the loaf gives out a resonant sound when you tap the sides and the bottom crust with your knuckles.

Leave it to cool on a rack, or lying across the empty tin. Bread should never be put away until it has cooled completely. As soon as it is wrapped or is put into a crock, the crust goes soft, so if I am baking bread in the evening, say for lunch the following day, I leave it uncovered overnight and until it is time to cut it. In this way the crust still retains some crispness.

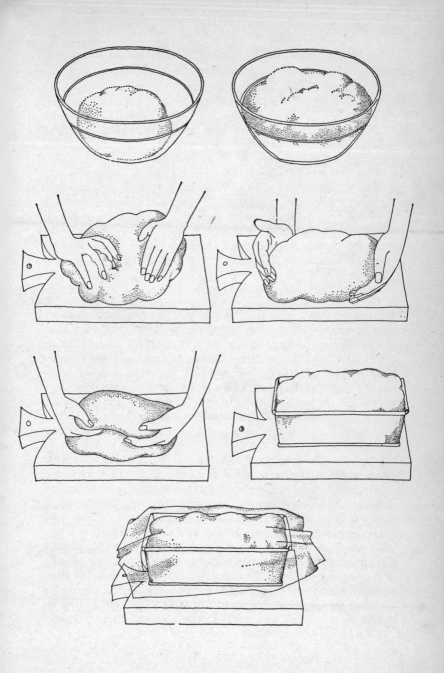

This type of bread is not good until it is quite cold, and in fact does not develop its full flavour until the day after it is baked.

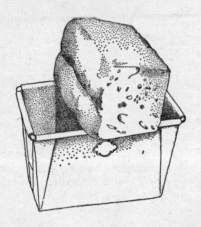

Notes: 1. In cold weather it will probably be necessary to find a warm place in which the dough can be left to rise. Don't overdo the heat, though. A temperature of 70°F or 21°C is quite high enough, 85° to 90°F or 30° to 32°C is as hot as the dough will take. Preferably the warmth should *surround* the bowl of dough. If it comes from one direction only, say from underneath via a radiator or from one side as from an open fire, the dough will start to cook at the bottom or side of the bowl, so that when you come to knead it, there will be hard lumps which will spoil the bread. A warm steamy bathroom is a good place for raising dough.

2. Anyone who is prepared to wait will find that in due course the dough ferments at a room temperature of 64° to 70°F or 18° to 21°C, and the resulting bread will be the better for the unhurried rising or proving process. It's really a question of arranging matters so that the dough suits *your* timetable, rather than the other way round.

Having given the dough a good start by warming the flour, mixing it with warm water, and covering it with a warm plate or dish, you can leave it overnight on the kitchen table, break it down and knead it early in the morning, put it into the warmed tin to prove for the second time, and bake it as soon as it has risen to the top of the tin. Or, after a very thorough kneading, the dough can be put back into the bowl for its second proving – until, say, midday. This time it will rise noticeably more than during the first proving period. Now you give it another kneading, mould it and let it prove for a third time in the tin. With each rising the dough improves in texture and is easier to handle. When it happens to suit me, this is the method I prefer. I find it produces the best bread, with a beautiful matured flavour and a good open texture. Incidentally, using the slow method, the amount of yeast can – in fact should – be halved. See note 4.

3. To make crusty loaves, that is any loaf baked without benefit of a confining mould or tin and therefore with an all-round crust, see the recipes for Coburg, bloomer and muffin loaves. To make quickly risen and baked bread see the method for baps and also the recipe for short-time dough.

4. When increasing the quantities of flour to make a batch of several loaves at a time, it is a mistake to increase the amount of yeast in the same proportion. It is indeed always a mistake to use more yeast than is strictly needed; 1 oz of bakers' yeast is ample for aerating up to $4\frac{1}{2}$ lb of flour over two 1-hour rising or proving periods; if the dough were to be left overnight it would be enough for 7 lb. Very often I make my dough with 40 oz of flour, $1\frac{1}{2}$ oz of salt and only $\frac{1}{3}$ oz of yeast. This is an overnight dough, given two rising periods and a final proving in the tins. It makes excellent bread which keeps uncommonly well – as always, the less yeast used the moister the loaf remains.

When baking with dried yeast, nearly everybody uses too much, the result being rather dry and uninteresting bread. Hence, I think, the prejudice against dried yeast among those who have been accustomed to bakers' yeast. Leaving the dough overnight I find that for 20 to 34 oz of flour *one teaspoon* of dried yeast is enough.

5. In my bread recipe there is a generous proportion of salt. For some people it may be a little too much, and the amount can be reduced to $\frac{1}{2}$ oz for 20 to 24 oz of flour. Less than that makes insipid bread. At the same time it must be remembered that too much salt inhibits the action of the yeast, makes for a tough crust, and won't in the least help the flavour of the bread, which should come from a combination of good flour or meal, yeast and salt in proper proportion, and unhurried fermentation.

If you have salt in coarse crystals rather than fine rock salt, put them into your measuring jug, pour a small quantity of hot water over them and leave them to dissolve before adding the rest of the warm water for mixing the dough. Coarse salt added directly to the flour will remain undissolved in the dough, like ice particles in an ice cream.

If you cannot easily buy pure sea salt or rock salt,[1] then use ordinary free-running salt. Although pure salt is always preferable, it is simply not worth paying the exorbitant prices asked for it in kitchen shops and fancy provision stores.

In the separate chapters on salt and yeast will be found more detail concerning the proportions of these ingredients in relation to rising or fermentation times, to the amount of flour used and to the temperature at which the dough is fermented.

6. The addition of a little fat to bread dough makes a moister and longer-keeping loaf. The proportion used should be very small, no more than just over $\frac{1}{2}$oz to 1 lb of flour. (Too much fat makes bread with a rather close crumb.) By far the best fat for the purpose is butter, which also helps to produce a silky crust of a fine golden colour. An equivalent proportion of thick cream serves much the same purpose. A tablespoon or two of light olive oil is another alternative and to my mind a much better one than the more commonly used lard.

When a dough is left to rise for a long period, as in the overnight system, it's a good idea to brush the top with oil, to prevent the formation of a crust or hard skin on the dough.

7. Milk is another good enriching ingredient for dough. But use it in moderation. Too much makes for a rather crumbly loaf.

Used half and half with water, or in the smaller proportion of one to two, milk goes into soft breads such as baps and into the dough for white rolls, and is important because when baked in a small domestic oven, the crusts of small loaves or rolls made from dough mixed with water only bake too hard; the milk prevents this.

8. A steamy oven is propitious to bread, particularly to the crust. For this reason some writers advocate that a tin of water be put on the lower shelf while the bread is baking. I have not found the system particularly helpful and have abandoned it. To be efficacious, the steam should be at very high pressure, injected into the oven in a fierce burst during the first few minutes of baking. Once the crust is formed the steam is withdrawn and the bread finishes baking in dry heat. In an ordinary domestic oven these conditions cannot be fulfilled, so the crust on home-made loaves is rarely as thin and crackly as it is on bread from an old-fashioned family bakery. When a batch of several loaves are baked at one time, however, a certain amount of steam is generated by the damp dough itself when the loaves go into the oven. This can be increased by the

1. Cheshire rock salt from Ingram Thompson of Liverpool is the one to go for.

spraying of water into cuts or slashes made in the crust, as explained in the next few paragraphs on how to make these cuts. It has to be remembered though that the cutting only works as it should on well-matured dough.

9. For bread made entirely with 100 per cent wholemeal the long-maturing method and the hard kneading are not suitable, particularly if the meal to be used is milled entirely from home-grown soft wheat. Several recipes for 100 per cent wholemeal loaves are given further on in this chapter, and others in the chapter on soda breads.

· THE CUTS ON THE CRUST ·

Cutting or slashing the surface of a loaf so that the dough underneath bursts open, and during baking pushes up to form a kind of secondary crust of varying colour and texture, gives certain loaves their characteristic and traditional appearance. The knack of slashing the dough needs practice. It needs also some experience with the feel of the dough itself.

For Coburgs, bloomers and other crusty loaves the cuts are made after full proof, in other words just before the loaves are set in the oven,

The cuts on a coburg are made in three strokes which open out the loaf during baking. This one opened out a bit too much.

whereas for pan or tin bread the cutting is more successful when done early on in the second proof stage. As the dough grows in the tin, the cuts spread with it.

For a split tin[1] one straight cut, the whole length of the loaf, is made about 10 minutes after the dough is shaped in the tin. It should be a deep cut, about half-way through the dough. But since dough takes diagonal cuts better than parallel ones, and the former make a nicer looking loaf,

1. See overleaf, and p. 198.

usually I make three slanting cuts, or when using a wide, squat, farm-house type of tin, three cuts each way, making a quadrille pattern. If the dough is at the right stage of maturity the cuts will open quickly, revealing the structure of the dough. By the time it has risen to the top of the tin and is ready to go into the oven, the cuts should be spread wide open. The dough should still feel springy and lively.

Instead of slashing a split tin loaf the dough can be put into the tin in two pieces which grow and merge as the loaf proves and bakes.

Some bakers, instead of cutting the dough for a split tin, mould it into two half loaves, as it were, placing these side by side in the tin. During proof the two pieces grow together but will still remain open at the top.

When cuts don't open, it is because the dough is too slack, or because it has been over-fermented, i.e. at too high a temperature for too long, or simply because it is not yet ready. By the time the dough is in the tins and you are waiting to get on with the baking, it's usually best to forget the cuts and bake the loaves plain when the dough reaches the tops of the tins. There is nothing wrong with a well risen, nicely domed plain top crust, and indeed that is how the majority of tin loaves are baked. The cutting simply opens up the dough and makes for a crustier crust, more of it, and a more varied texture. For times when it seems important to get the cuts to open properly, there *are* remedies to be applied to under-ripe and over-ripe dough. They are described in the recipe for a pan Coburg.

The long thick loaf we call a bloomer,[1] so similar to the French *bâtard*, is slashed diagonally after two rising periods, and just prior to baking, in evenly spaced deepish cuts. The cutting of round and pan Coburgs is described in the relevant recipes. There are many variations on the slashing of round loaves. One deep cut, straight across and slightly off

1. See the drawings of English loaves on p. 198.

centre, seems to have been traditional to the white loaf which appears over and over again in seventeenth-century Dutch, Flemish and French still-lifes. These loaves were, I think, the equivalents of our manchet bread of the same period, and the ancestors of our round dinner rolls which are still cut in the same way. Other, more complex, slashing is shown in the drawings of long French loaves and of a round *pain de campagne* on pp. 363 and 379. The chequerboard variation shown in the drawing is usually floured before the cuts are made. Once familiar in England, as well as in France, this was known as a college loaf – other

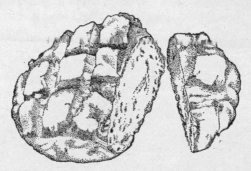

Chequerboard cuts give the maximum crust and plenty of variety. Eliza Acton called this a college loaf.

names for it were rumpy, underseller's Coburg and porcupine – and Eliza Acton describes the crust in detail in the passage quoted in the chapter on names and shapes of loaves. The petal cuts radiating from the centre of a loaf, as in the round *pain de campagne*, are easier to get right than the chequerboard cuts, which must not be made too deep, or the loaf becomes distorted in the baking.

English professional bakers don't use any special knife for making the cuts in their loaves. The French usually use razor blades of one kind or another. The essential is a sharp, short blade, say 4 inches or 5 inches for the average loaf. Use the knife decisively, making the cuts with firm clean strokes. Second thoughts are seldom successful. Once the dough has been cut it will show timid or wavering knife marks – provided, that is, that the cuts take at all – and the crust of the baked loaf will look like a map. And it is not much help at this stage in the life of the dough to attempt pressing and pulling and shoving it into a different shape. As French bakers say, '*le pain n'aime pas être tripoté*', bread dough doesn't like being messed around. What you can do to help the cuts to open out nicely as the loaf bakes is to spray them with water just before the bread is set in the oven. Even then it doesn't invariably work out, and tricks played by dough and crust are not confined to amateurs baking at home. Anyone who buys bread from an independent baker will have noticed that Coburgs and other crusty loaves are by no means always of uniform appearance and symmetry, some being better risen, more open and with a more enticing crust than their fellows. To the home baker this is a comforting sign that even an experienced professional is not always in complete control of his dough, which as one baker puts it when writing of the cottage loaf, sometimes elects to 'go on a journey of its own in the oven'.

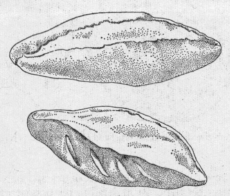

The cuts on two English Vienna-type loaves. The one with the single cut is simple to do. It used to be called a lemon loaf.

Notes: 1. If you have good kitchen scissors – to my mind as essential in any kitchen as sharp knives – they can often be used to very good effect for making the cuts in dough. For notching brioches and making cuts in any rolls, buns and so on, made from related soft, rich doughs, scissors are always a better implement than a knife.

2. The combined dough cutter and scraper shown in the drawing of the basic utensils for breadmaking (p. 242) is useful for dividing a batch of dough into loaf-size pieces and also for making very deep cross cuts on a round loaf. The alternative name of this utensil is the Scotch scraper. It is to be bought from bakery suppliers rather than from domestic kitchen shops.

· SHORT-TIME BREAD DOUGH ·

By increasing the proportion of yeast and adding a very small quantity of ascorbic acid as a dough-improver or maturing agent, fairly good bread can be made by the speeded-up or short-time method. It is a useful one to know.

Ascorbic acid can be bought from chemists, in tablet form. The proportion is only 25 mg to 1½ lb or 750 g of flour, so if possible buy it in 25 mg or 50 mg tablets. If you have to buy it in more concentrated form, such as 200 mg Redoxon tablets, it's quite easy to break off the appropriate fraction of the tablet.

To make two small loaves ingredients are 1½ lb of 81 or 85 per cent wheat-meal or strong plain white flour or a two-to-one mixture of white and 100 per cent wholemeal; 1 oz of fresh yeast; ½ oz of salt; one 25 mg tablet of ascorbic acid; approximately ¾ pint of water, or ½ pint of water mixed with ¼ pint of milk.

Equivalent metric quantities: flour 675 g, fresh yeast 30 g, salt 15 g ascorbic acid 25 mg (1 mg = ·0514 grain), water (or water and milk mixed) approximately 420 g. Tin size: two 0.5 kg tins.

Have the flour and salt ready warmed in a bowl. Put the yeast in a small bowl with a little warm water and the ascorbic acid. When this has dissolved mix the two to a cream. The water or water and milk for the dough should be at blood heat or a little over, say 100°F or 38°C. Make up the dough in the usual way. Mix and knead well. Cover the bowl, leave in a warm place (78° to 80°F, 26° to 27°C) for 10 to 15 minutes. This is the first rising, reduced from the usual 1½ or 2 hours to a fraction of that time.

Break down the dough. Knead it very thoroughly. This is important.

Divide and shape the dough into two loaves, put them into warmed greased 1 lb tins. If you wish make diagonal or cross cuts in the dough. Cover the tins, leave to rise for the second time. In about 45 minutes the dough will have sprung to the top of the tins.

Bake the loaves for 50 minutes at the usual temperatures, starting off at 450°F, 230°C, gas no. 8 for the first 15 minutes, reducing the heat at 15-minute intervals as for the basic loaf recipe on p. 256.

Notes: 1. Ascorbic acid is vitamin C. In breadmaking it is not used for its vitamin values, which are destroyed during baking, but for its work as an oxidizing agent and its resultant maturing effect on the dough. This is due to complex chemical interaction between the ascorbic acid and the components of the dough. They are explained, to those willing or able to grapple with the chemical terms of bread technology, in *The Short-Time Dough in Breadmaking*, a leaflet obtainable from the Flour Advisory Bureau, 21 Arlington Street, London SW1.

2. The short-time dough method outlined in the recipe given above is my own adaptation of the one suggested by the Flour Advisory Bureau. It produces quite good bread – provided that the flour or meal used is itself good, and the yeast fresh. What it lacks is that particular character, the savour, the scent, the bite, of bread made from dough slowly fermented with the minimum of yeast and a more generous allowance of salt. Although it is still superior to nearly all bought bread (most of which is made according to the commercial version of the same high-speed dough system), I would not myself want it as *daily* bread. And of course the high proportion of yeast adds quite a bit to the cost of making your own bread, or would if the method were used regularly rather than as an occasional expedient. It should, I think, be added that to some tastes a bland bread made from a rapidly matured dough is preferable to bread made from slowly developed, carefully ripened doughs, just as many people prefer or have become accustomed to anonymous immature Cheddar as opposed to the well-aged cheeses which have become a rare luxury sought after by people who like their food to have character.

3. Dried yeast, according to the Flour Advisory Bureau's leaflet, is not suitable for the short-time dough system. However, experiment by my American editor has shown that it works just as well as fresh yeast.

· WHOLEMEAL TIN BREAD ·

'Observe, brown bread is often recommended by medical men. When used as a matter of health, almost the only chance of succeeding, is by procuring the un-dressed meal, and making the bread at home. If bakers are applied to for brown bread they generally produce it by merely taking a portion of the regular dough, and sprinkling among it as much bran as will bring it to the colour required.'

Esther Copley, *The Complete Cottage Cookery*, 1849

Stone-ground 100 per cent wholemeal is in some ways – but only in some ways – simpler to deal with than white flour or finely ground brown flour from which the bran has been extracted. One hundred per cent wholemeal loaves to be baked in tins can be made with only one rising and very little kneading; the dough is improved by the addition of a small proportion of fat in the form of lard, butter, milk, fresh buttermilk or cream. Wholemeal loaves don't rise very much and require careful baking if they are not to be dry and brick-like, as those sold in health-food shops and wholefood restaurants so often are, or soggy and puddingy, as they will be if the dough is made too liquid, and since these wholemeals vary so enormously in the amount of liquid they will absorb it is virtually impossible to indicate the correct quantity of water to meal.

Given the erratic performance of wholemeals the following recipe is for guidance only, and given in quantities for one trial loaf to be baked in a 3 to 3½ pint tin, or for two smaller loaves.

1 lb 4 oz to 1 lb 6 oz of stone-ground 100 per cent wholemeal, ½ oz of yeast, ½ oz of salt, approximately ½ pint to 12 oz of water, 2 tablespoons[1] of buttermilk or thick cream or 4 of milk, fat for the tins, and extra meal for handling the dough.

Equivalent metric quantities: flour 550 to 600 g, yeast 15 g, salt 15 g, water approximately 280 to 340 g, 2 tablespoons of buttermilk or thick cream or 4 of milk, fat for the tins, extra meal for handling dough. Tin sizes: one tin of 1 litre capacity or two of 0.5 litre capacity.

First weigh out the flour. I find it best to start with the smaller quantity, keeping the extra 2 oz aside in case the dough turns out to be impossibly wet. Taking this precaution means that for next time one knows how much liquid to meal is needed. Warm the flour in its bowl for a few minutes in a very low oven, such as the simmering oven of a solid fuel cooker, or in the plate drawer of a gas or electric oven.

While the meal is warming – 5 to 7 minutes is ample – mix the cream or buttermilk, which in all probability will be ice cold from the refrigerator, with very warm water to make up a total of about 14 oz. Use a little of this to cream the yeast, then add the salt to the liquid. Grease or butter your warmed tin or tins. When the meal is warm to the touch, make a well in the centre, pour in the yeast, then about 10 oz of the warm liquid, and mix the dough with your hands. Add as much more liquid as will make the dough manageable. It must not be dry. If, on the contrary, it handles like a mud pie, as well as looking like one, dry it out a little with some of the extra meal, until you have a mixture which can be more

1. American tablespoons (½ fluid oz) and teaspoons (⅙ fluid oz) are used throughout. See chapter 'Weighing and Measuring Equipment', pp. 242–5.

easily handled. All that is necessary is to mix a fairly coherent dough which can be shaped and transferred to the tin or tins without difficulty.

Fill the warmed and greased tin or tins by about three-quarters, smooth the top surface of the dough as much as possible, cover with a damp cloth or a sheet of polythene and leave them in a really warm place until the dough has reached the tops of the tins. This should not take longer than 45 minutes – the dough, having been mixed with all ingredients well warmed, generates its own internal heat, which makes the yeast act well and quickly, even with an exceptionally coarse meal.

Have the oven ready heated, and bake the bread at 425° to 450°F, 220° to 230°C, gas nos. 7 to 8, for 15 to 20 minutes, then reduce the heat to 375°F, 190°C, gas no. 5, for another 15 to 20 minutes. By this time the loaf or loaves will have contracted and can be slipped out of the tins, but will not yet be quite cooked. Return them to the oven, upside down or on their sides, until they are ready, which is when the undersides are sufficiently baked to give out a hollow sound when tapped with the knuckles.

Leave them on their sides on a wire tray to cool, or balance them across the still warm empty tins, so that they are not subjected to a sudden draught of cold air.

Notes: 1. Although bread made from 100 per cent wholemeal rises very little in the oven and never looks spectacular it is most delicious, has a wonderfully sweet taste, and an irresistible smell of wheat – only, however, if the dough has been properly treated and correctly baked. It is, for example, a mistake to overdo the proportion of fat or cream. While a little is an improvement, too much will result in a crumbly loaf which will be difficult to cut. Overbaking and a hard crust, too stiff a dough and dry crumb are other very common faults in 100 per cent wholemeal bread. One way and another, it seems surprising that incorporated in so many published bread recipes one finds the claim that 100 per cent wholemeal bread is the easiest of all to make. To quote William Jago, author of several text books on breadmaking and its technology: 'As wholemeal contains the whole of the wheat berry, an analysis of the meal reveals a lower percentage of gluten and starch and a higher percentage of oil, mineral matter, fibre and protein. . . . Owing to its very unstable nature wholemeal should be fermented at as low a temperature as possible, and for a short time.'[1] Jago also advised that 'vigorous fermentation must be ensured by the employment of plenty of yeast'. Personally

1. *An Introduction to the Study of the Principles of Breadmaking*, 1889.

I don't find that an extra allowance of yeast makes any appreciable difference to the strength of the fermentation. Most people, however, do advocate an ounce of yeast to 1½ lb of wholemeal.

2. Anyone who finds it difficult to produce good bread from 100 per cent whole wheatmeal leavened with yeast may like to try chemically raised, or soda bread, which is very quick, easy and good, especially if mixed with buttermilk, as in the recipe given on p. 520.

3. For my 100 per cent stone-ground wholemeal bread I prefer to use the Irish meal milled from organically grown soft wheat of which details are given on p. 275. This particular wholemeal, which is more coarsely ground than most, and has a low gluten content, is stocked only by very few retailers in this country and, as already emphasized, meals vary so widely that the foregoing recipe will almost certainly need to be adjusted according to the meal you buy. Much depends upon whether it is milled from a blend of imported high-gluten and home-grown low-gluten wheats or whether it is an entirely home-grown product. The former gives more volume, the latter usually has a sweeter flavour.

In the light of these variations and also of the snags encountered when calculating larger quantities the following notes extracted from Walter Banfield's wonderfully informative and human book *Manna* (1937) should be of interest. They may also perhaps be of use to those who bake and sell home-made bread to health-food stores and wholefood restaurants.

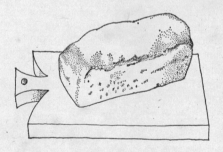

Wholemeals and wheatmeals

'The water capacity of meals from various sources afford an almost freakish range. A meal may take from 10 to 14 oz of water per lb of meal, and so it is impossible to indicate exactly the quantity of water which may be required.'

Stone-ground wholemeal loaves

'Select a genuine stone-ground, flavoury wholemeal. No white flour should be added, neither should a large-volumed loaf be the aim.'

'Stone-ground wholemeal 14lb, liquor about 1 gallon, yeast 4oz, salt 3½oz, moist sugar 2oz, lard 4oz. Straight dough. 1½ hours at 78 deg. F. or ½ hour at 70 deg. F using 8oz yeast.

'Yield 21 loaves scaled at 1lb 2oz.'

Crusty wholemeal loaves

'Stone-ground wholemeal 16lb, liquor about 9 pints, salt 3½oz, yeast 4oz, moist sugar 2oz, lard 4oz. Straight dough 2 hours at 78 deg. F.

'Proof time 15 minutes.

'Yield: 24 loaves at 1lb 2oz.

'A dough made from stone-ground meal takes longer to bake than the usual wheatmeal. A one-pound loaf requires thirty-five minutes and a two-pound loaf fifty-five minutes baking.[1] Large loaves are much easier to bake in long tins than in upright square tins.'[2]

Walter Banfield, *Manna*, 1937

· THE GRANT LOAF ·

Through her book *Your Daily Bread*,[3] and numerous other publications on sensible and wholesome diet, Mrs Doris Grant has taught hundreds of Englishwomen to mix and bake wholemeal bread by the easy method, with no kneading of the dough and one rising only. The Grant loaf is now part of English domestic bread-baking history. Nearly all household recipes for wholemeal loaves are based on this formula. Here is Mrs Grant's most recent version of the recipe in her own words:

'*3 lb stone-ground, wholewheat flour, 2 pints water at blood heat, 2 teaspoons salt – slightly more or less, according to taste, 3 rounded teaspoons Barbados sugar, honey or black molasses, 3 level British standard teaspoon measures dried yeast.*'

1. These are the times for professional bakers' ovens. In domestic ovens times are more like 45 minutes and 1 hour.
2. To the bakery trade square tins are extra deep – 4½ inch – rectangular tins. They are not geometrically square.
3. London, Faber, 1944.

Equivalent metric quantities: stone-ground wholewheat flour 1·5 kg, water at blood heat 1·20 litres, salt 15 g or more to taste, Barbados sugar, honey or black molasses 3 rounded teaspoons, dried yeast 3 level teaspoons. Tin size: three 1 litre tins. Equivalent oven temperature: 205°C.

'*Method:*

'Mix the salt with the flour (in very cold weather, warm flour slightly – enough to take off the chill). Place in a cup 3 tablespoons of the water at blood heat; the temperature is important – it is best to check with a cooking thermometer, which should register 35–38°C. Sprinkle the dried yeast *on top*. Leave for 2 minutes or so for the yeast to soak, then add the sugar, honey or black molasses. In about 10 to 15 minutes this should have produced a thick creamy froth. Pour this into the flour and add the rest of the water. Mix well – by hand is best – for a minute or so, working from sides to middle, till the dough feels elastic and leaves the sides of the mixing bowl clean; this helps to make a well-built loaf. Divide the dough which should be slippery, but not wet, into three 2-pint tins which have been warmed and greased. Put the tins in a warm place, cover with a cloth and leave for *about 20 minutes* or until the dough is within half an inch of the top of the tins. Bake in a fairly hot oven (electricity 400°F, Gas Regulo 6) for approximately 35 to 40 minutes.

'*Quantities for one loaf:*
1 lb flour   13 oz (a generous ½ pint) water at blood heat
1 scant teaspoon salt, or according to taste
1 rounded teaspoon Barbados sugar, honey or black molasses
1 level British standard teaspoon measure dried yeast*

'* *Method with fresh yeast:*
'Should you prefer to use fresh yeast, 1 oz is sufficient for three loaves. Mix in a small bowl with 2 rounded teaspoons Barbados sugar, honey or black molasses and add ¼ pint of the water at blood heat. Leave for 10 minutes or so to froth up before adding to the flour with the rest of the water. To make one loaf, use a scant ½ oz fresh yeast mixed with 1 rounded teaspoon Barbados sugar, honey or black molasses, and about ⅛ pint (roughly 8 tablespoons) water.'

Equivalent metric quantities for one loaf: wholewheat flour 450g, water at blood heat 350g, salt 1 scant teaspoon or to taste, Barbados sugar, honey or molasses 1 rounded teaspoon, dried yeast 1 level British standard teaspoon.

Doris Grant, *Your Daily Food*, 1973

Note: I hope that Mrs Grant's lesson of minimal yeast and sugar will be acted upon, and erroneous instructions on dried yeast packets ignored. I find though that 20 minutes rising time is on the short side, and can be taken as a minimum. The same applies to the salt quantities.

· HOLME MILLS WHOLEMEAL BREAD ·

'*Ingredients:*

2 lb wholewheat flour	1 teaspoon sugar
1 pint warm water	1 dessertspoon malt extract
1 level tablespoon dried yeast	1 dessertspoon salt'

Equivalent metric quantities: flour 900g, water 550g, dried yeast 1 level tablespoon, sugar 1 teaspoon, malt extract 1 dessertspoon, salt 1 dessertspoon. Tin size: two 0.5 kg tins. Equivalent temperatures in degrees C: oven 205°C. reduced to 180°C.

'*Method:*

'Put teaspoon of brown sugar and tablespoon of dried yeast in small bowl and add ½ pint warm water – blood heat – mix together and put in warm place until it becomes frothy. This can take 10–20 minutes. Measure 2 lbs flour into mixing bowl and keep warm. Mix salt and malt extract to remaining ½ pint warm water and keep warm until needed.

'Make a well in the centre of the flour, add the water, malt extract, salt solution, then the frothy yeast and mix well together by hand. Turn out onto a floured board and knead for about 3 minutes when you feel the dough change consistency. Divide dough into 2 × 1 lb greased tins, put tins in warm place, cover with a clean cloth and leave until dough has risen well over sides of tin. Place in top shelf of hot oven (400°F) for 10 minutes, then reduce heat (350°F) for further 30–40 minutes.

'When bread is properly cooked loaves should sound hollow when tapped underneath. Turn out to a wire tray and leave to cool.

'This amount should make two 1 lb loaves, plus 6 small rolls.'

The above recipe was given to me by Mr Jordan of Holme Mills, Biggleswade, Bedfordshire, who suggests also the following variations: 'Try using 1 lb wholewheat and 1 lb Jordan's strong white flour. Molasses, golden syrup or treacle can be substituted for the malt extract in this recipe, but we do not think the flavour is as good.'

· A WHOLEMEAL SCONE LOAF ·

This is a loaf to make when you have especially good, stone-ground, 100 per cent whole wheatmeal and a little thick very ripe cream to spare. As an occasional change it is most delicious.

1 lb of stone-ground 100 per cent whole wheatmeal; ½ oz of bakers' yeast; 4 tablespoons of thick cream, slightly sour (but without a hint of cheesey taste or smell); approximately ½ pint of warm water; 2 teaspoons of salt.

Equivalent metric quantities: flour 450 g, bakers' yeast 15 g, thick cream 4 tablespoons, water approximately 200 g, salt 2 teaspoons.

Put the flour in a big bowl, add the salt. Cream the yeast with a little of the warm water, stir the yeast into the flour, then mix in the cream, and finally enough water to make a dough which is not too dry.

Handle the dough lightly. Form it into a ball, cover it and leave it to rise for about 1½ hours.

Now re-shape the dough, kneading as little as possible.

Have ready a greased and floured baking sheet, put the ball of dough in the centre, flatten it a little, make four or six deep cross cuts, and leave it to rise a second time. Forty-five minutes to an hour should be sufficient. This bread does not rise very much, especially if you are using meal milled from soft home-grown wheat, so do not be misled into waiting all day for it to puff up like white bread; rather it will open out and spread somewhat.

Bake this loaf in the centre of a medium hot oven, 420° to 430°F, 215° to 225°C, gas no. 7, for approximately 45 minutes.

Although this bread keeps well it is at its best on the day it is baked. It is wonderful for breakfast or tea with blackberry or elderberry jelly, and also makes very good toast.

Note: The finest flavoured 100 per cent stone-ground wholemeal I have yet come across is Abbey brand, milled from their own organically grown wheat by the Cistercian monks at Mount St Joseph, Roscrea, Co. Tipperary. It is packed in 1 kilo and 2 kilo bags, and distributed by W. H. Mosse Ltd, Bennettsbridge, Co. Kilkenny, Eire. This meal is coarsely ground; it makes rather rough and rugged loaves with an incomparable flavour. It is excellent, too, for soda bread. Recipes are in the chapter on Soda Breads.

· TO MAKE A COBURG OR ROUND LOAF WITHOUT A TIN ·

I make these round loaves with *14 oz of strong plain unbleached flour, ¼ oz of fresh yeast, rather under ½ oz of salt, and slightly under 8 oz (1 cup U.S.) of warm water*. Also needed is a floured baking sheet or heatproof earthenware platter.

Equivalent metric quantities: flour 400 g, fresh yeast 10 g, salt rather under 15 g, water slightly under 225 g.

Mix the yeast to a cream with a little tepid water. Stir the salt into the flour, put the bowl, covered, into a very low oven for 5 minutes, just long enough to warm the flour. Mix the creamed yeast into it, add the tepid water. The right temperature is about 98° to 100°F, 37° to 38°C. Mix well and shape the dough into a ball. If it is too wet, sprinkle with a little more flour. Cover, and leave in a warm place to rise. The ideal temperature is from 70° to 75°F, 21° to 23°C.

In an hour to an hour and a half the dough should have doubled in volume and feel spongy and light. Scoop it up, and slap it down hard in the bowl or on a board. Repeat this three or four times. The more the dough is knocked down at this stage the better the loaf will be.

Now knead and roll the dough into a ball, place this in the centre of the floured baking sheet. At this stage – and it is an important one – fold the ball of dough all round, tucking the edges underneath, so that the uncooked loaf looks like a little, round, plump cushion. If this detail is omitted, the loaf will spread out flat. Getting the shape right is a knack which may take a few tries to acquire. The correct consistency of the dough also plays an important part. If it is too wet nothing will prevent it spreading, so if you have used too much water sprinkle in more flour as you shape the loaf. Try not to overdo the addition of flour, or the finished loaf will turn out patchy.

It is advisable to cover the dough while it is rising for the second time and the easiest way to do this is to invert a clean bowl over it. For example, quickly rinse and dry the bowl used for mixing the dough. Don't use it without cleaning it. An hour later it will be twice as difficult to wash. An alternative method is to put the shaped ball of dough upside down into the floured bowl, and cover it with a plate or a floured cloth.

Three-quarters of an hour should be long enough for the dough to double its volume once again. Remove the covering bowl. If necessary re-shape the loaf. (If you have used the method of proving the loaf upside down in a bowl, simply invert it on to the baking sheet.) With a sharp knife or scissors make three deepish cuts, one right across the loaf, the other two from the outer edges inward to the centre, so that they meet the first cut and form a cross.[1] As the cuts open the loaf is ready to go into the oven.

Have the oven heated to 450°F, 230°C, gas no. 8. Bake the loaf on the centre shelf for 15 minutes at this temperature, another 15 at 400°F, 205°C, gas no. 6, then turn it upside down and leave for 10 to 15 minutes with the oven turned off.

Cool on a rack.

Notes and variations: 1. If this loaf is baked plain, without cuts, it is called a cob, an old word meaning head. Basically, it is just the ordinary round loaf baked on the brick oven floor since the earliest times. A variation in cuts is a chequerboard pattern, called a 'rumpy', as in the drawing of a big crusty loaf on p. 265. Another way is just one cut, making a loaf which looks like a large roll. The latter is sometimes called a Danish cob. This was a common shape for the Dutch and Flemish white loaves of the sixteenth and seventeenth centuries. They were the equivalent of our manchets.

2. Any number of permutations on flour mixtures can be used for this loaf. I have given the recipe using all plain strong flour because that is the easiest flour for a beginner to work with. Eighty-one per cent or 85 per cent wheatmeal also makes good Coburgs and cobs.

3. Lightweight non-stick oven sheets are useful for the baking of hand-shaped loaves. These sheets are rather small, so it is a good idea to have two which fit side by side on the oven shelf.

4. An experienced breadmaker will know that 14 oz of strong plain bread flour can easily be leavened with $\frac{1}{4}$ oz of yeast only. If you need to hurry the dough, then use $\frac{1}{2}$ oz of yeast, but the slower rising with less yeast will make a better loaf. Alternatively, you can make two loaves, or one large one, with 28 oz of flour but still using only the $\frac{1}{2}$ oz of yeast.

5. Coburgs and cobs can be baked very admirably by the under-cover system described on p. 303.

1. See also instructions for cutting the crusts, p. 265.

· A PAN COBURG or DISH LOAF ·

This is made with an overnight dough, as described in note 2 of the basic loaf recipe (p. 260), and is baked in a rather shallow round tin, or an earthenware dish, with sloping sides. The dimensions of the tin I use – it came from Mathews, the bakery suppliers of 214 Borough High Street, London SE1 – are 7½ inches in diameter, 2½ inches deep, and with a capacity of 2½ pints or 5½ cups U.S. (see drawing on p. 207).

Another name for the pan Coburg is a cauliflower loaf, an accurately descriptive name provided that the dough has been properly matured so that in the oven it springs high out of the tin, the cuts opening and the dough spreading into a fine-looking head, almost the shape of a soufflé.

To make the dough use 1 lb 6 oz (22 oz) of 81 per cent or 85 per cent wheat-meal and 2 to 3 oz of 100 per cent wholemeal. If you happen to have a bag of malted meal such as Bermaline in the flour bin, add an ounce or two. The rest of the ingredients are ½ oz of yeast, ¾ oz of salt, approximately 12 oz (1½ cups U.S.) of water and milk mixed (two parts water to one of milk), and a tablespoon or two of olive oil for brushing the dough while it is rising overnight.

Equivalent metric quantities: 81 or 85 per cent wheatmeal 600 g, whole-meal 60 to 85 g, Bermaline or other malted meal (optional) 30 to 60 g, yeast 15 g, salt 20 g, water and milk mixed approximately 350 g, olive oil 1 to 2 tablespoons. Tin or dish size: diameter 18 cm, depth 7 cm, capacity 1·5 litres.

Make up the dough as for the basic loaf. After a first rising of 1½ to 2 hours, break it down, knead it well, brush the top with oil, cover it and leave it on the kitchen table overnight, or from the morning until the evening. The second time it rises the dough will have noticeably more volume than the first time. Break it down, knead it hard.

Have your tin or dish warmed and oiled. If the dish is an earthenware one, it is important that it be liberally greased; bread sticks to earthen-ware – glazed earthenware that is – much more tenaciously than it does to tin or steel.

Put your dough, moulded into a ball, into the dish or tin. At this stage it looks, for once, too much rather than too little for the dish. Sprinkle it with flour or wholemeal.

Now take a small sharp knife. Run it into the dough the whole way round the edge, and parallel to it, to the depth of about 1 inch. This cut frees the dough to spring above the mould. Next make your cross cuts, not too deeply, on the top of the loaf, as explained in the preceding recipe for a Coburg without a tin. If the dough has reached the right degree of maturity, these cuts will open out quite quickly, eventually spreading like wounds, revealing the interior structure of the dough and the tiny threads which form those graduations of colour and contrasts of texture in the baked crust which are characteristic of a loaf made from well-ripened dough and baked in a steamy oven.

Cover the shaped loaf with a deep inverted bowl or a sheet of polythene or a damp cloth, and leave it to prove for the third time.

In about 45 minutes to 1 hour the dough should have grown to the very top of the tin, and the cuts should have opened and spread with it. If they haven't it means either that the dough was too slack to take them or that it was not yet sufficiently matured. Should it have been left too long in too warm a room or have too much yeast and too little salt in it, the dough will be over-ripe and have no more life in it. That again will prevent the cuts from opening.

In the first case, easy enough to diagnose, go ahead and bake the loaf without further ado. The result will be a mushroom-shaped top rather than a cauliflower. In the second, the remedy is to break down the dough, re-knead it and leave it for a while – say 30 minutes – before re-shaping it, returning it to the tin and trying the cuts again. In the third case, the rescue operation would be a lengthy one. You would have to re-knead the dough with more flour, and a little extra water and salt[1] – in other words give it an injection of new life, so that gradually the dough grows springy and lively again. If you haven't time for this kind of rescue, or find it is not worth the trouble, just put the dough straight into the oven to bake. It will probably make perfectly good bread even if it isn't spectacular.

When the cuts *do* open, it's a good idea to spray them with water before consigning the loaf to the oven. The steam arising from them during the initial stage of baking helps in the formation of a good crust and a nice shape.

Baking times and temperatures are as for the basic loaf (see p. 258) – but once the cuts have spread and the crust has formed, turn the oven down. It is preferable to give the loaf a little longer in a slower oven than to let the crust get overbaked.

1. See Bloomer loaf (2), note 2.

· A BLOOMER LOAF (1) ·

Bloomer is the English name of the thick baton loaf, with diagonal cuts, common to most European countries. Baked in a domestic oven, it won't acquire the crackly crust associated with this type of loaf, but is still very good indeed. It is illustrated on p. 198.

1 lb of 81 or 85 per cent wheatmeal, 4 oz of strong plain flour, $\frac{1}{2}$ oz of yeast, approximately 12 oz of cold milk and hot water mixed in equal parts, $\frac{3}{4}$ oz of salt.

Equivalent metric quantities: 81 or 85 per cent wheatmeal 450 g, strong plain flour 120 g, yeast 15 g, milk and water mixed approximately 350 g, salt 20 g.

Make the dough in the usual way and give it two rising periods, of 2 hours and 1 hour respectively. When the second is completed and after hard kneading mould the dough into a square-ended boat shape, about 10 inches long and 5 inches wide. Turn it on to a floured earthenware platter or a baking sheet and give it 15 to 20 minutes to recover volume after the handling.

Reverse the shaped loaf and plump it up by tucking the dough under at the ends and sides. Using a short, sharp knife make five or six deep cuts at regular intervals along the loaf, cutting well on the slant rather than straight across. As the cuts open out, sprinkle water into them, and put the loaf into the oven at once. Bake it for 30 minutes at 450°F, 230°C, gas no. 8 and for another 15 to 20 minutes at 400° to 425°F, 205° to 220°C, gas no. 6 or 7. If at the end of this baking time the undercrust is still very soft, turn the loaf upside down and let it bake for another 10 minutes, but with the heat turned off.

As a variation, coarse salt crystals and dill or cumin seeds can be sprinkled on to the cuts just before the loaf goes into the oven.

· BLOOMER LOAF (2) ·

This is a loaf made with a long-rising dough, and demonstrates a very useful and successful method.

The dough is made as in the above recipe, with 1 lb of 81 or 85 per cent wheatmeal and $\frac{1}{4}$ lb of strong plain white flour, 12 oz of milk and water mixed, $\frac{3}{4}$ oz of salt, but only $\frac{1}{4}$ oz of yeast.

Equivalent metric quantities: 85 per cent wheatmeal 450 g, strong plain white flour 120g, milk and water mixed 350g, salt 20g, yeast 10g.

The flour is not warmed – unless the weather is exceptionally cold – but to get the dough off to a good start the mixing liquid should be well above blood heat – say just on 100°F, 38°C.

Having mixed the dough and kneaded it very well, cover it and leave it at cool room temperature – say 60° to 65°F, 15° to 18°C – for anything from 6 to 10 hours. Break it down, and knead it very hard and thoroughly. Again leave it at room temperature for a couple of hours, or longer if it happens to suit your timetable. (I have often left it for a whole morning for its second proving. Owing to the low yeast content it will not over-ferment unless the temperature is unusually warm. In this case there is an easy remedy. See note 2 below.)

Break down the dough again and repeat the tough kneading. Shape it into a loaf as described in the first bloomer recipe, leave it for a final proving or ripening on its floured baking sheet or platter for 20 to 40 minutes – again it is a question of suiting yourself. If you want to speed the final proving put the shaped loaf in a warm place, such as over the pilot light of a gas cooker, or wherever you normally put your dough to rise.

Now invert the loaf, re-shape it as necessary, then make the cuts as described in the first recipe; spray them with water and a scattering of salt crystals. Put the loaf in the oven to bake without delay. Temperatures and timing are as in the first recipe.

Notes: 1. The flavour of bread made on the slow-rising method is rather different from that of the routine, quickly risen loaf. The low yeast content, the tough kneading, the comparatively cool temperature all contribute to the maximum development of the gluten in the flour, and this gives the mature flavour which is so much appreciated in certain French breads such as the true *pain de campagne*. The keeping quality of this loaf is very high.

2. If you are making this type of bread dough in very warm weather, increase the quantity of flour to yeast by about half – over a long period ¼oz of yeast will easily aerate 2lb of flour; the extra flour can be added either when the dough is first mixed or, with an appropriate quantity of extra mixing liquid, at the end of the first rising period. This refreshes and feeds the existing dough and quickly gets the yeast to work again. Whichever method you decide to use, a little extra salt will be needed – say ¼oz – at the same time as the extra supply of flour.

3. The slow-rising dough can, of course, be used to make any shape of loaf; for example, the round shapes with cuts as shown in the drawings on pp. 265 and 379.

· BROWN OATMEAL BREAD ·

Oatmeal on its own would make a very flat loaf, but a small proportion mixed with a strong brown or white flour makes excellent bread with a wonderfully rich flavour.

The following recipe, similar to the one for a loaf made from Irish stone-ground 100 per cent wholewheat flour (p. 275) is very successful.

14 oz of wheatmeal, either Jordan's 85 per cent or Prewett's Millstone 81 per cent; 4 oz of Prewett's or Mayall's Pimhill medium oatmeal, stone-ground; ½ oz of yeast; ½ to ¾ oz of salt; a tablespoon or two of cream; ½ pint of water.

Equivalent metric quantities: wheatmeal 400 g, medium oatmeal 120 g, yeast 15 g, salt 15 to 20 g, cream 1 to 2 tablespoons, water 280 g.

Mix the two flours in a bowl, with the salt. Mix the yeast with a little warm water and cream. Stir it into the flour. Add the rest of the cream and water mixture, which should be warm but not hot.

Mix to a fairly moist dough and leave to rise for a couple of hours.

Break down the dough, knead it briefly, using a little extra oatmeal to dry it if necessary, form it into a round loaf, folds tucked underneath. Turn it upside down into a floured wooden or earthenware bowl,[1] and leave it to rise or prove a second time, for approximately 45 minutes. Turn it out on to a floured baking sheet or oiled earthenware platter. Now make about six fairly deep criss-cross cuts, with a sharp knife, so that the top of the loaf is chequered. As soon as the cuts open up, which should be almost immediately, put the loaf into the oven.

If possible bake by the under-cover method (see p. 303), at 425° to 450°F, 220° to 230°C, gas nos. 7 to 8, leaving the loaf under its cover for 20 minutes, then at gradually reduced temperatures for approximately 40 minutes, uncovered.

Although the volume of the loaf will be much increased by using the under-cover method of baking, oatmeal bread never rises as much as a loaf made entirely with wheat flour. The crust, though, is particularly successful.

1. See the recipe for Robert May's French bread, p. 313.

Notes and variations: 1. To a certain extent the oatmeal loaf provides an alternative for those who like a coarse and slightly crunchy bread but are unable to obtain a really good stone-ground 100 per cent wholemeal such as the Irish Abbey brand mentioned in the recipe on p. 275. If you have some coarse as well as medium oatmeal, a small amount – 2 or 3 tablespoons – can be added to the mixture, and the top of the loaf can also be sprinkled with a little.

2. Strong plain white flour can be mixed with oatmeal in the same proportions, and the dough mixed and baked in the same way as for the loaf described above.

· YORKSHIRE BROWN BREAD ·

The following notes are given by Miss Lizzie Heritage in the 1901 edition of *Cassell's Universal Cookery Book*. The different mixtures of flour are worth noting:

'The exact proportions differ, but a common recipe is a mixture of three and a half pounds of flour, with a pound each of rye flour and coarse bran. Sometimes a mixture of rye flour and white flour of the best quality and a small proportion of barley flour is used for bread, which is very satisfactory. The mode of baking is as in household or family bread. Small loaves and a moderate oven give the best results.'

It should be added that by small loaves Miss Heritage almost certainly meant 2 lb loaves. In those days few people bothered to bake any loaf smaller than that, and 4 lb loaves were more usual. In her recipe for household or family bread this excellent author uses 14 lb of flour and 3 oz of yeast (she called it dried, meaning what we call fresh). Total fermentation time was 2½ to 3½ hours, allowing a further proof for tin loaves. Out of this stone of flour the yield was either four large, six medium or eight small loaves, and the total estimated cost was 2s to 2s 3d 'on an average'.

· A GRANARY LOAF ·

This is made from the proprietary granary meal packed in 1·5 kg bags by Granary Foods Ltd of Burton-on-Trent. It is a mixture of wheat and rye meals with a proportion of wheatkernels (see p. 60). Directions for making up the bread are given on the bag, but I find the malt flavour rather too strong, and so usually mix a proportion of plain flour, either 81 per cent wheatmeal or strong white, with the granary meal, and prefer to add fat in the form of olive oil rather than the lard recommended by the packers.

Home-made granary bread stays fresh and moist for an unusually long time, is particularly well-liked by the young, and the dough is very good tempered, exceptionally easy to mix and bake; taken all in all it has much to recommend it, especially to beginners in bread-making. My recipe is for a pan Coburg[1] loaf, made as follows.

1 lb of granary meal, 4 oz of 81 or 85 per cent wheatmeal or strong plain unbleached flour, ½ oz of salt, ½ oz of yeast, 2 tablespoons of light olive oil, approximately ½ pint of water.

Equivalent metric quantities: granary meal 450 g, wheatmeal or strong plain unbleached flour 120 g, salt 15 g, yeast 15 g, light olive oil 2 tablespoons, water approximately 280 g.

Mix the two flours or meals very thoroughly. Either add the salt directly to the flour or dissolve it in the warm water, whichever method you prefer to use. If the weather is cold, warm the flour in the oven as explained in the basic loaf recipe, p. 256.

Cream the yeast with tepid water, mix it with the flour, make up the dough with the warm water; add the oil last. The dough will be very lithe and pliable, and will need little working or kneading at this stage. Form it into a ball, cover it, leave it to rise in the normal way, at room temperature in warm weather, in winter or whenever it is more convenient, over a pilot light or in some other warm place.

When the dough has at least doubled in bulk and is puffy, break it down, knead it for 2 or 3 minutes.

Have your round, sloping-sided tin or dish slightly warmed and well coated with olive oil or fat, put the ball of dough in the centre. Cover it, leave it for approximately 30 minutes, until it has filled the tin, and is beginning to rise above the rim. With a sharp knife make two deep cuts in the shape of a cross. These should start opening out immediately. Dough made with malted meal always takes the cuts most satisfactorily. Leave a few more minutes, until the dough has recovered its spring, before putting it into the oven.

Usually I bake this bread by the under-cover system,[2] putting it on a

1. See p. 278.   2. See p. 303.

low shelf, covered, with the oven turned on to 450°F, 230°C, gas nos. 8 or 9, but not preheated. The timing is approximately 45 minutes at this temperature, plus 20 to 25 minutes at 400°F, 205°C, gas no. 6, with the loaf uncovered. If you use an earthenware dish or mould it will probably be necessary to give the loaf a further few minutes on the underside, after it has been turned out of the mould. This is because earthenware makes for a much softer undercrust than does metal.

N.B. The Fahrenheit and Celsius temperatures given in this recipe are those registered low down in the oven, not, as is usual with equivalent electricity and gas temperatures, in the centre.

· VIRGINIA WOOLF BAKES BREAD ·

'She liked trying to cook too, but I always felt that she did not want to give time to cooking and preferred to be in her room working.

'But there was one thing in the kitchen that Mrs Woolf was very good at doing: she could make beautiful bread. The first thing she asked me when I went to Monks House was if I knew how to make it. I told her that I had made some for my family, but I was not expert at it. "I will come into the kitchen, Louie" she said "and show you how to do it. We have always made our own bread." I was surprised how complicated the process was and how accurately Mrs Woolf carried it out. She showed me how to make the dough with the right quantities of yeast and flour, and then how to knead it. She returned three or four times during the morning to knead it again. Finally, she made the dough into the shape of a cottage loaf and baked it at just the right temperature. I would say that Mrs Woolf was not a practical person – for instance, she could not sew or knit or drive a car – but this was a job needing practical skill which she was able to do well every time. It took me many weeks to be as good as Mrs Woolf at making bread, but I went to great lengths practising and in the end, I think, I beat her at it.'

From Louie Mayer's contribution to *Recollections of Virginia Woolf*, ed. Joan Russell Noble, 1972

Louie Mayer was Virginia and Leonard Woolf's cook at Rodmell in Sussex from 1934 until Leonard Woolf's death in 1969.

· COTTAGE LOAVES ·

Cottage loaves, as all professional bakers writing for their colleagues readily admit, are notoriously difficult to mould and bake, although I think that the main cause of my own difficulties with the making and baking of an English cottage loaf is the very particular and vivid memory I have of the cottage loaves of my childhood. It is the bread I remember best from those days, and it was the one we used for toasting in front of the coal fire in the nursery and later in the schoolroom. The loaves were large ones, and the topknots rather small, so the slices were irregular, and difficult to hold on the fork. The crumb was creamy and soft, the crust was always a bit scorched on one side, although it wasn't hard or tough. As I remember it, the topknot always leant to one side, in the way associated also with a brioche.

Our bread came from the village bakery, and I have since learned that the county of Sussex, where I grew up, was a region with a reputation for good, sweet-eating bread. This was probably because so many of the villages, in East Sussex particularly, were quite unspoiled, the shops retained their country character, the bakeries their old-fashioned ovens. It had been a region of many windmills and watermills too, so there was a tradition of bread flour milled from good locally grown wheat.

The loaf I remember, baked on the floor of a brick-built, side-flue oven, would be impossible to reproduce in a modern domestic gas or electric one. The nearest to be got to it, for anyone who feels like going to the trouble, is to use the following notes concerning the dough for a cottage loaf, its proving and moulding, and the assembling of the two separate pieces, which is the crucial point.

1. The dough should be a fairly stiff one – but not too stiff, or the loaf will be hard.

2. The dough must be well-risen but not over-proved, or it will collapse.

3. After the first rising and the breaking down of the dough, it should be divided into two pieces, the one for the topknot weighing approximately one-third, or a little more, of the total; to get the proportions right the first time it will be necessary, therefore, first to weigh the whole piece of dough, then to divide it and weigh both pieces to check that they are approximately accurate. After two or three attempts the weighing can be eliminated, but at first it is difficult to judge simply by sight and feel.

4. For the second rising or proving, the two pieces should be kept separate. Roll each one into a ball, turning the folds of the bottom piece under, those of the topknot *upwards*. Cover both pieces, so that no skin forms on the dough.

5. Before the second proving is complete, i.e. after about 45 minutes instead of the more usual hour, the assembling of the two loaves is done in the following manner: slightly flatten the top of the bottom loaf, make a small cross-shaped cut, as for a Coburg, approximately $1\frac{1}{2}$ inches across. Now flatten, slightly, the base of the topknot and perch it on the bottom loaf. The flattening of the two pieces of dough is the absolutely key point of the assemblage of a cottage loaf. Without knowledge of this small detail – the only publication in which I have ever seen it given is the late Walter Banfield's splendid book *Manna* (1937) – it is almost impossible to make a successful cottage loaf. Without a flat surface on which to rest the topknot, the bottom piece of the loaf simply collapses under the superimposed weight, so the two loaves re-merge into one.

6. With your thumb and first two fingers joined to make a cone shape, press a hole through the centre of the topknot down into the main body of the loaf. This operation (the bakers call it bashing) effectively joins the two pieces and also gives the entirely characteristic appearance to the loaf.

7. The joining of the two loaves is a danger point. If it is performed with too violent a hand, it causes a serious disruption in the dough, and may distort the shape completely.

8. The assembled cottage loaf should now be covered, preferably with an inverted pot or deep bowl, and left to recover after its handling, but not for too long, or it will spread and lose its shape before you get it into the oven. Ten minutes should be ample time for this final ripening but, if the dough is at all too slack and looks in the least bit like collapsing, put it straight into the oven. Do not, in any case, preheat the oven. Turn it to 450°F, 230°C, gas no. 8 or 9, immediately before putting in the loaf, on the lower shelf. As the oven heats up, so the loaf expands. I learned this method through talking to Louie Mayer – quoted above – about Virginia Woolf and her bread-baking. Mrs Mayer told me that for many years the cooking at the Woolfs' house at Rodmell was all done on an old Florence oil-fired cooker. The overhead plate rack was a good place to put the bread dough while it was rising. When ready to bake, the shaped loaf was put straight into the cool oven. As the heat built up the loaf grew. Mrs Mayer was not aware that there was anything unusual about the method. When the oil cooker was replaced with an electric one, she went on baking her bread in the same way and it still worked. I too found that

it worked quite well with my gas-fired oven, but with natural gas it is advisable to wait at least 5 minutes after lighting the oven, or the top crust of the loaf may get badly burned. In an electric oven the system works better, and can be applied to many other kinds of bread, always providing that the dough still has some spring left in it – in other words, as already explained, it must be slightly under-proved.

9. After 30 minutes, when the loaf has risen and taken shape, it is a good idea to cover it with a bowl – if you have one sufficiently deep – in order to prevent the crust becoming too hard and tough. But towards the end of baking time, uncover the loaf again to let out the steam and for any final browning of the crust which may be necessary.

I cannot say that, even with all these efforts and tricks, the cottage loaf of beloved memory emerges, but at least a loaf of approximately the correct shape and with a good flavour and excellent moist crumb can be produced.

10. The flours and the proportions I use are as follows:

1½ lb of strong plain unbleached flour, ½ lb of an 81 per cent wheatmeal such as Prewett's Millstone or Jordan's Country Cookbook bread flour, just over ½ oz of yeast, ¾ oz of salt, 1 pint or a little less of warm water. Very great care must be taken not to make the dough too slack.

Equivalent metric quantities: strong plain unbleached flour 675 g, 81 per cent wheatmeal 225 g, yeast just over 15 g, salt 20 g, water about 0.5 litre.

· POTATO BREAD ·

Usually associated with times of grain shortage, or with a need for strict economy in the kitchen, potato bread is also advocated by some nineteenth-century writers as being the best bread for toast. This is because a proportion of potato mixed with ordinary white flour makes a loaf which retains its moisture and is also very light. Dr A. Hunter, writing in a book called *Receipts in Modern Cookery; with a Medical Commentary,* first published in 1805, provided both a recipe, and in case it were needed yet more evidence of the English addiction to toast: 'lovers of toast and butter will be much pleased with this kind of bread. The potato is not here added with a view to economy, but to increase the lightness of the bread, in which state it will imbibe the butter with more freedom . . .' Well, there you have one way of increasing the consumption of butter. Today's dieticians would probably be aghast . . . but the bread *is* very good, and is one of my favourites – so I include the recipe here. Nobody is forced to make it into toast, buttered or otherwise – although it is true that it does make very good, light toast and is equally successful for fried croûtons.

To 1 lb of white flour, the proportion of potato is ¼ lb, mashed very smoothly, completely dry, and used while warm. Other ingredients are ½ oz of yeast, ½ pint of milk and water mixed, a minimum of ¾ oz of salt.

Equivalent metric quantities: white flour 450 g, potato 120 g, yeast 15 g, milk and water mixed 280 g, salt 20 g (minimum). Tin size: 28 cm by 10 cm by 8 cm deep, with a capacity of 1·5 litres.

Have the flour and salt ready in a bowl, the yeast creamed with a little water, and the milk and water warm in a jug.

When your potatoes (two medium sized ones will be ample) are cooked, peeled, sieved and weighed, mix them with the flour as if you were rubbing in fat, so that the two are very thoroughly amalgamated. Then add the yeast and the warm milk and water. Mix the dough as for ordinary bread. Leave until it is well risen, which will take rather longer than usual – anything up to 2 hours. Break it down, knead lightly, shape and put into a 2½ to 3 pint tin. Cover it with a damp cloth and leave until the dough reaches the top of the tin.

Bake in a moderately hot oven, 425°F, 220°C, gas no. 7, for about 45 minutes, taking care not to let the crust get too browned or hard.

Notes: 1. The tin I use for this loaf is a narrow straight-sided one, as for a sandwich loaf. Dimensions are 11 by 4 by 3 inches deep, with a capacity of 2¾ pints. The exact dimensions are not important, the reason for the shape being that I find potato bread makes good sandwiches, as well as good toast, and is also very useful for fried bread.

2. The covering with a damp cloth while the dough is rising for the second time is important. This dough tends to form a skin, which inhibits the loaf rising when put in the oven, and makes for a tough crust.

3. To cook potatoes to add to bread dough, I find the best way is to boil them in their skins, watch them carefully and, immediately they are cooked but *before* they start to disintegrate, pour off the water, cover the potatoes with a clean thick cloth, put the lid on the saucepan and leave them for a few minutes. This method produces the best results with our indifferent English potatoes. They will be easy to peel, and to sieve enough of them to make ¼ lb is very quick work, although it is obviously

more economical of effort to cook enough potatoes at one go to make potato cakes or potatoes browned in a frying pan.

4. A cheap recipe – it sounds like a war-time formula – for potato bread is given in a Penguin Education publication called *Our Daily Bread* (1973). Proportions are 1 lb each of flour and potatoes, 1 oz of yeast and a 'pinch' of salt. The author, Richard Tames, says 'it tastes not bad at all, but is somewhat heavy and dry'. This must be due to the method of mixing and baking. The potatoes are peeled before boiling (which would make them mushy) and no extra liquid is added to the dough, which is shaped into round loaves and baked on a floured tray. In her *English Bread Book* (1857), so often quoted in these pages, Eliza Acton gives the proportions of potatoes to flour for a potato loaf as 7 lb, weighed *after* cooking and peeling, to a gallon of meal or flour. This, again, is weight for weight, a gallon of flour being 7 lb. Miss Acton, like Dr Hunter, considers the bread excellently flavoured and light, 'one of the best varieties of mixed or cheap bread when it is made with care'. Its moisture-retaining properties, Miss Acton found, were second only to those of rice bread. But . . . *made with care*. Her potatoes are dry and warm when added to the flour, she specifies *more salt* than usual for ordinary bread and a lower temperature for baking. And should the potatoes be watery, you are to wring them dry in a cloth. There are times when I feel that Miss Acton is too good to be true. An unworthy thought, for so obviously, so transparently, she was utterly thorough, totally sincere in her anxiety to instruct, to pass on the knowledge she herself had acquired through such painstaking experiment. Her patience in recording every detail was phenomenal, and although our ovens and our domestic conditions are so far removed from those of the 1850s, Miss Acton's notes are still extremely instructive.

5. One point not mentioned by Miss Acton is that the mashed potatoes are particularly propitious to yeast growth. For this reason they were often used as the basis of a preliminary leaven which encouraged fermentation. The bakers' name for the potatoes they added to bread dough was 'fruit'.

· RICE BREAD ·

This is excellent bread for keeping, since the rice remains moist, and the texture is beautifully light and honeycombed. It is also a loaf which is very easy to mix and to bake.

Ingredients are 3 oz of rice (about ½ a U.S. cup) uncooked weight, three times its volume of water for cooking it, and for the dough 1 lb 2 oz of strong plain flour, ½ oz of yeast, ½ to ¾ oz of salt, rather under ½ pint of water, and fat for the tin. (If you use a larger saucepan you need extra water.)

Equivalent metric quantities: rice (uncooked) 85 g, three times its volume of water, strong plain flour 500 g, yeast 15 g, salt 15 to 20 g, water about ¼ litre, fat for the tin. Tin size: sandwich loaf tin of 1·5 to 2 litre capacity.

Put the rice in a thick saucepan of 1¾ to 2 pint capacity, cover it with 1½ cups of water. Bring it to the boil, cover the saucepan, leave the rice to cook steadily until the water is absorbed and little holes have formed all over the surface of the rice.

While the rice is cooking, weigh out and prepare all the other ingredients. Cream the yeast with a little warm water. Put the salt in a measuring jug and dissolve it in ¼ pint of very hot water, then add cold water to make up the correct quantity.

When the rice is cooked, and while it is still very warm, amalgamate it, very thoroughly, with the flour. Now add the yeast, then the salted water, and mix the dough in the usual way. It will be rather soft. Cover it and leave it to rise for 1 to 1½ hours, until it is at least double in volume, and bubbly.

Probably the dough will be too soft to handle very much, so it may be necessary to dry it out a little by adding more flour before breaking it down and transferring it – very little kneading is necessary – to a warmed and well greased tin or tins. For the quantity given I use a sandwich loaf tin of 3 to 3½ pint capacity. The dough should fill the tin by two-thirds. Cover it with a cloth or a sheet of polythene, leave it until it has risen above the top of the tin.

Bake the bread in the usual way, at 450°F, 230°C, gas no. 8, for 15 minutes, then at 400°F, 205°C, gas no. 6, for another 15 minutes, before turning the loaf out of its tin and returning it to the oven, on its side, for a final 15 to 20 minutes at the same temperature. If the crust shows signs of baking too hard and taking too much colour, cover the loaf with a large bowl or an inverted oval casserole.

Notes and Variations: 1. The variety of rice used is not, I think, of great importance. I always have Italian round-grained and Basmati long-grained rice in the house and have used both for bread. Those who habitually use only brown unpolished rice will know that it takes longer to cook and absorbs more water than white rice.

2. A recipe for rice bread was given to Eliza Acton by a clergyman's wife, who said that she had originally added the rice when flour was very expensive, and had found the bread made in this way 'so much improved by the addition that now we seldom omit it . . . we consider that the rice renders the bread lighter, and prevents the crust of it from becoming hard'.

The quantities given in the recipe quoted by Miss Acton[1] are 2 lb of rice to 28 lb of flour and ¼ pint of home-brewed yeast. This gave the high yield of 42 lb of bread, divided into ten loaves. The rice was cooked in 6 pints of water in a large covered dish or stoneware jar, in the oven, until the rice was very soft and swollen and the water absorbed.

3. Some ten years later, in 1867, Lady Llanover writing in *Good Cookery* gave a detailed description of the preparation of food cooked to be taken on a journey from South Wales to London. For the sandwiches two plump chickens were roasted, and rice bread specially baked the previous day. Lady Llanover held that rice bread was by far the best kind for sandwiches, and preserved the moistness of the chicken meat as well as its own. Her quantities were 1 lb of rice to 6 lb of flour, more than twice as high a proportion of rice as in the Acton formula; the proportions I use are closer to Lady Llanover's than to Miss Acton's.

4. Rice is now so expensive that using it for bread can scarcely be called an economy, except in so far as it does give exceptional keeping qualities to the loaf. It is hard to describe the flavour of rice bread; until it has been tried, it is also difficult to believe how delicious it is.

· PUMPKIN BREAD ·

This country recipe, which I have not tried, is entitled 'To make bread that will keep moist and good very long'.

'Slice a pompion, and boil it in fair water, till the water grows clammy, or somewhat thick; then strain it through a fine cloth, or sieve, and with this make your Bread, well kneading the dough; and it will not only encrease the quantity of it, but make it keep moist and sweet a month longer than Bread wetted with fair water only.'

The Family Magazine, London, 1741

1. *The English Bread Book*, 1857.

· A RYE LOAF ·

With very rare exceptions, such as certain types of German and Dutch pumpernickel, rye bread is always a mixture of rye and wheat flours, in varying proportions. The wheat flour may be 100 or 85 per cent wholemeal, or white, but should always be a flour strong in gluten content, since, although rye flour has its own gluten, it is of a kind which does little to aid the expansion of the dough, which is therefore difficult to stabilize.

Rye bread is often made on a leaven or sourdough starter, which gives it a characteristic sour taste, but is by no means essential. A dough of predominantly white flour with a small proportion of rye is very easy and straightforward. It makes a delicate and delicious bread especially good with smoked fish and white cheeses. It stays moist longer than wholemeal bread, and even when several days old is still good for cutting into thin slices, which makes it welcome to anyone who suffers from weight problems but is reluctant to renounce bread entirely.

For a small loaf to be baked in a tin of $1\frac{1}{2}$ to $1\frac{3}{4}$ pint capacity, proportions are 10 oz of strong plain flour, 2 oz of rye meal, $\frac{1}{2}$ oz of yeast, approximately 8 oz (well under $\frac{1}{2}$ pint) or 1 cup U.S. of tepid water, $\frac{1}{2}$ oz of salt.

Equivalent metric quantities: strong plain flour 280 g, rye meal 60 g, yeast 15 g, water approximately 225 g, salt approximately 10 g. Tin size: a tin of 1 litre capacity. Proportions for a larger loaf are: strong plain flour 450 g, rye meal 120 g, yeast 15 g, salt 15 g, water approximately 300 g. Tin size: a tin of 1·5 to 2 litre capacity.

Mix the yeast and a little water as usual. Blend the two flours together.
Put the salt into a measuring jug, dissolve it in a little very hot water. Make up the 8 oz with cold water.

Mix the dough and leave to rise as usual, for an hour or a little longer. If you have time, give the dough two risings and breakdowns instead of the usual one before shaping it and putting it in the warmed and greased tin.

With a sharp knife or scissors make an incision the whole length of the loaf, and widen this by pressing into it with the side of your hand. Sprinkle the top with rye meal.

When the dough has risen to the top of the tin, bake it in the centre of the oven, 450°F, 230°C, gas no. 8, for 15 minutes, then at 375°F, 190°C, gas no. 5, for another 15 minutes. Turn the loaf out of the tin and give it another 10 minutes with the oven lowered to 330°F, 170°C, gas no. 3, or even with the oven turned out.

Proportions for a larger loaf to be baked in a tin of 3 to 3½ pint capacity (1·5 to 2 litre) are: 1 lb of strong plain flour, 4 oz of rye meal, ½ oz of yeast, ½ oz of salt, a little over ½ pint of water. Oven temperatures are as above, but allow an extra 5 to 10 minutes' baking time.

In addition to keeping exceptionally well, this rye loaf can also be frozen very successfully.

Note: The rye meal I use, when it is obtainable, is Mrs Horsfield's which is stone-ground. Supplies are erratic. A more finely milled, much whiter, rye flour is marketed by Prewett's. This flour has less flavour than Mrs Horsfield's coarse brown meal, but is easier to work with. Allow a larger proportion, say 3 to 4 oz of rye flour to 9 or 10 oz of wheat-meal or wheat flour.

· SWEETENED RYE BREAD ·

Walter Banfield asserted that the best-selling rye bread for the English market is one sweetened with golden syrup.

His formula was for *equal proportions of rye flour and strong wheat flour, say 2½ lb of each. Other ingredients for this quantity are 2 pints of water, 1¼ oz of salt, 1½ oz of yeast, 5 oz of golden syrup, and optionally ½ oz of mixed spice.*

Equivalent metric quantities: rye flour and strong wheat flour 1·125 kg each, water 1·12 litres, salt 40 g, yeast 45 g, golden syrup 150 g, mixed spice 15 g (optional). For the starch paste: potato flour or rice flour 30 g, boiling water 0·5 litre.

The dough is made in the usual way, and left to rise for an hour and a half at 76°F, 24°C.

The loaves are made up – the quantities given will yield four large ones – in a cigar or torpedo shape and left to prove for the second time for 1¼ to 1½ hours. Before they are consigned to the oven, stab them with a fork in four or five places. This will help to prevent the natural cracking in the oven to which rye bread is subject.

If you like to attempt the varnished crust characteristic of rye loaves, make a starch paste with an ounce of potato flour or rice flour and a pint of boiling water and brush the loaves with this immediately before they are put in the oven, and again about 15 minutes before baking is complete. Oven temperature should be 425°F, 220°C, gas no. 7, reduced progressively to 400°F, 205°C, gas no. 6, and 375°F, 190°C, gas no. 5. Baking time is a good hour.

Note : Instead of golden syrup I prefer to use either honey, or black treacle or molasses.

· QUICK SOURDOUGH RYE BREAD ·

To make a modified and easy version of rye sourdough, Banfield suggests the following method :
Use the same ingredients as for the sweetened rye bread, but omitting the golden syrup, and optionally adding caraway or anis seeds. Weigh out half quantities of the flours and salt, mix them to a dough with warm water (and without yeast) and leave this to stand in a warm place for about 12 to 16 hours, until it gives out an agreeably sour smell.
Now make a straightforward bread dough with the remaining flours and salt and the yeast and water. Incorporate the soured dough. Leave to rise or prove for about an hour and a half. Break it down, knead it – adding caraway or anis seeds if you like them – and shape into loaves. Let them prove for at least an hour before putting them into the oven and baking them as for the sweetened rye bread.
I have made this version of sourdough rye, using half quantities, in the following proportions: *1 lb of rye meal to 1½ lb of strong wheat flour, either 85 or 100 per cent wholemeal, preferably a strong one.* (I find that equal quantities of rye and wheat flour make an almost impossibly sticky dough. Otherwise the method works very well and makes an excellent loaf.)

Equivalent metric quantities : rye meal 450 g, strong wheat flour 670 g, water 550 g, salt 20 g, yeast 20 g, caraway or anis seeds (optional).

· AMERICAN SOURDOUGH BREADS: A NOTE ·

There are several variations on the methods used to make sourdoughs, most American versions being made in three stages. A starter culture is made into a batter with flour and water or milk. When this ferments a portion of it is used to ferment a second sponge or leaven, and this in turn becomes the leaven for the dough proper. From making the starter to baking the bread takes about five days. I find the whole process rather unrewarding, but anyone who wants to try their hand at it will find recipes for both white and rye sourdoughs in James Beard's book *Beard on Bread*.[1]

James Beard tells me that San Francisco sourdough is something else again, that in fact it is in a class by itself, and a purely commercial class at that. Samples of this sourdough bread were sent to me by a San Francisco friend, Mr Charles Williams of Williams-Sonoma, the famous kitchen shop. One of the loaves airmailed to me survived the three or four days in transit remarkably well. It was still moist and remained fresh for another couple of days. It was very much akin to some of the good *pain de campagne* made on the old leaven system[2] and still to be found in French country bakeries. The San Francisco version appeared to be made from an 80 or 85 per cent wheatmeal, and was very genuine. I certainly wouldn't complain if we could buy bread as good in this country. The white version was not so good, and was rather like a very stale French *baguette* loaf. Somewhere along the line, yeast goes into these San Francisco sourdoughs, as indeed it does nowadays into most versions.

· BARLEY BREAD ·

Although, owing to its greyish crumb, barley bread may not look immediately appetizing, those who acquire a taste for it are likely to become addicts. I am one. It is an addiction which is not always easily satisfied. In London, barley meal is difficult to come by. Wholefood (as opposed to health-food) shops and bulk suppliers are the places to look for it. In agricultural areas supplies should be easier. Barley is extensively cultivated for animal food and for malting by the brewery trade. A corn chandler's is probably the best bet for buying barley meal, and in view of the small proportion of barley to wheat flour used for my barley loaves – bread made entirely of barley is rather heavy and dry – it would not be a formidable task to sift out the coarsest of the bran from the meal. Anyone who lives in the neighbourhood of an operative

1. New York, Knopf, 1973; London, Michael Joseph, 1976.
2. The system is described in the chapter 'Notes on French Bread'.

small-scale flour mill would surely be able to buy barley meal in, say, quantities of 7 lb at a time; in fact the best barley loaves I ever made were from meal obtained from Clapton Mills, Crewkerne, on the Dorset–Somerset border. This mill is still waterdriven, by the magnificent iron water wheel installed over a century ago; wheat, oats and barley are stone-ground, and various grades of wheatmeal for bread-making are packed for sale direct from the mill in 3 lb, 7 lb, 14 lb and 28 lb bags. The day I visited the mill, in September 1974, barley was being milled. I asked if I might have some of this meal for bread. Mr Lockyer, the miller, although mildly surprised, since his barley is milled for animal food, disappeared for a minute or two and returned with a large bag of freshly milled barley meal from which he had extracted the coarsest of the bran. This supply lasted me for several weeks of the following autumn and winter and, blended sometimes with strong white flour, sometimes with 85 per cent wheatmeal, made bread of remarkable quality and flavour.

The proportions of barley meal to white flour or farmhouse flour (i.e. 81 to 85 per cent wheatmeal) which go to make a good barley loaf can be varied according to taste. The two different ones I work from are:

(1) for the mildest-tasting bread, *1 lb of strong plain flour to 4 oz of barley meal, ½ oz of yeast, ¾ oz of salt, approximately 12 oz of water, 2 to 3 tablespoons of buttermilk, cream or creamy milk;* and (2) for a stronger, darker bread, *12 oz of 81 per cent wheatmeal or farmhouse flour to 4 oz each of 100 per cent whole wheatmeal and barley meal, with other ingredients as before.*

These quantities are for a large tin of 3½ pint capacity, and 4 inches in depth.

Equivalent metric quantities: (1) strong plain flour 450 g, barley meal 120 g, yeast 15 g, salt 20 g, water approximately 340 g, buttermilk, cream or creamy milk 2 to 3 tablespoons; (2) 81 per cent wheatmeal or farmhouse flour 340 g, 100 per cent whole wheatmeal 120 g, barley meal 120 g, other ingredients as in (1). Tin size: a large tin of 2 litre capacity, 10 cm deep.

Making up, raising of the dough, and baking of the loaf are as in the basic bread recipe on pp. 256 to 263, remembering that the two different flours or meals should be very thoroughly mixed, and that, when making bread wholly or with a proportion of coarse meal containing a quantity of bran, it is always – except in unusually hot weather – a help to warm the flour, or at any rate the mixing bowl, and equally the tin or tins in which the bread is to be baked.

Notes and variations: 1. To try just one small barley loaf, to be baked in a tin of 1¾ pint or 1 litre capacity, 3½ inches or 9 cm in depth, proportions are 8 oz or 225 g of strong plain or farmhouse flour to 4 oz or 120 g of barley meal, a generous ½ oz or 15 g of salt, ½ oz or 15 g of yeast, approximately 8 oz or 225 g (1 cup U.S.) of water and 2 tablespoons of buttermilk or cream. Baking time will be approximately as for a large loaf.

2. I have found it best to bake barley bread in tins, as opposed to making hand-moulded loaves. Using tins, a moister dough can be made, so the bread retains its freshness and its very characteristic aroma and flavour for three or four days, whereas a 'crusty' barley loaf bakes rather hard, and dries out quickly.

3. Barley bread is particularly good with English cheeses such as matured Cheddar, Cheshire, Wensleydale and Lancashire – when, and if, such commodities are to be found.

· BARLEY BREAD ON A LEAVEN ·

This is a Cornish recipe, from Mullion. I quote it for its interesting detail.

'To make the leaven mix a small quantity of barley flour with warm water into a dough. Form it into a round shape, like a pat of butter; make a dent in the centre with the thumb, about half-way through. Set the dough on a plate, cross it lightly twice, like a hot-cross bun, and fill the dent with warm water. Set it aside for a few days when the dough will have fermented and split like an over-ripe fruit. It is then ready for use instead of yeast to "plum" the bread, which is mixed in the usual way with warm water and a little salt.

'When the bread has been sufficiently kneaded, take a small piece of the dough and prepare it for leaven against the next baking day.

'Cover the newly mixed bread with a cloth and set in a warm place. When risen form into cone-shaped loaves and bake under a kettle on the hearth.

'The loaves were usually grouped in threes, and the soft crust, where the loaves touched each other, was called "kissing crust".'

Cornish Recipes Ancient and Modern, compiled by Edith Martin
for the Cornwall Federation of Women's Institutes, 5th edn, 1930
(first published 1929)

A RECEIPT FOR MAKING BREAD WITHOUT BARM,
· BY THE HELP OF A LEAVEN ·

The title of this recipe 'for making bread without barm' is misleading, since it is for bread made on the basis of a yeast or barm leaven, as opposed to the spontaneous leaven described in the 'salt-rising' bread recipe which follows it. Mrs Glasse's recipe, obtained by her from the Dublin Society, provides a good description of one of the most common methods of breadmaking, both domestic and professional, of the seventeenth and eighteenth centuries. It was used mainly, I think, for the coarser kinds of bread, mixtures of wheatmeal and rye, or of wheatmeal with only the outside bran bolted out.

'Take a Lump of Dough, about two Pounds of your last Making, which has been raised by Barm, keep it by you in a wooden Vessel, and cover it well with Flour. This is your Leaven; then the Night before you intend to bake, put the said Leaven to a Peck of Flour, and work them well together with warm Water. Let it lie in a dry wooden Vessel, well covered with a Linnen Cloth and a Blanket, and keep it in a warm Place. This Dough kept warm will rise again next Morning, and will be sufficient to mix with two or three Bushels of Flour, being worked up with warm Water and a little Salt. When it is well worked up, and thoroughly mixed with all the Flour, let it be well covered with the Linnen and Blanket, until you find it rise; then knead it well, and work it up into Bricks or Loaves, making the Loaves broad, and not so thick and high as is frequently done, by which Means the Bread will be better baked. Then bake your Bread.

'Always keep by you two or more Pounds of the Dough of your last Baking well covered with Flour to make Leaven to serve from one Baking-Day to another; the more Leaven is put to the Flour, the lighter and spungier the Bread will be. The fresher the Leaven, the Bread will be less sour.'

Recipe from the Dublin Society
Hannah Glasse, *The Art of Cookery Made Plain and Easy*, 1747

· SALT-RISING BREAD (1) ·

Like the barley bread on a leaven, p. 298, this is made on a spontaneous ferment, but with one ferment only and a relatively quick one, ready to use in about 6 hours, although sometimes it is left overnight. It is essential that the ferment or leaven be put in a jar or jug set in a big pan of water kept at a constant temperature. The following description of salt-rising bread and of the changes which occur as the leaven ferments explains much about leavens which might otherwise be obscure. The account was written by an American professional baker, who omits however the awful warnings given by James Beard[1] as to the terrible smell coming from the leaven as it ferments.

'Dough raised by spontaneous fermentation. New dough, as it contains both gluten and sugar, when moist, is capable of fermentation without adding any other substance. If simple flour and water be mixed and set aside in a warm place, after the lapse of several hours it will exhibit symptoms of internal chemical action, becoming sour from the formation of lactic acid, while minute bubbles appear, which are owing to a gas set free within the dough. The changes are irregular and uncertain on account of the property and condition of the constituents of the flour. They also proceed with greater or less rapidity at the surface or in intervals accordingly as the parts are exposed to the cooling and oxidizing influences of the air. Bread baked from such dough is sour, heavy, and altogether bad. Yet true vinous fermentation may be spontaneously established in the dough, by taking measures to quicken the action.

'If a small portion of flour and water be mixed to the consistency of batter (its half fluid state being favourable to rapid chemical change), and the mixture be placed in a jar or pitcher, and set in a vessel of water, kept at a temperature of from 100°F to 110°F; in the course of five or six hours decomposition will have set in, with a copious production of gas bubbles, which may be seen by the appearance of the batter when stirred. If this be now mixed and kneaded with a large mass of dough, moulded into loaves and set aside for an hour or two in a warm place, the dough will swell or "*rise*" to a much larger bulk; and when baked, will yield a light spongy bread. A little salt is usually added at first, which promotes the fermentation; hence, bread raised in this manner is called "*salt-rising*" bread. Milk is often used for mixing the flour, instead of water, and the product is then called "*milk-emptying bread*".'

J. Thompson Gill, *The Complete Bread, Cake and Cracker Baker*,
5th edn, Chicago, 1881

1. *Beard on Bread*, New York, Knopf, 1973; London, Michael Joseph, 1976.

· SALT-RISING BREAD (2) ·

'1 pt new milk   1 pt boiling water poured into
½ oz salt   the milk

'Thicken with flour; make a stiff batter and beat till very light; place the vessel containing the batter in a pan of warm water, let it stand 5 or 6 hours where it will keep warm, when the "emptyings" will be light. Put sufficient flour in a bread pan; scald part of the flour; cool it with water or milk sufficient to make the sponge (not too stiff); stir in the "emptyings", and place in a warm situation to rise; when light (in about an hour) mix into loaves; place to rise; prove, place in pans and let rise again.

'A little butter, ground ginger and soda or saleratus are often used in making the above.'

ibid.

· BREADBAKING IN THE AGA OVEN ·

Two of the four ovens of a large Aga range can be used for the simultaneous baking of a dozen loaves. The recipe quoted here is the one given in a leaflet supplied with the cookers in the 1920s.

'The even temperature of both the roasting and baking ovens is ideal for bread baking. Using both ovens, 12 2 lb loaves can be cooked at one time, i.e. six 2 lb loaves in each oven.

'A DAY'S BAKING

14 lb flour   6 pints (about) luke-warm water
14 teaspoonfuls salt   4 teaspoonfuls sugar
4 oz yeast   12 2 lb tins

Equivalent metric quantities: flour 6·25 kg, salt 14 teaspoons, yeast 120 g, water about 3·25 litres, sugar 4 teaspoons. Tin size: twelve 1 kg tins.

'*Method*
'Warm flour and salt, mix the yeast and sugar and put it to test in a warm place on the cooker, add tested yeast and water to flour, mix and knead very well. Cover with a cloth, and put to rise on the lid of the simmering plate, and leave till the dough is twice its original size. Knead again lightly and divide into twelve equal parts. Put the dough into greased tins and set to rise again. Bake for about 30 to 45 minutes in the roasting

and baking ovens. To brown and crisp the sides of the loaves it is a good plan to remove the loaves from the tins for the last ten minutes' baking.'

Another version of this recipe, dated 1933 and supplied to the late Ambrose Heath by Miss M. S. Frood, M.B.E., Warden of the Helena Club, London, gives 12 lb of flour, 12 teaspoons of salt, 3½ oz of yeast, 5 pints, approximately, of lukewarm water, 3 teaspoons of sugar.

The batch of dough is divided into five 2 lb tins and four 2½ lb tins. When risen for the first time, half the dough is kneaded, divided and put into the five smaller tins and left to rise for the second time.

The remaining portion of dough is now kneaded and divided into the four larger tins. The theory was that by the time this task was completed the dough in the first batch of tins would be ready to put in to bake in the top or hottest oven. After 30 or 40 minutes in the top oven, the tins could be moved to the lower and rather cooler oven to finish baking for another 15 to 30 minutes.

By the time the first batch is ready to be moved from the top oven, the second batch should be sufficiently risen to be put in to bake. It is left for 1 to 1¼ hours in the top oven, which will now be slightly cooler, so that there is no need to move the bread to the lower oven.[1]

Even if all this dovetailing didn't quite work out in practice, the theory is an excellent one and could well prove very useful today, to those who bake in gas and electric ovens as well as to the owners of Aga ranges. Division of the dough would have to be worked out to fit the capacity of the tins now available (few people would have 2 lb and 2½ lb tins), but this would scarcely present a difficulty. I would also suggest that for breadbaking in the Aga an oven thermometer is advisable.

As is so often the case with English bread recipes, however admirable in other respects, I find the proportion of salt far too small. One teaspoonful per pound of flour makes insipid bread. Of course, with so little salt the dough rises quickly. I prefer to give it more time, and have better bread at the end of it all. Also, unless using dried yeast, I would omit the sugar.

Equivalent metric quantities: flour 5·5 kg, salt 12 teaspoons or more to taste, yeast 100 g, water approximately 2·75 litres, sugar 3 teaspoons. Tin sizes: five 1 kg tins and four 1·5 kg tins.

1. This variation of the first recipe was published in Ambrose Heath's *Good Food on the Aga*, London, Faber & Faber, 1933. The book was basically a reprint of the author's *Good Food* (1932), with an introductory chapter on the upkeep and management of the Aga, and the special utensils made for use on the hot plates and in the ovens.

· UNDER-COVER BREADBAKING ·

'Loaves called "undertins" or "underpans" are those baked either on the oven bottom or on baking sheets, and covered with a long pan, which the loaf fills as it springs. They are generally made for sandwich bread . . . these loaves . . . are baked in an atmosphere much more impregnated with steam than any of the open-pan sort.'

The Bakers' ABC, ed. John Kirkland, 1927

Since it is so difficult in an ordinary household oven to create the steamy atmosphere required for the successful formation of a truly 'crusty' loaf, that is a loaf baked without benefit of a tin, and therefore crusty all round rather than just on the top, the 'undertin' method seemed to me to offer a clue worth following up. If a good loaf could be baked under an

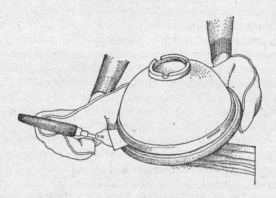

inverted tin, would it not be possible to apply the method to a crusty loaf, but using an earthenware or stoneware bowl or casserole instead of a tin? Experiment with this simple system proved enormously success-ful. The increase in the volume of a loaf baked for the first 15 to 30 or even 45 minutes under cover of a deep bowl is quite dramatic, the quality of the crust is much improved, and the crumb moist and evenly baked. What has happened is that the inverted bowl or casserole has become something like a small, domed, brick oven, a wonderful genera-tor of moist heat. Within its confines the yeast in the dough grows with great rapidity and, as the loaf expands, it is drawn upwards, rather than spreading only sideways, as so often happens if your dough is a moist one. Under the dome, the crust forms gradually, allowing the crumb to grow to its full extent before the yeast cells are killed, and this eliminates the fault which spoils so many home-made crusty loaves – a crust which has formed so rapidly that it has become overcooked and hard long before the crumb has had a chance to expand, the resulting loaf being poorly formed and small with a rock-like crust and heavy crumb.

Now, to experiment with the under-cover method the only piece of required equipment not necessarily used in bread-baking is a large deep earthenware or stoneware bowl, which must, it goes without saying, be heat resistant. I use an English earthenware bowl unglazed on the outside, and with an interior dark brown or white glaze. These bowls are made at the Devon pottery of Brannams at Barnstaple. English brown stoneware mixing bowls from the Pearson potteries at Chesterfield would also probably serve very well.[1] So would a large-capacity Pyrex glass bowl. For that matter, a large flower pot, if it is still possible to find one in old-fashioned terracotta rather than plastic, will do just as well, if not better, since it can be soaked in water before being inverted over the bread, and will then generate a steamier atmosphere than a stoneware bowl which is not so porous. Another alternative is a deep, straight-sided two-handled casserole of the stock-pot type. It should be clearly understood, though, that whatever bowl or pot is used must be large enough to make, of itself, a kind of oven within the oven; there must be space for the dough to expand, and the finished loaf is not supposed to *fill* the pot, although to a minor extent it will take on something of the shape of the pot used. For a loaf made with $1\frac{1}{4}$ lb of flour, the bowls I use are approximately 9 inches in diameter and $4\frac{1}{2}$ inches deep. Those I have mentioned are tough and will withstand the high temperatures needed for bread-baking; such bowls are however fairly heavy, so that a very large one will be cumbersome to manipulate – and it has to be borne in mind that, after 30 minutes or more in an oven at a minimum temperature of 400°F or 205°C, the bowl will be exceedingly hot, so it is not advisable to use one very much larger than actually needed.

To make one of these under-cover loaves, then, simply use any of the recipes given in this book for bread baked without a tin – say, the Coburg made with plain strong flour on p. 276, or the wheatmeal and oatmeal mixture on p. 282. Granary loaves and pan Coburgs are also very successful baked by this method.

1. But not the familiar cane-coloured English mixing bowls, which are not made to withstand high temperatures.

Mix the dough and leave it for its first rising in the ordinary way. Then, having broken down the dough, kneaded and shaped it on your baking sheet, or better, a flat earthenware platter,[1] heat resistant, cover it with the inverted bowl and leave it to rise for the second time.

About 5 minutes before you intend baking the loaf reshape it and cut or slash it in the way you prefer; as soon as the cuts open, replace the bowl or pot, and put all into the oven, heated to 450° to 465°F, 230° to 240°C, gas no. 8 or 9.

Leave the loaf for 30 to 35 minutes before removing the bowl to look at it. Make sure that you have a good thick cloth or oven gloves, and take the whole contraption, baking sheet, loaf and cover, from the oven before attempting to remove the cover or bowl. Slide a metal spatula or fish slice under the rim, tilting the bowl so that it is easy to lift it off. At this stage, depending upon the type of bread you are making and also upon your particular oven, the loaf should be very well grown while the crust will be only slightly coloured, or possibly not at all. Return the uncovered loaf to the oven, still at the same temperature.

After another 15 minutes, the crust should be golden, but may still be soft. In this case leave the loaf in the oven for another 10 to 15 minutes. At the end of the time the crust should be very beautiful, a mixture of gold and brown, with almost silvery patches where the cuts were made. The loaf will have shrunk a little while the crust has been baking to a proper crispness. If you prefer a soft crust, then leave the loaf covered throughout the whole of the cooking time, allowing an extra 10 to 15 minutes' baking time but at a reduced temperature.

Cool the loaf as usual on a rack. I find it a good idea to place the wire rack across the top of the bowl which is still warm from the oven. In this way the loaf cools gradually, instead of being subjected to a sudden draught of cold air.

Notes : Some months after I had started experimenting with this under-cover system of breadbaking, and after the foregoing description was written, I discovered from the works of John Kirkland and Walter Banfield, so frequently quoted in these pages, that professional bakers had long used a similar system of baking loaves for competition work. Their covering domes, or handled boxes, made of steel, were called

1. Baked on an iron or other metal sheet, the undercrust of this bread tends to become tough. An earthenware dish or platter – which should be very thoroughly greased or oiled – eliminates this fault, producing a soft undercrust. If it is too soft, give it a few minutes upside down in the oven at the end of baking time.

bonnets, a very descriptive term. The shape is rather that of a tall *marmite* or stock-pot, which in practice does rather better because the steel bonnets were tinny and rusted quickly. On the whole, though, I prefer an earthenware bowl or pot to a steel or other metal one, the disadvantage of a bowl being that it has no handles, and is heavy, so if you have a large enough earthenware stock-pot of the French *pot-au-feu* type, it makes an admirable baking cover.

In French cookery the bonnet would be called a *cloche*, a baking cover known, in varying forms, since prehistoric times, and still in use in many primitive parts of the world (see Plate 15). By my attempts to simulate conditions in a brick oven, all I had done, as I discovered, was to hit on a very ancient method of breadbaking and adapt it to a modern gas oven. The system is very successful, although it has its limitations in that unless you have an extra large oven it is feasible to bake only one large or two small loaves at a time. For those really interested in breadbaking, however, making the experiments is quite enlightening.

A bakers' steel bonnet for competition bread was especially successful with the tricky cottage loaf. Dimensions of the bonnet are 10 inches by 10 inches. For home baking an outsize fireproof earthenware stock pot or bowl makes much better bread.

· POT BREAD: THE SELF-SUFFICIENT WAY ·

'That some folks yet have a very primitive method of making bread I had well understood, but a visit paid a short time ago to the country disclosed, to my astonishment, what is, perhaps, the most primitive arrangement, and I think my readers will be interested in it; so here it is for them. It was early in the spring of the year, and they had been thrashing out their little stock of wheat with a FLAIL on the floor, and then it was separated, the chaff from the wheat, by simply lifting a shovelful of grains and dropping them again, the wind taking out the chaff, which was collected against a canvas stretched from uprights set in the ground. When they had cleaned it to their satisfaction, the wheat was collected in a sack and carried to the mill to be "ground". The chaff, hulls, and all waste was also collected and saved in a sack. Now, a few days later, the wheat was returned, ground to flour, together with the offal, or bran and pollard, as perhaps the majority of my readers know it by that name. The flour was in part turned out into a large red earthenware pan, some salt, yeast, and water added, and turned into dough by the industrious housewife. Now some of my readers have, no doubt, seen these large round pots, with three feet, which usually are swung upon a tripod stand, something like the witches' cauldron in "Macbeth," but not so large. That, however, is the shape. Now the "leese," or "chaff," is turned out of the sack upon the ground outside the house and set on fire. It burnt away briskly, till at last it consisted of only a heap of very hot ashes. This was swept aside with a broom, the prepared dough set in the centre on the earth, the pot turned down over it, and then the live embers piled over the pot; more fuel was placed upon it, and thus the bread was baked. When a portion was served for tea with some excellent fresh Devonshire butter, I had no hesitation in saying that I had never tasted sweeter bread. It was, indeed, perfection; and in this case you see the waste from the wheat had been utilised to cook it with, which, no doubt, contributed somewhat to its unique flavour. Of course it would be impracticable to feed London in this way, and so we will get along to more modern, and, let me hope, more profitable, methods.'

Frederick T. Vine, *Practical Breadmaking*, 1897

· WELSH PAN OR POT BREAD (1) ·

'Take three pounds and a half of brown flour (flour which has only had the coarser bran taken out of it), put it to rise with about two tablespoonfuls of barm, and, when risen, mix it and knead it in the usual manner;

then put it into an iron pot or a thick earthen pan, and turn it topsy-turvy on a flat stone, which should be placed on the ground in the middle of a heap of hot embers, made by burning wood, peat, or turf; cover the pot or pan entirely over with hot embers, leave it to bake, and when the ashes are cold take it out. This mode of baking produces most excellent bread, but of course it cannot be practised economically except where such rural operations are carried on as provide the necessary quantity of hot embers for other purposes within a convenient distance of the house.'

Lady Llanover, *Good Cookery*, 1867

· WELSH POT BREAD (2) ·

Elizabeth Clarke, in *The Valley*,[1] describes another method of Welsh pot baking: 'In the ordinary way Sian did her cooking on the peat fire, chastising it with sticks and bellows and embracing her cauldrons with hot turves. Even the bread was baked in a three-legged pot with a pyramid of smouldering peat raised about it. A loaf was sealed in with a ribbon of dough round the lid, and everyone said there was no crust half so sweet.' This author is writing of life in the 1920s on her grandmother's Radnorshire hill farm. The pot bread, Mrs Clarke recounts, was made just for the family. When a larger quantity was needed, as at a sheep shearing, or for Christmas, then the bread oven in the side of the chimney was heated with a burning faggot, and the baking was done there. The peat fire was used for boiling, and on the day a huge quantity of potatoes and a bag of peas went into the pot.

Many of these three-legged iron pots still survive in Wales. Several are to be seen in the various furnished kitchens on display at the St Fagans Folk Museum near Cardiff. See also Plate 21, and illustration on p. 218.

CORNISH POT BREAD ·

'Baking iron and kettle

'Heat baking iron to red heat. Heat kettle. Place bread or cake on iron,

1. London, Faber & Faber, 1969.

cover with kettle, surround with hot cinders and cover with burning furze and turf. Bake 1 to 1½ hours according to size.'

St Just Women's Institute. From *Cornish Recipes Ancient and Modern*, compiled by Edith Martin for the Cornwall Federation of Women's Institutes, 11th edn, 1934 (first published 1929)

· IRISH POT BREAD ·

In Ireland pot bread was baked in much the same way as in Wales. The old way still survives in isolated parts of the country. Soda bread baked in the pot is delicious.

· CUMBRIAN POT BREAD ·

In *Life and Tradition in the Lake District*,[1] William Rollinson describes a 'curious fireside cooking implement . . . a frying pan which could, with slight modification, be used for baking wheat bread'. On these occasions an iron ring two or three inches deep was placed inside the pan in order to increase the depth, and the lid was placed on top of this and the whole covered with burning peat.

· FLOWERPOT BREAD ·

Terracotta flower pots make admirable bread moulds. Anyone who still possesses some of these now nearly obsolete pots may like to try the following method. The best size of pot for a loaf is 5½ inches in diameter by 4½ inches deep.

First temper the pots for baking by coating them liberally outside and inside with oil and leaving them empty in the oven while bread or something else is baking at a fairly high temperature. Do this two or three times. Once they are well impregnated with oil the pots will need very little greasing, and the baked loaves will slip out of the pots without the slightest sign of sticking.

For two 14 to 15 oz loaves make your dough with 22 oz of 85 per cent wheatmeal or a mixture of wheatmeal, oatmeal and malted meal such as

1. London, J. M. Dent, 1974.

Bermaline or granary meal. For this amount of flour ½oz of yeast will be ample, plus ¾oz of salt, and for making up the dough 12 to 15oz of milk and water mixed.

Equivalent metric quantities for two 400 g loaves: flour 600 g, yeast 15 g, salt 20 g, milk and water mixed 340 to 400 g. Size of flower pot: two pots 13·5 cm in diameter by 12 cm deep.

When possible give this dough two risings of 2 hours each – or longer if it happens to suit your timetable – and a final proving of about 45 minutes.

The trick about making good flowerpot bread is to bake the loaves upside down. This is easier than it sounds: when the dough has fully risen for the second time, break it down, knead it very thoroughly and divide it into two equal pieces. Shape and fit each into a warmed and greased flower pot. There should be enough to fill the pots by just over half. Stand them upright in a warm place, covering them with damp cloths or sheets of polythene. Leave them for 30 to 45 minutes.

When the dough has risen to within 1½ inches of the tops of the pots, invert them on a baking sheet and put them, immediately, into the preheated hot oven to bake. Leave them for 30 minutes at 425° to 450°F, 220° to 230°C, gas nos. 7 to 8.

Now slip the loaves out of the pots and let them bake for another 10 to 15 minutes at reduced heat, 320° to 350°F, 160° to 180°C, gas nos. 2½ to 4.

Cool the loaves on a rack, or balance them across the empty flower pots.

Notes and variations: 1. What happens when the loaves are under the flower pots is that during the first few minutes of baking the dough springs up and fills the pot, producing a perfectly even and well formed loaf, whereas if the pot is put upright into the oven in the normal way the dough rises unevenly over the top, making an untidy loaf with a mushroom top which often sticks to the sides of the pot.

2. When baked under tins, bread emerges rather steamy and clammy, but when baked under earthenware pots, this fault doesn't occur. The loaves are nicely crusted and the crumb well honeycombed.

3. Cracked wheat or coarse oatmeal can be scattered at the bottom of the pots and on the sides before the dough is put in. This gives a nice finish to the loaves when they are turned out.

· PEGGY TUB BREAD

This is an interesting and useful old-fashioned system of raising dough, one of the best I have yet come across.

A peggy tub, also known as a dolly tub, was a wash tub with a hand-operated spinner or dolly and peg or four-legged peggy with a cross handle which drove the water through the linen to be washed. These dolly tubs, originally made of wood and subsequently of galvanized iron, were the forerunners of today's tumble-and-spin washing machines.

When not in use for their legitimate purpose wash tubs came in handy for a variety of household purposes such as the quick salting of a piece of meat, the raising of dough, and even the brewing of beer or country wines.

However, for making peggy tub bread you do not need a wash tub or any tub at all. A large bowl or a small bread crock or pancheon will do just as well.

The idea of peggy tub bread is that you can mix your dough, wrap it in a cloth, immerse it in a tub of cold water, and go out for the morning, or even all day. When you return to your dough, it has risen to the top of the tub and looks like a lovely fat soft pillow in its white cloth. You unwrap the dough, transfer it to a floured bowl or board, punch it down, knead it in the ordinary way, then mould it, either into tins or into round loaves which will be baked on an oven sheet. Leave the loaf or loaves in a warm place for 45 minutes to an hour, and bake them as for any other loaf.

Almost any dough can be used for peggy tub bread, including fat-enriched mixtures; and contrary to expectation the dough does not stick to the cloth, and is not difficult to knead, although it *is* more moist than dough raised in the normal manner.

The advantages of this slow-rising dough are obvious – and timing is by no means vital. Two hours in the tub will be enough, if that is what suits you, or you can mix the dough at night before you go to bed and it will be ready for kneading in the morning. The system is particularly useful in very warm weather when the dough would over-ferment if left too long. Immersion in cold water makes an infinitely more satisfactory dough than the system of leaving it in the refrigerator. In the cold water the dough rises slowly and evenly and doesn't get over-chilled, therefore you don't have to wait for it to warm up to room temperature. I have found that dough left in the refrigerator tends to produce tough dry bread with a poor volume. Water-risen dough produces moist and very well-expanded bread, particularly if you bake it by the under-cover method described on p. 303. It is instructive that some of the methods used by our ancestors, archaic though they may sound, still turn out to be more satisfactory than the newer fangles of our own age. One of the lessons I have learned from using the method of water-rising dough is that there are two moments only in the life of a loaf of bread, and the dough from which it is made, when it can with impunity be subjected to extremes of temperature: the first is the moment when the ripened and moulded dough is put into a very hot oven to bake; the second is if and when you consign the baked and cooled loaf to the freezer.

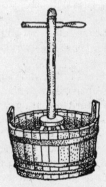

Wash tub with peggy or dolly.

· MUFFIN LOAVES ·

These are rather like soft rolls, but larger. They are made with a quick-rising dough, on much the same lines as the muffin mixture described on pp. 353–4.

1 lb of strong plain flour, ½ oz of yeast, ½ oz of salt, ¼ pint of milk and water mixed, 2 tablespoons of olive oil.

Equivalent metric quantities: strong plain flour 450 g, yeast 15 g, salt 15 g, milk and water mixed 280 g, olive oil 2 tablespoons.

GRAIN MILLING

1. A man kneels to crush grain, using a stone roller on a saddle-shaped stone or quern. Limestone figure, Egypt, sixth dynasty, 2250 B.C. Such querns probably go back to the earliest days of grain cultivation, c.8000 B.C. They are still in use in Mexico for grinding maize meal.

2. Grain-crushing bowl or mortar found in the Lebanon. Probably c.3000 B.C. The pounder or pestle would have been cone-shaped.

3. A woman crushes grain using a stone shaped like a short rolling pin. The quern is set in a big bowl standing on three legs, and the ground meal accumulates round the sides of the container. Terracotta figurine from Rhodes, mid fifth century B.C.

4 and 5. Probably the first rotary querns made their appearance in the Near East during the Neolithic or New Stone Age, 7000 to 3500 B.C. By the first century B.C. they were in general domestic use in Britain. Both these reconstructed querns are in the Jewry Wall Museum, Leicester, and can be worked by visitors. It should be appreciated, though, that querns were operated on the ground, not at table level.

6 (*below*). A Roman bakery of the first century A.D., uncovered at Pompeii in 1810. The grain was ground on the premises in the mills on the right of the photograph. The hourglass-shaped upper stones are hollowed to fit the corresponding cones of the fixed bedstones. The drawing on p. 27 shows how they were turned by slaves. On the left is the arched brick oven, prototype of the European bakers' oven for hundreds of years.

7. A farmer's wife rides to the mill with her sack of grain on her head. The windmill is of the early post mill type. Misericord on a choir stall in the chancel of Bristol Cathedral, 1520.

8 (*centre*). It is recorded of Clement Paston, fourteenth-century founder of the famous Norfolk family, that he had 'in Paston a five score or six score acres of land at the most ... with a little poor watermill running by the little river there'. His mill must have looked very like this one, portrayed by the artist of the Luttrell Psalter, executed in East Anglia, *c.* 1340. On the right of the picture are two eel traps.

9 (*below*). From the twelfth to the seventeenth centuries floating mills were familiar sights in European cities (p. 14). Detail from the frontispiece of a part-Flemish part-English MS. of the fourteenth century (Bodley 264).

10. Until the suppression of the monasteries by Henry VIII all religious houses, from Westminster Abbey down to the minor provincial priories, had their own grain stores, bakeries, brewhouses and mills. The little watermill at Michelham Priory in East Sussex, founded in the thirteenth century, was restored to working order in the mid 1970s. Visitors to the priory can buy the freshly ground flour and see the workings of a small mill much as it was five or six centuries ago.

A list of other recently restored mills open to the public is supplied by the Wind and Watermill section of the Society for the Protection of Ancient Buildings.

11(*left*). After every hundred or so hours of milling, the surfaces of the stones have worn down and must be regrooved or dressed. The 1930s millwright in the photograph is dressing a French burr stone in an Essex windmill. The grooves or furrows are cut to a complex pattern which ensures that the grain is distributed evenly as the stones revolve, and that it doesn't overheat. Both stones are dressed so that when the upper one is laid on the bedstone, the furrows cross each other at an angle.

12 (*right*). A Roman millstone found at Kirkby Bellars in Leicestershire. The stone is black lava from Andernach near Coblenz on the Rhine. For centuries lava stones were the most highly prized for the grinding of fine flour. This one, 20 ins in diameter, is rather large for a domestic hand mill, so would perhaps have come from an animal-turned mill.

BREAD OVENS

13 (*top*). Bakers at work in ancient Egypt. One man kneads dough, the second tends the stepped oven with its embryo chimney, shielding his face from the heat. Tomb model, Middle Kingdom, *c.*1900 B.C.

14 (*left*). A portable earthenware bread oven. While the bread was baking, a clay door would have sealed in the heat. Troad, from Dardanus. Early fifth century B.C.

15 (*right*). Portable earthenware cloche oven or cooking bell. This could be heated over a wood fire, then placed over the bread to be baked. Heat could be maintained either by live embers piled up round the cloche or by fire in a brazier underneath the bread. Modern versions of the cloche or *fourneau de campagne* are still practical, especially for caravan and camping cookery. The Athenian one illustrated is dated 500–480 B.C. It was found during the excavation of the Agora and is now housed in the Museum of the Stoa of Attalos.

16. A fifteenth-century French baker and a pastrycook at work. The baker is loading his oven with small white loaves, the equivalent of our manchets or paindemayn. These were the fine rolls eaten by those who could afford the best wheat flour with most of the bran sieved out. Note how the baker's assistant is moulding a fresh batch, one small loaf in each hand, just as professional bakers still mould round loaves today. Woodcut from *The Kalendar and Compost of Shepherds*, printed at Troyes, 1480. This almanac was subsequently much copied and an English translation appeared in 1518.

17. The local baker and his arched brick oven carved on a sixteenth-century misericord in the church of Estouteville-Ecalles, Normandy.

18. A gravel-tempered clay wall oven found in the Tudor part of a Welsh farmhouse at Llancafan, Glamorgan. These ovens, unique in Britain, were produced in the Devon potteries at Barnstaple and Fremington. Many were exported via Bideford to South and West Wales, Ireland, and in the seventeenth century to the American colonies. They were still being made in the 1890s. This one is 16 ins high at the crown and 16 ins across at the widest point. The walls are 1 in thick. It is one of the several preserved in the Welsh Folk Museum at St Fagans, Cardiff. Two others are in the Bideford Public Library and Museum.

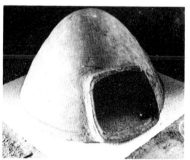

19. A terracotta bread oven originally in a farmhouse in the province of León, Spain, where many such ovens, built into the wall of the house, are still in use. This one, now in the possession of Anthony Denney, is 32 ins interior diameter and 20 ins high at the crown. The walls are 1 in thick. The doors of these ovens are always of wood, lined with tin on the inside, and with a wooden handle.

Ovens of the identical shape, on a larger scale and left free-standing for out-of-doors baking, are still to be seen in New Mexico.

20. Another Barnstaple oven, bearing the scars of restoration but with its clay door intact, preserved at the Colonial National Historical Park, Jamestown, Virginia. For more accounts of these ovens see pp. 177–9.

21. One of two main types of cast-iron cooking pot used for bread-baking on days when the oven was not fired, and in cottages and farmhouses where there was no wall oven. Many such pots are still used for bread in Wales, Ireland and the West Country. This one is 13 ins in diameter and 6½ ins deep. The Welsh Folk Museum, St Fagans.

22. The iron door of the original brick oven, probably *c.* 1790, built into the wall of the back kitchen of Ty Isaf, a small farmhouse at Taliaris, Carmarthenshire. The iron grate and the oven at the right, from the famous Shropshire foundry of Coalbrookdale, were installed in the open hearth at a later date, when the owners probably decided to use the iron side oven for baking their bread.

23. The same brick oven cleaned out and restored to use by the present owner of Ty Isaf. Although difficult of access owing to the Victorian range and grate, good bread can be baked in it. The photograph shows the wood and kindling ready for firing. Unless in frequent use, two hours is the minimum time to allow for a large brick oven to reach bread-baking temperature, but very little fuel is needed. Note the structure and curve of the oven roof. It is approximately 24 ins high at the crown, about 36 ins deep and the same in diameter. In the front kitchen of Ty Isaf is a hole in the side wall of the open hearth from which a small subsidiary oven, no doubt from a Devon pottery, has been removed.

24. A modern electric oven launched in 1971. Belling, the makers, claim that the fan system of circulating heat gives an identical temperature throughout the oven, eliminating the need to change the position of a batch of loaves during baking.

Warm the flour, mixed with the salt, in a covered heatproof bowl, in a low oven, 285°F, 140°C, gas no. 1. Five to seven minutes should be sufficient. While the flour is warming mix ¼ pint each of hot water and cold milk. With a little of this cream the yeast.

Mix the dough in the routine way, pouring the yeast into the centre of the flour, then adding the rest of the milk and water and working the mixture into a smooth, pliable dough. Finally add the olive oil. Form the dough, which will be fairly soft, into a ball. Cover the bowl. Leave the dough to rise until it has become very spongy and has at least doubled its volume.

Have ready a floured baking sheet or flat earthenware platter. Break down the dough, knead it for a minute or two on the baking sheet or platter. Form it into two nice plump little round loaves, folding the edges under, so that the loaves will hold their shape. Cover them with the rinsed dried bowl and leave them for about 15 minutes before putting them to bake in a fairly hot oven, 400° to 425°F, 205° to 220°C, gas nos. 6 to 7, preferably with the inverted bowl still covering them, for the first 15 minutes of baking. Remove the bowl and leave the little loaves to bake for another 15 to 20 minutes, until the crusts are well formed but not too hard.

Cool the loaves on a rack balanced across the bowl which will still be warm from the oven.

Notes and variations: This dough can be baked in a tin, preferably a rather shallow one, such as the round dish-shaped one or the shallow farmhouse shape, both shown on p. 207. Baking will take an extra 10 to 15 minutes, and there is no need to cover the loaf or loaves during the first quarter of an hour, although you achieve better risen and larger volume loaves if you do. In any case turn them out of their tins as soon as they will shake out easily, and finish the baking with the loaves lying on their sides.

· ROBERT MAY'S FRENCH BREAD ·

This is adapted from Robert May's recipe for 'French bread the best way', quoted on p. 375. Robert May's book *The Accomplisht Cook* was first published in 1660, the year of the Restoration of Charles II. A professional cook and the son of a professional cook, Adrian May, the very youthful Robert was partly trained in France, where he had been sent by one of his father's employers, Lady Dormer. Later, the younger May was apprenticed to Arthur Hollingsworth, cook to the Grocers' Hall and Star Chamber.

In the course of his long life Robert May became head cook and steward in several noble households, including that of the Countess of Kent, whose little book of receipts, published in 1653, two years after her death, is quoted a number of times in these pages.

Robert May's French bread is extremely simple, a total refutation – there are many others in this book – of the belief too hastily assumed by home economists, cookery journalists and cookery-book reviewers, that any recipe earlier than Mrs Beeton is impracticable today.

May's recipe starts off with a gallon of flour. That is, or was, about 7 lb. Reduce the quantity to 1 lb 2 oz. Next 'a pint of good new ale barm'. That one scarcely needs thought. We know that ½ oz of present day bakers' yeast is sufficient for up to 2 lb of flour. Then 'the whites of six new laid eggs well beaten in a dish'. This is a case of not dividing all the ingredients equally. Two whites are about the right quantity for 1 lb 2 oz of flour. New laid eggs are not quite so easy, but 'new laid' is really a way of saying 'fresh'. Then, 'well beaten in a dish' doesn't, I think, mean stiffly whisked because when Stuart writers intended this they wrote 'beaten to a snow' or 'to a high froth', so the whites are just beaten until they have *started* to froth, as for clarifying broth. The quantity of milk and water for 1 lb 2 oz of flour is, as we know, ½ pint, give or take a spoonful. Then there is salt and nothing else except those 'little wooden dishes'. These were used only to fashion or mould the loaves, not as baking moulds. French recipes of the period give similar directions for moulding special breads in wooden bowls, which were to be well floured to prevent the dough from sticking. (The system of moulding and proving bread upside down in cloth-lined baskets, still in use today in many French bakeries, must have been evolved later.) Alternatively, the loaves can be hand-shaped into 'rouls', into two small round loaves, or into one large one. I find the bread which results very good; it must be similar to the seventeenth-century manchet loaves described in the chapter on manchets, and since Robert May could well have learned this method during his apprenticeship in France – the egg whites in the dough differentiate it from most English 'French bread' recipes of the time – it might even be an example of the seventeenth-century *pain bénist*, the French equivalent.

To summarize the recipe, a worthwhile one:

1 lb 2 oz of flour – preferably a half-and-half mixture of unbleached white and 85 per cent wheatmeal; ½ oz of yeast; 2 egg whites; ½ pint to 12 oz of milk and water mixed, allowing for a rather larger proportion of water than milk, say six parts of water to four of milk; and ½ oz of salt.

Equivalent metric quantities: flour 500 g, yeast 15 g, egg whites 2, milk and water mixed 280 to 340 g, salt 15 g.

Warm the flour and salt; pour in the yeast creamed with a little of the warmed milk and water mixture. Add the egg whites, beaten in a small bowl until they are just beginning to froth. Pour in the remaining milk and water. Mix as for ordinary bread dough. Leave to rise until spongy and light. This will take 45 minutes to 1 hour, depending on the temperature of the ingredients when the dough was mixed.

Break down the dough, divide it and shape it into two round loaves – or long rolls if you prefer. Put them upside down on a floured wooden tray, board or flat earthenware platter. Cover with a sheet of polythene or a light cloth and leave them to recover volume. About 30 minutes should be long enough.

Turn the proved loaves right side up on to a baking sheet. Slash the tops with one slanting cut, rather off centre, or leave them uncut if you prefer. Bake as usual on the centre shelf of a hot oven, 450°F, 230°C, gas no. 8, for the first 15 minutes. Then, to prevent the crust getting too hard, cover the loaves with bowls (for this reason it is easier to make the loaves round rather than long, unless you have a large oval casserole which can be used as a cover). In another 15 minutes the loaves should be sufficiently baked.

I am not sure just what the egg whites do to this bread; whatever it is produces very good results. The loaf has a nice crumb, keeps well and can be re-warmed several times in a low oven so that the illusion of freshness remains rather better than with most kinds of bread. One large loaf will keep better than two small ones, and will take a little longer to cook.

It is worth noting that the moulding of round loaves in little wooden dishes as specified by May is not at all a fanciful idea. It is well known that the warmth of wood is propitious to the growth of yeast dough and, having tried the system, I can vouch for its efficacy. The bowl shape makes for a nicely rounded little loaf, there is no sticking problem – provided the bowls are floured – and, instead of turning the dough from one bowl to another, simply turn it, when proved for the second time, from the bowl to the baking sheet. It will emerge nicely rounded and ready for the oven. For a loaf of 1 lb 2 oz of flour I use a bowl of $7\frac{1}{2}$ inches diameter, approximately 4 inches deep. Any round loaf can be proved, like Robert May's, upside down in a floured wooden bowl. It is a sound and simple method; it should be used more often.

· ELIZA ACTON'S SUMMER BREAD ·

The following three recipes are quoted in full from *The English Bread Book* (1857). Although in some respects repetitive, the differences in detail are wonderfully informative. The first tells us in terms of the utmost precision how brewers' yeast was used, and in what quantity, and also explains the best method of making the dough in two stages but measuring the whole amount of flour into the bowl at one time instead of first making a sponge and subsequently incorporating the rest of the flour. Prior to the evolution of German or compressed yeast this was the usual method for household bread.

The second method gives us what came to be known as the 'straight dough' system, which means making up the whole bulk of flour into dough at the outset rather than in two separate stages. Nowadays we take this method for granted. When Eliza Acton was writing it was an innovation which represented a substantial saving of time and labour. The proportion of yeast needed in warm weather is, as Miss Acton proved, exceedingly small.

The third recipe is included for its notes on the preservation of German yeast for household use in pre-refrigerator days.

It will be noted that Miss Acton made her bread with so little salt that it is virtually salt-free. In this respect I cannot go along with her. I think I would find her bread insipid, however light and in other respects successful.

· SUMMER BREAD (1), JUNE 1856 ·

'Flour four pounds, mixed in a very large bowl with a teaspoonful of salt. The middle made hollow, and a single tablespoonful of brewers' yeast (which has been well watered for two days, and kept in a cool larder) very smoothly mixed with a pint of *cold* milk and water, – of which one part of three was new milk, and two were filtered water, – poured in, and stirred and beaten well with as much of the surrounding flour as made it into a stiff batter. On this a thick layer of flour was strewed, the spoon removed, and a large cloth twice doubled was laid over the pan, which was placed on a table in a north room. It was left for two hours, when the sponge had quite burst through the flour, and risen much; and was immediately made into a firm dough, with the addition to the sponge of about a quarter of a pint of *warm* water. In from half to three-quarters of an hour it was divided, and very lightly kneaded up into two loaves; put into shallow, round baking dishes,[1] previously rubbed with butter, placed on a tray, covered with a thick double cloth, and sent to the baker's oven, which was a quarter of a mile distant. This bread proved *excellent*.

'Flour, four pounds; salt, one teaspoonful; brewer's yeast (two days watered), one tablespoonful; *cold* milk and water, one pint: two hours. Warm water, one quarter of a pint; kneaded into firm dough: rising nearly three-quarters of an hour.'

Eliza Acton, The English Bread Book, 1857

· SUMMER BREAD (2), 4 JULY ·

'A gallon and a half of flour, and a dessertspoonful of salt, were made at once into a *firm*, well-kneaded dough with an ounce only (a pennyworth) of German yeast smoothly diluted with part of nearly five pints of weak milk and water, all of which was used *quite cold*. The pan, covered with a thick cloth, was then placed in a room without a fire, but with the door and windows closed, and left for two hours and a half, or rather longer. The dough, which was then perfectly light, was well kneaded a second time, and in half an hour afterwards was made up lightly into five loaves of different sizes and sent, in shallow pans, to a baker's oven. This bread was exceedingly good, and *very* light, proving the small quantity of yeast really required for use in general, during the summer months.

'Flour, one gallon and a half;[2] salt, one dessertspoonful; German yeast, one ounce; good new milk, full three-quarters of a pint; cold water, *exact* imperial measure, two quarts: rising two hours and a half to three hours. Kneaded down; rising again, half to three-quarters of an hour: five loaves. These, if of equal size, would not require, in a

1. Eliza Acton's bread pans were of thick earthenware, rather shallow, and with slightly sloping sides.
2. A gallon and a half of flour weighs $10\frac{1}{2}$ lb.

well-heated brick oven, more than an hour and a quarter's baking, perhaps rather less: in a common iron oven, more time might be needed for them.'

ibid.

· SUMMER BREAD (3), SEPTEMBER 1856 ·

'The ounce (or pennyworth) of German yeast with which this bread was made was brought in from a baker's late on the evening of Friday, Sept. 5th, and put immediately into an exact half-pint of cold filtered water, and remained undisturbed in a cool larder until about one o'clock on the following Monday. When the water was then gently poured from it, it was found to have settled at the bottom of the jug, and was perfectly sweet. It was mixed with three-quarters of a pint of water, *in addition* to that which was originally stirred to it, the whole being *fully milk warm*, and three pounds and a half (one quartern) of the best flour – purchased from a factor in Tottenham Court Road – with a large teaspoonful of salt, were kneaded up with it into a very smooth dough, which at the end of an hour had become exceedingly light. It was then again kneaded

A good way of cutting bread for sandwiches. From the *Illustrated London News, c.* 1900. Reproduced by permission of the Mary Evans Picture Library.

into a smooth mass, and left for nearly three quarters of an hour, when it was sent to a baker's oven, after being divided, into one small and one large loaf. It was well baked (in pans) and proved in every respect excellent bread, though rather less yeast would have been sufficient for it. I give these minute particulars to show that the German yeast may be preserved fit for use in the same manner as brewer's, when the weather is not excessively sultry. During part of the month of August last, when the heat was unusually intense, all kinds of yeast appeared to be more or less affected by it, and it was extremely difficult to obtain good bread in consequence. In such a case it is well to have recourse to unfermented bread.

'German yeast, one ounce, put into half a pint of cold *filtered* water (which was not changed) on Friday evening Sept. 5th kept in cool larder until Monday, September 8th, diluted altogether with one pint and a quarter of warm water, and mixed with one quartern (half a gallon) of flour, and one large teaspoonful of salt; left to rise one hour. Kneaded down; left three-quarters of an hour; divided and sent to oven. Bread very good and light.'

ibid.

Baps and Rolls

'The bap is the breakfast roll of Scotland. Properly made and properly handled it can justly be called noble . . .

'Flour, salt, lard, yeast, sugar, milk, water. These are the ingredients, but a reverential approach is an essential. Badly made, the bap can be horrid. You sift your pound of flour into a warmed bowl with a teaspoonful of salt, and you lightly rub in two ounces of lard. On the side, in another bowl, you mix an ounce of yeast with a teaspoonful of sugar until they become liquid, then you add half-a-pint of tepid water-and-milk mixed in equal proportions. This warmish liquid you strain into the flour, obtaining a soft dough. You cover this dough with a cloth, and

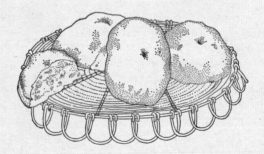

leave it in a warm place for about an hour so that it will rise. Then you lightly knead your dough, which you divide into oval pieces, say, about four-and-a-half inches long by about three wide. This makes a man-size bap. One hears of glazed baps, but they are unorthodox. "Floury baps" are the thing. You brush the tops with milk, as if to give a glaze, but you immediately dust them with flour, which you repeat just before you place them in the oven. But before doing this last you place the baps on a greased and floured oven-tray, and leave them for quarter-of-an-hour or so to prove. To stop the baps from blistering, you press a finger in their centres just before they go into the oven. This last should be fairly hot, and about twenty minutes should bake the man-size bap. The bap should go warm to the breakfast table.

'The sybarite, if his bap is too fluffy, pulls away and discards some of the inside before buttering each half and sticking them together again. The bap, I maintain, should be eaten this way. If you feel it is too large a handful to bite into, by all means cut it into pieces cross-ways. But don't attempt to tackle it as some people, for "politeness", treat a crisp roll – that is, broken and buttered in pieces. To this method the bap, somehow, doesn't seem to answer.'

Victor MacClure, Good Appetite My Companion, 1955

Most modern household recipes for baps are similar to Victor Mac-Clure's. Miss Elizabeth Craig, in *Scottish Cookery* (André Deutsch, 1956) gives precisely the same ingredients and proportions, although Miss Craig directs that the baps should be 'squarish' in shape. Miss Marian McNeill, author of *The Scots Kitchen* (1929) on whose authority so many authors have relied, gives an almost exactly similar recipe, while Lady Clark of Tillypronie, who died in 1900, has a note in her chapter on bread and scones to the effect that baps are made from flour, salt, yeast and water only. *No milk, butter or eggs*, Lady Clark says firmly. And adds 'the dough to be made very slack'.

Professional bakers evidently agree with Lady Clark, except that they seem to favour a half and half milk and water mix rather than plain water.

It is the latter method which I find the most successful, and leaving out the lard and the sugar – these ingredients are seldom absolutely necessary – I follow the rest of Mr MacClure's instructions exactly.

To sum up, my recipe goes like this:

1 lb of plain flour, ¼ pint each of tepid milk and water, 2 teaspoons of salt, 1 oz of yeast.[1] A little extra milk for brushing the baps, and flour from a sprinkler.

Equivalent metric quantities: plain flour 450 g, milk and water 150 g each, salt 2 teaspoons, yeast 30g, a little extra milk for brushing the tops of the baps, and flour for sprinkling.

---

1. See Note 1 below, p. 322.

Sift the salt into the flour, dissolve the yeast in the tepid milk and water mixture, see that it is well amalgamated, pour it on to the flour and mix lightly. If too stiff add a little extra milk. Cover the bowl. Leave to rise for about 1½ hours.

Flour a baking sheet. Break down the dough. Quickly divide it into eight or nine pieces. Form these into the oval shapes as described by Victor MacClure, and set them on the baking sheet, leaving as much space as possible between each. Cover them with a sheet of polythene to prevent a skin forming on the dough. Leave for 15 minutes to recover volume.

Have the oven ready heated to 425°F, 220°C, gas no. 7. Before putting the baps in to bake, brush the tops and sides with milk, then sprinkle them with flour. With a floury finger make a deepish impression in the centre of each bap. Then put them on the centre shelf of the oven. In 15 to 20 minutes they will be cooked, puffed up and pale golden. Shake a little more flour over them.

When possible, these baps should be made not more than 15 minutes before they are to be eaten. As Mr MacClure says, they are at their best while still warm from the oven. They can, however, be reheated in a gentle oven, or split and toasted.

Bap dough made with unbleached strong bread flour needs a little longer rising time than if made with soft household flour.

Quite often I find it very convenient to use this recipe in half quantities, just to make four or five baps instead of ordinary bread. Not that the dough is quicker or easier to mix than for a plain loaf – it hardly could be – but it needs less time to rise and to bake.

Notes: 1. Those with experience of the workings of yeast dough will know that ½ oz of fresh or 2 scant teaspoons of dried yeast to 1 lb of flour is quite sufficient, and that if the flour is warmed before the dough is mixed, rising will be very quick. A few minutes in a low oven does the trick.

2. Another name for baps is morning rolls, and the Scottish lady in my local bakery tells me that in her childhood her family called them fadge.

3. Baps vary a good deal in size and shape. Sometimes they are made no larger than 4 inches in diameter, sometimes they are oval, sometimes three-cornered. A large round soft-crusted and rather flat loaf is also called a bap loaf.

4. As a postscript I should like to quote again from Victor MacClure, this time on the way he enjoyed baps when a schoolboy: 'If not my earliest recollection of it, certainly my best is of having it stuffed with

Ayrshire bacon and a fried egg to eat while hastening to beat the bell for morning school. On these occasions it was still warm from the bakers' oven.'

· BREAKFAST BAPS ·

This recipe makes very small baps. It comes from Mr C. G. Lockyer of Clapton Mills, Crewkerne, Dorset, whose 85 per cent wheatmeal is stone-ground at the mills of which I have written in the recipe for barley bread on pp. 296–8.

'*Ingredients*

1 lb plain flour or ¾ wheatmeal and ½ white	1 teaspoonful sugar
2 oz lard	2 teaspoonfuls salt
¼ pint milk	3 teaspoonfuls dried yeast
¼ pint hot water	or 1 oz fresh yeast

Equivalent metric quantities : plain flour 450 g or wheatmeal 340 g and white flour 225 g, lard 60 g, milk 150 g, hot water 150 g, sugar 1 teaspoon, salt 2 teaspoons, dried yeast 3 teaspoons or fresh yeast 30 g. Equivalent oven temperature in degrees C : 205°C.

'*Method*

'Barely cover yeast with warm water and stand in a warm place for 5 minutes.

'Mix flour and salt, rub in lard.

'Add sugar to yeast, cream together until liquid, then add to milk and water, pour this into flour and blend to soft dough with wooden spoon, work into a lump, then leave covered in warm place till risen to double size (about one hour).

'Turn out on floured board and knead to smooth ball.

'Cut into 16 pieces, work each into a ball and place on a greased tin to rise in a warm place for 20 minutes.

'Bake for about 15 minutes in a hot oven, 400°F or 7 gas.'

· SOFT ROLLS ·

To make a dozen rolls ingredients are *1 lb of strong plain flour, ½ oz of yeast, ½ pint of milk, ½ oz of salt, a tablespoonful or two of cream for glazing the rolls after baking.*

Equivalent metric quantities: strong plain flour 450 g, yeast 15 g, milk 280 g, salt 15 g, cream for glazing 1 or 2 tablespoonfuls.

Mix the yeast to a cream with a tablespoon or two of tepid water. Warm the milk to blood heat (98° to 100°F, 37° to 38°C). Put the flour into a big bowl. Warm it. Mix in the salt, then the yeast, then the warm milk. Mix to a soft dough, form into a ball, cover and leave to rise for an hour.

Have ready a floured baking sheet.

Knock down the dough, knead it for a few seconds, sprinkle it with flour, shape it into a long thick sausage and divide it into twelve pieces as much of a size as possible. Form each piece into a small round roll. At this stage the rolls look very small. Remember that they will very nearly double in size.

Cover the rolls with a sheet of polythene or a light cloth. Leave them to rise for 15 to 20 minutes. Turn them the other side up on the baking sheet and with a small sharp knife or scissors make a cut across each roll. As the cuts open out put the rolls to bake in the centre of a preheated oven, 425°F, 220°C, gas no. 7, for 15 minutes. Lower the heat to 375°F, 190°C, gas no. 5, and leave for another 5 to 10 minutes.

When you have taken the rolls out of the oven, brush each with a little cream. These rolls are at their best when still warm, but they can be reheated.

N.B. The reason for using milk rather than water in this dough is that the former makes rolls with a softish crust, whereas an ordinary bread dough mixture tends to make rather tough rolls.

· BREAKFAST ROLLS or TEA CAKES, HOT ·

'Put about six handfuls of flour in a basin, half a pint of new milk, and a small piece of butter; warm the milk, which make hotter in winter than in summer; mix in a cup two ounces of German yeast with a little cold water; mix the yeast with the milk and butter, make a hole in the flour, pour the mixed milk and yeast into it, stirring it round until it is a thick batter; beat up one egg and mix into it; cover it over and keep it warm in your screen;[1] when it has risen a little mix it into a dough, knead it

1. A curved, burnished steel screen, often called a Dutch oven, the open side being set in front of the coal fire or the bars of a grate. Primarily intended for the roasting of meat suspended on a hook, the screen was also useful for many other purposes such as the toasting of cheese, bacon rashers and bread. Special hooks, containers

well, put it again in the screen, and when it has risen a good deal, take and form your rolls. They will take nearly half an hour, or according to the size you make the cakes; rub them over while hot with your paste brush dipped in milk.'

Frederick Bishop, *The Wife's Own Book of Cookery*, 1856

· VIENNA ROLLS ·

The dough for these delicious salty rolls is rich, but very easy to make and to handle.

For 1 lb of flour – half and half ordinary plain household and strong bread flour, or all strong plain – other ingredients are ½ oz of yeast, 1 level tablespoon of salt, ½ pint of milk and water mixed, ¼ lb of butter ; and, for strewing on the rolls when they are ready for baking, approximately 2 tablespoons of coarse salt and 2 tablespoons of cumin or caraway seeds, and a little milk or thin cream for brushing on the rolls.

Equivalent metric quantities : flour 450 g, yeast 15 g, salt 1 level tablespoon, milk and water mixed 280 g, butter 120 g. For the tops of the rolls : coarse salt 2 tablespoons, cumin or caraway seeds 2 tablespoons, a little milk or thin cream.

Mix the two flours and the salt, which should be very finely pounded. Warm the milk and water. Use a little of this mixture to cream the yeast. Stir this into the flour, then add the rest of the liquid and mix to make a fairly stiff dough, which will be lightened later by the addition of the butter.

Cover the dough and leave to rise for about 1½ hours, or until it is puffy and spongy.

Have the butter ready softened (it should be taken from the refrigerator well in advance) and divided into small pieces.

---

and racks were made for each of these different purposes. Many people also found that the screen, placed at the proper distance from the fire, was the ideal place for the raising of the dough. In the Scottish household of Lady Clark of Tillypronie, whose recipes are so often referred to or quoted in this book, all the yeast dough for bread, baps, rolls and muffins was put to rise in the meat screen. Some of the more elaborate screens had a separate compartment at the back, with a rack for warming plates. One of these can be seen in the kitchen of the Sir John Soane Museum in Lincolns Inn Fields.

Break down the dough, beat in the butter little by little, using your hands. When all is mixed in, sprinkle a little flour over the dough and shape it into a smooth ball, which you then flatten out into a neat rectangle. Divide this into about sixteen small pieces which are to be shaped into short sticks or small round rolls, or alternatively cut into triangles which are then rolled up like croissants but left straight instead of being shaped into crescents.

Put the prepared rolls on to non-stick baking sheets, cover them with a sheet of polythene and leave them to recover volume. Half an hour to 45 minutes should be ample.

Bake on the centre shelf at 375°F, 190°C, gas no. 5, for 15 minutes.

Now brush the rolls with the milk or cream, strew with the salt and cumin or caraway seeds and return to the oven for another 5 minutes.

· POTATO ROLLS ·

'Boil three pounds of potatoes, bruise and work them with two ounces of butter and as much milk as will make them pass through a colander.

'Take half or three-quarters of a pint of yeast, and half a pint of warm water, mix with the potatoes, then pour the whole upon five pounds of flour, and add some salt. Knead it well: if not of a proper consistence, put a little more milk and warm water, let it stand before the fire an hour to rise; work it well, and make into rolls. Bake about half an hour in an oven not quite so hot as for bread.

'They eat well toasted and buttered.'

Maria Eliza Rundell, *A New System of Domestic Cookery*, 1806

I have tried Mrs Rundell's recipe using approximately one-third of her quantities and making small round loaves instead of rolls. Like the potato bread given on p. 288, they were excellent, and kept exceptionally well.

For 1 lb of potatoes and 1½ lb of flour, you need about ¼ pint of milk, not much more than ¾ pint of water, ¾ oz of salt and 1 oz of yeast, although if you have time to leave the dough to rise for a couple of hours or more ½ oz will be ample. Remember that the mashed potato is particularly propitious as a fermenting ground.

Equivalent metric quantities: potatoes 450 g, flour 675 g, milk 150 g, water about 420 g, salt 20 g, yeast 30 g (or 15 g for a slow-rising dough).

· ABERDEEN ROWIES ·

The recipe for these flaky buns or rolls was given to me by an old friend, Mr William France, who has a nose for an authentic speciality. I have put the recipe into my own words because the Scottish cook from whom it originated had given very little detail, and until I had tried the recipe it was by no means clear.

In composition, rowies are not unlike croissants, although much less rich and consequently a great deal simpler and quicker to make. They don't look as showy as croissants but, for all their homely appearance, I prefer them in some ways, because they are light and small and surprising.

For twenty-four to thirty rowies ingredients are ¾ lb of strong plain flour, 6 oz of butter, ½ oz of yeast, rather under ¼ pint of tepid water, 2 teaspoons of salt, rice flour or cornflour for dusting the dough and the pastry board.

Equivalent metric quantities: strong plain flour 340 g, butter 170 g, yeast 15 g, tepid water rather under 280 g, salt 2 teaspoons, rice flour or cornflour for dusting the dough and pastry board.

Make an ordinary straight dough from the flour, salt and yeast and as much of the tepid water as will make the flour into a medium soft dough. Mix very well, and form the dough into a ball. Cover the bowl and leave the dough to rise for 30 to 45 minutes.

Have the butter ready divided into two parts, each cut into little cubes.

Break down the dough, knead it a little, put it on a floured pastry board (rice flour and cornflour are by far the best dusting flours, see pp. 70–71) and roll it out – or, if you prefer, pat it out by hand – into a rectangle about 10 inches by 8 inches (26 cm by 20 cm). On this spread the first portion of the little cubes of butter, as though making puff pastry. The butter should be cold but not too hard. Fold the dough over into three, then give it two or three turns, again as for puff pastry. Leave it to rest, wrapped in waxed paper, for 15 minutes, preferably in the refrigerator. Again, roll or spread the dough into a rectangle on the freshly dusted board. Repeat the process with the second portion of butter cubes. Again leave the dough to rest in the refrigerator for 15 to 30 minutes.

Finally, once more roll or press out the dough into a rectangle, making it as neat and even as possible. With a sharp knife make cuts along and across it, spacing them so that the dough is divided into twenty-four pieces, which probably won't be quite evenly sized. This is quite proper, and is part of the beauty of making rowies. There is no definitive shape for them. They emerge as nice high flaky knobs of uneven size and shape, and are much lighter cut in this way than when stamped out with a cutter or a glass. Some of the larger squares can be cut in half, making nice little triangular morsels.

Arrange the rowies on baking sheets or trays dusted with rice flour but not buttered. Cover them with a sheet of waxed paper or polythene and leave for 30 minutes, but not in too warm a place or the butter will start to melt before the rolls go into the oven.

Bake the rowies in a fairly hot oven, 425° to 450°F, 220° to 230°C, gas nos. 7 or 8, for 15 to 20 minutes, until they are pale gold.

Rowies can be rewarmed very easily and successfully. Put them in a low oven, under a cake tin or cover, for just 2 or 3 minutes. They are delicious for breakfast, with a little fresh cold butter. Each of these rowies is little more than a couple of mouthfuls, which makes them particularly endearing. They are a breakfast speciality.

Notes and variations : 1. Another name for Aberdeen rowies is Aberdeen butteries. One recipe I have for butteries specifies that the dough be 'torn into 18 pieces' rather than cut. As the recipe in question is for 1 lb of flour and $\frac{3}{4}$ lb of mixed butter and lard, the butteries would be much bigger as well as richer than Mr France's rowies.

2. In the original recipe self-raising flour is used for dusting the board. I found this puzzling until I realized that self-raising flour is drier and less sticky than ordinary flour, owing to the chemicals and the rice flour incorporated into it. But if you have rice flour proper, it is a better dusting flour.

3. Scottish professional bakers evidently make butteries by a different method, involving two separate doughs. A recipe is given in W. J. Fance's *Up-to-Date Breadmaking* (1968).

Manchets and Mayn
and Payndemayn

'Whit was his face as Payndemayn
His lippes rede as rose.'

> Geoffrey Chaucer, *Sir Thopas, c.* 1420

'Take creme or mylke, and brede of paynemayn, or ellys of tendyr brede.'

> From a recipe for *Creme Boylede* in *Two Fifteenth-Century Cookery-Books*,
> ed. Thomas Austin, 1888; reprinted 1964

And then take manged brede or paynman, and kutte hit in leches.'[1]

> From a recipe for *Payn Purdeuz*; ibid.

'I do love manchet bread, and great loaves the which be well moulded and thoroughly baked, the bran abstracted and thrown away, and that is good for all ages.'

> Andrew Boorde, *The Dyetary of Helth,* 1542

Because mention of them recurs so frequently in histories of English food and diet, and also because they do not quite fit into any other category, I have collected the manchet and its close relations into this separate chapter.

As can be seen from the quotations above, payndemayn, paynmayn, paindemayn – painmain, mayne, bread of mane, demesne or demeine bread were other spelling variations – was an early name for soft white bread; it was made from wheat flour as finely bolted and as white as was then feasible, and was the bread eaten by the rich, although probably only in relatively small quantity and as an alternative, or in addition, to more ordinary brown or yeomen's bread. I have discovered no record of the precise method of making payndemayn, but it seems likely that it was an enriched bread, perhaps made with milk, and butter or eggs, in the way sometimes specified in later recipes for manchet, as fine white

1. Slices.

bread had come to be known by the end of the fifteenth century, although since nomenclature doesn't change abruptly or tidily, for a while the two terms co-existed and were evidently interchangeable. The line from the second recipe quoted above is one of several examples to be found in these MS. cookery books. This recipe is particularly interesting, for *payn purdeuz* or *pain perdu* is still a much loved

Early manchets were always round and 'scotched about the waist to give them leave to rise'. Later, judging by pictorial evidence, they were cut on the top, and sometimes made long or oval.

French method of using up brioche or other fine rich bread by coating the slices in beaten egg, frying them in clarified butter and strewing them with fine sugar. The recipe has remained almost unchanged since the fifteenth century.

As to the derivations of the names manchet and payndemayn, there has been much speculation, some authorities claiming that mane was the Teutonic word for moon, and that the bread had originally been connected with some form of moon-worshipping rite; others, interpreting the same derivation in another way, think that it referred to the shape, like a half moon. A more likely explanation, and the generally accepted one, is that both words derived from the Latin *panem dominicum*, the Lord's bread, and that by the time this had been curtailed into manchet the word was an entirely English one, and unrelated to the French *manchette* or cuff. In this connection *The Oxford English Dictionary* tells us that 'at Rouen a ring-shaped cake of bread is known as *manchette*, but this name (which may be of recent origin) is obviously descriptive of shape, while the English word in early use denotes a certain quality of bread'. So much for nice neat interpretations; and certainly the French equivalent of the English manchet was not *manchette*, nor anything like it, but simply *pain mollet*, soft bread, or *pain bénist*, consecrated bread.

Two points about the English manchet of which we can be fairly certain are that the finest wheaten flour went into it, and that it was a relatively small loaf, sometimes weighing 1 lb, as specified in a recipe dated 1594 and quoted on p. 334, sometimes less than half that weight: 'eight ounces into the oven and six ounces out as I have been informed', wrote William Harrison, author of the *Description of England* (1577), so that however it was made up, whether round or long – usually, it seems, the former – compared with the usual household loaf the manchet was hardly more than a large roll and not considered a sufficient allowance of bread for one person at one meal. Indeed it was only the special part of the breakfasts and suppers of the rich. Here, in 1512,[1] are two of the Percy children, sons of the Earl of Northumberland, being served for breakfast with 'Half a Loif of household Brede, a Manchet, a Dysch of Butter'[2] plus two kinds of salt fish (this was for fast days; on flesh days they had a chicken or 'three mutton bones boyled') and two quarts of beer. Hearty eaters and drinkers, those boys. The elder was eleven years old at the time. The younger children, 'my Lady Margaret and Master Ingram Percy', in the nursery, were given the manchets and the fish or meat but not the household bread. Breakfasts and suppers allowed to the gentlemen and the maids of honour in royal households always included manchets and ale, and the flour for Queen Elizabeth's manchet bread was milled only from Heston wheat, at that time considered the finest, whitest and cleanest wheat in the whole country. It was grown on a tract of land between Heston near Hounslow and north to Harrow-on-the-Hill and Pinner.

If we are to believe fifteenth-century books of etiquette and manuals of instruction addressed to young men in the household service of personages of rank, the manner of cutting and presenting table bread was as important as the composition of the bread itself. John Russell, who had been Usher and Marshal to Humphrey, Duke of Gloucester, younger brother of Henry V, wrote or compiled a *Boke of Nurture*[3] in which he

1. *The Northumberland Household Book: The Regulations and Establishment of the Household of Henry Algernon Percy*, written *c.* 1512; new edn, 1905. See also Bibliography: Warner, p. li.

2. A dish of butter seems to have been about 1½lb.

3. *C.* 1480. Duke Humphrey was assassinated in 1477. Russell's book is believed to date from the following decade.

describes how a servitor, having first cut square trenchers from large, four-day-old coarse loaves – wooden and pewter trenchers were still uncommon – was then to prepare the table bread: 'furst pare the quarters of the looff round alle about, then kutt the upper crust for your soverayne', i.e. lord. In *The Boke of Kervynge*, printed by Wynkyn de Worde, *c.* 1508, and seemingly plagiarized from Russell, the instructions are amplified: 'take a loaf in your left hand and pare the loaf round about, then cut the over crust to your soverayne, and cut the nether crust, and void the paring, and touch the loaf no more after it is so served.' 'Do not put on the table a half loaf for one eating', enjoins another manual of the period; 'se that no lofe be more than an other'; again the insistence on that upper crust: 'let an upper slice of fine bread be taken off for the master'; and at the beginning as well as at the end of the meal, a ritual gesture to the poor: for three loaves of white bread wrapped in a cloth and presented at the nobleman's table 'a chet [coarse] lofe to the alms dish', directs *The Boke of Curtasye*,[1] and, 'when the end of dinner comes, let the servants take care to break up the bread on the table into pieces to be given to the poor'.

The white loaves and the 'fine' bread referred to in the fifteenth-century books of manners would have been, presumably, the equivalents of Chaucer's payndemayn. In what respect, if indeed in any, this bread evolved during the following century, as it became the more familiar manchet, we do not know. Neither milling nor baking methods had changed, but possibly there were more varieties of wheat, some yielding whiter flour than others, bolting had perhaps become more refined, and in the composition as well as in the size of manchet loaves there had always been variations. Sometimes the dough was made up with plain water, sometimes it was enriched with milk, butter and eggs, although in small proportions. In this form the manchet seems to have been the common ancestor, no less, of most of our breakfast breads, baps, tea cakes, muffins, soft rolls, even of lardy cakes and dough cakes, as well as of the eighteenth-century fine breads known as French rolls and French bread.

Although it is sometimes assumed that the emergence in cookery

1. All the works quoted date from the mid fifteenth and early sixteenth centuries. They are printed in *Manners and Meals in Olden Time*, generally known as *The Babees Book*, edited by Frederick Furnivall, M.A., published for the Early English Text Society, 1868.

books of recipes for 'French' bread coincided with the disappearance of the manchet, and that the two were more or less synonymous, for a long while they co-existed – just as payndemayn and manchet had co-existed – there is clear evidence that they differed in that the methods of baking them were distinct. Manchets, made from dough fermented for a comparatively short time, were baked in a cooler oven than was required for ordinary household bread. This was an important point. In some well appointed houses there was a separate oven for manchets, and whereas we know from the fifteenth-century manuals quoted above that the top crust of the white loaf was the choicest morsel, when it came to the eighteenth-century 'French' loaf or roll, invariably baked in a quick oven, the crust was so hard that it was chipped or grated off and discarded.[1] So when Hannah Glasse, giving a recipe for a boiled bread pudding,[2] notes that a 'French Manchet does best', she surely meant that a soft bread was needed, and when William Verral, author of *The Cook's Paradise* (1759), calls for 'some crusts of two or three manchets, or French rowls' for steeping in his vegetable soup, he seems to imply that they were two different things. By the end of the century, however, the manchet had disappeared from the cookery books and had been replaced by French rolls, but was by no means entirely forgotten. In *A London Family 1870–1900* (1946), Mrs M. Vivian Hughes, writing of life with her Cornish cousins, records that 'bread was made every day, in batches of a dozen manchet loaves. A manchet was a loaf moulded by hand, and not put in a tin.' In 1931 a correspondent writing to Miss Florence White[3] told her that 'manchant' was a term still used by Penzance bakers to distinguish a hand-moulded loaf from a tin loaf, and that 'the derivation is obvious'. The lady omitted to say what it was that was so obvious to her about the derivation.

Another pocket of country where the manchet tradition remained alive was the county of Surrey. Here it had become, as can be seen from the recipes quoted further on, a kind of flaky roll in which the basic dough was enriched with lard or butter, or half and half of each, treated

1. Examples of our eighteenth-century French roll and bread recipes are given on pp. 376–8.
2. *The Art of Cookery made Plain and Easy*, 1747.
3. *Good Things in England*, 1932. It was probably due to Miss White's work in the founding of the English Folk Cookery Association, and her collecting, collating and publishing of recipes sent in by correspondents from all over the country, that many other people became conscious at this period of the need to record customs and to preserve old recipes which were fast disappearing.

in the manner of puff pastry and divided into portions for baking. In one recipe the shape is still specified very definitely as round, while in another it is as 'you want it'.

Among seventeenth century recipes for manchet are two well known versions, Gervase Markham's, published in the early part of the century, and Lady Arundel's, given in the Countess of Kent's book which appeared in 1653. The earliest published recipe I have found dates from the end of the sixteenth century. At that time, as now, recipes were usually of much older origin than their published date, so the making of manchet according to the formula of 1594 may well go back to the early years of the century and the reign of Henry VIII.

· THE MAKING OF FINE MANCHET ·

'Take halfe a bushell[1] of fine flower twise boulted, and a gallon of faire luke warm water, almost a handful of white salt, and almost a pinte of yest, then temper all these together, without any more liquor, as hard as ye can handle it: then let it lie halfe an hower, then take it up, and make your Manchetts, and let them stande almost an hower in the oven. Memorandum, that of every bushell of meale may be made five and twentie caste[2] of bread, and every loafe to way a pounde besyde the chesill.'[3]

The Good Huswife's Handmaide for the Kitchen, 1594

1. A bushel was 56 to 60 lb.

2. A 'caste' of bread was two or three loaves according to size, two manchets being reckoned as one loaf. So in this recipe there would have been two loaves or four manchets to the caste, each weighing about 8 oz.

3. According to *The English Dialect Dictionary,* edited by Joseph Wright (1898), chesill or chisel in this context can only mean the middlings or offal sifted out of the ground meal during the second bolting, *after* the coarsest part of the bran had been discarded. The Dictionary quotes Best's *Farming Book* (1641): 'in every bushell of meale that commeth from the mill there is neare a pecke of chizell drossed out.'

The punctuation of the recipe is confusing, but the author must have meant that the 'good huswife' or her 'handmaide' should obtain 25 'caste' of manchets from a bushel of meal once the bran and the peck (14 lb) of chisel have been removed.

Another relevant instance of the use of the term chisel is given in the same Dictionary: 'when you get your corn grun, first comes the bran, then the chisel, then the fine flour.' The word seems to have been common in Northumberland, Yorkshire, Durham, Lincolnshire, Leicestershire, Kent and Sussex.

· MANCHET BREAD ·

'Now for the baking of bread of your simple meales, your best and principal bread is manchet, which you shall bake in this manner; first your meal being ground upon the black stones, if it be possible, which makes the whitest flower, and passed through the finest boulting cloth, you shall put it in a clean kimnel,[1] and opening the flower hollow in the midst, put into it of the best Ale-barm, the quantity of 3 pints to a bushel[2] of meal, with som salt to season it with: then put in your liquor[3] reasonable warm, and knead it very well together both with your hands, and through the brake,[4] or for want thereof, fold it in a cloth, and with your feet tread it a good space together, then letting it lie an hour or thereabouts to swel, take it forth and mould it into manchets, round, and flat, scorcht about the waste to give it leave to rise, and prick it with your knife in the top, and so put into the Oven, and make it with a gentle heate.'

Gervase Markham, The English Hus-wife, 1615

N.B. By 'the black stones' Markham must have meant the black emery or lava stones used in many flour mills. See p. 28 of the chapter on milling.

· LADY OF ARUNDEL'S MANCHET ·

'Take a bushel of fine wheat-flower, twenty Eggs, three pound of fresh butter, then take as much salt and barm as to the ordinary manchet, temper it together with new Milk pretty hot, then let it lie the space of

1. A wooden kneading or dough tub, also used as a salting tub.
2. A bushel was 56 to 60 lb.
3. The water or possibly mixture of water and milk used to make up the dough.
4. An early aid to the kneading of dough, which enabled the baker to push and roll with one hand while operating the brake by working a lever up and down with the other.

Another version of the brake or break was a long, stout, club-like pole clamped to the wall just above a low kneading table. It was operated by the baker sitting on the projecting end of the pole, as on a see-saw, or riding the break as the bakers called it. Such breaks were still to be found in use in bakeries as late as the 1890s. See p. 190.

half an hour to rise, so you may work it up into bread, and bake it, let not your Oven be too hot.'

The Countess of Kent, *A True Gentlewoman's Delight*, 1653

Lady Arundel's manchet is not as rich as it may sound. If a bushel really did mean 56 to 60lb of flour the allowance of eggs was less than one to every three pounds, and of butter less than one ounce to every pound. The significant ingredient is the milk specified for making up the dough. Together with the eggs and butter this would give the loaves a much softer crust than plain water, and would distinguish them from 'ordinary manchet'. Gervase Markham is less communicative on this point, saying simply 'liquor'. This is still the baker's term for the liquid, however composed, used to make up dough.

The 'pretty hot' milk in Lady Arundel's recipe presumably accounts for the very brief rising time. Her manchets would have been more like enriched baps or muffin loaves than ordinary rolls or bread.

The Lady Arundel credited with this manchet recipe was probably the one well known in her time for charitable works, ministrations to the sick and the giving of food and alms to the poor, while she herself lived very sparsely, and dressed always in plain black dresses of coarse material. Did she sometimes distribute her good white manchets among hungry families, or did even this saintly lady's bounty stop short at the giving of white bread to the poor?

*

From 1653 to 1932, the best part of three centuries, and manchet recipes are reappearing in print. They are more like dough cakes than straightforward white loaves, so it is curious that the name was attached to them. Here are two of the recipes, and a note concerning the continuing tradition, all quoted from *The Surrey Cookery Book*, compiled by Adeline Maclean and Evelyn Thompson, from recipes contributed by fifty-eight Surrey Women's Institutes. The Foreword was by Eleanour Sinclair Rohde, author of many famous gardening books, and herself a notable collector of old recipes. The book was published at Guildford in 1932.

· GUILDFORD MANCHETS ·

'Get 1 or 2 pounds of dough in the morning, then butter and lard as you use in puff pastry, and work similar. Be sure and sprinkle salt. Use dough the same morning, prove well before and after being on tin. Keep out of draught. Dock through centre only. Before baking wash over lightly with egg or milk. (N.B. Guildford Manchets were round in shape.)

'Another way now with dough is to mix and work well in similar to making a dough cake, butter and lard, very little salt as there is salt in the dough. Flour up enough to work in like making buns and prove well.'

Contributed by Mr J. H. Pope, Guildford

'*A Note*
'Manchets or Lardie Rolls still made by Mr King, Albury, the same as his father made before him.'

Both Mr Pope of Guildford and Mr King of Albury were no doubt good old-fashioned bakers, and their specialities would have been well known in their localities. If a customer wanted to buy the basic dough and make up her own dough cakes – a reversal of the system described by Flora Thompson in the passage about dough cake for harvest tea quoted on p. 424 – the bakers would have sold it, just as bakers in France used to sell dough to customers who wanted to make their own *pissaladière* or perhaps a special feast day cake.

The next recipe explains those 'lardie' rolls.

· LARDY ROLLS ·

'Take about 1 lb of Dough. Roll out in a flat Piece then spread on it a ¼ lb of Lard. Fold it over as you would Puff Paste and Roll it out 3 or 4 times, then Cut into the shapes you want it, take a Knife and Cross them over in a Diamond shape, then stand them on your Baking Sheet in a Warm Place then Bake in a good Brisk oven until they are nicely Browned. Do NOT let them RISE too much before baking.'

Contributed by the family of Poulter, Albury

These are interesting recipes, and how grateful we now are for their preservation, and how thankful to the ladies who compiled the little *Surrey Cookery Book* that they had the historical sense and good manners to leave the recipes exactly in the form in which they were sent in, so making them valid and credible. Those who bring recipes up to date, editing them to a standardized formula set out in the manner of a laundry list and without quoting the originals or the sources, are guilty, to say the least, of underestimating the intelligence of their readers, who are surely capable of understanding yesterday's and even the-day-before-yesterday's English. The old wording and the haphazard profusion of capital letters in the Poulter recipe and the economical phrasing of Mr Pope's directions are more informative on essential points, and far more revealing of the people who had used these recipes all their lives, than any amount of finicky detail. From Mr Pope we learn, for example, that Guildford manchets were docked through the centre and brushed over with milk, like baps; from the Poulter contribution we see very clearly that the recipe must have come from a family MS., that it was surely recorded over a century ago and that two of the characteristic points were the marking of the crust into diamond shapes and the avoidance of over-proving of the dough.

How much we should have lost had these recipes been translated into conventional cookery-book English. But the following recipe, which I have evolved and found useful and extremely easy does I think make manchets more resembling the seventeenth-century versions – in other words they are like large round rolls, each one made with 7 to 8 oz of dough.

For variations on lardy or dough cakes, see the chapter on fruit breads and spice cakes.

· MANCHETS, 1974 ·

1¼ lb (20 oz) of half and half 85 per cent wheatmeal and strong plain white bread flour, ½ oz of yeast, 1 level tablespoon of salt, 1 oz of softened butter, a little over ½ pint of milk and water mixed.

Equivalent metric quantities: half and half 85 per cent wheatmeal and strong plain white bread flour 550 g, yeast 15 g, salt 1 level tablespoon, softened butter 30 g, milk and water mixed a little over 280 g.

Warm the flour in a low oven for 7 to 10 minutes. Cream the yeast with a little milk. Dissolve the salt in ¼ pint of hot water, add milk to make up the ½ pint.

Add the creamed yeast to the warmed flour. Mix in the milk and water, stir to a dough. Work in the softened butter. The dough should be light, but not so much so that it is difficult to handle. Form it into a ball, as usual. Cover and leave to rise in a warm place. If the temperature is right (70° to 75°F, 21° to 23·5°C) and the flour was warm when the dough was mixed, 45 minutes, or at the outside 1 hour, will be long enough for the rising. As the old recipes tell us, manchet dough was not given a long fermentation.

Break down the dough, divide it into four equal pieces, form them into bun shapes, put them on a non-stick baking sheet or an oiled baking platter or tray. Cover them with a sheet of polythene, leave them to recover volume, which will take about 30 minutes. If they have spread, sprinkle them with flour and remould them. Make a deep cut down the centre of each manchet, and put them into the oven quickly, as the cuts start to open out.

Bake the manchets in the centre of a medium hot oven, 425°F, 220°C, gas no. 7, for approximately 30 minutes.

I find that the crust of these manchets is just about right, neither too hard nor too soft. The cut or crease down the centre means that the manchets can be easily broken apart. They should not be cut. They are delicious, not too soft, nor tough; they can be eaten while still warm or they can be reheated.

Variations: 1. Instead of butter, light olive oil can be used for manchet dough. Two tablespoons will be enough. The manchets then become small versions of the muffin loaves described on p. 312.

2. Instead of dividing the dough into four pieces, two round loaves or one large one can be made. In either of these cases, scoring them across in the diamond pattern as specified in the Poulter recipe on p. 337 makes a very attractive loaf.

· THE PENNY WHITE LOAF OF THE COOKERY BOOKS ·

The frequent recurrence in recipes of the seventeenth century, persisting until the latter part of the eighteenth, of directions to take 'a penny loaf', 'a penny white loaf', 'a penny French manchet', and so on with many variations in nomenclature, can probably be explained by the breakdown of the Assize Laws toward the end of the sixteenth century.[1]

It seems clear that by the time the Jacobean recipes were written the penny loaf had come to be understood, at any rate by the cookery

1. See p. 229.

writers and their readers, as Priced Bread, and from the recipes it is clear that, regardless of the fluctuating weights of Assize Bread, cooks knew that a penny white loaf – even if its actual cost was higher or lower – meant one made from the finest flour, enriched with milk and eggs, weighing from six to eight ounces, while an ordinary penny loaf meant one of slightly coarser flour milled from a secondary quality of wheat and weighing probably twice as much. The colours of the two breads would not have been enormously different but the former would have had a softer crumb. Still-life paintings of the relevant periods show very clearly what the different breads and rolls looked like. I suggest that anyone attempting to recreate the recipes of Jacobean and Georgian times try making small loaves from flour of 81 per cent or 85 per cent extraction mixed perhaps with a small proportion of unbleached white flour and enriched with milk and an egg or two. The recipes given in this chapter, and others on pp. 374 to 378, should provide plenty of clues. To use any of today's commercial white loaves in the old recipes would of course be an anomaly. To use coarse brown bread would be equally wrong. When brown bread is intended the recipes invariably indicate it.

· MANCHET GINGERBREAD ·

In the days when gingerbread was made from stale bread rather than from flour and treacle, manchets were the first choice.

'*To make Ginger bread.* Take 3 stale Manchets, and grate them: drie them, and sift them thorow a fine sieve: then adde unto them one ounce of Ginger, beeing beaten, and as much Cinamon, one ounce of Liquorice and Anniseedes being beaten together, and searced, halfe a pound of sugar, then boile all these together in a posnet, with a quart of claret wine, till they come to a stiffe paste with often stirring of it; and when it is stiffe, mold it on a table, and so drive it thin, and print it in your moldes: dust your moldes with Cinamon, Ginger, and Liquorice, beeing mixed together in fine powder. This is your Gingerbread used at the Court, and in all Gentlemens houses at festival times. It is otherwise called drie Leach.'

Sir Hugh Plat, *Delightes for Ladies*, 1609

Crumpets and Muffins

'If I sells three dozen muffins at ½d each, and twice that in crumpets, it's a werry fair day, werry fair; all beyond that is a *good* day.'

Henry Mayhow, *London Labour and the London Poor*, 1851

'Children are, in general, fondest of crumpets; but muffins are alone introduced at coffee-houses, etc. in London.'

The Family Receipt Book, London, 1853

To commence at the beginning, as the 1906 edition of *Mrs Beeton's Book of Household Management* said of bread storage, today's colloquialism or slang meaning of the word crumpet as a piece of skirt, any likely young woman, a girl with whom someone is having a passing affair, and other less polite interpretations, seems to have taken over from muffin, which once had the same or similar connotations. *The Oxford English Dictionary* quotes examples dating from 1856 and Miss Isabella Bird's observations during her travels in Canada: 'Every unmarried gentleman, who chooses to do so, selects a young lady to be his companion in the numerous amusements of the season ... when she acquiesces [she] is called a "muffin".' Another evocative one is attributed to a Major A. Griffiths, 1904: 'A pleasant *tête-a-tête* drive for many miles ... with your "muffin" by your side.' *The O.E.D.* concludes that the use of the word muffin in this sense is of Canadian origin.

Now for some slightly more literal interpretations of the two words:
'Muffin ... connected with old French *moufflet*, soft, said of bread.'[1]
'Muffin-worry *colloq.*, a tea-party ... an old ladies' tea party.'[2]
'The probable origin of the word crumpet is the Welsh *crempog*, a pancake or fritter. For some reason or other, probably because they are in some degree similar, and yet differing greatly, it is customary to

1. *The Oxford English Dictionary.*   2. ibid.

Muffins are on the left, crumpets on the right. And which are pikelets?

associate muffins with crumpets, it being a rare occurrence for either to appear at the table separately.

' Both are made of batter, both require re-cooking, and both are served hot and well buttered; yet there is so marked a difference between the two in flavour and constitution that most persons have a decided preference for one or the other.'[1]

Crumpets, or at least terrible travesties of them, can still be bought in England, although they are more commonly sold packeted by grocers or supermarkets than by bakers. Perhaps indeed they are delivered direct from a plastics recycling plant, and have never been near a bakery.

Muffins one rarely sees – although Sainsbury's sell packets of a thing they *call* a muffin – and hears about only when the spasmodic wave of nostalgia for bygone popular specialities breaks over the British Press and its cookery contributors, when there is much talk of the muffin-man and his bell from feature writers far too young ever to have heard that bell or eaten the wares which the muffin-man cried through the streets; at such times there is nearly always reference to the past glories of the British breakfast (I remember the muffin-man ringing his bell on Primrose Hill when I lived there in the 1930s; it was always at weekends and in the afternoon, in time for tea, so if you wanted them for breakfast you had to keep them until the next day) and also to a solitary surviving muffin-man who still supplies the occupants of Buckingham Palace.

Well, what are or were the crumpets and muffins which Mayhew's

1. *The Encyclopaedia of Practical Cookery*, ed. Theodore Francis Garrett, 1899.

muffin-man used to sell for a ½d each? What is the difference between them? Which have holes, which are baked in rings? Which are made from a pouring batter, which from a soft dough similar to the one used for baps and rolls? Is a pikelet the equivalent of a muffin or of a crumpet? What is the relation of an oatcake to either? Should muffins and/or crumpets be split and/or toasted or should they not? Are muffins and crumpets made from identical ingredients? If so, what are they? Flour, yeast, water, salt? Or flour and yeast plus milk, fat and eggs? Or flour, fat and eggs with a chemical raising agent? Anybody who knows the answers to more than two or three of these queries is wiser than I, although not necessarily more certain of their own beliefs than professional bakers, cooking-school teachers, contributors to Women's Institute recipe anthologies and such redoubtable authorities on English household cooking as Florence Jack, Florence White and Dorothy Hartley.

Because muffins and crumpets are among the most famous of English specialities – like so many, more talked about than actually experienced – I have thought it of interest to reproduce here some of the conflicting recipes, instructions and notes to be found in works directed at the household cook during the past century and a half, followed by a cross-section taken from books written by professional bakers of the nineteenth and twentieth centuries. The latter may well be useful to any reader needing recipes giving fairly large quantities, while those who would like simply to try an up-to-date workable recipe for a small amount would perhaps do best to skip the old recipes and turn at once to pp. 353 and 356. Incidentally, although both muffins and crumpets must be of considerably earlier origin, recipes for them do not appear to have reached the published cookery books much before the eighteenth century.

· MUFFINS AND CRUMPETS: THE HOUSEHOLD COOKS ·

To make muffins and oatcakes, 1747

'To a bushel of Hertfordshire white flour, take a pint and a half of good Ale Yeast, from pale Malt, if you can get it, because it is whitest; let the Yeast lie in Water all Night, the next day pour off the water clear, make two gallons of water just Milk-warm, not to scald your Yeast, and two Ounces of Salt; mix your water, Yeast and salt well together for about a Quarter of an Hour; then strain it and mix up your Dough as light as possible, and let it lie in your Trough an Hour to rise, then with your Hand roll it, and pull it into little pieces about as big as a large Walnut, roll them with your Hand like a ball, lay them on your Table, and as fast as you do them lay a Piece of Flannel over them, and be sure to keep your Dough covered with Flannel; when you have rolled out all your Dough begin to bake the first, and by that time they will be spread out in the right Form; lay them on your Iron; as one side begins to change Colour turn the other, and take great care they don't burn or be too much discoloured, but that you will be a Judge of in two or three Makings.

'Take Care the Middle of the Iron is not too hot, as it will be, but then you may put a Brickbat or two in the Middle of the Fire to slacken the Heat.

'When you eat them toast them with a Fork crisp on both Sides then with your Hand pull them open, and they will be like a Honeycomb; lay in as much Butter as you intend to use, then clap them together again, and set it by the Fire. When you think the Butter is melted turn them, that both sides may be buttered alike, but don't touch them with the Knife, either to spread or cut them open, if you do they will be heavy as Lead, only when they are quite buttered and done, you may cut them across with a Knife.'

Hannah Glasse, *The Art of Cookery Made Plain and Easy*,
4th edn, 1754 (first published 1747)

Although Mrs Glasse includes oatcakes in her heading for the muffin recipe, she does not again mention them, but that these two kinds of griddle bread were generally associated with the bakery trade of the time – for I cannot help thinking that Mrs Glasse obtained her directions from a professional baker – is shown by two recipes published some forty years later in *The Housekeeper's Instructor, or Universal Family Cook*, by W. A. Henderson, *c.* 1795. Having lifted Mrs Glasse's recipe almost word for word, Henderson, a professional caterer, then inserts one for oatcakes, stating that they are made in the same way as muffins, but with fine sifted oatmeal and using two gallons of water instead of three. The recipe doesn't work. I suspect that Henderson had never tried it, and there seems little point in quoting it here.

To make tea crumpets, 1769

'Beat two eggs very well, put to them a quart of warm milk and water, and a large spoonful of barm: beat in as much fine flour as will make them rather thicker than a common batter pudding, then make your bake-stone very hot, and rub it with a little butter wrapped in a clean linen cloth, then pour a large spoonful of batter upon your stone, and let it run to the size of a tea-saucer; turn it, and when you want to use them roast them very crisp, and butter them.'

Elizabeth Raffald, *The Experienced English Housekeeper*, first published 1769

Muffins, 1806

'Mix two pounds of flour with two eggs, two ounces of butter melted in a pint of milk, and four or five spoonfuls of yeast; beat it thoroughly and set it to rise two or three hours. Bake on a hot hearth, in flat cakes. When done on one side, turn them.

NOTE. Muffins, rolls, or bread, if stale, may be made to taste new, by dipping in cold water, and toasting, or heating in an oven, or Dutch oven, till the outside is crisp.'

Maria Eliza Rundell, *A New System of Domestic Cookery*, 1806

Muffins, 1817

'Take four pounds of flour, four eggs, a quarter of a pound of butter melted in a quart of milk, and ten spoonfuls of good yeast. Mix the whole, and beat it well; then set it to rise three or four hours. Bake on an iron plate, and when done on one side, turn them.'

Elizabeth Hammond, *Modern Domestic Cookery and Useful Receipt Book*, 1817

Well, one way of using your predecessors' recipes without seeming to be lifting them word for word is simply to halve or, as in Elizabeth Hammond's case, double the quantities.

Muffins, 1841

'Take 2 eggs, 2 spoonfuls of new yeast, and a little salt. Mix a little warm new milk and water into a quart of flour. Beat all well together, and let it stand to rise. Bake them for about 20 minutes, until of a light brown, either on a hot iron, or in shallow tin pans in a Dutch oven. When to be brought to table, toast them slightly on both sides, but not in the middle: then notch them round the centre, and pull them open with your fingers, without using a knife, and butter them.'

Emma Roberts in the revised edition of Mrs Rundell's
New System of Domestic Cookery, 1841

Crumpets, 1841

'Beat 2 eggs very well, put to them a quart of warm milk and water, and a large spoonful of yeast; beat in as much fine flour as will make them rather thicker than a common batter pudding; then make the stove hot, or the iron cover of a bain-marie very hot, and rub it with a little butter wrapped in a clean linen cloth; put a large spoonful of the batter upon the iron, and let it run within a ring to the size of a tea-saucer; turn them with the elastic blade of an old table-knife; and when you want to use them, toast them very quickly, but not too crisply and butter them.'

ibid.

The above two recipes are grouped under the heading of Breakfast Cakes, as are the Sally Lunn, Shrewsbury buckwheat cakes and various other such confections. These did not appear in the original edition of *A New System of Domestic Cookery*, although Mrs Rundell gave useful breadmaking instructions, recipes for yeast and hints on the detection of adulterations in bread.

The Muffin-man, 1851

'I did not hear of any street-seller who made the muffins or crumpets he vended. Indeed, he could not make the small quantity required, so as to be remunerative. The muffins are bought off the bakers, and at prices to leave a profit of 4d. in 1s. . . . The muffin-man carries his delicacies in a basket, well swathed in flannel, to retain the heat: "People likes them warm, sir" an old man told me, "to satisfy them they're fresh, and they almost always *are* fresh; but it can't matter so much about their being warm, as they have to be toasted again. I only wish butter was a sight cheaper, and that would make the muffins go. Butter's half the battle . . . My best customers is genteel houses, 'cause I sells a genteel thing. I like wet days best, 'cause there's werry respectable ladies what don't keep a servant, and they buys to save themselves going out. We're a great convenience to the ladies sir – a great convenience to them as like a slap-up tea."'

Henry Mayhew, *London Labour and the London Poor*, 1851

Then there was that cheerful bell, in my own youth regarded as a romantic survival, and in Queen Victoria's heyday as a very 'great convenience' to those households where muffins or crumpets were an important part of the winter tea-time ritual. It was by no means unanimously appreciated. A plaintive reference to it, quoted by *The Oxford English Dictionary*, was made in an 1830 issue of *Fraser's Magazine*. 'If the thin small voice of the muffineer's ring be justifiable,' it was asked, 'why is not the baker let loose upon us?' Some time later, in the 1840s, the muffin-man's bell was prohibited by Act of Parliament. As Mayhew recorded in 1851, 'the prohibition has been as inoperative as that which forbade the use of a drum to a costermonger'. In our own day the chimes of the ice-cream van have given rise to similar attempts at – and failures of – prohibition.

Scotch crumpets, c. 1880

'Make a thin batter of milk, flour, and water, and a *little* fresh yeast. From a small ladle, holding a sufficient quantity for 1 crumpet, the batter is poured on the heated iron plate, as you would a pancake into a frying pan.

'The crumpets are very soon sufficiently done on one side, and must be carefully turned.'

The above recipe comes from *The Cookery Book of Lady Clark of Tillypronie*, published in 1909, and compiled from note books kept during the period 1850 to 1900, when Lady Clark died. The recipe produces something more like small pancakes or what in the south we call drop scones – but yeast-leavened – than a thick honeycombed crumpet.

Muffins, 1899

'It has been claimed for the British baker that he alone can make a muffin; but it is almost to be feared, if this ever were so that the prestige has passed over to America, where muffins are made of various flours, and so light and digestible that it is a question if they are not rather an American dish.'

The Encyclopaedia of Practical Cookery, ed. Theodore Francis Garrett, 1899

Garrett was the author of a number of handbooks and treatises for professional cooks. Among his works was one entitled *Muffins and Crumpets*, so presumably the twenty-eight different muffin recipes he gives in his Encyclopaedia are his own. His English muffins are *cooked in rings*, in some cases on the griddle, others in the oven. Some versions have beaten egg whites incorporated into the batter, as for Russian blinis; one variation of the dough is – usefully – left to rise overnight, another is mixed with buttermilk and aerated with bicarbonate of soda, one is like a rich Yorkshire pudding batter made with cream, eggs and flour and no raising agent whatsoever. Further, he gives a recipe for a muffin cake which calls for cooked, split muffins soaked in a sugar syrup, layered with clotted cream, almonds and pistachios, the whole baked in a slow oven. Something of a muffin freak, Mr Garrett.

Yeast muffins and crumpets, 1914

'½ lb flour, 1 oz butter, 1 egg, ½ oz German yeast, 1 teaspoon sugar, ½ pint sweet milk, a pinch of salt.

'Sieve the flour and salt into a basin. Melt the butter in a small sauce-pan, add the milk, and let it become lukewarm over the fire. Put the yeast into a small basin with the sugar, and mix them together with a spoon until of a creamy consistency. Add the warm milk and butter to the yeast and sugar, mix well together, then strain into the centre of the flour. Add also the egg well beaten, and mix together for a few minutes. Cover the basin with a clean cloth, and set it in a warm place for 1½ hours to allow the mixture to rise. (On a chair by the side of the fire, or on the rack will do, provided the place is not so hot that it causes the mixture to cook on the sides of the basin.)

'*Crumpets*. Heat a girdle, and grease it with butter; drop on to it spoon-fuls of the above mixture, and brown first on one side and then on the other. Serve hot, buttered.

'*Muffins*. Grease some rings, and place them on a hot greased girdle; half fill them with the above mixture, cook and brown on one side, then remove the rings, turn the muffins, and cook and brown them on the other side. These are nice split, buttered, and served hot.

'Time to cook – crumpets, about 5 minutes; muffins 10 to 12 minutes. Probable cost 6d.'

Florence Jack, *Cookery for Every Household*, 1914

Florence Jack was Principal of the Edinburgh School of Domestic Arts, and as can be seen from Lady Clark's recipe on p. 347, Scotch crumpet recipes are rather different from English ones.

Muffins, 1932

'Muffins are served in the correct manner at the National Liberal Club, London.'

Florence White, *Good Things in England*, 1932

In Victorian clubs the 'correct manner' of serving the humble muffin seems to have attained almost the significance of a religious ceremonial, if not actually a sacrament. Sir Clough Williams-Ellis, creator of Portmeirion, now in his nineties, recently recalled how in his youth 'muffins would come in their heated covered silver dish along with salt cellar, china tea, cream and folded napkin, and be set down at my elbow by a club waiter still in the livery of the Regency, knee-breeches, silk stockings and buckled shoes . . . and all for no more than a shilling.'[1]

Scarborough muffins

Two recipes for these muffins are given by Miss Florence White. One came from 'the manuscript of Miss Wettin, the celebrated London confectioner' (no date given) while the second is sub-titled 'commonly called French rolls', and evidently derived from the same source, although noted by a different hand.

Both recipes call for eggs and milk, both instruct that the muffins be cooked in the oven.

Evidently Scarborough muffins differed rather from other English muffins. Yorkshire muffins generally seem to have been made from whatever bread or roll dough was going.

Lancashire Muffins

George Bellairs, writing of his Lancashire youth, describes Thursday baking days: 'it was considered disgraceful to buy bread from a shop . . . Once a week, early, the dough stood rising in the great earthenware mugs . . . When the tins were filled and in the oven, the residue of the dough was moulded into flat shapes and cooked on the bottom of the oven on a bakestone as muffins. The parsons, those clerical epicures,

1. 'Lament for the Vanishing Muffin', *House and Garden*, October 1974.

loved to save their visits till Thursdays, when they would be invited to a bite of new muffin and fresh butter.'[1]

Muffins, crumpets, 1954

'These are usually obtained from the bakehouse. Muffins must be fresh.'

Dorothy Hartley, *Food in England*, 1954

Miss Hartley adds that crumpets vary in size from a large dinner plate to 'small rather thick, very holey' crumpets made in the Midlands. Some are made with a proportion of brown flour.

All, according to this authority, should be toasted on both sides, the smooth side first, then the holey side, since it is the holes which provide the 'concavity' for the butter.

· MUFFINS AND CRUMPETS: THE BAKERY TRADE ·

From the professional bakers come further contradictory advice and information. On the whole, though, their hints and descriptions are more instructive than those of the domestic cookery writers.

Muffins, 1895

'The making of these used to be a special branch of the business, as special stones had to be erected and set in brick, but any baker now may make them by the aid of one of the gas muffin stones, which are clean, instantaneously heated and portable.

'Put $1\frac{1}{2}$lb of flour into a basin, add 1 oz of yeast made into a sponge, and a pinch of salt; let it rise, then form it into a very soft dough with half milk and water, let it rise in the basin, and beat it smooth; get ready a tray, spread it with flour about $2\frac{1}{2}$" in depth, make impressions in the flour with a smooth breakfast cup, take portions of the light dough out with a large spoon and put them into the flour impressions to rise; make the muffin-stone hot, let them cook on it for a few minutes, pass the palette knife under, turn them over on to the other side and bake likewise, keeping them of a light colour.'

Law's Grocer's Manual, 1895

1. 'Rough Epicures', *The Wine and Food Society Quarterly*, no. 58 (Summer 1948).

Crumpets, 1895

'Crumpets are also known as Pikelets, Light Cakes, Girdle Cakes etc. . . .

'It should be remembered that the batter for crumpets should always be a little thinner than for muffins . . .

'An alternative crumpet batter is made with 2 eggs to every quart of mixture. These can be baked in an oven in tin rings.'

ibid.

Muffins, 1898

'These are made much stiffer than crumpets though still soft, and are *baked without rings*.

'The flour will do to be stronger than in the case of crumpets . . . High-grade brands of English milled flour will do quite well . . .

'Muffins will, if properly turned out, be at least an inch thick, and display a nice white edge all round, the result of using a high-grade flour.'

Frederick T. Vine, *Saleable Shop Goods*, 6th edn, 1898

Muffins, 1908

'Muffins are essentially an old-fashioned fare . . . They are not now regarded as essentials on the tea tables of the present generation . . . The ordinary baker sells so few that it is not worth his while to keep a hot-plate for their manufacture . . . Considerable difficulty is experienced in making them of the required lightness and to the proper degree of holeyness.'

John Kirkland, *The Modern Baker, Confectioner and Caterer*, 1907

John Kirkland, Master Baker, regarded as *the* great authority of the first three decades of the twentieth century, goes on to describe the mixing and cooking of muffins. He uses hoops for baking them on the hot plate, asserts that the batter should be liquid, that the finished muffins must be full of holes, and that 'when done they should be light but tough, and although sufficiently cooked it is not intended that they should be eaten without previous toasting'. Kirkland adds that in a good many districts 'pikelets' is the name given to what are called muffins in others. Of crumpets he says it is not usual to bake them in rings 'although this is sometimes done'.

Muffins, *1927*

'Very light fermented cakes made of soft dough containing *only flour water yeast and salt.*'

The Baker's ABC, ed. John Kirkland, 1927

Crumpets, *1927*

'Round white cakes, holey on top, of equal thickness throughout, with a very thin or no crust or skin . . . The flour for crumpets should be rather soft, or, at least, not strong and tough. *They are made from flour, water, yeast, and salt only.*'

ibid.

Muffins and crumpets, *1929*

'Practice and judgement are required to make one proficient in muffin-making.

'Some persons now make muffins after the same formula as for tea cakes, namely, moulding one in each hand and pinning i.e. rolling out the size required, then proving and baking. I have tried that way more than once, but I cannot get the muffins to appear anything like what my experience teaches me a muffin should be. *Crumpets* are generally made by muffin-makers . . . Nothing but careful practice and particular attention to the whys and wherefores of both hot plate and batter will make a good muffin or crumpet maker.'

Robert Wells, *Bread and Biscuit Bakers Assistant*, 4th edn, 1929

Muffins, *1937*

'Many a muffin-man regards warm flour as his No. 1 secret.'

Walter Banfield, *Manna*, 1937

Crumpets, *1937*

'The batter requires attacking with vivacious turbulence.'

ibid.

Muffins, 1967

'Strong flour is required for muffins, otherwise a light open texture will not be obtained . . . a good muffin should be quite square at the edges, of a golden brown colour and, when broken, have a light open texture.'

Edmund Bennion, *Breadmaking*, 4th edn, 1967

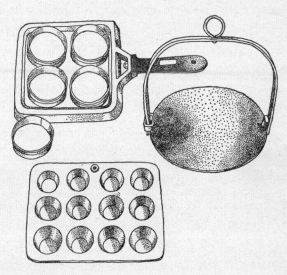

Square griddle with handle, cast aluminium. Tinplate hoops are 4 inches by 1 inch. Cast iron girdle with handle is for baking over a peat, wood or coal fire. In front is a sheet of American muffin pans or cups, 2 by 2 inches. We should call them pattypans.

Crumpets, 1967

'For crumpets an ordinary high-grade patent home-milled flour will give satisfactory results.'

ibid.

· ENGLISH MUFFINS, 1973 ·

The following is the recipe I have found the most successful of all that I have tried. It is based mainly on the one given by Walter Banfield, in his book *Manna* (1937).

1 lb of strong plain flour or 8 oz each of strong plain and ordinary house-hold flour, ½ oz of yeast, 1 level tablespoon of salt, ½ teaspoon of sugar, 2 tablespoons of olive oil, butter, clarified butter or good, clean lard (olive oil is my first choice), rather under ¾ pint of milk and water mixed. Rice flour[1] for dusting the moulded muffins.

Equivalent metric quantities: strong plain flour 450 g, or strong plain flour 225 g and ordinary household flour 225 g, yeast 15 g, salt 1 level table-spoon, sugar ½ teaspoon, olive oil, butter, clarified butter or lard 2 table-spoons, milk and water mixed rather under 420 g, rice flour for dusting.

First weigh out the flour, put it into a big ovenproof bowl, and if you are using two kinds mix them well. Put the bowl, covered, in a low oven, 285°F, 140°C, gas no. 1, for 7 to 10 minutes.

Meanwhile, mix the milk, water and olive oil or fat; warm them to blood heat. Use a little of this warmed liquid to cream the yeast and sugar.

When the flour is well warmed, take it from the oven, stir in the salt, add the creamed yeast, then the liquids. Using a wooden spoon, mix the dough well. Very quickly it will become coherent, elastic and smooth, but will be rather too soft for hand-kneading. Cover the bowl and leave the dough to rise, at room temperature – say 70°F, 21°C – for about 50 minutes.

Now break down the dough, divide it into seven or eight portions. Using rice flour for dusting, mould each piece into a round. Place these on a dusted baking sheet – again using rice flour, and if possible a non-stick sheet. Shape up the sides of the muffins so that they are even and squared. Cover the muffins with a cloth or a sheet of polythene, and leave them to recover volume for about 35 to 45 minutes. They should not be allowed to rise too much or they will lose their characteristic shape while cooking.

Have ready a griddle (I use one made of cast aluminium, 9 inches square, with a front handle. I find this far more satisfactory for gas cooking than the traditional iron girdle on which there is insufficient space and which tends to overheat in the centre), and just brush it, no more, with a scrap of butter or fat – this is unorthodox but necessary with aluminium.

1. See p. 71.

Warm the griddle over very low heat, and very carefully transfer the muffins one by one, using a wide thin palette knife or a fish slice, which can also be used to pat the sides of the muffins back into shape should they have become flattened or have spread as they were transferred.

Let the muffins cook *slowly* over *very moderate* heat allowing 8 to 10 minutes for each side.

When the first batch is cooked put them in a folded cloth, or transfer them to a low oven to keep warm, while the second batch is cooking.

Inevitably this second batch will be a little more risen and puffy than the first batch.

When fresh from the griddle muffins should be a good biscuit colour on the top and bottom, with a broad white band all round the waist; they should be 1½ to 2 inches thick, smooth and lightly crusted on the outside, honeycombed when split open. For the proper way to toast and eat muffins see Marian McNeill's description below.

Notes: The warming of the flour, prior to mixing, and the oil or fat give this muffin dough its character. It is easy to handle, and really does produce muffins as they should be. The dusting with the rice flour, which dries the surface of the muffins without making them sticky or patchy, is another important point. Cornflour, which is also a fine starch flour, can be used as an alternative. If the whole thing seems like rather too much of a production for a few muffins (which do go hard and tough very quickly – hence the toasting and buttering, and the hot-water-warmed and covered muffin-dishes of the Victorians) try the muffin loaves, made with the same dough, described on p. 312.

To toast muffins

'Muffins should not be split and toasted. The correct way to serve them is to open them slightly at their joint all the way round, toast them back and front, tear them open and butter the insides liberally. Serve hot.'

Marian McNeill, *The Book of Breakfasts*, 1932

*

· CRUMPETS, 1973 ·

To go back to 1937 and Walter Banfield's *Manna*, the following paragraph struck me as particularly relevant: 'Provided suitable flour is used, these honeycomby, labyrinthine structures are fairly simple to make. The idea that crumpets are difficult is not uncommon because if flour unsuitable for the process is used grotesque, unfair creations result. That is, one either makes good crumpets or very bad ones.'

Until I learned from Mr Banfield's book how a professional dough or batter for crumpets is – or was – made, my own efforts certainly came into the category of 'very bad ones'. Either the batter was much too liquid and ran out from under the hoops, or it was too stiff, and although fairly easily cooked on the griddle the resulting crumpets didn't have the characteristic 'honeycomby, labyrinthine' structure – they were what bakers call 'blind'.

Now, using a batter very similar to the muffin dough but much more liquid – note: the first is a dough, the second a batter – and adding, at the stirring-down stage, a little extra warm water in which a small quantity of bicarbonate of soda has been dissolved, the mixture works out just about right. The bicarbonate hint is given by Mr Banfield and also by John Kirkland.

So for 1 lb of flour, preferably half and half strong plain and ordinary household, allow ½ oz of yeast, 1 generous pint of milk and water mixed, 1 tablespoon of salt, 1 teaspoon of sugar, 2 tablespoons of oil. For the second mixing, ½ teaspoon of bicarbonate of soda, just over ¼ pint of warm water. For greasing the griddle and the rings, a scrap of oil or butter.

Equivalent metric quantities: flour (preferably half and half strong plain and ordinary household) 450 g, yeast 15 g, milk and water mixed 550 to 575 g, salt 1 tablespoon, sugar 1 teaspoon, oil 2 tablespoons. For the second mixing: bicarbonate of soda ½ teaspoon, warm water 150 g. For greasing the griddle and rings, a scrap of oil or butter.

Warm the flour in an earthenware bowl in a low oven for 5 minutes. Warm the oil, milk, water and sugar to blood heat. Use a little of this to cream the yeast.

Mix the salt with the warmed flour, stir in the yeast, pour in the liquid, stir the batter very well and vigorously – see Walter Banfield's memorable hint about attacking it with 'vivacious turbulence' – until it is smooth and elastic. Cover the bowl, leave the batter to rise at room temperature until the whole surface is a mass of bubbles and the mixture looks as if it were about to break. This will take 1½ to 2 hours.

Forestall the natural falling of the batter by beating it down yourself with a wooden spoon.

Dissolve the bicarbonate in the warm water and stir it into the batter.

Cover the bowl and leave the batter to recover, for about 30 minutes. This time put it in a rather warmer place, unless you need to delay the cooking of the crumpets, in which case use cold water for dissolving the bicarbonate and remove the bowl of batter to a cool place.

To cook the crumpets, grease the griddle *very* lightly, and have the rings ready (modern crumpet rings are 4 inches in diameter and ½ inch deep), also very lightly greased.

Put four rings on the griddle, pour enough batter into each to come almost to the top. Let them cook very gently until the top surfaces have formed a skin, which will take 7 to 10 minutes. By this time also there should be a mass of tiny holes. If the holes haven't appeared, the batter is too thick. Add more warm water or milk before cooking the next batch.

Once the crumpets have set it is easy to slip the rings off, and flip the crumpets over. They will need only 3 minutes more cooking; crumpets are *supposed* to be rather pallid and flabby-looking but very holey on the top surface, pale gold and smooth on the underside.

Keep the cooked crumpets warm in a folded cloth, or in a covered dish in the oven, while the rest are cooked.

The quantities given will make eight to ten crumpets, 4 inches in diameter and about ¾ inch thick. Because of the shallow rings it is scarcely possible to make them rise higher.

Personally, I find crumpets edible only when freshly cooked, warm and soaked in plenty of butter. Toasting makes them tough and alters the whole structure. I think it preferable to reheat them in a covered dish in the oven, with butter. When all is said – perhaps too much has been said – and done, crumpets are only yeast pancakes confined to rings and so made thick and of a uniform size.

Notes and variations: 1. I have also tried the crumpet batter without the oil, which is an unorthodox addition. The result was thinner crumpets with less volume and not so good a flavour.

2. For hoops or rings for crumpet batter, try kitchen shops or write to the manufacturers, T. Errington and Sons, Rodney Road, Portsmouth.

WELSH CRUMPETS, GRIDDLE CAKES or
· YEAST PANCAKES ·

These are cooked straight on the griddle or in a heavy iron frying pan, without rings. They are much like pikelets.

For 2 dozen very small pancakes or 1 dozen large ones, ingredients are ½ lb of ordinary household flour, or unbleached strong bread flour if you have it ; ¼ pint each of milk and water ; ½ oz of yeast ; 1 teaspoon of salt ; 1 whole egg ; ¼ oz of butter.

Equivalent metric quantities for two dozen small pancakes or one dozen large ones : ordinary household flour or unbleached strong bread flour 225 g, milk 150 g, water 150 g, yeast 15 g, salt 1 teaspoon, 1 whole egg, butter approximately 10 g.

Mix the milk and water. Warm them to blood heat. Use a little of the liquid to cream the yeast.

Dissolve the butter and the salt in the warm liquid, beat in the egg.

Add the yeast to the flour (to speed the rising, the flour can be warmed, as for ordinary crumpet batter), pour in the liquid and mix to a smooth batter. Cover and leave to rise.

In 1 to 1½ hours the batter should be thick and bubbly.

Warm your griddle plate or frying pan, brush it over with a scrap of butter.

If you are using a griddle, pour out three or four ladlefuls of the batter, spaced well apart. Yeast batters do not run like ordinary pancake batters, but stay put in neat little thin cakes. Let them cook rather slowly, until the top surfaces are a mass of tiny holes and have begun to set. Using a pliable spatula, flip them over and let the second side brown lightly. Each batch of the pancakes should be cooked in about 4 minutes. Keep them warm in the oven, or in a folded, warmed cloth, until all are done.

If you are using a frying pan or small pancake pan use more batter at a time and let it all but cover the surface of the pan. These will take a little longer to cook.

Eat the pancakes with butter and salt, or with bacon or small sausages, or as a sweet dish with brown sugar or honey.

In Welsh these griddle cakes or pancakes, as noted by Theodore Garrett (see p. 341), are called *crempog*, the equivalent of *krampoch*, the buckwheat pancakes of Lower Brittany.

· CRUMPET STREET ·

As a last word on the common present-day usage of the word crumpet, I quote Philip Oakes writing in the *Sunday Times* of 6 October 1974. (His words may be useful to future students of slang.) The subject is a play called *The Great Caper* by Ken Campbell. The play, the author told Philip Oakes, 'locates the crumpetstrassen of the world; thoroughfares where beautiful women can always be found . . . In London, King's Road Chelsea is the crumpetstrasse to note. In Munich it's the Leopold-strasse; in Rome via Botteghe Oscure . . . In Copenhagen you should try your luck on the Hans Christian Andersen Boulevard.'

Mr Campbell, added Philip Oakes, was not recommending pick-up points; he explained that the interest is purely aesthetic.

· PIKELETS ·

'Oatcakes were toasted and eaten with dripping, pikelets had butter and this was the rule.'

Alison Uttley, *Recipes from an Old Farmhouse*, 1966

Leicestershire pikelet, 1841

'Mix a pint of milk with flour sufficient to make a thick batter; add 4 eggs, 1 tablespoonful of good fresh yeast, a small quantity of nutmeg, and a little salt. The whole to be beaten up together for 10 minutes, then left to stand 2 hours to rise. Bake on a girdle-stone, and butter each while hot – laying 3 or 4 on the same plate.

'Those which are left to the following day should be laid separately on a clean cloth as they are baked, and when to be eaten, toast and butter them like crumpets.'

Maria Eliza Rundell, *A New System of Domestic Cookery*

First published in 1806, this book was edited and revised with additional recipes by Miss Emma Roberts in 1841. The above recipe is initialled by Emma Roberts.

Staffordshire pikelets for breakfast

'Orthodox pikelets come up as thick only as pancakes, piled up and buttered while hot on both sides; but they can be made as thick as a muffin, split, and buttered inside; they can also be served thin as toast, in a silver rack.

'½lb of flour to 1 oz German yeast melted in lukewarm milk and strained, a little salt, add 2 eggs and mix as for rolls, and let the sponge rise; keep it thin, and then divide into spoonfuls, and have the girdle very hot and buttered; it should run and be thin and baked in this state, a spoonful laid on the girdle at a time, turned on the girdle, quickly cooked (no sugar).'

The Cookery Book of Lady Clark of Tillypronie, 1909

'a pikelet is only the Yorkshire term for crumpet.'

Florence White, *Good Things in England*, 1932 (Miss White is quoting from a reader, a Mr Dupuis Brown, 1931)

Again, Miss Dorothy Hartley (*Food in England*, 1954) states that 'the pikelet is the Yorkshire–Lancashire version of the crumpet of medium size', and a Yorkshire-born Derbyshire-bred friend of mine said to me quite categorically: 'In Derbyshire and Yorkshire pikelets mean crumpets, the ones with holes.' Well, the ones with holes, yes, but in practice, since pikelets are cooked without rings, they are really rather more like ordinary yeast pancakes than crumpets. It is the confining of batter in rings or hoops and the consequent slow cooking necessitated which makes English crumpets distinctive from pikelets and other yeast-raised griddle cakes or pancakes. Edmund Bennion, author of *Bread-making* (4th edn, 1967), says that when finished the diameter of pikelets should be 6 inches. Another Derbyshire friend tells me, however, that no such law can be laid down, since in her part of the county, the south-west, *all* muffins, crumpets and similar yeast cakes, of whatever size, are pikelets. In *Food and Drink in Britain* (1973) Miss C. Anne Wilson says that pikelet was the west Midlands corruption of the Welsh *pyglyd* or *bara pyglyd*, also called pitchy bread.

· PIKELETS, 1974 ·

I make pikelets with the crumpet batter given on pp. 356–7, thinned down with the extra ¼ pint of water (or milk), but omitting the bicarbonate of soda, and increasing the quantity of yeast to 1 oz for 1 lb of flour.

Cook pikelets, if possible, on the griddle, as for Welsh crumpets, p. 358, and make them rather thicker.

· MUFFINS AND CRUMPETS: FINAL WORDS ·

'muffins and crumpets are very indigestible.'

E. H. Ruddock, M.D., *Essentials of Diet*, London, 1879

Indigestible as those crumpets and muffins may have been – according to Sir Henry Thompson they were also 'undesirable' and so was hot buttered toast – that didn't, nor perhaps will it ever, diminish their appeal to the young. The late Sir John Masterman, aged eighty-eight at the time his book was published, describes the lost Eden of the Oxford undergraduate:

'The height of luxury was reached in the winter afternoons . . . lying in a tin bath in front of a coal fire, drinking tea, and eating well-buttered crumpets is an experience few can have today.'

J. C. Masterman, *On the Chariot Wheel: An Autobiography*, London, Oxford University Press, 1975

'You don't get tired of muffins, but you don't find inspiration in them.'

George Bernard Shaw, *Man and Superman*, 1903

Notes on French Bread

'*Que Dieu m'accorde du pain avec des yeux et du fromage sans yeux.*' (French saying: 'God grant me bread with eyes and cheese without them.')

For nearly all English people who have ever set foot in France, the words 'French bread' evoke a golden-brown *baguette* or a long thin *ficelle*, the crust crisp and sweet with its characteristic leaf-shaped surface cuts, the crumb white and pitted with irregular holes, many of them very large. To us, the holes are part of the proper character of this kind of bread. To English bakers they are a sign of soft flour or faulty technique, or both. Bread that has holes so large is not suitable for buttering and, according to English bakers, bread's chief function is as a vehicle for butter (what makes them think that the clammy and flannelly stuff they sell sliced and wrapped can be buttered? Just try spreading cold butter on a slice of damp blanket), but the French don't find it necessary or desirable to butter their bread in the way we do. They don't have to put butter on it to make it edible. Another point is that the French do use a good deal of soft flour, because that is what is produced from the wheat grown in France. So they have long ago adapted their bread techniques to their flour. Or rather, what they adapted was the 'Vienna' technique, and this didn't happen until some time in the mid nineteenth century; it was the Viennese oven, with its steam injectors and its sloping floor, or sole, which was mainly responsible for creating the tradition of French bread as we know it today. English bakers, and indeed many of the older French ones, still call this type of bread 'Vienna' bread, the true French bread being the old round or cylindrical hand-shaped *pain de campagne* or *pain de ménage*, plump, and crossed with cuts so that when baked the crust is of many different shades, gradations and textures and the crumb rather open and coarse. It is this bread which is now enjoying something

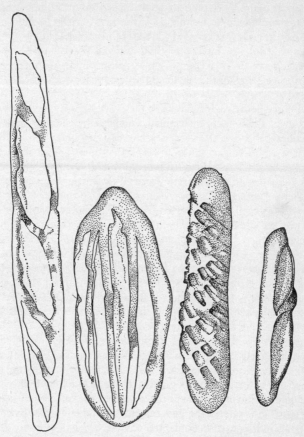

Four loaves bought in a Normandy bakery in the Calvados region, 1975. The one with the stripey cuts, second from the left, is *pain brié*, a speciality of the region. The name has nothing to do with the cheese. *Brié* means that the dough has been kneaded by a method based on the old hand-operated wooden brake (see note 4, p. 335). The dough is made on the leaven system, without yeast and with very little salt. It makes a very close-textured loaf. Note how the cutting on the third loaf – in Paris it is called a *polka* – resembles the English chequerboard-cut loaf shown on p. 265. The small long loaf is a *tire-bouchon* or corkscrew.

of a revival in France, perhaps because the Vienna type has not taken very kindly to the short-time dough maturing and the rapid mechanical kneading and moulding techniques of the 1970s, partly because a well-made *pain de campagne* keeps much better than *baguette* loaves, which is to say that it will stay moist for as long as two days, even three, whereas the long, crusty, thin loaf is, as we know, stale within an hour of emerging from the oven, and for the French three days is a long time to keep a loaf of bread.

In France housewives rarely bake their own bread;[1] they don't have to because, although French bread produced by the few large-scale mechanical bakeries is often very nearly as nasty as our own, in a different way, it is a rare village, however small, that doesn't have at least one operative bakery from which fresh bread will be available three or four times a day. And in towns of any size at all closing days and holidays for the bakers are staggered, as for pharmacies. Neither Sunday nor Monday is now the general closing day so that even if you find your favourite bakery locked and barred there will be others to choose from within easy walking distance. This is a point for English visitors to look out for. Don't assume, if you are buying food for a picnic and find the nearest bakery closed, that *all* bakers all over France are also closed that day. Inquiries will soon solve the problem, usually without resort to the self-service store, where the bread is nearly always stale and dry. The giant hypermarkets are a better bet. Sometimes their *pain de campagne* is surprisingly good.

A point you will also notice, if you buy an ordinary loaf of *pain de ménage* or a portion of one – in France this can always be asked for – is that the bakery shop assistant will weigh it before telling you the price. Behind this action, taken for granted by the French and all who are accustomed to buying bread in France, lie centuries of struggle between the French bakers and the governments of the country. An endless succession of decrees concerning the permitted weight of loaves offered for sale to the public, and – as in England – severe fines imposed on any baker selling underweight bread, were among the injustices which for at least 400 years harassed and infuriated the bakers who protested over and over again that, however meticulous the weighing of their dough prior to moulding and baking, it was a physical impossibility that each and every loaf emerge from the oven at a precise and pre-ordained

1. When they do it is because they want some kind of wholemeal, rye or other brown bread which is unobtainable from the baker. The health-food movement is gaining momentum in France.

weight. Very often an unfortunate baker would be prosecuted and fined through no fault of his own or intentional dishonesty on his part.

By 1781, just eight years before the Revolution, understanding of the factors governing the shrinkage of dough while baking was sufficiently far advanced for lengthy demonstrations on the part of the bakers to prove to officialdom that variation in the weight of the baked loaves was inevitable. At this moment the examining commission declared itself satisfied that it was unreasonable and a 'scientific heresy' to require of the bakers that their loaves reach a fixed and inalterable weight. Nothing, however, was done to alter the bread laws – it seems an extraordinary oversight that the Napoleonic régime failed to recognize the illogicality – until nearly sixty years later, when a government decree of 1839–40 granted the bakers freedom to sell their bread not by the loaf but by the kilo. The price per kilo might be, and usually was, controlled by the government, but the customer paid for precisely the number of kilos or fractions of kilos he bought. Except for certain small loaves in the *pain de fantaisie*, or fancy bread category, which are sold by the piece, the system still prevails in France.[1] For a time during the nineteenth century the English bread laws established the same or a similar system. During the First World War, it was decreed that our bakers must once more produce loaves baked to a fixed weight. For us that ruling still obtains. Hence that preoccupation with the exact weight of a household loaf, and therefore a high water content and underbaking to avoid shrinkage, which is one among many factors which make our bread what it is today.

Incidentally, if you find a particularly good bakery in France, it is worth buying a kilo or two of flour to bring home in the car. Ask for *farine panifiable*, type 55. The request may cause surprise, but is rarely refused. If it is, buy ordinary household flour, type 45. Since the percentage of strong flour in the blend for bread is small, the difference is not very great. For those interested in baking their own bread, it is an instructive exercise to try a loaf or rolls made with French flour. There is little hope of achieving anything like the crust of a real French loaf, but the taste *will* resemble that of French bread. French flour has a very characteristic flavour. It is milled from French home-grown wheat which yields a soft, or low-gluten, flour. For strength and volume, 10 to 20 per cent of high-gluten imported wheat is blended with the French product. The extraction rate of French bread flour is 70 to 75 per cent, much the same as our own. The colour of French flour for com-

1. In July 1978 the French government freed all bread prices.

mercial baking is, however, very different. This is because in France no artificial bleaching is permitted. So all French bread flour retains its natural rich creamy colour, as indeed does the English strong unbleached flour packed by several English mills for household bread-baking. The flavours of the two products are, however, different and distinct. They do of course vary according to the blend and the sources of the wheat, but as a generalization it is fair to say that French bread flours have a stronger and sweeter flavour of wheat than do our own blends. The strong flour we like yields a larger, more handsome loaf than would soft French flour. The volume of the loaf is achieved at the expense of savour. It has often been claimed – no doubt it will be again – in times of shortage of imported grain or during a national crisis, that bread made from a high proportion of our own soft wheat flour is finer in flavour than any produced by our present blends, which contain about 75 per cent of imported hard wheat. There is much evidence to support this claim, although flavour must always remain a subjective matter. One point is far from subjective. The whiter-than-white chemically treated flour foisted on the English public with the legal blessing and the financial aid of the British government would not be found legally acceptable in any other western European country, let alone in France where, with the sole exception of ascorbic acid[1] (vitamin C), the addition of chemical improvers to bread flour, as well as artificial bleaching, is absolutely prohibited.

It is then – and surely the point is obvious enough – the flour, its savour and its performance, which plays the greatest single part in creating the character of French bread. There are others, such as the water content, which is low. Soft flour, as all breadmakers know, absorbs less liquid than strong flour. When you buy bread in France you are not paying to carry home solidified water in your shopping basket. You are probably paying quite highly for the baker's time. In most French bakeries the maturing of the dough is still a comparatively lengthy process. It is one worth paying for.

After the flour, the most crucial aspect of French bread is its characteristic crust. This is achieved, first of all, by the cutting or slashing of the loaves immediately prior to baking. A practised hand, a particular knack and the correct thin curved blade, like an old-fashioned razor, are needed for this operation. Next, and more important, comes the fierce

1. Ascorbic acid speeds the ripening of the dough. The vitamin C is destroyed in baking.

burst of steam turned on the loaves as soon as they are set in the oven and the doors closed. This steam is injected into the oven by means of pipes, and is turned off after the first ten to fifteen minutes of baking. By this time the intense concentration of vapour in the oven has enveloped the whole batch of bread causing the dough to expand to its utmost capacity unhindered by the formation of a hard crust. The starch on the surface of the bread gelatinizes in the dry heat which succeeds the steam heat. Thus the natural gloss on the crusts starts to form. The cuts have opened (if they haven't it is because the dough was either insufficiently matured or too much so). The leaf-shaped scars in the dough form their own crust. In the dry heat these secondary parts of the crust bake pale and matt in contrast to the high colour, the gloss and shine on the ridges of the top crust and on the ends of the loaves. By the time baking is complete both the upper and under crusts have turned to browns and golds of innumerable variations and differing surface textures. As the baker unloads the batch from the oven, takes them into the shop and ranges them upright on the metal racks, the thin, fine crusts make a crackling noise even more enticing than the smell of wheat which assails your nostrils as you take the loaf of your choice from the rack and hand it to the shop assistant to be wrapped in the ritual, useless wisp of paper. This is crusty bread in the true and correct sense of the term. The drama of its baking and its delivery from the oven to the shop shelves is enacted three or four times every morning. Customers who buy from the same bakery day after day know that each oven-load of the morning's bread yields loaves with slightly differing characteristics, due to variations in the maturity or ripeness of the dough. There is also the agreeable choice between a loaf with a normal crust and a darker, more highly baked one – in spite of highly evolved ovens and controlled heat, baking is still sometimes uneven, so each loaf has its personality – and the diversity of shapes, long and wide, long and thin, short and wide, short and thin, round, cylindrical, in itself constitutes something of a *tour de force*.

Now this kind of baking is dependent upon experienced and skilled craftsmen as well as upon the materials and the tools. Although many English bakers use ovens similar to the French ones it is not to be expected, given English bread flour and primarily English methods of dough mixing and proving, that when they attempt French bread they will achieve anything much resembling the original article. Nor do they. I have yet to find in any English bakery claiming to sell French bread a loaf with a crust and its cuts, let alone its crumb and its savour, which could be taken for the authentic product. English French bread is a thing apart, an invention not so much, I fancy, of English bakers as of English food writers whose references to a 'crusty French loaf' tumble from their typewriters as automatically as those other meaningless clichés 'gourmet' and 'chef-prepared' and 'haute cuisine' are sprayed, as from aerosols, on to the labels of tinned and oven-ready or boil-in-the-bag frozen foods.

If professional bakers, with all the experience and equipment at their disposal, cannot succeed in producing an even passable imitation of a French *baguette* loaf, how much less are housewives going to be able to do so at home? Domestic ovens are simply not suitable for the baking of this type of bread, even had we the correct flour. That burst of all-enveloping high-pressure steam is not to be achieved, as is sometimes advised, by the placing of a bowl of water in the oven, nor by dropping a hot brick in the water, nor by making an oven shelf of quarry tiles. These improvisations may indeed help us to make better bread, with a less leathery crust and greater volume. So will the method of under-cover baking described on pp. 303–7. They will not help us to make *French* bread. And I wonder, even if they did so, would we be pleased? French bread as we understand it is good only when it is fresh. Within an hour or two of emerging from the oven it is already stale. The following day it is almost uneatable except as *pain grillé* or toast, which is indeed delicious, but hardly achieves the primary object of breadmaking.

How long the tradition of this kind of bread will survive even in France is a matter for speculation. As M. Rivière, a French Master Baker and miller, said to me: 'Wages increase continually. Our bakers work half the night and all the morning. There has to be fresh bread for every customer. If there is no new batch for the workers to take home for their midday meal they are aggrieved.' So far the big industrial bakeries have made little headway in France. But the bakers don't like the night work. It is difficult to see how they can continue to provide everybody with fresh bread so many times daily. In answer to questions, M. Rivière told me that the deterioration in the quality of French bread, so noticeable in recent years, is partly due to the increased use of mechanical kneading machines worked at high speed. This means shorter proving periods for the dough, a whiter appearance and a softer texture in the crumb of the baked loaf. Again, few bakers now could possibly afford the time or the staff to hand-mould their loaves. The job is done by a machine which divides a mass of dough into, say, four or five dozen long loaves of equal weight and uniform size all in one single movement. M. Rivière's own bakery, a relatively small one in the town of Honfleur, uses the modern methods, although he is careful to keep his mechanical kneader at medium speed so that the dough is not over-worked. He added that the present taste in northern France is for whiter and softer bread, so he does not make the *pain de campagne* now returning to favour in the central and southern parts of the country, more especially in remoter areas of the Auvergne, Limousin, eastern Burgundy, the Ardèche, the Drôme.

All in all, it will by now be clear why I am making no attempt here to provide a recipe for French bread as we know – or used to know – it, and why to me it is more realistic to concentrate on the baking of good English bread, for which we have the materials and the means at our disposal.[1]

✳

Although, as explained in the foregoing notes, it seems to me unreasonable to waste time attempting to make French bread with English bread flour and in the ovens of domestic cookers, there was a time when baking methods in France and England were much less disparate than they now are, and our love affair with French bread goes back a long way. Already in the reign of Edward I (1272–1307) the London bakers of white bread were making 'Light Bread known as French bread', also called puffe and pouf. From an Assay decree of 1288–9 we know that this French bread was made from flour of the same bolting as wastel, a bread of second quality, and that weight for weight its price was half that of a loaf of demeine or finest quality bread.[2] What was particularly light about the puffe bread of the thirteenth century is not clear. Possibly an improved method of managing the leaven, or piece of dough kept from the previous batch, had reached England from across the Channel. It must not be forgotten that at this period much of south-

1. My advice to anyone still determined to try their hands at French bread, whatever the difficulties, is to study the thirty-odd pages of instructions, with drawings illustrating the method, given by Julia Child in Volume 2 of *Mastering the Art of French Cooking*, published in London by Michael Joseph, 1977. Another famous American writer, James Beard, gives a recipe, with greater brevity, in *Beard on Bread*, also published by Michael Joseph (1977).

2. *Liber Albus* or *White Book of the City of London*, pp. 305–6.

western France still belonged to the English crown; there was a great deal of interchange between the two countries.

Demeine or demayne bread was the best quality which evolved into the manchets of the sixteenth and seventeenth centuries. The contemporary French equivalents of manchet loaves seem to have been made in much the same way as our own, except that when moulded the loaves were proved upside down on cloths or in wooden bowls, the latter system being described by several English writers giving recipes for French bread or the 'French rolls' which eventually replaced our manchet loaves. Today French loaves are still proved upside down, but in cloth-lined baskets, or simply on canvas cloths, instead of in wooden dishes.

One vital point which distinguished English bakers' methods from those of the French was in the use of ale barm or beer yeast. In England this seems to have been common from about the fourteenth century onwards. In France, until the middle years of the seventeenth century, only the finest white wheaten bread was commonly leavened with barm. Household bread was made on the spontaneous leaven system. This meant creating a leaven with flour and warm water, which was left in a large crock or a wooden trough until it started to ferment. To this leaven was added the rest of the flour and water. The original ferment leavened the whole batch. When this was made up and ready for moulding, a portion would be set aside and stored as leaven for the subsequent baking session. The method was much as it had been in biblical times; it was the one which eventually came to be known as the sourdough system.

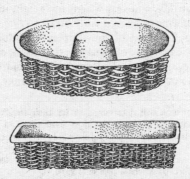

The canvas-lined baskets used at one time by all French bakers for proving their loaves are called *bannetons*. The round *couronne* basket is for a large ring loaf.

The use of ale and beer yeasts seems to have been introduced – or re-introduced, for it had been known to the Gauls in the Roman period – into France during the early seventeenth century by Flemish bakers, at that time known for their good light bread. Although bread leavened with yeast was admitted to be much more agreeable than any made on the natural leaven system, the French medical profession considered it unwholesome and injurious, if not positively poisonous. Even the passing of a parliamentary decree in 1670, allowing bakers to use yeast for their bread, applied officially only to *pains de luxe*, or small white wheaten loaves. Qualified though the decree was, at least one bread historian, Ambroise Morel,[1] considered the decision one of the most important in the whole history of the French baking trade, its effect being comparable only to that of the adoption, nearly two centuries later, of the Vienna baking system. The introduction of compressed grain yeast from Hungary (the equivalent of our German yeast) represented a third great landmark.

The importance of the use of yeast leaven lay not only in the alteration in the nature of the dough made by French bakers but in the great changes which it eventually brought about in the tastes and the bread-eating and breadmaking habits of the French. Hitherto, huge loaves, sometimes weighing as much as 16lb apiece, had been baked to last a household for several days. This household bread with its massive volume of close, hard crumb and relatively small area of crust remained acceptably fresh from one week's baking day to the next. The yeast-leavened bread, made in smaller loaves, often in long shapes instead of round, and with a higher water content and therefore a soft crumb but larger area of rather hard crust, had a more refined flavour and texture, but did not keep as well as the old sourdough type of bread. It became necessary for those who had acquired the taste to have fresh bread almost every day. In Paris, home-baked household bread was gradually abandoned in favour of bread bought from the bakeries. This bread was clearly not yet very much like French bread as we know it at its best today, but methods and understanding were progressing fast. It was for example at about this time – the middle years of the seventeenth century – that the long thick cylindrical loaves with a row of cuts across the crust, resembling our own modern 'bloomer' loaf, began to appear, and that bakers began to preoccupy themselves with the texture and the appearance of the crust which had become the most highly prized feature of the rich man's loaf.

1. *Histoire illustrée de la boulangerie en France*, 1924.

By the early decades of the eighteenth century, English domestic cookery writers were showing an increasing interest in French methods of breadmaking, surely a sign that French bread was acquiring a great reputation. There seems no cause to doubt that the English recipes for French bread given at this period were genuine, recorded in good faith and with practical experience. We may think them odd because they don't produce anything like French bread as we know it today, but when compared to their French counterparts across the Channel the recipes nearly always turn out to be for the enriched doughs used for the best or luxury bread at the same period in France. The dough was made up into round or long rolls – a good deal larger, clearly, than those of today – which were evidently deliberately baked in a 'quick' oven, so that the rolls developed a very hard crust which was then rasped or grated, or chipped with a knife, before being sent to table; chipping, says Hannah Glasse in 1747, 'makes the bread look spungy and of a fine yellow' while rasping 'takes off all that fine colour'; forty years later, W. A. Henderson, a professional cook and caterer, thought it more practical to rasp the crusts (see p. 378).

It was the system of fast baking and subsequent chipping of the crust, which continued in use until the 1920s, that distinguished English 'French' rolls and loaves from the earlier manchets, which were baked in a moderate oven, and must have been more like large versions of modern soft rolls. Eighteenth-century roll dough was also much more matured than manchet dough, which was a quick-rising one. The custom of rasping or chipping the crust of rolls does not seem to have been a French one. It was probably due to the differences in English and French eating habits and to our differing attitudes to bread. To the French the crust was a delicacy. It was used to dip into soup, or when stale to thicken it and add extra bulk.[1] To the English, then as now, the crumb of the loaf was the essential part. The grated crust was, presumably, thrown away, or perhaps given to the animals.

The following descriptions of French bread, and the recipes, give an interesting idea of how fancy bread, as French bread came to be known, developed in this country.

---

1. The old expression *faire tremper la soupe* meant to put slices or sups of bread into the pot and leave them simmering until the crumb became part of the soup while the crusts retained their identity. Achieving the correct consistency was quite an art.

· PAIN DE GONESSE ·

'Je suis roi de Gonesse et d'Ay.'
Henri IV of Navarre

Gonesse, a small town near Pontoise, about 35 kilometres north-west of Paris, was known from the thirteenth century until the time of the Revolution for the excellence of the bread made there and brought twice a week into the markets of Paris. Almost the entire population of Gonesse were bakers. Ay was, as it still is, one of the great wine-growing centres of the champagne country. So what Henri IV was saying was 'I am king of bread and wine'. Not that it should be inferred that he was bequeathing to posterity a useful puff for sparkling champagne. That wine was as yet unknown, and the wine of Ay enjoyed by Henri IV was probably red.

Two recipes for the bread of Gonesse were given by Nicolas de Bonnefons in *Les Délices de la campagne* (1654). It seems clear that the first is made on the basis of a spontaneous leaven. The second specifies the use of beer yeast. Here are the two methods:

'This bread is made both brown and white and in many sizes. You take six bushels[1] of flour, one of which you make into a leaven; at about eight o'clock in the evening, you add as much flour again; this is called refreshing the leaven; and the next morning, at sunrise, you make the dough, adding the remainder of the flour, which you make up very light, then you mould the dough and set it in wooden bowls well floured, for fear it will stick. When the dough has recovered, before putting the loaves in the oven you turn each into a second wooden bowl so that when they are turned out on to the peel the markings[2] will be on the top.'

'To make the small and light bread take one sixth of the flour you wish to use, make it into a leaven with very fresh beer yeast; and when the leaven is ready, re-work it with more flour as for the household bread and leave it to prove for the second time, then make it up very light, mould the loaves and put them on a cloth in which you make pleats [to form ridges] between each loaf, so that they will not touch, and you put them in the oven when they are ready.'

As a footnote to Nicolas de Bonnefons's recipes, it is interesting to find that Louis Liger, writing some fifty years later in *Le Ménage des champs*

1. A French bushel or *boisseau* of flour was much less than our own. According to La Varenne (see next recipe) it was 12 to 13 lb *without* the bran. The Paris pound was 16 oz, but in some districts only 14 oz.

2. Evidently the proving bowls were moulded or carved on the inside, probably with the figure of Christ.

(6th edn published in 1711), attributed the special qualities of various breads to the properties of the water in the localities concerned. He thought it futile to persist in attempts to imitate the bread of other districts, and cites the famed bakers of Gonesse as proof that it was not so much their skill as the water of the neighbourhood which accounted for the excellence of their bread: 'For all that the bakers of Gonesse may try to set up in Paris to make their bread, it will never be as good as it is in their native town; this has been several times proved.'

Two of Louis Liger's own recipes for bread are quoted further on.

· PAIN BÉNIST ·

Under this heading, meaning consecrated bread, two different methods are given in *Le Pastissier françois*, a famous and very rare volume printed by the Elzeviers at Amsterdam in 1655. Although no author's name is given on the title page, the book is generally attributed to François Pierre, known as La Varenne, head cook or steward to the Marquis d'Uxelles, who had already produced an equally well known volume called *Le Cuisinier françois*, published in 1651, to which the *Pastissier* is considered an obvious sequel.

La Varenne's second recipe is for a fine and delicate version of *pain bénist* (called in Paris a *cousin* and in other places a *chanteau*) and seems to be approaching what we know today as a brioche dough. The basis is a leaven prepared from 2 lb of fine flour. When this is ready it is kneaded into a dough made from another 4 lb of flour, warm milk, 1 lb of butter, and ½ lb of soft fresh white cream cheese – this would have been the equivalent of thick ripe cream, rather than cheese – plus, if you wished, three or four eggs beaten with a little milk. The prepared dough is to be shaped into one large *chanteau* or a *pain bénist*, gilded and docked when ready for the oven, and, owing to the richness of the dough, 'baked for longer than the first kind of bread', for which no more than a scant and surely very inadequate half hour is specified.

· TO MAKE FRENCH BREAD THE BEST WAY, 1660 ·

Next in chronological order comes Robert May's English recipe for French bread. As a very young man[1] May had been sent to France to

1. He was born in 1588 and so would have been in France in the early years of the seventeenth century. He was seventy-two when his book was published.

learn French cooking. Whether his French bread recipe is one learned there, or from the English City Guild and Star Chamber cook Arthur Hollingsworth to whom he was later apprenticed, or from one of the numerous grand and noble households in which he was subsequently employed, is entirely a matter for speculation. What is interesting is that it is an early one calling for the crusts of the rolls or loaves to be chipped.

'Take a gallon[1] of fine flour, and a pint of good new ale barm or yeast, and put it to the flour, with the whites of six new laid eggs well beaten in a dish, and mixt with the barm in the middle of the flour, also three spoonfuls of fine salt; then warm some milk and fair water, and put to it, and make it up pretty stiff, being well wrought and worked up, cover it in a bowl or tray with a warm cloth till your oven be hot; then make it up either in rouls, or fashion it in little wooden dishes and bake it, being baked in a quick oven, chip it hot.'

Robert May, *The Accomplisht Cook*, 1685 (first published 1660)

For a method of adapting this recipe to present-day conditions, and using a small quantity of flour, see pp. 313–15. Robert May's system makes very good little loaves.

Whereas Robert May clearly took the use of barm or ale yeast for granted, in France the attitude towards its application as a leavening agent for bread was still tentative even forty years after the government's decree sanctioning its use. The following two recipes although dated 1711 are probably of rather earlier origin.

· A WAY OF MAKING GOOD BREAD ·

'There are those who, to obtain light bread, make their leaven with fresh beer yeast, and when the leaven is ready, add water and more flour, re-work it and let it ferment a second time; then knead it up very light and when the loaves are moulded put them on a cloth; taking care that they do not kiss.[2]

1. A gallon was 7 lb.
2. Term used to denote loaves which touched at the sides during either proving or baking.

'When these sort of loaves, which are much more delicate than common bread, are put into the oven, it is well to observe that the oven be not so hot [as for common bread] since the heat is not required to last so long in order to perfect the baking.'

Louis Liger, *Le Ménage des champs,* 6th edn, 1711(first published 1700)

· ANOTHER WAY TO MAKE VERY DELICATE BREAD ·

'Sometimes, when in the Country, you have company to whom it is your pleasure to offer very special bread, and for this:

'You must take a bushel [12 lb] of the best and finest wheat flour you have; in the bolting sieve sift it as you wish, make up a quarter of it into a leaven, putting two full handfuls of new beer yeast if you have it, one handful of salt dissolved in hot water, and three *chopines* [1½ litres] of milk.

'One hour later, put in the rest of the flour, and work up the dough very light, and mould it and put it to prove in small wooden bowls, then you bake it in a reasonable hot oven; when it is baked you draw it out and leave it on its side to cool. One hour will be sufficient to bake it to perfection.'

ibid.

Now the English eighteenth-century writers take over. E. Smith, from whose book the next recipe comes, had fairly obviously learned from Robert May's recipe – his book was widely known and used – and had added the extra enrichment of egg yolks as well as whites. Henderson's recipe, written towards the end of the century, describes a quite different method of kneading and proving the dough.

· TO MAKE FRENCH BREAD ·

'Take half a peck[1] of fine flour, put to it six yolks of eggs, and four whites, a little salt, a pint of good ale yeast and as much new milk, made a little warm, as will make it a thin light paste; stir it about with your hand, but by no means knead it; then have ready six wooden quart dishes, and fill them with dough; let them stand a quarter of an hour to heave, and then

1. A half-peck was 7 lb.

turn them out into the oven; and when they are baked, rasp them: the oven must be quick.'

E. Smith, *The Compleat Housewife*, 15th edn, 1753
(first published 1727)

· FRENCH ROLLS ·

In this receipt the author seems to be using the term 'manchate' as descriptive of the size and perhaps the shape of the rolls. A dozen and a half out of a gallon of flour would have weighed about 9 oz each into the oven, perhaps 7 oz when baked.

'Put good, new, ale yeast in fair water over night, stirring it well, let it lie till morning, then pour the water from it and to a pint of it put a gallon[1] of flour, and a quantity of sweet milk, season it with salt and then strain it into your flour and work it into a lump, then let it stand a while to work of itself, then make it into manchate and let them stand a while to work and then put it into a quick oven for an hour; a gallon of flour makes a dozen and half.'

The Receipt Book of Elizabeth Raper, written 1756–70,
published by the Nonesuch Press, 1924

· TO MAKE FRENCH BREAD ·

'Lay at one end of your trough half a bushel[2] of the best white flour, and make a hole in the middle of it. Mix a pint of good small-beer yeast with three quarts of warm liquor, put it in, and mix it up well till it is tough; put a flannel over it, and let it rise as high as it will. When it is at the height, take six quarts of skimmed milk blood warm (the bluer the better, provided it is sweet) and a pound of salt. Instead of working it with your hands, as you would dough for English bread, put the ends of your fingers together, and work it over your hands till it is quite weak and ropey; then cover it over with a flannel, put your fire into the oven, and make it very hot. Observe, that when you take the dough out of the trough, you use your hands as before, or else you will not get it out till it falls, when it will be good for nothing. Lay it on the dresser,[3] and instead

1. A gallon was 7 lb.   2. A bushel varied between 56 and 60 lb.
3. The kneading table, often a removable board placed on the top of the dough trough, or the lid of the trough itself.

of a common knife, have one made like a chopping knife to cut it with; then make it up into bricks or rolls as you think proper. The bricks will take an hour and a half baking, and the rolls half an hour. Then draw them out, and either rasp them with a rasp or chip them with a knife, but the former is the most convenient, and is done with the greatest expedition. When you work it up with the second liquor, you may, if you please, break in two ounces of butter.'

W. A. Henderson, *The Housekeeper's Instructor, or Universal Family Cook*,
5th edn, *c.* 1795

THE ENGLISH FRENCH LOAF
· IN THE NINETEENTH CENTURY ·

In 1822 a London Bread Act laid down that the bread known in this country as French, made up in rolls, baked wholly crusty, in some cases rasped after baking, was to be designated as fancy bread. This meant that no fixed weight or price could be imposed for French rolls or their variants. At about this time the author of *The Cook and Housewife's Manual* (first published 1826) observed of French bread that 'all sorts of fine bread baked with milk, eggs, and butter receive this name'.

By mid-century, however, London bakers were evidently trying their hands at larger French loaves. Eliza Acton has the following observations to make on French bread and its adoption by London bakers. What she is describing seems to be the long broad cross-cut loaf still known in France as *bâtard*, and very similar in appearance to the 'London bloomer'. According to Félix Urbain Dubois[1] the name *bâtard* was originally descriptive of the dough, since it was made from a medium strong dough, neither too soft nor too firm. The *bâtard* has more volume and more crumb than the *baguette* or the *ficelle*.

'In France the usual form given to common bread is that of a *rouleau* or cylinder, which spreads and flattens a little in the baking. The loaves are sometimes two or three feet in length. One advantage of having them moulded thus is, that they are more perfectly and regularly baked than loaves of massive construction. Some few London bakers have adopted the French shape for their bread.'

Eliza Acton, *The English Bread Book*, 1857

1. *Boulangerie d'aujourd'hui*, 3rd edn, Paris, 1962 (first published 1955).

It is curious that although Eliza Acton knew, and described with her usual accuracy, one popular variety of French loaf, the 'French receipt for French bread' which she gives is for a dough enriched with butter and made up entirely with milk. The loaves, made *rouleau* shape, were to weigh one or two pounds each, and were to be rasped when they came from the oven – she sent them to the bakery, or so she implies – just as in all the recipes of her predecessors. An illuminating statement Miss Acton makes in her earlier and more famous book, *Modern Cookery* (1845), is that 'the best bread we ever tasted was made in great part with rye flour: this was in a provincial town in France'. That bread must have been the descendant of the traditional *méteil*, the mixed rye and wheat loaf of the French farmhouse since the Middle Ages. I have myself also found, in spite of the delicious qualities of the *baguette* loaf at its best, that *pain de campagne*, nowadays made with wheat flour, and often on the leaven system, can be much better. In small town and village bakeries in the Nivernais, in the Auvergne, in the Ardèche and in the Jura, I have found big round loaves so good and with a flavour and texture so unlike any others in their true savour and their incomparable scent that it is this bread that I would make, were it feasible, rather than any of the *baguette* type after which so many people hanker in vain.

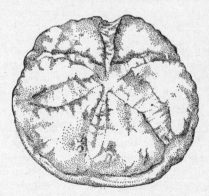

A large *miche* or *pain de campagne* made on a leaven, but yeast-boosted.

Eighteenth-century French writers sometimes appear to be obsessively preoccupied with the quality of the water used for bread. Modern bakers consider that this was no more than superstition. Sometimes I wonder if the earlier writers were not after all right. Staying in Carmarthenshire near Llandovery, where the water is very soft, I have found that I can make a better, more lively dough, than in London, where the water is notoriously hard. This is what the author or editor of a farmers' pocket dictionary[1] had to say on the subject:

'The goodness of bread depends often upon the quality of the water which goes into the mixing of the dough: as far as possible, the softest water should be used, because it penetrates more thoroughly than any other into the grains of the flour mixed with the leaven.

'It is claimed that rainwater is the best for fermenting and raising the dough, since it is often softer than spring or river water: it is certain that it is to the differences in water that must be attributed that exquisite taste found in certain breads and which others, although made with the same flour, have not.'

This author also notes that, to make good bread, it should be composed of two parts of flour to one of water. This is the normal proportion used in household bread. Mass-produced bread made from dough mixed at high speed in mechanical mixing vats contains a considerably larger proportion of water. Water, as Mr Tulliver, the miller of *The Mill on the Floss*, observes, 'is a very particular thing – you can't pick it up with a pitch fork'. The bakery plants, however, as a critic of factory bread said recently, can all but make water stand up.

*

By the beginning of the twentieth century, English and French bread-making techniques had parted company. It can be seen even from the pictures of French and Vienna 'French' loaves given in books of this period that the English bakers were making little attempt to produce

French roll pan. Long rolls baked in moulds are called *longuets*.

1. L'Agronome, *Dictionnaire portatif du cultivateur*, 1763.

authentically French bread. French rolls were still baked hard and the crust chipped:

'What are called French rolls, are rolls generally about 2 or 3 oz, baked in iron gutter-like open pans, four side by side. The rolls are crusty all round, but crumby at ends where they touch each other. Sometimes these rolls are baked very hard, then the burnt crust rasped off, as a method of making bread of a special and peculiar sweetness.'

The Bakers' ABC, ed. John Kirkland, 1927

Late eighteenth-century French walnut *huche* or bread hutch could be hung on the wall or used for carrying fresh bread from the farm kitchen to harvest workers in the fields. Many such cupboards, often on a large scale, are still to be found in the châteaux and farmhouses of Provence.

· LEAVENED BREAD: THE FRENCH METHOD ·

The French *pain de campagne* made on the old leaven system has been mentioned more than once in these notes. The following passage from one of William Jago's fine works on professional breadmaking explains how the dough was fermented.

'In France and other parts of the continent bread is made from leaven which consists of a portion of dough held over from the previous baking. The following description is given on the authority of Watts' *Dictionary of Chemistry*.

'A lump of dough from the preceding batch of bread is preserved; this weighs about 12 lbs, made up of 8 lbs of flour to 4 lbs of water, and is the fresh leaven (*levain de chef*). This fresh leaven after remaining for about 15 hours, is kneaded in with an equal quantity of fresh flour and water, and this produces the *levain de première*; again this is allowed to stand for some hours (about eight) and is kneaded in with more flour and water. After another interval of 3 hours, 100 lbs of flour, 52 of water, and about ⅓ lb of beer yeast are added; this produces the finished leaven (*levain de tout point*).

'The finished leaven weighs about 200 lbs, and is mixed, after standing 2 hours, with 132 lbs of flour, 68 lbs of water, ½ lb of yeast, and 2 lbs of salt. The dough thus formed is divided into two moieties; the one is cut into loaves which are kept for a time at a moderate temperature (77°F) and then baked. The bread thus produced is sour in taste and dark in colour. The remaining half of the dough is kneaded with more flour, water, yeast, and salt and divided into halves; the one quantity is made into loaves, which are allowed to ferment and are then baked; the other is subjected again to operation of mixing with more flour, etc, and working as before. The subdivision is repeated three times; the bread improving at each stage, and the finest and whitest loaves being produced in the last batch.

'In the more important towns this mode of bread-making is now largely supplanted by the use of distillers' yeast, and seems now to have largely given place to methods more nearly allied to Viennese and English processes.

'Leaven fermentation is due to the presence in the leaven of certain species of yeast, which grow and multiply in that medium. These induce alcoholic fermentation of the sugar of the flour.'

William Jago and William C. Jago, *The Technology of Bread Making*, 1921 (revised edition of the work which first appeared in 1911. This in turn was described by Jago as 'a development of the writer's former works on the same subject which appeared in 1886 and 1895'.)

William Jago senior was Senior Examiner in Bread-Making and Confectionery to the City and Guilds of London Institute for the Advancement of Technical Education and Cantor Lecturer on Modern

Development of Bread-Making. William C. Jago, his son, was a food manufacturing chemist.

It is interesting that Kirkland, in the revised, 1923 edition of his great work *The Modern Baker, Confectioner and Caterer*, first published in 1907, devoted a new section to various Continental breads, and provided descriptions and photographs of many Dutch and German loaves, but two only of French loaves. His opinion of French bread at that time was not high – he found Belgian bread to be of better quality and lower price – but admitted that the French seemed to be doing the best they could with the flour at their disposal. French wheat, he said, 'has a good deal of sweetness about it' and this accounted for the agreeable flavour 'in the main' of French bread. He observes also that 'the bulk of the bread baked in France recalls the best specimens of English bread made from blends into which entered a generous proportion of Norfolk or Cambridge flour', but made no effort to give directions for making French bread.

It appears to have been only after the 1939–45 War, and the end of rationing in 1954, that public demand, due no doubt to the increasing awfulness of our mass-produced bread, obliged bakers to attempt to imitate French bread or at least to use its name to denote a loaf baked in the form of a stick. The absurdities into which the attempts can lead them and their customers are well demonstrated by an incident in a London wholefood bakery where coarse brown bread only, whether whole wheatmeal, barley or rye, is produced. Seeing one very small, dried-out torpedo-shaped loaf, with a token scratch in the centre, I asked the young lady in charge what kind of bread this was, 'A French stick,' was her reply.

The Pizza and the Pissaladière

THE ONWARD (AND DOWNWARD) MARCH
· OF THE ENGLISH PIZZA ·

Although anglicized and only remotely related to the original, mass-market versions of the Neapolitan pizza have been with us since the 1950s. Although it was, I think, the Charles Forte snack bars of that period which first listed a substance under the name of pizza on a popular and cheap menu, it is only since the early seventies that the pizza has grown into big business for the English catering world. The time when the English pizza manufacturers were obliged to explain their product by describing it as Italian Welsh Rabbit were by that time long gone. So was the period of the late Mario Zampi, the film director who imported an Italian brick-built pizza oven, installed it in a Soho restaurant, turned it over to his brother and sister-in-law to run as a pizzeria – and failed to attract custom. There was nothing wrong with the pizzas served in the Zampi establishment. They were delicious and cheap, and indeed much superior to anything offered in today's pizza houses. But Mario Zampi's good idea was ahead of his time. In an Italian restaurant of those days the customers still wanted veal escalopes and spaghetti bolognese. A pizza and a glass or two of wine as a good midday or supper-time meal had little appeal for Londoners. In the days following the end of rationing,[1] people wanted to eat meat when they went out to a restaurant, and at that time they could afford to pay for it.

In the ten to fifteen years since Mario Zampi's venture – I think that it was the first of its kind – a generation of young people has taken to the hamburger heaven, the Golden Egg Bar and the pizza house, just as that of the 1950s took to the expresso coffee bar, and that of the 1960s to the steak house. In the pizza houses you may well get a pizza just as good as in many a native Neapolitan pizzeria – although that is not exactly an

1. Officially, this was in 1954.

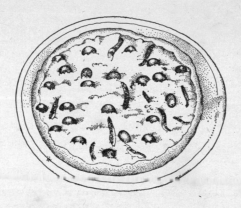

extravagant compliment – and all things considered the value provided in these establishments is fair. At the take-away counters and from the deep freeze cabinets a rather different deal is offered, and increasingly, the evidence shows, accepted.

The following extracts from magazines, newspapers and publicity handouts of the past five years show, briefly, the remarkable rise in popularity and price, although not necessarily in lightness and authenticity, of the English pizza.

'Alvaro's Pizza and Pasta, 39 Charing Cross Road, is open till 3 a.m., with a license till 1 a.m. every night . . . the place is dominated by the traditional kiln-shaped pizza oven. A pizza, or helping of pasta, a glass of wine and coffee cost around 10/-.'

Queen Magazine, June 1970

'Pizza Range Ltd, who started business some 10 months ago in a kitchen off Cricklewood Broadway, have moved into a fully modernised 4,700 sq. ft. kitchen at Lyon Industrial Estate, Watford. The firm provide a full range of pizzas, either individual or for caterers.'

Caterer and Hotel Keeper, 19 November 1970

'Pizza Range, Watford, Herts, is introducing its complete Pizza service . . . the pizzas are available in 7 ins. and 10 ins. rounds with five variations on a cheese and tomato topping. Recommended retail prices range from 13p up to luxury pizzas at 37p, with a colourful topping of mushrooms or mortadella, mozzarella, tomato, olives and pimiento.'

The Grocer, 24 April 1971

'In the words of Cook-Inn's managing director: "A whole new industry now in its infancy is about to expand rapidly." The menu should appeal to all palates ranging as it does from such national favourites as cottage pie and cod in batter to exotica like pizza and spare-ribs.'

Derek Cooper in the *Guardian*, 8 December 1971

'Selling about 20,000 pizzas a week, Peter Boizot is probably London's No. 1 pizza restaurateur. Now he tells me that besides new restaurants which he hopes to open whenever suitable sites are available, there are also facilities for franchising.

'And the cost? You can pay a maximum price of 68p, but one of the most popular types – there is a choice of 14 – with mozzarella and tomato, costs just 30p.'

What's On, 23 February 1973

'It's so easy . . . You just warm it up and it's ready to eat . . . with salad, with chips, or on its own . . .

'And to introduce you to Pizza Pie WE ARE GIVING YOU 10p OFF.'

Leaflet distributed by Eden Vale, valid until 30 April 1973.
Ingredients were listed as flour, cheddar cheese, Spanish peeled plum tomatoes, vegetable oil, Spanish onions, tomato purée, edible starch, baking powder, salt, skimmed milk powder, sugar, garlic, monosodium glutamate, herbs and spices.

Net weight 6 oz. Price in my local shop was 20p.

'Pizza squares are supplied by Pizza Range and measure 10 × 18 inches, costing 49p. In the takeaway each square divides into six portions and sells at 25p a portion plus chips.'

Photograph caption, *Caterer and Hotel Keeper*, 20 September 1973

'A Pizza Bar with a canopy simulating the ramparts of a castle is the focal point of the Argyle and Sutherland Highlander Inn, a new £70,000 luxury pub and restaurant opened . . . on a new housing estate at Eastham, Wirral, Cheshire.'

Caterer and Hotel Keeper, 6 December 1973

'*11th Pizza Express*
'Pizza Express, a private company formed in 1965, established a foothold in fashionable Chelsea, last week, when Mr Peter I. Boizot, prospective Liberal parliamentary candidate for Peterborough, opened his eleventh Pizza Express at 234 Kings Road. London.'

Caterer and Hotel Keeper, 30 May 1974

'The pizza, like the hamburger, has become part of our popular culture – an instant food which can be elevated, by a chef's invention, into a memorable treat.'

Peter Straub in an article entitled
'The Great British Pizza', *Nova*, September 1974

'Scots-American Mr. Bob Hamilton has converted the former Mascotte Restaurant, Brighton, into a pizzeria . . . Mr. Hamilton officially launched his pizzeria in Britain, using slogans like "I'm a pizza lover", "Peace and pizza", and "This country is going to pizzas".'

Caterer and Hotel Keeper, 6 February 1975

'Ten years ago today Peter Boizot, a salesman, opened a Pizza Express in Wardour Street[1] against the advice of the sceptics. "I was doing everything, including making the pizzas. I stayed open till 5 a.m. and took £27."

'Now he shuts at midnight and lives in Belgravia. He employs 150 people in a chain of 11 pizzerias . . . he was manning the oven again the other day trying out a new, very palatable pizza made from wholemeal.'

Peterborough in the *Daily Telegraph*, 27 March 1975

'In England pizzas . . . could claim even to be a serious rival to the dreaded cellophane-wrapped steak pie of motorway fame.'

Delia Smith in the *Evening Standard*, 11 April 1975

'LONDON'S NEW FOOD. SO CRISP, SO LIGHT
'2 giant slices of pizza with jacket potatoes   49p'

From the menu of the Pizzaland chain of restaurants, July 1975

The take-away pizza
'*Meal:* Pizza "Special". *From:* Pizzaland, Fleet Street, London, *Price:* 70p. *Weight:* 11 oz.

'The "Special" pizza – the most expensive – consisted of a bread dough base with a filling of bits and pieces of mushroom, bacon, onion, cheese, two olives, tomato and green pepper. It contained no seasoning at all, and the dough base stretched (and tasted) like rubber. The onions were raw, the bacon bits crisped almost beyond recognition and the whole mixture was sloppy.

'*Verdict:* Unappetising, and barely a meal for two even if they were hungry enough to eat it.'

Mary Collins in a report on take-away food shops,
Daily Express 13 September 1975

THE ITALIAN PIZZA AND
· THE FRENCH PISSALADIÈRE ·

In colloquial Italian the word pizza denotes a pie of almost any kind, savoury or sweet, open or covered, and with a basis of any variety of pastry or of leavened dough, and to the English-speaking world a pizza means a flat, round, open pie with a filling of tomato and onion topped with melting cheese.

1. This is the site of the original Zampi pizza restaurant referred to on p. 384. It was the adventurous Mr Boizot who bought the Zampi brothers' premises, and, in a different era, made a success where they had failed.

In short, the pizza which has travelled the world, reached almost every deep freeze cabinet in Europe and America, become a mainstay of the take-away food counters, and is manufactured by the ton in the food-processing factories, was originally the Neapolitan interpretation of an ancient method of dealing with a piece of bread dough in a rough and ready fashion, strewing it with a few onions, a handful of salt sardines or anchovies, or a sprinkling of pork scrapple left from the rendering down of lard. To us the pizza may be indissolubly associated with the tomato, but it did of course exist long before tomatoes were cultivated in Europe. Something like it was familiar to the Greeks and to the Romans, probably the early Arabs had a version of it – they certainly have one now – and the Armenians claim that they invented it (perhaps they did); there are variations to be found in Spain where it is called *coca*, meaning a kind of cake, and in Provence where it was once known as *pissaladeira*, and has now all but merged with the universal pizza. In eastern France the quiche of Lorraine, almost as much a victim of current fashion and factory production as the pizza, was originally made on a basis of bread dough, and a quiche was not committed exclusively to a filling of bacon and cream and eggs. It could be, and often was, the basis for a spread of fresh plums or cherries, which baked to a delicious sticky, sugary mass. This brings it all nearer home, to our own lardy cakes and fruit-enriched doughs. For surely, anywhere there was leavened bread there was likely to be left-over dough, to be quickly made up and baked to provide something cheap and filling for children, for the poor, the hungry.

What seems extraordinary is that so many people in so many places can be induced into paying so high a price for something so simple and cheap to make at home and so difficult to reproduce in mass-market terms as the Neapolitan pizza. Even taking into consideration your own time and work plus the cost of the oven fuel, a home-made pizza is something of a bargain, making the mass-produced 'pizza pie' – many are made with a baking powder dough, not a yeast-leavened one, hence their incredible toughness – seem rather more of a confidence trick than most products of its kind. This is probably because being an alien import with an unfamiliar name it contains a built-in mystique. Equivalent prices for a hot cheese sandwich or a take-away portion of cottage pie would soon meet with resistance.

Now, it must be said that the authentic Neapolitan pizza was – and is – heavy going, and lies uneasy on any but the most robust of stomachs. It became popular because it was cheap, and the original *pizzeria*, or pizza house, furnished with its own brick oven in which every pizza was baked to order, was a refuge – if rather a noisy one – where the hungry and hard-up could eat their hefty round of cheese-topped pizza and drink a glass or two of cheap wine for the equivalent of a few pence. As late as 1950 the pizzeria was an almost exclusively southern Italian institution. The beehive-shaped brick oven installed in the pizzeria was a conscious survival, or revival, of the ancient, traditional bread oven, and it was then rare to find a pizzeria north of Rome, whereas now there must be one or more in almost every town throughout the Italian peninsula.

Along the Mediterranean coast, west beyond Genoa and across the borders of Provence a different version of pizza was to be bought from the bakeries. It was baked and displayed for sale in huge rectangular iron oven trays from which the customers could buy slices at the same time as they bought their morning bread. On the Ligurian coast this pizza was known as a *sardenara*, because originally salted sardines were part of the top dressing, the basis of which was onion and tomato. In Provence between Nice and Marseilles the *pissaladeira*, very similar to the *sardenara*, owed its name to *pissala*, a brined and potted mixture of small-fry peculiar to the coasts of the County of Nice and of Provence. By the time I first encountered the *pissaladeira*, in the 1930s, anchovies had taken the place of the *pissala*, and there were basically two kinds of dressings for the bread dough, one mainly of onions stewed in olive oil, with black olives added, the other with tomatoes, anchovies and, again, black olives. A third, called *anchoïade*, was an anchovy and garlic mixture. This one is now nearly always made on a basis of ready cooked, fresh and thick bread slices, but is much nicer spread on the raw dough and then baked. None of these versions featured the cheese of the Neapolitan pizza.

These variations, then, are the ones upon which I base my own pizza mixtures: onion, tomato, anchovy, black olives, in varying proportions and not necessarily all at once, but always cooked in olive oil and flavoured with oregano, the wild marjoram of Italy. Sometimes, but not invariably, garlic goes into the mixture. I don't include any top dressing of chewy cheese. The pizza manufacturers, evidently believing it to be an essential selling point, use either processed Cheddar or a specially developed 'pizza Mozzarella'. Both seem to me quite pointless. The mass-market product would be better as well as cheaper without them.

The dough I use is what the Italians would call *casalinga*, a household dough rather than a baker's basic bread dough, which means it is made rather lighter, with an egg or two and olive oil – or butter if you prefer it – so that what it amounts to is a very modified form of brioche dough.

Once you have acquired the knack of making this dough – it was through the pizza that I first discovered how easy it is to work with yeast – it is no trouble whatever to make a pizza in any size or form you please.

One word of advice, though, as to the filling or dressing for the dough. A great many English people make the mistake of thinking that the more oddments added in the way of bits of sausage, bacon, mushrooms, prawns and anything else that comes to hand, the better the pizza will be. In fact the reverse is true. The black olives for example, can be eliminated – it is now very difficult to find the right kind, and it is better not to attempt any substitute for them. There *is* no substitute. But you *can* use a few extra anchovies, which are more easily obtainable. And tomato is not obligatory any more than is cheese. Just onions, if you like them, slowly, slowly stewed in olive oil, and with a final addition of anchovy fillets before the dough goes into the oven, make an excellent pizza. For those allergic to onions, a tomato filling without them is perfectly feasible. There is really no problem and not many rules. The idea is, basically, that what you spread on the dough sinks *into* it, amalgamates itself with, and becomes an integral part of, the bread as it bakes. A mass of bitty things won't do this. They will just stay on top of the dough, toughen and probably burn as the pizza cooks. It is insufficient understanding of the nature and behaviour of leavened dough which causes English cooks to attempt so many non-viable additions and substitutions. Or is it the English propensity for treating every basic dish, so long as it is a foreign one, as a dustbin for the reception of left-overs?

The first recipe which follows is for an 8 inch pizza baked in a tart tin. For those unfamiliar with yeast leavened dough and its workings, this is the easiest way to start, and the best way to ensure that a presentable pizza will be produced at the first attempt. Those who are already practised in dough-making will probably prefer to go straight on to the other recipes for pizzas baked on a larger scale, either on a shallow, rectangular oven tray or on a large, flat, round platter. These are so very much cheaper in proportion than the smaller tart-tin version that they come nearer to fulfilling the original purpose of the pizza.

· LIGURIAN PIZZA OR SARDENARA ·

For a pizza to be baked in a 7 to 8 inch shallow tart tin with a removable base, ingredients and quantities are as follows:

For the filling: *1 lb of ripe tomatoes, or half and half fresh and Italian tinned tomatoes, 2 small onions, 2 cloves of garlic, salt, sugar, freshly milled pepper, dried oregano (the Italian name for wild marjoram), olive oil, one 2 oz tin of flat anchovy fillets in olive oil, a dozen very small black olives.*

For the dough: *¼ oz of yeast, 2 tablespoons of milk, ¼ lb of plain white flour – strong bread flour for preference, 1 whole egg, 2 tablespoons of olive oil, 1 teaspoon of salt.*

Equivalent metric quantities, for the filling: *tomatoes ½ kg, small onions 2, garlic 2 cloves, salt, sugar, freshly milled pepper, dried oregano, olive oil, anchovy fillets one 50 g tin, very small black olives 12;* for the dough: *yeast approximately 10 g, milk 2 tablespoons, plain white flour 125 g, 1 whole egg, olive oil 2 tablespoons, salt 1 teaspoon. Tin size: a 20 or 22 cm shallow tart tin with a removable base.*

To make the dough: Put the yeast into a cup with the milk. Mix it to a cream. Put the flour into a bowl with the salt, warm it for 4 or 5 minutes – no longer – in a very low oven; add the yeast mixture, then the whole egg and the olive oil. Mix all well together, then with your hands work the dough rapidly until it is smooth. Form it into a ball. Shake a little extra flour over it. Cover the bowl. Put it in a warm place and leave for 1½ to 2 hours until the dough is well risen and very light.

To make the filling: Pour boiling water over the tomatoes, leave them a couple of minutes, then slip off the skins. Chop the tomatoes roughly. Peel the onions, slice them into the thinnest possible rounds. Peel the garlic cloves. Crush them with the flat of a knife.

Into a heavy 10 inch frying pan or sauté pan put enough olive oil to cover the surface. Let the oil warm over low heat then put in the onions. They should stew gently, without frying, for about 7 minutes. Add the crushed garlic cloves, then the fresh tomatoes. With the pan uncovered, increase the heat, so that the water content of the tomatoes evaporates rapidly. Add seasonings of salt and a very little sugar. When the fresh tomatoes have reduced almost to a pulp add the tinned ones if you are using them. There is no need to chop them. Simply spoon them into the pan with some of their juice and crush them with a wooden spoon.

Cook for a further few minutes, until the sauce has again reduced. Taste for seasoning – not forgetting that the olives and anchovies will provide extra salt – and scatter in a scant teaspoon of oregano. The basis of the pizza filling is now ready. The olives and anchovies are added when the dough is spread with the tomato mixture and is all but ready to cook.

Prepare the olives by removing the stones with an olive- or cherry-stoner and halving them, or, if they are very small, simply rub them between thumb and first finger and push the stones out. (In Provence the bakers do not bother to stone the olives; the kind they use are so small it would not be feasible to do so.)

To make the final preparations for cooking the pizza: Brush the tart tin, or a round iron sheet with slightly raised rim, or an earthenware plate of similar shape and size, with olive oil.

Break down the dough, which should have doubled in volume and feel puffy and soft, sprinkle it with flour so that it does not stick to your hands, reshape it into a ball which you put into the centre of the oiled tin. With your knuckles gently press out the dough until it fills the tin.

Turn the oven on to fairly hot, 425° to 450°F, 220° to 230°C, gas nos. 7 to 8, and have a baking sheet ready on the centre shelf.

Now spread the dough with the warm tomato mixture, break the anchovy fillets into inch-long pieces and arrange them at random on the top. Season them with a little black pepper from the mill. Scatter the black olives among the pieces of anchovy, add a final extra sprinkling of oregano and olive oil.

Leave the prepared pizza on the top of the stove for about 10 minutes, until the oven is really hot and the dough has started to rise again. Now slip the tin into the oven, leave it for 15 minutes, then decrease the heat to 375°F, 190°C, gas no. 5, and cook for another 10 to 15 minutes. Alternatively, leave the oven at the same temperature and simply move the pizza to a lower shelf. If the filling begins to look dry, cover it with a piece of oiled foil or greaseproof paper.

Serve your pizza hot, with the base of the tart tin still underneath it, the whole on a flat serving platter.

These quantities should be enough for four people for a first dish, while for the hungry young, who will probably prefer to make a whole meal off a pizza and perhaps a salad, an 8 inch pizza will just about do for two.

After one or two tries, the confection of a pizza becomes so easy that any intelligent cook will be able to make it almost without reference to a recipe.

Notes and variations: 1. The olive oil in the dough mixture gives an excellent and light texture but, for those who do not habitually use olive oil (substitutes will not do) and so might have to buy it specially, butter or thick ripe cream can perfectly well be used. Allow approximately 1½ oz of softened butter, or 4 tablespoons of cream.

oil, it pays to use a good brand,
e, with a true taste of the olive.
illing. Here, again, anyone who
and onions in butter – although
me an important feature of the
ged, for reasons of economy or
est to go for one which has the
undnut oil is probably the best

, which becomes like an old boot
the version made with enriched
ted. Cover it with greaseproof
ow oven.

le the quantity of flour without
nple to aerate ½ lb of flour), 1 egg
ons of olive oil, so while you are
or one large one.

is, you need only one and a half
, but twice the number of olives

elf to put two tins side by side,
is left waiting to be cooked while
the oven.

Produces acceptable result
but rather more like rich
short crust pastry - rather
too cake-like for my taste
- prefer them made with
the standard ½/½ bread
mix: no egg & virtually
no oil or fat or milk

· A LARGE RECTANGULAR PIZZA ·

Anyone who has made the foregoing pizza a few times, and gained confidence, may like to try baking it in the original Provençal or Italian manner, without benefit of an enclosing tin or at least using one with only a very shallow rim. Once accustomed to working with yeast dough it is if anything easier to make it in this way, and it is notably more economical. Proportionately less dough and less filling are required and, provided the dough is well made and fully 'ripened', there is no reason whatever for the pizza to be heavy. It is this maturing of the dough at the two crucial stages, after its initial mixing, and then when it is spread out on the tray or baking plate, which makes a light, well-risen and worthwhile pizza.

Italian tin-lined copper tray, for a large rectangular pizza.

The following quantities will yield twelve or more good sized portions weighing about 4 oz each, from a rectangular pizza baked on a shallow oven tray or a baking sheet measuring approximately 14 by 12 inches. I suggest this baker's shape of pizza, more like the Provençal than the Neapolitan version, because it is economical of oven space and more practical for home-baking than half a dozen or more round pizzas.

For the dough: *1 lb of strong plain flour or 1 lb 2 oz of household flour, ½ oz of yeast, 2 teaspoons of salt, ¼ pint of milk, 3 to 4 fluid oz of olive oil, 1 whole large egg or 2 small ones.*

Put the flour with the salt in a bowl and warm it in a low oven for a few minutes. Warm the milk. Pour a little over the yeast and leave it to stand until it can be easily stirred into a cream.

Make a well in the centre of the warmed flour, pour in the yeast, then the warm milk. Break in the egg or eggs, then add about half the olive oil. Mix all to a dough, adding the remainder of the oil as it may be needed, until you have a good, manageable, lithe dough, neither too firm nor too soft, which can be shaped into a ball which will come away easily from the bowl, leaving it clean. Cover the dough. Leave it to rise in a warm place for about 2 hours or until it is at least double in bulk, and spongy.

For the filling: *2 lb of tomatoes altogether, made up of half and half fresh and tinned (or now that fresh ripe tomatoes have become almost a luxury, use only the tinned kind), 2 average size onions, 3 large cloves of garlic, olive oil for cooking the onions, seasonings of salt, sugar, freshly milled pepper and dried oregano. For the final dressing of the pizza, anchovy fillets from two 2 oz tins, about 20 small black olives, a little extra olive oil and oregano.*

Equivalent metric quantities for twelve portions weighing about 125 g each, for the dough: *strong plain flour 450 g or household flour 500 g, yeast 15 g, salt 2 teaspoons, milk 150 g, olive oil 85 to 125 g, eggs 1 large or 2 small;* for the filling: *tomatoes 1 kg, onions 2 average size, garlic 3 large cloves, olive oil for cooking the onions, salt, sugar, pepper, dried oregano;* for the final dressing: *anchovy fillets two 50 g tins, small black olives 20, extra olive oil and oregano. Baking tray or sheet measuring approximately 36 cm by 30 cm.*

Prepare the filling exactly as for the recipe on p. 391.

When the dough is ready – and if it has risen before you find it convenient to make the pizza simply break it down, re-shape it into a ball, cover it and leave it to rise for a second time; it will come to no harm – spread your baking tray or sheet with a film of olive oil.

Put the ball of dough in the middle of the tray and spread it gently with your hands. You may think that there is too little dough to fill the tray, but as you work it across the surface of the tray, it grows in a very reassuring way. If you are using a flat baking sheet, turn the dough very slightly at the edges, to make a little rim, while if it is a shallow tray you are filling, press the dough lightly up the sides. After the considerable working to which you have now subjected the dough, it is advisable to leave it to rest for a while, covered with a sheet of polythene or a floured cloth. About 15 minutes should give the dough time to recover and to start growing again.

Spread the warm tomato mixture over the dough. If you are using a flat sheet leave a small margin of uncovered dough all round the edges of the pizza; in the case of a tray, spread the filling right to the edges and into the corners. The filling will not and should not be very thickly spread. Sprinkle a little extra oregano over it, then spread on the anchovy fillets, each one torn in half. They don't have to form a rigid pattern, and look best if arranged diagonally and well spaced from corner to corner of the rectangle.

Scatter the olives, stoned and halved, between the anchovy fillets. (It is easier and quicker, I find, to rub the stones out of the olives than to use an olive-stoner. For a pizza the olives are not supposed to look as if they have been turned out of a mould, like buttons.)

Before putting the pizza into the oven, trickle a little olive oil over the dressing, so that it will remain moist during baking.

Temperature of the oven and baking times are as for the pizza on p. 391: centre shelf, 425° to 450°F, 220° to 230°C, gas nos. 7 to 8, for 15 minutes, and 375° to 400°F, 190° to 205°C, gas nos. 5 to 6, for 15 minutes.

Serve the pizza cut into portions, straight from the tray if it is suitable, or arranged on a heated platter.

It is very easy to reheat separate portions of this pizza. Sprinkle a few drops of olive oil over the tops, and protect them with a piece of grease-proof paper.

· A LARGE ROUND PIZZA ·

If you possess or can lay hands on a 12 inch flat oven platter, of rough or glazed earthenware, it is easy and cheap to make a pizza large enough for 7 to 10 ample helpings.

Make the dough with ½ lb of strong flour, ¼ oz yeast, 1 whole large egg, approximately 10 tablespoons of milk, 2 tablespoons of olive oil, 2 teaspoons of salt. Extra olive oil will be needed for the dish.

The filling can be the tomato and onion mixture described in the first pizza recipe given on pp. 391–3, using one and a half times the quantity (see the notes concerning the increase of quantities, on p. 393), or a variation in the Middle Eastern manner. This one is made with meat, spices, garlic and a good deal of tomato, as follows:

6 to 8 oz of cooked or raw minced lamb, a small onion, 2 or 3 cloves of garlic, one 8 oz tin of peeled tomatoes, salt, olive oil, and seasonings of ground cinnamon, cumin, cloves and pepper. In Armenian and Lebanese cooking the seeds of a plant called sumach are much used as a spice and should go into this mixture. They are hard to come by in this country.[1] It is because, for most of us, the filling must be made without

1. Try Greek and Levantine provision shops.

this spice that I call it 'in the Middle Eastern manner'. The dough is also different from the Levantine one.

To cook the filling, melt the chopped onion in olive oil. Add the meat and let it brown gently; put in the peeled and crushed garlic cloves, salt, a level teaspoon each of cinnamon and ground cumin, a half teaspoon of ground cloves, or of mixed sweet spice, and the same of freshly ground black pepper. Add the tomatoes from the tin, cover the pan and simmer gently until the juice from the tomatoes has evaporated and the whole mixture is fairly thick. Taste it for seasoning. It should be really well spiced, so may need more pepper and perhaps extra cumin. A teaspoon or two of sugar may be needed, and a little dried mint can also be added.

Having mixed the dough and left it to rise until very light and puffy, oil your large platter and spread the dough on it, taking it right up to the edges. Leave it, covered, for 15 minutes, until it has returned to life. Spread the warm filling over it. There should not be too thick a layer. Again leave the prepared pizza for 10 to 15 minutes before putting it into the oven, at the usual temperature for pizza, 425°F, 220°C, gas no. 7. Cooking times are also as usual, 15 minutes at high temperature, and another 15 at 375° to 400°F, 190° to 205°C, gas nos. 5 to 6, or alternatively at the original temperature but on a lower shelf. In either case it is a good idea to cover the pizza with a piece of oiled greaseproof paper at half time, as the filling should not dry out.

This is an excellent pizza, in some ways the best of all, and if you have lamb left from a joint it provides a splendid way of using it, and at very little cost.

Equivalent metric quantities, for the dough: *strong flour 225 g, yeast approximately 10 g, 1 whole large egg, milk approximately 10 tablespoons, olive oil 2 tablespoons, salt 2 teaspoons, extra olive oil for the dish;* for the filling: *cooked or raw minced lamb 200 to 250 g, 1 small onion, garlic 2 or 3 cloves, 1 250 g tin peeled tomatoes, salt, olive oil, ground cinnamon, cumin, cloves and pepper, ground sumach seeds (if obtainable), 1 teaspoon each sugar and dried mint (optional). Flat oven platter, of rough or glazed earthenware, 32 cm in diameter.*

Quiches with Yeast Dough

As already explained in the introductory notes to my chapter on the pizza and its variations, the quiche of eastern France, the pissaladière of Provence and the pizza of southern Italy had common origins in that all were by-products of bread-baking and based on leavened dough. For the rest, just as the pissaladière and the pizza were spread with the oil, the salt fish, the onions and the olives of the south, quiche fillings were the everyday ingredients of the farms of Lorraine and Alsace: rich cream, unripened white cheese, home-cured pork. For sweet quiches there were the orchard fruits of the region, plums, cherries, greengages, little yellow mirabelles, sugared and spiced with cinnamon, or flavoured with locally distilled kirsch or other fruit alcohol.

Sometime during the nineteenth century the quiche moved up into the world of the professional pastrycooks of Paris. In Jules Gouffé's beautiful and very aristocratic *Livre de pâtisserie* (1873) there are several quiche recipes (he calls them kiches) made on a basis of the finest puff pastry, with rich fillings of cream and eggs – 5 eggs, a pint of cream, a pinch of salt, 2 little nuts of butter, nothing else – of rice cooked in cream, of parmesan, eggs and cream, of fine noodles either sweetened or with cheese; and always the double cream. These kiches were served as hot *entremets*, i.e. a savoury or sweet course for luncheons. Despite refinements such as Gouffé's rich puff pastry, the tradition of more homely yeast-leavened doughs remained very much alive in the eastern provinces of France, and had perhaps owed a good deal, originally, to Jewish, Polish, German and Austrian cooking. My recipe for a cream cheese quiche on an enriched leavened bread dough also owes a good deal to these old traditions, but the more fanciful of my two quiche recipes, the Roquefort one, owes only the quiche part of its name to Lorraine. The idea for it came from the Aveyron in central France, via an American musician who lives in Paris, who in turn had the recipe from the oyster-seller in his local market. This lady used a routine flan pastry base. I found it unsatisfactory and somehow unbalanced. The Roquefort filling, though, about which I had had doubts, proved original and delicious. So I tried it out on the same leavened dough I use for pizza, enriched with cream rather than with olive oil or butter. Those who like Roquefort will find it, I think, well worth trying. It is also useful to know that whereas only 5 oz of flour and 2 oz of cream or butter go into the leavened dough, enough short pastry to contain the same amount of filling would require nearly twice that quantity of both.

· TARTE AVEYRONNAISE OR ROQUEFORT QUICHE ·

For the yeast pastry: 5 oz of plain, preferably unbleached, bread flour, ¼ oz of bakers' yeast, 1 whole egg, 1 teaspoon of salt, 3 tablespoons of thick ripe cream or unsalted butter.

For the Roquefort filling: 3½ to 4 oz of Roquefort, 2 whole eggs, 4 tablespoons of milk, 3 tablespoons of thick cream, seasonings of nutmeg, freshly milled pepper, and salt if necessary. Roquefort is a salty cheese, and needs very little seasoning.

A 10 inch removable-base tart tin or two 6 to 7 inch tins.

Equivalent metric quantities, for the yeast pastry: plain unbleached bread flour 125 g, bakers' yeast approximately 10 g, 1 whole egg, salt 1 teaspoon, thick ripe cream or unsalted butter 3 tablespoons; for the Roquefort filling: Roquefort 100 to 120 g, eggs 2, milk 4 tablespoons, thick cream 3 tablespoons, nutmeg, pepper, salt if necessary. Tin size: a 26 to 28 cm removable-base tart tin or two 16 cm tins.

To make the pastry: Cream the yeast with a couple of tablespoons of tepid water. Warm the flour in a bowl, add the salt, then the whole egg and the creamed yeast. Mix all the ingredients into a light dough. Add the cream (or butter, softened but not melted) and with your hand beat the dough into a soft batter. Dry this by sprinkling it with a little flour, form it into a bun, cover the bowl with a plate or cloth. Leave in a warm place for approximately 2 hours, until the dough has doubled in volume and is light and spongy. Break it down, sprinkle again with flour, re-shape into a bun. Unless you are going to use the dough at once, cover the bowl again, and this time leave it in a *cold* place – not the refrigerator – until next day.

To mix the filling: Mash the cheese to a paste. Add the cream. Stir rather gently until the two are amalgamated. Beat the eggs and the milk – the blender can be used for this operation but *not* for mixing the cheese and cream – and amalgamate the two mixtures. Gentle stirring with a fork or spoon is necessary now, and there is no cause for worry if there are a few recalcitrant lumps of cheese in the filling. They will smooth themselves out during the cooking. On the other hand, over-vigorous whisking can curdle the cream and the cheese, a minor disaster which does not affect the flavour but results in a rather flat filling when the quiche is cooked.

When the time comes to cook the quiche, butter and flour the tin, work the dough into a ball, put this into the centre of the tin. Sprinkling the dough with flour from time to time, press it out gently with your knuckles until it covers the base of the tin. Leave it, covered with a sheet of polythene or paper, and in a warm place, for about 25 minutes, until it has again become very pliable and is sufficiently risen to be gently pressed out again to line the sides of the tin.

To bake the quiche: Have the oven turned to 425°F, 220°C, gas no. 7. Spoon the filling into the dough-lined tin, and put this quickly on to a baking sheet on the centre shelf of the oven.

Bake for 15 minutes before reducing the oven heat to 375°F, 190°C, gas no. 5, covering the filling with buttered paper and cooking the quiche for another 10 minutes.

Serve quickly, before the filling sinks.

There should be enough for four to six people, depending upon whether the dish is to be eaten as a first, a main or a savoury course, and upon what else is to be offered.

Correctly cooked, and eaten hot and fresh, this Roquefort quiche is one of the most delicious things I know. Given the present price of Roquefort cheese it is also something of a luxury.

Notes: 1. There is a good case for the use of two small tins for this quiche, rather than one large one. It is a question of synchronization. In small tins the yeast pastry and the fillings are ready at precisely the same moment, whereas in one big tin the filling tends to cook more quickly than the dough. To a certain extent this depends upon your oven. It is in any case a wise precaution to use the buttered greaseproof paper covering as directed.

2. Roquefort varies a good deal in quality. If it is very strong use a little less, and make up the difference with extra cream or milk.

3. It is not easy to suggest a substitute for Roquefort, which is unique as a cheese. It has to be remembered that it is made from ewes' milk, and that blue cheeses made from pasteurized cows' milk are totally dissimilar in flavour and texture. Possibly the best one to use instead of Roquefort would be Bresse Bleu. This is milder and rather cheaper. There is also a creamy Danish cheese called Blue Castello which makes a lovely filling. I have not found English blue cheeses very successful for this dish, but experiment is always worth while and could well result in something really interesting in the way of a dish based on one of our own cheeses. I have, for example, had quite good results using a well-matured farmhouse Cheddar.

· CREAM CHEESE QUICHE ·

Although not quite so interesting as the Roquefort quiche, this is a good deal cheaper and has the advantage that the ingredients are very easy to come by.

The pastry: _For one 10 to 12 inch removable-base tart tin or earthenware pizza dish the ingredients for the yeast pastry are 5 oz of plain flour, preferably strong bread flour, ¼ oz of yeast, ¼ teaspoon of salt, 3 tablespoons of thick ripe cream, 1 whole egg._

Make the pastry as for the Roquefort quiche, and either use it as soon as it has doubled in volume (which will be after 2 hours in a warm place) or break it down and keep it in a cold place until next day.

Butter the tin, sprinkle it with flour, pat out the dough to fill the base of the tin, and having covered it with a sheet of polythene leave the dough in a warm place to rise until it has re-acquired sufficient elasticity to stretch easily up the sides of the tin. This will take about 15 minutes if the pastry is being used after its first rising, anything from 30 to 45 minutes if it is a next-day operation.

The filling: _5 to 6 oz of cream cheese such as Gervais_ demi-sel (_each square packet of this cheese weighs approximately 2½ oz) or Raine's double cream cheese_ (not _cottage cheese from the big dairy combines; this skim-milk product is too poor in fat content and too acid for successful cooking), 2 generous tablespoons of grated Parmesan, 2 tablespoons of cream, 10 tablespoons of milk, 2 whole eggs, salt, freshly milled pepper, freshly ground nutmeg._

These quantities should make approximately ¾ pint of filling.

To mix the filling, all the ingredients except the cream can be blended in one go in an electric mixer or with a wooden spoon in a mixing bowl. Seasonings are to taste, meaning that the tasting part is essential. Stir in the cream, gently, when all other ingredients are smoothly blended.

To cook the quiche: Turn the oven to 425°F, 220°C, gas no. 7, and check that your baking sheet is ready on the centre shelf. Pour the filling into the pastry-lined tin, put it in the oven at once and leave for 15 minutes.

Prepare a square of buttered greaseproof paper which will cover the quiche, and after the first 15 minutes decrease the heat to 375°F, 190°C, gas no. 5, put the paper over the quiche and cook for another 10 minutes.

Serve quickly, and remember that a good protective oven glove is essential when it comes to pushing up the base of the tin – upon which you leave the quiche for serving – to separate it from the frame. This done, place the quiche and its base on a flat tart plate.

Again, this size of quiche will be enough for four to six people depending upon capacity, appetite and the rest of the meal.

Equivalent metric quantities, for the pastry: *plain flour 150 g, yeast approximately 10 g, salt ½ teaspoon, thick ripe cream 3 tablespoons, 1 whole egg;* for the filling: *cream cheese 150 to 170 g (see above for suitable cheeses), grated Parmesan 2 generous tablespoons, cream 2 tablespoons, milk 10 tablespoons, 2 whole eggs, salt, freshly ground pepper and nutmeg. Tin size: one 26 to 28 cm removable-base tart tin or earthenware pizza dish.*

Notes and variations: Quiches made on a basis of yeast pastry are very easy to reheat. Simply cover them with lightly buttered greaseproof paper and warm them through in a very moderate oven.

A variation on the white cheese quiche can be made by omitting the Parmesan and using 6 oz of smoked bacon rashers (rinds removed) cut into little slivers, fried until the fat runs, then arranged in circles on the pastry before the egg and white cheese mixture is poured in. This brings us back almost to the original quiche of Lorraine, which was simply cream or fresh white cheese and smoked bacon baked on bread dough. Gruyère cheese was not, and is not, one of the ingredients of a true quiche lorraine as it is known in its native province.

Sausage in Brioche Crust

· SAUSAGE IN BRIOCHE CRUST ·

For this excellent dish a large coarsely cut sausage weighing about 1 lb is first poached, or cooked in the oven, then wrapped in a brioche dough and baked.

In France the sausage used is a Lyonnais speciality, the *cervelas*, for which the sausage meat is brined, so that when cooked the inside is an appetizing pink – from the saltpetre – rather than the dead-looking grey of the traditional English sausage. And of course there is no bread filling in the French product. It is pure pork meat, sometimes lightly spiced, sometimes truffled.

Although it is difficult to get the right type of sausage in England, the time may well come when it will be obtainable from enterprising pork butchery specialists; alternatively it could be made at home[1] without too much difficulty, and there are other possibilities such as the Italian *cotechino* to be bought in Soho shops, or the English luncheon suasage made by Harrods butchery department from pure fresh pork meat without additional bread or rusk. Both these sausages will weigh 12 oz to 1 lb, although the Italian variety may be a little heavier.

For the brioche dough, which is made in the morning for the evening, or in the evening for the next day's lunch, ingredients are.

8 oz of strong plain flour, ½ oz of yeast, a teaspoon each of salt and sugar, 3 tablespoons of milk, 4 oz of butter, 3 large eggs. For glazing the crust, a little cream.

Equivalent metric quantities : a large coarsely cut sausage (see above for suitable types) about 400 to 500 g; for the brioche dough: strong plain flour

---

1. See Jane Grigson's admirable *Charcuterie and French Pork Cookery*, London, Michael Joseph, 1967; Penguin Books, 1970.

225 g, yeast 15 g, salt 1 teaspoon, sugar 1 teaspoon, milk 3 tablespoons, butter 125 g, 3 large eggs, a little cream for glazing the crust.

Sprinkle the salt into the flour. Warm the flour very slightly, by putting it in its bowl in a cool oven for a few minutes. Cream the yeast with the sugar and the milk, made just tepid. Soften the butter by putting it on a plate or in a bowl standing over a saucepan of hot water. None of these warming operations must be overdone.

Make a well in the flour. Pour in the yeast. Break in the eggs. Stir all together and mix to a paste. It will be rather sticky. Beat in the softened butter, using your hands. The dough will now be smooth and shiny. If it is too liquid, incorporate a little more flour. Form the dough into a ball, sprinkle it with flour, cover it and leave it in a warm – not too warm – place to rise until it has just about trebled in bulk and looks very light and spongy. Now break it down and knead it for a minute or two. Return it to a clean floured bowl. This time put the bowl in a *cold* place so that the dough remains quiescent overnight or for several hours.

Two hours or so before you intend making the dish, bring the dough back into the warm kitchen, so that it will come back to life slowly, while you deal with the sausage, which must be wholly cooked *before* it is wrapped in the brioche dough.

The easiest and least messy way to cook the sausage is to put it in a moderate oven and let it bake slowly, uncovered, at 330° to 350°F, 170° to 180°C, gas nos. 3 or 4. An English sausage will take 45 minutes to an hour to cook by this method. When it is cooked through – but not overcooked so that it shrinks – let it drain on paper towels, and leave it to cool a little before attempting to peel off the skin.

An Italian *cotechino* takes much longer to cook, and is best gently simmered in water to cover it, for about 2 hours. For this I use a narrow, rectangular, enamelled cast-iron pâté terrine in which the sausage fits neatly, or, if cooking more than one at a time, a small fish kettle (the kind known as a trout kettle) or an oval cocotte. Any of these can be used in the oven or on the hotplate.

When the sausage is ready, turn the dough on to a non-stick baking sheet or floured iron sheet, work it into a ball, pat it or roll it out into a rectangle, sprinkling it with flour as you do so. Put the skinned sausage in the centre, draw up the sides and ends of the dough, and dipping your fingers in cold water, pinch the seams together along the top and at the ends so that the dough entirely encloses the sausage, forming a nice plump bolster.

Using the back of a knife mark the top of the dough in a diamond pattern, then leave it for 10 to 15 minutes, just long enough for the dough to recover from the handling. Before putting it in the oven brush the dough with a little cream, to give a nice finish to the crust when it is baked.

Cook the sausage in the centre of a fairly hot oven, 425°F, 220°C, gas no. 7, for 20 to 25 minutes, until the crust is a good golden colour.

Slide the sausage on to a hot serving dish and leave it for 2 or 3 minutes before taking it to the table and carving it. The best way to do this is to start at the centre and work outwards towards the ends, cutting thick slices.

Sausage in brioche is always served as a hot first course, usually at the midday meal. No vegetable, salad or other accompaniment is ever served with it.

Notes: 1. The dough for this crust is a rather firmer one than that used for a brioche baked in a mould, which is too liquid to be handled with ease.

2. When mixing brioche dough take great care not to overheat any of the ingredients. The flour and milk should be just warmed, the butter softened so that it can be easily incorporated into the batter. If it is melted or 'oiled' it will separate from the flour, and a heavy dough will result.

3. The sausage should be warm when wrapped in the dough. If it is cold the dough will not adhere to it while baking, and when cut the slices of sausage will separate from the crust.

4. The joining of the seams of the dough with cold water when wrapping the sausage is important. If this step is omitted the dough will open during baking. This won't affect the taste but rather spoils the look of the finished dish.

5. The sausage should be completely cooked before it is wrapped in the crust. During the brief baking required for the brioche dough, the heat penetrates the crust sufficiently to make the sausage hot but does not allow for extra cooking.

6. Should your sausage weigh more than 1¼lb, make rather more dough, say 10oz or 280g of flour, 5oz or 150g of butter, 5 tablespoons of milk. It will not be necessary to add extra yeast or eggs.

7. A good dish to follow a sausage in brioche crust is something which has been slowly cooking low down in the oven while the sausage was baking, say a gratin of vegetables such as courgettes and tomatoes which can be transferred for its final browning to the centre or top shelf of the

oven after the sausage has been taken out. A chicken baked slowly in a covered pot or in foil is another possibility. Or perhaps, for a simple but still ample meal, follow the hot sausage with a good fresh green salad, and finish with cheese or a compote of fruit.

· EXCELLENT BREAD CRUST FOR HOT PIES OR TARTS ·

'Roll out square a pound of good white dough which is just ready for the oven; make four ounces of butter into a ball, put it in the centre of the paste, fold the corners well over it, and roll it out lightly two or three times, folding the ends always into the centre. Use it immediately.

'Meat well seasoned, and folded in it in the form of a turnover, and baked about half an hour answers well.'

Eliza Acton, *Modern Cookery*, 3rd edn, 1845

Miss Acton qualified her instructions for this bread crust – the recipe disappeared from later editions of her book – by adding that she had used it only with a dough made with milk. With common dough she suggests that an additional ounce, or even more, of butter be allowed.

Yeast Leavened Pancakes and Oatcakes

In the past, one of the great points about leavened pancakes and all the tribe of griddle cakes was that they provided a means of using meals and flours such as barley, buckwheat, oatmeal, which were not suitable for bread proper. In cottages and houses lacking an oven, bread was in any case baked on a griddle or a hearthstone or bakestone. Pancakes, pikelets, oatcakes, barley cakes, Welsh light cakes were just another form of bread. Today these delicious, homely specialities, where they survive at all, are usually made with baking powder, or have been refined and commercialized as a form of biscuit. The old recipes, using a coarse grade of meal and a yeast leavening, produce much more attractive and more authentic results. To be sure, most of the recipes call for a proportion of wheat flour to be mixed with the barley or the oatmeal. The wheat flour makes for a lighter and more manageable batter, without swamping the flavours and enticing smells of oatmeal and barley meal. These pancakes and bakestone cakes are incomparably good with bacon, or just with butter. A griddle or girdle for cooking oatcakes and yeast pancakes is in no way essential. I find that I can achieve thinner and more evenly cooked pancakes using an iron frying pan. Sometimes I use my blini pan – there is a drawing of one on p. 408 – so the pancakes or barley cakes come out very small and neat, but properly speaking most Welsh and English griddle cakes should be quite large, about the size of a tea plate, very thin, riddled with tiny holes. (In the Lake District and in some parts of Yorkshire, oatcake cooked on the bakestone was called riddle bread. Descriptions of the methods of making it are on pp. 409–11 and pp. 529–31.) These old country recipes are very practical and useful and they are simple enough to learn. They make cheap treats, too. And one of the joys of all yeast-leavened pancake batters is that they are so good tempered. They can be stored in the fridge for three or four days and can be brought back to life over and

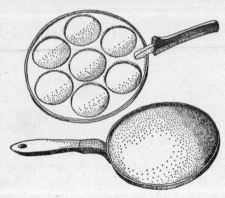

Finnish non-stick pan for blinis and other yeast pancakes, and French cast iron *galettière* or shallow pancake pan.

over again, simply by being transferred from the refrigerator to a warm kitchen, stirred vigorously and left until bubbly once more. Some yeast-leavened pancakes, barley among them, improve with keeping.

· WELSH OATMEAL PANCAKES ·

Ingredients: ¼ lb of fine oatmeal, ½ lb of plain unbleached flour, ½ oz of bakers' yeast, 1 teaspoon of salt, 1 whole egg, a tablespoon or two of butter-milk, 1 pint of water.

Equivalent metric quantities: fine oatmeal 125 g, plain unbleached flour 225 g, bakers' yeast 15 g, salt 1 teaspoon, 1 whole egg, buttermilk 1 or 2 tablespoons, cold water 550 g.

The oatmeal should be put to soak overnight (or in the morning for the evening) in 1 pint of cold water.

Next morning, mix the yeast and buttermilk (the commercial butter-milk now widely available does very well) to a thin cream. Put the plain flour in a bowl with the salt. Strain the oatmeal but keep the water.

Mix the oatmeal with the flour, break in the egg, add the yeast mixture, stir all together. Thin the dough with about ½ pint of the oatmeal water, and stir. The dough or batter should be thin enough to drop off the spoon, but not too runny.

Cover the bowl and leave in a warm place (the ideal temperature is 70° to 75°F, 21° to 23·5°C) for 1½ to 2 hours, until risen and bubbly.

To cook the pancakes use an iron griddle or a shallow, heavy iron frying pan, heated and rubbed with a scrap of butter or fat.

Pour in about 1 ladleful of batter (i.e. the equivalent of 2 tablespoons) and let it spread. Each pancake should be about 7 inches in diameter and very thin. Cook rather slowly until the pancake is full of tiny holes and firm enough to turn with a pliable spatula. The underside needs only a few more seconds. Keep warm in the oven while the rest are cooked.

The quantities given should make twelve very thin pancakes. They are delicious with bacon, or simply with butter, and can be reheated very successfully.

If the batter is not all used at once, it will keep in a covered bowl in the refrigerator. The way to bring it back to life is explained in the final paragraph of the introductory note on p. 407.

· LANCASHIRE OATCAKES ·

'Itinerant vendors brought round crumpets and oatcakes. The latter were thin wafers of oatmeal paste cooked on a bakestone. They were delivered soft and damp and hung up in the kitchen until they dried, crisp and firm, to be eaten with butter.'

George Bellairs, 'Rough Epicures', *Wine and Food,*
no. 58 (Summer 1948)

· YORKSHIRE RIDDLE BREAD ·

'Riddle bread was made like a batter and cooked on the old bakestone, or "bak-stun", a slate slab, very smooth, under which a fire was kindled. Nowadays an electric stove hot-plate can be used in place of the "bak-stun".

'Country people would make a full week's supply of Riddle Bread all at once, and would help themselves to it from the fleeak when required. White bread was only eaten on Sundays as a treat.

'*Method:* Take a quantity of pin-head oatmeal and mix it with warm water and yeast to form a thick porridge. Leave overnight in a warm room. Next morning, salt to taste and place spoonsful on to the hot bak-stun and spread the mixture with a wooden paddle shaped like a

Scotch hand. As the bread cooks, bubbles rise and give it its character-istic appearance. The cakes should not be turned, but should be browned on one side only. When cooked, hang them on the creel whilst still warm and use when needed.

'Many old records of the West Riding describe the batter being trans-ferred to the bake-stone by means of a "throwing motion" so that the batter spread out evenly in a long oblong. To do this throwing well was an expert's task.'

Through Yorkshire's Kitchen Door, the Yorkshire Federation of Women's Institutes, 31st edn, n.d. (first published 1927)

An interesting early nineteenth-century description of Yorkshire oatcakes or haver cakes is quoted in the chapter on unleavened bakestone cakes and breads, and the two methods, leavened and unleavened, seem to have been traditional to different districts. Originally the leavening was not ale yeast but a spontaneous leaven made from an oatmeal sour-dough. The way this was prepared is described in detail by Mrs Esther Copley, reporting on oatcakes or 'aver bread' in *The Family Economist*, November 1850:

'Mix a little oatmeal into a stiff paste – two tablespoonfuls of dry meal will be amply sufficient for a gallon – leave it in a warm place, free from dust, until it becomes sour, when it is converted into leaven. With this the first batch of dough is to be prepared. Afterwards the dough pan is never washed, but the batter that adheres to it becomes leaven, and suffices for the next batch. The pan must be kept in a dry place and free from dust, and if it be deemed fitting occasionally to wash the pan, fresh leaven will be required. Yeast is not approved for the purpose, nor any of the chemical preparations more recently adopted for bread.

'*Method of preparing*. Twelve hours, or thereabouts, is a proper time to allow from making the dough or batter to baking it; it is therefore generally convenient to take it in hand overnight.

'If fresh leaven, incorporate it well with the oatmeal, and mix with a sufficient quantity of water to bring to a stiff batter considerably stiffer than would be suitable for pancakes, yet not nearly so stiff as to be fit for rolling, like a pie-crust. In fact it should just admit of pouring or dipping with the ladle.'

Mrs Copley, whose information had been 'obtained from one York-shire native and confirmed by another accustomed from infancy to observe the process and partake of the result' goes into two closely printed pages of detail as to the necessary utensils – the riddle or bach-board, the ladle, the oatcake turners or spitals, the bakestone, and the 'bread-flegg' or drying rack – and tells us that 'the cakes are sometimes eaten new, being buttered the instant they are removed from the hot stone, and very nice they are, much superior to crumpets; but this is a sort of luxury not generally allowed by frugal housewives. The usual plan is to reserve them for occasional use, and if well baked they will keep good for months, and even years.'

· THE OATCAKES OF THE STAFFORDSHIRE POTTERIES ·

'On Saturday nights my mother used to send me out to buy the oatcakes for Sunday breakfast . . .

'The shop stood half-way down the hill, the bottom of its bow window level with my eyes. It was open for business at 7.30 but always I got there half an hour early to watch the oatcakes being made. Looming above me, his belly bulging in a striped apron, the oatcake man would test the heat of his bakestone – a black iron plate which sent the thermals shimmering to the ceiling – and from a tall white jug he would pour out 12 liquid pats of oatmeal which spat and bubbled on the metal.

'There was an instant, mouth-watering smell of toasted oatmeal as the mixture crisped at the edges. One by one, the oatcakes would be flipped over, then with both sides done they would be stacked in a tender, tottering pile beside the bakestone. I would buy 12 and bear them home, clasped to my chest like a hot and fragrant poultice.

'When I left the Potteries oatcakes disappeared from my life and the loss was insupportable. I searched everywhere but soon found that they were an intensely local delicacy, unheard of north of Leek, unimagined south of Banbury. Most shops think of oatcake as an oatmeal biscuit. But the oatcakes of my childhood were soft oatmeal pancakes, delicious with butter and honey, delectable with bacon and eggs.'

Philip Oakes, writing in the *Sunday Times*, 15 December 1974

My recipe is adapted slightly from the one supplied by Philip Oakes, which came originally, he said, from the North Staffordshire *Evening Sentinel*.

To make sixteen to eighteen 6 to 7 inch oatcakes or pancakes, quantities are ½ lb each of fine oatmeal and plain bread flour (I use 85 per cent wheatmeal, but white will do), ½ oz of bakers' yeast, 2 teaspoons of salt, approximately ¾ pint each of warm milk and water. A little fat will be needed for the frying pan.

Equivalent metric quantities for sixteen to eighteen 15 to 18 cm oatcakes or pancakes: fine oatmeal 225 g, plain bread flour 225 g, bakers' yeast 15 g, salt 2 teaspoons, warm milk and water approximately 420 g each, fat for the frying pan.

Put the oatmeal and the wheatmeal into a bowl with the salt. Cream the yeast with a little of the warm milk and water mixture. Stir it into the flours, add the rest of the liquid and with a wooden spoon beat the mixture into a batter. If it is too thick add a little more warm water. Cover the bowl and leave to rise for an hour or so.

Make the oatcakes as for pancakes. I like them very thin and curling at little at the edges. Oatcakes can be kept warm and soft in a folded cloth; and if you want to make them in advance and reheat them in the pan or in a slow oven, dampen the cloth so that they remain moist.

· BARLEY PANCAKES ·

The batter for these pancakes is made in the same way as the one for Elizabeth Hammond's buckwheat cakes on pp. 416–17, but they are cooked differently. Instead of being made into small thick cakes, the batter is cooked in a 7 or 8 inch pan and spread very thin. They are excellent eaten by themselves with melted butter and salt, or reheated with a filling of cheese, as explained below.

To make the pancakes, ingredients are 3 oz each of strong plain flour and barley flour (I use Mrs Horsfield's Welsh barley meal or flour, obtainable in many wholefood shops), ½ oz of yeast, salt, ¾ pint of milk, 4 eggs.

Equivalent metric quantities: strong plain flour 85 g, barley flour 85 g, yeast 15 g, salt, milk 420 g, eggs 4. Pan size: a pancake pan, 18 or 20 cm top diameter.

Warm ½ pint of the milk. Put the two flours together in a bowl, add a heaped teaspoon of salt, mix well. Cream the yeast with a little of the warmed milk, add it to the flour, then mix to a batter with the rest of the ½ pint of milk. Cover the bowl and leave to rise for an hour or a little longer, until the batter is spongy and bubbly.

Beat in the eggs and then the remaining ¼ pint of milk, which does not have to be warmed. Again cover the bowl and leave the batter to rise for the second time, for another hour, or longer if necessary. As Elizabeth Raper[1] wrote in a memorable phrase, and in a different context, 'less won't do it, more won't hurt it'. This maxim could be applied to so many of the processes in yeast cookery that it could almost have been used as the title for this book.

To cook the pancakes, put the smallest scrap of butter in your pan, warm it and pour in one scant ladleful of the batter. Tip the pan so that the batter spreads evenly. Let it cook, not too fast, until tiny holes appear all over the top surface and you see that it is firm enough to turn with a pliable spatula. The underside needs only a few seconds in the pan.

The quantities given go a long way. The batter will make a dozen or more very thin 7 inch pancakes, and need not all be used at once. If anything the batter improves with keeping. See introductory note on p. 407.

Barley pancakes with cheese

To convert six to eight of these pancakes into a cheap, easy and very attractive lunch or supper dish, have a ¼lb block of Cheddar cheese cut into sticks about 1 inch wide. Put two of these portions of cheese on each pancake, seasoning with freshly ground black pepper and nutmeg, arrange them one on top of the other in a shallow round gratin dish. Pour over them a little melted butter.

Put in the centre of a moderately heated oven for about 15 minutes, until the cheese begins to melt and the pancakes are well heated through.

Notes and variations: 1. I find that after the initial mixing, barley pancake batter sometimes needs a little extra salt.

2. The cheese used for the filling does not have to be Cheddar. Other English cheeses, such as Double Gloucester, Lancashire or Wensleydale do very well. So does a soft melting cheese such as Port Salut or Bel Paese. I invented these cheese-filled barley pancakes myself, so there is no sacred tradition involved.

3. Barley flour has a very particular flavour, earthy and rather primitive. I like it very much, but it is not to everyone's taste.

1. *The Receipt Book of Elizabeth Raper*, written 1756–70, published by the Nonesuch Press, 1924.

· BLINIS ·

Blinis are the Russian version of pancakes made with a yeast batter. Traditionally, buckwheat flour[1] is used, and the pancakes are eaten with salt herring, or caviar for the rich and showy, plus sour cream and melted butter.

Speaking for myself, and heretically, I find that a half and half mixture of buckwheat and white flour or even all white flour makes a much lighter, if less authentic, batter. And as for the embellishments, these are a matter of taste, of what you can afford and of what is available. Not everybody likes salt herring, and even those accustomed to luxuries may feel that fine Beluga caviar is better on its own than spread on pancakes and doused with sour cream. My own impression is that the caviar is swamped by the cream. A good compromise is the salmon roe sometimes called 'red caviar' or *keta*, which seems just right with the pancakes and the cream. At present prices it is still a luxury. At least it is a genuine one whereas the black substance known as lump-fish roe which often does duty for caviar in sandwiches and cocktail canapés is, to my mind, worthless. If you can get good bacon it is delicious with blinis. So is simple melted butter with a few anchovy fillets chopped into it. Smoked cod's roe softened with cream cheese is another possibility. In short, the idea is something salt, plus cold thick sour cream, plus hot melted butter – although if you have something fat, such as bacon, you will hardly need butter and cream as well.

The size of the blinis is an essential point. They are rarely larger than about 4 inches in diameter, sometimes an inch smaller; they should be about half as thick as an English crumpet. Special pans with divisions in which some half dozen little pancakes can be made simultaneously are available on the English market. (See the illustration on p. 408.)

If you have no special pans, blinis, like all yeast pancakes, can be cooked on a griddle or in one of the shallow French cast-iron pans used for Norman or Breton pancakes. Since yeast batter does not spread like ordinary pancake batter, three or four little blinis can be made at the same time in one of these pans. They will not be so regular in form as blinis made in a special pan, but they will be just as good.

Ingredients for about twenty-five yeast pancakes of 4 inch diameter are: ½ *lb of flour, either half and half buckwheat and plain strong bread*

1. Obtainable from many health-food stores.

flour, or all strong white flour ; ½ oz of yeast ; ½ pint of milk ; ¼ pint of sour cream ; 2 large or 3 average eggs ; 1 teaspoon of salt.

Equivalent metric quantities for about twenty-five blinis of 10 cm diameter : half and half buckwheat and plain strong bread flour, or *all strong white flour, 225 g ; yeast 15 g ; milk 280 g ; sour cream 150 g ; eggs 2 large or 3 average ; salt 1 teaspoon.*

Put the flour in a big bowl. Add the salt. Warm the milk barely to blood heat. Mix the milk and yeast together. Separate the eggs. Stir the yolks and the cream into the milk and yeast mixture. Set aside the whites. Pour the yeast mixture into the flour and stir until you have a thick batter. If at this stage there are a few lumps in the batter it is of no consequence.

Cover the bowl, leave in a warm place for approximately 1 hour until the batter is spongy and bubbly.

Now whisk the egg whites to a stiff froth – as for a soufflé – and fold them into the batter. Cover the bowl again and leave the batter to rise once more, for another hour or even longer.

To make the pancakes, brush the little pans with a scrap of melted butter and set them over medium heat. Pour a small ladleful of batter into each division. The batter sets immediately it comes into contact with the heat. In a few seconds holes appear in the top surface. Turn the blinis and let them brown on the underside. Keep each batch warm (with a little melted butter poured on them) in the oven while the rest are cooked.

Blinis are eaten as a first – or only – course, with hot melted butter in a jug or sauce boat, cold thick sour cream in a bowl and another bowl of chopped salt herring, or caviar, or a dish of bacon rashers cut into strips and grilled, fried or baked in the oven while you are cooking the blinis.

If you prefer them as a sweet course blinis are good with cinnamon butter, or with a little rich jam such as black cherry or plum – or with clotted cream, or even with apple purée.

Notes: 1. The batter for blinis can be kept overnight in the refrigerator and removed to a warm place to rise for an hour or so before it is to be cooked.

2. Provided they have not been overcooked in the first place, blinis can be reheated quite successfully. Put them in a very moderate oven, protected with buttered paper, for a few minutes.

3. Alternative proportions of flour for the batter are: 6 oz of strong plain white to 2 oz of buckwheat.

4. The sour cream in the batter can be replaced with buttermilk, or even yogurt, so long as it is not too sharp-tasting.

5. An alternative method of cooking blinis is to bake them in a medium hot oven in small shallow iron pans or in the heavy black cast-iron handled pans especially made for blinis. These have recently appeared on the market here and have divisions for four blinis. They are sold in the shops as 'egg pans'. Blinis cooked in the oven are thought by many people to be better than those made in the more orthodox manner.

· BOCKINGS ·

Under this curious name, a derivative of buck or buckwheat, a recipe for buckwheat pancakes leavened with yeast appears in *Modern Domestic Cookery and Useful Receipt Book* by Elizabeth Hammond, first published in 1817.

Buckwheat pancakes appear rarely in English cookery books. When they do, it is usually in the form of a recipe derived from American sources, and leavened only with baking powder. Yeast-leavened buckwheat pancakes were, however, obviously known in the Midland counties of England in the eighteenth century. Variations on Elizabeth Hammond's recipe are to be found in one or two of her contemporaries' books, and another is given among the traditional recipes in the Shropshire Women's Institute cookery book.[1] Here is the Hammond recipe:

'Mix six ounces of buck-wheat flour, with half a pint of warm milk and two spoonsful of yeast, place it before the fire about an hour to let it rise; then mix eight eggs well beaten, and as much milk as will make the batter the usual thickness for pancakes; then fry them in the same manner.'

· ENGLISH BUCKWHEAT PANCAKES ·

I thought Elizabeth Hammond's description of bockings so interesting that I could not resist trying a modified version, using half and half buckwheat and white flour, with four instead of eight eggs. Although in texture rather more resembling the Welsh crumpets, for which the

1. *Shropshire Cookery Book, c.* 1955.

recipe is given on p. 358, than Russian blinis, the pancakes produced by this formula are really excellent.

Weigh 3 oz each of buckwheat and plain household flour, and put in a large bowl with a teaspoon of salt. Warm ½ pint of milk to blood heat. use a little of this to mix ½ oz of yeast to a thick cream, stir this into the flour, then add the rest of the milk. Stir as for a batter. Cover the bowl, and leave to rise for approximately an hour, or until the batter is bubbly.

Now beat in 4 whole eggs, and a very little extra milk – rather under ¼ pint, as the batter should not be *too* thin.

Cover and leave to rise again, which will take another hour or so.

Make into small pancakes rather as for blinis.

Four eggs to such a small amount of flour may sound very odd proportions. In fact these pancakes are extraordinarily good, not at all heavy, and perhaps at their best with butter and brown sugar.

Equivalent metric quantities: buckwheat 85 g, plain household flour 85 g, salt 1 teaspoon, milk 280 g, yeast 15 g, eggs 4, extra milk – rather under 150 g.

· YEAST LEAVENED BATTER FOR FRITTERS ·

Leavened pancake batter, slightly thinned down, is excellent for fritters, sweet or savoury. The following ancient recipe for apple fritters shows that the tradition is a very old one. It is worth reviving.

'*Fretoure.* Take wheat flour, Ale yest, Safroun, & Salt, & bete alle to-gederys as thikke as thou schuldyst make other bature in fleyssche tyme; and then take fayre Applys, & kut hem in maner of Fretourys, & wete hem in the batoure up on downne, & frye hem in fayre Oyle, & caste hem in a dyssche; & caste sugre ther-on, & serve forth.'

Two Fifteenth-Century Cookery-Books, ed. Thomas Austin, 1888, reprinted 1964

Dumplings and Doughnuts

Yeast dumplings, rarely encountered nowadays, were a by-product of domestic bread-baking. A portion of dough from the main batch would be kept back when the loaves were moulded preparatory to going into the oven, and when the time came to prepare the evening meal the dumplings would be boiled in a big pan of water while a stew was simmering on the hob or perhaps in the oven from which the bread had been taken. The heat in the old bread ovens lasted a long time and it was wasteful not to make use of it for cooking something which needed slow heat like potatoes. Boiled yeast dumplings made a stew go further, and were good fillers for hungry children and outdoor workers. Today they may seem rather too filling, but it is interesting to know how they were made and eaten. The following is Hannah Glasse's recipe.

· YEAST DUMPLINGS, 1747 ·

'First make a light Dough as for Bread, with Flour, Water, Salt and Yeast, cover with a Cloth, and set it before the Fire for half an Hour; then have a Sauce-pan of Water on the Fire, and when it boils take the Dough, and make it into little round Balls, as big as a large Hen's Egg; then flat them with your Hand, and put them into the boiling Water; a few Minutes boils them. Take great Care they don't fall to the Bottom of the Pot or Sauce-pan, for then they will be heavy; and be sure to keep the water boiling all the Time. When they are enough, take them up (which they will be in ten Minutes or less), lay them in your Dish, and have melted Butter in a Cup. As good a Way as any to save trouble, is to send to the Baker's for half a Quartern of Dough (which will make a great many) and then you have only the Trouble of boiling it.'

The Art of Cookery Made Plain and Easy, 1747

It should be added that a very large and wide pan such as a preserving pan is needed for boiling dumplings in any quantity. If they are crowded together in a confined space they will merge during boiling and turn into a doughy mass. I find also that dumplings which start off the size of a 'large Hen's Egg' swell up far too big, and also take much longer – more like 25 minutes – to boil than Hannah Glasse's 10 minutes, so it is best to make the dumplings the size of a small egg and boil them for about 20 minutes.

Mrs Glasse's half quartern or $1\frac{3}{4}$lb of dough certainly will make a great many dumplings, about forty.

· NORFOLK DUMPLINGS ·

'It was a dinner Nesset loved. First came Norfolk dumplings, light as puff-balls, made with real brewer's yeast, floating in rich brown hare gravy. Then jugged hare with red-currant jelly, roast potatoes, turnip-top salad, mashed swede, turnips and leeks, hot apple-pie, and thick yellow cream. After that came home-baked bread and cheese and russet apples.'

Mathena Blomefield, *The Bulleymung Pit: The Story of a Norfolk Farmer's Child*, Faber, 1946

It is curious that yeast dumplings are always associated with the East Anglian counties – particularly Norfolk – since they were made pretty well wherever the baking of household bread flourished, and wherever there were hungry families to feed. The old brick ovens did of course survive intact in East Anglia for longer than in most other English agricultural regions, and with them the old traditions and routines of cooking and baking were kept going until the 1939–45 War and the years of shortages and rationing put an end to them. If housewives make dumplings at all nowadays they make them with a chemical raising agent, and they add suet in an effort to lighten them. I am not alone in finding that this doesn't really work. 'How can you reconcile a baking powder with a bakers' yeast?' wrote a Norfolk patriot, Mr Arthur Pendle,[1] discussing the yeast dumpling versus the chemically aerated version. The 'true Norfolk dumpling, made with flour, baker's yeast and salt' is steamed or boiled and produces 'the aristocrat of the dinner table. Few homes', continued Mr Pendle, 'now have bread baked in ovens in the kitchen wall and . . . few have a truly Norfolk dumpling.' This agreeable

1. 'Dumplings and Dialect', the *East Anglian Magazine*, September 1961.

yeast-dumpling enthusiast considers that the suet dumpling is a pretender, and belongs over the Suffolk border on the southern side of the river Waveney. There I think he is underestimating past generations of Suffolk housewives. Allan Jobson,[1] writing of his Suffolk grandmother's weekly baking day, has a very different tale to tell:

'Dumplings also came off the dough . . . pieces about the size of a small fist were broken off and boiled for twenty-five minutes in salted boiling water. They were excellent with rich gravy from the joint . . . There were also floaters, made from the dough. These were rolled flat and cut into pieces the size of a tea saucer and the thickness of a crumpet. They were slid into boiling water, and served to take the edge off an appetite, since they were eaten before the meat with treacle or sugar.'

· TO MAKE A BARM PUDDING ·

I have not attempted the following recipe from Elizabeth Raffald's *Experienced English Housekeeper*, published in 1769; I quote it for its charm, but it has practical advice to offer too.

'Take a pound of flour, mix a spoonful of barm in it, with a little salt, and make it into a light paste with warm water, let it lie one hour then make it up into round balls, and tie them up in little nets, and put them in a pan of boiling water, do not cover them, it will make them sad, nor do not let them boil so fast as to let the water boil over them, turn them when they have been in six or seven minutes, and they will raise through the net and look like diamonds, twenty minutes will boil them; serve them up, and pour sweet sauce over them.'

· DOUGHNUTS ·

'Doughnuts, now there's something good. Why don't you write about doughnuts? People will pay for a good quality doughnut. Of course they're nicer when you can put the jam in before frying them.'

George Ort, Master Baker, of Leighton Buzzard,
talking to the author, 1975

'One of my jobs in the bakery was to fry the doughnuts before I went to school in the morning.'

Rita Ensing, daughter of a London Master Baker,
talking to the author, 1974

1. *An Hour-Glass on the Run*, 1959.

Frankly, doughnuts are not for me. I have never made them, and haven't eaten them since schooldays. Nowadays I avoid deep fried food of all kinds, from chips to everything in batter, with the occasional exception of some alluring little Chinese morsel – but then Chinese cooks, like Italians, are exceptionally good at deep frying. For those likewise talented here is a reliable doughnut recipe.

Dough Nuts

'1 lb flour	2 whites of eggs
1 oz bakers' yeast	3 oz butter
8 fluid oz (1 cup U.S.) of sweet milk	1 oz sugar
3 yolks of eggs	Some jam'

'Sieve the flour into a good-sized basin, add a pinch of salt, and make a well in the centre. Put the yeast and sugar into a smaller basin, and mix them together with a teaspoon until of a creamy consistency. Melt the butter in a small saucepan, add the milk, and, when lukewarm, pour over the yeast, and strain into the centre of the flour. Add the eggs, yolks and whites, well beaten, and mix from the centre outwards, forming a nice light dough. Beat with the hands from 10 to 15 minutes, then cover the basin with a cloth, and set it in a warm place to rise from 1½ to 2 hours. When well risen, turn out the dough on to a floured board, knead lightly until free from cracks, and then roll out to about ¾ inch in thickness. Stamp out in rounds with a cutter.[1] Put a small teaspoonful of red jam in the centre of half of these, and brush over the others with a beaten egg. Place two together, one with jam and the other without, and press the edges well where they join. Fry these, a few at a time, in boiling fat, allowing them to cook until they are about double their original size, and are nicely browned. Lift out, drain on paper, and sprinkle well with sugar, or with sugar and ground cinnamon mixed. Dough nuts should be used when they are quite fresh.

'*Note* – Care must be taken to have the fat sufficiently hot: it should be quite still, and a blue smoke should be seen rising from it. Allow the fat to reheat before putting in a second lot of dough nuts.

'Time to cook, 10 to 12 minutes. Probable cost, 8d.'

Florence Jack, *Cookery for Every Household*, 1914

1. Doughnut cutters, ingenious and cheap little gadgets, can be bought at most well-stocked hardware shops and kitchen gadgets counters of department stores.

Equivalent metric quantities : flour 450 g, bakers' yeast 30 g, milk 225 g, egg yolks 3, egg whites 2, butter 85 g, sugar 30 g, jam.

*

At one time doughnuts were evidently a great speciality of the Isle of Wight. I have come across a number of recipes for this variation in Victorian and Edwardian books. It is interesting to note that in the following version candied peel replaces the more familiar jam.

· ISLE OF WIGHT DOUGHNUTS (1) ·

'1 gallon of flour,[1] 1 pound of butter rubbed well into it; pour in one teacupful of good ale yeast (not bitter), and put it to rise; mix and knead it as you would bread, and add 6 well beaten eggs, ¾ lb of sifted sugar, 1 grated nutmeg, and a little warm milk. The dough must not be mixed too soft at first or it will be too soft to roll up subsequently. Leave it again by the fire to rise for an hour or two. Then take out small lumps of dough, the size of a smallish orange, insert into the centre of each a piece of candied peel and some currants (some grated lemon rind also is a great improvement), and roll it up securely. Have ready a deep pan of boiling lard, and be sure that it is quite boiling when the doughnuts are put in; let them be completely covered with the lard, and boil 15 minutes over a slow fire. Take out, set to drain on paper, and let them get cool gradually and not stand in a draught. Dust over with sifted sugar. These are first rate.'

From St Lawrence Women's Institute, in *The Isle of Wight Cookery Book*, 5th edn, *c.* 1930

Equivalent metric quantities : flour 3 kg, butter 450 g, ale yeast 1 teacup, eggs 6, sugar 340 g, nutmeg 1, milk, candied peel, currants, lemon rind.

· ISLE OF WIGHT DOUGHNUTS (2) ·

Eliza Acton's recipe for Isle of Wight doughnuts specifies brown sugar, allspice, cinnamon, cloves and mace for sweetening and spicing the dough. Miss Acton's cooking time is 7 minutes only, and she adds the following notes:

1. A gallon is 7 lb.

'When they are made in large quantities, as they are at certain seasons in the island, they are drained upon very clean straw. The lard should boil only just before they are dropped into it, or the outsides will be scorched before the insides are sufficiently done.'

Modern Cookery, 1855 edn (first published 1845)

Regional and Festival Yeast Cakes and Fruit Breads

'The chief delicacy at these [harvest] teas was "baker's cake", a rich, fruity, spicy dough cake, obtained in the following manner. The housewife provided all the ingredients excepting the dough, putting raisins and currants, lard, sugar and spice in a basin which she gave to the baker, who added the dough, made and baked the cake, and returned it, beautifully browned in his big oven. The charge was the same as that for a loaf of bread the same size, and the result was delicious.'

Flora Thompson, *Lark Rise to Candleford*, 1945

Not one among the collection of English regional cookery books in my possession is without its quota of recipes for some local yeast cake or fruit bread speciality. From Cornwall to Norfolk, from Sussex to Cumberland, from the Channel Islands to the North Riding of Yorkshire, from Anglesey to the Isle of Wight, the recipes have been preserved, recorded and published, often owing to the initiative of the ladies of the Women's Institutes, sometimes by other local organizations collecting recipes and publishing their modest volumes to raise money for the restoration of a church, for a new village hall, for a hospital, for a playing field.

In no branch of English cookery is there a richer variety of recipes than in the making of cakes, scones and bread; it is of extraordinary interest to discover how large a proportion of these recipes is for yeast-leavened spice cakes and breads; it is also easy to see how many more there must have been before the days of the chemical raising agents and baking powders which replaced fresh yeast in so many households, for it is obvious enough from the composition of many modern English fruit cakes that they were originally yeast-leavened and subsequently adapted to the use of baking powder. Others, such as the baker's or dough cake referred to by Flora Thompson in the passage quoted above, could not be easily adapted, so in households where bread was no longer made, dough was bought from the baker and used as a basis in which to incorporate the dried fruit, butter or lard, sugar and spice. Other households, where there was no bread oven, or where the fuel to heat it was too expensive, managed things the other way round, and took their fruit and spices to the dough, as described by Flora Thompson. To the humble village family of which she was writing the delicious, sugary, fruit-enriched dough cake was a rare treat.

Writing of the evolution of cakes and of their composition in the twentieth century, H. D. Renner, in *The Origin of Food Habits* (1944), observes that 'so marked has been the change that in America and also in England, the cakes of the early nineteenth century made with yeast would if produced today, be now considered uneatable'. This seems to me an astonishing statement for a responsible author to make. Mr Renner had surely never eaten a lardy cake, a Yorkshire tea cake, a currant loaf, a Sally Lunn or even a hot cross bun, and certainly could not have made any attempt to interpret into practical working terms any of the recipes for those 'early nineteenth century cakes made with yeast'. Had he studied them with any care Mr Renner would have seen, first, that scores of those recipes date back far earlier than the nineteenth century, some to Elizabethan times and possibly earlier, and next, that many of them survive in the twentieth century and are so taken for granted that perhaps not everybody appreciates that such familiar confections as the common currant bun are made from no more than a batch of ordinary yeast-leavened dough enriched with a little fat and dried fruit. Indeed, when dealing with the old recipes it is sometimes difficult to make the modern distinction between bread and cake, proportions in the old formulas very often producing something between the two. What is certain is that many of them turn out to be confections of remarkable distinction and delicacy. On this level alone, numbers of recipes among those which have been all but forgotten are worth reviving. There are other reasons which could be just as forceful. One point worth remembering is that yeast-leavened dough or pastry requires a good deal less flour for the same volume of finished cake, bun or whatever you like to call it, than ordinary doughs and cake batters. Fewer eggs are needed, and in most cases less fat or butter. So from the point of view of diet as well as of saving in cost the yeast-leavened cakes, fruit breads and pastries have distinct advantages over those made by what are considered more modern methods and with more modern ingredients. Over and over again, using the older recipes in this book, it has been just those modern methods and ingredients which have begun to appear to me crude and out of date. One of the most marked differences, even in yeast cake recipes which have probably descended from mother to daughter for generations, is the startling increase in the proportion of sugar as well as of fruit to flour which has crept in over the past century or so. This question is gone into more fully on pp. 428-9.

*

The problem in choosing recipes for English spice and fruit cakes is the quite remarkable number of variations on record. Nobody could possibly try them all. Mrs Johnstone, the lady who sheltered behind the pseudonym of Mistress Margaret Dods when she published *The Cook and Housewife's Manual* in 1826, put the matter very neatly, if with an audible note of despair, in a footnote: 'Every country town, village, and rural neighbourhood in England, Scotland and Ireland, has its favourite holiday cake, or currant loaf . . . we do not pretend to give receipts for all of these – the formula is endless – and they are all good.'

As typical of its kind Mrs Johnstone gives a recipe for what she calls 'Irish Brade breached', adding that the word breached means spotted or freckled. So, for that matter, does the similar word *brith* in bara brith, Welsh currant bread – *bara* is bread – the composition of the Welsh version being much like the Irish one given by Mrs Johnstone. It would be unthinkable to omit bara brith from a chapter on national and regional fruit breads, so both Irish and Welsh versions are included.

Another national cake, the Scotch Christmas Bun, is very different and much richer, being a fruit mixture – raisins, currants, candied peel, almonds and spices – encased in a yeast-leavened and butter-enriched dough, the whole moulded into a large round cake. I have seen it also in a tall, narrow, pie shape, and in a long, slab cake form, but these are commercial adaptations of the real thing. The Scotch Bun is a kind of Christmas pudding in a crust, and as rich as it sounds; the old recipes quoted in the following chapter differ little in composition from Florence Jack's twentieth-century version, although the latter is more clearly explained. Curiously, the seventeenth-century Countess of Rutland's recipe for Banbury cake, quoted on p. 447, would have produced a cake much like the Scotch Bun, pieces of the yeast dough being mixed in with the fruit filling as well as making the outer cover or crust. This cake was made for the festivities at the marriage of the Countess of Rutland's daughter. It must have been a noble sight. The Banbury cakes of the eighteenth century seem to have been rather different, although still yeast leavened. The modern version is something else again. Both are described on p. 448.

From the Lake District, and from Northumberland, Yorkshire, Shropshire, Derbyshire, Lancashire, Guernsey, and Cornwall, come other interesting variations on fruit bread recipes. Several are quoted later in this chapter, the delicious and beautifully simple Cornish saffron cake being almost my own favourite. But the Countess of Kent's seventeenth-century spice cake comes a close second. Again, this one is more bread than cake; with the recipe reduced to manageable proportions it has proved of unexpected finesse. And there are so many more: Edwardian country house 'luncheon cakes', for example, and a delicious spice cake to be made from the same batch of dough mixed for hot cross buns, and a Devonshire cake which is a subtle variation of the Cornish saffron cake. Then there are the lardy or dough cakes, spiced, rich in fat and fruit, crunchy with sugar. I have kept recipes for these to a minimum. They are a dietician's nightmare. Weight watchers must stay far away from them, and to schoolchildren they could become perilously compulsive.

Very far, then, from being 'uneatable', these old yeast cakes and fruit breads are all too tempting. Making a choice of the recipes has been a slow process, first of accumulation and then of elimination. It was difficult to avoid overprofusion.

*

Confusion between breads, cakes, tea cakes and buns has presented another problem, and one I have attempted to solve by assembling the smaller, individual cakes or buns into a separate chapter, even when the dough or batter from which they are made may be identical with that used for a large cake or loaf. On the whole the latter are the more satisfactory. They keep better than small buns, they cut economically and neatly, and they are very often more sightly than the individual versions which tend to get out of control and grow – or, worse, shrink – into unexpected shapes when moulded by inexperienced hands. And unless far too great a proportion of our cooking lives is to be spent acquiring the tricks of the baking trade, inexperienced is what most of us are going to remain. When all is said and done, it is the making and baking of ordinary good daily bread which is the main preoccupation of this book. The more fancy confections should perhaps be seen as sidelines, by-paths fascinating to explore, techniques extraordinarily satisfactory to understand, so that now and again it is possible to re-create in some measure the treats and the festive luxuries of our ancestors, and to discover for ourselves how good and worthwhile those luxuries were and still are.

*

One of the points I have looked out for when making a selection of recipes for this chapter, as indeed throughout this book, has been the quantities in which the recipes are given, so that, although there may be repetition of the theme, there is little in the *amount* which will be produced by any given recipe. For some, a recipe based on 3½ lb of flour may be too much, for others, cooking for a family or for a special festivity, it will be right. Those who need these confections in small quantities only will find plenty of recipes based on just ½ lb to 1 lb of flour. Some recipes call for a high proportion of sugar, others for very little. It is in this respect that discrepancies are most marked, some of the modern recipes allowing, as noted above, more than is necessary, and certainly far more than would have been used even a hundred years ago. For example, I have come across a modern Yorkshire spiced loaf in which there is 1 lb of sugar as well as 3 lb of fruit to 2 lb of flour. This is almost solid sweet matter held together by flour, eggs and fat, while the Yorkshire spice loaf, on p. 454, although eggless, contains 2 lb 3 oz of fruit and ½ lb of sugar to 2½ lb of flour. Compare these proportions with those given in Frederick Bishop's recipe for breakfast cake, published in 1856, and probably therefore of much earlier origin, in which the proportions are 3 lb of fruit and only ½ lb of sugar to 7 lb of flour. Admittedly, he adds a quarter pint of brandy, but that was presumably to assist the cake's keeping qualities, since he notes that it will remain good for three months. I think it important to bear in mind that in recipes containing a high fruit content the amounts of additional sugar could be drastically reduced, and in many cases eliminated entirely.

Not all the modern versions of the old recipes are over-sugared. The lardy cakes are moderate in this respect, and the Northumbrian harvest tea cake on p. 463, an interesting plaited loaf, is barely sweetened at all.

Proportions of yeast are also uneven, but with mixtures enriched with fruit and fat this is a frequent inconsistency, owing to the different methods by which the dough may be raised. In cases where the amounts seem either inadequate or excessive I have added my own notes.

· SPICE MIXTURES, FLAVOURINGS, SPICED SUGARS ·

All Housekeepers, in the Country especially, should lay in their Groceries at best hand, and be provided with store of Nutmegs, Cinnamon, Ginger, Cloves, Mace, Jamaica Pepper, Long Pepper, Black pepper, etc.'

The Family Magazine, London, 1741

'The flavouring of cakes is a delicate branch of the baker's art, requiring the exercise of his nicest faculties . . . A little too much flavour is often nauseating, whereas not enough is very unsatisfactory.'

J. Thompson Gill, *The Complete Bread, Cake and Cracker Baker*,
5th edn, Chicago, 1881

A blend of mixed sweet spices is used to flavour a great many of the cakes, fruit breads and buns described in this book. A bought blend of 'pudding' or 'cake' spice is satisfactory only up to a point, in that the spice packers and retailers force the customer into buying far too large a supply at one time, so that the spices have lost their aromas long, long before the jar is used up. It becomes almost impossible to judge how much to use to produce the required flavour. The remedy is to blend and grind one's own mixture, in sufficient quantity to last for just a few weeks. Using a small electric coffee mill kept especially for spices nothing is easier than to have always to 'best hand' a store of freshly ground mixed spice.

The sweet spices are cinnamon, nutmeg, cloves, ginger, to which coriander seeds and mace are sometimes added. Pepper in some form – white, black, Jamaica (allspice) – is nearly always included in sweet spice blends, since it helps to bring out and also to hold the aromas of the other spices. By using white peppercorns instead of black or the milder allspice berries, an excellent blend can be achieved, one that has good lasting qualities. The pepper must not be overdone, though; there should not be enough for it to be apparent once the cakes or buns are cooked. Cloves too should be kept in small proportion. They are very expensive, and very powerful, so there should be little temptation to use too many. On the other hand, without cloves a mixed spice blend tends to be rather feeble. Cinnamon is a highly important ingredient, and one that, once ground, quickly loses its potency. (Try grinding a piece of cinnamon bark on its own. When freshly ground it is almost overpowering, and even difficult to recognize as cinnamon. Next day it is tamed. A fortnight later it has faded.)

· SWEET SPICE BLEND ·

The following formula is one I have worked out and have used frequently for spicing hot cross buns, currant loaves and many of the cakes for which recipes are given in this book.

Proportions are: two parts of nutmeg; two parts of white or black peppercorns or, for those who like a milder blend, allspice berries; one part of cinnamon bark; one part of whole cloves; one part of dried ginger root.

In both manageable and easily measurable terms this means ¼ oz each of nutmeg (i.e. 1 large nutmeg) and white peppercorns or allspice berries (approximately 3 level teaspoons), ⅛ oz of cinnamon bark (one 6 inch stick), $\frac{1}{8}$oz of whole cloves (2 scant teaspoons, about 30 cloves), $\frac{1}{8}$oz of dried ginger root (a piece about 2 inches long).

To the above mixture a fraction of freshly ground cumin seed can be added. This is particularly successful for hot cross buns. But make this addition only as and when the spice is to be used. Ground cumin quickly loses its aroma.

Although I find that my small and very ancient Mouli coffee mill does not grind spices as finely as the mixtures of commerce, it does reduce them to a powder quite fine enough for the spicing of cakes.

To keep home-ground spices, turn them, as soon as the mixture is ground, into small glass jars with well-fitting stoppers, preferably of ground glass, and store the jars in a cupboard. They should be kept away from the light, not left out on shelves or racks in the kitchen. Remember to label them, putting the date as well as the blend. In this way there will be no confusion, and less danger of stale spices being used.

· A FRENCH BLEND ·

An old French '*épices douces*' or mild spice mixture for pastrycooks is the formula given in La Varenne's famous *Pastissier françois*, first published in 1655. The spices are the same as in my own blend, the proportions being two parts of ginger to one each of pepper, cloves, nutmeg and cinnamon.

· A CORIANDER BLEND ·

This is a useful variation on the first sweet spice mixture: 1 teaspoon each of white peppercorns and whole cloves, 2 teaspoons of coriander seeds, about half a nutmeg, $\frac{1}{2}$ inch of cinnamon bark and a piece of dry ginger root about the size of a finger nail.

· A BLEND FOR SCOTCH CHRISTMAS BUN ·

This is given by Emma Roberts in her revised 1841 edition of Mrs Rundell's *A New System of Domestic Cookery*, and advised specifically for the spicing of the fruit for a Scotch Bun: 1 drachm ($\frac{1}{16}$oz) of cloves, 1 large nutmeg, $\frac{1}{2}$oz of allspice berries, $\frac{1}{2}$oz of dried ginger root.

· TO MAKE CLOVE OR CINNAMON SUGAR ·

'Lay peeces of sugar in close boxes amongst stickes of cinnamon, cloves, etc. and in a short time it will purchase both the taste and sent of the spice.'

Sir Hugh Plat, *Delightes for Ladies*, 1609

· VANILLA AND ALMOND FLAVOURINGS ·

It may be noticed that neither vanilla sugar, vanilla essence nor vanilla in any form is called for in any recipe in this book. This is because vanilla has not, or should not have, any place in cakes and breads flavoured with other spices and enriched with fruit. Vanilla, true vanilla that is to say, is an exquisite flavouring on its own, but quarrels with other strong flavours. As for synthetic vanilla essence, it is sickeningly all-pervading, and ruins everything into which it goes. Almond essence, provided it is the true, concentrated essence of bitter almonds, can be used in yeast tea cakes and buns, but is very difficult to find in this country. When you do find it, remember that it is very strong and must be used in the smallest quantities. Imitation almond flavouring is as repulsive as artificial vanilla.

· ADAPTING TRADITIONAL RECIPES: A NOTE ·

Nobody will deny that there's a certain monotony, not to put it too unkindly, about our English yeast dough specialities. The sugar, the butter, the lard, the currants and the candied peel, the caraway seeds and the sweet spices recur in a thousand recipes, each one only a slight variation on the last. Many of them originated as a spin-off from the weekly household bread-baking, when a portion of dough was kept back to be made into a bread-cake with lard and sugar and currants, to be baked in time for the children's tea. I think that sometimes we should take out these old recipes, give them a good shake, put them to work on a different job, inject them with a completely new lease of life.

Suppose, for example, that olive oil were to be substituted for the lard added to a basic bread dough for one of these tea-time cakes, and that, once it was rolled and divided into rounds or squares, or made into rolls or bap shapes, it were to be spread with cooked onions or anchovy fillets or a freshly made tomato sauce, then quickly baked, what would you get? It's as obvious as that. These dough specialities of ours are simply the sugary equivalents of the pizza and other savoury breads of Italy and the Mediterranean countries. So why don't we take a leaf or two out of the cookery books of those countries and turn some of our over-sweetened and too-rich dough cakes into the cheese and other savoury morsels more acceptable today?

The Italians, for example, have an agreeable method of making *pizzette* or miniature pizzas which can be offered with wine or the vermouth aperitifs they like so much. Such little things are infinitely adaptable. If you have once mastered the making of a good light dough from one of the recipes in the pizza chapter, all you need to do is to stamp out small rounds with a cutter, spread them with the fillings of your choice – two or three different ones can be used – and bake them for 15 minutes. (These *pizzette* also make a nice and original first course for lunch.)

Then there are plenty of ways of enclosing a slice of cheese or other savoury filling, such as a home-made sausage meat, in a small roll of dough or in a bap type of roll, or of making a spinach and cream cheese mixture – rather as for ravioli – and using it as a filling for small covered pies made with yeast pastry, as described for Windermere and Ulverston Fair cakes. And don't forget Mrs Raffald's delightful instructions to 'toast a light wigg' and pour hot melted cheese over it. There are also the galettes described in the recipe quoted from Lizzie Heritage on p. 492; they are very good as they are, that is, as a kind of dried fruit pizza, and I think the recipe would be equally successful with cheese and little pieces of bacon, or pork cracklings – the Genoese have a flat bread with cracklings, salt and oil; another version is strewn with fennel seeds.

The caraway seeds in wigg cakes are a reminder of how good are many of the central European brown and rye breads spiced with dill or aniseeds, and of what an excellent combination they make with cheese and wine. There's no need, therefore, to confine dough cakes and the like to white flour. Some of them can be made with 81 or 85 per cent wheatmeal. I don't see why we should not bring about a welcome renewal of our old recipes, forget that the English tradition is to have everything as sweet and as white as possible, and branch off in another direction.

· BAKING DAY IN AN EAST SUSSEX FARMHOUSE ·

'Wednesday was baking day. It was a day of days, when all the baking of the week, of bread and cakes, and pastry for tarts and puddings and heaven knows what else was done in the big brick oven. First a large fire was lighted in the oven itself; "two faggots and three bats" was the prescription, bats being mighty logs. At seven o'clock a shaving of wood which had been dipped in brimstone and set alight by a tinder, was applied to the faggots, and the fire would be carefully tended until the wood was consumed and the ashes were red hot. They were then spread evenly over the oven, so that the bricks on its floor should be evenly heated.

'A critical moment having come, when the temperature of the oven was precisely to Grandma's liking, and the flour had been duly prepared and was at hand, the ashes were scraped out, the oven was swept with the green brooms supplied by the "broom squire",[1] these having been dipped in water, and then all was ready, as Grandma would say, to "set in".

'The flour was made from wheat grown on the farm, and mixed with boiled potatoes, these having been rubbed through a colander and softened by milk, and a special yeast was used, made from a receipt of the miller's wife. Large loaves and small were first baked, and they would keep fresh for a week or more. Always the bread was kept for three days before it was served at table, so that it should last the longer. Then came the turn of the cakes and pies. Twenty of them at least would be at hand to go into the great red hot oven after the bread. Beef pies, mutton pies, pork pies – and then the tarts. These were made from the fruits of the garden and hedgerows, according to the season. Through most weeks of the year the famous apple turnovers were made, each a foot long. The early spring was the time for the equally famous sorrel pies of Stantons.

'Glorious were the cakes, and infinite their variety. Large and plain household cakes were made more or less haphazard, or by guesswork as to quantities, but the superior cakes were made with the same care a doctor might bestow on the mixing of dangerous drugs. Receipts, old and trusty, were followed to the letter, and nothing but the best and freshest butter, milk, cream, eggs and fruit went to the making of the rich and luscious whole.

1. The name given to the travelling merchant who made and sold the green brooms used for sweeping out the oven.

'The loaves of bread would be ranged round the back and sides of the oven; next would be set the large superior cakes, then the pies, and in front of these the little cakes and pastries. Among the cakes would be those called fleedy, which Grandma's daughters make to this day: concocted from what is called the fleed of pigs flesh, and resembling the Hampshire lardie cakes. Such cakes needing little baking would be taken from the oven by a quick sleight of hand, and the door banged to again, so that no iota of heat should be wasted.'

Marcus Woodward, *The Mistress of Stantons Farm*,[1] 1938

· THE VILLAGE BAKERY: PREPARING THE CAKE HOOPS ·

'Cakes went into the oven after the bread had been removed; they required a gradually declining heat. The square or oblong cakes were baked in separate tins; but most of the round cakes were baked in round hoops of tin placed on a long iron tray. Before the tins were ready to receive the cakes they had to be greased, and for this purpose a spare tin was kept filled with lard and a piece of cloth ready in it. This tin was placed in the oven for a few minutes, in order to melt the lard, and then every tin and hoop was quickly wiped round inside with the cloth. Large sheets of paper were placed on the iron trays and a strip of paper was placed around the inside of each tin hoop. To line the hoops with paper the baker first cut the strips to the right size and then, twisting them with a quick movement around his left hand, dropped them into place. The whole operation was completed in about two minutes. The standard cake was the plain "dough" cake; but twice a week a rather more elaborate selection was produced – madeiras, plain buns and a few more tasty varieties. From time to time there was an order for a Christmas or wedding cake ... Our own pies were often baked in the bakehouse oven; but I never remember seeing a joint of any kind cooked in it and was rather surprised, when I went to live in Somerset, to find that it was a common practice in the villages to have joints cooked at the local bakehouse.

'I never learnt any baking; my jobs in the bakehouse were always of a very simple nature. One I liked very much was removing the round cakes from their tin hoops on the long trays. In nearly every case a little of the cake had oozed out between the hoop and the tray and this I was allowed to eat. It was very sweet and crisp and formed a nice snack at about

1. Stantons Farm was at East Chiltington, five miles from Lewes.

eleven o'clock in the morning, which was about the time the men knocked off for a few minutes rest and a mouthful of bread and cheese.'

H. S. Joyce, *I was Born in the Country*, 1946

The author is writing of his father's bakery in a village on the Dorsetshire Stour. He recounts that he was nine years old at the period he describes.

· ENGLISH CURRANT BREAD ·

Although not a recipe with any specific regional association, this is a typical English spiced fruit bread, made with $\frac{3}{4}$ lb of strong plain flour, $\frac{1}{2}$ oz of yeast, $\frac{1}{4}$ pint of milk, 2 oz of butter, 1 oz of soft brown sugar, 4 oz of currants, 1 egg, 1 teaspoon of salt. Spices are powdered cinnamon, mace, allspice and nutmeg in equal quantities plus a very small proportion of ground cloves. The total maximum quantity should be 2 level teaspoons. Ready-mixed pudding or cake spice can be used, but anyone who grinds their own spices will find that the mixture suggested for hot cross buns, on p. 430, gives an immeasurably better flavour and aroma. One teaspoonful of this mixture, or a maximum of $1\frac{1}{2}$, will be ample. For glazing the loaf: 2 tablespoons of cream or milk mixed with 2 of sugar, heated together in a small pan.

Put the flour in a bowl. Mix in the salt, sugar and spices. Warm the milk. With a little of it mix the yeast to a cream. Add the softened butter to the rest of the warmed milk.

Make a well in the flour, pour in the yeast, then break in the egg; mix all to a lithe dough with the milk and butter. Finally, add the warmed currants, mixing them carefully so that they are well distributed throughout the dough.

Cover the bowl and leave the dough to rise for $1\frac{1}{2}$ hours.

Have ready a warmed and buttered loaf tin of $1\frac{1}{4}$ pint capacity. Break down the risen dough, knead it very lightly for a few seconds. If it is too wet, sprinkle in a little more flour. Put the dough in the prepared tin, cover it, let it rise for 30 to 45 minutes, until it reaches the top of the tin. Bake in the centre of a fairly hot oven, 425°F, 220°C, gas no. 7, for 15 minutes, then reduce the heat to 375°F, 190°C, gas no. 5, move the loaf to a lower shelf and bake for another 15 minutes. As soon as you take the tin from the oven, brush the top of the loaf with the hot milk and sugar glaze. Leave for a few minutes before turning the loaf out of the tin. Stand it across the tin to cool.

Notes: 1. Because of the spices and the brown sugar, this currant loaf comes out a nice pale coffee colour. If you prefer a whiter loaf, use caster sugar.

2. Those who dislike white flour will find that 81 or 85 per cent wheatmeal can be substituted with perfect success.

3. The best shape of tin to use for this, and most other fruit bread, is a rather shallow wide one, such as the farmhouse shape shown in the drawing on pp. 207 and 425.

4. The above recipe makes only one medium size loaf. To make it on a larger scale increase the quantities to 2¼ lb or 1 kg of flour, 1¼ oz or 35 g of yeast, 12 oz or 340 g of currants, 2 oz or 60 g of sugar, 2 eggs, 6 oz or 170 g of butter, ½ to ¾ pint or 280 to 420 g of milk, 2 teaspoons of salt and 3 level teaspoons of spice. These amounts should fill two loaf tins of 3¼ pint or 1¾ litre capacity.

Equivalent metric quantities: strong plain flour 340 g, yeast 15 g, milk 150 g, butter 60 g, soft brown sugar 30 g, currants 120 g, eggs 1, salt 1 teaspoon; spices: *powdered cinnamon, mace, allspice and nutmeg in equal quantities, plus a very small proportion of ground cloves, total quantity not more than 2 level teaspoons;* for glazing: *cream or milk 2 tablespoons, mixed with sugar 2 tablespoons. Tin size: loaf tin with a capacity of 0·75 litre.*

· BARA BRITH ·

This is the famous speckled or fruit bread of Wales, of which there are a great many versions. This one, without eggs, is based on a recipe given in *A Welsh Welcome*,[1] a small collection of Welsh dishes published by the Wales Gas Board. I have reduced the proportion of sugar, as the fruit already provides its own sweetening, and use the home-blended spice mixture given on p. 430. The result is a really delicious fruit bread.

1 lb of strong plain bread flour or 85 per cent wheatmeal, ½ oz of yeast, 3 oz of butter, ¼ pint of milk, 2 oz of soft brown sugar, 3 oz each of currants and seedless raisins, 1 oz of candied peel, 1 teaspoon of salt, ½ teaspoon of mixed sweet or pudding spice.

1. Fifth revised edn, 1969 (first published 1953).

Equivalent metric quantities: strong plain bread flour, or 85 per cent wheatmeal, 450 g; yeast 15 g; butter 85 g; milk 150 g; soft brown sugar 60 g; currants 85 g; seedless rasins 85 g; candied peel 30 g; salt 1 teaspoon; mixed sweet or pudding spice ½ teaspoon. Tin size: a loaf tin of 1·5 litre capacity.

Put the flour and salt in a heat-proof bowl and warm it in the oven for a few minutes.

Warm the milk in a small saucepan. Pour a little over the yeast to cream it. Cut the butter in small pieces and melt it in the warm milk. Pour the creamed yeast into the warmed flour. Mix to a fairly light dough with the milk and butter. Cover and leave to rise until doubled in bulk. If all the ingredients, and the bowl, were warm when the dough was mixed this will take only 30 to 40 minutes, at normal room temperature.

Now put the dried fuit, chopped candied peel, sugar and spice into a small bowl or on an ovenproof plate and warm it in the oven.

Work the fruit mixture into the dough, using your hands. As always with fruit bread, try to ensure that the fruit and sugar are well and evenly distributed. If the dough seems too stiff, add just a little extra milk.

Put the mixture into a *warmed* and well-buttered loaf tin, of 2½ to 3 pint capacity. Pat it into shape, so that it is evenly spread in the tin. Cover with a sheet of polythene or a light cloth and leave until the dough has risen to the top of the tin. This will take 1 to 1½ hours.

Bake on the centre shelf of a medium hot oven, 400° to 425°F, 205° to 220°C, gas nos. 6 or 7, for 20 to 30 minutes, covering the top with a piece of foil or greaseproof paper during the final 10 minutes of cooking.

Leave the loaf to cool a little before attempting to turn it out of the tin.

Bara brith is eaten with butter, although when it is fresh, butter is unnecessary and the loaf is nicer without it.

Notes and variations: 1. The relatively short baking time produces a loaf which is moist and not overbaked on the top, a common fault with fruit breads.

2. Instead of the candied peel, a few dried apricots can be used. Half a dozen will be ample. They should be cut into very small slivers. Modern dried apricots will not need to be softened in water.

3. A sweeter, richer version of bara brith, for a 3 to 3½ pint tin, specifies 3 lb or 1,350 g of flour, ¾ lb or 340 g each of sugar and lard or butter, 1 lb or 450 g each of currants and raisins, ¼ lb or 120 g of candied peel, ½ teaspoon of pudding spice, 2 eggs, salt, milk, 1 oz or 30 g of yeast.

4. The raisins are characteristic and should not be omitted or replaced by other fruit. In Wales, all the grocery shops sell pound packets of ready-mixed fruit – raisins, sultanas, currants and chopped peel.

5. In Wales, or at any rate in South and West Wales, bara brith is to be bought in bakeries and markets. Examples I have bought have not been creditable. Most of them are chemically aerated, not yeast-leavened. Housewives use mainly self-raising flour, the result being cake rather than bread. One useful trick to know is the way they leave the fruit steeping overnight in cold tea, so that it is well plumped up by the time the bara brith is mixed.

· BARMBRACK ·

This is the Irish version of spice bread. The recipe comes from Helen Edden's *County Recipes of Old England*, published by *Country Life* (1929). An almost identical recipe is in Lady Harriet St Clair's *Dainty Dishes* (1866). The allowance of caraway seeds seems to be enormous; I would reduce it by at least half and include instead a small proportion of mixed sweet spices.

'½ *quartern of dough, 6 oz sugar, 4 eggs, 2 oz of caraway seeds, ¼ lb butter.*

Equivalent metric quantities: dough 780 g, sugar 170 g, eggs 4, caraway seeds 60 g, butter 120 g.

'Melt the butter and beat it into the dough with the sugar, then beat in the eggs one at a time, and lastly the caraway seeds. Make into a round loaf or put in a large cake tin and let it rise, then bake about 40 minutes.'

Notes and variations: 1. A half-quartern or quart of flour is 1¾ lb or 780 g; to make a half-quartern of leavened dough about 1¼ lb or 550 g of flour is needed, with ½ oz or 15 g of yeast, 10 to 12 oz or 280 to 340 g of water and ¾ oz or 20 g of salt.

2. Currants are often added to the dough for barmbrack.

3. Originally, barmbrack was baked in a pot over a peat fire like ordinary bread, and it is still traditionally made in a round cake shape rather than in a loaf tin.

4. Recipes for barmbrack with chemically aerated dough abound in cookery books. To call this version barmbrack seems rather sad, since its name so clearly means that it was originally a bread fermented with barm or ale yeast.

· IRISH BRADE BREACHED ·

'To as much flour as will make two quartern loaves[1] put a half-pound of melted butter. Make the dough with fresh yeast, and when it has risen, mix in a half-pound of beat sugar, a half pound of currants, picked, cleaned, and dried; the same quantity of stoned raisins; a few sweet almonds blanched and chopped, and some candied orange-peel sliced.

'Mould and bake the loaves. They may be of any size.'

> Mistress Margaret Dods, *The Cook and Housewife's Manual*,
> 4th edn, 1829 (first published 1826)

According to the author, this speckled bread was the holiday cake of Munster. In a footnote she adds that the loaves should be baked in a dome-shaped fluted mould or Turk's-cap, but 'look still more imposing at holiday times, formed like large respectable household loaves'.

· CORNISH SAFFRON CAKE ·

Cornish saffron cake is really a spiced bread, delicate and light, and usually made without eggs. My recipe was evolved from several variations given in *Cornish Recipes Ancient and Modern*, compiled by Edith Martin and first published in 1929 by the Cornwall Federation of Women's Institutes, and from two other variations in a more recent and equally enterprising collection called *Devonshire Flavour*, published in 1970 by the Exeter branch of the Y.W.C.A.

It was from a recipe given in the latter book and attributed by Professor Arthur Hutchings[2] to his Aunt Polly that I learned a valuable detail which no other recipe had made clear: that the little bits of saffron in the infusion which colours the cake are not strained out. This piece of information tells us that the good West Country cooks of the past used, and understood the advantages of, whole saffron filaments as opposed to ready-powdered saffron. Perhaps also it was a case of proper pride in the use of the best ingredients, just as at one time the specks of vanilla were left in ice cream to show that it had been flavoured with the bean rather than with essence. Further, Professor Hutchings adds that 'the true saffron yeast cake of the West Country should not be confused with travesties sold under the same name. They are not yeast cakes and they

1. In other words, about 7 lb of flour.
2. Professor of Music at Exeter University.

often have no saffron, but are coloured yellow and have a disgusting sickly taste of vanilla and far too much sweetening.' Having myself encountered those false, shameful saffron cakes when attempting to track down authentic West Country dishes, I can sympathize with the Professor's anger at the debauching of this fine old speciality, familiar to him since childhood.

The proportions I give here make a 2lb cake to be baked in one rectangular loaf tin of approximately 3 pint capacity or in two smaller farmhouse-type tins, as in the drawing on p. 207, each of 1¼ to 1½ pint capacity.

To 1 lb of plain flour, other ingredients are ½ oz of yeast, ¼ lb of butter or the equivalent in thick heavy cream, 2 oz of caster sugar, 2 oz each of sultanas and currants, rather over ¼ pint of milk, 1 teaspoon of salt, a scant saltspoon each of freshly grated nutmeg, powdered cinnamon and mixed sweet spice, approximately ½ teaspoon of saffron filaments. For glazing the cake an extra 2 tablespoons of milk and 1 tablespoon of sugar.

Equivalent metric quantities: plain flour 450 g, yeast 15 g, butter or thick cream 120 g, caster sugar 60 g, sultanas 60 g, currants 60 g, milk rather over 150 g, salt 1 teaspoon, grated nutmeg, powdered cinnamon and mixed sweet spice a scant saltspoon each, saffron filaments approximately ½ teaspoon, extra milk 2 tablespoons and sugar 1 tablespoon (for glazing). Tin size: one rectangular loaf tin of approximately 1·5 litre capacity, or two smaller farmhouse-type tins each of 0·75 to 1 litre capacity.

First prepare the saffron, and the yeast. Take about half the ¼ pint of milk and heat it to boiling point. Put the saffron filaments on an ovenproof saucer or small plate, place in a hot oven for about 5 minutes. Crumble the filaments into a coffee cup, pour a little of the hot milk over them and leave to infuse. Within 10 minutes the saffron will have dyed the milk a beautiful pale marigold colour.

Pour the remainder of the heated milk – which by this time will be only lukewarm – over the yeast and mix it to a cream.

Weigh out the flour, sugar, sultanas, currants and butter or cream.

Put the flour, sugar and salt into a warmed mixing bowl. Sprinkle in the dry spices. Stir in the creamed yeast. Now beat in the softened butter or the cream. This is best done with your hands. When it is well amalgamated, add the saffron infusion and the remainder of the milk. A little extra may be needed. Much depends upon the flour. The dough should be soft but not runny. Finally mix in the warmed currants and sultanas and make sure that they are well distributed throughout the dough. Cover the bowl, leave the dough to rise for a couple of hours, or longer if it is more convenient.

When the dough has at least doubled in volume, break it down very lightly, sprinkle it with flour, transfer it to the warmed and buttered tin, pat it into shape and leave it to rise for the second time. This is a slow-rising dough and will take a minimum of 45 minutes to an hour to return to life and reach almost to the top of the tin. When sufficiently risen, bake the cake in the centre of a fairly hot oven, 375° to 400°F, 190° to 205°C, gas nos. 5 to 6, for 15 minutes, then move the tin to the lower shelf and leave it for a further 10 to 15 minutes at the same temperature.

As soon as you take the cake from the oven, brush it with the heated sugar and milk glaze. Leave it for about 15 minutes before turning out of the tin.

Saffron cake is at its best eaten when freshly baked and just cooled, although it *can* be reheated in a very low oven. It is for this reason that it is important not to overbake it in the first instance. This particular cake makes an original and subtle accompaniment to a glass of sweet Sauternes or any dessert wine of your fancy. A Madeira or the charming Italian soft white Orvieto called *amabile* would be other possibilities.

Notes: 1. Saffron cake freezes well.

2. An interesting piece of information concerning saffron cake was given to me by a reader, Mrs Havard, of Llandysul in Cardiganshire, Wales.

'In North Cardiganshire,' writes Mrs Havard, 'where the lead mines were worked early this century, the Cornish miners who came to work there had brought with them a taste for saffron cake. This has become a traditional recipe in the area around the Nantymuch Dam in the Plynlimon range, as has also a large "Cornish Pasty" made with Welsh ham instead of with fresh meat.

'I have happy memories of visits to an aunt on a farm in those hills, of afternoons picking winberries and coming back to both these treats, the Pasty made on a huge blue-patterned willow dish . . .'

· DEVONSHIRE CAKE ·

This recipe, adapted from one given by T. F. Garrett in his *Encyclopaedia of Practical Cookery* (1899), is a variation on Cornish saffron cake, and produces a similar saffron and fruit bread, very light and good. It is a particularly useful recipe because the dough, leavened with only a very little yeast, can be left to rise overnight, or for about 8 to 10 hours.

1 lb of strong plain flour, ¼ oz of yeast creamed with a little water, ¼ lb of thick solid cream¹ or butter, a generous half teaspoon of saffron filaments, ¼ lb of currants, 1 tablespoon of chopped candied citron peel or ginger in syrup or a mixture of the two, 2 oz of sugar, 2 whole eggs, ¼ pint of milk, 1 teaspoon of mixed sweet pudding spice, 1 teaspoon of salt.

Equivalent metric quantities: strong plain flour 450 g, yeast approximately 10 g, thick cream or butter 120 g, saffron filaments ½ teaspoon, currants 125 g, candied citron peel or ginger in syrup or a mixture 1 tablespoon, sugar 60 g, eggs 2, milk 150 g, mixed sweet pudding spice 1 teaspoon, salt 1 teaspoon. Tin size: two tins of 1 litre capacity each or one large tin of 1·5 to 2 litre capacity.

Mix the prepared yeast, slightly warmed flour and cream to a dough and prepare the saffron as for Cornish saffron cake. Beat the eggs in the milk with the saffron infusion, leaving in the filaments. Warm the currants very slightly. Add these and the chopped peel or ginger and the sugar to the dough. Moisten with the beaten egg and milk and sprinkle in the spice and salt. The dough should be fairly stiff. Cover the bowl. Leave overnight to rise. Next morning break down the dough and knead it briefly. Warm and butter two tins of 1½ pint capacity each. One large tin of 3 to 3½ pint capacity can also be used.

Turn the dough into the tins. Cover them and leave until the dough rises to the tops. This takes approximately 1 hour in warm weather, anything up to 2½ hours in winter.

Bake as for the Cornish saffron cake in a fairly hot oven, 375° to 400°F, 190° to 205°C, gas nos. 5 or 6, for the first 15 minutes, and for another 10 to 15 minutes, with the tops protected by paper, at 350°F, 180°C, gas no. 4.

The tops of the cakes can be glazed in the same way as the Cornish version.

Leave the cakes in their tins for about 10 minutes before turning them out on to a rack to cool.

1. In the original recipe clotted cream is specified. When using ordinary double cream, allow 4 to 5 fluid oz.

Notes and variations: 1. This excellent method of preparing dough for fruit breads can be used for many of the recipes in this chapter on occasions when it is more convenient to leave the dough overnight than for a short period.

2. Instead of candied citron or stem ginger, the grated peel of a large lemon makes a delicious flavouring.

3. The baking time given for this cake is intentionally on the short side, so that it can be re-warmed under a bowl or cover when needed. I have found that if anything the cake is better when re-warmed after a few days – up to a week but not longer – than when freshly baked. The small proportion of yeast used in this mixture and the long, slow rising account for its keeping qualities.

SAFFRON CAKES
OF THE SEVENTEENTH, EIGHTEENTH AND
· NINETEENTH CENTURIES ·

Of course, saffron cake has not always been made in a loaf tin, since this type of tin was a nineteenth-century development, nor has it always been regarded as an exclusively West Country speciality. In the seventeenth and eighteenth centuries cakes similar to the modern Cornish version were called simply saffron cakes or perhaps just 'an excellent cake' as in the seventeenth-century Digby recipe quoted on p. 446. A good eighteenth-century example is Hannah Glasse's saffron cake reproduced below. This comes from her *Compleat Confectioner*, first published *c.* 1760, some twelve years after her more famous *Art of Cookery Made Plain and Easy*. As so often, Mrs Glasse rather overdoes the spicing of her saffron cake, specifying ¼ oz of mixed cloves and mace plus no less than 3 oz of caraway seeds, a pennyworth each of cinnamon and saffron and a pound of sugar to a cake made with 3½ lb of flour. I don't know how much cinnamon or saffron could be bought for a penny at that period. Probably considerably more than we would now think necessary. And although there is no fruit in this recipe a pound of sugar to 3½ lb of flour was still an ample allowance for Mrs Glasse's day. I have often wondered whether Mrs Glasse did not have family interests in the East India Company or with the West Indies spice and sugar trade, and hence always had these commodities at her disposal. The lavish quantities she used, plus her preoccupation with recipes for foods suitable for carrying on long sea voyages, her efforts to imitate mango and other Indian chutneys and her recipe for a chicken curry – one of the first to appear in print in England[1] – all seem to point to some such connection.

In mitigation of her heavy hand with the spices, Mrs Glasse does suggest that you may leave out the caraway seeds, and says, not for the only time in her recipes, that she prefers to omit them. It is clear that she did not really care for them, so their inclusion must have been the taste of the day – the beginnings perhaps of the seed-cake mania of the later years of the eighteenth century.

By the nineteenth century, the saffron cake has become 'the famous saffron cake'. A recipe for this, noted in the Gibson/Pegus MS.,[2] differs from most in that it specifies stiffly whisked egg whites to be added to the risen dough just before the cakes, which are to be baked 'on a Paper', are set in the oven. The quantities given in this recipe – again there is no fruit – are based on about 12 lb of flour, 2 lb of butter, one only of sugar, and 14 eggs. Apart from saffron the only spice is caraway seeds. Reduced to manageable quantities, the Gibson recipe, which has some affinity with the Bath cakes and buns of the eighteenth century, should produce excellent straightforward saffron tea cakes or one larger cake.

· SAFFRON CAKE ·

'Take a quarter of a peck [3½ lb] of fine flour, a pound and a half of butter, three ounces of carraway seeds, and six eggs; beat well a quarter of an ounce of cloves and mace together very fine, a pennyworth of cinnamon beat, a pound of sugar, a pennyworth of rose water, a pennyworth of saffron, a pint and half of yeast, and a quart of milk; mix all together lightly with your hands thus; first boil the milk and butter, scum off the butter, and mix it with the flour and a little of the milk, stir the yeast into the rest, and strain it; mix it with your flour, put in your seed and spice, rose water, tincture of saffron, sugar, and eggs; beat all up with your hands very lightly, and bake it in a hoop or pan, minding to butter the pan well; it will take an hour and a half in a quick oven; you may leave out the seed if you chuse it, and I think it the best,'

Hannah Glasse, *The Compleat Confectioner*, 1772 (first published *c.* 1760)

1. In *The Art of Cookery Made Plain and Easy*, 1747.
2. See the recipe for a common plumb cake, p. 460.

· TO MAKE THE FAMOUS SAFFRON CAKE, *c.* 1810 ·

'Take 7 quarts [12¼ lb] of Flour, 2 pounds of fresh Butter, one pound of Sugar, rub the Butter and Sugar in the Flour with an ounce of Carraway seeds, a quarter of an ounce[1] of Saffron, steep it the night before in sack or Milk, the Saffron to be first dried and finely powdered. Then take 14 eggs, beat the yolks of them by themselves, take a pint and a half of good fresh Barm, making a hole in the middle of the flour, mix the yolks and Saffron together, and put it into the hole after the Barm, and then cover them with the flour, set it by the fire till it rises, whip up the whites and work it to a light paste, bake them on a Paper, prick them to the bottom.'

The Gibson/Pegus MS.[2]

· TO MAKE AN EXCELLENT CAKE ·

'To a peck [14 lb] of fine flower, take six pounds of fresh butter, which must be tenderly melted, ten pounds of Currants, of Cloves and Mace, half an ounce of each, an ounce of Cinnamon, half an ounce of Nutmegs, four ounces of Sugar, one pint of Sack mixed with a quart at least of thick barm of Ale (as soon as it is settled, to have the thick fall to the bottom, which will be when it is about two days old) half a pint of Rosewater, half a quarter of an ounce of Saffron.

'Then make your paste, strewing the spices, finely beaten, upon the flower. Then put the melted butter (but even just melted) to it; then the barm, and other liquors: and put it into the oven well heated presently.

'For the better baking of it, put it in a hoop, and let it stand in the oven one hour and half.

'You Ice the Cake with the whites of two Eggs, a small quantity of Rose-water, and some Sugar.'

The Closet of the Eminently Learned Sir Kenelm Digby Knight Opened, 1669

1. This is a very lavish allowance – too lavish – for 12 lb of flour. Even Sir Kenelm Digby, in the next recipe quoted, specifies only 'half a quarter of an ounce' to his 14 lb of flour, and ⅛ oz is still a large quantity.

2. More details about the Gibson/Pegus MS. and another recipe from it will be found on p. 460.

The Digby recipe is a richer version of today's saffron cakes. Quantities are not difficult to reduce to manageable proportions. Divide very roughly by six and for the main ingredients you arrive at 2½ lb of flour, 1 lb of butter, approximately 1½ lb of currants and about 3 oz of sherry. The saffron and spices would be reduced to ½ teaspoons and the rosewater to 2 tablespoons. An ounce or more of modern yeast would be needed for so rich a mixture, and a mixture of milk and water to replace the liquor of the ale-barm. Sugar could be omitted altogether, for Sir Kenelm's recipe specifies only 4 oz, less than 1 oz per pound of flour, and the currants supply ample sweetening.

Equivalent metric quantities: flour 1·125 kg, butter 450 g, currants approximately 670 g, sherry about 85 g, cloves, mace, cinnamon, nutmeg and saffron ½ teaspoon each, rosewater 2 tablespoons, yeast 30 g, milk and water mixed.

THE COUNTESSE OF RUTLANDS RECEIPT
OF MAKING THE RARE BANBURY CAKE WHICH WAS
SO MUCH PRAISED AT HER DAUGHTERS (THE RIGHT
· HONOURABLE THE LADY CHAWORTHS) WEDDING ·

'Take a peck[1] of fine flower, and halfe an ounce of large Mace, half an ounce of Nutmegs, and halfe an ounce of Cinnamon, your Cinnamon and Nutmegs must be sifted through a Searce,[2] two pounds of Butter, half a score of Eggs, put out four of the whites of them, something above a pint of good Ale-yeast, beate your Eggs very well and straine them with your yeaste, and a little warme water into your flowre, and stirre them together, then put your butter cold in little Lumpes: The water you knead withal must be scalding hot, if you will make it good past, the which having done, lay the past to rise in a warme cloth a quarter of an hour, or thereupon; Then put in ten pounds of Currans, and a little Muske[3] and Ambergreece[4] dissolved in Rosewater, your Currans must be made very dry, or else they will make your Cake heavy, strew as much Sugar finely beaten among the Currans, as you shall think the water hath taken away the sweetnesse from them: Break your past into little pieces, into a kimnell[5] or such like thing, and lay a layer of past broken

1. Fourteen pounds. 2. A fine silk or lawn sieve.
3 and 4. Perfumes which were to be bought from apothecaries and spice merchants.
5. A wooden salting or butter tub.

into little pieces, and a Layer of Currans, until your Currans are all put in, mingle the past and the Currans very well, but take heed of breaking the Currans, you must take out a piece of past after it hath risen in a warme cloth before you put in the Currans to cover the top, and the bottom, you must roule the cover something thin, and the bottom likewise, and wet it with Rosewater, and close them at the bottom of the side, or the middle which you like best, prick the top and the sides with a small long Pin, when your Cake is ready to go into the Oven, cut it in the midst of the side round about with a knife an inch deep, if your Cake be a peck of Meale, it must stand two hours in the Oven, your Oven must be as hot as for Manchet.'[1]

The Compleat Cook, 1658 (first published 1655)

A recipe very similar to the Countess of Rutland's is given by Gervase Markham in *The English Hus-wife* (1615), so this version of Banbury cake must have been current during the first half of the seventeenth century. It is interesting to compare it with the one given by Miss Dorothy Hartley in *Food in England* (1954). Miss Hartley's recipe is for small cakes, with a filling of currants, candied peel, allspice, cinnamon, butter and honey encased in very fine flaky pastry. These cakes, Miss Hartley tells us, were carried around all hot and crisp and fresh, in specially made chip baskets, wrapped in white cloths; they were very light and flaky, and 'crunchy crusted'.

· BANBURY CAKES ·

This is the eighteenth-century version of Banbury cakes, very different from the Countess of Rutland's, but still yeast-leavened. There is no sign of the pastry casing of the modern version or of the seventeenth-century leavened paste. In fact it is a spiced fruit bread much like a dozen others described in this book.

'Take half a peck [7 lb] of fine flour, three pounds of currants, a pound and a half of butter, a quarter of a pound of sugar, a quarter of an ounce of cloves and mace, three quarters of a pint of ale-yeast, and a little rose-water; boil as much milk as will serve to knead it, and when it is almost cold put in as many carraway seeds as will thicken it; work all

1. A small loaf made of the best and whitest flour then obtainable. See pp. 329–40. Manchets were baked in a rather cooler oven than was required for ordinary household bread.

together at the fire, pulling it to pieces two or three times before it is made up.'

Mrs Charlotte Mason, *Mrs Mason's Cookery or The Ladies' Assistant*,
a new edition, 1786

· SCOTCH BUN ·

The Scotch Bun, also called Black Bun, seems to bear a close resemblance to the seventeenth-century Banbury cake as made in the recipe attributed to the Countess of Rutland. First a butter-enriched, leavened bread dough is made. Then a rich fruit mixture as for a Christmas cake or mincemeat is prepared from currants, raisins, candied peel, almonds and sweet spices.

The prepared dough is now divided into two pieces, one-third being kept for the outside of the bun, the remainder being used for mixing with the fruit. In Emma Roberts's recipe, 1841 (see p. 450), extra yeast

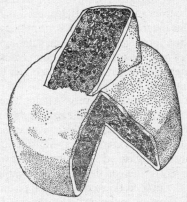

The Scotch Black Bun should be about 3 inches deep, with a thin casing of yeast pastry.

is added at this stage, to the fruit and dough mixture only, which is then made up into a big round bun (I wonder about the efficacy of the extra yeast). The reserved dough is spread out in a flat round, the fruit bun placed in the centre, and wrapped in the dough. The whole affair is then again rolled out to the desired thickness and is made ready for baking, in a hoop, in a mould or, as in Emma Roberts's recipe, in a protective binding of thick paper. A remarkable confection, no richer than mince pies and less so than a Christmas cake, since there are no eggs in the mixture, and at any rate in the Roberts recipe, no extra sugar, while the proportion of butter is 6 oz to the pound of flour.

In the more modern version, quoted from Florence Jack's *Cookery for Every Household* (1914), the method is slightly different, the dough is sweetened and there are eggs and treacle in the fruit filling. The later version seems to me less interesting, but it is included here because, as in all Florence Jack's recipes, there is useful detail and directions are very clear. Miss Jack was principal of the Edinburgh College of Domestic Arts, and later wrote an excellent small volume of simple cookery for publication by the Good Housekeeping Institute.

· A RICH SCOTCH BUN ·

'To four pounds of flour (half a peck Scotch) stone and cut two pounds of raisins, and clean two pounds of currants. Take six ounces of orange-peel, the same of citron, and of almonds, blanched and cut; mix all these together. Take one drachm[1] of cloves, a large nutmeg, half an ounce of allspice, and the same of ginger, pound them, strew the spice on the fruit, and mix them very well. Make a hole in the flour, break in nearly a pound and a half of butter, pour warm water on the butter to soften it a little; then work the flour and butter together, spread the paste, and pour in half a pint of good yest; work it up very well until the paste is light and smooth. Cut off about a third part of the paste for the sheets, spread out the rest of the paste on the table, put the fruit on it, pour about a gill of yest over the fruit and paste, and work the fruit and paste very well together. Then make it up round; roll out the sheet which was reserved in a circular form, lay the bun on the middle, and gather the sheet round it; roll it out to the desired thickness, run a fork through in different parts down to the bottom, and pinch it on the top. Flour double gray paper and put the bun upon it, give it a cut round the side, put a binder of double paper round it to keep it from running too thin in the oven. Bake in a moderate oven.'

Emma Roberts's recipe, from the extensively revised 65th edition
of Mrs Rundell's *New System of Domestic Cookery*, 1841.
It was Miss Roberts who was responsible for the new recipes and the revisions
in this excellent edition of Mrs Rundell's work, first published in 1806

1. One-sixteenth of an ounce.

Miss Roberts's Scotch Bun recipe, signed with her initials,[1] derives from Mrs Frazer's *Practise of Cookery, Pastry and Confectionery*, published in Edinburgh (1791), but Miss Roberts reduced Mrs Frazer's proportions of fruit from $7\frac{1}{2}$ lb to an almost austere $4\frac{3}{4}$ lb to the same quantity of flour (4 lb), and cleared up confusions over the measurements. Mrs Frazer gave these in Scotch pints and gills which at the period differed substantially from English ones.

Although so often called a Christmas bun, the Black Bun is made much more for New Year, or Hogmanay. It should be at least 3 inches high, and the pastry casing should be 'something thin' just as described in the Countess of Rutland's Banbury cake recipe. Incidentally, Victor MacClure, some of whose delightful Scotch recipes and descriptions of the food of his childhood are quoted in this book, thinks that the method of encasing the rich fruit mixture in fine pastry dough reached Scotland via the cooks of Renaissance Italy. I am sure he is right, but I think that the origin of such pies goes back further, to Arab cooking and the marvellous spiced meat and fruit pies which are still a part of the great tradition of Moroccan pastrycooks.

· SCOTCH BUN ·

'*Dough.*

2 lbs. flour.	1 oz. yeast.
6 oz. butter.	2 tea-cupfuls of cold milk.
6 oz. sugar.	A pinch of salt.

'*Inside of Bun.*

$1\frac{1}{2}$ lb. above dough.	1 lb. sultanas.
1 oz. mixed spice.	$\frac{1}{2}$ lb. candied orange peel.
$\frac{1}{2}$ tea-cupful treacle.	$\frac{1}{4}$ lb. sweet almonds.
2 lbs. currants.	2 eggs.

'*Cover.* – 1 lb. 2 oz. of above dough.'

Equivalent metric quantities, for the dough: *flour 900 g, butter 170 g, sugar 170 g, yeast 30 g, cold milk 2 teacups, salt a pinch;* for inside of bun: *about 675 g of the dough; mixed spice 30 g, treacle $\frac{1}{2}$ tea-cup, currants 900 g, sultanas 450 g, candied orange peel 225 g, sweet almonds 120 g, eggs 2; for cover: 500 g of the dough. Tin size: cake tin or hoop 20 to 22 cm in diameter.*

1. These were omitted from later editions.

'First prepare the dough. Sieve the flour and sugar into a basin, and rub in the butter until free from lumps. Cream the yeast in a small basin with the salt, and pour in the milk. Strain this into the centre of the flour, &c., and work all together with the hand, adding a little more milk if necessary. The dough should be rather soft. When it is well kneaded, put it in a clean dry bowl, cover it with a thick cloth, and leave it in a warm kitchen overnight.

'Next day prepare the centre of the bun. Take 1½ lb. of the dough, and put it into a basin. Mix the spice with the treacle, and add them to the dough with the eggs well beaten, the almonds blanched, but not cut, the currants and sultanas picked and cleaned, and the orange peel finely shred. Mix all well together in a basin, and then knead on the baking board until very stiff. Mould the mixture with a little flour in a 7-inch hoop, and leave it for a short time.

'*Cover.*—Take 1 lb. 2 oz. of the dough, and knead it well on the board, using extra flour if too soft. Then take three parts of this dough, and roll it into a round. Lift the inside part of the bun on to this, and draw the dough up the sides to reach the top. Brush the edges with beaten egg, and roll out the remainder of the dough from the top. Press the top round on, and make it very neat. Turn the bun upside down in an 8-inch hoop, and prick it all over with a fork, making a few holes go right through to the foot. Brush over with egg, and bake in a good moderate oven. Just before moving the bun from the oven, brush it over with a little gelatine dissolved in water with a lump of sugar.

'. . . The above quantities will make a 6-lb. bun.

'Time to bake, about 2 hours. Probable cost, 3s. 6d.'

Florence Jack, *Cookery for Every Household*, 1914

· SELKIRK BANNOCK ·

'2 lb bakers' dough, ½ lb butter, ½ lb lard, ½ lb sugar, ½ lb sultanas, ½ lb currants, ¼ lb [candied] orange peel.'

Equivalent metric quantities: dough 900 g, butter 225 g, lard 225 g, sugar 225 g, sultanas 225 g, currants 225 g, orange peel 120 g.

'Work the lard and butter into the bakers' dough, add sugar, sultanas and finely chopped orange peel and knead well. Place the dough in a buttered tin and allow to stand in a warm place for about 30 minutes to rise, and bake in a moderate oven.'

'Cereals', ed. André L. Simon, Section IV of *A Concise Encyclopaedia of Gastronomy*, London, the Wine and Food Society, 1943

Notes: As can be seen from the ingredients, a Selkirk bannock is almost as rich in fat and fruit as the Scotch bun, and much sweeter, which makes it into a luxury version of lardy cake. The recipe given above was credited to the Scottish Women's Rural Industries publication, *Farmhouse Recipes*, 1938.

· CUMBRIAN CHRISTMAS BREAD ·

'1¾ lb flour, 3 oz lard, 6 oz sugar, 4 oz currants, 8 oz raisins, 4 oz sultanas, 1 tablespoon black treacle, 2 oz mixed peel, 2 eggs, 1 teaspoon spice, 1 teaspoon salt, 1 oz yeast.'

Equivalent metric quantities: flour 780 g, lard 85 g, sugar 170 g, currants 120 g, raisins 225 g, sultanas 120 g, black treacle 1 tablespoon, mixed peel 60 g, eggs 2, spice 1 teaspoon, salt 1 teaspoon, yeast 30 g, milk and water mixed.

'Put the flour and salt into a warm bowl and stand by the fire to warm. Rub in the lard. Cream the yeast in a basin with a teaspoon of sugar. Beat the eggs well and add sufficient warm milk and water to make three quarters of a pint, including the eggs. Stir in the yeast and mix well.

'Make a well in the middle of the flour and pour in the mixture. Set to rise half an hour in a warm place, then knead well and add all the fruit, sugar, etc, warmed.

'Mix well and leave to rise for two hours; then put into two loaf tins. Rise for twenty minutes more and bake for one hour fifteen minutes in a moderate oven.'

Lakeland Cookery, Clapham via Lancaster, the Dalesman Publishing Co. Ltd, 1969; compiled from recipes supplied by readers of *Cumbria*

N.B. I have not tried the above recipe. The cooking time seems excessive, but otherwise it reads well and should produce a good, moist, rich, fruit bread.

· GUERNSEY GÂCHE ·

A commercially produced version of this famous speciality sent to me from Guernsey proved rather dry and quite undistinguished. The following eighteenth-century recipe, which I have not tried, should make something more like the genuine article. It comes from *Guernsey Dishes of Bygone Days* (1971), one of several delightful small collections of MS. receipts put together, edited and printed by Mr J. Stevens Cox, F.S.A., of the Toucan Press, Mount Durand, St Peter Port, Guernsey, Channel Islands. This recipe for *gâche* is attributed to Mrs Louisa Helmot and derives from an eighteenth-century version.

'*1½ lb wholemeal flour (some recipes give plain white flour), ½ lb of Guernsey butter, 2 eggs, 4 oz candied orange peel, 1 lb sultanas, ¼ pint Guernsey milk, 2 oz yeast, pinch of salt, 2 oz dark brown sugar.*'

Equivalent metric quantities: wholemeal (or plain white) flour 675 g, Guernsey butter 225 g, eggs 2, candied orange peel 120 g, sultanas 450 g, Guernsey milk 150 g, yeast 60 g, pinch of salt, dark brown sugar 60 g.

'Wash fruit, dry it. Cream butter with the sugar, add eggs, then mix with the flour, warm the milk, add the yeast and a pinch of salt. Then make a depression in your dough and pour in the milk with added yeast and mix well, adding fruit as you mix, and knead as you do bread. Leave to rise 2 hours, in a warm room, then knead again. Grease cake tin and put in prepared Gâche.

'Cook for 1 hour in a moderate oven until golden brown.

'Currants can be used instead of sultanas if that is your taste.'

· YORKSHIRE SPICE LOAF (WITHOUT EGGS) ·

'*2½ lb of flour, 2 oz of yeast, 1 lb of large raisins, 1 lb of currants, 3 oz of candied peel, ¾ lb of butter, ½ lb of Demerara sugar, a little grated nutmeg, 1½ teaspoons of ground cinnamon, 1 teaspoon of ground cloves, warm water.*'

Equivalent metric quantities: flour 1·25 kg, yeast 60 g, large raisins 450 g, currants 450 g, candied peel 85 g, butter 340 g, Demerara sugar 225 g, a little grated nutmeg, ground cinnamon 1½ teaspoons, ground cloves 1 teaspoon, warm water.

'Make like bread, with the flour, water, and yeast only, adding the sugar and butter before leaving it to rise. When it has risen add the fruit. Put into tins. Leave to rise 3 hours. Bake in a moderate oven.'

The Imperial Cookery Book, arranged by Mrs C. H. Milburn, Hull, 1913; recipe contributed by Miss Earle, Hull

· SIMNEL YEAST CAKE ·

At one time simnel cakes were made with a yeast-leavened dough and baked with a layer of almond paste in the centre of the cake. The dough was spiced and enriched with eggs, butter and dried fruit, so that the old simnel cake was another variation of spice cake rather like the one described in the Countess of Kent's recipe on p. 457.

Simnel cakes made on a basis of yeast dough were gradually superseded by ordinary cake batters, and the strip of almond paste or marzipan moved from the centre to the top of the cake, which was originally made for Mothering Sunday. Nowadays it has become associated with Easter. Below is a Victorian recipe for simnel cake made with yeast dough.

'*Required: half a pound of flour, ten ounces of currants, four ounces each of fresh butter, candied peel and caster sugar, two eggs, some milk and spice as below and half an ounce of dried yeast [i.e. compressed or what we now call fresh yeast]. Cost, about 2s. 6d.*'

Equivalent metric quantities: flour 225 g, currants 280 g, butter 120g, candied peel 120g, caster sugar 120g, eggs 2, milk 150g, mixed spice 1 teaspoon or cinnamon 1 saltspoon mixed with $\frac{1}{4}$ of a small nutmeg (grated), compressed yeast 15g; for the almond paste: ground almonds 225g, icing sugar 450g, rose water.

'Make a dough with the flour and yeast, after dissolving the latter in a gill [$\frac{1}{4}$ pint or 5 oz] of lukewarm milk and adding a spoonful of the sugar; this is to be put to rise for an hour, then mixed with the fruit and eggs, and the creamed butter and spice; the latter may be all mixed spice, when about a teaspoonful will be wanted, or the fourth of a small nutmeg can be grated and mixed with a saltspoonful of cinnamon.

'The materials are to be well worked in, and the dough left to rise for another hour in a warm place, covered. Then put half of it in a tin lined with a few folds of buttered paper, and insert a layer of almond icing half an inch thick; the remainder of the cake mixture goes in next. It is then ready for baking for a couple of hours or so in a steady oven.'

Notes: 1. This recipe – it comes from *Cassells' Universal Cookery Book* by Lizzie Heritage, first published 1894 – is fairly typical of a period when fruit cakes were becoming increasingly rich and sweet. The two hours' baking is excessive for a cake made with a total of only 2 lb of ingredients.

2. The almond paste for the centre of the cake was made with ½ lb of ground almonds and 1 lb of icing sugar worked together in a heavy saucepan over a very gentle heat, and with the addition of a few drops of rose water. No eggs were needed for this version of almond icing; it was left to get cold and then rolled out.

3. I find that the most satisfactory way of adapting the Victorian recipe is to make a slightly less rich mixture, in quantities which yield enough for two 6 to 7 inch or 16 to 18 cm round cake tins, about 2½ inches or 7 cm in depth. So the proportions I use are 1 lb or 450 g of flour, 8 oz or 225 g of currants, 3 eggs, ¼ lb or 125 g of butter, 2 oz or 60 g of brown sugar, 2 oz or 60 g of chopped candied peel, 1 tablespoon of chopped preserved ginger, ½ oz or 15 g of bakers' yeast, 1 teaspoon of mixed sweet spice, 7 oz or 200 g of milk, a teaspoon of salt.

For the almond paste, I buy two 8 oz or 227 g packets of ready-made pure marzipan (sugar, almonds and glucose syrup only). Although a little more expensive than home-made almond paste, this is usually more satisfactory; it is not too easy to achieve the right texture.

To make and prove the cake mixture follow Lizzie Heritage's directions, and to get the almond paste to the right size for the tins, knead the marzipan until it is pliable, roll or press it out on a board, invert a cake tin over the paste and cut round the tin with a sharp knife.

The cakes are quite sufficiently baked in 25 to 30 minutes at 425°F, 220°C, gas no. 7.

To minimize the risk of the two halves of the cake separating at the almond paste layer as the cake is turned out, leave it in its tin to cool and set for about 15 minutes.

· THE COUNTESS OF KENT'S SPICE CAKES ·

Here are two seventeenth-century recipes, both from the Countess of Kent's little book, posthumously published in 1653. Probably the recipes in the Countess's notebook go back to a much earlier date, for these spiced cakes were well known to the Elizabethans; indeed, towards the end of Elizabeth I's reign, a decree issued by the Clerk of the Markets to the bakers of London forbade them to 'make, utter, or sell by retail . . . any spice cakes, buns, biscuits, or other spice bread . . . except it be at burials, or on Friday before Easter, or at Christmas . . .'[1]

1. The decree is more fully quoted in the introduction to the chapter on yeast buns and small tea cakes.

The reason for the ban, made in other cities, and more than once, was that spice bread, cakes and buns did not conform – it was probably impossible to make them do so – to the weights of loaves laid down by the bread laws.

To Make a Spice Cake

'Take one bushel[1] of Flower, six pound of Butter, eight pound of Currans, two pints of Cream, a pottle[2] of Milk, half a pint of good Sack, 2 pound of Sugar, 2 ounces of Mace, 1 ounce of Nutmegs, 1 ounce of Ginger, twelve yolks, 2 whites, take the Milk and Cream, and stir it all the time that it boils, put your hot seething milk to it and melt all the Butter in it, and when it is blood warm, temper the Cake, put not your Currans in till you have made the paste, you must have some Ale-yeast, and forget not Salt.'

The Countess of Kent, *A True Gentlewoman's Delight*, first published 1653

To Make a Cake

'Take half a peck[3] of flower, two pound and a half of Currans, 3 or 4 Nutmegs, one pound of Almond paste, 2 pound of Butter, and one pint of Cream, three spoonfuls of Rosewater, three quarters of a pound of Sugar, half a pint of Sack, a quarter of a pint of Yest, and six Eggs, so make it and bake it.'

ibid.

At a preliminary reading the first of the Countess of Kent's recipes appears extremely lavish, and the second quite modest in comparison. In fact a more careful study of the proportions shows that the second cake is rather richer than the first, and, since the second one is more easily transposed into manageable quantities for today's household cookery, this is the one I have adapted, using approximately one-third of the original amount, as follows:

The Countess of Kent's Spice Cake or Bread, 1973

2¼ lb of plain unbleached flour, 1 oz of bakers' yeast, 2 teaspoons of salt, ¼ pint of cream, ¾ pint of milk, ¼ lb of caster sugar, 3 eggs, ¾ lb of currants,

1. Fifty-six pounds. 2. Four pints or half a gallon.
3. Seven pounds.

6 oz of ground almonds mixed to a paste with a tablespoon or two of rose water, ½ lb of butter, 1 nutmeg grated or 3 teaspoons of mixed pudding spice, 3 fluid oz of light sherry.

A little extra butter for the tins, and milk and sugar for glazing the cakes.

Equivalent metric quantities: plain unbleached flour 1 kg, bakers' yeast 30 g, salt 2 teaspoons, cream 150 g, milk 420 g, caster sugar 120 g, eggs 3, currants 340 g, ground almonds 170 g, rose water 1 or 2 tablespoons, butter 225 g, nutmeg 1 (grated) or mixed pudding spice 3 teaspoons, light sherry 85 g. Butter for the tins, milk and sugar for glazing. Tin size: two wide loaf tins of about 1·75 litre capacity.

Put the flour, salt and sugar into an extra large mixing bowl and put it to warm in the oven for a few minutes. Mix the yeast with the cream, warmed. Have the milk also warmed to blood heat. Stir the yeast into the flour; add the milk, then the whole eggs. Mix all to a light dough. Cover and leave to rise, until it is at least doubled in volume and looks spongy. This will take about 1½ hours.

Have ready all the other ingredients. The butter should be cut into small pieces and put in a warm place so that it is easily malleable, and the ground almonds mixed with the rose water.

Break down the dough, knead it lightly, then work in the butter, the almond paste, the warmed currants, the spice and the sherry. At this stage the dough requires thorough and careful kneading, so that all ingredients are well and equally distributed throughout the mass.

Now the dough is put into a warmed and buttered tin or tins. In the old days a cake hoop would have been used, but I find it more convenient to use two large, rather wide loaf tins of 3¼ pint capacity. There will be sufficient dough to fill each tin by about two-thirds. Cover them with a cloth and leave them for 15 to 25 minutes, until the dough has risen almost to the tops of the tins and is perfectly light and springy.

Bake in the centre of a moderately hot oven, 375° to 400°F, 190° to 205°C, gas no. 5 or 6. After 15 minutes cover the tops of the loaves with a double sheet of greaseproof paper, and bake for another 30 minutes, or until a fine skewer plunged into the centre of the loaves comes out quite clean.

As soon as the loaves are taken from the oven brush the tops with a thick sugar and milk glaze (see p. 436 and use double quantities) but leave them in the tins until they have contracted sufficiently to be turned out quite easily. Leave them on a cake rack to cool completely. Store the loaves in an airtight tin.

This is a delicious and delicate tea or breakfast bread, to be eaten with or without butter. The almonds give the bread a wonderful flavour and help to keep it moist.

· ICING FOR A SPICE CAKE (1) ·

Sometimes these leavened fruit and spice cakes were iced or frosted. The formula given in a little book contemporary with the Kent volume is a simple sugar glaze:

'Against you draw the cake from the oven have some Rose Water and Sugar finely beaten, and well mixed together to wash the upper side of it, then set it in the Oven to dry, when you draw it out, it will shew like Ice.'

The Compleat Cook, 1658 (first published 1655)

· ICING FOR A SPICE CAKE (2) ·

Here is another, more modern, frosting, from the manuscript receipt book of Ann Hendren, who seems to have been the housekeeper to a Mr Goff at Hale Park in Hampshire from 1787 onwards. Her receipts were copied out, with slight variations, by her son Patrick from an earlier MS. left in the house by Elizabeth Unthank, wife of a former Goff. This MS. was dated 1742, so the recipes would be about a century later than those of the Countess of Kent. Although in composition much richer in eggs, butter and fruit (it is called plumb cake) than the Kent spice cake, the quantities given for the cake to be frosted are considerably smaller, being based on 3 lb of flour.

'If you frost this cake take a pound of Double refined Suggar, pounded and sifted thro a silk sieve, take 2 or 3 white of Egg beat them up in a Delf bowl, mix yr. suggar in it by Degrees, beating it continually till all yr. suggar is in, if it should be too dry, add some more whites, beat it up very well, you must not make it too thin, but fine and smooth, and also thick, when yr. cake comes out of the oven, you must let it ly a little before you put on the Frosting, then lay yr. frosting on smooth with a knife on top and side till all is on, then set in yr. oven, till yr. Frosting is a little hard, so keep for use.'

· A PLAIN PLUM CAKE, *c*. 1760 ·

'2 pound of flour, 6 ounces of butter, 5 ounces of sugar, a pound and quarter of currans, some spice, a little salt, 5 or 6 spoonfuls of yest, mix with warm milk, this makes three cakes. You may bake them in tin pans.'

The Receipt Book of Elizabeth Raper, written 1756–70,
published by the Nonesuch Press, 1924

· TO MAKE A COMMON PLUMB CAKE, *c*. 1810 ·

'Take 3 pounds of flour, well dried, and half a pound of melted Butter, half a pint of good Ale Yeast, four eggs, a pint and a quarter of thick Cream, 6 ounces of Sugar, half a nutmeg grated; let your liquor be blood warm when you mix them together. Melt the Butter into the Liquor, strain it into the flour and sugar, then mix them all together very well and beat it before the fire till it will come clean from the bowl; let it stand before the fire to rise, when the Oven is ready mix well into it 3 pounds of Currants rubbed and picked very clean – then put into a small sized Hoop, well buttered an hour and a quarter will bake it.'

The above recipe, like the 'famous saffron cake' quoted on p. 446, is from a family manuscript receipt book (the Gibson/Pegus MS.) in the possession of Mrs Caroline Simmonds of Littleover, Derby. Mrs Simmonds, who very kindly typed out the entire MS. for me, and who has allowed me to publish these recipes, tells me that the MS. has been in her family since the book was started in 1802. It belonged to her 'great-great-great-grandmother, who lived in Ceylon; she was born a Layard, a Huguenot family . . . The book runs from 1802 to 1886 though the bulk of the receipts are pre-1820. I know this by internal evidence of a marmalade recipe "very badly copied by my Willie, 1823". This is the third hand in the book.'

The recipes quoted come near the beginning of the book, so would be among the earliest.

· YORKSHIRE SPICE BREAD, *c*. 1960 ·

'*Ingredients*
3½ lb flour   ½ lb sugar
1 lb lard or butter   1 lb currants
2 oz yeast   ⅛ oz cinnamon
1½ gills¹ new milk   3 oz candied peel'
2 eggs

Equivalent metric quantities: flour 1·5 kg, lard or butter 450 g, yeast 60 g, milk 225 g, eggs 2, sugar 225 g, currants 450 g, cinnamon 1 scant teaspoon, candied peel 85 g. Equivalent oven temperature in degrees C: 150° to 160°C.

'*Method.*
'Warm the flour and rub into it three quarters of the fat. Cream yeast and add with warm milk and eggs. Beat in the sugar, currants, cinnamon and peel and the remaining fat, and continue to beat for about ten minutes. Leave to rise in the tin until twice its original size. Bake in a moderate oven at 300°–325°F for one–one and a half hours.'²

From Skelton-on-Ure, in *Through Yorkshire's Kitchen Door*,
the Yorkshire Federation of Women's Institutes, 31st edn, n.d.
(first published 1927)

· LARDY CAKES AND HARVEST CAKES ·

Based on bread dough, oozing with fat, sticky with sugar, often further enriched with dried fruit, lardy cakes – as already noted in the introduction to this chapter – are just about as undesirable, from a dietician's point of view, as anything one can possibly think of. Like every packet of cigarettes, every lardy cake should carry a health warning. It should also be remembered that originally these cakes were intended as special celebration cakes, made only at Harvest time and perhaps for family festivals. It was only when sugar became cheap, and when the English taste for sweet things – particularly in the Midlands and the north – became more pronounced, that such rich breads or cakes were made or

1. A gill is ¼ pint imperial or 5 fluid oz.
2. Bake in two 8½ × 3 inch square tins.

could be bought from the bakery every week. That said, here are the recipes. I have chosen only those in which the proportions of sugar and fat to flour are moderate. I'm afraid this doesn't make them less fattening or less tempting.

When using home-made pork lard (and it must be pork lard, not vegetable fat) rather than the bought variety, it is advisable that it be very cold and hard before starting to work it into the dough; it is also advisable to cool the dough in the refrigerator between turns, as for puff pastry. Remember that the flavouring of mixed sweet spice is important to lardy cakes. A final and useful piece of advice comes from a little book of Hampshire recipes:[1] '. . . the secret of a good lard cake is to turn it upside down after baking so that the lard can soak through.' The true Hampshire lardy cake, adds the author, has no fruit. This relates them to the Surrey lardy rolls and Guildford manchets given in the chapter on manchet bread.[2]

· SUFFOLK HARVEST CAKE ·

'The harvest-cake, or biscuit, called by some a bever-cake, was only made at that season. For this a portion of dough was taken off the bread and put in a basin, mixed with lard, two eggs, sugar, raisins, candied peel and nutmeg. This was all thoroughly mixed by hand and left for a time; then baked in a tin, either in biscuit form or as a slab.

'Fatty-cake was yet another form, made from a lump of dough rolled out flat, then spread with lard, sprinkled over with sugar, and doubled over. This rolling out, larding, sugaring and doubling over was repeated several times before shaping the dough into a cake for the oven. These simple bulging-sided cakes, oozing with burnt sugar, were particularly toothsome as I very well know, since grandmother taught her daughters these tasty bits in cookery. Dough was also shortened down with lard to make crusts for chicken or meat pies.'

Allan Jobson, *An Hour-Glass on the Run*, 1959

1. Kate Easlea, *Cooking in Hampshire Past and Present*, 1974; Paul Cane Publications Ltd, 39 Above Bar, Southampton, Hampshire.
2. If you can't lay hands on pure pork lard, don't attempt lardy cakes.

· NORTHUMBERLAND LARDY CAKE ·

'*Ingredients:*

for the dough:	pinch of salt
8 oz flour	for the filling:
¾ gill of milk[1]	2 oz lard
½ oz yeast	2 oz sugar
1 teaspoon sugar	2 oz currants'
1 egg	

Equivalent metric quantities, for the dough: *flour 225 g, milk 120 g, yeast 15 g, sugar 1 teaspoon, eggs 1, pinch of salt;* for the filling: *lard 60 g, sugar 60 g, currants 60 g. Tin size : 20 cm cake tin.*

'*Method:*

'Sift together flour and salt and leave in a warm place. Cream the yeast with sugar,[2] add the egg and warmed milk and mix with the flour to make a soft dough.

'Leave in a warm place and when the dough has doubled its bulk roll out onto a floured board. Divide the filling into two portions and spread one half onto two-thirds of the dough then fold into three as for flaky pastry and roll out again. Spread the remainder of the filling, refold and roll out twice, finally shaping to fit an eight inch cake tin. Allow to rise and bake in a hot oven for thirty to thirty-five minutes.'

Peggy Howey, *The Geordie Cook Book*, 1971

· NORTHUMBRIAN HARVEST TEA CAKE ·

'1 lb plain flour	2 oz butter
½ teaspoon salt	1 egg
1 oz yeast (fresh or ½ oz dried)	1 tablespoon currants
1 oz sugar	little grated nutmeg
¼ pint warm milk (good measure)	2 teaspoons lemon peel'

Equivalent metric quantities : plain flour 450 g, salt ½ teaspoon, fresh yeast 30 g or dried yeast 15 g, sugar 30 g, warm milk 150 g, butter 60 g, eggs 1, currants 1 tablespoon, grated nutmeg, lemon peel 2 teaspoons. Equivalent oven temperature in degrees C : 220°C.

1. Just under a quarter of a pint.   2. I prefer to omit the sugar.

'*Method*

'1. Warm the flour and salt in a large earthenware bowl.

'2. Warm the milk in a saucepan, add the butter, stirring until it melts, remove from the heat, cool, and beat in the egg.

'3. Mix together the yeast and a little of the sugar until they are liquid. If using dried yeast, add this to the lukewarm milk mixture and proceed as follows.

'4. Add the sugar to the flour and salt. Make a well in the centre of the flour and stir in the milk and yeast. Mix well to a soft dough and leave to stand in a warm place until it doubles its size.

'5. Cut this into three portions. Form each of these into a three-stranded plait. Dampen the edges to secure the ends of the plait. To make ordinary teacakes divide the mixture into six pieces and form into rounds.

'6. Place on a baking sheet, leave to prove in a warm place for 10–15 minutes.

'7. Bake at Gas mark 7, Electric mark 425 for 15 minutes or until golden brown.

'*Background*

'These plaits were served at farmhouses at harvest-time when many well-earned celebrations took place.'

Patricia Donaghy, *Northumbrian and Cumbrian Recipes*, 1971

The currants, nutmeg and lemon peel given in the list of ingredients are not mentioned again in this otherwise carefully explained recipe. I think that they should go into the mixture at stage 4, after the milk and yeast. When creaming fresh yeast, I omit the sugar.

· BREAKFAST CAKE ·

'To half a peck [7 lb] of flour, rub in a pound and a half of butter; add three pounds of currants, half a pound of sugar, a quarter of an ounce of nutmeg, mace, and cinnamon together, a little salt, a pint and a half of warmed cream or milk, a quarter of a pint of brandy, a pint of good ale yeast, and five eggs; mix all these well together, and bake in a moderate oven.

'This cake will keep good for three months.'

Frederick Bishop, *The Wife's Own Book of Cookery*, 1856

· DOUGH CAKE FOR BREAKFAST

'On Sundays we had breakfast in the Front Room, a dough cake with currants or carraway seeds being an invariable part of the breakfast. One slice each – that was all. Bread and butter (or when one was old enough to be allowed a knife, "bread and dab-it" – butter dabbed on with every mouthful – for we got butter direct from local farmers) made the rest of the meal.'

George Sturt, *A Small Boy in the Sixties*, 1927

George Sturt was writing of his childhood in the Surrey town of Farnham. His father was a wheelwright, his mother ran a small stationers' shop. Here is a Surrey recipe for dough cake:

1 lb dough, ½ lb lard or butter, ½ teaspoonful spice, ¼ lb sugar, ¼ lb currants.

'Beat all in your Dough let Rise then Bake in a fairly Hot oven.'

The Surrey Cookery Book, 1932. Contributed by the family of Broomer, descended from the Broom Squires[1]

Equivalent metric quantities: dough 450 g, lard or butter 225 g, spice ½ teaspoon, sugar 120 g, currants 120 g.

· LUNCHEON CAKE ·

'Perhaps four or five courses for luncheon . . . in case the set menu of that meal failed to satisfy, there were always cheese and biscuits, "luncheon cake" and port, followed by coffee, to make good any deficiency.'

Clough Williams-Ellis, *Architect Errant*, Constable, 1971

In modern cookery books giving recipes for what are called 'English country house dishes', luncheon cakes still make an appearance. They are almost always perfectly ordinary fruit cakes, with the occasional seed cake for a change, or now and again a richer cake with the name of some once-famous London club attached to it – in these establishments luncheon cakes were indeed a great feature, and must have gone down

1. For the explanation of this apparently mysterious note see the extract from *The Mistress of Stantons Farm* on p. 434.

nicely with a glass of Madeira, the nomenclature deriving, perhaps, from the days when luncheon was a mid-morning, light meal.

North of the border, if *The Cookery Book of Lady Clark of Tillypronie* (1909) is anything to go by, luncheon cakes were more like the fruit breads of the seventeenth and eighteenth centuries. In the chapter devoted to cakes, no less than twelve recipes are described specifically as luncheon cakes. Of these, ten are for yeast-leavened mixtures, some of them being in composition more in the nature of the Italian panettone or the Austrian kugelhopf than of the English fruit cake. One or two are not unlike Cornish saffron cake without the saffron. The following is one of these, of which Lady Clark notes that it is 'small and very light'; it is dated 1866.

Small though it may have been for Lady Clark's household, I have made it still smaller by halving her quantities. My ingredients and method of mixing and baking the cake are exactly as described by Lady Clark.

To ½ lb of plain flour, the other ingredients are 2 oz each of butter and caster sugar, 2 small eggs, ½ oz of bakers' yeast, 6 tablespoons of milk, 1 oz of sultanas, 1 oz of candied citron peel.

Equivalent metric quantities: plain flour 225 g, butter 60 g, caster sugar 60 g, eggs 2 small, bakers' yeast 15 g, milk 6 tablespoons, sultanas 30 g, candied citron peel 30 g. Tin size: 0·5 litre capacity.

Rub the butter into the flour, add the sugar. Dissolve the yeast in the warmed milk; beat the eggs in a bowl. Add both to the flour mixture, mix lightly to a soft dough. Stir in the sultanas and the candied peel, cut into very small pieces. The fruit should be as evenly distributed throughout the dough as possible.

Turn the dough into a warmed and buttered 1 pint capacity tin (I use a loaf tin as in the illustration on p. 425 but a small round tin would do equally well). The tin should be half full. Cover it, and leave the dough to rise in a warm place until it has reached the top of the tin, which will take about 1½ hours.

Bake the cake in the centre of a moderate oven – Lady Clark directs that it should be a slack oven – 350°F, 180°C, gas no. 4, for approximately 45 minutes, covering the top with paper after the first 15 minutes.

Leave the cake in the tin for 10 minutes before turning it out on to a cooling rack.

· SALLY LUNN or SOLEILUNE CAKE ·

There are dozens of versions of this famous tea cake or, as Eliza Acton[1] calls it, 'rich French breakfast cake'; the variations are mainly in the proportion of eggs and butter to flour, although Miss Florence White[2] asserts that it is incorrect to use butter either in the composition of the cake or for spreading on it when it is cooked, and advises good rich cream for the dough and scalded cream (i.e. clotted or Cornish cream) for spreading on it when baked and split.

There are also numerous methods of baking the cake – in one large hoop, in two or more smaller ones to produce muffin-size cakes, in a cake tin, or shaped by hand and put into the oven on a baking sheet. This latter method would be difficult with today's Sally Lunn recipes, which produce too soft a dough for hand-shaping. Earlier recipes made a firmer, more bread-like mixture. Another possibility is to use a decorated kugelhopf or turban mould, like that shown in the drawing on p. 211. This produces an effective-looking cake, and if it is then no longer quite an English Sally Lunn – well, Miss Acton does quite firmly call it a French cake.

As for the name, Miss Dorothy Hartley's[3] explanation that Sally Lunn and solimemne, as Miss Acton calls it, are both corruptions of the French *soleil lune*, or sun and moon cake, sounds reasonable enough, and disposes of the picturesque legend[4] that one Sally Lunn, a West Country Molly Malone, cried the cakes in the streets of eighteenth-century Bath, and that a baker and musician called Dalmer bought her business *and* composed a song in her honour. In his *Up-to-Date Breadmaking* (1968), however, Mr W. J. Fance asserts that Sally Lunn in fact had a pastry-cooks' shop in Lilliput Alley in Bath.

My recipe for a Sally Lunn is simple, not very rich and relatively quick.

Ingredients are ½ lb of strong plain flour, ½ oz of yeast, 2 tablespoons of tepid milk, a teaspoon of salt, 4 oz of thick cream, 2 whole eggs, a little grated lemon peel or a half teaspoon of mixed sweet spice.

For the glaze: 1 tablespoon each of milk and sugar.

For preparing the cake tin – an ordinary plain English 6-inch tin, 2½ to 3 inches deep – a little butter and flour.

1. *Modern Cookery*, 1845. 2. *Good Things in England*, 1932.
3. *Food in England*, 1954.
4. Quoted, from *The Gentleman's Magazine*, 1827, in *The Oxford English Dictionary*.

Equivalent metric quantities: strong plain flour 225 g, yeast 15 g, tepid milk 2 tablespoons, salt 1 teaspoon, thick cream 120 g, eggs 2, a little grated lemon peel or mixed sweet spice ½ teaspoon, milk 1 tablespoon and sugar 1 tablespoon (for the glaze), a little butter and flour for the cake tin. Tin size: a 16 cm tin, 7 to 8 cm deep.

First put the yeast in a cup with the tepid milk. There should be just enough warm milk to cover it. Leave it for a few minutes until the yeast starts to work.

Meanwhile weigh out the flour, sprinkle in the salt and the grated lemon peel or spice. Add the yeast mixture, then the cream and the eggs. Mix all the ingredients together to make a thickish batter, *just* stiff enough to form into a bun shape.

Have ready the buttered and floured tin. If you have a non-stick tin, it is a more practical proposition, and this preparation is eliminated.

Transfer the ball of dough to the tin, sprinkle it with flour, cover it and leave it in a warm place until it has risen to the top of the tin. This will take from an hour to an hour and a half, but longer if the cream in the dough was very cold when used. Warming the tin before preparing it and putting in the dough will help to speed the rising.

As soon as the dough has risen transfer the cake to a fairly hot oven, 400° to 425°F, 205° to 220°C, gas nos. 6 or 7, and bake for 15 minutes. The top should be a pale gold, not browned.

In a small saucepan heat the sugar and milk for the glaze until it boils. While it is still in its tin brush the top of the cake with the hot glaze, which will give it a beautiful, almost mirror-like, shine.

As soon as the cake has cooled sufficiently for it to come away easily from the sides of the tin, turn it out.

At this stage, it is traditional to slice the cake into two or even three layers, spread these with clotted cream or softened butter, put the whole thing together again and eat it while it is still warm.

Personally, I find that when freshly cooked this kind of brioche-type cake – or perhaps a better description would be an extra-light leavened Victoria sponge cake – is much nicer without the spread of butter or cream. It is so delicate, and so light, that a slice or two goes beautifully with a fruit dessert such as a cooked apple dish or baked apricots, and even instead of biscuits or wafers with an ice cream, fruit fool or syllabub. The time to toast and butter the cake is next day when it has already begun to get dry.

I think that this is the place to add that at what was in the sixties and early seventies one of the most attractive and truly French restaurants in France, La Mère Brazier's on the Col de la Luère above Lyon, where the menu changed little and every dish – among them always one of those fat white Lyonnais chickens poached in broth, totally plain – was skilfully chosen and presented with great simplicity, the desserts offered were *fromage frais à la crème*, apple tart with crisp pastry a good deal thinner than a plate, and invariably a slice of very fine and light brioche. That brioche very much resembled our Sally Lunn cake – without the clotted cream, which was replaced by the fresh milk cheese with fresh, thick, ripe cream.

Notes and variations: 1. To make Sally Lunns on a larger scale, double all the quantities with the exception of the yeast, allow a little longer rising time, and make two 6 inch cakes rather than one large one.

2. Just to see what the result would be, I have tried out Florence White's theory about making Sally Lunn with clotted cream. Apart from the extra cost which was considerable, and the extra rising time which was nearly 3 hours because the cream was ice cold when the dough was mixed, there appeared to be little difference in the finished result. In the old days of unpasteurized cream and true farmhouse-produced clotted cream no doubt there would have been a very noticeable difference in flavour.

3. Mrs Rundell, author of the immensely popular *New System of Domestic Cookery* (1806), giving a recipe for 'excellent rolls', a simple dough enriched only with a little milk and butter, appends the following note: '. . . if made in cakes three inches thick, sliced and buttered, they resemble Sally Lunns as made at Bath . . . the addition of a little saffron, boiled in half a teacupful of milk, makes them remarkably good.' Mrs Rundell surely knew what she was talking about. She lived all her married life – over thirty years – in Bath. As with most enriched doughs and tea breads, no doubt the composition and the size of Sally Lunns varied, as is still the case, according to locality and to individual fancy. Meg Dods,[1] for example, required that they be made into 'cakes the size of a large plate'. Her quantities were ½lb of butter, 2lb of flour, 1 pint of warm milk, ¼ pint of yeast.

4. In *Le Livre de pâtisserie* (1873), Jules Gouffé, one of the most celebrated of French nineteenth-century chefs and cookery writers, gives a recipe for '*Solilem*' made with 1 kg of flour, 8 eggs, 2 decilitres of cream, 30g each of yeast and sugar, 20g of salt and 250g of butter. He

---

1. *The Cook and Housewife's Manual*, first published 1826.

directs that the batter or dough be well whisked, and kept very soft, if necessary by the addition of milk. His solilems are cooked in small oval moulds. When turned out, they are sliced transversely, melted butter is poured over them and the little cakes reconstituted.

· A PLAIN LUNCHEON OR TEA CAKE ·

This is very much like a Sally Lunn. It is baked in a shallow round cake tin, and is very good and light.

To make a cake which should be ample for six to eight helpings, ingredients are ½ lb of strong plain flour, ¼ to ½ oz of yeast, approximately 4 tablespoons of milk, 2 tablespoons of sugar, 1 teaspoon of salt, 2 oz of butter or 4 tablespoons of thick cream, 1 egg.

For glazing the cake, a tablespoon each of milk and caster sugar.

Equivalent metric quantities: strong plain flour 225 g, yeast 10 to 15 g, milk approximately 4 tablespoons, sugar 2 tablespoons, salt 1 teaspoon, butter 60 g or thick cream 4 tablespoons, eggs 1; milk 1 tablespoon and caster sugar 1 tablespoon (for glazing). Tin size: 18 cm in diameter, 3·5 cm deep.

Put the flour into a bowl with the salt and sugar.

Mix the yeast to a cream with a little water.

Warm the milk and mix it with the softened butter or the thick cream.

Make a well in the flour, break in the egg and add the yeast. Mix lightly, then add the warm milk and the butter. With your hands, knead all the ingredients into a soft and pliable, not liquid, dough. Sprinkle with more flour if necessary, and form into a ball. Cover and leave to rise for approximately 1½ hours – less when the weather is very warm.

Have ready a round, straight-sided tin, 7 inches in diameter by 1½ inches deep, warmed and buttered.

Break down the dough, knead it very lightly and briefly, re-shape it into a ball, put this in the centre of the tin, and with your knuckles press it out until it covers the surface and is evenly spread.

Cover with a cloth, or a sheet of polythene, leave until the dough has risen to the top of the tin. This will take from 45 minutes to an hour. With scissors or a sharp knife, make four deep cuts in the dough, radiating out from the centre. Leave for another 10 minutes or so until the dough has once more puffed up.

Bake the cake in the centre of a hot oven, 425°F, 220°C, gas no. 7, for
10 minutes, then move it to the lower shelf and reduce the heat to 375°F,
190°C, gas no. 5, for another 10 minutes.

As soon as the cake is taken from the oven, brush it over with the milk
and sugar mixture, which gives the crust a beautiful shining glaze.

Leave a few minutes before turning the cake out of the tin.

Like all English tea cakes and French brioche confections, this one is
best eaten as soon as it has cooled, with or without butter as you please,
but can be reheated under a tin or bowl in a slow oven.

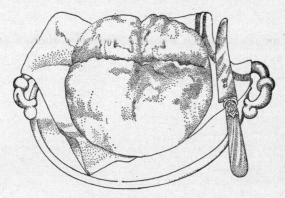

A typical plain breakfast cake or teacake.

· A PLAIN CAKE ·

'As made at Winkinhurst, Sussex.

'1½ lb flour, ½ lb sugar, ¾ lb butter, 1 egg, ¾ oz yeast, a little nutmeg.

'Rub butter and sugar very fine in the flour. Put in a warm tin and set
it to rise, the same as you would bread; it may take an hour or two. Then
put it in a nice hot oven and bake.

'This cake was made in the days when bread was baked in a brick oven,
and was baked along with the bread.'

M. K. Samuelson, *Sussex Recipe Book, with a Few Excursions into Kent*, 1937

*Equivalent metric quantities: flour 670 g, sugar 225 g, butter 340 g,
eggs 1, yeast 20 g, a little nutmeg.*

· AN ORDINARY CAKE TO EAT WITH BUTTER ·

'Take two pounds of flour, and rub into it half a pound of butter; then put to it some spice, a little salt, a quarter and half of sugar, half a pound of raisins stoned, and half a pound of currants; make these into a cake, with half a pint of ale-yeast, four eggs and as much warm milk as you see convenient; mix it well together; an hour and half will bake it. This cake is good to eat with butter for breakfast.'

E. Smith, *The Compleat Housewife*, 1727

Yeast Buns and Small Tea Cakes

'A bun may be defined as a small, soft, plump, sweet, fermented cake.'

The Bakers' ABC, John Kirkland, 1927

'The variety and names of buns are determined by the skill and ingenuity of the bakers.'

ibid.

Bath buns, hot cross buns, spice buns, penny buns, Chelsea buns, currant buns – all these 'small, soft, plump, sweet, fermented' cakes are English institutions. Very stodgy ones, too, if you buy them from the bakeries, and to be avoided by anyone mindful of their weight and, in particular, of the obesity problems of so many of today's English children. Just occasionally, though, it is agreeable to be able to bake some of these old English specialities at home, to discover what they were really like – how much lighter, how much more character and individuality they had than the stereotyped products turned out by the commercial bakeries. Made at home, Bath buns and spice buns are by no means heavy, and hot cross buns, well spiced and fresh from the oven, are entirely delicious. None of these buns should be more than very lightly sweetened, and the fat content is not high.

The most interesting of the recipes is perhaps the simple spiced fruit bun, the original of our Good Friday hot cross bun without the cross. These spice buns first became popular in Tudor days, at the same period as the larger spice loaves or cakes, and were no doubt usually made from the same batch of spiced and butter-enriched fruit dough. For a long time bakers were permitted to offer these breads and buns for sale only on special occasions, as is shown by the following decree, issued in 1592, the thirty-sixth year of the reign of Elizabeth I, by the London Clerk of the Markets:

'That no bakers, etc, at any time or times hereafter make, utter, or sell by retail, within or without their houses, unto any of the Queen's subjects any spice cakes, buns, biscuits, or other spice bread (being bread out of size and not by law allowed) except it be at burials, or on Friday before Easter, or at Christmas, upon pain of forfeiture of all such spiced bread to the poor.'[1]

Captain BUN Quixote attacking the OVEN.

For four generations the Chelsea Bun House belonged to a family called Hand. One of them became an officer in the Staffordshire militia. Inevitably he was nicknamed Captain Bun. From a print dated 4 January 1773; Chelsea Public Library.

If anybody wanted spice bread and buns for a private celebration, then, these delicacies had to be made at home. In the time of James I, further attempts to prevent bakers from making spice breads and buns proved impossible to enforce, and in this matter the bakers were allowed their way. Although for different reasons, the situation now is much as it was in the late seventeenth century, spice buns appearing only at Easter

1. Stow's Survey of London, 1598, ed. John Strype, 1720, Vol. 2, ch. xxiv, p. 441.

– not, to be sure, on Good Friday when the bakeries are closed, but about a fortnight in advance, so that, as I was told in 1972 by my local bakery, 'people can buy them and put them in their freezers ready for Easter'. The mass-market bakers, it seems, go even further, at any rate if the following item from a *Sunday Times* 'Diary'[1] is anything to go by:

'For the first time, in my experience, the air of Camden Town is not filled with a sickly sweet, asphyxiating vapour reminiscent of the deadly chlorine gas attacks of the First World War.

'What has happened? Could it be the ABC Bread Factory is not baking its usual batch of five million hot cross buns?

'No, it's not. I am indebted to a *Sunday Times* printer who tells me he was asphyxiated in Basildon by hot cross buns last January. Nowadays, you see, they bake them months ahead, then freeze them.'

And those asphyxiating vapours? Spice essences? Synthetic flavourings? Let them remain the secret of the bakery plants. When you make your own spice buns, you find that the 'vapours' and the scent of spices coming from the oven are so enticing as to be irresistible. And, since there is no need to restrict the making of these delicacies to Easter time, it seems best to start with a recipe for the ordinary spice bun. To make the whole process as easy as possible, it is worth investing in a couple of inexpensive bun sheets which make the shaping, apportioning and spacing of the dough so simple a matter.

· SPICE BUNS ·

To make twenty to twenty-four buns quantities are: 1 lb to 1 lb 2 oz plain flour, preferably strong, 1 oz of yeast, 4 oz of currants, a level teaspoon of salt, approximately ½ pint of milk, 2 oz of soft light-brown sugar, 2 oz of butter, 2 teaspoons of mixed sweet spice (usually allspice, nutmeg, cinnamon and cloves, but many variations are possible; see note 2 below), 2 whole eggs.

For glazing the buns: 2 tablespoons of milk taken from the half pint in the main recipe, and 2 tablespoons of caster sugar.

For preparing the bun trays, unless you have the non-stick variety, a little extra butter and flour are needed.

Equivalent metric quantities: plain, preferably strong, flour, 450 to

1. On 22 April 1973.

500 g, yeast 30 g, currants 125 g, salt 1 level teaspoon, milk approximately 280 g, soft light-brown sugar 60 g, butter 60 g, mixed sweet spice 2 teaspoons, eggs 2 ; (for glazing) milk 2 tablespoons (taken from the 280 g in the main recipe) and caster sugar 2 tablespoons ; extra butter and flour for the bun trays.

First warm the milk to blood heat and use a little for creaming the yeast.

Warm the flour in a big bowl. Add the salt, sugar and spices. Make a well in the centre, pour in the creamed yeast, then add the softened butter, the whole eggs, one at a time, and the rest of the milk, or as much of it as can be absorbed by the dough, which should be soft but not too liquid. Stir or mix by hand until all the ingredients are well amalgamated. Finally, add the currants, and mix them in carefully, so that they are well and evenly distributed throughout the dough.

Cover the bowl and leave the dough to rise for about 2 hours, or until it is at least double in volume, light and puffy.

Now break down the dough, knead it briefly and, using a tablespoon, fill the prepared bun moulds to two-thirds only of their size, doming up the dough to achieve the right plump and rounded shape. Smooth each one over with a palette knife.

Cover the trays with a sheet of waxed paper or polythene and leave them in a warm place – a steamy atmosphere is ideal for buns – until the dough has recovered from the moulding and once more grown and doubled in volume. They should feel soft and light to the touch.

Bake the buns in the centre of a fairly hot oven, 375° to 400°F, 190° to 205°C, gas nos. 5 or 6, for 15 to 20 minutes.

Just before they are ready to come out of the oven, boil the milk and sugar glaze until it is bubbly and syrupy. Brush the buns with this glaze while they are still hot, giving them two successive coatings. Provided that the dough was well matured and baked at the right moment, the crusts will be fine and soft, and the glaze will not turn tacky or sticky but will form a fine shining mirror-like finish to the buns.

Notes and variations: 1. The brown sugar combined with the spices gives the finished buns a brownish crumb which to me seems part of their charm, but, taking into account the public mania for white bread, even in the case of fancy goods such as buns, the bakers at one time decided that it would be more advantageous to use white sugar and a more or less colourless spice essence instead of powdered spices. The essence was also cheaper and less trouble.

2. A formula for a spice blend composed of cinnamon, nutmeg, cloves, ginger and white peppercorns, to be made in small quantity from whole spices ground in an electric coffee mill, will be found on p. 430. Those who make spice buns and cakes only on rare occasions will probably prefer to use a bought 'pudding' spice, which should be perfectly adequate.

For spice buns I find that a very small proportion of ground cumin added to whichever blend of spices is chosen gives a wonderfully warm and attractive flavour, unorthodox but well worth trying.

· HOT CROSS BUNS ·

'Perhaps no cry – though it is only for one morning – is more familiar to the ears of a Londoner, than that of One-a-penny, two-a-penny, hot-cross buns on Good Friday.'

Henry Mayhew, *London Labour and the London Poor*, 1851

'One for the poker,
Two for the tongs;
Three for the dust-pan,
Hot Cross Buns!'

Good Friday rhyme recorded by Allan Jobson
in *An Hour-Glass on the Run*, 1959

Under the heading 'Hot and Cross' the *Daily Telegraph* published in March 1972 a letter from a reader asking if the time had not come for a re-naming of the Good Friday bun, since it was now the consumer who was hot and cross 'being expected to pay $2\frac{1}{2}$p each for what cost only half that amount before the introduction of decimal currency'.

The remedy for this trouble – and surely by now the hot and cross, or rather frozen and cross, bun costs a good deal more than $2\frac{1}{2}$p – would be to make the buns at home. There may not be a great saving in money, but in terms of temper and enjoyment the benefit is very great, and it does seem entirely wrong that for even such a simple thing as a spiced bun we should put ourselves at the mercy of the bread and cake factories and their deep freezes.

The recipe for hot cross buns is exactly as for the spice buns above, except that a little less milk should be used for making up the dough, so that the mixture is slightly firmer. If the dough is too soft, it will not take the cross cuts, which are made after the moulded buns have recovered volume and when the dough looks well-grown. The cuts are made fairly deep, with the back of an ordinary table knife, or with a thin wooden or metal spatula. As soon as they have opened out, the buns are ready for baking, as ordinary spice buns, but hot cross buns always remain rather flattened, because although the dough may be made stiffer than for a simple bun, it is still a soft dough which will not completely regain shape and volume after the cutting.

To emphasize the cross, some bakers superimpose strips of candied peel or little bands of ordinary pastry. Both these methods involve unnecessary fiddling work. Neither, in my experience, is successful. There is no need to worry overmuch about the exactitude of the cross. You have made the symbolic gesture. That is what counts.

Notes: 1. Spice buns and hot cross buns can be reheated in a very moderate oven, and they are delicious split and lightly toasted. It is really rather a treat to have fresh, well-spiced hot cross buns for breakfast during the Easter weekend.

2. Hot cross buns are not invariably spiced, so they can be made just simply as currant buns, using the same dough and the same proportions of currants and sugar, brown or white. But unless the buns are being made for children who may dislike spices it is a pity to leave them out. Without spice, currant buns are rather dull.

· TEA BUNS ·

'½ pint milk	2 oz sugar
2 oz butter	2 oz currants or sultanas
1 egg	1 lb flour
1 oz yeast	pinch salt'

Equivalent metric quantities : milk 280 g, butter 60 g, eggs 1, yeast 30 g, sugar 60 g, currants or sultanas 60 g, flour 450 g, pinch of salt.

'Warm milk and butter and then add beaten egg. Beat yeast and sugar to warm. Mix with fruit, flour and salt to a light dough.

'Put to rise.

'When risen make into about 28 small buns and allow to rise again.

'Bake in hot oven – 20 min. (Reg. 6).

'When cool, brush over with thin white icing.'

The above recipe was passed on to me in 1974 by Mrs Broadbent, an old lady living in the Isle of Wight, who heard that I was working on a book about English yeast cookery. Her recipe makes nice, simple little fruit buns.

· BATH BUNS AND CAKES ·

'These Bath-buns are almost the same preparation as the Brioche cakes so much eaten and talked of in Paris.'

Mistress Margaret Dods, *The Cook and Housewife's Manual*, 4th edn, 1829 (first published 1826)

'The comestible known as the Bath Bun and now sold everywhere throughout the kingdom . . . is a sweet bun of a somewhat stodgy type, and is popularly supposed to constitute, with a little milk, the average form of luncheon taken by mild curates.'

Frederick Hackwood, *Good Cheer*, 1911

'A solitary porter shuffles along the platform. Yonder, those are the lights of the refreshment room, where all night long, a barmaid is keeping her lonely vigil over the beer-handles and the Bath buns in glass cases.'

Max Beerbohm, *Yet Again*, 1923

What happened, then, to the Bath bun? Remembering the hefty, sticky, sugary Bath buns of school days, I would, until recently, have agreed with Frederick Hackwood's verdict, except that I would have substituted school children's elevenses – and indeed the rail travellers' refreshment – for curates' luncheons. Now, having tried the recipes from cookery books of the latter half of the eighteenth century, when Bath buns and cakes were great favourites, I see that Margaret Dods was perfectly correct in relating them so closely to the brioche. Her own recipe allows for a half pound of butter, four eggs and four ounces of sugar to a pound of flour and a 'glassful' of yeast. For cakes she added caraway seeds, while the smaller buns were strewn with 'sugar carraways'. I think that somewhere along the line Bath cakes, which were very light, delicate tea cakes, developed into or became indistinguishable from Sally Lunns, while the bun version was down-graded by the bakers into the amorphous, artificially coloured, synthetically flavoured and over-sugared confections we know today. This London Bath bun should, I believe, be distinguished from the Bath bun of Bath and the West Country, said to be still at least shapely and neatly rounded if not precisely light.

Could the Great Exhibition of 1851 have been responsible for the London Bath bun? During the five-and-a-half-month run of that great show, I learn from Anthony Bird's *Paxton's Palace*,[1] six million visitors consumed between them the impressive total of 943,691 Bath buns. It is easy to visualize the overworked bakers supplying the Exhibition at some point abandoning the business of hand-shaping thousands of buns every morning and simply throwing the dough anyhow on to their oven trays. Certainly it was said at the time that the Crystal Palace refreshments were of such poor quality and served in so slovenly a manner that they barely even reached railway buffet standards.

The recipe I use for Bath buns is based on the one given by Elizabeth Raffald in *The Experienced English Housekeeper*, first published in 1769. This recipe differs from the Dods version chiefly in that it has no eggs:

'Rub half a pound of butter into a pound of flour, and one spoonful of good barm, warm some cream, and make it into a light paste, set it on the fire to rise, when you make them up take four ounces of carraway comfits, work part of them in, and strew the rest on the top, make them into a round cake, the size of a French roll, bake them on sheet tins, and send them in hot for breakfast.'

Mrs Raffald's proportions and method work perfectly, and produce an excellent dough, although cream in addition to a large proportion of butter does seem rather over-lavish, so I use milk instead of the cream. Caraway comfits, so often specified in recipes of the period, were sugar-coated caraway seeds, a sweet which has long disappeared but which must have been something like the tiny aniseed balls still made in France. Nowadays the comfits are omitted from Bath buns, and to the best of my knowledge so are caraway seeds, but little chips or nibs of crystallized sugar are still traditionally strewn over the finished cakes.

To make twelve Bath buns, then, you need 1 lb of white flour – whether ordinary household or strong bread flour is not important – ½ oz of yeast, ½ lb of butter, ½ pint of milk, a teaspoon of salt, 2 tablespoons of sugar, and for glazing and decorating the buns a little extra sugar and milk, plus 2 tablespoons of white sugar crystals, made from roughly crushed white candy sugar or coffee sugar. (The little sugar nibs used in bakeries and pastry shops are available only to the trade.)

Equivalent metric quantities: white flour 450 g, yeast 15 g, butter 225 g, milk 280 g, salt 1 teaspoon, sugar 2 tablespoons; for glazing: extra milk and sugar, plus white sugar crystals 2 tablespoons.

1. London, Cassell, 1976.

Warm the milk very slightly, pour a little over the yeast, then rub the softened butter into the flour, into which you have already mixed the salt and sugar. Add the creamed yeast, then mix to a light dough with the milk. Cover the bowl, leave in a warm place for about 1½ hours, until the dough has risen very high and is extremely light and puffy.

Have ready a buttered and floured baking sheet or, better still, a non-stick sheet which requires no preparation.

At well-spaced intervals on the baking sheet put rounded tablespoons of the dough. Smooth over the top of each bun with a palette knife. Leave the buns, covered with a sheet of polythene or a cloth, for about 15 minutes, so that the dough recovers its spring, before putting them into a moderately hot oven, 375°F, 190°C, gas no. 5.

They will take 15 to 20 minutes to bake, and during the process will puff up, spread and become almost joined together. If they are un-evenly shaped, and some more square than round, there is nothing to worry about. After they have been glazed and sugared simply break them apart. If possible, eat these buns while they are still warm from the oven.

To glaze and sugar the buns

Put 2 tablespoons of caster sugar and 1 of milk into a very small saucepan. Heat the mixture and brush it over the buns as soon as they are taken from the oven. Have ready the sugar crystals, roughly pounded in a mortar. Strew a few of them over each bun as soon as they have all been brushed with glaze.

· TO MAKE THIRTY-NINE BATH BUNS ·

'Take one pound of flour, the rinds of three lemons grated fine, half a pound of butter melted in a coffee-cup of cream, a teaspoonful of yeast and five eggs. Add one pound of powdered loaf sugar. Work well. Let it stand to rise, and it will make thirty-nine Bath buns.'

Quoted by Marcus Woodward in *The Mistress of Stantons Farm*, 1938

I don't know how you'd get thirty-nine buns out of the quantities given in the above recipe – they'd have to be very small ones – and I think the yeast must have been measured in one of those deep Victorian teaspoons which easily held an ounce. I like the runic title. 'Thirty-nine Bath Buns' should surely be a children's game or the name of a country dance.

Equivalent metric quantities: flour 450g, rinds of 3 lemons (grated), butter 225g, cream 1 coffee-cupful, yeast about 30g, eggs 5, loaf sugar 450g.

· CHELSEA BUNS ·

'There's a charm in the sound, which nobody shuns
Of smoking hot, piping hot, Chelsea Buns.'

Eighteenth century song

The famous Bun House of Chelsea was probably built towards the end of the seventeenth century or in the early years of the eighteenth. It was a large establishment, situated near Sloane Square in what was then Jews Road, later the Pimlico Road, and within easy reach of the river. Evidently a bakery, pastry cooks' and refreshment shop combined, the Bun House provided tables at which the customers could sit down to eat their cakes and buns fresh from the oven. In its early days the Bun House was renowned chiefly for its hot cross buns, sold in massive quantities on Good Fridays and during the Easter celebrations, when great crowds flocked to Chelsea expressly to visit the Bun House. Caroline of Ansbach, Queen of George II, was a frequent visitor to Chelsea during the early years of the reign (he succeeded in 1727), going there by water – tradition has it that she, her family and the King himself visited the Bun House on many occasions. Possibly, then, the popularity of the Chelsea bun, as distinct from the older and more famous Good Friday buns, dates from the days of Hanoverian royal patronage, although already in the days of Queen Anne, Swift, staying at Chelsea for a change of air, reported to Stella how 'Rrrrrrare Chelsea buns' were cried in the streets, and how the one he bought for a penny was stale, adding, not surprisingly, 'I did not like it.'[1]

A century after Swift's brief stay in Chelsea, the Bun House was still flourishing. For four generations it was in the ownership of a family called Hand (see illustration on p. 474) and according to Chambers's *Book of Days* 'families of the middle classes' would still walk a considerable way to taste the delicacies of the Chelsea Bun House.[2] Demolished in 1839, the original Pimlico Road Bun House was re-created in Sloane Square for a brief period in 1951 as part of the Festival of Britain celebrations.

1. *Journal to Stella*, 2 May 1711.
2. Chambers's *Book of Days*, Volume 1, 1869.

'It is singular', wrote Sir Richard Phillips,[1] an addict of the original Chelsea buns, 'that their delicate flavour, lightness and richness, have never been successfully imitated . . . for above thirty years I have never passed the Bun House without filling my pockets.'

Sugary, spicy, sticky, square and coiled like a Swiss roll, the Chelsea bun as we now know it is a pretty hefty proposition. That it can be very usefully adapted to smaller scale needs was demonstrated to me in the letter quoted further on. So it is worth knowing the principle on which Chelsea buns are made. Recipes vary considerably in detail, but the basic bun dough is fairly constant.

First prepare a simple bun dough, as for the Bath buns on p. 480, but with the addition of eggs and a flavouring of grated lemon peel and a teaspoon of ground cinnamon or mixed sweet spice. Keep the dough fairly stiff. When it has risen for the first time, break it down, knead it well, divide it into two equal portions. Roll each into a rectangle. For a dough made with 20 oz of flour, 2 eggs, ½ lb butter, approximately ¼ pint of milk, ½ oz of yeast, a teaspoon of salt, and 2 tablespoons of sugar, have ready the following ingredients:

3 oz of currants, 3 oz of brown sugar, 3 oz of butter, 1 oz of caster sugar; milk and sugar for a glaze, as described on p. 481.

Equivalent metric quantities: flour 550 g, eggs 2, butter 225 g, milk approximately 150 g, yeast 15 g, salt 1 teaspoon, sugar 2 tablespoons; for spreading on the dough: currants 85 g, brown sugar 85 g, butter 85 g, caster sugar 30 g; milk and sugar for a glaze.

Spread each rectangle of dough with an equal quantity of butter cut into small knobs, warmed currants and brown sugar.

Fold the rectangles in three, as for puff pastry, give them one turn, then roll them out again into rectangles approximately 8 inches by 10 inches. Now roll up each piece of dough firmly, like a jam roll. Seal the edges with water. Cut these rolls into slices from 1 to 2 inches thick, according to the size you need your buns to end up, remembering that by the time they have been proved and baked they will have doubled in volume.

Arrange the slices in even rows on a greased baking sheet – seven to a row used to be the rule of professional bakers – with a space of about 1 inch in between each bun. The spacing is important, for during the proving period, and as the buns grow in volume, so that they almost

1. *A Morning's Walk to Kew.* 1817.

merge, they begin to assume the characteristically square shape. (If they are too far apart they remain round.) When they are all but touching, sprinkle them with the caster sugar. They are now ready for the oven. Bake them for 15 minutes at 425°F, 220°C, gas no. 7. During baking the merging process is completed. As soon as you take the buns from the oven, brush them with the hot milk and sugar glaze. Separate them only after they have cooled for a few minutes.

Here is the promised suggestion for adapting Chelsea buns to suit tastes less than robust; it comes from a lifelong friend, the painter Arthur Lett Haines, who has always had interesting and beautifully imaginative ideas about food. He writes: 'I like Chelsea buns. But find them rather large and bucolic. So make them very small, exaggerate the quantity of fruit, chopped small, and serve them no larger than big petit fours, coated with royal icing

1. lemon-flavoured and peppered with a crushed pistachio
2. royal icing flavoured with Angostura and sprinkled with poppy seeds.'

Now that seems to me a most admirable approach to the problem of re-creating a speciality which would otherwise have little place in our lives today. It would be agreeable to think that the delicate flavour and lightness described by Sir Richard Phillips might one day be restored to the Chelsea bun.

· WIGS or WIGGS ·

'Some wax dronk in lent of wygges and craknels.'

More, *Dyaloge*, ii, xi, 1529

'Home to the only Lenten supper I have had of wiggs and ale.'

Samuel Pepys, *Diary*, 8 April 1664

'In London the various sorts of common buns make whigs little regarded; where, indeed, the name of them is now far from generally known . . . they are often made into a large round cake crossed, so as easily to be divided into quarters; this however is quite discretional.'

The Family Receipt Book, London, 1853

Although there is evidence that wygges, wigges, wiggs, wigs or whigs were known in England at least as far back as the fifteenth century, recipes for them seem not to have appeared in print until some three centuries later. By this time, these yeast-leavened and spiced tea cakes were obviously no longer the Lenten speciality they had once been. They were light and sometimes 'very rich'.

Butter, sugar, flour, milk and yeast are the basic ingredients. Some recipes call for eggs, some for sack[1] as well; among the spices specified are ginger, nutmeg, mace and cloves; occasionally currants are included, while caraway seeds seem to have been a constant. As so often, Hannah Glasse's recipes – she gives several variations – are the richest in the quantity and variety of ingredients, while Elizabeth Raffald, writing some thirty years later, gives just one rather terse recipe for 'wigs', a good, quick and practical one, with 'seeds' as the only spice.

Not one of the eighteenth-century ladies gives us a clue as to the shape of these wiggs – it was taken for granted that readers knew what they should look like – but since wigg is said to derive from *weig*, an old Teutonic word meaning wedge, it seems fairly obvious that the cakes should be triangular, and the note from *The Family Receipt Book* quoted above confirms this.

Curiously, these excellent little spice cakes disappeared from most of the nineteenth-century cookery books. Neither Eliza Acton nor Mrs Beeton mentions them, while Cassell's *Dictionary of Cookery*, that extraordinary late Victorian compendium, gives a recipe which turns out to be, word for word, Mrs Raffald's.

In the early 1930s Miss Florence White, writing in *Good Things in England*, tells us that 'whigs' were still then made at the Red House Restaurant, Bath, and at Hawkshead, in Cumberland, where the poet William Wordsworth went to school. Miss White directs that 'whigs' 'can be made up into any shape you please', but are 'usually made into large round cakes, crossed so as to be easily divided into quarters', while Miss Dorothy Hartley, in *Food in England* (1954), gives two recipes, one dated 1900, in which 'whigs' are baked on saucers or plates.

Here is Elizabeth Raffald's recipe from her *Experienced English Housekeeper* (1769).

'*To make light Wigs*. To three quarters of a pound of fine flour put half a pint of milk made warm, mix in it two or three spoonfuls of light barm, cover it up, set it half an hour by the fire to rise, work in the paste four ounces of sugar, and four ounces of butter, make it into wigs with as little flour as possible, and a few seeds, set them in a quick oven to bake.'

1. Sweet sherry, in our terms.

Except for the substitution of ½ oz of bakers' yeast for the three spoonfuls of light barm, Mrs Raffald's recipe needs little adaptation. I have used it much as it was written over two centuries ago.

Although caraway seeds are not among my own addictions, they were very popular as a flavouring for English cakes, buns and biscuits during the eighteenth, nineteenth and early twentieth centuries, and it seems right that they should go in to these particular tea cakes, for their use was probably symbolic of the spring sowing of wheat, and this may explain the appearance of wiggs or other seed cakes in Lent. So I use a modest amount of caraway – about 2 teaspoonfuls – to Mrs Raffald's ¾lb of flour. No harm in putting more if you like the flavour to predominate. I find it an improvement to add also a very little ground ginger and mixed sweet spice – about ½ teaspoon of each – since these too appear to have been traditional flavourings for wiggs; occasionally an old recipe specifies mixed sweet spice, or nutmeg, mace and cinnamon only, without the caraways.

So: *¾ lb of flour (ordinary plain household flour can be used), ½ oz of bakers' yeast, 6 fluid oz of warm milk, 4 oz each of caster sugar and softened butter, 2 to 3 teaspoons of caraway seeds, ½ teaspoon each of ground ginger and mixed sweet or 'pudding' spice.*

Equivalent metric quantities: flour 340 g, milk 170 g, bakers' yeast 15 g, caster sugar 125 g, butter 125 g, caraway seeds 2 to 3 teaspoons, ground ginger ½ teaspoon, mixed sweet or 'pudding' spice ½ teaspoon.

Put the flour in a bowl, dissolve the yeast in the warm milk and mix with the flour to a light dough. With your hands beat in the softened butter, then add the sugar and spices. Cover the dough and leave in a warm place to rise for about 2 hours.

Break down the dough, which should be very light and bubbly. If it is too slack, sprinkle in a little extra flour, and, again using more flour to make the dough easy to handle, divide it into two pieces. Pat these out into rounds, either on a floured baking sheet or in two warmed and buttered 7 to 8 inch sponge tins. The latter is the easier and neater method. (The Prestige factory produces useful aluminium sponge tins with loose bases.)

Make four cross cuts on each round, so that the two cakes will divide easily, when baked, into a total of sixteen wedges. Now leave the dough, covered, for about 20 minutes, to recover from the handling and cutting.

Bake the cakes in a moderately hot oven, 375° to 400°F, 190° to 205°C, gas nos. 5 or 6, for 15 minutes.

Sometimes wiggs, like Bath buns, were strewn with coarsely broken sugar, just prior to baking. I find they are nicer without this extra trimming. They are best eaten warm, and can be reheated in a very low oven.

Notes: 'To stew cheese with light wiggs' is the heading of another of Mrs Raffald's recipes. For this a plateful of cheese, with a glass of red wine poured over it, was melted in front of the fire. You were then to 'toast a light wigg', pour over it two or three spoonfuls of hot red wine, put it in the middle of your dish, lay the cheese over it and serve it up.

Evidently Mrs Raffald, or the Warburton family for whom she cooked, was fond of stewed cheese and wiggs. Another recipe is for cheese with ale poured over it, melted before the fire until like a light custard, then poured over toasts or wiggs.

Odd though it sounds, the slightly sweet, spicy wiggs and a mature English Cheshire or Lancashire cheese (the ones Mrs Raffald would have known best – she was a north country woman) go extraordinarily well together.

· CORNISH SPLITS ·

'*1 lb flour; 1 oz butter; ½ oz yeast; ½ oz castor sugar; ½ pint tepid milk; salt.*'

Equivalent metric quantities: flour 450 g, butter 30 g, yeast 15 g, caster sugar 15 g, milk 280 g, salt.

'Cream the yeast and sugar together until they are liquid, then add the milk; sieve the flour and quarter teaspn. salt into a basin. Melt the butter gently, add it and the milk, etc., to the flour and mix all into a smooth dough. Put the basin in a warm place, to let the dough rise, for ¾ hour. Then shape it in small round cakes and place them in a floured baking tin. Bake in a quick oven for from 15 to 20 minutes. Split and butter them. Serve very hot. Or may be left until cold, then split and butter them, or split and eat with cream, jam or treacle.

'Splits eaten with cream and treacle are known as "thunder and lightning".'

Kathleen Thomas, *A West Country Cookery Book*, 1961

· DEVONSHIRE CHUDLEIGHS ·

According to Miss Thomas these are made in the same manner as the Cornish splits above, but are smaller.

· YORKSHIRE CAKES (1) ·

'Take three pounds of flour, a pint and a half of warm milk, four spoonsful of yeast, and three eggs, beat the whole well together, and let it rise; then form your cakes, and let them rise on the tins before you bake, which must be in a slow oven.

'Five ounces of butter may be warmed in the milk if agreeable.'

Elizabeth Hammond, *Modern Domestic Cookery and Useful Receipt Book*, 1817

· YORKSHIRE CAKES (2) ·

The following nineteenth-century recipe for plain Yorkshire tea cakes comes from *The Mistress of Stantons Farm* by Marcus Woodward (1938):

'Dry a pound and a half of flour before the fire, beat up an egg with a spoonful of good new yest and add to these three quarters of a pint of new milk just warmed, strain the whole through a sieve into the flour, mix it lightly into a dough and let it rise by the fire for an hour. Make it up into cakes about the size of a large saucer, put them on a tin and let them stand before the fire for a little while before they are set into the oven. Half an hour will bake them, the oven should only be moderately hot.'

MRS TASHIS' LITTLE PUDDINGS

'To nine eggs put a pint of cream and mix it pretty stiff with flower, put in three spoonsful of yeast; and then let it stand two hours to rise; grate in the Peel of one Lemmon and some sugar. Put it into tins. A quarter of an hour will bake them; if you pleas, you may put in a little lemon juice.'

Receipt Book of Mrs Ann Blencowe *1694*,
with an introduction by George Saintsbury,
published by Guy Chapman, the Adelphi, London, 1925

A publisher's note tells us that Ann Blencowe was born in 1656, daughter of John Wallis, mathematician and cryptographer. She married John Blencowe in 1675.

Mrs Blencowe's receipt book includes some interesting recipes, well written and accurately observed. There is one for a 'Delma', which, although it mystified George Saintsbury, is simply Turkish *dolma* or the

Greek *dolmádes*, vine or cabbage leaves stuffed with rice and meat, very much as we know them today. From the recipe for Mrs Harvey's pancakes we learn that when they are done, they are to be turned out 'upon ye wrong side of a pewter plate', which seems admirably practical. As for Mrs Tashis, how I wish Mrs Blencowe had given us a clue as to her identity and nationality. Her 'little puddings' are quite delicious, perfectly easy to adapt, and turn out rather like a lemon-flavoured brioche. I have never seen another recipe quite like it, and it has become a particular favourite.

Mrs Tashis' little puddings are baked in dariole moulds. They look rather like babas.

This is how I make the little puddings:

½ lb of strong plain flour, a scant ½ oz of yeast, 4 to 6 tablespoons of thick cream, 3 average size eggs, or 2 large ones, 3 oz of caster sugar, 1 rough-skinned lemon for grating. Butter for the moulds.

Equivalent metric quantities: strong plain flour 225 g, yeast 15 g, thick cream 4 to 6 tablespoons, eggs 3 average or 2 large, caster sugar 85 g, lemons 1 (rough-skinned), butter for the moulds. Tin size: eight dariole moulds, height 8 cm, top diameter 8 cm, or one large mould or bread tin of 2 litre capacity.

Put the flour and sugar in a bowl, cream the yeast to a paste with warm water, add it to the flour, then put in the cream and the eggs. Grate in the lemon peel. Mix lightly, to the consistency of a batter. Cover it and leave to rise for approximately 1 hour, or until it is very light and spongy.

Butter eight dariole moulds (the shape which we call castle pudding tins, approximately 3 inches high, and 3 inches in diameter at the top) and spoon the batter into them, until they are just about half full.

Place the moulds on a baking sheet, cover them with a piece of polythene, leave them for approximately 45 minutes, until the batter has risen just to the top of the tins.

Put them in the centre of a fairly hot oven, 375° to 400°F, 190° to 205°C, gas nos. 5 or 6. As Mrs Blencowe says, 'quarter of an hour will bake them'.

Leave them to cool a little before turning them out of the tins on to a cooling rack.

The shape of the little puddings or brioches will be rather like that of babas, with a mushroom-like head, beautifully golden-brown.

Notes and variations: 1. If you prefer, or if you have no dariole moulds, the batter can be baked in one large 3 to 3½ pint mould or bread tin. The procedure and the oven temperature are the same as for the 'little puddings', but after 10 minutes' cooking, cover the top of the cake with paper and move it to the lowest shelf of the oven for a further 5 to 10 minutes.

Leave the cake in the tin for 5 minutes before inverting it on to a cake rack to cool. Made in this fashion the little puddings become Mrs Tashis' lemon cake, tea cake, or just Mrs Tashis' cake . . . A slice or two, served warm, goes wonderfully well with a fruit sorbet, a plain apple purée or pears baked in wine.

2. Ordinary household flour instead of strong bread flour can be used for this batter, but the volume of the finished cake or little puddings will be smaller, and the texture not quite so open and light.

· GUERNSEY BISCUITS ·

A mid-nineteenth-century recipe given by Mr J. Stevens Cox in his *Guernsey Dishes of Bygone Days* (1971).[1] Guernsey biscuits are not what we call biscuits but are more like wiggs or soft, butter-enriched rolls.

'4 lb of flour, 1 lb of Butter, 2ᵈ worth of Barm set the leaven to rise an

1. St Peter Port, the Toucan Press.

hour before you add the Butter – when the Dough is done, let it rise before the fire, one hour, then make your biscuits and bake them in a rather quick oven – if you like you may add a few Carraways – and lay them on a table or slab for 2 hours before baking.'

From the recipe book of Augusta Diana Lane, dated January 1843

N.B. Mrs Lane forgot, I think, to mention that milk or water would be needed to make up the leaven, for 2d worth of barm would hardly have been enough to moisten 4 lb of flour, even given the pound of butter added later. At any rate, today, using bakers' yeast, say a generous ounce, to 4 lb of flour, it would be necessary to mix the flour with milk or a mixture of milk and water. In the sense intended in Mrs Lane's recipe, a leaven is simply an ordinary dough or sponge, so the normal proportion of a half pint of liquid per pound of flour is about right. Baking time, for biscuits made up in 3 oz to 4 oz rounds, would be 15 to 20 minutes at 425°F, 220°C, gas no. 7.

Equivalent metric quantities: flour 1·8 kg, butter 450 g, bakers' yeast 30 g, milk or milk and water mixed 1,120 g, caraway seeds (optional).

· SOFT BISCUITS ·

'The Soft Biscuit is made properly only in Aberdeen and the N.E. of Scotland. It looks like a round roll or flattish bun, and has a depression made in the centre. A good variety of nursery rusk is made with a Soft Biscuit toasted for half a minute till it sizzles and gives off a pleasant baking aroma; it is then broken up into small pieces (not too small), hot milk is poured over it and plenty of sugar.'

Mrs E. M. L. Douglas, of Innerleithen, in a contribution to *A Concise Encyclopaedia of Gastronomy*, London, the Wine and Food Society, 1943

The dough for soft biscuits is made, according to Miss Marian McNeill, with 3 oz of melted butter and a tablespoon of sugar to every pound of bakers' dough. It is formed into flattened buns about 3 to 4 inches in diameter, left to prove a second time and baked in a medium hot oven.

It is interesting that these soft biscuits are common to Scotland and Guernsey, and that the term biscuit as applied to a soft product was retained in these places, and in America, whereas in England it has completely died out. I have seen buns or biscuits corresponding to Mrs Douglas's description in Flemish and Dutch paintings. One painter in particular, Floris van Schouten, who flourished in the early decades of the seventeenth century, painted these biscuits over and over again, as indeed he painted manchet loaves, Delft dishes of butter and a variety of silver or pewter salt cellars.

Equivalent metric quantities: to 450 g of bakers' dough, melted butter 85 g, sugar 1 tablespoon.

· PLAIN GALETTES ·

'Required: a pound and a half of light bread dough, two ounces of sugar, the same of currants and raisins, a little spice, two ounces of fat of any kind (dripping is nice) and an egg – cost, about 6d.'

Equivalent metric quantities: bread dough 670 g, sugar 60 g, currants 60 g, raisins 60 g, spice, fat 60 g, eggs 1.

'The above ingredients are blended and the dough left to rise after mixing; it is then made into balls the size of an orange; these are flattened a little and snipped round the edges with scissors; the incisions are rather deep; this adds to the lightness. Then put them on a baking tin with half an inch of space between, and "prove" over hot water for ten minutes. Cover with a thin cloth.

'Bake in a hot oven about twelve to fifteen minutes, and glaze them; return to the oven for a minute to set, and serve hot or cold with butter.

'*Note:* Any of the richer doughs can be used, and the fruit, etc. increased for better galettes. Very rich galettes resemble shortbread. A galette the size of a dinner plate may be made: but the snipping must not be omitted, and it may be gashed a time or two.'

Lizzie Heritage, *Cassell's Universal Cookery Book*,
1901 (first published 1894)

Miss Heritage's galettes are really a kind of flat lardy cake, the snipping of the dough round the edges giving them a characteristic appearance. I have made them and found them very good indeed.

In the next recipe, for plum heavies, the Sussex version of lardy rolls, the ingredients are almost identical to those in the galettes.

· SUSSEX PLUM HEAVIES ·

The following recipe is the Sussex version of lardy rolls:
'One pound dough, 2 oz lard, 3 oz currants, 2 oz brown sugar. Work all together with your lard until thoroughly mixed, and make into buns, not flat. Bake in a fairly hot oven for about 15 minutes.'

Equivalent metric quantities: dough 450 g, lard 60 g, currants 85 g, brown sugar 60 g.

M. K. Samuelson, *Sussex Recipe Book, with a Few Excursions into Kent*, 1937

· YEAST SOULE CAKES ·

'" Three pounds flour, quarter pound butter (or half pound if the cakes are to be extra rich), half pound sugar, two spoonsful of yeast, two eggs, allspice to taste, and sufficient new milk to make it into a light paste. Put the mixture (without the sugar or spice) to rise before the fire for half an hour, then add the sugar, and allspice enough to flavour it well; make into rather flat buns, and bake."'

Equivalent metric quantities: flour 1,350 g, butter 125 g (or 250 g), sugar 225 g, yeast approximately 50 g, eggs 2, allspice, milk.

'This is the recipe of Mrs Mary Ward, who is known to be the last person who kept up the old custom of giving "Soul Cakes" at Pulverbatch. She died in 1853 at the age of 101.'

Shropshire Cookery Book, compiled by
the Shropshire Federation of Women's Institutes, *c.* 1955

· ULVERSTON FAIR CAKES ·

'These cakes were made at Whitsuntide and Martinmas for the Hiring Fair at Ulverston.

'1 lb flour, ¼ lb butter, ½ lb lard, a pinch salt, ½ oz fresh yeast, 1 dessertspoon sugar, ½ cup warm water.

'Rub fat into dry ingredients, make a well in the centre and put in the yeast with the half cup of warm water and bind together. Roll out very thin and cut into 4 or 5 inch squares. Place a tablespoon of the following mixture on half the squares, damp the edges with water, cover with the remaining pastry squares and pinch together round the edges.

Filling mixture: 1 lb currants, ½ lb soft brown sugar, 2 oz candied peel, finely chopped, a pinch of nutmeg, a pinch of allspice, 1 teaspoon rum.

'Mix all together and make a little softer with water or cold tea. Bake in hot oven until golden brown.'

Equivalent metric quantities: flour 450 g, butter 125 g, lard 225 g, pinch of salt, fresh yeast 15 g, sugar 1 dessertspoon, warm water ¼ cup; for the filling: currants 450 g, soft brown sugar 225 g, candied peel 60 g, pinch of nutmeg, pinch of allspice, rum 1 teaspoon.

Lakeland Cookery, Clapham via Lancaster, the Dalesman Publishing Co. Ltd, 1969; compiled from recipes supplied by readers of *Cumbria*

· BURTERGILL WINDERMERE CAKES ·

The following recipe is obviously another version of the Ulverston Fair cakes above. Both bear some relation to the seventeenth-century Countess of Rutland's Banbury cake as well as to the Scotch Christmas bun.

'*Ingredients*

3 oz butter	2 oz sugar
4 oz lard	1 oz yeast
1¼ lb plain flour	2½ gills warm milk

'Filling

5 oz currants	Cassia,[1] to taste'
1 oz castor sugar	

Equivalent metric quantities: butter 85 g, lard 120 g, plain flour 550 g, sugar 60 g, yeast 30 g, warm milk 350 g; for the filling: currants 150 g, caster sugar 30 g, cassia to taste. Equivalent oven temperature in degrees C: 230°C.

'*Method*
'Rub butter and lard into flour, adding sugar. Raise the yeast with the milk and beat into the dry ingredients. Set to rise. When risen turn on to

1. A spice resembling cinnamon, which can be used instead.

baking board. The bowl should be left clean. Cut into eighteen pieces and roll out as eighteen teacakes. Into the bowl put currants, sugar and the cassia if liked, and mix together. Share this equally on nine of the cakes, then place the remaining nine on top, one on each. Set to rise. When risen bake for seven minutes in a hot oven (450°F or Regulo 7). To prepare for table split and butter generously and heat until piping hot.

'*Note:* These are really double tea cakes with a fruit stuffing.'

Through Yorkshire's Kitchen Door, the Yorkshire Federation of Women's Institutes, 31st edn, n.d. (first published 1927)

French Yeast Cakes

Anyone already familiar with English yeast cakes such as Sally Lunns, some of the many varieties of tea cake and perhaps the Scottish Aberdeen rowies will easily perceive the affinities as well as the differences between our own specialities and the renowned, much loved brioches, savarins and croissants of France. On the whole, the French versions are richer in butter and eggs, the manner of making and working the dough or batter is usually more complex, less yeast is used, the rising takes longer, and the final shaping of the dough, and often the finishing touches, call for more patience and expertise than do our own more homely buns and tea cakes.

Although a few of the more practised cooks among French housewives do make their own yeast cakes, many more tend to buy them from the professional pastrycooks and bakers, and do not grudge the often very high prices charged for these specialities. Given the cost of butter in France, prices could not be anything but high – and made with substitutes, as for example croissants often are, they are not worth buying. Brioches bought from the bakers, on the other hand, are usually well made, and although expensive, the larger ones especially are good value because they stay fresh and soft for much longer than do the little top-knotted breakfast brioches. Returning home at the weekend from a visit to Normandy during the autumn of 1974, it was a treat to see the special Saturday displays of outsize brioches in the windows of *pâtisseries* and *boulangeries* in even the humblest of villages and the most bleak of small towns on the route from Rouen to the coast. The *charcuteries* too are crammed with specialities at the weekend (crammed with customers too). At the bakery of a one-street village where parking was easy, we stopped to buy several varieties of bread to bring home, one of them the oddity called *pain brié*, particular to the Pont Audemer district of Normandy – it is drawn on p. 363 – plus three large and splendid brioches. When we broke into one of these the crumb was so yellow it looked too good to be true. True it was, though. No cheating there. A taste of delicious butter, fresh, fresh eggs . . . and not a trace of the artificial flavouring, harmless colouring matter, separated milk solids or any other of the glum ingredients which cloy and spoil so many of our own cakes and pastries even when bought from expensive and reputable bakeries.

It is very easy to make brioche dough at home. If you do not possess or cannot find the fluted brioche moulds used by French pastrycooks it really does not matter. Ordinary cake tins or ring moulds will do very well and, for smaller brioches, dariole or castle pudding tins like those illustrating the recipe for Mrs Tashis' little puddings on p. 489 are much easier to use than the individual fluted moulds which have become 'traditional'. 'Traditional' in this case means nineteenth-century. Brioches originated as soft and light white loaves, enriched with butter and eggs, but much less so than those we know today. They were baked without moulds. Looking at Chardin's beautiful paintings of brioches[1] you can see that he has quite clearly defined the notches round the base of his cottage-loaf-shaped confections, which are handsome and tall but not tidy like a moulded cake. So I think that in the eighteenth century, and at the time that poor, foolish Marie Antoinette is supposed to have said, when told that the people of Paris were rioting for bread, 'qu'ils mangent de la brioche', the composition of the cake must have been simply that of an enriched bread much like that of our own Bath buns and Sally Lunns, also made at that period without benefit of moulds or tins, although paper bands were sometimes wrapped round them for baking. Certainly it would not be possible to bake today's liquid brioche batter without an enclosing mould, but when it is to be used as an outer wrapping or crust for a fillet of beef or a large sausage[2] then the brioche mixture is made with fewer eggs and less butter, or it would be impossible to handle.

In a sense, both the savarin and the Alsatian kugelhopf, which also belongs to Austrian, Jewish, Polish and German cookery, are variations on brioche dough, although the different methods by which each is mixed and the variations in proportion of the ingredients produce totally individual results. A savarin, like its close relation the baba, is much more honeycombed and spongy than a brioche; a kugelhopf is

1. Two of the most famous, a wedding brioche with a spray of orange blossom stuck in the topknot, and another which is part of a dessert with cherries and a goblet of wine, are in the Louvre.

2. There is a recipe for sausage baked in brioche crust on p. 403.

smoother and more cake-like, enriched with raisins, of great finesse and delicacy. The savarin and the baba become soft and squashy when they are soaked after baking in rum- or kirsch-flavoured syrup; the kugelhopf is always presented with a snowy powdering of icing sugar, and sometimes for Easter the cake is baked in the shape of a fish instead of in the otherwise obligatory tall, round, decorated mould with its high central funnel.

There are, of course, many regional yeast cakes still to be found in France, most of them baked, as in England, for feast days: Twelfth Night, New Year's Eve, Easter, Whitsun, the local village fête day, the name day of the patron saint of the parish church. Here I am giving recipes only for those very few which have become familiar to us in England, through travel, proximity, interchange of cooks, professional and amateur. Some of these specialities, such as the savarin, we admire and find difficult to achieve; others have marked similarities to our own old favourites, often to the point when it is obvious that they have a common ancestry. The fifteenth-century curiosity, for example, called '*rastons*', quoted on p. 500, is just one instance of an apparently Anglo-French confection, a kind of vol-au-vent made from a yeast-fermented dough. Did it come to us from across the Channel? Was it of our own invention? Or was it of more distant origin? Italian, Spanish, Levantine? In those days there were fewer boundaries in Western European cooking than there are today. National preferences were far less firmly crystallized; and it must not be forgotten how much European cookery owes to the Arab influence (the Arabs were skilled pastrycooks long before the Italians took over) and to the peoples of the Near East and Asia Minor; it was they who originated so many of the dough-making and baking traditions which have descended to us, they who first supplied the fruit, the spices, the sugar and the flavourings we now regard as our own.

One attractive and popular French bakery speciality, the *petit pain au chocolat* so much beloved by French children, has never, so far as I know, crossed the Channel. In view of our national addiction to chocolate it is curious that we have not adopted this simple little recipe. I do not remember ever having seen even a description of it in any English cookery book. I give it here in its simplest and I think best form, an enriched bread or roll dough wrapped round a stick of coarse cooking chocolate and baked until the chocolate is just about to melt. This is the way I remember it from over thirty years ago in Paris. The difficulty now – in England it is an impossibility – is to find the crude, rather gritty chocolate of those days. Chocolate processing techniques have reached so refined a stage that the remembered texture has gone, and with it some of the character. Just as with bread.

· BRIOCHE ·

The dough for a brioche is rich in butter and eggs, and the rising processes are rather different from those customary in English yeast cooking.

I am giving here a simplified recipe, in quantities for one large brioche cake to be made in the traditional French brioche mould, fluted and with steeply sloping sides.[1] The one I use measures 20 cm or 8 inches at the top, is 10 cm or 4 inches deep and has a capacity of just over 1 litre or 2 pints. I don't attempt to make this large brioche cake with a topknot, but simply make a cut in the centre of the dough before the brioche goes into the oven. This is much easier than the topknot system; it makes a little hat on the cake, rather like the one on a well-risen soufflé. Very little yeast is needed in a brioche dough because it is given three risings over a long period, part of it in a cold place.

Quantities are 10 to 12 oz of flour, depending on whether you use strong bread flour or ordinary household flour; 5 to 6 oz of unsalted butter; 3 whole eggs; ¼ oz of yeast; 1 tablespoon of sugar; 1 teaspoon of salt; 2 tablespoons of milk.

For the glaze: 2 tablespoons each of milk and sugar.

Equivalent metric quantities: strong bread flour 280 g or household flour 340 g, unsalted butter 150 to 170 g, eggs 3, yeast approximately 10 g, sugar 1 tablespoon, salt 1 teaspoon, milk 2 tablespoons; for the glaze: milk 2 tablespoons and sugar 2 tablespoons.

Dissolve the yeast in the milk, just warmed. Add the salt and sugar to the flour and then pour in the yeast. Beat in the eggs, one at a time.

The *softened*, but not melted, butter should be ready. With your hands incorporate it into the dough, which at this stage will become very soft and almost too liquid. When all ingredients are thoroughly amalgamated, cover the bowl and leave the dough to rise for 2 to 2¼ hours, until it is light, bubbly and spongy.

Now break it down and transfer it to a clean, cold bowl. Cover it and leave it for several hours – preferably overnight – in a cool place, but not

1. See illustration p. 211.

in the refrigerator. The dough will continue to rise, but very slowly. In the morning it will once more be light and spongy.

Butter your tin, taking great care that all the fluted sides are well coated. The easiest, tidiest and most efficient way to do this is to melt a little piece of butter in a small pan and use a pastry brush for buttering the tin.

Having broken down the dough, beat it until it feels springy, transfer it to the tin and leave it to rise once more. It may take as long as 3 hours before it reaches the top of the tin. As this point, using a small, sharp knife held almost flat to the dough, make a fairly deep circular incision, about $1\frac{1}{2}$ inches from the sides of the tin. Now leave the dough to recover for a few minutes – 5 to 7 minutes should be enough – before putting the brioche on the centre shelf of the oven, preheated to 375°F, 190°C, gas no. 5, to bake. It will take no more than 20 to 25 minutes to cook.

Have ready the glaze, boiled in a very small pan until it is thick and syrupy. Brush it over the top surface of the hot brioche, which should then be returned to the oven for a couple of minutes.

When the brioche is baked and glazed, it should be well risen in the tin, with the centre-piece breaking away from the main part. The glaze will give a beautiful shining finish. French pastrycooks use yolk of egg to glaze their brioches. I find that the milk and sugar system gives a more appetizing glaze.

· RASTONS ·

I quote the following fifteenth-century recipe for its remarkable interest. It seems to be a cross between a brioche and a kind of early vol-au-vent, made with egg-enriched, sweetened and leavened dough, the centre cut out after baking, the crumb part mixed with clarified butter then put back into the crust and the whole re-warmed in the oven. I have so far found no explanation of or derivation for the curious name, but in another published MS. of about thirty years later,[1] a very similar recipe is given under the name of Rostand, meaning presumably, roasted or toasted. In old French, *rôtir*, to roast, was spelt with an 's', and slices of fried, grilled or toasted bread were called *rostis de pain*.

'Take fayre Flowre, & the whyte of Eyroun,[2] & the yolke a lytel; than take Warme Berme, & putt al thes to-gederys, & bete to-gederys

1. *A Noble Boke off Cookry*, ed. Mrs Alexander Napier, published 1882.
2. Eggs.

with then hond tyl it be schort & thikke y-now, & caste sugre y-now, ther-to, & lat reste a whyle; than kaste in a fayre place in the oven, & late bake y-now; & then with a knyf cutte yt round a-bove in maner of a crowne, & kepe the cruste that thou kyttyst; and than pyke al the cromys withynne to-gederys, and pike hem smal with thin knyf, & save the sydys & al the cruste hole with-owte; & than caste ther-in clarifyd Boter, & Mille[1] the cromes & the botere to-gederes, & kevere it a-gen with the cruste, that thou kyttest a-way; than putte it in the ovyn agen a lytil tyme; and than take it out, and serve it forth.'

Two Fifteenth-Century Cookery-Books, ed. Thomas Austin, 1888, reprinted 1964

Even more interesting than the above recipe is the next one, a six-teenth-century version of restons. The dough is rich in eggs and butter, and spiced with cinnamon, ginger, cloves and mace. The manner of moulding the restons after the fashion of an 'Ackorn broad above, and narrow beneath' seems to describe the modern dariole or castle-pudding shape, and the size 'the bignes of Ducks egges' is the same. Most illuminating of all is the startling way in which the language and the manner of writing a receipt have changed since the mid fifteenth century.

The proportions of the receipt are a problem. Ten egg yolks and 'a dishfull' of butter (thought to be $1\frac{1}{2}$ lb at this period) to a quart or $1\frac{3}{4}$ lb of flour would make a dough much too soft to handle. Again, five dishes of butter clarified would be a very large amount for moistening the restons when baked and sliced. Possibly the quart of flour should have been a quartern or half-gallon.

· TO MAKE GOOD RESTONS ·

'Take a quart of fine flower, lay it on a faire boord, and make an hole in the middest of the flower with your hand, and put a sawcerfull of Ale Yest therein, and ten yolkes of Egges, and put thereto two spoonefuls of Synamon, and one of Ginger, and a spoonfull of Cloves and Mace, and a quarterne of Sugar fine beaten, and a little Safron, and halfe a spoone-full of Salt. Then take a dishfull of Butter, melt it and put into your flower, and therwithall make your paste as it were for Manchets, and mould it a good while and cut it in peeces the bignes of Ducks Egges, and so moulde everye peece as a Manchet, and make them after the fashion

1. Mix.

of a Ackorn broad above, and narrow beneath. Then set them in an Oven, and let them bake three quarters of an howre. Then take five dishes of Butter and claryfie it clean upon a soft fire then drawe foorth your Restons foorth of the Oven, and scrape the bottoms of them faire and cut them overthwart in foure peeces, and put them in a faire charger and put your clarified butter upon them. Then have powder of Synamon and Ginger readie by you, and Sugar very fine. And mingle them alto-gether, and ever as you set your peeces thence, together cast some of your sugar, Synamon and Ginger upon them, and when you have set them all by, lay them in a faire platter, and put a little butter upon them, and cast a little sugar upon them, and so serve them in.'

The Good Huswife's Handmaide for the Kitchen, 1594

The traditional earthenware kugelhopf mould is glazed inside, unglazed outside. The ring mould and charlotte tin can both be used for brioche-type cakes.

· SAVARIN ·

The basic ingredients for a savarin are the same as those which go into a brioche, the proportions also being very similar. The methods of pre-paration and the cooking of the two mixtures are, however, rather dif-ferent; from the finished results it is hard to believe that these two famous confections stem from mixtures so similar, for while a brioche is rather close in texture and has affinities with both bread and pastry, a savarin is open, spongy, almost honeycombed, an effect achieved by the method of beating and mixing the dough, or rather the batter, a savarin mixture being much more liquid than a brioche dough.

A liberal dose of kirsch-flavoured syrup, administered while the savarin is still warm from the oven, softens the cake and makes it deliciously spongy although still light and elegant. It is an admirable cake for a dinner party, a wedding feast, a celebration of any kind.

The authentic savarin mould still used by French professional pastry-cooks is a plain ring approximately 2 inches deep, domed on the under-side and with a central tube a good $\frac{1}{2}$ inch higher than the sides of the tin. It is illustrated on p. 211. A deeper, fluted mould (although this belongs more properly to the baba and the kugelhopf) can also be used for a savarin.

Ingredients for a savarin to be cooked in a 2 pint mould and sufficient for six people are:

8 oz of white flour, preferably strong bread flour, 1 teaspoon of salt, $\frac{1}{4}$ oz of bakers' yeast, a scant $\frac{1}{4}$ pint of milk, 2 teaspoons of sugar, 3 eggs, 3 oz butter.

For the syrup: $\frac{3}{4}$ lb white sugar, $\frac{3}{4}$ pint water, 8 to 10 tablespoons of kirsch or rum if you prefer. (This seems a lavish amount. I do think that the flavour of kirsch or rum should predominate over the sugar in the syrup – but some may prefer it with less alcohol.)

Equivalent metric quantities: white, preferably strong, flour 225g, salt 1 teaspoon, bakers' yeast approximately 10gm, milk a scant 150g, sugar 2 teaspoons, eggs 3, butter 85g; for the syrup: white sugar 340g, water 420g, kirsch or rum 8 to 10 tablespoons. Tin size: a ring mould of 1 litre capacity.

To prepare the batter for the cake, first sieve the flour into a large bowl and add the finely pounded salt. Warm the milk to blood heat. Mix it gradually with the yeast and sugar in a separate bowl. Stir the yeast and milk mixture into the flour. Break the eggs into the yeast and flour mixture. Mix all together, by hand, or, if you find it easier, with a wooden spoon. At this stage the batter may be slightly lumpy. This is of no consequence. The lumps will disappear when the mixture has risen. Cover the bowl with a floured cloth, leave it in a warm place (for example, on top of the stove with the oven turned on at 330°F, 170°C, gas no. 3) for about 45 minutes to an hour, until the batter has doubled in volume and looks spongy and bubbly.

Now melt the butter. Reserve a spoonful for coating, with a pastry brush, the inside of the savarin tin. Remember also to flour the tin.

Add the rest of the butter, tepid, to the flour and yeast batter. With a sturdy wooden spoon or spatula beat the mixture for close on 5 minutes.

The batter thickens as you beat it. Now ladle it into the tin, filling it just under half full.

Put the tin in the same warm place used for the initial rising of the batter and leave for another 40 minutes or so, until the batter has risen to the top of the tin. Have the oven heated to 375°F, 190°C, gas no. 5, and put the savarin in its mould on an iron baking sheet in the centre of the oven.

Bake for 25 minutes.

Remove from the oven. Leave to cool for 2 or 3 minutes. Have ready a large and deepish round dish. Into this turn out the cake, shaking the tin slightly, and if necessary running a palette knife round the edges if the cake is stuck at any point. Now pour a proportion – about one third – of the prepared syrup (see below) over the cake. Leave it for 10 to 20 minutes. Put another large plate or dish over the top and invert the cake and its syrup. Leave until it is time to get your meal ready. Turn the cake once more so that it can be presented with the characteristic rounded side uppermost. Serve the remainder of your syrup separately in a jug or sauce boat.

A savarin tends to loose its lightness and spring when kept and should, ideally, be eaten the day it is cooked, although it can be re-warmed in a low oven provided the syrup has not already been poured over it.

The deep golden brown crust characteristic of a brioche is not an attribute of the savarin, which should remain smooth and of a beautiful even pale gold colour. This effect, however, is obtained only when the mould used is a thick and heavy one, and when it is correctly buttered and floured prior to the baking. I think that the temptation to fill the centre of the savarin with whipped cream and fruit is one to be resisted. The attractive shape of the cake is lost when the centre is filled, and a gooey mixture spoils the texture.

To prepare the syrup: Put the sugar and water in a heavy saucepan, preferably of untinned copper or cast aluminium. Since the melting point of tin is lower than the boiling point of sugar, a tinned pan should never be used for any kind of sugar boiling, confectionery or jam-making.

Boil the sugar and water for 10 to 15 minutes, until it will fall from the spoon (use a long-handled stainless steel or aluminium basting ladle or spoon) in drops like a thick syrup. For a syrup, such as this one for savarin, which is to receive additional kirsch or other liqueur, remember that the initial syrup should be a little thicker than usual to allow for the thinning out caused by the additional liquid – the kirsch – which is to be added as soon as the syrup has been removed from the heat and has stopped bubbling. Do not thereafter re-cook the syrup, or the flavour and aroma of the kirsch will be lost.

Notes on the making of a savarin: 1. The point of a mould with an inner funnel higher than the sides is immediately perceived when the batter rises in the tin. If the funnel is too low, the batter may rise over the top and overflow. When using a tin in which the funnel has not the requisite height, the matter can be rectified by the improvisation of an extra little chimney made from a piece of greaseproof paper slipped into the funnel as you place the savarin on the oven sheet for baking. This paper chimney can be removed as soon as the cake has set into its correct shape.

2. The syrup should always be poured over the savarin while the latter is tepid. If the cake has been baked the day before it is required, when the moment comes to make the final preparation, cover it with paper and warm it in a slow oven for a few minutes. Pour the syrup, also tepid, over the savarin as directed above.

3. When brushing the tin with melted butter remember about the funnel as well as the inner walls. The more evenly the tin is buttered, the easier it will be to turn out the cake, and the better the finished appearance.

4. Should it be available, slightly sour, thick cream is every bit as good as butter for savarin and brioche doughs. Allow the same quantity in fluid ounces and add it to the batter without heating it.

· RUM BABA ·

Babas are made with the same yeast batter or dough as a savarin, usually with the addition of a small quantity of sultanas. Allow 2 oz to a dough made with ½ lb of flour, and add them after the butter has been beaten in.

The babas are baked in dariole or castle pudding moulds – that is, plain, flower-pot shaped tins, usually 3 inches in diameter by 3 inches high.

Fill the buttered tins by a little less than half, and leave the batter to rise only until it has reached about two-thirds up the tin. Bake the babas in the centre of a moderately hot oven, 350° to 375°F, 180° to 190°C, gas nos. 4 or 5, for about 15 minutes. They should rise and puff up like soufflés, but unlike soufflés they do not fall.

Leave for a few seconds before sliding them out on to a cooling tray.

The syrup for babas is made with rum, sugar and water in the proportions of $\frac{1}{2}$ lb of sugar, $\frac{3}{4}$ pint of water and 8 to 10 tablespoons of rum. For the method see p. 504 of the savarin recipe.

When the time comes to serve the babas, warm them gently in the oven. Pour the syrup over them. Babas are always presented lying on their sides, in a small deep plate.

A batter made with $\frac{1}{2}$ lb of flour will yield nine to ten babas cooked in 3 inch tins. This is the conventional and traditional size. I find it rather large, and smaller dariole moulds are difficult to find. The batter can, of course, be cooked in one large (2 pint) mould, plain or fluted, but deeper and narrower than the ring used for a savarin.

Equivalent metric quantities: for a dough made with 225 g of flour, allow 60 g of sultanas; for the syrup: sugar 225 g, water 420 g, rum 8 to 10 tablespoons. Tin size: dariole moulds 8 cm high, 8 cm in diameter, or one large, deep, mould of 1 litre capacity.

· KUGELHOPF ·

Kugelhopf is an Austrian, German, Polish, Alsatian and Jewish cake. There are several variations in the spelling – kougloff, kuglof, kougelhopf – just as there are in the composition and the manner of preparing the batter. The shape of the cake varies little. It is made in a tall round mould with a central funnel and decorative markings. Some of the old copper kugelhopf moulds to be seen in museums in Strasbourg and Nancy are huge and magnificent; these must have been heirlooms used on festive occasions and handed down from mother to daughter for generations. More ordinary moulds were of earthenware, glazed only on the interior. Some fine old specimens of these may also be seen in the same museums in Alsace and Lorraine, and the potteries of the region still make them. They are decorative and appealing but difficult to use because in earthenware the cake tends to stick. The most practical moulds now obtainable in England are the German aluminium ones, siliconized on the interior, which are imported by an old-established wholesaler's firm and well distributed to kitchen shops throughout the country. There is a drawing of this kugelhopf mould on p. 211.

As with many Continental yeast cakes, the composition of the kugelhopf is very similar to several of our own, but the manner of mixing the batter is more complex.

Ingredients for a 2 to 2½ pint mould are ½ lb of strong plain flour, ½ oz of yeast, a scant ¼ pint of milk, 3 oz of butter, 2 large whole eggs or 3 small ones, ¼ lb of stoneless raisins, 1 oz of caster sugar, 1 level teaspoon of fine salt, the grated peel of a small lemon.

A little extra butter is needed for the tin, and about 3 tablespoons of icing sugar for dusting the cake when it is turned out of the tin.

Equivalent metric quantities: strong plain flour 225 g, yeast 15 g, milk a scant 150 g, butter 85 g, eggs 2 large or 3 small, seedless raisins 120 g, caster sugar 30 g, fine salt 1 level teaspoon, grated peel of 1 small lemon; extra butter for the tin; for dusting the cake: icing sugar 3 tablespoons. Tin size: 1 kugelhopf mould of 1 to 1·5 litre capacity.

First make a sponge. That is, in a warmed bowl mix about 2 oz of the flour with the yeast dissolved in 4 tablespoons of the milk, just warmed. On the top of this liquid batter pour the rest of the flour, without mixing it in. Cover the bowl. Leave it in a warm place until the batter breaks through the top layer of flour. This will take from 30 to 45 minutes.

Now amalgamate the batter and the top layer into a dough, mixing it gradually and thoroughly. Beat in the eggs, one at a time, adding a little more warm milk, and the salt and sugar. (While you are mixing the batter it is a good idea to put the raisins into a low oven to warm, as also the tin.) Now, first using your hands and then a whisk, beat in the softened butter, little by little, at the same time adding more of the milk.

Kugelhopf batter should be very elastic, so at this stage requires beating. I use a wire coil whisk. I find this very effective for cake and pancake batters. Others prefer a thick wire balloon whisk. And if the batter were being mixed on a large scale, it would obviously be more practical and quicker to use the electric blender.

When the butter is thoroughly amalgamated, and the batter of thick pouring consistency – if all the milk has not been used, add the remainder now – grate in the lemon rind and stir in the warmed raisins. This must be done by hand or with the whisk. The electric blender would break and cut the fruit.

Now butter the warmed tin, using a pastry brush, and making very sure that all the indentations of the mould, the central funnel and the top rim receive their thin coating of butter.

Pour the batter into the tin, which should be filled by a half to two-thirds. Cover it with a sheet of polythene or a coarse cloth, and leave it until the batter has risen to the top of the tin, which may take from 45 minutes to over an hour, depending upon the temperature. Using a warmed tin, and at a temperature of 70° to 75°F, 21° to 23·5°C, an hour should be amply sufficient.

Bake the kugelhopf on the centre shelf of the oven, preheated to 425°F, 220°C, gas no. 7, for approximately 25 minutes.

Leave the cake to cool for 10 minutes before turning it out of the tin on to a wire rack placed over a plate. Dust it with the icing sugar, using either a flour shaker or a dry pastry brush – the old-fashioned bunch of goose feathers is the perfect brush for icing sugar – which you dip into the sugar and then shake over the cake, which should be quite white, as if powdered with freshly fallen snow.

If you use icing sugar only rarely, it will almost certainly be caked into lumps when you take the packet or jar from the cupboard. The easy way out of this trouble is to put the sugar in the electric coffee grinder and swiftly reduce it back to its powder form.

Notes and variations: 1. Sometimes almonds are used to decorate a kugelhopf. The blanched, skinned and split almonds are put into the indentations of the buttered mould, and in this case the mould must be cold so that the butter has set and formed a coating to which the half almonds will stick. About 15 almonds will be needed for a 2½ pint mould. If almonds are to be used the grated lemon peel is usually omitted from the batter.

2. If an earthenware mould is used the cake takes up to 10 minutes longer to cook, as the thickness of the walls slows up the penetration of the heat.

3. If the cake is made with ordinary household or pastry flour instead of strong bread flour, use a little extra – up to 2 oz – and 1 extra egg.

4. Such is the popularity of the kugelhopf in Alsace that every year in June the little town of Ribeauvillé holds a fête in its honour, with brass bands, the full folklorique treatment, a great *concours* for the best kugelhopf baked by a local housewife, and plenty of the delicious white wines of the country to help down all the cake.

PETITS PAINS AU CHOCOLAT
· (Chocolate Rolls) ·

In France, in my youth, there were *petits pains au chocolat* which consisted of a bar of melting chocolate encased within a roll of bread warm from the oven. These could be bought from bakeries in the early morning, at the same time as the new, fresh bread was on sale.

When I allowed myself time, I could stop to buy a *pain chocolat* to eat in the tram on which I travelled from Passy to the Boulevard Saint-Michel to attend lectures at the Sorbonne. The chocolate in those rolls– I have remembered it all my life – was of that rough and gritty quality which no longer exists in France because the chocolate merchants have perfected their machinery to the point where all their products emerge smooth, bland, shining and uniform. And nowadays, the bakers use their second-best flaky pastry or third-quality croissant dough to make their *pains chocolat*.

Now flaky pastry and croissant dough made with inferior ingredients are both pretty deadly. They accord ill with everything and most especially with one's stomach. How would one want a pillow of pastry, sticky rather than flaky, wrapped round a very sparse little piece of fast congealing chocolate, and for breakfast into the bargain? Even the best flaky pastry or the finest croissant is all wrong with the chocolate – too rich, too grand.

I learn from old French books on bread that *petits pains au chocolat* were indeed made with a modified form of bread dough, one very much like the mixture used for English rolls and Scottish baps. With this dough, and the best cooking chocolate to be found, the formula does recapture something of the appeal of those *pains chocolat* of long ago.

For 8 chocolate rolls make a dough with ½ lb of white bread flour, a teaspoon of salt, ½ oz of bakers' yeast, approximately ¼ pint of warm milk and water mixed. For the filling you need 4 oz of chocolate.

Equivalent metric quantities: white bread flour 225 g, salt 1 teaspoon, bakers' yeast 15 g, warm milk and water mixed approximately 150 g. For the filling 125 g of chocolate.

Mix the dough as for baps (p. 321) but with rather less liquid; it must be more of the consistency of ordinary bread dough, so that, when the time comes to form the rolls, it is easy to handle.

Leave the dough to rise in the ordinary way. Have ready eight ½ oz sticks of chocolate. As most chocolate is now sold in 3 oz or 85 g packets, for 8 rolls you will need to buy two packets, unless you can lay hands on 250 g (½ lb) slabs of imported chocolate.

When the dough has doubled in volume, break it down, knead it very little, divide it in half, then in quarters, then eighths. Roll or pat each piece out on a floured board, into rectangles of a size to fit round your chocolate bars, which you place on your rectangle of dough. Fold over first the ends, then the sides, making a neat parcel of each. Press the joins together carefully, and brush the rolls with milk. Leave them on a floured baking sheet to recover shape and volume. As for baps, about 15 to 20 minutes should be sufficient.

Bake the rolls in a medium hot oven, 400° to 425°F, 205° to 220°C, gas nos. 6 or 7, for 15 to 20 minutes.

To make the rolls shiny after you take them from the oven, brush them with a thick sugar and milk glaze, as for saffron cake (p. 436).

Chocolate rolls are, obviously, at their best a few minutes after you have taken them from the oven. But they can be reheated low down in a low oven, for a few minutes. The chocolate bar inside the roll *must* be just melting.

When they are well made with the right dough and good chocolate these rolls are still, to me, one of the most enchanting of all chocolate confections. Who invented them? Certainly somebody who knew something about chocolate – and about children, and about the rightness of certain combinations – more than grand chefs knew when they worked themselves into ecstasies about that most terrible of aberrations, a beautiful juicy pear blanketed in sticky chocolate sauce and whipped cream.

Note: It is high time to dispel the myth that Menier chocolate is the best for cooking purposes and for sweet dishes. All cooking chocolate manufactured in England under license – and that includes Menier – is much of a muchness. I don't think it's possible to recommend any one brand, but the German Bensdorp, the Belgian Côte d'Or and the Swiss Lindt, each imported direct from its country of origin, are among the better ones available in Britain. Like any good chocolate today, these brands are all expensive.

· CROISSANTS ·

I have only limited tolerance towards all the rolling and folding and turning involved in puff pastry. It is a process which gives me no pleasure. As in effect a croissant dough is just a yeast-leavened puff pastry I don't often embark on making croissants. When I do, I use the recipe from Julia Child's *Mastering the Art of French Cooking*, Volume 2.[1] It is a long recipe, and that I have used it a couple of times with success proves that it is also a pretty foolproof one. I have to admit, though, that at the end of it all I do tend to suffer from combat fatigue, and question whether croissants are really worth all the production involved. However, now that at last Volume 2 of Mrs Child's extraordinary work is published in England (and before long will surely appear in paperback), those who are keen enough to have a try, and who have an aptitude for pastry-making, will be able to consult her croissant recipe direct. For a telescoped method, I suggest the following professional baker's recipe, which does of course assume that the reader knows all about the rolling out and folding of puff pastry. The author uses very slightly less butter to flour than is specified by Julia Child, gives the dough three turns to her four, and suggests only 30 minutes' resting period between turns where Mrs Child orders $1\frac{1}{2}$ hours (it's a rest for the dough, not for the cook who probably needs it just as much), and a final proof period of 1 hour at 75°F (23°C).

I suggest that for a first try Mr Fance's recipe below could be used in half quantities, which should make twenty to twenty-four croissants.

'Flour (strong) 2 lb 4 oz, salt $\frac{3}{4}$ oz, sugar 3 oz, yeast 1 oz, milk approx 1 lb 8 oz [i.e. 24 fluid oz], butter for rolling in, 1 lb.'

Equivalent metric quantities: strong flour 1 kg, salt 20 g, sugar 85 g, yeast 30 g, milk approximately 670 g, butter 450 g.

'Make a flying ferment [i.e. a preliminary sponge or batter] with the milk, yeast, sugar and 6 oz of flour. Weigh up the other ingredients and make up a dough with the salt and the balance of the flour. The dough should be soft and well developed.

'Allow to rest for 30 minutes then roll the dough into a rectangle. Cover half the surface with the butter and fold the other half over on to the top. Give three half-turns, resting between turns if the dough toughens.

'When the dough is ready for finishing, it should be rolled out in a rectangle about $\frac{1}{8}$ in thick and cut into strips 8 in wide, then cut into triangles to obtain a many-storied structure, allowing the dough pieces to roll up on themselves many times.

'The pieces are placed on to warmed and lightly greased baking sheets in the form of a crescent and egg washed. They are again egg washed

1. New York, Knopf, 1970; London, Michael Joseph, 1977.

after proof, before baking at 470°F (243°C). The prover must not be too hot or the butter will melt and spoil the flaky structure.'

W. J. Fance and B. H. Wragg, *Up-to-Date Breadmaking*, 1968

Notes: A few details should, I think, be added to the above recipe.

1. The triangles of dough are rolled from the broad base towards the extended point; when rolled this point should come out on the top of the straight roll; with the next movement the ends are bent inwards to shape the crescent, and the point then comes to the front of the croissant.

2. As Mr Fance indicates, professional bakers have a proving box or cupboard heated to a controlled temperature, so to them the final rising or proving of the croissants is no problem. In a centrally heated domestic kitchen it is best to find a cool place for them, cover them with a sheet of polythene, and allow a good hour or longer for them to regain full volume before they go into the oven. It is preferable to delay the proving process rather than to allow them to get warm enough for the butter to run.

3. I find that in a small domestic oven 470°F (243°C) is too hot for the baking of croissants, and that 12 to 15 minutes at 425° to 450°F, 220° to 230°C, gas nos. 7 to 8, with the tray on the shelf above centre, is about right. When there is more than one trayful it is advisable to bake them in two batches.

4. If you don't want all the croissants at once it is perfectly feasible to freeze some of the batch. They can be frozen either uncooked, at the full proof stage, or after baking and as soon as they have cooled.

5. *Please* don't use any fat but butter for croissants.

· PLUM GALETTE ·

This is made rather in the same way as a pizza or a cream cheese quiche, but with a firmer dough, and a filling of fresh fruit.

For the dough: 5 oz of strong plain flour, ¼ oz of yeast, 1½ oz of butter or thick cream, a teaspoon of salt, 1 whole egg.

For the filling: 1½ lb of plums, sugar, mixed sweet spice.

Equivalent metric quantities, for the dough: *strong plain flour 150 g,*

yeast approximately 10 g, butter or thick cream 45 g, salt 1 teaspoon, eggs 1;
for the filling: *plums 0·75 kg, sugar, mixed sweet spice. A flat earthenware
dish of about 26 cm diameter.*

Make the dough as for the cream cheese quiche on p. 401.

While the dough is rising (which will take approximately 2 hours),
prepare the plums. Make a cut down the natural division of each, and
put them in a fireproof bowl or deepish dish. Strew sugar over them. It
is impossible to specify the exact quantity. This depends upon the type
of plum and its relative ripeness. The safest course is to start with very
little. More can always be added, and too much will make all the juices
run out and leave the fruit itself soft and wet.

Put the prepared fruit, uncovered, in a low oven, 300° to 330°F, 150°
to 170°C, gas nos. 2 or 3, for 30 to 45 minutes. Again it is impossible to
give exact timing. The aim is not to cook the fruit completely but to
soften it, so that the stones can be extracted, and also so that some of the
juice, which would be excessive if the fruit were cooked directly on its
dough base, will flow out so that it can be used later.

Have ready a well-buttered, flat earthenware dish, as for a pizza, of
about 10 inches in diameter.

When the dough has risen and the fruit is ready, with the stones
removed, break down the dough in the usual way, shape it into a ball,
put it in the centre of the buttered dish and with your knuckles pat it out
into a disc of 8 to 10 inches in diameter. At first it looks as though it
could not possibly stretch to this size. As you work it, it spreads very
satisfactorily. Cover it with a sheet of waxed paper or polythene, or a
cloth, and leave it for about 10 minutes to recover volume before
spreading the plums, skin sides down, over the entire surface. Strew a
little sugar over them, and a sprinkling of mixed sweet spices, or just
plain powdered cinnamon if you prefer it. This spicing makes an extraordinary difference to the flavour of the fruit.

Bake in the centre of a hot oven, 425°F, 220°C, gas no. 7, for 15
minutes, then cover the top with paper and cook for another 10 minutes.
Finally, add the reserved plum juice, and return the galette to the oven
for another 5 to 7 minutes.

This is a simple and rough dish, and when well made it is quite
delicious.

Among the best plums to use for the galette are the small egg-shaped
variety called quetsch or, in English greengrocers' terms, switzens. In
France it is often made with the beautiful little golden mirabelle plums.

Apricots make another alternative, so do cherries. These last should not be cooked first, but they must be stoned.

These galettes can of course be made in tart tins. They can also be re-warmed quite successfully, in a low oven and protected with paper.

Soda Breads

'A light touch and speed in making and baking have almost all to do with success here. Half a dozen people following the same recipe might produce very variable specimens of bread. Though nice for a change, it is not so wholesome or satisfying as ordinary bread.'

Lizzie Heritage, *Cassell's Universal Cookery Book* 1901 (first published 1894)

Quickly made breads, griddle cakes and scones aerated with bicarbonate of soda and cream of tartar or tartaric acid became popular in Ireland, Scotland and England well over a hundred years ago. The properties of chemical raising agents had been appreciated early in the nineteenth century, and experiments with commercially practical formulas had been successful during the 1850s and earlier – one baking powder, Millers (the name was not, I think, a coincidence), first appeared in 1847 – but it was only from the 1860s onwards that ready-mixed baking powders and self-raising flours began to make a serious impact on household baking.

At first, chemical mixes seem to have been used mainly to lighten home-made biscuits, girdle scones, oatcakes, and other bakestone products which had previously been made without benefit of any aerating agent. It was only later, after they had been much advertised as 'yeast powder', 'dried yeast', 'yeast substitute', that housewives began to think that chemical mixtures could indiscriminately replace fresh yeast in their tea cake, spice cake and bread recipes. It was, to say the least, misleading to use the terms 'dried yeast' or 'yeast powder' in connection with chemical raising agents. Even the brand names, for example Easteleine[1] and Yeatmans, were calculated to cause confusion through association or suggestion. At the period, German or compressed yeast, much like the bakers' yeast we know today, was increasingly replacing the old ale yeasts and barms, and was very generally

1. In some parts of the country east was another word for yeast.

known, although incorrectly, as dried yeast. So the confusion was doubly compounded. That confusion still, to a great extent, exists. Many household cooks have not the faintest idea of what baking powder can or cannot do, or of the reason for the mixture in these powders of bicarbonate of soda with cream of tartar or tartaric acid. It is necessary for a cook either to understand the function of these chemicals or to avoid them altogether, for it is all too easy to use them incorrectly, to overestimate their powers as raising agents, or to wreck the taste of scones or bread by overdoing the soda or omitting the acid element.

An ordinary cake tin inverted over soda bread while it's baking helps it to rise and makes a lighter loaf. The flatter one is more traditional.

Especially, it seems to me, it is a mistake to put much faith in the kind of advertising which used to tell us that with the aid of baking powder we could make pastry and cakes with less butter, and puddings without eggs.

Baking powders are, in effect, mixtures of alkali and acid. When mixed with water or milk the two enter into chemical reaction and form carbonic acid gas which immediately starts working on the dough. As soon as the liquid has liberated the carbonic acid gas the dough should go into the oven, or the gases will have escaped. The bicarbonate of soda is the alkaline element. The acid is the cream of tartar or tartaric acid. Both these are fruit acids derived principally from grapes. In baking powders the alkali and acid are usually mixed in proportions of three parts of soda to two of cream of tartar, a further three parts of starch in the form of rice flour, cornflour, potato flour or arrowroot being added to keep the mixture dry, and to prevent the two chemicals acting upon each other before needed.

It will be seen from these proportions that when you buy baking powder you are paying for a deal of extraneous matter – the rice, maize or potato flour – which you do not need, and which is in no way going to add to the success of a bread or scone dough. So it is more satisfactory to buy the bicarbonate and the cream of tartar separately, from a chemist, and in small quantities so that they can be used as and when needed. It is important, though, to mix the two together very thoroughly before sifting them into the flour, and to remember also that when acid buttermilk or sour milk or treacle are specified in a recipe for soda bread or scones, these supply the necessary acid element, so the cream of tartar is usually omitted or the proportion reduced by half, but that when sweet milk is used the proportion of cream of tartar is not affected.

In addition to cream of tartar some baking powders contain tartaric acid, which acts more rapidly than cream of tartar, providing an initial boost to a dough or cake batter, leaving the cream of tartar to continue its aerating work. Blends containing both acids are known as double-action baking powders; they are often called for in American recipes.

For bread made with 100 per cent whole wheatmeal many people consider chemical aeration just as effective as yeast leavening, and there are those who think it is superior. It is true that well-made Irish soda bread, baked over a peat fire and with meal ground from soft Irish wheat unblended with imported high gluten grain, is unsurpassed for flavour. The drawback with these breads, even when made in ideal conditions, is that they quickly become dry, so are only at their best when freshly baked. With that proviso, soda breads or dairy breads as they were once called – presumably because of the buttermilk which often goes into them – are extraordinarily good and useful. Everybody who cooks, in however limited a way, should know how to make a loaf of soda bread. Rapidly mixed, immediately consigned to the oven or the griddle, the demands of this kind of dough are the very reverse of those made by yeast-leavened bread doughs. High-speed action rather than patience, quick, light handling instead of hard kneading and tough treatment, are necessary when it comes to baking powder doughs. And if, after all possible care has been taken, your soda bread still seems rather more like cake than bread in texture and in the way it cuts, that is what soda bread is called in most parts of Ireland – cake or 'a cake of bread', whereas a loaf of bread is one bought from the bakery.

Recipes for chemically aerated fruit cakes and spice breads are reduced to a minimum in this book. They are not, to my mind, as successful or useful as straightforward soda breads and bakestone cakes. They tend to be dry and crumbly, lacking the distinction of texture and the characteristic flavours of the old spice cakes made on a basis of yeast-leavened and matured dough; they are more expensive, requiring more flour and a larger proportion of eggs – very often more fat as well – to arrive at the equivalent volume of dough.

Where flours and meals for soda breads are concerned, there is no point in using strong bread flours. In England, however, many of the flours and meals sold for household bread – that is, wholemeals, wheatmeals and unbleached white flours – are milled from blends of high gluten imported wheat and soft home-grown grain. One of the few firms marketing a softer 81 per cent wheatmeal (which they recommend for pastry) is Prewett's, and, as I have already written elsewhere in this book, the Irish Abbey brand 100 per cent wholemeal, when you can find it, makes a coarse-textured and particularly excellent soda bread. A certain quantity of home-produced flour, stone-milled from wheat organically grown under the auspices of the Soil Association, is coming into the wholefood shops, and this too is admirable for chemically aerated breads. It would be wrong, though, to get the idea that strong meals and flours won't do at all for soda bread. They will. It is just that they are rather wasted on this type of loaf.

When self-raising flours are used for breads and scones then no further chemicals are needed. Some recipes, however, do advocate the addition of small proportions of baking powder or soda and cream of tartar, the theory being that self-raising flours are all-purpose blends and that when used for plain breads and scones are the better for a boost. This is just what makes them unsatisfactory.

The acid content which helps aeration is already present in self-raising flour so although extra acid in the form of sour milk won't do any harm, sweet milk is more satisfactory for doughs and batters based on self-raising flour.

An unbleached self-raising flour is packed by Prewett's.

Soda-bread mixes, needing only water or milk to make them up into dough, need not be scorned. They can be useful for times when good wholemeal is hard to find. It is worth looking out for a mix made on a basis of authentic stone-milled Irish whole wheatmeal. A mix made with Abbey meal is marketed by W. H. Mosse of Bennetsbridge, Co. Kilkenny. The same firm also packs a white soda-bread mix. White soda bread always has a cake-like texture, and the bread made from a mix is no exception. It can be useful in an emergency, and like so many stop-gap breads makes agreeable toast.

· CULTURED BUTTERMILK ·

Buttermilk is an important and useful ingredient of many soda breads and scones. In 1970 cultured buttermilk was launched on the British market by one of the big dairy combines. The rival organization quickly followed suit. It is now widely distributed, fairly easy and relatively cheap to buy and keeps well in the refrigerator. Cultured buttermilk, however, is not a new invention. The following formula was published in *The Bakers' ABC* (1927):[1]

'If about 3 oz of ordinary flour is carefully scalded with 1 qt. of boiling water, and about ½ oz malt flour and ½ pt. fresh milk added when the scalded liquor cools, lactic fermentation starts spontaneously, and in two days, if the liquid has been kept warm, it is in the condition of an artificial buttermilk, answering all the purposes for scone-making, etc.

'A fresh mixing can be stocked with a quantity from a previous making, and a supply kept up, much in the same way as barm is made.'

1. Ed. John Kirkland.

· IRISH WHOLEWHEAT SODA BREAD ·

This is quickly made and delicious while fresh.

1 lb to 1 lb 4 oz of 100 per cent whole wheatmeal; 1 level teaspoon of bicarbonate of soda; 2 level teaspoons of salt; approximately ½ pint of slightly sour buttermilk[1] or milk sour enough to be just solid but without the slightest hint of a mouldy or acrid smell; 2 to 4 tablespoons of warm water.

Equivalent metric quantities: 100 per cent whole wheatmeal 450 to 550 g, bicarbonate of soda 1 level teaspoon, salt 2 level teaspoons, slightly sour buttermilk or milk approximately 280 g, warm water 2 to 4 tablespoons. Covering tin size: two deep cake tins, 16 to 18 cm in diameter.

Sift the salt and the bicarbonate very carefully throughout the mass of meal. Add the cold buttermilk or sour milk and mix to a dough, adding the warm water if the mixture is too dry.

Quickly divide the dough into two pieces, form them into nice round buns as tall as you can make them, place them on a non-stick baking sheet or a floured iron sheet. The alternative method of shaping the loaves is to make them rather flatter, like a scone, then make a deep cross cut, so that each loaf when baked will divide easily into four parts. Cover each loaf with a deep 6 inch or 7 inch cake tin. Put them immediately on the shelf above the centre of a hot oven, preheated for 5 minutes at 425° to 450°F, 220° to 230°C, gas nos. 7 or 8, and bake for 30 minutes. Remove the tins and leave the loaves for another 10 to 15 minutes, until they have formed brown but not overbaked, crusts.

This bread is at its best when just cooled, but reheats successfully by the usual method, i.e. low down in a very moderate oven, and covered with a tin or bowl, for 7 to 10 minutes.

Notes and variations: 1. If you cannot lay hands on buttermilk and have no sour milk, add 2 level teaspoons of cream of tartar to the bicarbonate of soda, and mix the dough with half fresh milk and half water. The cream of tartar provides acid in place of the sour milk or buttermilk. Should you have a little sour cream, say 2 to 4 oz, to hand, use this made up to the right quantity of liquid with water. A little butter, up to 1 oz, can also be added.

1. See pp. 128 and 519.

2. The reason for making two small loaves rather than one large one is that, using 100 per cent wholemeal, small loaves bake better than large ones.

3. Many people who live alone would like sometimes to make their own bread, but may feel that it is wasteful and expensive to do so, and perhaps that it involves too much effort just for themselves. Soda bread offers a solution. If only one small loaf is needed, halve all quantities exactly.

4. While a loaf of soda bread is baking just above the centre shelf of the oven, something else can be cooking lower down, so that the heat need need not be wasted.

5. The cake tin inverted over the bread while it is cooking helps it to rise a little – wholewheat soda bread never rises very much – and also to remain moist and not form too hard and dry a crust. It is an old dodge, helpful in today's gas and electric ovens.

6. Different wholewheat meals give varying results. As I have written in other chapters in this book, the Irish wholewheat meal milled at Roscrea in County Tipperary is the one I use when I can get it. The savour of the wheat in bread made from this very coarsely milled meal is beyond compare. Other stone-milled meals which I have tried on numerous occasions over a long period, and using various methods, tend to produce either rather pudding-like or very dry loaves. If the first of these faults proves to be the case with the meal you are using, then it is a good idea to try making the bread with a proportion of finer flour, say $\frac{1}{4}$lb of either 85 per cent wheatmeal or white flour to $\frac{3}{4}$lb of wholewheat meal. If your bread is too dry, next time incorporate an ounce or so of butter into the dough.

7. Whole wheatmeal bread makes incomparable toast. Cut rather thick slices and toast them lightly. It is almost more a question of re-warming the bread than of toasting as it is usually understood. As the slices warm and take colour, all the original aroma of the wheat returns.

8. It is very important to remember that, unlike yeast dough, any mixture made with chemical raising agents should go into the oven just as soon as the dough is mixed. This is because the effervescing of the raising agent starts from the moment it comes into contact with the acid and liquid which go into the dough, so if this is left to stand, the raising agent will not do its work.

· IRISH WHEATMEAL SODA BREAD ·

This recipe comes from Gracie McDermot who cooks for Derek Hill, the painter, in Co. Donegal, Eire. I have often eaten Gracie's soda bread. It is delicious. I give the recipe as she told it to Derek Hill.

'1 cup of white ordinary flour, 2 cups of wheatmeal (81 per cent or 85 per cent) flour, ½ teaspoon of salt, 1 full teaspoon of baking powder, buttermilk.

'Blend all loosely and make a well in the middle into which slightly less than a cup of buttermilk is poured. Work it all with your fingers and put the resulting "cake" on to a buttered griddle. Bake for 10 minutes at full heat[1] till bread rises and slightly browns, then lower heat and bake an extra 25 minutes.'

The wheatmeal Gracie uses comes from the Ballisodare Mills, Ballisodare, Sligo, Eire.

· WHOLEWHEAT AND OATMEAL SODA BREAD ·

The following recipe was given by Sir Henry Thompson, the Victorian surgeon and dietician, in his *Food and Feeding*, a work which was first published in the 1880s, and ran into many editions. Sir Henry considered that whole wheatmeal mixed with fine Scotch oatmeal and fat in the form of milk or butter makes the most nutritionally excellent bread to be found anywhere. By no means bigoted in his views, Sir Henry was prepared to admit that bread made from fine white flour 'especially at Paris and Vienna' was unrivalled for delicacy, texture and colour. At the same time he appreciated the natural flavour of the wheat in wholemeal bread 'in place of the insipidity characteristic of fine flour'. He recommended that, in view of the difficulty of obtaining good whole wheatmeal in London, the meal be ground at home in a domestic hand mill. I find the mixture of wheatmeal and oatmeal most delicious, and the system of baking the bread in rings (sponge tins serve just as well) is very successful; it makes for rather tidier and neater loaves than does the more usual method of hand shaping.

'Take two pounds of the well-ground wheat meal described, and add

1. Derek Hill notes 'in our oven', i.e. a solid fuel range fired with peat. Full heat would probably be about 450°F, 230°C.

half a pound of fine flour, or, better still, the same weight, or more if preferred, of *fine* Scotch oatmeal. Mix thoroughly with a sufficient quantity of baking powder[1] and a little salt; then rub in two ounces of butter and make into dough – using a wooden spoon – with cold skimmed milk or milk and water,[2] soft in consistence, so that it can almost be poured into the tin ring, which gives it form when baked. In this manner it is to be quickly made into flat cakes (like tea-cakes), and baked on a tin, the rings used being about an inch high and seven or eight inches in diameter, each enclosing a cake. Put them without delay into a quick oven at the outset, so that the external surface may be instantly hardened or sealed to prevent the gas formed by the baking powder from escaping, otherwise the result will be a dense, thin, and heavy cake instead of a light and spongy one. This is a cardinal point in the process which is often overlooked. When the object is accomplished, which will occupy some five or seven minutes, the temperature should be lowered to complete the process gently and completely.'

Equivalent metric quantities: whole wheatmeal 900 g, fine flour or fine oatmeal 225 g, bicarbonate of soda 2 teaspoons, cream of tartar 3 teaspoons, salt, butter 60 g, skimmed milk or milk and water mixed. Tin size: rings or tins about 2·5 cm high and 18 or 20 cm in diameter.

Sir Henry Thompson, *Food and Feeding*, 12th edn, 1901 (first published *c*. 1882)

· MANX BARLEY BREADS ·

In a book of recipes[3] from the Isle of Man, Suzanne Woolley tells us that 'barley flour is particularly tasty if pan-roasted before making it into a dough. This gives the bread a moist cake-like consistency.'

'The traditional Manx way of making barley bread was to mix the finely ground meal with water into a dough which was kneaded into thin round cakes. The cakes, which were clapped flat between the hands, were known as *berreens*. They were baked on the griddle or in a pot-oven.'

· BARLEYMEAL BONNAG ·

'¾ *lb barleymeal,* ¼ *lb plain flour, 2 oz lard or margarine, 1 small teaspoon each of baking powder, cream of tartar, and salt,* ½ *pint of buttermilk.*'

1. I use 2 teaspoons of bicarbonate of soda and 3 of cream of tartar.
2. Half and half milk and water makes better bread than all milk.
3. See n. p. 524.

Equivalent metric quantities: barleymeal 340 g, plain flour 120 g, lard or margarine 60g, baking powder, cream of tartar and salt 1 small teaspoon each, buttermilk 280g.

'Put barleymeal, flour and salt in a bowl and rub in the fat. Mix baking powder and cream of tartar with the buttermilk. Add the liquid mixture to the dry ingredients and mix to a soft dough. Shape into two or three loaves and bake in a moderate oven for an hour. To make sweet loaves add currants to the mixture and sprinkle the loaves with sugar.'[1]

Mrs Woolley adds that the barley in grain form was dried on a hot hearth or a stone heated over a turf fire, and then ground in a quern or handmill made of granite. But in 1647 Lord Derby, whose family owned the island, ordered the destruction of all handmills, so that people would be forced to use the lord's mills.

· WHITE BUTTERMILK BREAD ·

This is made by the same method as whole wheatmeal soda bread, proportions of salt and bicarbonate of soda to flour being identical. Depending upon the flour used, which if possible should be an unbleached one, the quantities of buttermilk and water may vary slightly; and, as always with white flour, the volume of the loaf will be greater than that of one made with whole wheatmeal.

Oven temperature and baking time are as for the wholewheat soda loaf, except that the second stage, after the covering tin is removed, may take a little longer.

Reheating of a white buttermilk loaf under a covering tin in a low oven is quite satisfactory, but chemically raised white bread is inevitably more cake-like than its wholewheat counterpart. It is worth trying the experiment of baking a loaf of each, side by side in the oven, and putting them on the table at the same meal, in order to discover which is the more popular.

· ENGLISH CHEMICALLY AERATED WHITE BREAD ·

Walter Banfield (*Manna*, 1937) gives an interesting version of soda bread, made on a short-time lactic ferment. Banfield claims that white

1. Suzanne Woolley, *My Grandmother's Cookery Book*, Douglas, Isle of Man, Shearwater Press, 1975.

bread, chemically aerated, is rarely as good as it should be because the flour is given no chance to mature. Even the brief maturing of part of the flour in fresh milk makes, so he asserts, a vast difference, the result being moist light loaves instead of the more usual heavy, close-grained, pinhole-textured white soda bread. The recipe, which I have not tried, specifies soft flour.

For the lactic batter, 3 pints of fresh cold milk, 3 lb of soft home-milled flour. Mix the milk and flour, cover the bowl and leave it at a temperature of 70°F, 21°C, for 30 minutes.

To make up the bread dough add 2¼ lb to 2½ lb of flour – again a soft or medium-soft one, 1 oz of salt, 5 oz of lard, 2 oz of golden syrup and 4 oz of baking powder, made up in the proportion of 2 to 1, meaning two of cream of tartar to one of baking soda.

Banfield goes on to say that 'the dough can be observed rising . . . a vesicular thread-like structure of ripe dough is clearly seen', and the ferment puts such life into this dough that it should only be used in small batches, or it will be partially lost before the loaves can be made up and consigned to the oven.

For baking the bread Banfield used 'long square tins with a sheet tin covering', and suggests that the dough be cut down the centre to assist the loaf to spread and fill the tin well. Small coburgs and baton shapes can also be baked from this dough 'provided they are well cut, and that the oven is humid'.

Baking temperature should not be higher than 425°F, 220°C, gas no. 7.

The above summary of Banfield's instructions may well prove useful to those who prefer white soda bread to brown. Probably the method could also be applied to wholemeal mixed with ordinary soft white household flour.

Equivalent metric quantities, for the lactic batter: *milk 1·75 litre, soft flour 1·35 kg;* for the bread dough: *soft flour 1 kg to 1·12 kg, salt 30 g, lard 150 g, golden syrup 60 g, baking powder 120 g.*

SPICE AND FRUIT CAKES or
· BREADS LEAVENED WITH BAKING POWDER ·

The following three recipes seem to be typical of scores of English recipes in which the original raising agent was barm or fresh yeast, and which were adapted to the use of baking powder. As in many of the more modern recipes in the chapter on yeast cakes, the proportions of sugar and fruit to flour seem very high. The sugar could be substantially reduced.

The custom of eating cheese with these spiced fruit breads or cakes, as noted in the recipe for sour-milk cake, is a very good one. The cheese should, preferably, be a Wensleydale, a Cheshire or a well-matured Lancashire – if and when to be found.

· NORTH RIDING BREAD ·

'1 lb plain flour, ½ teaspoon salt, 4 teaspoons of baking powder, 6 oz of currants, 1 tablespoon of treacle, ½ pint of milk, 4 oz of lard, 6 oz of Demerara sugar, 6 oz of raisins, 3 oz of mixed peel, ½ teaspoon of almond essence.

'Sift plain flour with salt and baking powder. Rub in lard and sugar. Mix in raisins, currants and mixed peel. Stir in treacle, almond essence, ½ pint milk, or less, mix all to a soft dough. Divide into two small tins and bake at 375°F or gas no. 5 for about 1 hour.'

Equivalent metric quantities: plain flour 450 g, salt ½ teaspoon, baking powder 4 teaspoons, currants 170 g, treacle 1 tablespoon, milk 280 g, lard 120 g, Demerara sugar 170 g, raisins 170 g, mixed peel 85 g, almond essence ½ teaspoon. Equivalent oven temperature in degrees C: 190°C.

Ryedale Recipes, 2nd printing, Pierson Smith Enterprises
('Westland', Westfields, Kirbymoorside, York), 1968

· SHOOTING CAKE ·

Originally, I included this recipe here because of its ingredients. The lemon makes it unusual, in more ways than one. It supplies the necessary acid element in soda cakes and as a flavouring it takes the place of spices. It has since proved most successful.

'1 lb of flour, ½ lb brown sugar, 1 lb raisins, ½ lb butter, 2 eggs, peel and juice of 2 lemons, 2 teaspoons of carbonate of soda mixed with warm milk.'

Equivalent metric quantities: flour 450 g, brown sugar 225 g, raisins 450 g, butter 225 g, eggs 2, peel and juice of 2 lemons, bicarbonate of soda 2 teaspoons, warm milk.

'Rub butter into flour and add other ingredients; beat eggs with a little warm milk; dissolve soda in a little warm milk; then mix well together, and bake two hours in a slow oven.'

Ulster Fare, the Belfast Women's Institute Club, Belfast, 1946

I cannot help thinking that two hours' baking for a cake containing just three pounds of ingredients would be excessive. It would be a good idea to try the cake in half quantities and for a shorter cooking time.[1]

· SOUR-MILK CAKE ·

'This cake resembles spice bread in flavour, but is made differently The recipe originally came from Brawby in the North Riding. Like so many of the fruit loaf recipes in the North this cake should be eaten with cheese and is especially associated with Christmastide.

'*Ingredients*

½lb butter	1 teaspoon mixed spice
1lb flour	(optional)
½lb sugar	1 tablespoon syrup
½lb currants	1 teaspoon bicarbonate of soda
2oz peel	About 1 pt sour milk to mix'[2]

Equivalent metric quantities: butter 225g, flour 450g, sugar 225g, currants 225g, peel 60g, mixed spice (optional) 1 teaspoon, syrup 1 tablespoon, bicarbonate of soda 1 teaspoon, sour milk approximately 550g.

'*Method*
'Rub the butter into the flour and add the other dry ingredients. Warm the syrup and pour into the centre. Mix to a fairly soft dough with sour milk. Bake in either two bread tins or in a deep slab cake tin for about one hour. Use a moderate oven.'

Contributed by Folkton and Flixton W.I. to *Through Yorkshire's Kitchen Door*, the Yorkshire Federation of Women's Institutes, 31st edn, n.d. (first published 1927)

1. I now make the cake with ½lb flour, ¼lb Demerara sugar, ¼lb raisins, ¼lb butter, 2 eggs, peel and juice of one lemon, 1 level teaspoon bicarbonate of soda. Bake in 6½ to 7 inch round tin, 3 ins. deep, for 50 minutes at gas no. 5, 375°F, 190°C.
2. Nowadays it is best to use buttermilk or home-made yogurt.

Bakestone Cakes or Breads

'Oates termed by Galen the Asses and Horses provender, are of the like nature with Barly, but more astringent, especially being old and thorough dry. Had Galen seen the oaten cakes of the North; the Janocks[1] of Lancashire, and the Grues of Cheshire, he would have concessed that Oates and Oatmeal are not only meat for beasts, but also for tall, fair and strong men and women of all callings and complexions.'

Dr Thomas Muffett, *Health's Improvement*, written *c*. 1595, published 1655

Most of the recipes in this section are included for their great historical and regional interest. Oatmeal and barley meal make the best and finest-flavoured bakestone breads or cakes – the terms are interchangeable – and until late in the eighteenth century oats and barley, and in the Midland counties rye, were the staple cereals of large areas of the British Isles. In Yorkshire and Northumberland, on the hill farms of Cumberland and Westmorland, oatcakes in one form or another were the daily bread of the agricultural population. Wheat bread was for Sundays and probably had to be bought on market day from the nearest town. Even in quite large towns there were few bakeries (as late as 1804 there was still not one public bakery in Manchester), but every household had a bakestone or a griddle. In Scotland it was only the bakers who made wheaten loaves, the housewives who made oatcakes, barley bannocks and girdle scones. In Wales, again, barley and oats were both used for bakestone breads; barley meal is now rarely to be found outside health-food stores, but Welsh housewives still use their bakestones for oatcakes and potato cakes. In Ireland a supper of bacon rashers and potato cakes made by Gracie, the cook whose oatcake recipe is on p. 531, was always such a treat that I've tried many times to reproduce it. Without success. Perhaps one needs the smell of the peat as well as the good Irish potatoes – and a light hand like Gracie's.

1. According to *The Bakers' ABC* (ed. John Kirkland, 1927), jannock was a Lancashire term for wheaten flour bread made on a leaven, as well as for oaten bread or cake.

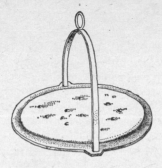

I have not attempted here to give descriptions of the many versions of Scots oaten cakes and barley bannocks or of the ancient traditions and rites connected with them. These would make an absorbing study. In her splendid book *The Scots Kitchen* (1929), Miss F. Marian McNeill devotes fifteen pages to the subject, and includes recipes for both girdle scones and the oven-baked version, and for oatmeal, white, drop and treacle scones. I would have liked to include a few scone recipes in this chapter, but once you start on scones where do you stop?

So I would advise any reader interested in such recipes to turn to Miss McNeill. Her oatcakes and scones have nothing of the tea shop and the tourist board about them. They are the real thing. There are also in *The Scots Kitchen* a number of lovely things to be made with oatmeal – gingerbread, pancakes, cream-crowdie. We could make more use of oatmeal in our cooking.

· YORKSHIRE OATCAKES ·

A detailed description of the making of oatcakes and the manner of storing them was written by George Walker for his remarkable work *The Costume of Yorkshire*, published in 1814:

'With perhaps the exception of some parts of Lancashire, it is almost exclusively made in the West Riding of Yorkshire, and constitutes the principal food of the labouring classes in that district. It is a very thin cake, composed of oatmeal and water only, and by no means unpalatable, particularly while it is new. The mixture is made of a proper consistence in a large bowl, and measured out for each cake by a ladle. As the price of an oatcake is invariably one penny, the size of the ladle of course depends upon the rate of meal in the market.

'Some dry meal is sifted upon a flat board, and a ladle full of the mixture poured over it. The cake is formed and brought to a proper size and thickness by a circular horizontal movement of the board. It is then laid upon what is termed the backstone, or hot hearth, to bake, which does not require many seconds of time, and afterwards placed upon a cloth to cool. An inverted chair frequently serves this purpose. The cakes are then hung upon a frame, called a Bread Creel, suspended from the ceiling of almost every cottage in the district.

'The people in the neighbourhood of Huddersfield are fond of what they term Browiss, which is oatcake supped in broth or gravy.'

George Walker adds that the local name of this species of bread is 'Haver Cake which must undoubtedly be a corruption of the German haber or hafer, and not derived, according to Johnson, from the Latin *avena*'.

Accompanying the above description is Walker's fine coloured illustration of the process of oatcake-making. The board on which the oatcake is formed seems to have a shallow round depression in the centre (rather as described by Celia Fiennes when she saw oatcakes or clap bread being made at Kendal in the Lake District) so that a tidy, round oatcake would be formed as the operator turned the board in 'a circular horizontal movement'. The bakestone is a slate or iron slab set over a fixed brick-built hearth adjacent to the fireplace but not part of it, and with a fire burning underneath; a chair lying on its side is draped with a cloth upon which several oatcakes are spread out to dry. More are shown draped over the bread creel, a kind of hammock of narrow slats slung between cross bars suspended from the ceiling. This is another version of the Welsh bread cart or crate and the bread shelves shown in the illustrations on pp. 218 and 224. According to the Yorkshire Federation of Women's Institutes, the bread creels were eventually replaced by wooden laths for the airing of clothes. No doubt those too have now become obsolete, but how practical they were. Two versions of Yorkshire riddle bread, oatcake or haver cake, one leavened with yeast and the second, a much older recipe, based on oatmeal sourdough, are described in the chapter on yeast-leavened pancakes and oatcakes.

The men of a Yorkshire regiment, the 33rd Foot, raised during the American War of Independence in the neighbourhood of Halifax, were known as the Haver-cake lads. According to Walker this was because the regiment's recruiting sergeants always preceded the party with an oatcake impaled on their swords. 'Till very lately', wrote Walker, 'the gallant Lord Wellington was the Colonel of this regiment.'

· KENDAL OATCAKES or CLAP BREAD, 1698 ·

'. . . they mix their flour with water so soft as to rowle it in their hands into a ball, and then they have a board made round and something hollow in the middle riseing by degrees all round to the edge a little higher, but so little as one would take it to be only a board warp'd, this is to cast out the cake thinn and so they clap it round and drive it to the edge in a due proportion till drove as thinn as a paper, and still they clap it and drive it round, and then they have a plaite of iron same size with their clap board and so shove off the cake on it and so set it on coales and bake it . . . if their iron plate is smooth and they take care their coales or embers are not too hot but just to make it look yellow it will bake and be as crisp and pleasant to eat as anything you can imagine.'

Celia Fiennes, *The Journeys of Celia Fiennes*, ed. C. Morris, 1947

'As we say of all sorts of bread there is a vast deale of difference in what is housewifely made and what is ill made, so this if its well mixed and rowled up and but a little flower on the outside which will drye on and make it mealy is a very good sort of food; this the sort of bread they use in all these countrys . . . it made me reflect on the description made in scripture of their kneading cakes and baking them on the hearth when ever they had company come to their houses, and I cannot but think it was after this manner they made their bread in the old tymes especially those Eastern Countryes where their bread might be soone dry'd and spoil'd.'

ibid.

DONEGAL OATCAKE or

· *A bannock of bread and a sheetful of crumbs* ·

Donegal oatcake, like its Scottish counterparts, is a mixture of oatmeal and water bound with a very little fat. According to local tradition it was toasted on an iron stand called a breadiron, also known as a harnen (hardening) stand. The oatcake was put on the stand to toast very slowly for several hours at some distance from the open peat fire. The process is really more of a drying-out operation than toasting proper.

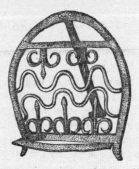

Irish breadiron or oatcake stand from a cottage in County Donegal. It is 16 inches high by 15 inches across.

The beautiful and typically Celtic iron stands – there are many different patterns – have fallen into disuse and the Irish country people seldom nowadays make their delicious oatcakes.

The recipe I use is the one given me by Gracie McDermot, whose soda bread recipe is on p. 522. Gracie usually cooks her oatcake in a very slow oven on the peat-fired range, but she also showed me how the breadiron was used to toast a bannock.

Ingredients are fine oatmeal, 1 lb; salt, 2 teaspoons; fat (butter, lard), 1 to 2 oz; boiling water, approximately ¾ pint.

Equivalent metric quantities: fine oatmeal 450 g, salt 2 teaspoons, butter or lard 30 to 60 g, boiling water approximately 420 g. Tin size: a baking tin at least 30 by 20 cm.

Put the oatmeal into a mixing bowl, the salt and fat into a measuring jug. Over the latter pour boiling water. Stir until the fat and salt are dissolved. Pour this mixture into the oatmeal. A little more or a little less water may be needed to mix the oatmeal into a pliable cake, which at this stage resembles nothing so much as a mud pie. This is now left overnight, or at least for several hours, until it is dry enough to press out, very thin and flat, into an ungreased baking tin. For a pound of oatmeal, a tin of at least 12 by 8 inches is needed. After a little practice at making oatcake, you find that it can be pressed out almost as thin as card, and then two tins – or baking sheets – will be needed.

Before baking the oatcake leave it again to dry out for an hour or two. Press it once more and even out the top with a palette knife or spatula.

Put the tin or tins at the bottom of the slowest possible oven (265° to 285°F, 130° to 140°C, gas nos. ½ or 1) and leave them for a minimum of 3 hours and longer if it happens to be convenient. Too high a temperature will ruin oatcake; the longer the drying out at a very low temperature, the better it will be.

Break the oatcake into wedges and eat it for breakfast or tea with cold creamy butter. It is wonderfully good also with fresh cream cheese.

Oatcake keeps well and can be reheated – always at a minimum temperature – as often as you please.

The only disadvantages of oatcake are the speed with which it disappears, and the crumbs left scattered all over the table and the floor after an oatcake meal. Gracie McDermot told me that in her childhood oatcake was known as the 'Moon and Stars', the round oatcake or bannock toasted before the peat fire on the iron being the moon and the 'sheetful of crumbs' the stars.

· WELSH OATMEAL BREAD or OATCAKE ·

'Much oatmeal bread was eaten in the old days, the baking of which was an important event. In some cases great quantities were made at a time – as much as three winchesters[1] were used and three bakestones were used simultaneously on the spacious hearthstones, under the shadow of the old big open chimney . . . Oatcake thus baked . . . was the staple form of bread used on many farms.'

Miss R. M. Evans, *Transactions of the Cardiganshire Antiquarian Society*, vol. xii, 1937

N.B. Miss Evans was writing of Cardiganshire customs in the seventeenth and early eighteenth centuries.

· WELSH OATMEAL CAKES ·

The following description of the making and baking of Welsh oatcakes differs somewhat from other descriptions I have seen and from verbal accounts I have been given. Quite certainly, however, it was written from first-hand knowledge and observation. Lady Llanover, although not of Welsh origin, was born at Llanover in Monmouthshire, South

1. A Winchester bushel was 60 lb.

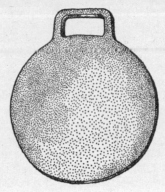

Massive cast iron bakestones are used in Wales for baking oatcakes (bara ceirch) and Welsh round cakes.

Wales, and lived there all her life. The methods she describes were no doubt those of her own region, probably of her own household.

'Make a stiff paste with oatmeal and water or skim milk; then form it into balls with the hand about the size of small eggs; then shape with the hand round and round to the size of a small cheese-plate or large saucer; when one oat-cake is formed the right shape and thickness, turn it and shake dry oatmeal all over it; then take another, put it in the middle of the oat-cake you have made, and form that in the same manner upon the first made; when well tempered, turn it, and shake dry oatmeal all over it, and proceed in the same way until you have got eighteen oat-cakes one on the other, remembering that each must be turned, and that dry oatmeal must be put between every one, and they must be turned and re-turned, and shaped with the hand, until they are all of the same texture, as thin as is possible without breaking. When dry enough to put on the bake-stone (heated to the required point which practice alone can teach), bake them one at a time; have a clean cloth folded to the proper shape, and press the cake down flat on the bake-stone, where it should remain until it is of a nice light brown colour. The upper side of the cake is to be glazed before it is taken off the bake-stone; the glaze is made with egg and milk, and a little sugar is generally added, but that is only a matter of taste; some persons like a little sugar mixed with the oatmeal of which the cakes are made. As each cake is taken off the bake-stone it is laid across the rolling-pin that it may dry in a hollow shape; and as each cake becomes hard and crisp, they are again put one on the other, and are always served and kept in a pile. The rolling-pin *must not* be used in making these cakes, all must be done with the hand, and they must be flattened and worked round and round with the hand until they are almost as thin as a wafer. Great skill and dexterity, as well as practice, are necessary to make these cakes well, which when once attained, the process is very quickly executed. The *thin Welsh-oat cake* is particularly wholesome, and often agrees with invalids of weak digestion better than bread; they are sometimes eaten with cold butter or cheese, or eaten dry with milk or tea.'

Lady Llanover, *Good Cookery*, 1867

Welsh oatcakes were sometimes broken up or crushed with a rolling pin and mixed with buttermilk to make a kind of porridge called *siot*. Another such mixture was *brywes*, made with oatmeal, breadcrumbs, salt and a little bacon fat or dripping, moistened with boiling water and left to stand until the oatmeal was soft and swollen. *Brywes* and *siot* were the breakfast foods – and sometimes the midday meal and the supper, too – of many Welsh families, of farm labourers and quarry workers in times of scarcity, and like Scotch oatmeal porridge, were understood by country people long before such things as breakfast cereals in packets were even heard of.

· THICK WELSH BARLEY CAKE ·

'Put the baking stone on, will you? I will make milk cakes for supper.'

Richard Llewellyn, *How Green was My Valley*, Michael Joseph, 1939

'Take fine barley meal and make into a stiff dough with skim milk; roll out to the size of a small bakestone, about three-quarters of an inch thick, and bake.

'It is eaten with cold butter.'

Lady Llanover, *Good Cookery*, 1867

· THIN WELSH BARLEY CAKE ·

'Mix fine barley meal and milk together to the consistency of batter, and pour slowly on the bakestone out of a jug until it has formed a circle the size of a small plate, then let it bake slowly. It ought to be very thin but soft, like a pancake or a pikelate; it is likewise eaten with cold butter.'

Lady Llanover, *Good Cookery*, 1867

· SINGING HINNIES ·

'The singing hinnie was so called as, when the butter and the cream melted during the baking, it sizzled on the hot girdle and was thought to be singing.

'*Ingredients:*

½ lb plain flour	1 teaspoon baking powder
2 oz butter	½ teaspoon salt
2 oz lard	milk and sour cream'
1 oz currants	

Equivalent metric quantities: plain flour 225 g, butter 60 g, lard 60 g, currants 30 g, baking powder 1 teaspoon, salt ½ teaspoon, milk and sour cream.

'*Method:*

'Rub fat into flour, add other dry ingredients, mix to a soft dough with a little milk and sour cream. Roll out and bake both sides on a hot girdle.

'In order to turn these without breaking into pieces, a pair of singing hinnie hands were used.'

Peggy Howey, *The Geordie Cook Book*, 1971

Another version of Singin' Hinny, given in *Farmhouse Fare*,[1] specifies 2 oz of ground rice added to ¾ lb of flour, 2 oz of sugar, 1 oz of lard, 3 oz of currants, 1 teaspoon of salt, 2 of baking powder and ¼ pint of liquid, half cream and half milk.

Equivalent metric quantities: ground rice 60 g, flour 340 g, sugar 60 g, lard 30 g, currants 85 g, salt 1 teaspoon, baking powder 2 teaspoons, cream and milk mixed (half and half) 150 g.

When rolled out the dough is pricked all over with a fork before it is baked on a fairly hot girdle.

1. Recipes contributed by readers to *The Farmer's Weekly*. First published 1935, 6th edn, Countrywise Books, 1963.

The contributor of the recipe, Miss Mary T. Bell of Northumberland, adds that the cake can be cut in half or in quarters for greater ease in turning, and that it is delicious split, buttered and eaten hot.

· A WELSH TEA, MACHYNLLETH, 1888 ·

'Tea-time was fixed for 4 o'clock, because our only possible return train started at 5, and it would never do to hurry a meal. A cup of tea would certainly have been welcome, but behold there was a real sit-down affair. The main dish was "light cakes". This famous Welsh concoction is a kind of pancake, made with flour and eggs and buttermilk. You eat them hot, with sugar and butter, the very thing for a winter tea after a long tramp. But for a summer afternoon, hard upon such a massive dinner! The cook kept sending in fresh relays, straight from the pan, and they were piled on our plates, with the warning, "Remember there's a journey before you". I could only be thankful that the train started too early to permit a supper to follow.'

M. Vivian Hughes, *A London Girl of the Eighties*, 1936
(Part 2 of *A London Family 1870–1900*, 1946)

· WELSH LIGHT CAKES ·

'Take 3 teacupfuls of flour and mix it with buttermilk till of the consistency of batter. Then put $\frac{3}{4}$ teaspoonful of carbonate of soda. Pour the mixture on to the girdle (which will have been rubbed with bacon fat) in small quantities, size of half a crown.'

Dorothy Allhusen, *A Book of Scents and Dishes*, revised edition 1927
(the recipe is credited to the late Hon. Mrs William Stanley, Penrhos, Anglesea)

· WELSH CAKES ·

The Welsh cakes made nowadays by housewives, and also to be found in bakeries and food markets throughout south and mid Wales, are much as described in Mrs Stanley's recipe above, except that currants are usually added, and sometimes a little mixed spice. I have also had them flavoured with lemon peel. A typical recipe is the one given me by a friend who made them for me in her little farmhouse near Llandeilo, Carmarthenshire. The small size is characteristic and attractive, although sometimes they are made in one large cake as big as the bakestone.

Rub 6 oz of butter into 9 oz of plain flour. Work in 1 whole large egg, 3 oz each of currants and sugar, ½ teaspoon of mixed sweet spice (or grated nutmeg), ½ teaspoon of baking powder.

Equivalent metric quantities for cakes 1 to 2 cm thick and 7 to 8 cm in diameter: butter 170 g, plain flour 250 g, eggs 1, sugar 85 g, currants 85 g, mixed sweet spice or grated nutmeg ½ teaspoon, baking powder ½ teaspoon.

Roll or pat out the dough to a thickness of ½ inch. With a cutter or small glass stamp out rounds 3 inches in diameter. Bake the cakes on the griddle or *planc*, as the Welsh call it, or in a lightly buttered iron frying pan. They are quickly cooked, and should be soft, not crisp. When well-made, Welsh cakes are light and short. I find them delicious. Sometimes they are eaten with a little butter, although when fresh I find them better without it.

Welsh cakes are also known as 'round cakes', and according to a leaflet published by the Welsh Folk Museum at St Fagans, Cardiff, an alternative method of cooking them, favoured in the Vale of Glamorgan, was to bake them in a Dutch oven in front of 'a clean, red fire'. To achieve the same effect using a modern cooker, Minwel Tibbott, author of *Welsh Fare*,[1] suggests baking the cakes in a shallow tin in a low position under a hot grill. Bake on both sides until golden brown.

· POTATO SCONES ·

'Before leaving the subject of scones, I must mention what in boyhood was a wonder and, properly-made, remains so. The potato scone.

'You mash half-a-pound of cold boiled potatoes, as mealy as possible, with a pinch of salt. Into this you work a heaped tablespoonful of sifted flour, and you make a stiffish dough with the addition of milk. This you roll out very thinly – less than an eighth of an inch – on a floured board, and cut into rounds about the size of a (generous) teaplate. The rounds are pricked with a fork, and are put on a hot girdle for about five minutes, being turned over when half done. Little brown blisters rise on both sides of the scones. You squash them with a spatula or the flat

1. The Welsh Folk Museum, St Fagans, Cardiff, 1976.

of a knife. The supposedly sybaritic way is to serve the potato scones hot off the girdle, buttered and rolled up. But I, for one, like them better cold, though as soon after baking as possible, rolled up with unmelted butter spread over inside.'

Victor MacClure, *Good Appetite My Companion*, 1955

· POTATO CAKES ·

'Take some freshly boiled mealy potatoes and rub them through a sieve or vegetable presser while still hot. Add salt and a small piece of butter. Then roll out rather thinly, using a little flour, barley meal, or fine oatmeal to prevent the mixture sticking. Cut out rounds, and cook the cakes on a hot greased girdle until brown on both sides. Serve hot spread with butter.

'Cold cooked potatoes can also be used, but the scones will not be so light.'

Florence Jack, *Good Housekeeping Cookery Book*, 1925

The cast iron hanging pan for griddle cakes and scones was called a Scotch frying pan, but was also used in many rural areas of England and Wales. It was made by the famous ironfounding firm of Izons.

Toast

'No bread. Then bring me some toast!'

Punch, 1852

'"Toast" said Berry, taking the two last pieces that stood in the rack. "I'm glad to get back to toast. And a loaf of brown bread that isn't like potter's clay."'

Dornford Yates, Adèle & Co., Ward, Lock, 1931

It isn't only fictional heroes to whom toast means home and comfort. It is related of the Duke of Wellington – I believe by Lord Ellesmere – that when he landed at Dover in 1814, after six years' absence from England, the first order he gave at the Ship Inn was for an unlimited supply of buttered toast.

In *The Origin of Food Habits* (1944), H. D. Renner makes an attempt to explain the English addiction to toast. 'The flavour of bread', he says, 'can be revived to some extent by re-warming and even new flavours are created in toasting.' This is very true, but leaves the most important part unsaid. It is surely the *smell* of toast that makes it so enticing, an enticement which the actuality rarely lives up to. In this it is like freshly roasted coffee, like sizzling bacon – all those early morning smells of an intensity and deliciousness which create far more than those new flavours, since they create hunger and appetite where none existed. Small wonder that the promise is never quite fulfilled. 'Village life', Renner continues, 'makes stale bread so common that toasting has become a national habit restricted to the British Isles and those countries which have been colonized by Britain.' Surely England was not the only country where villages were isolated and bread went dry and stale? I wonder if our open fires and coal ranges were not more responsible than the high incidence of stale bread for the popularity of toast in all classes of English household. For toasting bread in front of the fire and the bars of the coal-burning range there were dozens of different devices – museums of domestic life are crammed with them, Victorian cookery books show any number of designs – as many as there are varieties of electric toaster in our own day; apart from toasters for bread, there were special racks for toasting muffins and crumpets, and special pans for toasting cheese. And, as recorded in the recipe for potato bread given on p. 288, there were, in the nineteenth century, eminent medical men writing grave advice as to the kind of bread which, when toasted, would absorb the maximum amount of butter. That buttered toast goes back a long way in English life, and was by no means confined to country places where fresh bread was a rarity is shown by the following quotation: 'All within the sound of Bow Bell', wrote Fynes Morison in *Itinerary*, Volume 3 (1617), 'are in reproch called cochnies, and eaters of buttered tostes.'

Buttered toast is, then, or was, so peculiarly English a delicacy – and I use the term delicacy because that is what in our collective national memory it still is – that the following meticulous description of how it was made, at least in theory, reads poignantly indeed. It is from the hand of Miss Marian McNeill, author of that famous work *The Scots Kitchen*, on this occasion writing in an enchanting volume, long out of print,[1] called *The Book of Breakfasts*, published in 1932:

'Sweet light bread only a day old makes the best toast. Cut into even slices about quarter of an inch thick. It may be toasted under the grill, but the best toast is made at a bright smokeless fire. Put the slice on a toasting-fork and keep only so near the fire that it will be heated through when both sides are well browned. Move the toast about so as to brown evenly. Covered with an earthen bowl, toast will keep warm and moist.

'If very thin, crisp toast is desired, take bread that is two days old, cut it into slices about three-eighths of an inch thick, and toast them patiently at a little distance from a clear fire till delicately browned on both sides. With a sharp knife divide each slice into two thin slices, and toast the inner sides as before. Put each slice as it is done into a toast rack.

'For hot buttered toast, toast the bread more quickly than for ordinary toast, as it should not be crisp. Trim off the crusts and spread the toast liberally with butter that has been warmed but not allowed to oil. Cut in neat pieces, pile-sandwichwise, and keep hot in a covered dish over a bowl of hot water. Use the best butter.'

I have my own childhood memories of toast-making in front of the schoolroom fire. Although I fancy that more toast fell off the fork into the fire and was irretrievably blackened than ever reached our plates, I

1. Since writing the above, *The Book of Breakfasts* has been reprinted by Reprographia (Edinburgh, 1975).

can recall the great sense of achievement when now and again a slice did come out right, evenly golden, with a delicious smell and especially, as I remember, with the right, proper texture, so difficult to describe, and so fleeting. Only when it was hot from the fire and straight off the fork did that toast have the requisite qualities. Perhaps young children are better qualified than grown-ups to appreciate these points. And perhaps that is why buttered toast is one of those foods, like sausages, and potatoes baked in their skins, and mushrooms picked from the fields, which are never as good as they were.

Nowadays my toast is usually made on one of those ridged metal plates which goes over a gas flame or an electric burner. This produces crisp toast, very different from the kind made in front of the fire, but in its way almost as good. These lightweight metal toasters are very cheap. There is no need to buy an expensive iron one. Rye bread or 100 per cent whole wheatmeal bread both make excellent toast, but for buttered toast a light white bread is best. I prefer to make this kind of toast under the grill, electric toasters being machines with which I cannot be doing. In this I must be in a very small minority, for electric toasters are one of the most popular of all wedding presents, and in May 1975 *Which?* published a report on no fewer than thirteen different electric toasters. 'Some like it well done,' declared *Which?*, 'others pale brown; some like it done slowly to give a crisp finish, others done quickly so it's still soft inside.' All of these pronouncements are no doubt correct, as indeed is the statement that 'you don't want your piece of toast to be black in the middle and white round the edges'. That is to say, I don't. But I know plenty of people who actually *like* their toast to be charred. Perhaps they prefer it charred at the edges and white in the middle, and I'm not sure how this would be achieved. Another of the report's dictums, 'however you like your toast, you want all pieces to be more or less the same', is one I don't agree with, perhaps fortunately, for it is not easy to get all your pieces more or less the same. Unless, that is, you have a caterers' toasting machine and caterers' sliced bread which between them produce what I call restaurateurs' toast, that strange substance cut in triangles and served with the pâté, and for breakfast, in all English hotels and restaurants. This English invention has in recent years become popular in France where, oddly enough, it goes by the name of toast, as opposed to real French toast which is called *pain grillé*, and is just what it says, grilled bread. That brings me back to the toast-making device I myself use, the metal plate or grill over the gas burner. Part of the charm of the toast produced on this device is that every piece is different, and differently marked, irregularly chequered with the marks of the grill, charred here and there, flecked with brown and gold and black . . . I think that the goodness of toast made in this way does depend a good deal on the initial quality of the bread, and the way it is cut. Thin slices are useless, and I don't think that white sliced bread would be very successful – there is too much water to get rid of before the toasting process starts, and steamy bread sticks to the toaster. Thickish slices are best, preferably rather small ones which can be easily turned with grill tongs. Like most other toast, this kind is best straight from the grill. 'If allowed to stand and become sodden, dry toast becomes indigestible. From the fire to the table is the thing', wrote the delightfully named Lizzie Heritage in *Cassell's Universal Cookery Book* (first published 1894). And if the toast is to be buttered, I suppose we must remember Marian McNeill's 'use the best butter'. What *is* the best butter? Unsalted, some would say. I'll settle for any butter that's good of its kind. The very salt butter of Wales can be perfectly delicious eaten with the right kind of toast (no marmalade for me), and here is Flora Thompson[1] describing toast with salt butter and celery, and toast with cold boiled bacon. Toast-resistant though I am, she makes me long for that fresh hot toast and crisp celery, a wonderful combination, and how subtle:

'In winter, salt butter would be sent for and toast would be made and eaten with celery. Toast was a favourite dish for family consumption. "I've made 'em a stack o' toast as high as up to their knees", a mother would say on a winter Sunday afternoon before her hungry brood came in from church. Another dish upon which they prided themselves was thin slices of cold, boiled streaky bacon on toast, a dish so delicious that it deserves to be more widely popular.'

· TOAST AND ALE: CHRISTMAS MORNING ·

'Then there was the smell of hot toast and ale from the kitchen, at the breakfast hour.'

George Eliot, *The Mill on the Floss*, 1860

1. *Lark Rise to Candleford*, 1945.

· ANCHOVY TOAST AND ALE ·

'The Reverend Doctor Gaster found himself rather queasy in the morning, therefore preferred breakfasting in bed, on a mug of buttered ale and an anchovy toast.'

T. L. Peacock, *Headlong Hall*, 1816

· TOAST: UNKIND CUT ·

'As to toast, it may fairly be pronounced a contrivance for consuming bread, butter, firing and time.'

Esther Copley, *The Complete Cottage Cookery*, 1849

· DRIPPING TOAST ·

'I had toasted four rounds of bread which my mother put on the end of the fork as piece after piece was browned.

'There is good dripping toast is by the fire in the evening. Good jelly dripping and crusty, home-baked bread, with the mealy savour of ripe wheat roundly in your mouth and under your teeth, roasted sweet and crisp and deep brown, and covered with little pockets where the dripping will hide and melt and shine in the light, deep down inside, ready to run when your teeth bit in.'

Richard Llewellyn, *How Green was My Valley*, Michael Joseph, 1939

· RAILWAY TOAST ·

In December 1975 British Rail's catering department announced that toast would henceforward cost buffet car passengers 11p a slice. The then cost of a 12-slice white loaf was 15p, so British Rail was in effect selling it for £1.32.

No doubt British Rail assumed that the national devotion to toast is unshakable, and that the public will put up with anything and pay anything to get it. British Rail was clearly right. There was no public protest or outcry.

· TOAST MELBA ·

'I remember one of those afternoons, at tea-time, I complained about the toast in Escoffier's hearing. "Toast is never thin enough to suit me," I said. "Can't you do something about it?"

'As usual Escoffier and Ritz took such a remark with absolute serious-ness. They discussed the problem of thin toast. "Why not," said Ritz, "toast thin slices of bread once, then cut it through again, and again toast it?" And with Escoffier he retired to the kitchens to see if it could not be done. The result was Escoffier's justly famous *toast Melba*. When they brought out on the lawn a plate full of the thin, crisp, curled wafers, Escoffier said, "Behold! A new dish, and it is called *toast Marie*." But as I ate it I tried to think up another name. Marie was far too anonymous to suit me.

'During that year Melba had returned from America very ill. She was staying at the Savoy where she was a much-indulged invalid. I had heard Escoffier discuss her *régime*. Dry toast figured on it . . . "Call it *toast Melba*," I said.

'And so it was done. I was the first to taste *toast Melba;* Madame Melba herself had to wait until the following day!'

Marie Ritz, *César Ritz, Host to the World*, 1938

You may or may not care for Melba toast, but there is something wonderfully pleasing in the picture evoked by Madame Ritz of the most celebrated chef and the most brilliant hotelier in all Europe getting together to make a few slices of thin toast and the result ending up with the name of a world-famous prima donna on a diet.

And was it then the alliance Escoffier–Ritz–Melba which was initially responsible for the idea of that restaurateurs' toast which subsequently became such a plague? Somewhere along the line things seem to have got a bit muddled. In the first place, Escoffier surely did not invent, nor claim to have invented, the method of slicing a piece of toast in half and then toasting the untoasted sides – see Marian McNeill's recipe quoted above – and the next awkward point is that Melba toast nowadays is usually understood to consist of thin, thin slices of bread toasted or rather dried in the oven until they curl round. Certainly it's a much easier and rather more successful method than all that slicing business.

· PULLED BREAD ·

In the eighteenth and early nineteenth centuries 'pulling' bread was a fashionable way of producing crisp and crunchy pieces of bread to be eaten with cheese. The crumb of a newly baked loaf was torn into rough lumps, put back into the oven, and left until all the pieces were beginning to crisp on the outside but were still soft within. In effect, this was a form of toast.

I am not very seriously suggesting that anyone should bake a loaf especially to make pulled bread. There are times though when it may be a saving grace to know about pulled bread. For example, suppose that you have baked a loaf which turns out to be undercooked in the centre. Then you tear the crumb into pieces, put these pieces on a baking sheet or earthenware platter, and let them bake in a medium hot oven for about 10 to 15 minutes, until they are golden-flecked or pale toast coloured. They look and smell appetizing and fresh, and because they are not uniform each piece has a slightly different texture and its own character. They are really delicious and, I think, much more interesting than toast. It is worth trying pulled bread with pâté. It's quite a revelation.

To be good, pulled bread must be sufficiently salted; and it must have good texture and a little scrunchy bite. Soft baps and muffin loaves make good pulled bread.

According to Mr John Scade, author of a chapter on the local traditions of English breads, the names and shapes of loaves, and the different varieties of tea cakes, baps and buns, contributed to Ronald Sheppard and Edward Newton's *The Story of Bread* (1957), pulled bread is or was at that time still served 'at dinners and banquets from shallow napkin-covered baskets'.

· BREAD FOR POTAGES ·

'The best way of ordering your bread in Potages, is thus. Take light spungy white French-bread, cut only the crusts into tosts. Tost them exceedingly dry before the fire, so that they be yellow. Then put them hot into a hot dish, and pour upon them some very good strong broth, boiling hot. Cover thus, and let them stew together. Gently, not boil; and feed it with fresh-broth, still as it needeth. This will make the bread swell much, and become like gelly.'

The Closet of the Eminently Learned Sir Kenelm Digby Knight Opened, 1669

Bibliography and
Further Reading List

Acton, Eliza: *Modern Cookery for Private Families*, London, Longmans Green, 1845; 3rd edition (revised) 1845; revised edition 1855. *The English Bread Book*, London, Longmans Green, 1857. *The Best of Eliza Acton*, ed. Elizabeth Ray, introduction by Elizabeth David, London, Longmans, 1968; Penguin Books, 1974.

Agriculture, Fisheries and Food, Ministry of: *Food Standards Committee Second Report on Bread and Flour*, London, H.M.S.O., 1974. *Manual of Nutrition*, London, H.M.S.O., 1970.

Agriculture, Fisheries and Food, Ministry of: *Food Standards Committee Review of Food Labelling. Part 2. Exemptions from ingredient listing and generic terms*, FSC/REP/69B, London, H.M.S.O., September 1977. (In this report the Committee recommended that *no* food be exempted from ingredient listing. As far as bread and flour confectionery are concerned the Committee's findings are meeting with much opposition.)

L'Agronome: *Dictionnaire portatif du cultivateur*, 2 vols., Paris, 1763.

Allen-Gray, Dorothy: *Fare Exchange*, London, Faber & Faber, 1963.

Allhusen, Dorothy: *A Book of Scents and Dishes*, revised and enlarged edition 1927, first published 1926, London, Williams & Norgate.

American School of Classical Studies at Athens (c/o Institute for Advanced Study, Princeton, New Jersey, U.S.A.): *Pots and Pans of Classical Athens. Excavations of the Athenian Agora*, Picture Book No. 1, 3rd printing 1964.

Ashby, M. K.: *Joseph Ashby of Tysoe, 1859–1919: A Study of English Village Life*, Cambridge University Press, 1961; Merlin Press, 1974.

Ashley, Sir William: *The Bread of our Forefathers*, Oxford, the Clarendon Press, 1928.

Austin, Thomas (ed.): *Two Fifteenth-Century Cookery-Books: Harleian MS. 279 (c. 1430) and Harleian MS. 4016 (c. 1450) with extracts from Ashmole MS. 1439, Laud MS. 553, and Douce MS. 55*; published for the Early English Text Society by the Oxford University Press, London, 1888; reprinted 1964.

Banfield, Walter: *Manna*, London, Maclaren & Sons, 1937.

Batten, M. I.: *English Windmills*, Volume 1, on behalf of the Society for the Protection of Ancient Buildings, London, the Architectural Press, 1930.

Beard, James: *Beard on Bread*, New York, Alfred Knopf, 1973; London, Michael Joseph, 1976.

Beeton, Isabella: *Mrs Beeton's Book of Household Management*, London, 1861. *See also* Senn, Herman.

Bennett, H. S.: *The Pastons and their England*, London, 2nd edition, Cambridge University Press, 1932.

Bennion, Edmund: *Breadmaking*, 4th edition, London, Oxford University Press, 1967.

Best, Henry: *Rural Economy in Yorkshire in 1641*, ed. C. B. Robinson, Surtees Society, xxxiii, 1857.

Bishop, Frederick: *The Wife's Own Book of Cookery*, London, Ward, Lock, 1861.

Blencowe, Ann: *Receipt Book of Mrs Ann Blencowe 1694*, with an introduction by George Saintsbury, London, the Adelphi, Guy Chapman, 1925.

Bonnefons, Nicolas de: *Les Délices de la campagne*, Paris, Pierre Deshayes, 1654.

Boorde, Andrew: *The Dyetary of Helth*, 1542.

British Fermentation Products Ltd, Felixstowe, Suffolk: *The Story of Yeast*, n.d. (14-page booklet).

Bulleid, Sir Arthur and Gray, H. St George: *The Lake Villages of Somerset*, 6th edition, revised by the author, the Glastonbury Antiquarian Society, 1968; first published 1924.

Burkitt, Denis P.: 'Some Diseases Characteristic of Modern Western Civilisation', *British Medical Journal*, 3 February 1973. *See also* Painter.

Burnett, John: *Plenty and Want*, London, Nelson, 1966; Penguin Books, 1968.

Cassell's Domestic Dictionary, c. 1880.

Child, Julia and Beck, Simone: *Mastering the Art of French Cooking*, Volume 2, New York, Alfred Knopf, 1970; London, Michael Joseph, 1977.

Clark, Lady: *The Cookery Book of Lady Clark of Tillypronie*, ed. Miss C. F. Frere, London, Heinemann, 1909.

Cleave, T. L., Campbell, G. D. and Painter, N. S.: *Diabetes, Coronary Thrombosis and the Saccharine Disease*, 2nd edition, Bristol, Wright, 1969; first published 1966.

Cobbett, William: *Cottage Economy*, first published 1821–3; with additions of 1831 and Mrs Cobbett's recipes for using Indian corn, first published 1846; London, Peter Davis, 1926.

Compleat Cook, The, London, printed by E.B. for Nath. Brook at the Angel in Cornhill, 1658; 1st edition, 1655. *A Queen's Delight*, printed by R. Wood for Nath. Brook at the Angel in Cornhill, 1658.

Constable: *John Constable's Correspondence. The Family at East Bergholt 1807–1837*, edited with an introduction and notes by R. B. Beckett, Suffolk Records Society, Volume IV, 1962.

Copley, Esther: *The Complete Cottage Cookery*, London, William Wosley, 1849.

Cornish, W. J.: *The Naturalist on the Thames*, London, 1902.

Curwen, Dr E. Cecil (F.S.A.): 'Querns', *Antiquity*, June 1937, Vol. XI, pp. 133–151. 'More About Querns', 1941, Vol. XV, pp. 15–30.

Daniel, Albert: *The Reasons Why: Practical Answers to Everyday Bakehouse Questions*, London, Maclaren & Sons, 1959.

David, Elizabeth: *Italian Food*, London, Macdonald, 1954; Penguin Books, 1963. *French Provincial Cooking*, London, Michael Joseph, 1960; Penguin Books, 1964. *Spices, Salt and Aromatics in the English Kitchen*, London, Penguin Books, 1970.

Digby, Sir Kenelm: *The Closet of the Eminently Learned Sir Kenelm Digby Knight*

Opened, 1669; newly edited with introduction, notes and glossary by Anne Macdonell, London, 1910.

Dods, Mistress Margaret (Christine Isabel Johnstone): *The Cook and Housewife's Manual*, 4th edition, revised and enlarged, Edinburgh and London, 1829; first published 1826.

Donaghy, Patricia: *Northumbrian and Cumbrian Recipes*, Newcastle-upon-Tyne, Oriel Press Ltd, 1971.

Drummond, J. C. and Wilbraham, A.: *The Englishman's Food: A History of Five Centuries of English Diet*, revised and with a new chapter by Dorothy Hollingsworth, London, Jonathan Cape, 1957; first published 1939.

Dubois, Urbain: *Boulangerie d'aujourd'hui*, 3rd edition, Ouvrages d'Urbain Dubois, augmentés et tenus à jour par Félix Urbain-Dubois, Éditions Joinville, 48 rue Monsieur le Prince, Paris 6e, 1962; first published 1955.

Dufour, E.: *Traité pratique de panification, française et parisienne*, 4th edition, 1957; published by the author, Villeneuve-les-Bordes, Seine-et-Marne, 1937.

Eagle Range Co.: *The History of the Coal Devouring Cooking Range and its Progeny, Smoke and Fog, and the Remedy*, by the author of *Hot Water Supply*, *c.* 1895.

Emmison, F. G. (F.S.A., F.R.H.S.): *Tudor Food and Pastimes*, London, Ernest Benn Ltd, 1964. *Elizabethan Life: Home, Work and Land*, from *Essex Wills and Sessions and Manorial Records*, Chelmsford, Essex Record Publication No. 69, 1976.

Ewart Evans, George: *Ask the Fellows Who Cut the Hay*, London, Faber & Faber, 1956. *The Farm and the Village*, London, Faber & Faber, 1969.

Fairrie, Geoffrey: *Sugar*, Liverpool, Fairrie & Co. Ltd, 1925.

Fance, W. J. and Wragg, B. H.: *Up-to-Date Breadmaking*, London, Maclaren & Sons, 1968.

Fiennes, Celia: *The Journeys of Celia Fiennes*, ed. with an introduction by Christopher Morris, London, the Cresset Press, 1947.

Francatelli, Charles Elmé: *A Plain Cookery Book for the Working Classes*, London, *c.* 1862.

Frazer, Mrs: *The Practise of Cookery, Pastry and Confectionery*, Edinburgh, 1791.

Furnivall, Frederick J. (ed.): *The Babees Book* (includes Hugh Rhodes' *Boke of Nurture*, John Russell's *Boke of Nurture*, *c.* 1480, Wynkyn de Worde's *Boke of Kervynge*, *c.* 1508, and *The Boke of Curtasye*), Early English Text Society, 1868.

Garrett, Theodore Francis (ed.), *The Encyclopaedia of Practical Cookery*, 8 vols., London, 1899.

Glasse, Hannah: *The Art of Cookery Made Plain and Easy*, London, 1747; 9th edition 1765 with additions, as printed in the 5th (1755) edition. *The Compleat Confectioner*, London, 1772; first published *c.* 1760.

Good Huswife's Handmaide for the Kitchen, The, imprinted at London by Richard Jones, 1594.

Gottschalk, Dr Alfred: *Histoire de l'alimentation et de la gastronomie depuis la préhistoire jusqu'à nos jours*, 2 vols., Paris, Éditions Hippocrate, 1948.

Grant, Doris: *Your Daily Bread*, London, Faber & Faber, 1944; *Your Daily Food*, London, Faber & Faber, 1973.

Grant, James: *The Chemistry of Breadmaking*, London, 1912.

Gribbin, H.: *Vienna and Other Fancy Breads*, London, Maclaren & Sons, *c.* 1900.

Hackwood, Frederick: *Good Cheer*, London, 1911.

Harris, Gertrude: *Manna: Foods of the Frontier*, San Francisco, 101 Productions, 1972.

Harrison, William: *Description of England*, 1577 and 1587.

Hartley, Dorothy: *Made in England*, London, Methuen, 1939. *The Countryman's England*, London, Batsford, 1935; 2nd edition, revised, 1942–3. *Food in England*, London, Macdonald, 1954. *Water in England*, London, Macdonald, 1964.

Heritage, Lizzie: *Cassell's Universal Cookery Book*, London, Cassell & Co., 1901; first published 1894.

Howey, Peggy: *The Geordie Cook Book: Recipes from Northumberland and Durham*, Newcastle-upon-Tyne, Frank Graham, 1971.

Hughes, M. Vivian: *A London Child of the Seventies*, 1934: *A London Girl of the Eighties*, 1936; *A London Home in the Nineties*, 1937; published in one volume as *A London Family 1870–1900*, Oxford University Press, 1946; reprinted 1947.

Hugill, J. A. C. (ed.): *Sugar*, London, Cosmo Publications and Tate & Lyle Ltd, 1949.

Jack, Florence B.: *Cookery for Every Household*, Edinburgh, T. C. and E. C. Jack, 1914. *Good Housekeeping Cookery Book*, London, 1925.

Jago, William: *An Introduction to the Study of the Principles of Breadmaking*, London, The British Baker, 1889.

Jago, William and William C.: *The Technology of Breadmaking*, revised edition, Liverpool, the Northern Publishing Co., 1921; first published 1911.

Jekyll, Gertrude: *Old English Household Life*, London, Batsford, 1925.

Jenkin, A. K. Hamilton: *Cornish Homes and Customs*, London, Dent, 1934.

Jewitt, Llewellyn: *The Ceramic Art of Great Britain*, London, 1883.

Jobson, Allan: *An Hour-Glass on the Run*, London, Michael Joseph, 1959.

Jones, Tom: *Henry Tate 1819–1899. A Biographical Sketch*, London, Tate & Lyle Ltd, 1960.

Joyce, H. S.: *I was Born in the Country*, London and Glasgow, Art and Educational Press, 1946.

Kent, Countess of (Elizabeth de Grey): *A True Gentlewoman's Delight*, 1653.

Ketteridge, Christopher and Mays, Spike: *Five Miles from Bunkum. A Village and its Crafts*, London, Eyre Methuen, 1972.

Kirkland, John: *The Modern Baker, Confectioner and Caterer*, 6 vols., London, Gresham Publishing Co., 1907; new and revised edition, 4 vols., 1923. (Ed.) *The Bakers' ABC*, London Gresham Publishing Co., 1927.

La Varenne, François Pierre: *Le Pastissier françois*, Amsterdam, Louis Ct. Daniel Elzevier, 1655. Nouvelle Edition avec une Introduction de Maurice des Ombiaux, Paris, Dorbon-Aine, 1931; edition limited to 400 copies.

Law, James T.: *Law's Grocer's Manual*, Liverpool, 1895; 2nd edition, London, c. 1902.

Liber Albus, The White Book of the City of London, compiled 1419 by John Carpenter, Common Clerk, and Richard Whittington, Mayor; translated from the original Latin and Anglo-Norman by Henry Thomas Riley, 1861.

Liger, Louis: *Le Ménage des champs et le jardinier françois*, 6th edition, Paris, 1711.

Llanover, Lady: *The First Principles of Good Cookery*, London, 1867.

MacClure, Victor: *Good Appetite My Companion*, London, Odhams Press, 1955.

McCance, R. A. and Widdowson, E. M.: *Breads White and Brown: Their Place in Thought and Social History*, London, Pitman, 1956.

McNeill, F. Marian: *The Scots Kitchen*, Edinburgh, Blackie, 1929. *The Book of Breakfasts*, London, Alexander Maclehose, 1932; reprinted by Reprographia, Edinburgh, 1975.

Markham, Gervase: *The English Hus-wife*, London, 1615; a new edition 1653.

Marshall, Rosalind K.: *The Days of Duchess Anne: Life in the Household of the Duchess of Hamilton 1656–1716*, London, Collins, 1973.

Mason, Charlotte: *Mrs Mason's Cookery, or The Ladies' Assistant*, originally published from the manuscript collection of Mrs Charlotte Mason, a professed housekeeper, etc.; a new edition, London, 1786; first published 1773.

May, Robert: *The Accomplisht Cook*, London, 1660; 5th edition 1685.

Mayhew, Henry: *London Labour and the London Poor*, 1851.

Moelwyn-Hughes, Ronw: *Cheap Bread*, London, Benn, 1930.

Monckton, H. A.: *A History of English Ale and Beer*, London, The Bodley Head, 1966.

Morel, Ambroise: *Histoire illustrée de la boulangerie en France*, Paris, Syndicat Patronal de la Boulangerie de Paris et de la Seine, 1924.

Muffet, Dr Thomas: *Health's Improvement or Rules Comprising and Discovering the Nature, Method and Manner of Preparing All Sorts of Food Used in This Nation*, corrected and enlarged by Christopher Bennett, Doctor in Physics, London, 1655.

Napier, Mrs Alexander (ed.): *A Noble Boke off Cookry ffor a Prynce Houssolde or Eny Other Estately Houssolde*, reprinted verbatim from a rare MS. in the Holkham Collection, London, 1882.

Noble, Joan Russell (ed.): *Recollections of Virginia Woolf*, London, Peter Owen Ltd, 1972.

Oxford Book of Food Plants, London, Oxford University Press, 1969.

Painter, Neil S.: 'Aetiology of Diverticular Disease', *British Medical Journal*, 17 April 1971, p. 156. 'Irritable or Irritated Bowel', correspondence in *British Medical Journal*, 1 April 1972, p. 46.

Painter, Neil S. and Burkitt, Denis P.: 'Diverticular Disease of the Colon: A Deficiency Disease of Western Civilisation', *British Medical Journal*, 22 May 1971, p. 450.

Paston Letters. See Bennett, H. S.

Patent Office: *Abridgement or Specifications Relating to Cooking, Breadmaking, and the Preparation of Confectionery*, Part I, 1634–1866, Part II, 1867–1876; published 1873 and 1882.

Peate, Iorwerth: *Tradition and Folk Life: A Welsh View*, London, Faber & Faber, 1972.

Pennant, Thomas: *Tours in Wales 1778–81*, 1782.

Pinto, Edward H.: *Treen and Other Wooden Bygones. An Encyclopaedia and Social History*, London, G. Bell & Sons, 1969.

Plat, Sir Hugh: *Delightes for Ladies*, 1609; first published 1602; reprinted with introductions by G. E. and K. R. Fussell, London, Crosby Lockwood, 1948.

Pococke, Dr Richard: *The Travels through England of Dr Richard Pococke 1750*, Camden Society Publications, 1888 (new series No. 42).

Raffald, Elizabeth: *The Experienced English Housekeeper*, London, 1769.
Raper, Elizabeth: *The Receipt Book of Elizabeth Raper*, written 1756–70; edited by her great-grandson Bartle Grant, with a portrait and decorations by Duncan Grant, London, the Nonesuch Press, 1924.
Renner, H. D.: *The Origin of Food Habits*, London, Faber & Faber, 1944.
Reynolds, John: *Windmills and Watermills*, London, Hugh Evelyn, 1970; reprinted with corrections, 1974.
Ritz, Marie: *César Ritz, Host to the World*, London, Harrap, 1938.
Roberts, Emma. *See* Rundell.
Rundell, Mrs Maria Eliza: *A New System of Domestic Cookery; Formed Upon Principles of Economy*, a new edition, corrected, London, 1807; first published 1806; 65th edition remodelled and improved, by the addition of nearly one thousand entirely new receipts (contributed by Miss Emma Roberts), 1841; *Modern Domestic Cookery Based on the Well-known Work of Mrs Rundell*, 1851.
Russell, John: *Boke of Nurture. See* Furnivall.

St Clair, Lady Harriet: *Dainty Dishes*, Edinburgh, 1866.
Samuelson, M.: *Sussex Recipe Book, with a Few Excursions into Kent*, London, Country Life, 1937.
Scade, John: *Cereals*, London, Oxford University Press, 1975 ('Value of Food' series).
Scurfield, George and Cecilia: *Home Baked*, London, Faber & Faber, 1956.
Senn, Herman, *The New Century Cookery Book*, London, 1901. (Ed.), *Mrs Beeton's Book of Household Management*, London, Ward, Lock, 1906.
Sheppard, Ronald and Newton, Edward: *The Story of Bread*, London, Routledge & Kegan Paul, 1957.
Smith, E.: *The Compleat Housewife or Accomplish'd Gentlewoman's Companion*, 15th edition, with additions, 1753; first published 1727.
Society for the Protection of Ancient Buildings, 55 Great Ormond Street, London WC1N 3JA: Paul N. Wilson, *Watermills: An Introduction*, 1956; revised edition 1973. Paul N. Wilson, *Watermills with Horizontal Wheels*, 1960. David Luckhurst, *Monastic Watermills. A Study of the Mills within English Monastic Precincts*, n.d.
Soyer, Alexis: *Shilling Cookery for the People*, London, 1855.
Stevens Cox, J. (ed.): *Guernsey Dishes of the 18th Century, Guernsey Gâche* and *Guernsey Dishes of Bygone Days*, the Toucan Press, Mount Durand, St Peter Port, Guernsey, 1966, 1969 and 1971.
Stow, John: *Survey of London*, 1598; ed. John Strype, 2 vols., 1720.
Strong, L. A. G.: *The Story of Sugar*, London, Weidenfeld & Nicolson, 1954.
Sturt, George (George Bourne): *A Small Boy in the Sixties*, introduction by Arnold Bennett, London, Cambridge University Press, 1932; first published 1927.

T.A.C.C. Report. *See* Technology Assessment Consumerism Centre.
Tames, Richard: *Our Daily Bread*, London, Penguin Education, 1973.
Technology Assessment Consumerism Centre (T.A.C.C.): *Bread. An Assessment of the Bread Industry in Britain*, Intermediate Publishing Ltd (P.O. Box 6, Kettering, Northants.), 1974.

Thomas, Kathleen: *A West Country Cookery Book*, Wheaton of Exeter, 1961.

Thompson, Flora: *Lark Rise to Candleford*, London, Oxford University Press, 1945: Penguin Books, 1975.

Thompson Gill, J.: *The Complete Bread, Cake and Cracker Baker*, 5th edition, Chicago, Confectioner and Baker Publishing Co., 1881.

Thompson, Sir Henry (F.R.C.S.): *Food and Feeding*, 12th edition, London, 1901; 3rd edition 1884; first published *c.* 1882.

Tibbott, S. Minwel: *Welsh Fare*, National Museum of Wales, Welsh Folk Museum, St Fagans, Cardiff, 1976 (English translation of *Amser Bwyd*, 1974).

Torr, Cecil: *Small Talk at Wreyland*, Series I, II and III, Cambridge University Press, 1918, 1921, 1923; combined edition, Bath, .Somerset, Adams & Dart, 1970.

Trevelyan, G. M.: *Illustrated English Social History*, 4 vols., London, Longmans Green, 1949–52; Penguin Books, 1964.

Tull, Jethro: *Principles of Tillage*, 1751.

Uttley, Alison: *Recipes from an Old Farmhouse*, London, Faber & Faber, 1966.

Vince, John: *Discovering Watermills*, 2nd edition, Princes Risborough, Shire Publications Ltd, 1976.

Vine, Frederick T.: *Practical Breadmaking*, London, Baker and Confectioner, 1897. *Saleable Shop Goods*, 6th edition, London, Baker and Confectioner, 1898. *Savoury Pastry*, London, Baker and Confectioner, 1900.

Wailes, Rex: *The English Windmill*, London, Routledge, 1954. *Horizontal Windmills*, paper read at the Science Museum, London, on 3 April 1968 – excerpt from *Transactions of the Newcomen Society*, vol. xl, 1967 and 1968.

Wales Gas Board: *Croeso Cymreig. A Welsh Welcome: Recipes for Some Traditional Welsh Dishes*, 5th revised edition, Cardiff, 1969; first published 1953.

Walker, George: *The Costume of Yorkshire*, 1814.

Walsh, J. H. (F.R.C.S.): *A Manual of Domestic Economy Suited to Families Spending from £100 to £1000 a Year*, new edition, London, 1861; first published 1856.

Warner, the Reverend Richard: *Antiquitates Culinariae* or *Curious Tracts Relating to the Culinary Affairs of the Old English*. Includes *The Forme of Cury*. A roll of ancient English cookery, compiled about A.D. 1390, by the master cooks of King Richard II.

Warren, C. Henry: *Corn Country*, London, Batsford, 1940.

Watkins, C. Malcolm: *North Devon Pottery and Its Export to America in the 17th Century*, United States National Museum Bulletin 225, Smithsonian Institution, Washington, D.C., 1960.

Whatman, Susanna: *The Housekeeping Book of Susanna Whatman 1776–1800*, ed. Thomas Balston, London, Geoffrey Bles, 1956.

White, Florence: *Good Things in England*, London, Jonathan Cape, 1932.

White, Gilbert: *Gilbert White's Journals*, ed. Walter Johnson, London, Routledge & Kegan Paul, 1931; reprinted Newton Abbot, Devon, David & Charles, 1970.

Williams, James: *Give Me Yesterday*, Gwasg Gomer, Llandysul, Cardiganshire, 1971.

Williams, W. Mattieu: *The Chemistry of Cookery*, 3rd edition, London, 1898; first published 1885.

Wilson, C. Anne: *Food and Drink in Britain from the Stone-Age to Recent Times*, London, Constable, 1973; Penguin Books, 1976.

Winchester, Barbara: *Tudor Family Portrait*, London, Jonathan Cape, 1955.

Wine and Food Society: *Cereals*, Section IV of *A Concise Encyclopaedia of Gastronomy*, compiled under the editorial direction of André L. Simon, London, 1943. In his Foreword André Simon acknowledges the Society's debt 'to Professor Sir Jack Drummond, who has contributed . . . the entry which we consider the most important of all: *Bread*'.

Women's Institutes, Federations of: *Cornish Recipes Ancient and Modern*, compiled by Edith Martin, Truro, 1929; 5th edition, 1930; 11th edition, 1934. *The Isle of Wight Cookery Book*, 5th edition, Newport, I.O.W., *c.* 1930. *Shropshire Cookery Book*, Shrewsbury, *c.* 1955. *Through Yorkshire's Kitchen Door*, 31st edition, York, n.d.; first published 1927. *The Surrey Cookery Book*, compiled by Adeline Maclean and Evelyn Thompson, Guildford, 1932.

Woodward, Marcus: *The Mistress of Stantons Farm*, London, Heath Cranton, 1938.

Y.W.C.A.: *Devonshire Flavour: A Devonshire Treasury of Recipes and Personal Notes*, Exeter, 1970.

Index

Abbey, stone-ground wholemeal, 283, 518, 519

Aberdeen: butteries, 328; rowies, 327–8; soft biscuits, 491–2

Abridgement or Specifications Relating to Cooking, Breadmaking and the Preparation of Confectionery, 553

Accomplisht Cook, The, 313–16, 341, 374–5, 553

Acidity, importance of in bread, 110

Acids, in chemical aerating of mixtures, 517, 519

Acton, Eliza: on aniseed, 146; *Best of Eliza Acton*, 100, 549;
  on bread: college loaves, 201, 265; cottage loaves, 203; crust for hot pies or tarts, 406; French, 378–9; home-made, 160, 191, 246; potato, 72, 290; rice, 71, 292; summer, 316–19; whole wheatmeal, 49;
  on brewer's yeast, 99–100, 316–17; on doughnuts, 422–3; *English Bread Book, The*, xiii, 49n., 146, 161, 175–6, 185, 191, 201, 203, 290, 292, 316–19, 549; on German yeast, 100, 317–19; on ginger, 146n.; on milk in dough, 127; *Modern Cookery for Private Families*, 99–100, 146n., 160, 186, 246, 379, 406, 422–3, 467, 549; on ovens, 161, 175–6, 186; on Sally Lunn cakes, 467; on sending bread dough to bakers' ovens, 161–2, 185, 209; on tins for bread, 209

Acts, Bread, 230–31, 378

Additives, 33–4, 36, 52–3, 57, 59, 61, 191, 366

Adulteration, 191–2

Aerated bread, 91, 125

Aerated Bread Company, 37, 125, 475

Aeration, chemical, 439, 516, 518, 521, 534–5

Aga oven, breadbaking in, 167, 301–2

Aga range, 167

Agene, 33

Agriculture, Fisheries and Food, Ministry of, publications, 549

Albionette cooker, 164

Ale: barms, 98–9, 101, 335, 370, 375; toast and, 543

Aleurone skin, 48

Alexandrian bread, 145

Alkalinity, 517

Allen-Gray, Dorothy, *Fare Exchange*: 549; on fermentation, 106

Allhusen, Dorothy, *A Book of Scents and Dishes*: 549; on Welsh light cakes, 537

Allied Bakeries, 36, 125, 195

Allspice, 144–5

Almond flavouring, 432

Almond paste, 456

Almonds, 135, 151, 508

Alsatian kugelhopf, 498, 508

Alum, 192–3

Aluminium ware, 211, 215

American: active dry yeast, 117; all-purpose unbleached flour, 61; cornmeal, 70; Graham flour, 61–2; measures, conversion of, 243–4; muffin pans, *353*; sourdough breads, 295–6; spoons, measuring, 243, 269n.; wheat, 10, 16, 52

Anatto, 147

Anchoïade, 389
Anchovy: pizza, 389; toast, 544
Andernach lava stones, 28
Angelica stems, candied, 135
Animal feed, 32, 48, 69, 73, 88
Aniseed, 145, 433; balls, 480
Antiphanes, on baking pans, 209
Antiquitates Culinariae, 555
Apricots: dried, 135, 136, 437; in galettes, 514
Arab pastrycooks, 498
Arachide oil, 131
Aristophanes, on pot-baked loaves, 210
Armenian pizza, 388
Art of Cookery Made Plain and Easy, The, 99, 167, 299, 333, 343-4, 418, 445n., 551
Arundel, Lady, manchet of, 335-6
Ascorbic acid, 57, 267-8
Ashby, Miss M. K., on wood oven door, 177
Ashley, Sir William, *The Bread of our Forefathers*, 549
Ask the Fellows Who Cut the Hay, 172-4, 551
Assay of bread, 229, 369
Assisa Paris, 227
Assize bread, 226-30, 339-40
Athens, American School of Classical Studies at: *Pots and Pans of Classical Athens*, 549
Atta, 72
Austin, Thomas, 329, 417, 501, 549
Australian grain, 16
Aveyron, 398, 399; *tarte aveyronnaise*, 399-401
Avoirdupois pound, 238
Avoirdupois–U.S.–metric conversion table, 235

Baba, 498; rum, 505-6
Babees Book, The, 332n., 551
Bacon, 433
Baguette loaf, 204, 362, 379
Bakeries: independent, 115; in shops, 195-6; suppliers of, 278; village, 43, 180-85, 435-6; surviving, 183-5

Bakers, 158, 229; brown flour, 32, 57-8; in France, 46; steel bonnet, 305-6; wheatmeal, 57-8; white bread flour, 11, 56-7; wholefood, 59; wholemeal, 59; wholewheat flour, 59; yeast, 93, 106-10; unwillingness to sell, 111-12
Bakers' A.B.C., 65n., 128, 197, 303, 352, 381, 473, 519, 552
Bakestone, 528, 530, *534*; bread and cakes, 518, 528-9; Irish, 531-3; Kendal, 531; Welsh, 532-8; Yorkshire, 529-30
Baking: home, J. Williams on, 39; in an East Sussex farmhouse, 434-5; industry, bought by millers, 36-7; microwave, 88; powder, 516-18; bread and fruit cake leavened with, 517, 525-7; double-action, 517; sheets, non-stick, *216*; temperatures, 239-40, 258, 270; 'under', 155-6, 210, *516*, 520; *see also* Breadbaking
Ballisodare Mills, 522
Balloon yeast, 96
Balston, Thomas, 138, 255
Banbury cake: Countess of Rutland's, 427, 447-8, 494; 17th century, 447-8; 18th century, 448-9; 20th century, 448
Banfield, Walter, *Manna*, xii; on: bread, 191, 197, 206, 271-2, 294-5, 305; cottage loaf, shaping of, 287; holes in, 126; crumpets, 356-7; dough, 97, 109; ice in, 126; quarter-sponge system, 107-8; earthenware pots for bread, 209; gluten, 45; molasses, 143; muffin dough, 354-5; salt, 121, 123-4; soda bread, 524-5; sugar, 141; tins, square, variety of sizes, 216; wheat germ in cottage loaf, 82
Bannetons, 370
Bannocks, 68-9; barley, 64, 528; Selkirk, 452-3
Baps, 75, 321-3; breakfast, 323; Scots, 320-23
Bara brith, 426, 437-9

Barbican House Museum, Lewes, 18
Barley, 528; bannocks, 64, 528;
　bread, 62, 64, 156, 296-8; with cheese,
　　298; on a leaven, 298; Manx, 523;
　　and wheatmeal, 63;
　cakes, 407; Welsh, thick and thin,
　　535-6;
　common, *63*;
　meal, 62-5, 156; bonnag, 523-4; buy-
　　ing, 296-7; pastry, 64;
　naked, *5*;
　pancakes, 412-13; with cheese, 413
Barm, 91, 97, 106, 299; ale, 98-9, 101,
　335, 370, 375; pudding, 420
Barmbrack, 439
Barnstaple: Brannams of, 222, 304;
　ovens, 157, 177
Baskets: canvas-lined, *370*; cloth-lined,
　314, 370; linen and straw, 219;
　proving, 314, 370
Bâtard loaf, 264, 378
Batch loaf: Scottish square, 107-8, 199;
　in Wales, 199
Bath, 467, 485
Bath buns, 473, 479-81; Beerbohm,
　Max, on, 479; glazing and sugaring,
　481; at the Great Exhibition (1851),
　479-80; Hackwood, Frederick, on,
　479; London, 479-80; to make, 39,
　481-2
Bath cakes, relationship to Sally Lunns,
　479
Baton loaf, thick, 280
Batten, M. I., *English Windmills*, 549
Batter: aerating, 126;
　yeast-leavened, 358; for crumpets,
　346, 348, 351, 352, 356-7, 358; for
　fritters, 417; for pikelets, 359-61;
　see also Pancakes *and* French yeast
　cakes
Beard, James, *Beard on Bread*, 126, 296,
　300, 369n., 549
Beaufort, Duke of, 230
Beck, Simone, 369n., 511, 550
Beer yeast, 370-71
Beerbohm, Max, *Yet Again*, on Bath
　buns, 479
Beet sugar, 142
Beeton, Isabella, *Mrs Beeton's Book of*

Household Management, 549, 554; on
　ovens, 162-3, 166, 170, 189
Beetroot in bread, 72
Belfast Women's Institute Club, 527
Belgian bread, Kirkland's opinion of,
　382
Belgian Côte d'Or chocolate, 510
Bell, cooking, 156, 306, *Plate 15*
Bell, Mary T., 537
Bellairs, George, on muffins, 349-50;
　on oatcakes, 409
Belling fan ovens, 166-7
Bemax, 81
Bennett, Dr Christopher, xvii-xviii
Bennett, H. S., *The Pastons and their
　England*, 549
Bennion, Edmund, *Breadmaking*: on
　muffins, 353; on pikelets, 360; on
　yeast, 92, 97
Bensdorp chocolate, 510
Bermaline: bread, 205; malted meal, 58,
　74
Best, Henry, *Rural Economy in Yorkshire
　in 1641*, 550
Best of Eliza Acton, 100, 549
Best's Farming Book, 334n.
Besun, 72
Bever-cake, 462
Bicarbonate of soda, 516-17, 520
Bideford, ovens, 157, 177
Bins: bread, 223;
　flour: brown Japanned steel, *217*;
　　metal, 219
Bird, Anthony, *Paxton's Palace*, on Bath
　buns, 480
Birk Hall bread, 103
Birmingham, 176
Biscuits for Bakers, 190
Biscuits: Guernsey, 490-92; soft, 491-
　492
Bishop, Frederick, *The Wife's Own Book
　of Cookery*: on breakfast cake, 428-9,
　464; on breakfast rolls, 324-5
Black buns, 449
Black treacle, 143, 295
Blacksmiths, 214
Bleaching of flour, 32-3
Blencowe, Ann, *Receipt Book of*, on Mrs
　Tashis' Little Puddings, 489-90

Blinis, 414–16;
    pans for, 416; Finnish non-stick, 216,
    408
Blomefield, Mathena, on Norfolk dump-
    lings, 419
Bloomer, Amelia, 202
Bloomer loaf, 201–3, 264, 280–82
Board, oatcake, 530
Bockings, 416
Boizot, Peter, 386, 387
Boke of Curtasye, The, 332, 551
Bolland, Jean, xi
Bolting: cloths, 30; machine, 23
Bolting the flour, 30–31
Bonnag, barleymeal, 523–4
Bonnefons, Nicolas de, *Les Délices de la
    campagne*, on bread, 373–4, 550
Bonnet, bakers' steel, 305–6, *306*
Bonyon, Thomas, 13
Book of Breakfasts, The, 355, 541, 553
Book of Scents and Dishes, A, 537, 549
Boorde, Andrew, *Dyetary of Helth*, on:
    bran, 48–9; manchet bread, 329; mas-
    lin bread, 65; saffron, 148
Bordyke bread, 100
Bornholm Island, 67
Boscawen, Mrs Edward, 230
Boulangerie d'Aujourd'hui, 378, 551
Boyes, April, xi
Brade breached, Irish, 426, **440**
Brake, wooden, *190*, 335, 363
Bran, 32, 48, 81; Boorde, Andrew, on,
    49; in bread, 50, 80;
    coatings, 47; pigmentation of, 10;
    in diet, 35, 48–9, 78–80;
    fibre, 48; importance of, 78;
    Graham, Dr Sylvester, and, 78; tea,
    49
Brannams of Barnstaple, 222, 304
Brannan's thermometers, 244–5
Branscombe, 183–4
Braudel, F., on oats, 67, 69
Brazier, Mère, restaurant of, 469
Brazil sugar, 142
Brazilian bread, Sir Francis Drake and,
    xvii
Bread Acts, 230–31, 378
Bread: additives, 33–4, 36, 52–3, 57, 59,
    61, 193; adulteration of, 191–2;

aerated, 91, 125; Alexandrian, 145;
    Assay of, 229, 369; Assize, 226–30,
    339–40; bakestone, *see* Bakestone;
    barley, 62, 64, 156, 296–8; on a leaven,
    298; with cheese, 298; Manx, 523;
    and wheatmeal, 63;
basic loaf, 256–63; batch or Scotch
    pan, 107; batched, 199; bloomer loaf,
    201–3, 264, 280–82; bran in, 48–9,
    50, 61, 78–80; Brazilian, xvii; British,
    most chemically treated in Europe, 56;
    brown, 35–6, 57, 73, 74, 204–5, 227–8;
    Liebig on, 78; oatmeal, 282–3;
    Yorkshire, 283;
buttermilk, white, 75, **524**; cart,
    Welsh, 530; caste of, 334n.; cheate,
    xxi;
chemically aerated, 517; English
    white, **524**–5;
choice of, 35–40; clap or riddle, **531**;
    consumption of, 3–5;
Cornish: barley, 298; kettle, 155–6,
    308–9; pot, 308–9
crates, Welsh, 223, 530; creel, 224,
    530;
crust, 128, 261; chipping and rasping,
    372, 375; cuts on, 263–6; for hot
    pies or tarts, 406;
Cumbrian Christmas, **453**; pot, 309;
currant: English, **436**–7; Welsh (bara
    brith), 426, **437**–9; wheatmeal, 437;
    cutting for sandwiches, *318*; demayne
    or demeine, 329, 370; Dutch, 206, 208,
    293; egg-whites in, 313, 315; fac-
    tories, 38, 88, 108, 191–6; fancy, 197,
    365, 372, 378; fat in, 262, 269–70;
    flavour of: water and, 380; yeast and,
    110–11, 281;
flowerpot, 73, 205, 210, 309–10;
    freezing of, 224–5; French, *see* French
    bread;
fruit, **436**–40; with cheese, 426;
    dough for, 426, 439, 444;
Genoese flat, **433**; German, 206;
    grain, 3–16; granary, 60, 153, 283–5;
    griddle-cooked, 64;
home-baked, 46; cost of, 246–51; salt
    in, 120, 123, 261, 302, 316; wheat-
    germ, 81–2;

home-baking, 170–74, 255–6; hutch, French, *383*; ingredients, lack of legislation covering listing of, 59;

Irish: brade breached, 426, 440; 'cake', 518; pot, 309; spice, **439**; wheatmeal soda, 517, **522**; wholewheat soda, **520–21**;

Italian, 121; laws, 230–31;

leavened: with baking powder, 517, 525–7; French method, 381–2;

malt, 60, 153, **154**, 205;

manchet, 329, 335; French equivalents of, 370; Queen Elizabeth's, 331; *see also* Manchets;

milk in, 127–8, 262; Ministry of Agriculture advertisement for, *c.* 1930, 87;

mixes, 74–5, 118; moulds and tins for, 206–16; muffin loaves, 75, **312–13**;

North Riding, 526; oaten, 68;

oatmeal: brown, 282–3; Welsh, **533**;

ovens, *see* Ovens: pans, 221–2, 317n.;

payn puffe, 369; payndemayn, 329–340; peggy tub, 126, **311–12**;

penny loaf, 340; white, 339–40;

pitchy, 360;

pot, 210, **307–9**; Cornish, 155–6, **308–309**; Cumbrian, **155–6**, **308–9**; Irish, 309; the self-sufficient way, **306–7**; Welsh, **307–8**;

for potages, 546; potato, 103, **288–9**; price regulation, 226–30; priced, 230, 339; proprietary brands of, 37; puffe, 369; pulled, 546; pumpernickel, 206, 293; pumpkin, **290**; quality of, 191–3, 195; re-baking, 225; Regulations, 57; rice, 290–92; riddle, 407, **409–11**, 531; root vegetables in, 72–3; round loaf, 276–7;

rye, 65–7, 72, 205, 293–4; caraway in, 67; glaze for, 294–5; home-baking, 66–7;

sourdough, 67, **295**, 296; spiced, 67; spicing, 433; sweetened, **294–5**; toast, 542;

salt in, 108, 119, 120–21; salt-rising, **299–301**; serving, 15th century, 331–332; smell of while baking, 195–6;

soda, 271, 515–27, **516**; barleymeal, **523**; bonnag, **523–4**; English chem-

ically aerated white, **524–5**; flour for, 74, 518;

Irish: wheatmeal, 517, 519, **522**; wholewheat, **520–21**;

mixes, 74–5, 519; undercover, 521; white, buttermilk, **524**;

wholewheat, 520–22; with oatmeal, **522–3**;

sourdough, 156; American, 295–6; rye, 67, **295**, 296; spiced, 67, 433;

soya flour in, 72;

spice: chemically aerated, 518; Cornish, **440–42**; Irish, **439**; yeast in, 516;

Yorkshire, **461**; without eggs, 428, **454**;

spices for, 144; storage of, 221–5, 371;

summer, Eliza Acton's, 316–19; texture of, 126; Thomas's, Mrs, 103;

tins, 206–9; under-tin, 210; Welsh currant (bara brith), 426, **437–9**;

Welsh pan, **307–8**; Welsh pot, **307–8**;

wheat and rye, 53; wheat-germ, 81–2;

wheatmeal: in basic loaf, 256–63; 'brown' bread confused with, 58; 81 per cent or 85 per cent, 32, 35, 36; flavour of, 53–4; Irish soda, **522**; oatmeal in, 69; term to be outlawed, 58;

white, 34, 37–8, 79, 193; buttermilk, 75, **524**; English chemically aerated, **524–5**; traditional demand for, 5–6; whiteness all, 26;

wholemeal, wholewheat: additives, permitted, 59; confusion of with 'brown' and 'brownish', 58–9; content of legal, 34, 36, 53; cost of, 249–50; flavour of, 49; Grant's, Doris, **272–4**; Holme Mills, **274–5**; loaves, crusty, 275; and oatmeal, soda, **522–3**; oatmeal in, 69, 249; scone loaf, 275; tin loaf, **268–72**; toast made from, 521, 542;

without barm by the help of leaven, 299; workers' strike, 192;

Yorkshire: brown, 283; North Riding, 526; riddle, 407, **409–11**;

spiced, **461**; without eggs, 428, **454**;

see also Dough; Loaves

Bread. An Assessment of the Bread Industry in Britain, 36n., 56, 59, 554

Bread and Biscuit Baker's Assistant, 114, 352

Bread and Flour Regulations, 35n., 59

Bread Industry in Britain, T.A.C.C. Report on, 36n., 56, 59, 554

Bread of our Forefathers, The, 549

Breadbaking, 159–61, 258; in the Aga oven, 167, 301–2; in brick ovens, 167–177, 434–5; cool-oven system, 165–6; cost of, 246–51; in gas oven, 127–8, 166–7, 187–90; in electric oven, 166–7, 188–9; in iron oven, 158–9, 161–4; in oil-fired cooker, 164–5; temperatures, 258, 270; undercover, 155–6, 210, 277, 284–5, 303–6, 309–10; *see also* Cookers; Home-baking; Ovens; Ranges

Breadiron, 53

Breadmaking, 92, 96, 353, 360, 550

Breadmaking: bakestone system, 518, 528–9; butter in, 127, 128, 130, 262; Chorleywood process, 37, 88, 108, 195;
French, 364, 366–71, 382; the best way (1660), 374–5;
instant dough method, 193–4; lard in, 130–31; liquids in, 125–32; Muffett, Thomas, on, xviii–xxi; slow-rising method, 106–7, 238–9, 261, 268, 280–281; sponge and dough method, 107–108, 110; straight-dough system, 316; Sussex, 434–5; in wash tub, 126, 311–312; water in, 125–7; yeast quantities, 96, 98–9, 106, 109, 115, 261, 270–271

Breads White and Brown: Their Place in Thought and Social History, 552

Breakfast: baps, 323;
cake, 428–9, 464, 465; rich French, 466;
dough cake for, 465; rolls, hot, 324–5

Breedon, Leicestershire, 27

Brewers' Book, The, 92n.

Brewers' yeasts, 95, 98–100

Brewing, muscovado sugar in, 142

Brick loaves, 199, 204

Brick ovens, 156, 158; fuel for, 158, 161,

174–6, 183; with iron doors, 176; renewing the lining, 182–3; in use, 167–77, 180–85, 286, 434–5; with wooden doors, 176

Bridge-house, the granaries and ovens of, 14

Bridgewater, 3rd Duke of, 15–16

Bright wheat, 4

Brightwell-cum-Sotwell, 184n.

Brindley, James, 15

Brioche: crust, sausage in, 403–6, 498; dough, home-made, 403, 405, 497–8; moulds, 211, 216, 497; *pain perdu*, 330

Brioches, 496–7, 499–500; Bath buns and, 479; lemon-flavoured, 150; Sally Lunn cake and, 469; savarin and, 502; Mrs Tashis' Little Puddings and, 489

British Fermentation Products Ltd, *The Story of Yeast*, 550

British Medical Journal, 78

British Rail's toast, 544

Brittany, 358

Broadbent, Mrs, on tea buns, 478

Brook, Nath, 550

Bronze Age, 155

Broomer family, 465

Browiss, 530

Brown, Mr Jo, of B.F.P., xii

Brown bread, 35–6, 57, 73, 74, 204–5, 227–8; Liebig on, 78; oatmeal, 282–3; Yorkshire, 283

Brown flour, 35, 72; bakers', 32, 57–8

Brown sugar, 141–2

Browne, Sir Thomas, *Of the Divisions of the Seasons*, on grain, 3

Brunswick loaf, 200

Brywes, 535

Bucher, M. Bob, xii

Buckman, J., *Materials of Roman Querns*, on puddingstone, 27

Buckwheat, 73; flour for blinis, 414; in France, 73–4;
pancakes, 358, 416; English, 73, 416–417; yeast-leavened, 416

Bulleid, Sir Arthur and Gray, H. St George, *The Lake Villages of Somerset*, 550

Bun House, Chelsea, 474, 482

Bun sheets, non-stick, 216

Buns:
  Bath, 473, 479–81; Beerbohm, Max, on, 479; glazing and sugaring, 481; at the Great Exhibition 1851, 479–480; Hackwood, Frederick, on, 479; London, 479–80; to make, 39, 481–482;
  Chelsea, 482–3, 484–5;
  Christmas, 451, 494; Scotch, 427, 431;
  hot cross, 152, 473, 475, 477–8; limitation of sales 1592, 473–4; reheating, 478;
  Scotch, 449, 449–52; black, 449, 451; Christmas, 427, 431; spice blend for, 431;
    Jack, Florence, on, 450, 451; Roberts, Emma, on, 449, 450, 451; spice, 473–4, 475–7; tea, 478–9; yeast, 473–84
Bunyan, John, 13, 214
Burkitt, Denis P., and Painter, N. S., on fibre and diverticular disease, 78–9
Burnett, John, *Plenty and Want*, 550
Burr stones, 26; mill, French, 26, 29, 44, 50; shown at Great Exhibition 1851, 26n.
Burtergill Windermere cakes, 494–5
Bushels, 228, 237; French, 373n., Winchester, 533n.
Butter: cakes to eat with, 472; dish, dishfull, dysch of, 331 and n., 501–2; in dough, 127, 128, 130, 262; Welsh, 543
Buttered toast, 541–3
Butteries, Aberdeen, 328
Buttermilk, 128, 271, 517; acid, 517; bread, white, 75, 524; cake, 156; cultured, 519

Cake bread, Irish, 518
Cake hoops, 212–13, 435–6
Cake icing, 139–40, 151
Cakes: baba, 498; bakestone, *see* Bakestone;
  Banbury: Countess of Rutland's, 427, 447–8, 494; 17th century, 447–8; 18th century, 448–9; 20th century, 448;

barley, 407, 535–6; bever, 462;
breakfast, 428–9, 464, 465; rich French, 466;
Burtergill Windermere, 494–5; buttermilk, 156; chemically aerated, 518; Cornish saffron, 440–42; Devonshire, 427, 442–4;
dough, 424–7; for breakfast, 465; cream in, 129, 443n.;
flavouring of, 429, 432; flour for, 54, 56; French yeast, *see* French yeast cakes; freezing, 442;
fruit: with cheese, 526; leavened with baking powder, 525–7; Rebecca Price's, 213;
girddle or girdle, 60, 358, 407, 516; singing hinnies, 536–7;
Guernsey *gâche*, 453–4;
harvest, 461; Northumbrian, 463–4; Suffolk, 462;
haver, 69, 410, 530; kugelhopf, 498, 506–8;
lardy, 130, 427, 429, 461–2; fat in, 462; Hampshire, 462; health hazard from, 461; Northumberland, 463; sugar in, 461;
large and small, 428; lemon, 490;
luncheon, 427, 465–6; plain, 470–71; moulds and tins for, 211, 212–16; muffin, 348; ordinary, to eat with butter, 472; plain, 471; plum, plain, 460; plumb, 137, 459, 460–61; potato, 539; quantities in recipes for, 428; regional and festival, 424–72; rye, Danish, 67; saffron, *see* Saffron cake; Sally Lunn, 129, 150, 467–70, 479; eggs in, 133; saffron in, 147;
salt in, 123–4; savoury, 432–3; shooting, 526–7; Simnel, yeast, 455–6; soleilune, 467–70; solimemne, 467; soule, 493; sour-milk, 527; spice, *see* Spice cakes; sponge, Victorian, 468; Tachis, Mrs, of, 490; tea, *see* Teacakes; Ulverston Fair, 433, 493–4; Welsh, *see* Welsh cakes; wheatmeal, 433;
wiggs, 129, 433, 484–7; with cheese, 433, 487; saffron in, 147; sugar on, 487;

Cakes (continued)
Windermere, 433, 494–5;
yeast, 424; moulds and tins for, 211, 212–16; regional and festival, 424–472;
Yorkshire, 488, 530
Calstock, clay or 'cloume' ovens of, 157, 177
Cambridgeshire, 172
Campbell, G. D., 78, 550
Campbell, Ken, on Crumpet Street, 359
Canadian wheat, 9, 10, 11, 51
Canals, 15–16
Candied peel, 135
Cane sugars, 141
Caramel, permitted colouring in bread, 36
Caraway: comfits, 480; in rye bread, 67; seeds, 145, 433, 445, 486
Cardiganshire, 442
Cardiganshire Antiquarian Society, Transactions of the, 62, 219
Carmarthenshire, 40, 380, 538
Caroline, Queen (of George II), 482
Carpenter, John, 552
Cart, Welsh bread, 530
Cartland, Barbara, on white bread, 79
Cassell's: Book of the Household, 165; Dictionary of Cooking, 485; Domestic Dictionary, 29, 78, 550; Universal Cookery Book, 283, 433, 455–6, 492, 516, 543, 552
Cassia, 150
Caste, of bread, 334n.
Casters: spice, English silver, 144; sugar, 140
Caterer and Hotel Keeper, 385, 386, 387
Cauliflower loaf, 201, 278
Caviar, 414
Celery with toast, 543
Celsius–Fahrenheit temperature conversion table, 239
Ceramic Art of Great Britain, The, 157, 177–80, 552
Cereals, 195, 546, 554
Ceres Bakery, 59
Ceres Mail Order Organization, 43
Cervelas, 403

Chambers' Book of Days, on Chelsea Bun House, 482
Chanteau, 374
Charcuterie and French Pork Cookery, 403
Chard, 176
Chardin: brioches painted by, 497; eggs, in his paintings, 134
Charlotte moulds, 211, 216, 497
Chaucer, Geoffrey, on Payndemayn, 329
Cheap Bread, 16, 553
Cheate bread, xxi
Cheese: with barley bread, 298; barley pancakes with, 413; Cheddar, maturity of, 268, 401; Gruyère, 402; for quiches, 398–402; Roquefort alternatives, 401; savouries, 433; with sour-milk cake, 527; with spice fruit bread or cakes, 526; wigg cakes with, 433, 487
Chelsea Bun House, 474, 482
Chelsea buns, 482–3, 484–5
Chemical aeration, 439, 516, 518, 521, 524–5
Chemically aerated white bread, English, 524–5
Chemistry of Breadmaking, 237, 551
Chemistry of Cookery, The, 55, 154, 168, 192, 555
Chequerboard cuts, 265, 363
Cherries in galettes, 514
Cheshire cheese, wiggs with, 487
Cheshire rock salt, 122–3, 262
Chick-pea flour, 172
Child, Julia, and Beck, Simone, Mastering the Art of French Cooking, 369n., 511, 550
Chinese weights, 228n.
Chisel, chissel, meaning of, 334n.
Chlorine bleaching, 32
Chocolat, petits pains au, 499, 508–10
Chocolate: for cooking, 510; rolls, 499, 508–10
Chollahs, 146, 205
Chorleywood Bread Process, 37, 88, 108, 195
Christmas: bread, Cumbrian, 453 bun, 451; Scotch, 427, 431; goose pies, 64

Chudleighs, Devonshire, 487
Chupattees, 72
Cinnamon, 149; sugar, 432; water, 151
Citron, candied, 444
Citrus fruits, peel of, 135
Clap or riddle bread, 531
Clapton Mills, Crewkerne, Dorset, xii, 31, 297
Clark, Lady, of Tillypronie, *Cookery Book of*, 102–6, 550; on baps, 321; crumpets, 347; luncheon cakes, 466; pikelets, 360; screens, use of for raising yeast dough, 325n.; yeast, 102–106
Clarke, Elizabeth, *The Valley*, on Welsh pot bread, 308
Clay ovens, 156, *Plates 18, 19, 20*; Cornish, 157, 177–9
'Clayed' sugar, 142
Cleave, T. L., and Campbell, G. D., *Diabetes, Coronary Thrombosis and the Saccharine Disease*, 550; on bran, 78
Clébert, Jean-Paul, *The Gypsies*, on maize cake, 70
Cloche, or cooking bell, 156, 306, *Plate 15*
Clove, sugar, 432
Cloves, oil of, 151
Coal, ranges, 163–4, 187–8; *Eagle*, 162, 188
Cob loaf, 200, 277; as term of abuse, 200; Welsh, 200
Cobbett, William, *Cottage Economy*, 550; on breadbaking, 159, 601; his hand-mill, 42
Coburg loaf, 200, 263, 276–9; pan, 201, 278–9
Coca, 388
Coeliacs, xxi
Cohen Report, 34n.
Coke of Norfolk, 6
College loaf, 201, 265
Collier, Gerald, of Branscombe, 183–4
Collins, Mary, 387
Comfits, caraway, 145
Communal ovens, 159
Compleat Confectioner, 441, 445, 551
Compleat Cook, The, 65, 459, 550

Compleat Housewife, The, 135, 212, 376–377, 472, 554
Complete Bread, Cake and Cracker Baker, 119, 555
Complete Cottage Cookery, 161, 175, 185–186, 268, 544, 550
Concise Encyclopaedia of Gastronomy, 84n., 452, 491, 556
Cones, 71
Constable, Abram, 22, 25
Constable, John, on watermills, 19, 22, 25
Cook and Housewife's Manual, 212, 378, 426, 440, 469, 479, 480, 551
Cook-Inn, 386
Cookers: electric, 166–7; gas, 161, 166, 189; oil-fired, 164–5, *165*
Cookery for Every Household, 221, 348, 421, 450–51, 552
Cooking in Hampshire Past and Present, 462
Cook's Paradise, The, 373
Cooper, Derek, 386
Copley, Esther: on breadmaking, 161, 175, 185, 186; on brown bread, 268; *The Complete Cottage Cookery*, 161, 175, 185, 268, 544, 550; *The Family Economist*, 410; on oatcakes, 410; on toast, 544
Cord-wood, 175
Coriander spice blend, 431
Corkscrew loaf, *363*
Corn Country, 26, 80, 180, 176, 555
Corn oil, 131, 393
Corn prices, 228
Cornflour, 67, 70–71, 355
Cornish, W. J., on mills, 15
Cornish barley bread, 298
Cornish clay oven, 157, 177–9
Cornish clotted cream, 129
Cornish Homes and Customs, 156, 552
Cornish: kettle bread, 155–6, 308–9; pasty, 442; pot bread, 155–6, 308–9; pot ovens, 178
Cornish Recipes, Ancient and Modern, 178–9, 298, 308–9, 440–42, 556
Cornish saffron cakes, 427, 440–42
Cornish spice bread, 440–42
Cornish splits, 487

Cornmeal, 69–70, 355; American, 70

Cornstarch, 67, 70–71

Cornwall: 'baking under', 155; Phoenicians and, 148

Cost of home-baked bread, 246–51

Côte d'Or chocolate, 510

Cotechino, 403, 404

Cottage loaves, 203, 286–8; brick and pan, 204

Country Cookbook flour, 53; flavour of bread made from, 54

Country Recipes of Old England, 439

Couronne basket, 370

Cowslip vinegar, 151

Craig, Elizabeth, *Scottish Cookery*, on baps, 321

Craig, Thurlow, on ovens, 187

Cranks wholefood restaurant, 54

Crates, Welsh bread, 223, 530

Cream, 129; cheese quiche, 398, 401–2; clotted, 129, 443n.; in dough, 127, 129, 262, 443n.; soured, 128; of tartar, 516–17, 520

Creel, bread, 224, 530

Crempog, 358

Crispbread, 67

Crocks, 222; earthenware, 219, 221–2, 223; stoneware, 221; terracotta, 222–3

Crocus sativus, 147

Croeso Cymreig. A Welsh Welcome: Recipes for Some Traditional Welsh Dishes, 437, 555

Croissants, 496, 510–12

Crumbly loaves, 262

Crumby or crummy loaves, 108, 199

Crumpet: colloquial meanings of, 341; origin of word, 341–2; street (coll.), 359; Yorkshire and Derbyshire term for, pikelet, 360

Crumpets:
batter for, 352, 356; Banfield on, 356; bicarbonate of soda in, 356–7; breakfast cakes, grouped with, 346; children fond of, 341; composition of, 342; confusion of, with muffins, 341–343; flour for, Edmund Bennion on, 353; Garrett, T. F., on, 358; girdle or griddle for, *353*; indigestibility of, 361; Masterman, Sir J. C., on eating

them in his bath, 361;
and muffins, 341–61, *342*; differences from and similarities with, 343, 351;
pikelets, known as, 351; in Derbyshire and Yorkshire, 360;
recipes for:
by household cooks, 343–50; Hannah Glasse 1747, 323–4; Elizabeth Raffald 1769, 344–5; Emma Roberts 1841, 346; Lady Clark of Tillypronie *c.* 1880, 347; Elizabeth David 1973, 356–7;
by professional bakers, 350–53; J. T. Law 1895, 351; Florence Jack 1914, 348; T. F. Garrett 1927, 358;
printed, late appearance of, 343;
rings or hoops for, 216, 353, 357; Scotch, 347, 348; sold by muffin man 1851, 346; tea, 347; texture of, 356–7; travesties of, now to be bought, 342; Welsh, 358

Crust: bread, 128, 261; for hot pies or tarts, 406;
chipping or rasping, 333, 372, 375; cuts on, 263–6; pan Coburg, 278–9; effects on of: butter, 130, 262; ice and iced water, 126; long fermentation, 110; milk, 127; salt, 261; steam, 262;
of French bread, 366–7; for toasts, 546–7;
of manchets, for soup, 33; upper, cutting of, in 15th century, 332, 333

Crusty loaves, 199–200, 261, 263, 303–6; wholemeal, 272

Crystal Palace, Bath buns sold there, 480

Cuisine Anglaise, La, 188–9

Cuisines of Mexico, The, 70

Cuisinier françois, Le, 374

Cumberland goose pies, 64

Cumbrian Christmas bread, **453**; pot bread, **309**

Cumin seeds: in hot cross buns, 431, 477; on rye bread, 67; in spice mixture, 145, 431

Cupboards, bread and food storage, 223

Curious Tracts Relating to the Culinary

Affairs of the Old English, 555
Curly loaf, 203
Currant bread: English, 436–7; Welsh (bara brith), 426, **437** 9; wheatmeal, 437
Currants, 136–7
Curwen, Dr E. Cecil, on querns, 17, 18, 28
Cutter and scraper, dough, 266
Cutters, sugar, *139*
Cypriot loaves, 205

Daily Express, 387
Daily Telegraph, 387, 477
Dainty Dishes, 439, 554
Dalen, Dr Gustav, 167n.
Daniel, Albert, *The Reasons Why: Practical Answers to Everyday Bakehouse Questions*, 550
Danish: loaf, 200; cob, 277; rye cakes, 67; yeast, 112
Daren flour, 74
Dariole moulds, 216, *488*
Dates, 136
Dauglish, Dr, 91, 125
David, Elizabeth: *French Provincial Cooking*, 550; *Italian Food*, 550; *Spices, Salt and Aromatics in the English Kitchen*, 550
Délices de la campagne, Les, 373–4
Delightes for Ladies, 143, 149–50, 340, 432, 553
Delma, 489
Demeine (demayne) bread, 329, 370
Demerara sugar, 142
Derbyshire: millstone grit, 26, 29; pikelets, 360
Devon ovens, 155–7, 177, *Plates 18 and 20*
Devonshire: cake, 427, **442–4**; Chudleighs, **487**; ovens, 155, 156, 157
Devonshire Flavour: A Devonshire Treasury of Recipes and Personal Notes, 440, 556
De Worde, Wynkyn, *Boke of Kervynge*, 332, 551
Dictionary of Chemistry, 241, 382
Dictionary of Cooking, 485
Dictionnaire portatif du cultivateur, 380

Diet, bran and wheat-germ in, 35, 48–9, 78–80
Digby, Sir Kenelm, 550; on: ale barm, 98; dried fruit, 137; cake hoops, 212; icing, 139–40; saffron cake, 16, 69, 446–7; toast, 547
Dill, 145; in rye bread, 67, 433
Discovering Watermills, 29, 555
Dish, dishfull or dysch, of butter, 331 and n., 501–2
Dish loaf, 276–7
Distilleries, yeast, 95–6
Diverticular disease, 78–9
Docker, 200
Dods, Margaret, 426, 551;
  Cook and Housewife's Manual, on: Bath buns, 479, 480; French bread, 378; Irish fruit bread, 212, **440**; Sally Lunn cakes, 469
Dolly tub, *311*
Dolma, 489
Dolmades, 489
Domo yeast, 95, 97
Donaghy, Patricia, *Northumbrian and Cumbrian Recipes*, 551; on harvest tea cakes, 463–4
Donegal oatcake, **531–3**
Dorsetshire: mills, 31; village bakeries, 181–2, 425–6
Dough: Banfield on, 96, 107–8, 109; brioche, home-made, 403, 405, 497–8; brushing with oil, 262; butter in, 127, 128, 130, 262;
  cake, 424–7; for breakfast, **465**; cream in, 129, 433n.;
  casalinga, 389–90; chemically aerated, 439; Chorleywood process, 37, 88, 108, 195; cream in, 127, 129, 262, 443n.; cutter and scraper, 266; dried fruit in, 135–6; fermented, from hard and soft wheat, 11; fruit bread, 426, 439, 444; lard in, 127; milk in, 127–8, 262;
  mixing, 106, **107–8**, *253*, **257–8**, *259*, 260–61, 434; oil in, 131, 433; pancheon, *253*; peggy-tub system, 126, 311–12;
  polythene cover for, 315; sandwich, 433; sending to bakers' ovens, 161–2,

Dough (*continued*)
185; short-time, 267–8; slashing of, 263–6, 366–7; slow-rising, 106–7, 238–9, 261, 268, 280–81; sponge and dough method, 107–8, 110; straight-dough system, 316; sugar in, 429; temperatures, 125–6, 238, 260, 276; Fahrenheit-Celsius conversion table, 239; thermometers, 244–5; trough: lid, *171*; pronunciation of, 171; water in, 125–7, 380; water-risen, 312; *see also* Breadmaking

Doughnuts, 420–21, 421–2; Isle of Wight, 422–3

Douglas, Mrs E. M. L., 491

Doulton storage crocks, 221

Drummond, Professor Sir Jack, 556

Drummond, J. C., and Wilbraham, A., *The Englishman's Food: A History of Five Centuries of English Diet*, 551

Dublin Society, 299

Dubois, Félix Urbain, *Boulangerie d'Aujourd'hui*, 551; on *bâtard* bread, 378

Dufour, E., *Traité pratique de panification française et parisienne*, 551

Dumplings, yeast, 418–20; barm pudding, 420; Glasse, Hannah (1747), 418–19; Norfolk, 419–20

Durum wheat, 10, 78

Dusting flours, 71, 72, 328

Dutch bread, 206, 208, 293

Dutch ovens, 324n.

Dutch yeast, 95, 117

Dyetary of Helth, 48–9, 65, 148, 329, 550

Eagle range, *162*, 188

Eagle Range Co., *The History of Coal Devouring Cooking Range and its Progeny, Smoke and Fog, and the Remedy*, 551

Earthenware:
bowls, 215, 304, 306; greasing, 278; crocks, 219, 221–2, 223; moulds, 209–210, 214–15, 216, 230; ovens, 157, 177–80; pancheon, *253*; pans, 317n.

Easlea, Kate, *Cooking in Hampshire Past and Present*, on lardy cakes, 462

East Anglia, 170–74, 419

Easteleine, 516

Edden, Helen, *County Recipes of Old England*, barmbrack recipe, 439

Eden Vale, 386

Edmonds, on Greek loaves, 209–10

Egerton, Francis, 3rd Duke of Bridge-water, 15–16

Egg pans, 416

Eggs, 133–4; whites of, in bread, 313, 315

Egypt: bakers at work in, *Plate 13*; lime-stone figure from, *Plate 1*

Egyptians, ancient, 17–18, 90, 145

Electric cookers and ovens, 128, 166–7, 188–9, 287–8

Electricity-gas oven temperature conversion table, 240

Eliot, George, on: Christmas morning, ale and hot toast, 543; watermills, 19, 25, 380

Elizabeth, Queen, manchet bread of, 331

Ellesmere, Lord, 540

Elstow, John Bunyan and, 13, 214

Emmer wheat, 9

Emmison, F. G.: *Tudor Food and Pastimes*, 551; *Elizabethan Life*, 551

Encyclopaedia of Practical Cookery, 89, 95–6, 442–3, 551

English Bread Book, The, 49n., 146, 161, 175–6, 185, 191, 201, 203, 290, 292, 316–18, 549

English: buckwheat pancakes, 73, 416–417; chemically aerated bread, white, 524–5; currant bread, 436–7

English Hus-wife, The, 28n., 227n., 335, 448, 553

English savarin mould, *211*

English silver spice caster, *144*

English Windmill, The, 555

English Windmills, 549

Englishman's Food, The: A History of Five Centuries of English Diet, 551

Ensing, Rita, xii, 71, 203, 420

Ergot, 65

Errington, T., and Sons, 357

Escoffier and toast Melba, 545

Essentials of Diet, 361

Essex: home-baking in, 170–74; village bakeries in, 182–3

European Economic Community, wheat prices and, 88

Evans, Miss R. M., on: barley bread, 62; meal storage, 219; oatcake, 533

Evelyn, John, *Diary*, on saffron, 147

Evening Standard, 387

Ewart Evans, George: *Ask the Fellows Who Cut the Hay*, 172–4, 551; on breadbaking, 172–4; *The Farm and the Village*, 27n., 551; on mining, 26–7

Experienced English Housekeeper, The, 212, 344–5, 420, 433, 480–81, 485–7, 554

Extraction rates, 31, 33, 53, 55, 76, 81; myth of, 34–5

Factories, bread, 38, 88, 108, 191–6

Fahrenheit–Celsius temperature conversion table, 239

Fairrie, Geoffrey, *Sugar*, 138, 142n., 551

Family Economist, the, 410

Family Magazine, on: pumpkin bread, 292; spice, 429

Family Receipt Book, The, on: crumpets and muffins, 341; wiggs, 484–5

Fan ovens, 166–7

Fance, W. J., and Wragg, B. H., *Up-to-Date Breadmaking*, on: butteries, 328; croissants, 511–12; Sally Lunn, 467; yeast, 109

Fancy bread, 197, 365, 372, 378

Fare Exchange, 106, 549

Fareham pottery, 223

Farine de maïs, 70

Farine panifiable, 365

Farm and the Village, The, 27n., 551

Farmer's Weekly, 536n.

Farmhouse: bread flour, 535; tin loaf, 199

Farmhouse Fare, 536

Farmhouse Recipes, 452–3

Farming Book, 334n.

Farnham, 465

Fats in bread, 262, 269–70

Fécule de pommes de terre, 72

Felin Geri mill, 31

Fennel seeds, 145, 433

Fermentation, 89–91, 93; potato mash, 72, 103, 290; slow, 97, 98, 100, 106, 109, 280–81; spontaneous, 90, 299–300; temperatures for, 109, 260, 270, 281

Fermented dough from hard and soft wheat, 11

Fermipan yeast, 117

Ferté-sous-Jouarre, La, 26

Festival yeast cakes, 424–72

Feudalism, 24, 40–41

Fibre: bran, lack of in our bread, 48, 78–80; crude, 57, 248; dietary, medical findings concerning, 78–80, 248; *see also* Bran

Ficelle loaf, 362

Fiennes, Celia, *The Journeys of Celia Fiennes*, 551; on oatcakes, 530, 531

Fife, David, 10

Figgys, 137

Figs, 137

Finger loaves, 205

Finnish non-stick pan, 216, *408*

First Principles of Good Cookery, 155, 214, 292, 307–8, 533–6; 552

Flatford Mill, 25

Flavouring essences, 151–2

Flemish bakers, 172

Florence cooker, 164–5

Flour Advisory Bureau, 38, 47, 79, 268

Flour, ageing of, 33–4; American all-purpose unbleached, 61; barley, 54, 56, 62–5; bin, brown japanned steel, 217; bleaching, 32–3; blended, 46, 51–2, 53, 55, 74–5; bolting, 30–31; bread: bakers' white, 11, 56–7; buying, 50–88, 364–5; farmhouse, 53–55; Prewett's, 51–2, 67, 75, 294, 518, 519; proprietary brands, 74; strong plain white, 55–6;

brown, 35, 72; bakers', 32, 57–8;

chick-pea, 172;

composition of (table), 248–9; Cohen Report on, 34n.;

dusting, 71, 72, 328;

extraction rate, 31, 33, 53, 55, 76, 81; myth of, 34–5;

French, 62, 305–6; Graham, 61–2;

Flour (*continued*)
gram, 72; high-gluten, 11, 45, 52, 56, 61; home-baking, 45–6; household, 60–61; labelling laws, lack of, 59; lentil, 72; Millstone, 54; for muffins, 352, 353, 355; National, 34, 82–8; old dry measures for, 237–8; Order 1953, 33–4; patent, 75–7; potato, 67, 72; quantities, 246; Regulations, 57, 58, 59; rice, 71, 75, 328; self-raising, 74–76, 328, 439, 516, 519; sifting, 30; soda bread, 74, 518; soft-wheat, 11, 46, 51, 362, 365–6, 518; soya, 72; stone-ground, 26, 29, 31, 51, 54, 518; storage of, 34–5, 217–20; straight-run, 77; subsidized, 34, 247; Vienna, 76; wheatmeal, 52–3, 106, 518; bakers', 57–8; and rye, 53;
white, 30–33, 46, 55–6, 218;
 bakers', 11; quality of bread made from, 56–7;
 home-baked bread from, 46; strong plain, 55–6; unbleached, quality of bread made from, 57; with wheat germ, 58;
wholemeal, 36, 59, 50–53; composition of, 248–9;
wholewheat, 48, 51; bakers', 59; meal, 50–52;
see also Milling; Oatmeal; Rye meal, etc.

Flowerpot bread, 73, 205, 210, **309–310**

Folkton and Flixton Women's Institute, **527**

Food and Drink in Britain from the Stone-Age to Recent Times, 360, 555

Food and Feeding, 42–3, 191–2, 361, 522–3, 554

Food in England, 350, 360, 448, 467, 485, 552

Food, its Adulterations and the Methods for their Detection, 71

Food Ministry leaflet 1944, **85**

Food Standards Committee: Second Report on Bread and Flour, 36, 58, 549; *Review of Food Labelling, Part 2*, 549

Forte, Charles, 384

Francatelli, Charles Elmé, *A Plain*
Cookery Book for the Working Classes, 160–61, 551

France: ale yeasts in, 371, 375; bakers in, 46; beer leaven in, 370; bleaching banned in, 33; bread storage in, 223, 371; breadmaking in, 364, 366–71, 382; buckwheat in, 73–4; buying bread flour in, 364–5; cornmeal in, 70; dried yeast in, 117; flour in, 62, 365–6; handmills in, 43–4, *44*; health food movement in, 364n.; mills in, 26, 29, 43–4, *44*, *50*; Pissaladière, 389–90; price and weight control in, 365; savarin mould in, *211*; yeast leaven in, 371, 375, 382; *see also under* French

France, William, 327

Fraser's Magazine, 347

Frazer, Mrs, *Practise of Cookery, Pastry and Confectionery*, 451, 551

Freezing: bread, 224–5; cake, **422**; yeast, 113–14

Fremington, 177

French blend of spices, **431**

French bread, 129, 201, 205, 362–72; *baguette*, 204, 362, 379; *bâtard*, 264, 378; butter and, 362; buying, 364; crust, 371–2; prices freed, 365n.;
 English-made, 365, 367, 369–70; 'French stick', 381; 19th century, 378–80;
 recipes, 372; Robert May 1660, 313–16, 374–5; E. Smith 1753, 376–7; W. A. Henderson 1795, 377–8;
fancy, 365; *ficelle*, 362; flour, 365–6; home-made, 365, 368, 369n., 371; Kirkland's opinion of, 382; leavened, the old method, 381–2; Liger, Louis, recipe of, **375–6**; *longuets*, 380; manchets and, 332–3; *méteil*, 379;
pain: *bénist*, 314, 331, **374**; *brayé et coiffé*, 204; *brié*, 363, 416;
 de campagne, 223, 265, 296, 362–4, 369, 381–2; large round, *379*;
 de Gonesse, 373–4; *grillé*, 368, 542; *de ménage*, 362–4; *mollet*, 331; *perdu*, 330;
payn puffe, 369; *payn purdeuz*, 329, 330; *polka*, *363*; *rouleau*, 378–9;

slashing of, 366–7; *tire-bouchon, 363*; 'Vienna', 362, 371, 380

French: brioche mould, *211, 216, 497*; burr stone mill, 26, 29, *44, 50*; bushels, 373n.; charlotte mould, *211, 216*; *huche, 383*; leaven system, 381–2; manchet, 333, 370; pancakes, 73–4; pan for, *408*

French Provincial Cooking, 550

French roll pan, *380*

French rolls, 372, 377, 381

French yeast cakes:
brioches, 496–7, 499–500; Bath buns and, 479; dough for, home-made, 403, 405, 497–8; lemon-flavoured, 150; moulds for, *211, 216, 497*; *pain perdu*, 330; Sally Lunn cake and, 469; sausage in crust of, 403–6, 498; savarin and, 502; Mrs Tashis' Little Puddings and, 489;

croissants, 496, 510–12; *petits pains au chocolat*, 499, 508–10; plum *galette*, 512–14; rastons, 498, 500; regional and festival, 498; restons, 501, 502; rum baba, 505–6;

savarin, 498, 502–5; moulds for, *211, 216*, 503

Frere, Miss C. F., 550

Fritters, yeast-leavened batter for, **417**

Frohń, Maurice, 37

Fromage, blanc or *frais*, 129

Frood, Miss M. S., on bread, **302**

Fruit:
bread, 436–40; with cheese, 526; dough for, 426, 439, 444;
cakes: with cheese, 526; chemically aerated, 439; leavened with baking powder, **525–7**; Rebecca Price's, 213;
cleaning, 136–7; dried, 134–7, 439

Frumenty, 73

Frying pan, Scotch, *539*

Fuel for brick ovens, 158, 161; 174–6, 183

Furnivall, Frederick (ed.), *The Babees Book*, 332n., 551

Gâche, Guernsey, 453–4

Gaillard Senior, La Ferté, 26

Galettes, 433; plain, **492**; plum, **512–514**

Galettière, cast iron, *408*

Garrett, T. F.: on Devonshire cake, **422–3**; *Encyclopaedia of Practical Cookery*, 89, 95, 97, 442–3; *Muffins and Crumpets*, 347–8; on Welsh crumpets, 358; on yeast, 89, 95, 97

Gas: cookers, 161, 166, 189; natural, 288; ovens, 128, 164, 166, 187–90, 288

Gas–electricity oven temperature conversion table, 240

Gaskell, E. S., 227n.

Gauze, miller's, 30–31

Genoese flat bread, 433

Gentleman's Magazine, The, 467

Geordie Cook Book, The, 463, 536, 552

George II: brown bread and, 49; at Chelsea Bun House, 482

Gerard, John, *Herball*, on: barley, *5, 63*; oats, *68*; rye, *66*; saffron, 147; starch corn, *8*; wheat, *4*

German Bensdorp, chocolate, 510

German bread, 206

German names, anglicized, 200–201

German pumpernickel bread, 206, 293

German yeast, 94

Gibson/Pegus, MS., 102, 445, 446, **460**

Gills, 230

Ginger, 146; dried, in root form, 146; 'stem', 135, 146, 444; yeast, 102–3, 146

Gingerbread, 67; manchet, **340**

Girdle or griddle:
cakes, 68, 358, 407, 516; singing hinnies, 536–7;
for crumpets, *353*; scones, 528

Give Me Yesterday, 39, 63, 126, 555

Glasse, Hannah: on ale yeast, 99; *The Art of Cookery Made Plain and Easy*, 99, 167, 299, 333, 343–4, 418, 445n., 551;
on bread, 99, 299; French, 372; *Compleat Confectioner*, 444, 445, 551; on French manchet, 333; on muffins and oatcakes, 343–4; on ovens, 167, 190; on saffron cake, 444, 445; on wiggs, 485; on yeast dumplings, **418–419**

Glastonbury, 9, 27

Gluten, xxi; Banfield on importance of, 45; extract, 46; -forming protein, 10; -free diet, xxii;
   -high flours and meals, 11, 45, 51, 52; in Midlands and North, 61; for puff pastry, 56; ripening of, 110; in rye, 65; water-absorption of, 61;
   lack of: in National loaf, 84; in oatmeal, 67

Goddisgoode, 92

Golden Syrup, 143, 294

Gonesse, *pain de*, 373–4

Good Appetite My Companion, 320–23, 451, 539, 552

Good Cheer, 56, 479, 551

Good Food Guide 1974, 54

Good Food on the Aga, 302

Good Housekeeping Cookery Book, 450, 539, 552

Good Huswife's Handmaide for the Kitchen, 334, 502, 551

Good Things in England, 129, 330, 349, 360, 467, 469, 485, 555

Goose pies, 64

Gottschalk, Dr Alfred, *Histoire de l'alimentation et de la gastronomie depuis la préhistoire jusqu'à nos jours*, 155, 551

Gouffé, Jules: *Le livre de cuisine*, 184; *Le livre de patisserie*, 184, 398, 469; on ovens, 184; on quiches, 398; on Solilem cakes, 469–70

Graham, Sylvester, 61

Graham meal and flour, 61–2

Grain: Australian, 16; bread, 3–16; history of cultivation of, 6–13; measures, 238; milling of, 15, 17–44; pounding, 17; transport of, 14–16

Grain race, 16

Gram flour, 72

Gram, liquid, 234

Granary loaf, 60, 153, 283–5; meal, 60, 283; mix, 118

Grand Junction Canal, 16

Granose salt, 123

Grant, Doris, *Your Daily Bread*, 551; on wholemeal bread, 272–4; *Your Daily Food*, 273

Grant, James, *Chemistry of Breadmaking*, 237, 551

Grant loaf, 272–4

Grapes, dried, 136

Gray, H. St George, 550

Great Exhibition of 1851, 26, 479–80

Greek: cooking bell, 156; *dolmades*, 489; loaves, 71, 98, 202–3, 205, 209; weights, 228n.

Gribbin, H., *Vienna and Other Fancy Breads*, 205, 551

Griddle, *353*, 528;
   cakes, 68, 358, 407, 516; hanging pan for, *539*
   square, *353*

Griddle-cooked bread, 64

Grigson, Jane, *Charcuterie and French Pork Cookery*, 403

Grill, toast under, 542–3

Grinding: Roman, 19, 28; stones, 26–30, 77; wheat, Thomas Muffet on, xx; *see also* Handmills; Milling; Millstones

Grocer, 385

Groundnut oil, 393

Gruyère cheese, 402

Guardian, 192

Guernsey biscuits, 490–92

Guernsey Dishes of Bygone Days, 454, 490, 554

Guernsey Dishes of the 18th Century, 554

Guernsey Gâche, 554

Guernsey *gâche*, 453–4

Guildford manchets, 336–7, 338

Gwynne, Félicité, xi

Hackwood, Frederick, *Good Cheer*, 56, 551; on Bath buns, 479

Haines, Arthur Lett, on Chelsea buns, 484

Hamilton, Bob, 386

Hamilton Palace, 214

Hammond, Elizabeth, *Modern Domestic Cookery and Useful Receipt Book*, on: buckwheat pancakes, 416; muffins, 345; Yorkshire cakes, 488

Hampshire lardy cakes, 462

Hampshire House Bakery, paper bags for, *250*

Hand family, 474, 482

Hand milling, 18–19, 40–44

Handmills, 19, 41–3, 524; buying, 43; modern French, 43–4, *44*; Victorian household, *41*

Hanging pan, *539*

Harnen stand, 531

Harris, Gertrude, *Manna: Foods of the Frontier*, 551; on ginger, 70

Harrison, William, 6; on bread, 172; on grain-growing, 11–12; on manchets, 331

Harris's of Wrecclesham, 223

Harrods, 403

Hartley, Dorothy: *The Countryman's England*, 552; *Food in England*, 350, 360, 448, 467, 485, 552; *Made in England*, 552; on muffins and crumpets, 350; on pikelets, 360; on potteries, 215; on saffron cake, 448; on tinkers, 214; on 'whigs' (wiggs), 485; *Water in England*, 551

Harvest cakes, 461; Northumbrian, **463**–464; Suffolk, 462

Harvey, Mrs, 489

Hassell, Dr A. H., *Food, its Adulterations and the Methods for their Detection*, on cornflour, 71

Havard, Mrs, 442

Haver cake, 69, 410, 530; lads, 530

Hawkshead, 485

Health-food stores, 112, 122

Health foods, 123, 364n.; *see also* Diet

Health's Improvement or Rules Comprising and Discovering the Nature, Method and Manner of Preparing All Sorts of Food Used in This Nation, xvii–xxii, 137, 139, 528, 553

Heat radiation, 168

Heath, Ambrose, *Good Food on the Aga*, on bread, **302**

de Heem, his paintings, eggs and lemons in, 134

Helmont, Louisa, on Guernsey *gâche*, 454

Henderson, W. A., *Universal Family Cook*, on: French bread, 372, **377**–8; muffins and oatcakes, 344

Hendren, Ann, on spice cake icing, 459

Henri IV of Navarre, on bread and wine, 373

Hepworth, Walter, 97

Herball, 4, 5, 8, 63, 66, 68, 147

Here's Health, 79n.

Heritage, Lizzie, *Cassell's Universal Cookery Book*, 552; on *galettes*, 433; plain, **492**; on Simnel yeast cake, 455–6; on soda bread, 516; on toast, 543; on Yorkshire brown bread, 283

Hesiod, *Works and Days*, on bread, 202

Heston wheat, 331

Hill, Derek, xi, 522

Histoire de l'alimentation et de la gastronomie depuis la préhistoire jusqu'à nos jours, 155, 551

Histoire illustré de la boulangerie en France, 371, 553

History of English Ale and Beer, A, 89, 111, 553

Hofels, Pure Foods Ltd, 43

Hog and Wheatsheaf design, *250*

Hollingsworth, Arthur, 375

Holme Mills, xii, 53, 80; wholemeal bread, 274–5

Home Baked, 92, 219, 554

Home-baked bread, 46; cost of, 246–51; French, 365, 368, 369n., 371; rye, 66–67; salt in, 120, 123, 261, 302, 316; wheat-germ, 81–2

Home-baking, 170–74, 255–6; flour for, 45–6

Honey, 151, 295

Honeycakes, 67

Hoops: cake, 212–13, 435–6; crumpet, *353*, 357; expanding, 213; paper, 212; steel, *213*; tinplate, 213; wood, 212

Horizontal Windmills, 20–21, 555

Horsfield, Mrs, 294

Hot-bread shops, 195–6

Hot cross buns, 152, 473, 475, **477**–**8**

Houghton Regis, 214

Household flour, 60–61

Household handmill, Victorian, *41*

Housekeeper's Instructor, The, 344

Housekeeping Book of Susannah Whatman 1776–1800, 255, 386, 555

Hovis, 37, 58, 74, 81, 205

Howey, Peggy, *The Geordie Cook Book*, 552; on lardy cakes, **463**; on singing hinnies, 536

Huche, French walnut, *383*

Huddersfield, 530

Hughes, M. Vivian: on breadbaking, 163, 255–6; *A London Child of the Seventies*, 551; *A London Family 1870–1900*, 104, 163, 333, 552; *A London Girl of the Eighties*, 537, 552; *A London Home in the Nineties*, 104, 255–256, 552; on manchets, 333; on Welsh tea at Machynlleth, 537; on yeast, 101, 104

Hugill, J. A. C. (ed.), *Sugar*, 138, 552

Hunsbury, Northamptonshire, Iron Age Settlement, 18, 27

Hunter, Dr A., *Receipts in Modern Cookery; with a Medical Commentary*, on potato bread, 288–**9**

Huntsman, Maris, 88

Hutchings, Professor Arthur, on saffron cake, 440

Ice, iced water, in bread dough, 125–7

Icing: cake, 139–40, 151; for a spice cake, 459; sugar, 139–40, 141

Imperial Cookery Book, The, 454

Ingram Thompson and Sons Ltd, salt processors, 123, 262n.

Introduction to the Study of the Principles of Breadmaking, An, 270n., 552

Irish: brade breached, 426, **440**; bread-iron, *532*; 'cake' bread, 518; pot bread, 309; potato cakes, 528; soda bread, 517, 519, **520–21**; spice bread, **439**; stone-ground wholemeal, 271, **272**, 282; Abbey brand, 275, 283, 518, 519; stone-milled meal, storage of, 217, 218; wheatmeal soda bread, 517, 529, **522**; wholewheat, **520–21**; meal, 521; soda bread, 520–21

Iron Age querns, 18, 27

Iron: bakestone, *534*; cauldron, 210; hoops, 212–13; kitchen ranges, 158, 161–4, 166, 208–209; oil and gas-fired, 164;

ovens, 158–9, 161–4, 166, 185–8; doors of, 176; pans, 214; pots, three-legged, 306; side-oven, 161, 185–8

Isle of Wight Cookery Book, The, 556; on doughnuts, **422**; on National Mark flour, 82, 84

Isle of Wight doughnuts, **422–3**

Israelites, 90

Italian bread, 121

Italian *cotechino*, 403, 404

Italian Food, 550

Italian panettone, 466

Italian pizza, 387–90

Italian Welsh rabbit, 384

Jack, Florence, 348, 450; on bread storage, 221; *Cookery for Every Household*, 221, 348, 421, 450–51; on doughnuts, 421; *Good Housekeeping Cookery Book*, 450, 539, 552; on muffins and crumpets, 348; on potato cakes, **539**; on Scotch buns, 450, **451**; on Scotch Christmas bun, 427

Jackman, Brian, 183

Jago, William, xii, 382–3; on French bread, 381–2; *An Introduction to the Study of the Principles of Breadmaking*, 270n., 552; *The Technology of Breadmaking* (with William C. Jago), 381–2, 552; on wholemeal, 270

Jamaica pepper, 144

Jannock, 528n.

Jekyll, Gertrude, *Old English Household Life*, 552

Jenkin, A. K. Hamilton, *Cornish Homes and Customs*, 156, 552

Jenkins, J. Geraint, *Life and Tradition in Rural Wales*, 218

Jewitt, Llewellyn, *Ceramic Art of Great Britain*, 157, 177–80, 552

Jewry Wall Museum, Leicester, 18, 27

Jobson, Allan, *An Hour-Glass on the Run*, 552; on buying flour, 39–40; on dumplings, 420; on harvest cakes, 462; on hot cross buns, 477; on ovens, 137, 167; on sifting currants, 137; on village grocer, 133; on yeast, 97

Johnson, Walter (ed.), *Gilbert White's Journals*, 13, 555

Johnstone, Mrs (Margaret Dods), *The Cook and Housewife's Manual*, 212, 378, 426, 440, 469, 479, 480, 551

Jones, Rev. D. Parry, *Welsh Country Upbringing*, on grates, 185

Jones, Tom, *Henry Tate 1819–1899*, 552

Jones, Wendy, xii

Jordan, Mr W., xii, 53, 80, 275

Joseph Ashby of Tysoe: A Study of English Life, 177, 549

Journal de Genève, 7

Joyce, H. S., on: village bakery, 181–2; white bread, 80

Jugs, measuring, 242

Kalderash, 70

Keats, John, on barley bread, 65

Kendal oatcakes, 530, **531**

Kennedy, Diana, *The Cuisines of Mexico* and *The Tortilla Book*, 70

Kent and Co., 43 and n.

Kent, Countess of, *A True Gentlewoman's Delight*, 314, 336, 552; on spice cakes, 427; on manchets, **335–6**

Ketteridge, Christopher, and Mays, Spike, *Five Miles from Bunkum*, 45, 552; on breadbaking, 170–72, 183

Kettle bread, Cornish, 155–6, **308–9**

Kiches, *see* Quiches

Kimnel, 335

King, Mr, of Albury, 337

Kirkland, John, xii, 351; *Bakers' A.B.C.*, 65n., 128, 197, 303, 352, 381, 473, 519, 552;
on bread, 197, 210, 303, 305; French, 381; Parthian, 126–7;
on buns, 473; on buttermilk, 128, 519; on malt extracts, 153; *The Modern Baker, Confectioner and Caterer*, 126–127, 153, 156, 210, 351, 381, 552; on muffins, 351–2, 356; on ovens, 156; on rye meal, 65

Kirsch-flavoured syrup, 502–3

Kitchen ranges, iron, 158, 161–4, 166, 187–8, 208–9; oil and gas-fired, 164

Krampoch, 358

Kugelhopf, 466, 498, 508; moulds, *211, 216, 497,* 506

Labelling laws for flour and bread: lack of, 35, 59; recommendations concerning, 549

Labour Government, 39

Lady Bountiful's Legacy, 170, 187

L'Agronome, *Dictionnaire portatif du cultivateur*, on soft water for bread, 380

Lake villages, 9, 27

Lake Villages of Somerset, The, 550

Lakeland Cookery, on: Cumbrian Christmas bread, 453; Ulverston Fair cakes, 493–4

Lancashire: cheese, wiggs with, 487; muffins, 349–50; oatcakes, 408–9

Lane, Augusta Diana, 491

Lard, 127, 130–31; home-made, 462

Lardy cakes, 130, 427, 429, 461–2; fat in, 462; Hampshire, 462; health hazard from, 461; Northumberland, **463**; sugar in, 461

Lardy rolls, 337; Sussex, **493**

La Varenne (François Pierre), on: bread, 373n., 374; *Le Pastissier françois*, 374, 553; spice blend, 431

Lava stones, 28–9

Lavender, 151

Law, James T., *Law's Grocer's Manual*, 552; on buckwheat, 73; on malt, 65; on mixed spice, 152; on muffins, 350; on stoning raisins, 136; on yeast, 91, 95

Leaven, 89–90; barley bread on a, 298; bread without barm by the help of a, 299; Muffett, Thomas, on, xx; potato, 102;
spontaneous, 370; St Paul on, 80

Leavened bread, French method, 381–2

Lebanon, grain-crushing bowl found in, *Plate 2*

Leicestershire pikelet, **359**

Lemon: cake, 490; loaf, *266*; peel, 150

Lemons, 150–51, 444; grating, 150

Lentil flour, 72

Lester, Fred, *Looking Back*, on breadbaking, 180–81

Lewes, 24

Liber Albus, The White Book of the City of London, 227, 369, 552

Lickley, Mrs, of White Mill, Carmarthen, 40

Liebig, J. von, 78, 91

Liger, Louis, *Le Ménage des champset le jardinier français*, 552; on bread, 373–374, 375–6

Light cakes, Welsh, 407, 537

Ligon, Richard, *A True and Exact History of the Land of Barbadoes*, on muscavadoes, 141

Ligurian pizza, 389, 391–3

Lindt chocolate, 510

Liquid measurements, metrication of, 234–5

Liquid/solid measures, conversion table, 235

Liquids in breadmaking, 125–32

Lisbon sugar, 142

Liverpool salt, 123

Livre de cuisine, Le, 184

Livre de pâtisserie, Le, 184, 398, 469

Llanover, Lady, *The First P rinciples Good Cookery*, on: barley cake, 535–6; bread: pot, 155, 210, 307–8; rice, 71, 292; oatmeal cakes, 533–5; ordering boiling pots, 214

Llewellyn, Richard, on baking stone, 535; on toast, 544

Loaves: *baguette*, 204, 362, 379; *bâtard*, 264, 378; batched, 199; baton, thick, 280; bloomer, 201–3, 264, 280–82; brick, 199, 204; *brié*, 363, 496; 'brown', 'brownish', 36, 58; Brunswick, 200; cauliflower, 201, 278; cob, 200, 277; Coburg, 200, 263, 276–7; pan, 201, 278–9; college, 201, 265; corkscrew, *363*; cottage, 203, 286–8; brick, 204; pan, 204; crumbly, 262; crumby *or* crummy, 108, 199; crusty, 199–200, 261, 263, 303–6; wholemeal, 272; curly, 203; Cypriot, 205; Danish, 200, 277; dish, 276–7; English, *197*; shapes and names of, 197–205; farmhouse tin, 199; *ficelle*, 362; finger, 205; granary, 60, 153, 283–5; Grant, 272–4; Greek, 71, 98, 202–3, 205, 209; lemon, 266; malted, 60, 153, 154, 205; manchet, 329, 335; muffin, 75, 312–313; National, 33–4; penny, 226, 340; white, 339–40; plaited, 205, 429; porcupine, 201, 265; Roman, 98, 126–7, 202, 210; round, 276–7; sandwich, 210; scone, wholemeal, 275; Scottish batch, 199; shapes and names of, 197–205; sisterbrick, 199; slashing, 263–6; sliced, 193, 205; supermarket, 88; tin, 199, 263–4; English, *197*, 197–205; farmhouse, 199; pan Coburg, 278–9; split, 199, 263–4; wholemeal, 268–72; *tire bouchon*, *363*; for trenchers, 332; undersellers', 201, 265; undertin, 303; underweight, punishment for, 227; Vienna-type, 266; French, 362, 371, 380; weights of, 226–32; Welsh cob, 200; wrapped, 37, 193; Yorkshire spiced, 428, 461; without eggs, 428, 454; *see also* French bread

Lockyer, C. G., xii, 31, 297; on baps, 323

London: Bath bun, 479–80; Bread Act 1822, 231, 378; mills of, 14, 40; Museum, 212

London Child of the Seventies, A, 552

London Family 1870–1900, A, 104, 163, 333, 552

London Girl of the Eighties, A, 537, 552

London Home in the Nineties, A, 104, 255–6, 552

London Labour and the London Poor, 49, 342–3, 346–7, 477, 553

Longuets, 380

Luckhurst, David, *Monastic Watermills. A Study of the Mills within English Monastic Precincts*, 554

Luke, Sir Harry, on caraway, 145
Luncheon cake, 427, 465–6; plain, 470–471
Luncheon sausage, 403
Lunn, Sally, 467
Lydgate, John, on weights and measures, 226

McAllister, Bryan, 192
McCance, R. A., and Widdowson, E. M., *Breads White and Brown: Their Place in Thought and Social History*, 552
MacClure, Victor H., *Good Appetite My Companion*, 552; on potato scones, 539; on Scotch buns, 451; on Scots baps, 320–23
McDermot, Gracie, xii, 522, 528, 532–3
McDougalls, 37, 60–61
Mace, 151
Machynlleth, 537
Maclean, Adeline, and Thompson, Evelyn, *The Surrey Cookery Book*, 465, 556; on manchets, 336–7
McNeill, F. Marian: on baps, 321; *The Book of Breakfasts*, 355, 541, 553; *The Scots Kitchen*, 321, 529, 553; on soft biscuits, 491; on toast, 541; on toasting muffins, 355
Maize meal, 69–70
Maldon salt, 122
Malt, 64, 153; bread, 60, 153, 154, 205; extracts, 46, 64, 153–4
Malted meals, 58, 74
Malting, 64–5
Manchet:
bread, 329, 335; Queen Elizabeth's, 331;
common ancestor of many specialities, 332; gingerbread, 340; Lady of Arundel's, 335–6
Manchets, 314, 329–40; early, *330*, 334; French, 333; Guildford, 336–7, 338; making of fine, 334; penny white loaf and, 339–40; 1974 recipe, 338–9
Manitoba wheat, 9, 51
Manna, 45, 82, 96, 107–9, 121, 123–4, 126, 141, 143, 191, 197, 205, 209, 216, 271, 287, 294–5, 305, 354–7, 524–5, 549

Manna: Foods of the Frontier, 146, 551
Manners and Meals in Olden Times, 332n.
Manual of Domestic Economy Suited to Families Spending from £100 to £1,000 a Year, 41, 42, 57, 58, 187, 555
Manx barley bread, 523
Mapleton's granary meal, 60, 283
Marie Antoinette, Queen, 497
Marigold vinegar, 151
Maris Huntsman wheat, 88
Markham, Gervase: on Banbury cake, 448; on black stones, 28, 335; on bread, 227–8; *The English Hus-wife*, 28n., 227n., 335, 448, 553; *Maison Rustique: or The Countrey Farme*, 814; on manchet bread, 335; on saffron cake, 448
Marquis wheat, 10
Marshall, Rosalind K., *The Days of Duchess Anne. Life in the Household of the Duchess of Hamilton 1656–1716*, 214, 553
Martin, Edith, *Cornish Recipes Ancient and Modern*, on: barley bread, 298; pot bread, 308–9; saffron cake, 440–442; underbaking, 178–9
Maslin, 53, 65
Mason, Charlotte, *Mrs Mason's Cookery, or The Ladies' Assistant*, 553; on saffron cake, 448–9
Mastering the Art of French Cooking, 369n., 511, 550
Masterman, J. C., on crumpets, 361
Mathews, bakery suppliers, 278
May, Robert, *The Accomplisht Cook*, 553; on French bread, 313–16, 374–5
Mayer, Louie, xi, 165, 285, 286
Mayhew, Henry, *London Labour and the London Poor*, 553; on brown bread, 49; on hot cross buns, 477; on the muffin-man, 342–3, 346–7
Mayn, 329–40
Mays, Spike, 45, 170–72, 183, 552
Meal, storage of, 35, 217–20
Meare, Somerset, 9, 28
Measurements: metrication of, 232–6; of moulds and pans, 236
Measures, 232; dry, 237–8; grain, 238; half-peck, 237, 376n.; metrication of,

Measures (*continued*)
232–6; solid/liquid, conversion table, 235

Measuring equipment, *242*; jugs, 242

Measuring spoons, 243–4, 269n.

Melba toast, 545

Mendip Hills, 28

Menier chocolate, 510

Mère Brazier's restaurant, 469

Merle and Reitich, *Domestic Dictionary*, 170

Méteil loaf, 379

Metrication, 232; linear measurements, 236; liquid measures, 234–5; weights, 233–5

Mexico, maize meal and pancakes in, 70

Miche, 379

Michelham Priory watermill, *Plate 10*

Microwave baking machinery, 88

Milburn, Mrs C. H., *The Imperial Cookery Book*, on Yorkshire spice loaf, 454

Milk: in dough, 127–8, 262; sour, 128, 517; sweet, 519

Mill on the Floss, 19, 25, 380, 543

de Mille, Cecil B., 18

Miller, N. W., 64n.

Millers and Flour Order 1953, 33–4

Millers, 22; British bakery industry bought by, 36–7; extraction rate myth and, 34–5; gauze, 30–31; independent, 24, 25; malpractices alleged, 30, 42

Millet, 73

Millilitres, 234

Milling, 17–44; feudal, 24, 40–41; government control of, 33–4; hand, 18–19, 40–44; history of, 17–33, 40–44; roller, 25, 32, 34, 39, 54, 80–81; stone, 26–30, 39, 54, 77

Milling of Wheat, 48n.

Mills, 19–26; floating, 14, *Plate 9*; French burr stone, 26, 29, *44, 50*; household, 18–19, *41*, 42–3, *44*; made illegal, 40–41

Roman, 19, *27*; surviving, 40; *see also* Handmills; Watermills; Windmills

Millstone, 26, 29; burr, 26, 29; dressing, 30; flour, 54; grit, 26, 29

Millstones, *Plates 4 and 5*; dressing, *Plate 11*; Roman, 18, 28, *Plate 12*; yield from, 29

Millwrights, 30

Mirabelle plums, 513

Mistress of Stantons Farm, The, 434–5, 481, 488, 556

Modern Baker, Confectioner and Caterer, The, 126–7, 153, 156, 210, 351, 381, 552

Modern Cookery for Private Families, 99–100, 146n., 160, 186, 246, 379, 406, 422–3, 467, 549

Modern Domestic Cookery Based on the Well-known Work of Mrs Rundell (ed. Emma Roberts, *q.v.*), 554

Modern Domestic Cookery and Useful Receipt Book, 345, 416, 488

Moelwyn-Hughes, R., *Cheap Bread*, 16, 553

Molasses, 60, 143, 295

Monastic Watermills. A Study of the Mills within English Domestic Precincts, 554

Monckton, H. A., *A History of English Ale and Beer*, 89, 111, 553

Moore, Denis, xii, 202

More's *Dyaloge*, on wygges, 484

Morel, Ambroise, *Histoire illustrée de la boulangerie en France*, 371, 553

Morison, Fynes, on toast, 541

Moschus moschiferus, 149

Mosse, W. H., 519

Moulds and tins: for bread, 206–16; brioche, *211*, 216, *497*; buying, 215–216; for cakes, yeast-leavened, *211*, 212–16; Charlotte, *211*, 216; dariole, *216, 488*; earthenware, 209–10, 214–215, 216, 230; fancy, 216; fluted, *211, 497, 503*; iron, 212–13; kugelhopf, *211*, 216, *497, 506*; ring, *211, 497*; savarin, *211*, 216, 503; terracotta, *211*; wooden, 315; *see also* Hoops; Tins

Muffet, Thomas, *Health's Improvement or Rules Comprising and Discovering the Nature, Method and Manner of Preparing All Sorts of Food Used in This Nation*, xvii–xxii, 553; on oats, 528; on sugar, 137, 139

Muffin:
  bell, 342, 346–7; attempted prohibition of, 347;
  cake, 348; colloquial meanings of, 341;
  man, 342–3, 346; his No. 1 secret, 352;
  hoops, 351, *353*; loaves, 75, 312–13; pans, American, *353*
Muffineers, 149
Muffins: breakfast cakes, grouped with, 346; butter and, 361; cornmeal, 355; and crumpets, 341–61, *342*; dusting for, 71; familiarly associated with crumpets, 341–2; flour for, 352, 353, 355; griddle for, 353; indigestibility of, 360; Lancashire, 349–50; Mayhew, Henry, on, 342–3, 346–7; nomenclature of, confused with crumpets and pikelets, 341–3, 351, 360; and oatcakes, 344; olive oil in, 131; and pikelets, 351, 360; price sold at (1851), 346;
  recipes for, by household cooks, 343–350; Hannah Glasse 1747, **343–4**; Mrs Rundell 1806, **345**; Elizabeth Hammond 1817, **345**; Emma Roberts 1841, **345**; Elizabeth David 1973, **353–5**;
  by professional bakers, 350–53; J. T. Law 1895, **350**; T. F. Garrett 1899, 347–8; (and crumpets) Florence Jack 1914, **348**; Robert Wells 1929, **352**; Walter Banfield 1937, **354–5**; Edmund Bennion 1967, **353**; not published before 18th century, 343;
  Scarborough, 349; served at London coffee houses, 341; served at National Liberal Club, 349; Shaw, G. B., on, 355; similarities with and differences from crumpets and pikelets, 343, 351; sold at Sainsbury's, 342; tea, 347, 352; to toast, 355; Williams-Ellis, Sir Clough, on, 349
Muffins and Crumpets, 347–8
Mullion, 298
Munich, 168
Muscatel raisins, 136

Muscovado sugar, 141–2
Musk, 149
Musk-scented sugar, 149–50
My Grandmother's Cookery Book, 523

Naked barley, 5
Nan, 72
Napier, Mrs Alexander (ed.), *A Noble Boke off Cookry ffor a Prynce Houssolde or Eny Other Estately Houssolde*, 501, 553
National Association of British and Irish Millers, 48n.
National Bakery School, 82
National Federation of Women's Institutes, 73
National flour, 34, 82–8
National Liberal Club, muffins correctly served at, 349
National loaf, 33–4
National Mark flour, 82–4; advertisement, *83*
Nevill, H. W., Ltd, 194
New Century Cookery Book, The, 554
New System of Domestic Cookery, A; Formed Upon Principles of Economy, 10–11, 99, 101–3, 130, 168, 186, 208, 326, 345–6, 359, 431, 449, 450, 451, 469, 554
New Twentieth Century Cookery Book, 162
Newton, Edward, 45, 180, 194–5, 546, 554
Nightingale, Mr, of Leahurst, 103
Noble, Joan Russell (ed.), *Recollections of Virginia Woolf*, 553
Noble Boke off Cookry ffor a Prynce Houssolde or Eny Other Estately Houssolde, 501, 553
Nollekens and his Times, 144, 148
Non-stick pans, 216; Finnish, 216, *408*
Norfolk, 172; dumplings, **419–20**
Norman, Jill, xi
Normandy, 223–4, 496
North Riding bread, 526
Northumberland Household Book, The, 331n.
Northumberland lardy cakes, 463

Northumberland and Cumbrian Recipes, 463–4, 551
Northumbrian harvest cakes, 463–4
Nutmeg grater, 148; pocket, *149*
Nutmegs, 148, 151
Nutrients, 52n., 59
Nutrition, Manual of, 549

Oakes, Philip, 359, 411
Oatcake: board, 530; stand, *532*
Oatcakes, 68, 344, 528; Donegal, 531–3; Kendal, 530, 531; Lancashire, 408–9; muffins and, 344; in Scotland, 528–9; Staffordshire Potteries, 411–12; Welsh, 69, 528, **533–5**; yeast-leavened, 407; Yorkshire, 410–11, 529–30
Oaten bannocks, 69
Oaten bread, 68
Oatmeal, 67–9; bread, Welsh, **533**; brown bread, 282–3; cakes, Welsh, **533–5**; muffins, 68; pancakes, Welsh, 408–9; and wholewheat soda bread, 522–3
Oats, 528; common, *68*; rolled, 69
Oglander, Brig.-Gen. Cecil Aspinall, on weights of loaves, 230
Oil: arachide, 131; brushing dough with, 262; corn, 131; in dough, effect of, 131, 433; of cloves, 151; groundnut, 393; in muffin dough, 131; olive, 131, 262, 393, 432; peanut, 131; prevents formation of skin on dough, 262; sesame seed, 131; sunflower seed, 131
Oil-fired cooking stove, 164–5, *165*
Olive oil, 131, 262, 393; in teacakes, 432
Orange-flower water, 151
Origin of Food Habits, The, 425, 540, 554
Ort, George, xii, 154, 420
Orvieto wine, saffron cake with, 442
Our Daily Bread, 79n., 290, 554
Oven sheets, lightweight non-stick, 277
Oven thermometers, 245
Ovens, *Plates 13–24*; Acton Eliza, on, 161–2, 175–6, 186; Aga, 167, **301–2**; Barnstaple, 157, 177, *Plates 18 and 20*; Beeton, Mrs, on, 162; Belling, 166, 167, *Plate 24*; Bideford, 157, 177, *Plates 18 and 20*; bread, 155–90;

brick, 156, 158, *Plates 22 and 23*; fuel for, 158, 161, 174–6, 183; with iron doors, 176; renewing the lining, 182–3; surviving, 183–5, 190; in use, 167–77, 180–85, 286, 434–5; with wooden doors, 176;
Calstock, 177;
clay, 156; Cornish, 157, 177–9; Spanish, *Plate 19*;
communal, 159; cool, 165–6; depth of, 164; Devon, gravel-tempered clay, 155, 156, 157, 177, *Plates 18 and 20*; Dutch, 324n.; earthenware, 157, 177–180; electric, 128, 166–7, 188–9, 287–288; fan, 166–7; floors of, tiled, 156, 163; Fremington, 177; French, *Plates 16 and 17*;
gas, 128, 164, 166, 187–90, 288; natural, 288;
history of, 155–67; iron, 158–9, 161–164, 166, 185–8; of oil stores, 164–5, *165*; pastry, 184, 189; at Pompeii, *Plate 6*; pot, Cornish, 178; Roman, 156, *Plate 6*; steamy, 170, 184, 261;
temperature of, 239–40, 258; electricity–gas conversion table, 240; judging, 169–70;
see also Cookers; Ranges
Oxford Book of Food Plants, 553
Oxford mills, 15

Pain: bénist, 314, 331, **374**; *brayé et coiffé*, 204; *brié*, 363, 496;
de campagne, 223, 265, 296, 362–4, 369, 381–2; large round, **379**;
de Gonesse, 373–4; *grillé*, 368, 542; *de ménage*, 362–4; *mollet*, 331; *perdu*, 330
Painter, Neil S., and Burkitt, Denis P., 553; on fibre and diverticular disease, 78–9
Pan bread, Welsh, **307–8**
Pan Coburg loaf, 201, **278–9**
Pan cottage loaf, 204
Pancakes:
barley, 64, 412–13; with cheese, **413**; batter for: aerating, 126; for fritters, **417**;

Blencowe, Ann, on, 489; blinis, 414–416;

buckwheat, 358, 416; English, 73, 416–17; yeast-leavened, 416

French, 73–4; Mexican, 70; pans for, *408*; Welsh, 358; Welsh oatmeal, 408–409; on wrong side of pewter plate, 489; yeast, 358; yeast-leavened, 407–417

Pancheon, earthenware, *253*

Panettone, 466

Pans: blini, 416; bread, 221–2, 317n.; earthenware, 317n.; egg, 416; French roll, *380*;

frying: hanging, *539*; Scotch, for scones and griddle cakes, *539*;

iron, 214; muffin, American, *353*; non-stick, Finnish, 216, *408*; for pancakes, *408*

Paraffin cookers, 164

Parisian barm, 101

Parthian bread, 126–7

Pasta, 77

Pasteur, Louis, on yeast, 91

Pastissier françois, Le, 374

Paston, Clement, *Plate 8*

Paston, Margaret, asks for sugar, 138

Pastons and their England, The, 549

Pastries: flour for, 54, 56; savoury, 432–433

Pastry: barley-flour, 64; Cornish, 442; oven, 184, 189; puff, 210; for quiches, 398; yeast-leavened, 426, 510

Pastry-making, stone-milled flour for, 54

Pâté, pulled bread good with, 546

Patent flours, 75–7

Patent Office, 75; *Abridgement or Specifications Relating to Cooking, Breadmaking, and the Preparation of Confectionery*, 553

Pattypans, *353*

Paul, St, 90

Payn puffe, 369

Payn purdeuz, 329, 330

Payndemayn, 329–40

Peacock, T. L., on anchovy toast, 544

Peanut oil, 131

Pearson potteries, 304

Peate, Iorweth, *Tradition and Folk Life*, 553

Peel, candied, 135

Peels, wooden, *169*, **182**

Peggy tub, *312*; bread, 126, 311–12

Pendle, Arthur, 'Dumplings and Dialect', 419

Pennant, Thomas, *Tours in Wales*, 553; on canals, 16

Penny loaf, 226, 340; white, 339–40

Pepper, 144–5; Jamaica, 144

Pepys, Samuel, on wiggs and ale, 484

Persian water and windmills, 21

Peterborough (*Daily Telegraph*), 387

Petits pains au chocolat, 499, 508–10

Phillips, Mrs Margaret, xii

Phillips, Sir Richard, on Chelsea buns, 483

Phoenicians, 148

Pikelet, corruption of Welsh *pyglyd*, 360

Pikelets, 358, 407; batter for, 359; correct diameter of, 360;

equivalent of:

crumpets, 351; in Derbyshire and Yorkshire, 360;

muffins and all yeast cakes in S.W. Derbyshire, 360

Leicestershire 1841, **359**; 1974 recipe, 361; Staffordshire, for breakfast, 360

Pimento berry, 144

Pinto, Edward, *Treen and Other Wooden Bygones: An Encyclopaedia and Social History*, 176–7, 553

Pissala, 379

Pissaladeira, 388, 389

Pissaladière, 389–90

Pitchy bread, 360

Pittard, Professor Eugene, on origins of agriculture, 7

Pizza, 384–97; Armenian, 388; bars, 386; copper tray for, *394*; dough, oil in, 131, 433; Eden Vale, ingredients of, 386; English, onward and downward march of, 384–7; Express, 386; French, 389; frozen, 385; home-made, 388–9; houses, 384–7; Italian, 387–90; large rectangular, **393–6**; large round, **396–7**; Ligurian, 389,

Pizza (*continued*)
391–3; meaning, 387–8; pie, 386; take-away, 385, 387
Pizza Range Ltd, 385, 386
Pizzaland, 387
Pizzeria, 386, 389
Pizette, 433
Plain Cookery Book for the Working Classes, A, 551; poor value, 160–61
Plat, Sir Hugh, *Delightes for Ladies*, 553; on clove sugar, 432; on manchet gingerbread, 340; on molasses, 143; on spiced sugar, 149–50
Pliny, 126–7, 210
Plum: cake, plain, 460; *galette*, 512–14; heavies, Sussex, 493; pudding, 137
Plumb cake, 137, 459, 460–61
Plums, 137, 513
Pococke, Dr Richard, *The Travels through England of Dr Richard Pococke 1750*, 553; on pot ovens, 178
Polegate tower mill, *23*
Polenta, 69–70
Polka bread, *363*
Polythene to cover dough, 315
Pompeii, mills and oven, *Plate 6*
Pope, J. H., manchets of, 336–7, 338
Poppadums, 72
Poppy seeds, 146
Porcupine loaf, 201, 265
Pork crackling, 433
Pot bread, 210, 307–9; Cornish, 155–6, 308–9; Cumbrian, 309; Irish, 309; the self-sufficient way, 306–7; Welsh, 307–8
Pot ovens, Cornish, 178
Pot querns, 18–19
Potages, bread for, 546
Potato: bread, 103, 288–90; cakes, 528, 539; flour, 67, 72; leaven, 102; mash, as fermenting agent, 72, 103, 290; rolls, 326; scones, 538–9; starch, 72
Potatoes, 72, 159, 289
Pots: earthenware, 209–10; terracotta, 309; three-legged iron, 306, 308
Pots and Pans of Classical Athens. Excavations of the Athenian Agora, 549
Potters, 156, 177, 214–15

Poulter family, manchets of, 337, 338
Practical Breadmaking, 89, 155, 160n., 191, 201, 306–7, 555
Practise of Cookery, Pastry and Confectionery, 451, 551
Prewett's bread flour, 51–2, 67, 75, 294, 518, 519
Price, Rebecca, MS. Receipt book, on cake hoops, 212–13, 212n.
Price regulation bread, 226–30
Priced bread, 230, 339
Prices and quality, 122
Prunes, 136
Pudding-stick, 135
Puddingstone, 27
Puddings, Mrs Tashis' Little, 150, 488–490, *489*
Puff pastry, 510; for quiches, 398
Puffe-bread, 369
Pulled bread, good with pâté, 546
Pumpernickel, 206, 293
Pumpkin bread, 290
Punch, on toast, 540
Pyrex ware, 242

Quality: of bread, 191–3, 195; and price, 122
Quarterns, 231
Quarter-sponge system of dough mixing, 107–8
Queen Magazine, 384
Querns, 17–19, 28
Quetsch plums, 513
Quiches: Blue Castello, 401; Bresse Bleu, 401; Cheddar, 401; cream cheese, 398, 401–2; Gouffé, Jules, on, 398; Lorraine, 388, 398, 402; reheating, 402; Roquefort, 398–9, 399–401; sweet, 398; *tarte aveyronnaise*, 399–401; with yeast dough, 398–402

Raffald, Elizabeth, *The Experienced English Housekeeper*, 554; on barm pudding, 420; on Bath buns, 480–81; on cake hoops, 212; on crumpets, 344–5; on wiggs, 433, 485–7
Railway toast, 544
Railways, 16
Raising agents, 516–17

Raisins, 136, 439; Muscatel, 136; stoning, 136

Rake, ash-clearing, *169*, 182

Ranges: coal, 163-4, 187-8; Eagle coal-fired, *162*, 188; iron kitchen, 158, 161-164, 166, 208-9; oil and gas-fired, 164

Rank Hovis McDougall, 37, 74, 195

Rank, J., Ltd, 37

Raper, Elizabeth, *Receipt Book of Elizabeth Raper*, 554; on French rolls, 377; on plum cake, 460

Rastons, 498, 500

Reasons Why, The: Practical Answers to Everyday Bakehouse Questions, 550

Receipts in Modern Cookery; with a Medical Commentary, 288-9

Recipes, modernized, 432-4

Recipes from an Old Farmhouse, xix, 359, 555

Red Fife wheat, 10

Redoxon tablets, 267

Refrigerator, bread storage in, 225

Regional and festival yeast cakes, 424-472; French, 498

Renner, H. D., *The Origin of Food Habits*, 554; on toast, 540; on yeast cakes, 425

Restons, 501, 502

Reynolds, John, *Windmills and Watermills*, 21, 554

Rhodes, figurine found in, *Plate 3*

Rhodes, Hugh, *Boke of Nurture*, 331-2, 551

Rice, 71, 291; bread, 290-92; flour, 71, 75, 328

Riddle bread, 531; Yorkshire, 407, 409-411

Riley, Henry Thomas, 553

Ring mould, *211*, *497*; *see also* Hoops

Rippingille cooker, 164

Ritz, Marie, *César Ritz, Host to the World*, 554; on Melba toast, 545

Rivière, M., xii, 368

Roberts, Emma, 186, 359; on brick ovens, 186; on muffins, 345; on Scotch buns, 449, 450, 451; on spice blend, 431; *see also* Rundell, Maria Eliza

Roll pan, French, *380*

Rolled oats, 69

Roller milling, 25, 32, 34, 39, 54, 80-81

Rollinson, William, *Life and Tradition in the Lake District*, on pot bread, 309

Rolls: Aberdeen rowies, 327-8; breakfast, hot, 324-5; chocolate, 499, 508-510; croissants, 496, 510-12; fadge, 322;

French, 372, 377, 381; *petits pains au chocolat*, 499, 508-10;

lardy, 337, 493; morning, 322; potato, 326; saffron, 148; soft, 323-4; Sussex lardy, 493; Vienna, 325-6; *see also* Baps

Roman: agriculture, 9; grinding, 19, 28; loaves, 98, 126-7, 202, 210; mills, 19, 27; millstones, 18, 28; ovens, 156; watermills, 19

Root vegetables in bread, 72-3

Roquefort quiche, 398-9, **399-401**

Roscrea, Tipperary, 521

Rose water, 151

Rosemary, 151

Rostis de pain, 501

Roughage, 80

Rowies, Aberdeen, **327-8**

Royal Institution, 168n.

Ruddle's Brewery, Rutland, 64n.

Ruddock, E. H., *Essentials of Diet*, on muffins and crumpets, 361

Rum baba, 505-6

Rumford, Count, 168n.

Rumpy loaf, 265

Rundell, Maria Eliza: *Modern Domestic Cookery Based on the Well-known Work of Mrs Rundell* (ed. Emma Roberts, *q.v.*), 554; *A New System of Domestic Cookery: Formed Upon Principles of Economy*, 345-6, 554; on American flour, 10-11; on butter, 130; on muffins, 345; on ovens, 168, 186; on pikelets, 359; on potato rolls, 326; on Sally Lunn cakes, 469; on Scotch buns, 449, 450, 451; spice blend, 431; on tin loaves, 208; on yeast, 99, 101-3

Rural Economy in Yorkshire in 1641, 550

Russell, John, *Boke of Nurture*, 551; on serving bread, 331–2

Rutland, Countess of, *The Compleat Cook*, on saffron cake, 447–8

Rye, 66:
bread, 65–7, 72, 205, 293–4; caraway in, 67; ergot in, 65; home-baking, 66–7;
sourdough, 67, 295, 296; spiced, 67;
spicing, 433; sweetened, 294–5; toast, 542; varnishing, 294–5;
cakes, Danish, 67; meal, 65–6, 294; wheatmeal and, 53

Ryedale, Recipes, 526

Ryvita, 67

Saccharomyces cerevisiae, 92

Saddle quern, 17

Saffron, 147, 440; buns, 147; Boorde, Andrew, on, 148;
cake, 147, 444–7; Cornish, 427, 440–442; Devonshire, 427, 442–4; Digby, Sir Kenelm, on, 446–7; freezing, 442; Gerard, John, on, 147; Gibson/Pegus, in 1810, 446; Glasse, Hannah, in 1760, 444, 445; 17th, 18th and 19th centuries, 444–445; travesties of, 440–41;
Evelyn, John, on, 147; whole filaments, 147, 440

Saffron-Walden, 147, 172n.

Sage, 151

Sailing ships' grain cargoes, 16

St Clair, Lady Harriet, *Dainty Dishes*, 554; on barmbrack, 439

St Fagans, Cardiff, 157, *218*, 219, 308, 538

St Just Women's Institute, 309

St Kea Women's Institute, 179

St Lawrence Women's Institute, 422

Saintsbury, George, 489

Saleable Shop Goods, 133, 151–2, 555

Sally Lunn cakes, 129, 150, 467–70, 479; eggs in, 133; saffron in, 147

Salt, 119–24;
in bread, 108, 119; home-baked, 120, 123, 261, 302, 316;
in cakes, 123–4; Cheshire, 122–3;
crystal, 123; Granose, 123; Liverpool, 123; prices of, 122; proprietary, 121; pure, 121–3, 261; quantities for bread, 120–21; rock, 122–3, 261; sea, 122, 123; storage, 124; and yeast action, 119–20, 121

Salt-rising bread, 229–301

Salter's spring-balance kitchen scale, 241

Samuelson, M. K., *Sussex Recipe Book, with a Few Excursions into Kent*, 554; on plain cake, 471; on Sussex plum heavies, 493

San Francisco sourdough, 67

Sandoe Books, xi

Sandwich loaves, 210

Sandwiches: cutting, *318*; potato bread, good for, 289; rice bread, good for, 292

Sardenara, 389, 391–3

Saunders, Dr A. P., 10

Sausage: *cervelas*, 403; in brioche crust, 403–6, 498; *cotechino*, 403, 404; English, 404; luncheon, 403

Savage, Elizabeth, xi

Savarin, 498, 502–5; moulds, *211*, 216, 503

Savouries, 432–3

Savoury Pastry, 76, 555

Scade, John, *Cereals*, 195, 546, 554

Scales, 241

Scarborough muffins, 349

Schouten, Floris van, 492

Science Museum, S. Kensington, 31

Scissors, dough slashing with, 266

Scofa meal, 74

Scone loaf, wholemeal, 275

Scones: aerated, 516; girdle, 528; hanging pan for, *539*; potato, 538–9

Scotch bun, 449, 449–52;
Christmas, 427; spice blend for, 431 Emma Roberts's recipe, 449, 450, 451

Scotch crumpets, 347, 348

Scotch frying pan, *539*

Scotch scraper, 266

Scotland:
bannocks in, 64, 452–3; oatcakes and, 528–9;

dough-making in, 108; soft biscuits of, 491

Scots baps, 320–23

Scots Kitchen, The, 321, 529, 553

Scottish Cookery, 321

Scottish loaves, 199

Scottish pints, 232

Scottish Women's Rural Industries, *Farmhouse Recipes*, on Selkirk bannocks, 452–3

Screen, steel, 324–5n.

Scurfield, George and Cecilia, *Home Baked*, 92, 219, 554

Sea salt, 122, 123

Seistan windmill, 20–21

Self-raising flour, 74–6, 328, 439, 516, 519

Selkirk bannocks, 452–3

Seminolo di grano duro, 77

Semolina, 32, 55, 77

Semolina meals, 77–8

Senn, Herman (ed.): *Mrs Beeton's Book of Household Management*, 162–163, 166, 170, 189, 554; *The New Century Cookery Book*, 187, 188, 554; *New Twentieth Century Cookery Book*, 162; on ovens, 162–3, 166, 170, 187–9

Sesame seeds, 131, 146

Shakespeare, William, on cob loaves, 200; on grain, 11

Shaw, George Bernard, on muffins, 361

Sheffield, 158

Sheppard, Ronald, and Newton, Edward, *The Story of Bread*, 45, 180, 194–5, 546, 554

Shilling Cookery for the People, patronizing and long-winded, 160–61

Shooting cake, 526–7

Shops, bakeries in, 195–6

Short-Time Dough in Breadmaking, The, 268

Shropshire Cookery Book, 416n., 493, 556

Shropshire Women's Institute, 416

Side-oven, iron, 161, 185–8

Sifting of ground grain, 30

Silk, miller's, 30–31

Simmond's, Caroline, xii, 460

Simnel yeast cake, 455–6

Simon, André L. (ed.), 'Cereals', in *A Concise Encyclopaedia of Gastronomy*, 556; on Selkirk bannocks, 452; on wartime bread, 84n.

Singing hinnies, 536–7

Siot, 535

Sir John Soane Museum, 188, 325n.

Sisterbrick loaves, 199

Skidmore, Jenny, xii

Smith, Delia, 387

Smith, E., *The Compleat Housewife or Accomplish'd Gentlewoman's Companion*, 554; on cake with butter, 472; on cake hoops, 212; on French bread, 376–7; on pudding-stick, 135

Smith, John Thomas, *Nollekens and his Times*, on spices, 144

Smollett, Tobias, on breadmaking, 40, 191

Snow, aerating with, 126

Society for the Protection of Ancient Buildings, xiii, 25n., *Plate 10*; publications of, 554

Soda bread, 271, 515–27, *516*; barleymeal, 523; bonnag, 523–4; English chemically aerated white, 524–5; flour for, 74, 518; Irish: wheatmeal, 517, 519, 522; wholewheat, 520–21; mixes, 74–5, 519; undercover, 521; white buttermilk, 524; wholewheat and oatmeal, 522–3

Soft biscuits, 491

Soft rolls, 323–4

Soil Association, 518

Soleilune cake, 467–70

Solid and liquid measure conversion table, 235

Solimemne cakes, 467

Soule cake, 493

Soup, bread for, 372

Sour milk, 128, 517; cake, 527

Sourdough bread, 156; American, 295–296; rye, 67, 295, 296; spiced, 67, 433

Soured cream, 128

Soya flour, 72

Soyer, Alexis: aerial cooking stove of,

Soyer, Alexis (*continued*)
161n.; *Shilling Cookery for the People*, 554
Spain, *coca*, 388
Spice blends, 430–32, 477; coriander, 431; French, 431; Scotch Christmas bun, 431; sweet, 430–31
Spice boxes, 148–9
Spice bread: chemically aerated, 518; Cornish, 440–42; Irish, 439; yeast in, 516;
Yorkshire, 461; without eggs, 428, 454
Spice buns, 473–4, 475–7
Spice cakes, 456; banned, 456–7; with cheese, 526; Countess of Kent's, 456–459; icing for, 459; leavened with baking powder, 525–7; yeast in, 516
Spice caster, English silver, *144*
Spice essence, 151
Spiced sugars, 149–50
Spices, 144–50; for bread, 144; ground, 148, 150, 431; mixed, 144–5, 430–32; quantities required, 445–6, 446n.; storage, 148–9, 429, 431; sweet, 144
Spices, Salt and Aromatics in the English Kitchen, 550
Spillers French, 38n., 195
Spillers Ltd, 37
Spit-roasting, 158
Split tin loaf, 199, 263–4
Splits, Cornish, 487
'Spon' barm, 101
Sponge cake, Victorian, 468
Sponge and dough method, 107–8, 110
Spoons, measuring, 243–4, 269n.
Spring-balance kitchen scale, 241
Springhill Bakery, Dinton, 59
Springhill Farms (Dinton) Ltd, 44
Staffordshire, 411; pikelets for breakfast, 360; Potteries' oatcakes, 411–12
Stanley, Mrs William, 537
Starch corn, *8*
Steamy oven, 170, 184, 261
Steel: bonnet, *306*; hoops, *213*; measuring jugs, 242
Stevens, Cox, J.: on Guernsey biscuits, 490; *Guernsey Dishes of Bygone Days*, 454, 490, 554; *Guernsey Dishes of the 18th Century*, 554; *Guernsey Gâche*,

554; on Guernsey *gâche*, 454
Stone-ground meal, 26, 29, 31, 51, 54, 518; storage of, 217, 218;
wholemeal, 271, 272, 282; Abbey brand, 275, 283, 518, 519; loaves, 272
Stones: burr, 26, 29; dressing, 30; grooving, 29; milling, 26–30, 39, 54, 77; pounding, 17
Stoneware: bowls, 304; crocks, storage in, 221
Storage: bread, 221–5, 371; cupboards, 223; meal and flour, 35, 217–20; salt, 124; spices, 148–9, 429, 431; sugar, 138, 140; yeast, 89–90, 92–3, 106, 112–14
Story of Bread, The, 45, 180, 194–5, 546, 554;
Story of Sugar, The, 554
Story of Yeast, The, 550
Stour canal, 25
Stow, John, *Survey of London*, on restrictions on bun sales, 473–4; on watermills, 14
Straight-dough system, 316
Straight-run flour, 77
Straub, Peter, 386
Strike, bread workers', 192
Strong, L. A. G., *The Story of Sugar*, 554
Sturt, George, *A Small Boy in the Sixties*, 554; on breakfast dough cake, 465
Subsidized flour, 34, 247
Suffolk, 420; harvest cake, 462; home-baking in, 170–75
Sugar, 138, 142n., 551, 552
Sugar, 134–5, 137–42: beet, 142; box, japanned tin, *140*; Brazil, 142; brown, 141–2; cane, 141; caster, 141; 'clayed', 142; clove or cinnamon, 432; cube, 141; cutters, *138*; Demerara, 142; in dough, 429; fruit and, 429; health hazard from, 142; icing, 139–140, 141; in lardy cakes, 461; Lisbon, 142; loaves, 138–9, *138*; muscovado, 141–2; musk-scented, 149–50; price of, 140; refineries, 138; sifting, 139; spiced, 149–50; storage, 138, 140;

white, 141; with yeast, 111, 116, 257, 426

Sultanas, 136, 137

Summer bread, Eliza Acton's, **316–19**

Sunday Express, 187

Sunday Times, 51, 411, 475

Sunflower-seed, 131

Surrey, manchets, 333–4, **336–7**; dough cake, 465

Surrey Cookery Book, The, 336–7, 465, 556

Sussex, 286; baking day in a farmhouse, 434–5; lardy rolls, 493; plum heavies, 493; village bakeries in, 43, 80–81

Sussex Recipe Book, with a Few Excursions into Kent, 471, 493, 554

Suzanne, Alfred, *La Cuisine Anglaise*, on gas ovens, 188–9

Sweet spice blend, **430–31**

Sweet spices, 144

Sweetened rye bread, **294–5**

Swift, Jonathan, on Chelsea buns, 482

Swiss Lindt chocolate, 510

Switzens, 513

Symond's Yat, 27

Syrup: Golden, 143, 294; kirsch-flavoured, 502–3

Tablespoons, American, 243, 269n.

T.A.C.C. Report, *see* Technology Assessment Consumerism Centre

Tames, Richard, *Our Daily Bread*, 79n., 554; on potato bread, 290

Tartar, cream of, 516–17, 520

Tartaric acid, 516–17

Tarte aveyronnaise, **399–401**

Tashis, Mrs, Little Puddings of, 150, *488*, 489–90

Tate & Lyle's Golden Syrup, 143, 294

Tate Sugar Company, 141

Tea buns, 478–9

Tea crumpets, 347

Teacakes: hot, 324–5; Mrs Tashis', 490; Northumbrian harvest, 429, 463–4; plain, 470–71; small, 484–95

Teaspoons, American, 243

Technology Assessment Consumerism Centre: *Bread. An Assessment of the Bread Industry in Britain*, 36n., 56, 59, 554

Technology of Bread-making, The, 381–2, 552

Temperatures: dough, 125–6, 238, 260, 276; Fahrenheit–Celsius conversion table, 239; fermentation, 109, 260, 270, 281

oven, 239–40, 258; electricity–gas conversion table, 240; judging, 169–70

Terracotta: crocks, 222–3; moulds, 211, 309; oven, Spanish, *Plate 19*

Tharffe cakes, 68

Thearion, 209, 215

Thermometers, 244–5

Thomas, Kathleen, *A West Country Cookery Book*, 554; on Cornish splits, 487; on oven temperature, 169

Thompson, Benjamin, Count Rumford, 168n.

Thompson, Evelyn, 336, 556

Thompson, Flora, on: dough cake, 337, 424; toast and celery, 543

Thompson, Sir Henry, *Food and Feeding*, 555; on bread, 191–2; on crumpets and muffins, 361; on handmills, 42–3; on soda bread, 522–3

Thompson Gill, J., *The Complete Bread, Cake and Cracker Baker*, 555; on cake-flavouring, 429; on fermentation, 300; on salt, 119

Through Yorkshire's Kitchen Door, 410, 461, 495, 527, 556

Tibbott, S. Minwel, *Welsh Fare*, 538, 555

Tiger yeast, 97

Tiled oven floor, 156, 163

Timbs, John, 169, 170, 187

'Times' yeast, 105

Timothy White's, 216

Tin hoops, 212

Tin loaves, 199, 264; farmhouse, 199; pan Coburg, 278–9; split, 199, 263–4; wholemeal, 268–72

Tinkers, travelling, 214

Tins, 206, *207*, 444;
bread, 206–9; early use of, 208 and n.; buying, 215–16; fancy, 216; hinged cake, *213*; non-stick, 216; quality of,

Tins (*continued*)
216; removable-base, 216; shiny, 216; *see also* Moulds and tins

Tinsmiths, 214

Tire-bouchon loaf, *363*

Toast, 203, 540–45; and ale, 543; anchovy, 544; bacon, cold boiled, with, 543; best butter for, 543; buttered, 541–3;
  with celery, 543; 'Cockneys, eaters of', 541
  dripping, 544; grilled, 542–3; Melba, 545; *pain grillé*, 368, 542; for potages, 546–7; potato bread, good for, 288; pulled bread, better than, 546; railway, price of, 544; Renner, H. D., on, 540; rye bread, 542; in soup, 564–7; Thompson, Flora, describes, 543; unkind cut, 544; Wellington, Duke of, fondness for, 540; white bread, 542–3; whole wheatmeal, 521, 542

Toasters, 540–41, 542; electric, *Which?* report on, 542

Toasting muffins, 355

Torr, Cecil, 555; on grain, 3

Tortilla Book, The, 70

Traditional recipes, adaptation of, 432–3

Traherne, Thomas, *Centuries of Meditations*, on wheat, 7

Traité pratique de panification française et parisienne, 551

Transport, grain, 14–16

Treacle, 517; black, 143, 295

Trenchers, loaves for, 332

Trevelyan, G. M., *Illustrated English Social History*, 555; on bread, 6

Triticum compactum, 9

Triticum vulgare, 7

Troy weights, 228–9

True Gentlewoman's Delight, A, 314, 336, 552

Tull, Jethro, *Principles of Tillage*, 555

Turkish *dolma*, 489

Turog flour, 74

Two Fifteenth-Century Cookery-Books, 329, 417, 501, 549

Ulster Fare, 527

Ulverston Fair Cakes, 433, 493–4

Undercover breadbaking, 155–6, 210, 277, 284–5, 303–6, 309–10

Undercover method, flowerpot, 73, 205, 210, 309–10

Underseller's loaves, 201, 265

Undertin loaves, 303
  Granary Foods Ltd, 60, 283

Universal Family Cook, 344, 372, 377–378

Unstead, R. I., *Living on Pompeii*, 27

Unthank, Elizabeth, 459

Up-to-Date Breadmaking, 109, 328, 467, 511–12, 551

Uttley, Allison, *Recipes from an Old Farmhouse*, 555; on dough, xix; on pikelets, 359

d'Uxelles, Marquis, 374

Valor Perfection cooker, 164

Vanilla flavouring, 432

Vegetables in bread, 72–3

Vegetarian fats, 132, 284

Vegetarian Society, 132

Velasquez, eggs and lemons in his paintings, 134

Verral, William, *The Cook's Paradise*, on manchets, 333

Victoria and Albert Museum, 208n., 250

Victorian household handmill, *41*

Vienna and Other Fancy Breads, 205, 551

Vienna: flour, 76; 'French' loaves, 362, 371, 380; rolls, 325–6

Vienna-type loaves, *266*

Village bakeries, 180–85; Dorset, 181–2, 435–6; Essex, 182–3; preparing the cake hoops in, 435–6; surviving, 183–185; Sussex, 43, 180–81

Vince, John, *Discovering Watermills*, 29, 555

Vine, Frederick, T., xii; *Biscuits for Bakers*, 96, 190; on bread, 191, 199, 201; on eggs, 133; on muffins, 351; on pot bread, 155, 306–7; *Practical Breadmaking*, 89, 155, 160n., 191, 201, 306–7, 555; *Saleable Shop Goods*, 133, 151–2, 555; *Savoury Pastry*, 76, 555; on spices, 151–2; on Vienna flour, 76; on white bread, 160

Violets, syrup of, 151

Virgin barm, 101
Vitamins, 33–4, 52, 267
VitBe bread, 205
VitBe flour, 74
Vol-au-vent, 498, 500

Wailes, Rex: *The English Windmill*, 555; *Horizontal Windmills*, 20–21, 555
Wales: barley in, 6; batch loaf in, 199; bread storage in, 223; cob loaf in, 200; Gas Board, *Croeso Cymreig. A Welsh Welcome: Recipes for Some Traditional Welsh Dishes*, 437, 555; mills in, 31, 40; tea at Machynlleth 1888, 537
Walker, George, on oatcakes, 529–30
Walsh, J. H., *A Manual of Domestic Economy Suited to Families Spending from £100 to £1000 a Year*, 41, 555; on brown bread, 57, 58; on handmills, 42; on ovens, 187
Warburton family, 487
Ward, Mary, 493
Warner, the Reverend Richard, *Antiquitates Culinariae or Curious Traces Relating to the Culinary Affairs of the Old English*, 555
Warren, C. Henry, *Corn Country*, 555; on bread, 26, 80; on ovens, 176, 180
Wartime National flour, 84–8; Government poster 1917, *86*; Ministry of Food leaflet 1944, *85*
Wash tub: breadmaking in, 126, *311–12*; with peggy or dolly, *311*
Water: aerated, 125; in Australia and U.S.A., permitted limit of in bread, 127; in breadmaking, 125–7; distilled from flowers, 151; in English bread, no law governing content of, 127; iced, 126; scented, 151; soft, 380; wheel, 19; in wholemeal and wheatmeal, 127
Watermills, 14, 19–20, 24; Constable, John, and, 19, 22, 25; in Domesday Survey, 20; horizontal, 19; from Luttrell Psalter, *Plate 8*; machinery of, *24*; Michelham Priory, *Plate 10*; monastic, 554
Watermills: An Introduction, 554
Watermills with Horizontal Wheels, 554

Waterways, inland, 14, 15
Watkins, C. Malcolm, *North Devon Pottery and Its Export to America in the 17th Century*, 157, 555
Watts' Dictionary of Chemistry, on French leaven, 382
Wedgwood, Josiah, piecrust dishes, 230n.
Weighing equipment, 241
Weighing and measurement, 238, 243
Weights: avoirdupois–metric conversion of, 233–5; Chinese, 228n.; of loaves, 226–32; troy, 228–9
Weights and Measures Act 1878, 231
Wellington, Duke of, 530, 540
Wells, Dilys, on flour and bread quality, 79
Wells, Robert, *Bread and Biscuit Baker's Assistant*, on: muffins and crumpets, 352; testing compressed yeast, 114
Welsh:
  bakestone, *534*; cakes, 533–8;
  bread cart, 530; bread crates, 223; butter, 543;
  cakes, 537–8; barley, thick and thin, 535–6; light, 407, 537; oatmeal, 533–5;
  cob loaf, 200; crumpets, 358; currant bread (bara brith), 426, 437–9; oatcakes, 69, 528, 533–5; oatmeal bread, 533; oatmeal pancakes, 408–9; pan bread, 307–8; pot bread, 307–8; potato cakes, 528
Welsh Country Upbringing, 185
Welsh Fare, 538, 555
Welsh Folk Museum, St Fagans, 157, 223, 538
Welsh Welcome, A: Recipes for Some Traditional Welsh Dishes, 437, 555
West country: barley in, 6; earthenware ovens in, 157, 177–80
West Country Cookery Book, A, 169, 487, 554
West Indies sugar, 138, 142
Weston, Garfield, 36
Whatman, Susannah, *The Housekeeping Book of Susannah Whatman 1776–1800*, on sugar storage, 138, 140
What's On, 255, 386, 555

Wheat: amber, 10; American, 10, 16, 52;
Bright, 4; Browne, Sir Thomas, on, 3;
Canadian, 9, 10, 11, 51; cracked, 73;
durum, 10, 78; emmer, 9; feed,
48; flour, with barley or oatmeal,
407;
germ, 32, 34, 46, 80–82; bread, home-
made, 81–2; in bread and in diet,
78–80; Jordan's, 82; in proprietary
bread flours, 74;
grain, structure and content of, 47, 48–
49; hard, 10, 45, 86; Harrison, William, on, 6; Heston, 331; history of,
7–13; Manitoba, 9, 51; Maris
Huntsman, 88; Marquis, 10; Muffett,
Thomas, on, xx; origins of, 7; pigmentation of bran coatings, 10; prices,
E.E.C. and, 88; red, 10, 13; Red Fife,
10; replaces rye and mixed crops, 6;
soft, 82, 86, 88; flavour of, 11, 52;
flour, 11, 46, 51, 362, 365–6, 518;
Torr, Cecil, on, 3; Traherne, Thomas,
on, 7; transport of, 14–16; varieties of,
9–10, 88; white, 10, 13; White, Gilbert, and, 11–13; Yeoman, 10, 83;
yields, 88, 230
Wheatmeal:
bread, 32, 35, 277; basic loaf, 256–63;
chemically aerated, 517; oatmeal in,
69; with rye, 53; soda, 517, 519,
522; toast, 521, 542;
cakes, 433;
flour, 52–3, 106, 518; bakers', 57–8;
and rye, 53;
water in, 127
Which?, 37, 542; Good Food Guide 1974,
54
Whisks, 507
White, Florence, Good Things in England,
555; on clotted cream, 129; on man-
chants, 333; on muffins, 349; on pikelets, 360; on Sally Lunn cakes, 467,
469; on 'whigs' (wiggs), 485
White, Gilbert: on grain growing, 11–13;
Journals, 13, 555; Natural History of
Selborne, 11
White Book of the City of London, 227,
369, 552
White bread, 5–6, 34, 37–8, 79, 193;

buttermilk, 75, 524; soda, chemically
aerated English, 524–5
White Mill, Carmarthen, xii, 40
Whittington, Richard, Mayor, 553
Wholefood organizations and stores, 38,
54, 59, 296
Wholemeal, 81, 227; bakers', 59;
bread, 36, 59, 69, 249, 271, 522; cost
of, 249–50; Grant's, 272–4; Holme
mills, 274–5;
flour, 36, 59, 50–53; composition of,
248–9;
loaves, crusty, 272; low-gluten, 111;
scone loaf, 275;
stone-ground, 51, 271, 272; Abbey
brand, 275, 518;
storage of, 219; tin bread, 268–72;
water in, 127; wheatmeal and,
58
Wholewheat:
bread, 35–6, 49, 520–21, 522; oatmeal
in, 522–3;
flour, 48, 51; bakers', 59;
meal, 50–52, 521; home-made, 522–3;
soda bread, 522; Irish, 520–21; with
oatmeal, 522–3;
toast, 521, 542
Widdowson, E. M., 552
Wife's Own Book of Cookery, The, 324–5,
428–9, 464, 550
Wiggs or wigs, 129, 433, 484–7; light,
with stewed cheese, 433, 487; saffron
in, 147; sugar on, 487
Wilbraham, A., 551
Williams, Charles, 296
Williams, James, Give Me Yesterday,
555; on home-baking, 39, 63, 126
Williams, W. Mattieu, The Chemistry of
Cookery, 555; on bread, 55, 154, 192;
on ovens, 168
Williams-Ellis, Sir Clough, Architect
Errant, 465–6; on luncheon cake, 465;
on muffins, 349
Wilson, C. Anne, Food and Drink in
Britain from the Stone Age to Recent
Times, 555; on pikelets, 360
Wilson, Paul N.: Watermills: An Intro-
duction, 554; Watermills with Hori-
zontal Wheels, 554

Winchester, Barbara, *Tudor Family Portrait*, 556

Winchester bushels, 533n.

Winchester mills, 25

Windermere cakes, Burtergill, 433, **494–495**

Windmills, 14, 20–26, *Plate 7*; Constable, John, and, 22; hazards of, 22; horizontal, 21; interior of (Polegate tower mill), *23*; Seistan, *20*

Windmill and Watermill Section of the S.P.A.B., xiii, 25n., *Plate 10*

Windmills and Watermills, 21, 554

Wine and Food Society, *A Concise Encyclopaedia of Gastronomy*, 84n., 452, 491, 556

Wine and Food Society Quarterly, The, 350n.

Wine yeasts, 98

Women's Institutes, 424;
    Federations of, 73, 178n., 309, 410, 493, 556; *Cornish Recipes Ancient and Modern*, 178–9, 298, 440, 556; *The Isle of Wight Cookery Book*, 82, 84, 422, 556; *Shropshire Cookery Book*, 416n., 493, 556; *The Surrey Cookery Book*, 336–7, 465, 556; *Through Yorkshire's Kitchen Door*, 410, 461, 495, 527, 556;
    see also under place names

Wooden: bowls, 315; brake, *190*; hoops, 212; oven doors, 176; peels, *169*, 182

Woodward, Marcus, *The Mistress of Stantons Farm*, 556; on baking, 434–435; on Bath buns, 481; on Yorkshire cakes, 488

Woolf, Virginia, breadmaking by, 164–5, 285

Woolley, Suzanne, *My Grandmother's Cookery Book*, on Manx barley bread, 523

Woolworths, 216

Wragg, B. H., 109n.

Wrapped loaf, 37, 193

Wrecclesham, pottery at, 223

Wright, Joseph, 334n.

Wroxeter, Shropshire, 27

Wygges, *see* Wiggs

Yates, Dornford, on toast, 540

Yeast, 89–118; Acton, Eliza, on, 99–100, 316–19; ale, 98–9, 371; American active dry, 117; bakers', 93, 106–10; bakers unwilling to sell, 111–12; Balloon, 95, *96*; beer, 97, 370–71; Bennion, E., on, 97; bread flavour and, 110–11; brewers', 95, 98–100; buns, *see* Buns; buying and storing, 111–12, 116–18; cakes, *see* Cakes *and* French yeast cakes; Clark of Tillypronie, Lady, recipes for, 102–3, 104–6; compressed, 94, 101, 106–10, 516–17; freezing of, 113–14; sugar not needed with, 111; to test, 114; cultivation, 92–3; in Denmark, 112; distilleries, 95, 97; domo, 95, 97; dough, pancheon for, *253*; dried, 94, 114–17, 261, 268, 516–17; bread mixes blended with, 75; buying, 116–17; granular, using, 114–116; measuring, 115; quantities to use, 115; reactivating, 116; storing, 117–18; dumplings, 418, **419–20**; barm pudding, **420**; Dutch, 95, 117; Fermipan, 117; and the flavour of bread, 110; food for, 91–93; freezing of, 113–14; French, 371, 375, 382; Garrett, Theodore, on, 97; German, 94; ginger, 102–3, 146; growth, 97; potato mash and, 290; sugar and, 92; of Hepworth, Walter, of Harwich, 97; history of, 89–93; home-made, 101; explodes, 104; Hughes, M. Vivian, and, 104; killed by heat, 111; Liebig and, 91; from malted rye, 97; manufacture of, 93–6; nature of, 91–2, 94–102; pancakes, 358; pans for, *408*; patents, 100–101; Paris Faculty of Medicine and, 90; Pasteur and, 91; powder, 516; puff pastry, 510; quantities, 97, 98, 99, 106, 109, 115, 277, 281; for wholemeal bread, 261, 270–71; reproduction of, 97; Rundell, Mrs, recipe for, 99, 101–3; salt and, 121; in

Yeast (*continued*)
   spice cakes, 516; storing, 89–90, 92–3, 106, 112–14; substitutes, chemical, 516; sugar and, 111, 426; Tiger brand, 97; 'Times', 105; using, 257; wine, 98
Yeast-leavened: batter for fritters, 417; buckwheat pancakes, 416
Yeatmans' baking powder, 516
Yeoman wheat, 10
Yogurt, 128
Yorkshire, bread creel, 224; brown bread, 283; cakes, 488, 530; Federation of Women's Institutes, 410, 461, 527, 530; grate, 161; haver cakes, 410–411, 530; muffins, 349; North Riding bread, 526; oatcakes, 410–11, 529–30; pikelets, 360; riddle bread, 407, 409–411; sour-milk cake, 527; spice bread, 461; without eggs, 428, 454;
   33rd Foot Regiment, 530
Your Daily Bread, 91, 272–4, 551
Y.W.C.A., *Devonshire Flavour: A Devonshire Treasury of Recipes and Personal Notes*, 440, 556

Zampi, Mario, 384, 387

MORE ABOUT PENGUINS
AND PELICANS

Penguinews, which appears every month, contains details of all the new books issued by Penguins as they are published. From time to time it is supplemented by our stocklist, which includes around 5,000 titles.

A specimen copy of *Penguinews* will be sent to you free on request. Please write to Dept EP, Penguin Books Ltd, Harmondsworth, Middlesex, for your copy.

In the U.S.A.: For a complete list of books available from Penguins in the United States write to Dept CS, Penguin Books, 625 Madison Avenue, New York, New York 10022.

In Canada: For a complete list of books available from Penguins in Canada write to Penguin Books Canada Ltd, 2801 John Street, Markham, Ontario L3R 1B4.

In Australia: For a complete list of books available from Penguins in Australia write to the Marketing Department, Penguin Books Australia Ltd, P.O. Box 257, Ringwood, Victoria 3134.

Penguin Cookery Handbooks for 1979

THE VEGETABLE GROWER'S CALENDAR

David Mabey

David Mabey shows how to maintain a continuing supply of fresh vegetables whatever the season, with practical advice on simple and traditional outdoor gardening.

VEGETABLE COOKERY

Nika Hazelton

An A-Z of vegetables, both fresh and dried, with their history, ways of keeping and preserving, their nutritional value and a host of exciting recipes.

THE FARMHOUSE KITCHEN

Mary Norwak

A bevy of recipes (with notes on their historical origins) which includes all the traditional country occupations such as pickling, bread-making and home brewing as well as delicious fish and meat dishes, sauces, puddings, sweets and cakes.

FRUIT IN SEASON

Marian Denny

This collection of recipes will help you make the most of seasonal gluts without always falling back on apple pie. Some of the recipes are old favourites, like Lemon Meringue Pie and Summer Pudding; others, like Grape and Cream Cheese Flan, and Peaches with Chestnut Sauce, you may be trying for the first time.

Penguin Cookery Handbooks for 1979

THE HOME GARDENER'S COOKBOOK

Clare Walker and Gill Coleman

Designed to help all amateur gardeners and allotment holders to use their vegetable and fruit crops to the full, particularly when they have problems such as glut, misshapen, overripe or underripe produce, this book gives lots of different methods of cooking, preserving, freezing and storing.

COOKING FOR A BABY

Sylvia Hull

A book for mothers who do not want to feed their babies on fattening, processed baby foods. The recipes are varied, approved by a nutritionist and a paediatrician, and suitable for babies from the age of four to five months.

MORE EASY COOKING FOR ONE OR TWO

Louise Davies

Once again Louise Davies has written an ideal book for those cooking for one or two. Full of ideas and recipes, it aims at good nutrition with the minimum of cooking effort. The type is large and clear and Tony Odell's line drawings are used to illustrate cooking techniques.

and

The Penguin Guide to Real Draught Beer   *Michael Dunn*
The Wines of Germany   *Cyril Ray*
Friends of the Earth Cookbook   *Veronica Sekules*
Step-By-Step Chinese Cookery   *Georges Spunt*
La Cuisine du Comté de Nice   *Jacques Médecin*
Pots and Pans   *Gertrude Harris*
Outdoor Cookery   *Claudia Roden*

MEDITERRANEAN SEAFOOD

Alan Davidson

Mediterranean seafood can be as baffling as it is delicious – so Alan Davidson has, in a scholarly and amusing style and with the help of illustrations, catalogued the edible marine life of the Mediterranean and labelled it in several languages. British and American readers will find that the 200 recipes are skilfully presented so as to show how easily the native flavour of Mediterranean seafood can be brought into more northerly homes.

Arranging the dishes country by country, from the *Suquillo de Pescadores* of Spain and the famous *Anchoïade* and *Bouillabaisse* of Provence to the Greek *Ochtapódi Krassáto* – octopus in red wine – the author also includes rarer recipes from such places as Istanbul, Alexandria and Bizerta, and describes them with the quixotic charm of the true enthusiast.

MASTERING THE ART OF FRENCH COOKING

Volumes 1 and 2

Simone Beck, Louisette Bertholle, Julia Child

'The most instructive book on fine French cooking yet written in the English language' – Elizabeth David

A practical guide to *haute cuisine*, with hundreds of clear and precise recipes for cooking in the classic French style.

'Essential reading for anyone wishing to produce ambitious and entertaining dishes in the French manner' – *Wine and Food*

'Has been described as being the best book about French cooking in English ... I agree' – Ambrose Heath in the *Guardian*

THE COOKERY OF ENGLAND

Elisabeth Ayrton

'Both a history of English food, from the days when we were esteemed better cooks than the French, and a book of recipes that will extend the repertoire of the Cordon Bleu cook without being too extravagant or too complicated for the novice . . . this is a lovely book which could restore pride to our English kitchens' – *The Times Literary Supplement*

A TASTE OF THE COUNTRY

Pamela Westland

'A garden is a lovesome thing, God wot' – and all the lovelier for providing such a wealth of good food on our back doorsteps.

An ardent advocate of home produce, Pamela Westland has assembled a variety of suggestions and recipes for dealing with the fruits of your labours. She begins by listing the crops you can grow and how to deal with them, and includes mouthwatering recipes for jams, jellies and chutneys. She devotes a chapter to home brewing and wine-making, and demonstrates how cheap, simple and versatile yogurt is. She gives a wide choice of breads, cakes and buns to try, and finally discusses the best ways to store the lot in a home freezer.

THE PENGUIN BOOK OF JAMS, PICKLES AND CHUTNEYS

David and Rose Mabey

'An excellent book; practical, personal and suggestive, every recipe's clearly the result of real experience and written with great charm' – *The Times*

JANE GRIGSON

FISH COOKERY

There are over 50 species of edible fish; and Jane Grigson feels that most of us do not eat nearly enough of them. If anything will make us mend our ways, it is this delightful book with its varied and comprehensive recipes, covering everything from lobster to conger eel, from sole to clam chowder. Many of her dishes come from France, others are from the British Isles, America, Spain, Italy – any country where good fish is cooked with loving care and eaten with appreciation.

CHARCUTERIE AND FRENCH PORK COOKERY

Ever since Charles Lamb stated that there was no other taste comparable to that of roast pork, the pig has never looked back. And it is hoped that this book – the first of its kind – will further its popularity in the English kitchen. Together with a guide to *charcuterie* and a host of French pork dishes, it gives new and unusual information on the history and growth of this art. Certain to delight both adventurous housewife and diffident traveller to France, this book allows you to make a true pig of yourself.

GOOD THINGS

Bouchées à la reine, civet of hare, Mrs Beeton's carrot jam to imitate apricot preserve, baked beans Southern style, wine sherbet . . .

These are just a few of the delicious and intriguing dishes in *Good Things*: Jane Grigson is a firm believer in the pleasure food gives. Echoing the great chef Carême – 'from behind my ovens, I feel the ugly edifice of routine crumbling beneath my hands' – she emphasizes the delights and solaces of a truly creative activity.

and

ENGLISH FOOD
THE MUSHROOM FEAST

ELIZABETH DAVID

Elizabeth David is well known for the infectious enthusiasm with which she presents her recipes.

'She has the happy knack of giving just as much detail as the average cook finds desirable; she presumes neither on our knowledge nor on our ignorance' – Elizabeth Nicholas in the *Sunday Times*

MEDITERRANEAN FOOD

A practical collection of recipes made by the author when she lived in France, Italy, the Greek Islands and Egypt, evoking all the colour of the Mediterranean but making use of ingredients obtainable in England.

FRENCH COUNTRY COOKING

Some of the splendid regional variations in French cookery are described in this book.

FRENCH PROVINCIAL COOKING

'It is difficult to think of any home that can do without Elizabeth David's *French Provincial Cooking* ... One could cook for a lifetime on the book alone' – *Observer*

ITALIAN FOOD

Exploding once and for all the myth that Italians live entirely on minestrone, spaghetti and veal escalopes, this exciting book demonstrates the enormous and colourful variety of Italy's regional cooking.

SUMMER COOKING

A selection of ummer dishes that are light (not necessarily cold), easy to prepare and based on the food in season.

SPICES, SALT AND AROMATICS IN THE ENGLISH KITCHEN

Elizabeth David presents English recipes which are notable for their employment of spices, salt and aromatics. As usual, she seasons instruction with information, explaining the origins and uses of her ingredients.